P9-CKY-155

DATE DUE

NO 12'98			
MY 27'99			
JE 10'99			
JA 29'07			
MY - 1'09			

DEMCO 38-296

ATOMIC
SPACES

Peter Bacon Hales

UNIVERSITY OF ILLINOIS PRESS

Urbana and Chicago

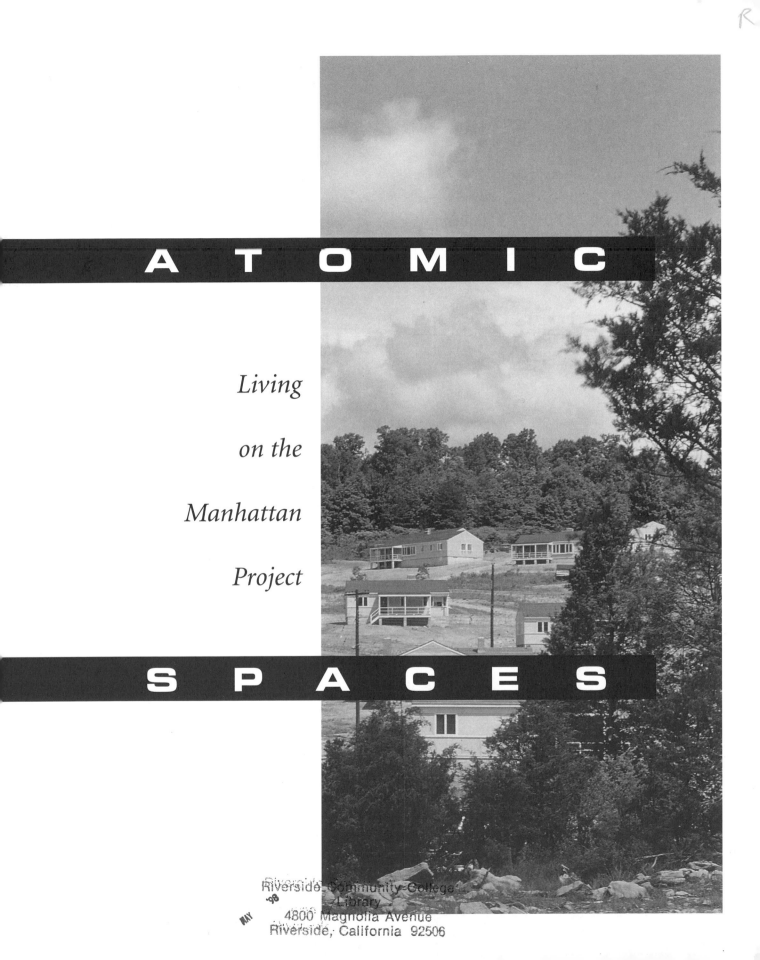

ATOMIC

Living

on the

Manhattan

Project

SPACES

Riverside Community College
Library
MAY '98
4800 Magnolia Avenue
Riverside, California 92506

QC 773.3 .U5 H35 1997

Hales, Peter B.

Atomic spaces

© 1997 by Peter Bacon Hales
Manufactured in the United States of America
C 5 4 3 2 1

This book is printed on acid-free paper.

Library of Congress Cataloging-in-Publication Data

Hales, Peter B. (Peter Bacon)
Atomic spaces : living on the Manhattan Project / Peter Bacon Hales.
p. cm.
Includes bibliographical references and index.
ISBN 0-252-02296-3 (cloth : alk. paper)
1. Atomic bomb—United States—History. 2. Manhattan Project
(U.S.)—History. 3. United States. Army. Corps of Engineers.
Manhattan District—History. I. Title.
QC773.3.U5H35   1997
304.2—dc21
97-4614
CIP

For Barbara, Taylor, Molly

New lives, new hope

CONTENTS

In a cabinet of an office in the Oak Ridge facility of the Department of Energy is a file containing a photograph that has lost its caption and so seems at first to float without anchor in time or place (fig. 1). An 8 x 10" glossy, it presents with diffident specificity a chair, a man, and behind the man a map of the world.

Like everything within it, the photograph is standard issue. Made (we assume) by an army photographer as a publicity shot, it describes the geography of a military bureaucracy, bland and efficient. Only the map seems suggestive. It is pocked by push-pins, marking sites of some sort, locations.

To immerse ourselves in the picture and its context, to seek its meanings, is to enter into unexpected complexities. The year is 1945; the man is an officer in the Manhattan Engineer District—that section of the U.S. Army Corps of Engineers responsible for building and running the Manhattan Project and hence for bringing atomic holocaust to the globe. The pins on the map show the locations of various facilities of the Manhattan District: medical, manufacturing, research, assembly, stockpiling, deployment, targeting, and the like. From this multitude of sites and people, resources and possibilities, suggests the picture, came the unity of will needed to win this war.

This photograph might seem the quintessence of the Manhattan Project's history as we have come to understand it since those early August days of 1945 when the planes banked away from roaring upsurges of destruction at Hiroshima and Nagasaki, when an American president warned that the enemy had "reaped the whirlwind," and when Americans danced and sang in the streets to celebrate the end of the war. In its mundaneness, it proposes a reassuring narrative to a nation and a world confronted with a terrifying new form of warfare and mass destruction: it celebrates the very matter-of-fact confidence with which, the myth tells us, American scientists, government figures, military planners, GIs, and ordinary citizens all cooperated to bring forth this decisive new instrument of moral vengeance and apply it, in the name of peace and freedom, to end old tyrannies and control new ones. In this regard, the picture is a marvelous foil, for the man who sits before the camera seems so uneasy in his role as hero, the environment too bland for remarkable acts and great moments. Yet the map is there—an implicit and crucial backdrop to the scientific and military achievements of the Manhattan Project.

This is a story about the birth of America's atomic spaces, their creation by military fiat and necessity, their occupation by people, buildings, and social networks, their consolidation into a new type of cultural environment, penetrating work, leisure, environment, language, and belief, and present even today as a significant, if surreptitious, strain of American culture.

This is a history of that atomic culture. The Manhattan Engineer District—the formal term for the wartime Manhattan Project—occupied three main sites and more than a hundred smaller ones, from Alamogordo, New Mexico, to Trail, in British

FIG. 1 Captain O'Sullivan with map, 1945. Courtesy National Archives.

Columbia, and included secret locations in places like Rochester, New York; Ames, Iowa; and Berkeley, California. At the three principal sites—Oak Ridge, Tennessee; Los Alamos, New Mexico; and Hanford, Washington—the District employed as many as 125,000 people at one time, hundreds of thousands over the years between 1942 and 1946. These were vast sites (one nearly as large as a state), hidden in mountains and mesas, or set in desert lands fortified by layers of walls, fences, security patrols, guards. They became American communities as the District built its factories and towns and set up its systems of authority and regulation, in order to invent and manufacture the most destructive and dangerous weapons in the history of humankind.

The Manhattan District began by carving out spaces; in these spaces it constructed streets, houses, factories, all the requirements for modern social life. Into these spaces came workers and their families, and their behavior had to be regulated. The result was a new sort of social landscape, a cultural environment that melded the peculiar needs of the Project and the particular beliefs of its military-industrial rulers with the broader currents of American tradition.

Most communities emerge from an admixture of planning and inadvertency, mingling tradition and novelty, developing a history or histories, interconnecting with their surroundings, drawing from them and influencing them in turn. This was only marginally the case with the Manhattan Engineer District and its cultural geography. Somewhere between an army base and a utopian social experiment, the MED as a whole and each of its three principal sites joined a small handful of American planned communities of the twentieth century. At Oak Ridge, the District's planners hired the architectural firm of Skidmore, Owings, and Merrill, primarily because of SOM's involvement with utopian housing and building programs of the Depression era. SOM responded accordingly, though the result was not an architect's or planner's utopia. At the Hanford, Washington, site, the District contractor, Du Pont, and District planners concurred in hiring a small local architect to create a planned community-within-a-community. There, too, the architecture of utopia set itself within the harsh landscape of military expediency.

These impulses toward utopian planning had to accommodate the military planning models. General Leslie R. Groves, shadowy director of the MED, had made his career by studying—and building—military bases, simultaneously spartan grids of self-sacrifice to the will of the state and intrusive environments of individual and social management and regulation.

Groves's most recent construction project was a different kind of extension of the modern social landscape, the largest ever undertaken by the military: a giant multisided model of a bureaucracy-as-fortress—the Pentagon. His influence on the Pentagon had been to ruthlessly enforce efficiencies of scale and mass-regulation to keep the project on time and budget. Its influence on him had been to provide a paradigm for imagining military bureaucracy mapped out as space and symbol.

Groves himself represented a larger tradition of military bureaucracy devoted to the manipulation and transformation of American spaces to the goal of greater efficiency and the control of nature, imbedded within the Army Corps of Engineers. The Manhattan District was but one part of this powerful legacy, and Groves was but one among the thousands of corps officers, engineers, veterans, contractors, and companies that carried the long tradition of the corps into the novel world of atomic weapons invention, production, and deployment.

The physical landscapes manufactured by the District formed one manifestation of a complex and evolving ideology blending corporate capitalism, government social management, and military codes of coercion and obedience.

The District's goal was not to produce communities but to produce weapons in and from those communities. To do this required the labor and commitment of civilians: atomic scientists, pipe fitters, concrete pourers, housewives, musicians, writers, engineers, social workers; expatriate European Jews, Okies and Arkies, African Americans (then, they were Negroes, or "colored people"), Hispanos, American Indians; farmers and city folk; men, women, and children. Their coming changed the District even as the District changed them.

Here physical landscape and social landscape blur into something larger and more amorphous—culture. Within its own boundaries, the Manhattan Project suppressed the larger climate of cultural heterodoxy with its special form of order, forged and justified by the extraordinary circumstances of the last great war. District officials largely recognized the ways this incursion of people, traditions, and beliefs threatened their program; they sought, more or less directly, to eradicate that threat where possible, and to redirect it where necessary. This they did in the spheres of law and regulation, in a broad campaign of intercession in everyday life I call (rather ironically) social work. They did this also through the programs devoted to ensuring secrecy and security on the project. And they did it through the invention, manipulation, and transformation of languages, spoken and written but also visual, gestural, and symbolic.

The Manhattan Engineer District created a new form of American cultural landscape with one Herculean goal in mind: the manufacture of an atomic superweapon in time to use it on the Japanese. The goal was achieved, and the forces that resulted still buffet us. But I have chosen in this book to look at a different set of consequences, less visible, less spectacular, but in their own way perhaps as important and influential. Having begun a cultural geography of the Manhattan Project, I have ended by suggesting some of the ways the project intruded into American life and influenced the world we live in. This is an ending I have left deliberately sketchy. My goal when I began this book was to draw on a mass of unexamined or underexamined evidence to propose new interpretations of this most important event in recent American cultural history, and I hope to leave a broad swath of open space around my own project. And so I have ended the story at the moment when the Manhattan Engineer District melted into other, broader streams of American and global cultural history, leaving my own photographs of the sites as a deeply personal residue and allowing others to debate the implications of that final (and continuing) transformation from past to present.

It is the conceit of this book to propose the Manhattan Project as a geographical enterprise, defined by space as reality and as metaphor. I have written a cultural history of three places and the consequences of their occupation by a wartime project. The webs that connected those places and gave their occupants a shared reality are not necessarily clear or easy to describe. Wherever possible, I have looked straight at the thing itself—the landscape, the program, the factory, house, room, person, act, voice, speech, word. I take these things as significant—as signifying the larger patterns and imperatives that drove the individuals who created these environments. To stare long and hard at one artifact is to be led in widening spirals out to the largest enterprises of the District, and when we do that, we see the ways in which the atomic culture it engendered and sought to control drew from precedents and prefigured so many of the underlying, and often unspoken, imperatives of our present.

Already we have begun this work, looking at that photograph of a man, a chair, a map. The task is the same with memos, with regulations, orders, letters, events: to apply techniques drawn from the analysis and interpretation of literature, the arts, anthropology, as well as the methods of the more traditional historian, to the scraps and fragments left to us.

Most of the materials of the Manhattan District are hidden in plain view, rendered insignificant by their sheer number, the chaotic condition of their origins, and their eventual dismemberment and storage, the inevitable encryption that results when security officials selectively declassify government documents and, having declassified them, dislocate and disguise the historical record. In each file there might be memos, letters, forms, plans—the residues of a powerful and complex bureaucracy. Most are written in a language hard to understand at best, often utterly incomprehensible without knowledge of physics, of business, of military codes, of all the surrounding contexts that make up the Manhattan District. But translation is not enough. The work of interpretation requires not just the sifting of facts but something close to a poetics of historical evidence. Then we can begin to understand what it was that Eisenhower feared as "the military-industrial complex": a new and immensely powerful consortium of institutions ranging across the worlds of business, government, and the military, devoted to self-perpetuation and eventual colonization of the American democracy. And we can see the sources of a painful environmental legacy that confronts us today and that will shadow us for decades, perhaps centuries, to come.

Today, the atomic spaces of the Manhattan Engineer District are legendary deserts of toxic horror. Nothing seems safe, no one immune. These are the physical traces of the Project: noxious regions, injured workers and bystanders, stockpiles of weapons and tanks of untreatable wastes. This is what is often called the poisonous legacy of the Manhattan Project. It is the stuff of news, and has been for some years. The newspapers tell of government-sponsored radiation poisoning—whether of retarded children in state homes, hospitalized patients in prestigious medical institutions, or "down-winders" breathing the air and drinking the milk tainted by the making and testing of atomic weapons. Politicians, reformers, and journalists have found, again and again, the fallout of the atomic era. The dangers that today threaten to eat a larger and larger share of federal dollars in order to isolate, neutralize, and rectify are the consequence of the larger constitution of the District as an ideological and social system, and also a system of belief.

The Manhattan Project lies at the center of our mythology, whether we know it or not. It is one of the origin myths of the atomic age. Nature and technology, science and faith, fear and arrogance: these dualities, central to our uneasy sense of ourselves, come together on the three sites of the Manhattan Engineer District, and in the enterprises of war and invention for which they were made.

Central it is, and yet the Project is also disappearing from the consciousness, and the conscience, of our cultural and moral life. We are in danger of forgetting. But if we do, it will be a peculiar forgetting, the sort that comes when things become so deeply imbedded in everyday discourse, and yet are so painful, ambiguous, and complex that they seem a part of the ground upon which we stand to survey the world and measure our place within it.

And so I have written this story of the spaces and places where the myth came into being, and of the people who transformed those spaces and then occupied a new sort of America, forged in wartime but extending far beyond it.

In the years since the Project ended, we might think that its special purpose and special nature had disappeared from around us, overwhelmed by peacetime prosperity. But this has not happened. Instead, the Manhattan District opened its fences and took down its walls, while exporting its own systems of belief, its artifacts, and its geography into the many streams of American life.

These are large and uneasy issues. They lie beneath the everyday circumstances that make up the atomic culture. For this is a story of lands, sacred lands, taken and altered. It is a story of men and women, buildings, work, pleasure, punishment, language, food, bodies, and out of all of these, consequences.

ACRES	TRACTS	INTEREST ACQUIRED	COST	STATUS ACQUISITION COMPLETED
3,599.70	35	FEE SIMPLE	$57,255.00	IN CONDEMNATION
45,666.80	1	PERMIT	NONE	4-8-43
40.00	1	LEASE	$600.00 P.A.	IN CONDEMNATION

INVENTION

N

COUNTY ___
DIVISION _ SO
DISTRICT __ A
SERVICE CO
USING AGEN
_25_ MILES
____ MILES

TRANSP

__ NONE
No. 4
NONE
NONE

ACRES OWNE
ACRES LEAS
ACRES LEAS
ACRES TRAN
ACRES DONA
ACRES BY PI

ACRES SOLD
ACRES TRANS
ACRES EXCHA
ACRES OTHER

PROJECT BOUND
TATE OR PROV
COUNTY LINE—
PROPERTY LINE
LAND-GRANT L
CITY, VILLAGE,
CEMETERY, SMA
TOWNSHIP & RA
SECTION LINE—

LOS ALAM
A
LOS A
RECOMMENDED
APPROVED
CAPT,
COMPILED W. S.
DATE BY

SANDOVAL

NEW MEXICO

STATE INDEX

A-4

SECRET

Deeds of property need to be read like poems. Legal descriptions, land appraisals are full of stories about the hollows and ridges, the mesas and mountains, the wastes and the rivers. Words, signatures, and seals on paper, they promise to define the legal boundaries of lands. Instead, they reinforce the imprecision of spaces, the way the lands flex and shrink over time. Beneath their dry words lie the histories and myths of lands, men, and women.

Consider this one, made for the U.S. military in the summer of 1942. "Gross Appraisal Proposed Site for Kingston Army Camp Kingston, Tennessee" is its title, its language that of officialdom, bland and bureaucratic:

> Pursuant to instructions from Lt. Col. M. J. O'Byrne, Director of Real Estate Section, War Department, Ohio River Division, Cincinnati, Ohio, and in compliance with a telephone request from Col. O'Brien, Washington, D.C. on July 23, 1942, the undersigned proceeded to Knoxville, Tennessee the same day for the purpose of making a Gross Appraisal of an area totaling 83,000 acres of which 3,000 acres is owned in fee simple or by permanent easement by Tennessee Valley Authority.[1]

ORIGINATION 1

A seventy-seven-word sentence, dry and precise, half-full of names and dates, it marks the beginning of something—of the Manhattan Engineer District, a military entity taking land, space, people, folkways, and stories, remaking them into a new and different physical and cultural landscape, from which a new weapon of war will emerge.

This particular opening sentence anticipates the story of the Manhattan Project as it is told by the U.S. Army. If we look closely, we notice that it moves in two directions—backward to the military origins of the District, and forward to the site itself; back again to the definite world of the telephone on the desk, and forward to the Tennessee town of Knoxville—hot and humid on that day, with the inevitable chance of rain. Its author doesn't yet dig into the earth to see its loaminess or seek stone markers where county lines are drawn. Instead, he pauses to describe a topography of power that maps his authority "to make a preliminary evaluation and study of the land together with all improvements thereon."[2]

The author is Orrin Thacker Jr., a land surveyor for the Army Corp of Engineers. The corps has sent him on a mission of surveillance, to get the lay of the land and assess the mood of its people. He knows what is coming—the expropriation of some or all this land, the eviction of its people, and its conversion to some military purpose.

Thacker is, in some sense, a local. He comes from the region, and there are Thackers living within the parcel he surveys. His charge is to walk the land and feel its value. His task is not entirely happy. And so we might see in this opening sentence some subtle reluctance to take responsibility for the chain of events his work will set in motion. He is doing this work "pursuant to instructions."

When Orrin Thacker's report reaches down into the specifics of his survey, the language shifts. He begins to walk along the boundaries of a portion of that ridged land you might see as you head out of Knoxville along U.S. 70, "Beginning at a point in the south right-of-way line of the Southern Railroad (Knoxville-Harriman Division) northeastwardly from Elverton in Roane County, Tennessee, where Oxier Creek and County Road crosses said railroad at the old Pop Edwards place; thence northeastwardly." It is a region about to be claimed for a "demolition range" and, much later, to be renamed.[3]

Already, in the first steps of this surveyor's trek, we sense the site resisting its situation in the world of military accuracy. Oxier Creek meanders along and its meanderings change from year to year with floods and droughts, the felling of timber along one farmer's boundary, or the damming of a tributary to provide a cattle draw—it is not yet a waterway under the control of the Army Corps of Engineers. A man, now dead, once a homesteader, has refused to loosen his hold on his lands; even Orrin Thacker, operating under the authority of Colonel O'Brien, must invoke his name in order to find the place where "Oxier Creek and County Road crosses said railroad."

Striving to provide an unerring physical description, only there for a day or two, Thacker has found it necessary to call on the locals for help. He has been drawn into the net of their language, of their kinship patterns. They have told him something of their story; he has accepted it and passed it on, thereby imbedding the cultural within in the topographic.

"The old Pop Edwards place" is not an exception. Every part of Thacker's land description mixes the precision of some landmarks with the fluidity of others; the spot "where State Highway #61 crosses said railroad" must compete with the point "where said highway crosses Poplar Creek at or near the place now or formerly owned by Frank Jones." One moves "on a line that follows the general direction of Brush Fork Creek . . . more or less to Dossett Station."

In the end, imprecision wins. After tracing a circuit that begins at a far southwestern point of a parallelogram roughly defined by railroads, creeks, farmhouses, county lines, highways, churches, and towns, after working in interrupted straight lines, but also "on a slight curve or arc to the right, crossing Clinch River through Poplar Creek Island and continuing in a northerly direction beyond in all approximately four miles," the surveyor finds himself having come "more or less, to the place of beginning, containing 83,000 acres, more or less."[4]

Official histories of the Manhattan Project tend to begin with scientific discovery and military necessity. The land and its people, their histories together, rarely appear, except perhaps as necessary sacrifices. But this is a history of land and people; what disappears from military history is at the center of our quest.

Already we have walked with Orrin Thacker along the boundaries of the first of three physical sites that were to be the locations of a vast new industrial production system. Located in eastern Tennessee, along the Clinch River above its absorption by the Tennessee, this site ran northeasterly approximately fifteen miles along state route 61, keeping a distance of about five miles from the nearest towns—Kingston (population 880), Harriman (population 5,620), Oliver Springs (population 855), and Clinton (population 2,761). The rocks that undergird this site were portions of a series of northeastward-trending formations of limestone, dolomite, shale, and sandstone, reported Thacker. The result was a set of "well-defined ridges" of sandstone; as Thacker slid down the ridges, his feet knocked off chips of soft stone, which caromed down the hillsides before reaching the limestone-defined narrow valleys through which wandered a host of small streams. These waterways poured into the Clinch, which tended first southeastward, then southwestward, then westward, defining three sides of the site. In places occupied for some time by the Clinch, rich bottomland fields had emerged, often flooded but excellent for croplands and pasture. The rest consisted of more or less rugged hills angling upward, some gradually, most sharply. Of the eighty-three thousand acres, fifty thousand were timberland—too steep to tolerate farming or grazing, or not yet cleared because of the general poverty of the region and the glacially slow pace of its development.[5]

About nine hundred separate tracts lay within the boundaries Thacker defined in the summer of 1942. Eleven hundred families lived there, most of them occupying single farms, a few occupying the tiny "hamlets" like Wheat, Tennessee, that clustered along the four state and federal roads paralleling the diagonal vector of the Clinch. Two railroads—the Southern, and the Louisville and Nashville—passed along the northern edge; the L&N dipped into the site at its northernmost point.[6]

Significantly, more dead than living souls occupied what was to become the Clinton Engineer Works of the Manhattan Engineer District. Thacker found forty-eight cemeteries within the space. The bodies of some six thousand men, women, and children were interred there, and there were more (Thacker estimated as many as a thousand) in inaccessible areas, in family plots on farms and parcels of land. Like "the old Pop Edwards place," these burial grounds signified the encrustations of tradition and history that comprised the culture of this place—not yet even an official site, still made up of places claimed by historical events, natural transformations, and human incursions. Like the living occupants, these pasts would have to be defeated, uprooted and moved, and it would be a costly process, only marginally successful.

In the back of his report, Thacker added an appendix. It contained between eleven and thirty numbered photographs he had made or assembled during his surveillance.[7]

These were pictures that evoked things forbidden in the written text. They showed an industrious farming region, with traditional clapboard farmhouses dating back into the nineteenth century, surrounded by large barns and outbuildings. Picture after picture showed fields of rye, of hay, of tobacco, their custodians standing in their midst, harvesting, sampling, or posing with examples of the crops. The composite image presented a prosperous region, rich in community values and traditions—a cohesive traditional American community, full of the symbols of a nostalgic American rural past.[8]

Photo 11011-C shows a man in a shirt and tie standing in a deep field of head-tall rye. Number 7692-F is a scene of agricultural richness (fig. 2), two white men pausing in the work of forking hay from one of a row of haystacks. Typed on the bottom: "River Bottom Hay Field—Knox County Near Reservoir Area." Number 11006-E shows an open-sided structure made of poles and roofed with galvanized roofing sheets. In front of it, a ceramic jug sits upon a primitive table. Inside, in the shadows, a man in work clothes drinks from a dipper. Beyond the springhouse, two men and a boy rest; behind them, we can see the good fields and a well-made barn. A horse grazes by the springhouse, shaded by the same tree that protects the structure. Thacker inscribed this picture, "Numerous Good Springs Abound in Area."

These are not neutral captions. They collaborate with the idyllic pictures contained

FIG. 2 *Field of Rye—Roane County*. Photographer unknown (Orrin Thacker?). Courtesy National Archives.

within the photographs' edges. The resulting images resonate with each other, invoking the mythologies of American rural life, the land and its dwellers—myths that reach back to the origins of the American experiment.

The District's plans for the region had nothing to do with these webs of culture, history, and myth. The area was selected because it was in the direct service area of the Tennessee Valley Authority. Army officers seeking a site for a giant, supersecret enterprise looked at the TVA as both a resource and a precedent. At its simplest, the TVA offered the huge amounts of electrical power that scientists and engineers were predicting would be required to alchemize raw uranium ore into weapons-grade material. The Tennessee site seemed particularly appropriate because the TVA had already done so much of the work necessary to this new endeavor. It had appropriated land, resettled peoples, adjusted a backward population to a new future as industrial workers laboring in factories whose processes they would never understand and whose products would never be theirs to own or use.

A final note in Thacker's report reflected the tension between two pictures of the region and, by extension, of American values more generally—between a pastoral, individualistic, democratic past, and a bureaucratic, efficient, authoritarian and technocratic future. Thacker reported that the residents of his landscape "seemed anxious and eager to cooperate" in the war effort; from this, he concluded that "there will be no difficulty encountered in acquiring property in this area." But he also worried that the District's policies would do harm to these people and their landscape. He urged the District to find appraisers "familiar and sympathetic with the people in this area."[9]

Or perhaps his comment reflected his allegiance to his employers. Perhaps he understood how easily the District might turn eagerness into anger, docility into resistance. In either case, his comment was premonitory. The District represented the new America, but the old America still retained its powers.

Due west of the Tennessee hills, the land flattens for a time. In the summer of 1942, one might travel west on U.S. 70, past Nashville and the end of Tennessee to U.S. Route 66, and then into other states: first Arkansas, then Oklahoma, and into Texas. By the end of those long days and nights, the land has utterly changed—it is flat in a new way, and even the cattle differ from those grazing the hills along Black Oak Ridge. The air, still hot, is dry and full of wind blowing upward from Mexico. Then, after Amarillo, one enters New Mexico.

In the fall of 1942, Maj. John H. Dudley was entrusted by a consortium of military, government, and scientific authorities with finding a site upon which to assemble a small, closed scientific colony where some eighty scientists could work in uninterrupted fashion on the theories and practicalities behind a new weapon to be manufactured back in Tennessee. Dudley arrived at Los Alamos, New Mexico, by a circuitous route; he was looking through the West because his superiors had determined that the West was remote, its spaces large, the population sparse, the land cheap, the whole of it pockmarked by regions ripe for acquisition and development, where "the ownership and estimated value of land and speed of acquisition" offered the potential for a quick incursion, a successful land sortie.[10]

Dudley and his superiors were only the latest in a long string of warriors who had come to conquer the region. To look at the site one might have wondered what was so valuable about it. It was stony ground, made of dust and ashes from a gigantic volcanic explosion hundreds of thousands of years before, carved into islands by the force of rivers, covered by tough grasses on the flatter lands and Ponderosa pines along the slopes, and chiseled into bare rock faces where erosion left slopes too sharp for growth.[11]

Dudley had come here seeking a contradiction. The site the District needed had to be "inaccessible," yet convenient to scientists and their families, bulldozers, electrical generators, even cyclotrons. It had to be a place on the edge between wilderness and civilization—a place on the frontier.[12]

Dudley's excursions to the regions north and west of Santa Fe took him into an area gripped by the romance of the West and the mythology of the frontier. In the 1880s, publicists for the Santa Fe Railroad boasted that their trains ran through these lands at night to spare the sensitive rider the indignity of staring out at its endless wastes. By the end of the 1890s, the influence of the hotelier Fred Harvey had changed all that. Harvey arranged for Indians dressed in breech-clouts to pose for the Kodaks of tourists bound to or from the Grand Cañon of the Colorado or the Painted Desert. By the end of the First World War, when a neurasthenic Easterner named Edith Warner first escaped into "the mesa and the aspen all golden on the Sangres," the area had become dotted with guest ranches offering redemption from urban illnesses, for a fee. In Santa Fe one might pause to taste the exotica of the expatriate life, where escapees of the East, artists and writers and photographers (and also "artists" and "writers" and "photographers"), had bought adobe dwellings and tried their best to decorate them as if they were Pueblo Indian dwellings at San Ildefonso or Acoma or Taos.[13]

Edith Warner was the quintessential transplanted romancer. Driven from the East by ill-health—weakness, depression, the symptoms of a lingering mental disorder of unpredictable prognosis—she eventually settled at age thirty-five in an abandoned house on the Rio Grande River, where the Denver and Rio Grande Railroad's short-line tourist trains stopped to drop off freight for the Los Alamos Ranch School for Boys. Between 1928 and 1942, she became a fixture of the region, gradually turning the house into a living museum of the aesthete's Southwest.

Insinuating herself into the insular Pueblo community at San Ildefonso, Warner went native. Warner's dreams—"to bridge the gulf of racial heritage" and have the Pueblos call her "one of us," to enter a pantheistic landscape where mesas became "ancient beings who have seen much," to "feel very small and of little worth in the presence of great spaces and deep silence, but not afraid"—were the fantasies of an expatriate on this picturesque frontier.[14]

The Los Alamos mesa that rose above Edith Warner's home was, for her and for many expatriates like her, a landscape of spiritual power, the embodiment of that passive merging with nature that they had sought. Paradoxically, it was also the location for another redemptive fantasyland: the Los Alamos Ranch School. Founded in 1917, it was the brainchild of Ashley Pond. City-bred in Detroit ("a delicate boy," his daughter called him), Pond grew up in boarding schools, the disappointing scion of a wealthy and driven father. An enlistee with Teddy Roosevelt's Rough Riders during the Spanish-American War, Pond collapsed before seeing action and was sent West "to recover his health."[15]

Pond's life seemed destined to burlesque that of his erstwhile commanding officer. He concluded that his destiny was to found a school where "city boys from wealthy families . . . could regain their heritage of outdoor wisdom at the same time that they were being prepared for college and the responsibilities which their position in life demanded."[16]

To run his school, Pond found an able counterpart in A. J. Connell, a man of action who shared his vision. Connell's background lay within that same strain of American masculine mythos. He had been a forest ranger, an administrator for the Boy Scouts; he had a strong belief in discipline, in the virtues of hardship, uniforms, horses, and collective work. His boys shared studies; they slept outside in screened communal sleeping porches the year round. At times they awoke to find their cots dusted with snow. Upon arrival, each boy was requisitioned a horse, his responsibility for the duration of his education. At the Ranch School, students wore the summer Boy Scout uniform—short-sleeved shirt, shorts, knee socks, sensible shoes, a neckerchief—throughout the year, though the temperature rarely rose above seventy and occasionally dipped below zero. Periodically, they dressed in full "cow-boy regalia" to be shown off to visitors or parents on visiting days and graduation. On camping and pack trips, Connell sometimes ordered that his charges ride, work, and sleep naked.[17]

The boys' experience at Los Alamos would leave them comfortable with the underlying philosophy of masculine pantheism shared by many of the most prestigious institutions of male America. And Connell's acolytes were destined for those institutions. Costs at the school kept all but the most respectable of upper-class families out of the tiny clique—tuition and housing ran $2,400 per year in the Depression thirties, and every boy was required to buy a riding outfit for $380.[18]

The Los Alamos School combined its manly pantheism with a harsher and more mechanistic ideology drawn from the factories and cities. Connell had a deep commitment not only to woodcraft but to industrial management practices. Like the assembly-line factories of the urbanized East and Midwest, the Los Alamos Ranch School became a production facility, its every activity broken down into independent units, to be performed with maximum efficiency, under the omniscient eye of the supervisor. And this practice extended beyond the machine of the school to the machine of the boy. A rigorous program of monthly testing measured each part of the body, and the results, computed on the basis of the Taylor system of industrial efficiency, were posted to foster "a spirit of competitiveness."[19]

This man-as-machine aspiration might seem oddly out of place for a site where boys farmed their own small plots of land, rode horseback, and slept outdoors. But the larger ideology of which Connell's small school was but a part drew these inconsistencies into a whole. The pantheism, rural nostalgia, desire for transcendental experience, and Thoreau-like struggle to achieve a simplified relation to life were, at the Ranch School, forms of preparation, rather than the goal itself (fig. 3). Inducted into manhood, Connell's boys would leave the atavistic realm of the Ranch School and go forth to the mechanistic world of their fathers' urban factories and banks and stock brokerages. As a Ranch School recruitment brochure put it, "the speed of modern life in and near the large centers of population depletes the nervous energy of youth— that energy on which, in the next generation, they and their country must depend."

FIG. 3 Two Los Alamos Ranch School students ride the high meadows. T. Harmon Parkhurst. Courtesy Los Alamos Historical Museum.

The school would replace that energy and teach the boys how to move into a more harmonious relation with the machine-world. Is it any surprise that a number of the officers in the Manhattan Engineer District would be graduates of its tiny, adolescent predecessor?[20]

The rest of the privately owned land, slightly more than half of it, belonged not to privileged expatriates but to twenty-nine Pueblo and Hispano farmers, sheepherders, and ranchers with small holdings, primarily acquired by homesteading. Because they were not "authentic," in nostalgic Anglo terms—that is, not reservation-dwelling, potterymaking Indians, but small-time capitalists, cultural halfbreeds who eked out their livings on marginal lands—these residents of the mesa hardly existed in the Western mythology invented by the emigrés who surrounded them. The better lands of the valleys and the flatlands by the river were already occupied or leased to more prosperous, mostly white ranchers. The arduous process of herding sheep and cattle up into these summer grazing lands, the primitive huts and "dilapidated log shacks, barns and fair fences" (to quote from Manhattan District appraiser Bernie White's *Preliminary Real Estate Report*) that the small ranchers shared with their sheep and dogs, the crude diet to which they resorted, were all byproducts of poverty and marginality, not conscious choices. And though they formed the majority of residents expatriated by the acquisition of Site Y, as the Los Alamos location was known to insiders, Major Dudley barely noted them in assessing the locale.[21]

Then there was the final, and largest, landholder of all: the federal government. Bernie White's appraisal, released on November 21, 1942, never detailed the area already under government ownership, though that was one of the primary advantages cited by his superiors when they directed him to the region. The government owned more than fifty thousand of the fifty-four thousand acres needed by Dudley and White's employers, all of it part of the Santa Fe National Forest and administered by the U.S. Forest Service as timberland of such marginal value that no one could be persuaded to cut it.[22]

Reading White's report, one might gain only the barest insight into the interlocked relationship between the marginal landholders and the national lands. For the Forest Service, lands weren't pristine stands of timber. They were grazing lands, and access to them required forest grazing permits that went to the owners of property immediately surrounding the government's land. All of the federal land up there was claimed by grazing permits, permits held by the Ranch School, by Anchor Ranch (the other large, white-owned homestead on the mesa), by the twenty-nine landholders, and by others who had managed to win permits. To take these lands would be to remove from these permit holders a significant part of their livelihood (in some cases all of it), for the alternative to low-cost grazing permits was to lease grazing rights from the Baca Land Company. This company controlled most of the surrounding lands, offered the rancher's equivalent to sharecropping (a ruthless Anglo form of the old Spanish scheme known in the region as *partido*), and as a result had already taken over most of the small ranches that had depended upon it for grazing grounds. White estimated the value of the Forest Service permits at $7,600, but his estimate was far below the actual worth.[23]

Three other parcels of land appeared on the appraisal (fig. 4). At the eastern edge of the site was Bandelier National Monument, home to a rich trove of archaeological

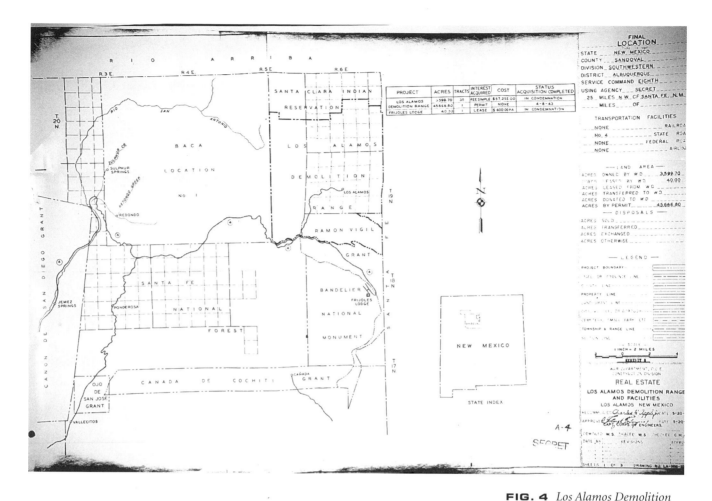

FIG. 4 *Los Alamos Demolition Range and Facilities.* Manhattan District History, National Archives.

remnants. A second corner of the site, to the southeast, cut off a portion of a sacred Pueblo burial ground. Unlike the cemeteries that dotted the Oak Ridge site, however, this burial ground received no further attention from the appraiser. No funds were allocated for the purchase of this area, nor for the moving of graves or ceremonial objects.[24]

Finally, there was the game refuge. The U.S. Forest Service had designated the mesa a game protection area, limiting hunting rights and monitoring wildlife activity. "Deer, bear, and wild turkeys are abundant," White reported. The game refuge, the sacred burial grounds, the archaeological sites: all of these were physical extensions of the more ephemeral, and more powerful, histories that permeated every part of the topography. Neither White nor Dudley—nor, eventually, the physicist and project director J. Robert Oppenheimer or his military superior, Gen. Leslie R. Groves—took any further notice of these historical and ecological functions of the site. None of the reports discussed the potential effects of sudden, extensive urban development, or weapons development and experimentation, on the landscape, the ecology, the natural and human histories of the Pajarito Plateau. These advance men were looking for a site that could be isolated by a perimeter fence and, by such isolation, disentangled from its surroundings so thoroughly that the site could disappear from human memory for the duration of the war.

But Dudley and the others missed much with their intent focus on a landscape of secrecy. Los Alamos was both virgin land and settled territory. It offered the illusion of free land, but the appearance deceived. Like Oak Ridge, it was both topography and landscape.

There is another American West far outside the picturesque pine-scented mesas of New Mexico's central regions. Head west and you would come to a place where the annual rainfall is far beneath Los Alamos's 18.5 inches. There the land flattens and its breaks are more violent. Holes open up in the earth; one comes across them unexpectedly, traveling across the flatlands. The geologists and geographers of the twentieth century knew this region as the Great Basin. A century before, a portion of this land also had a more dramatic and legendary name: it was the Great American Desert. This was the stony hell through which one passed seeking the green paradise of the Pacific coast. Explorers of the nineteenth century debated its usefulness; encountering this wide band of inhospitable terrain, a few argued for its potential once people came to tame it, or its utility as scenery. Most declared it wasteland.

Few then could imagine how far north the desert ran—how its diagonal stretch reached through Utah and Nevada, into Idaho and Oregon, upward into Washington, all the way to the Canadian border. Near the top edge was the Columbia River, fast flowing, icy cold. As the Columbia heads west toward the sea, defining much of the southern border of the state of Washington, on either side are sagebrush flats, some with small stands of windblown trees; if you followed it upstream, past Kennewick, beyond where it is fed by the Snake and the Yakima Rivers, traveling the circuitous state roads built to carry cattle and crops to market, you would reach the Grand Coulee Dam. Between Kennewick and the Grand Coulee is a further stretch of the Great Basin called the Yakima Valley—west of the Rockies, east of Mount Rainier and the Cascades—where the winds blow in great sweeps, lifting dust and the topsoil of failed dry farmers, and you may drive for an hour without seeing more than a dozen trees.

In the wide, shallow peninsula formed by the Columbia's riverbed, the blacker topsoil of the valley gives way to sandy sagebrush country. In the eighteenth century, it was home to a tribe of Indians known as the Chemnapum. The tribe gathered wild vegetables in the spring, harvested whitefish on the Yakima, and retreated to the mountains in the summer. Probably the first European-American to see this section of the country was Meriwether Clark, who left the rest of the Lewis and Clark expedition to reconnoitre northward. He saw nothing to impress him with the possibilities of settlement and returned to the expedition.[25]

By the end of the nineteenth century, most of Lewis and Clark's territory had been occupied. But settlement and dry farming did not succeed here, despite recurrent bursts of optimistic predictions. The rainfall, less than nine inches a year, came mostly in the winter, often in the form of mist or snow.[26]

Those who attempted to dry farm found the results exactly opposite those predicted by Cyrus Thomas, the infamous U.S. Geological Survey agronomist who announced (in a widely quoted passage of the official USGS report for 1873) that "the Americans bring the rains with them"—a statement quickly recast by journalists and boosters as "rain follows the plow." Instead, deep plowing broke up the surface soil and, after seeding, the small shoots would come up only to wither in the brutal, rainless sunny months. Then the winds came. Routinely blowing as high as forty miles an hour, they would sweep across the furrows, picking up the soil and blowing it into giant clouds of dust. Few settlers survived there for long, and those who did treated the region as grazing land. One homesteader reported in her diary the difficulties—tomato plants hard-frozen in late March, when the temperature in the kitchen of her farmhouse stood at twenty degrees; winds so strong they knocked over the windmill, breaking the mounting bolts and bending the pipe over on itself.[27]

Irrigation changed all that. When a man named Haynes floated down the Columbia from Vantage in a rowboat sometime in the early 1890s, he saw a possibility for settlement if the waters of the Columbia could be transported over the high banks and onto the land inside that inverted capital C between Umatilla and Wenatchee.[28]

The first larger-scale irrigation projects began in 1903 and included programs of the Northern Pacific Company and the Federal Reclamation Agency. But these grand schemes bore little fruit. Instead, it was a group of entrepreneurs, led by Judge Cornelius H. Hanford, that brought water and farming together in the region.[29]

Hanford, Washington, was the booster community owned and operated by the Hanford Power and Irrigation Company. Following the lead of the Northern Pacific, the company recruited businesses and, where none could be recruited, ran the essential and profitable ones with salaried employees. Beginnings were small—in January 1908, the only building in Hanford was a long barracks housing the irrigation workers who were putting in the ditch and pipe. By April of that same year, the first issue of the first local newspaper, the Hanford *Columbia*, described two hotels, a livery stable, and a variety of businesses. Judge Hanford's plan was to develop the entire region, profiting from land sales, from irrigation charges, from running the businesses, and from speculating in the rising value of lands as settlement ate up the best acreage. His rivals in the White Bluffs Company, an enterprise begun by his former business associates, competed on all these grounds, founding the town of White Bluffs at about the same time.[30]

Advertising throughout the Northwest, the rival companies touted an idyllic landscape combining a dry, sunny climate—perfect for those with health problems—with the economic opportunities vital to attracting dreamers and utopians of every stamp. The land companies presented the region as ideal for intensively irrigated fruit orchards, and for high-priced exotic crops like peppermint and melons. Settlers could buy townsites for their homes, and separate areas nearer the existing irrigation ditches for their orchards and fields. Many who arrived that first year lived in tents while they planted their fruit trees and waited for the water to run down the ditches.[31]

Nothing came quite that easily; by the end of 1909, problems had forced consolidation of the two rival companies, capital reorganization of the resulting corporation, damage payouts to landowners, and reconstruction of many of the ditches. Once they received their water, the farmers had their abilities tested to the limit. Many had never farmed before; many failed to take the advice of the irrigation companies that they plant exotic fruit, choosing apple orchards instead—apples were, after all, the staple orchard fruit of the state. Often undercapitalized, usually inexperienced, these farmers saw their dreams of flourishing farms and a new life disappear.[32]

In 1919, with the end of World War I, the area found itself once again the focus of grand land schemes, this time by the state of Washington, which promised a utopia where veterans "and also industrial workers, and other American citizens desiring a rural life, may settle upon and become owners of small improved farms and farm laborers' allotments." The government provided land, irrigation pumps, deep wells, outbuildings, even houses.[33]

The White Bluffs–Hanford Land Settlement Project was founded upon the Western version of the yeoman myth that runs through American culture from Jefferson to the country-and-western present: of the small farmer's fruitful (and profitable) settlement of the nation in small holdings, where children played behind white picket fences after classes in one-room schoolhouses and before the chores, while mother baked pies and father plowed the rich fields or tended the apple-laden orchards. The program even promised something approaching guaranteed wealth to its participants. It published a leaflet quoting W. H. Keal of White Bluffs, who reported that he averaged twelve tons of potatoes per acre, harvested one hundred crates of strawberries from a third of an acre at $3.50 per crate, and raised one and a half tons of onions on one-eighth of an acre. The combination of ready land, readymade quarters, and the assurance of abundant water, combined with the testimonials of men like Keal, drew a wild variety of settlers.[34]

The "soldier settlement project" (as locals called the scheme) ended in 1926, when the state of Washington auctioned off its final portions of the land and its share in the irrigation district and water rights. In the end, the scheme had not been as successful as its marketing promised. Many of the plots lay empty. City dwellers hungering for escape, veterans buying their first plots of land, discontented failures at other trades and in other regions: these were not the ideal pioneers for a region requiring patience, expertise, and endless work to make a go of it. The fortunate ones had tended to combine their small "soldier farms" into larger plots of eighty acres or more, hiring laborers to tend and pick the fruit.[35]

By the onset of the Depression, the site supported a strange hodgepodge of land uses. Still-productive twenty-acre "soldiers' plots" checkerboarded with abandoned apple orchards where the water limits set by the Hanford Company had turned out to be insufficient for the porous soil, or where inept farmers had destroyed their own trees. Other areas, never developed, remained flat sagebrush land, mimicking the broad expanses of rangeland that predominated in the regions beyond the reach of irrigation canals. Three small towns—White Bluffs to the north, Hanford in the center, and Richland to the south—served as nodes for the region. The native Indian tribe, the Wanapum, continued to traverse between wilderness and settlements, working as migrant laborers during harvest periods, fishing for whitefish on the Yakima, traveling to the mountains in August to fish and to pick and preserve huckleberries, moving from one to another of their inherited tribal grounds while still remaining at the margins of white culture.[36]

By 1933, the Depression threatened the region once again. The irrigation district had to be saved by New Deal programs; individual farmers retrenched or retreated. Adelaide Kolar remembered her father's struggles as one of the "industrial workers" drawn to the agrarian project (he had been a coal miner). The Depression required him (and many others) to take a job in town in order to pay his irrigation costs. Annette Heriford recalled that her father worked as a guard for the irrigation district to supplement his dwindling orchard income.[37]

Harry Anderson's father, Edmund, owned a plot about a mile and a half from White Bluffs. He also operated the White Bluffs movie house. During the thirties, the elder Anderson purchased a movie camera and began to make "shorts" of events in the area to be shown along with the national releases at his movie house. His shorts featured a number of community rituals: groundbreaking for the Community Hall; local picnics, especially on the Fourth of July; races (including three-legged races, dads' races, kids' races, and family contests, obviously all part of various public celebrations); swimming on "The Bathing Beaches of the Mighty Columbia" (as his title card joked); men working together building an irrigation viaduct.[38]

The small size of the community, the relative hardships shared by all, the economic straits of both the region and its occupants, all resulted in a tight-knit mutual-aid society memorialized in Ed Anderson's movies. Anderson didn't just run the theater and make the local movies; he also drove the school bus. One man recalled that his father had helped to build the Hanford school; he himself, while still a child, worked with his father laying the floor of the gymnasium. Orchard operators were also ministers, school teachers, county commissioners—virtually any job that might be considered to benefit the community in general was a part of the community work shared out by all.[39]

The thirties became the forties, and Anderson's movies reflected the broader transformation of the region as war approached and the economy recovered. The resolution of financing problems by the Priest Rapids Irrigation District meant a new stability for the region. Profits from electricity sales enabled the district to line the rest of its ditches, making irrigation pumping more efficient and water proportionally less expensive. The failure of the apple growers had provided a telling lesson for those who remained and those who took up abandoned lands; now the predominant crops were the higher-yielding exotic fruit, like cherries and apricots, or other cash crops like mint and herbs. Fruit growers, like all farmers in the region, benefited when the Milwaukee Line built a new spur, guaranteeing easy access to markets. The war, with its demand for increased agricultural production, promised a new era of prosperity. There were better prices for crops but also severe competition for fewer and fewer laborers, as the workforce was siphoned off, into the armed forces and into high-paying defense industries. For many farmers and orchardists, the war meant higher hopes, but it did not necessarily bring them back to farms and orchards they had temporarily abandoned or cut back in darker times. Many who had found wage-jobs in Pasco or Kennewick continued to work there, reassured that, when the time came, they could return to their farms and orchards, but unable yet to move back. For family orchardists, maintaining the orchards often depended upon sons now drawn off to war or to the shipyards along the Washington and Oregon coast. Many people remained in town, leaving the orchards underattended and the fields fallow, waiting the end of war and the return of sons and daughters for whom the lands would be a patrimony.[40]

Army site-selection officials arrived at Hanford in the late fall of 1942; their picture of the region differed markedly from that of the residents. The surveillance of Hanford occurred in stages. The first took place in committees, where representatives from the Du Pont corporation, the scientific community, and the military argued out the site-selection criteria—pondering questions of electrical power availability, contiguous square area, access to rail freight lines, low land costs, distance from communities "greater than 1,000." At the next stage, the selection process moved to local offices of the district engineers, where low-level employees of the Army Corps of Engineers wrestled with the difference between abstract requirements and actual lands: how to determine just what *was* a community; should White Bluffs and Hanford be separated or consolidated? And then the officials inspected the chosen lands.

To those who had lived on the land for decades, "the site" lay not as one might see it from the air, but as an accretion of memories and symbols of ownership, of love and hope, failure and tragedy, of everyday sounds redolent of significance, like the rustle of grasses, or the crack of ice a homesteader heard one spring morning when "the thermometer in the kitchen read 20."

For them, 1942 was a time of hope and possibility. Bessie Whitwer spoke of the stability promised by the community and its visible symbols: "a good grade school, high school, two churches, a recreation hall, grange, tavern, hotel, two general stores, a post office and a fire bell."[41] Esther Krug recalled that "our father shared with other pioneers of the Valley an unshakable faith that big things were bound to happen there someday."[42] Economic circumstances confirmed this, in the small events of higher crop yields and better prices, of more money available for dry goods and for theater tickets at Ed Anderson's movie house, of newcomers moving into the region and making fallow plots successful. Jerome Clark's family was finally "doing better; our soft fruit was giving us income enough to put in pressure water, sink and cabinets" in the kitchen and bathroom of their house.[43]

The cold touch of white porcelainized cast iron on a new kitchen sink, the hush of water coming from faucets: these are realities of great power to those who experience them. But the physical evidence honored by the representatives of corps and corporation came from a different order of magnitude, from the monuments produced by the power projects that sat roughly equidistant upriver and down from the residents' hardwon Priest Rapids dam and its irrigation district.

Upstream was the Grand Coulee Dam; begun in 1933 and completed in 1941, it was the largest public works project in the world, dwarfing even the pyramids. It was designed and built by the Reclamation Agency, inheritors of the mantle of the 1902 Reclamation Act and lately committed to generating power as well as providing irrigation. Downstream from Hanford was the Bonneville Dam, begun and completed at about the same time as the Grand Coulee but different from it in many respects. Certainly it was not as grandiose—it was not meant to symbolize the entire New Deal philosophy in a single concrete monument to the conquering of nature by technology. Instead, it was a more matter-of-fact project, a low hydroelectric dam, built by the Army Corps of Engineers.[44]

The two dams did share with each other, and with the Tennessee Valley Authority, a bureaucratic vision of lands and people that was fundamentally at odds with the picture held by residents of those regions. This conflict between American utopias was at the heart of all three sites of the Manhattan District. At Hanford and at Oak Ridge, the embodiment of the new prototype could be found in a physical sweep of immense dams, holding back the flow of rivers, producing power, transforming the land. This was a vision seen from above—far above.

FIG. 5 *View across the Plain, Looking Southeast toward Hanford.* Manhattan District History, National Archives.

Officials came to look over Hanford from an airplane droning over the site. Peering down through the window of a small-engine plane, Col. Franklin T. Matthias, reconnoitering for the Army Corps of Engineers, could not observe the communities of Hanford, White Bluffs, and Richland. He flew high above the settled farmlands where ranchers and fruit growers had invested so heavily in the reality and the myth of their blooming desert. But it was winter; no apple trees bloomed, no crops waved gently in the wind, no children played and swam along the banks of the Columbia. What Matthias saw conformed to the photographs the appraisers had made (fig. 5)— he wrote in his report that it was "an area with almost no people, very undeveloped." Matthias's conclusion that the site was "perfect" assured that it would be selected. On January 2, 1943, the area engineer sent out his report declaring Hanford the chosen location for a plutonium production facility of as-yet unimagined magnitude. "The entire area," he wrote in his report, "is sandy waste land with no vegetation or trees other than sagebrush, [is] locally known as 'scab-land' and is valueless."[45]

The Manhattan Engineer District was a military entity. It was a subset of the Corps of Engineers, U.S. Army. Its origins reflected its complex mandate: to conquer not just political enemies, but physical ones; to turn scientific discovery into a tool for the control of nature, and the control of nature into a tool for war.

The District's ideological antithesis was the scientific community that helped to bring it into being, the loosely organized collective of physicists and mathematicians who recognized in an obscure set of theories, experiments, and developments the possibility of a new and unimaginably powerful weapon of war.

The world of modern "pure" science, and particularly particle physics, evolved in a sort of blissful, excited isolation from the realms of the useful. A particular problem might look "promising": what dictated the quality of promise was determined by the peer group, by the suggestions of one's mentor, by the internalized dictates of the discipline, inculcated through the entire experience of the academy within which one had been trained. Research moved *away* from each new discovery rather than toward a practical end.

Mathematics and physics were the purest of the pure sciences—least connected to the worlds of pragmatics, of production and consumption, of engineering and industry, or of material progress as it appeared in the advertisements of corporations like Du Pont.

INCORPORATION   2

The American physicist Richard Feynman came to understand this well when, graduating from MIT in the late 1930s, he went job hunting: "At that time nobody knew what a physicist even was, and there weren't any positions in industry for physicists. Engineers, OK; but physicists—nobody knew how to use them. It's interesting that very soon, after the war, it was the exact opposite."[1]

Feynman ended up getting a job as a "research chemist" instead. Like most of his comrades, however, Feynman lasted only a short time in the world of products and profits. His understanding of what was important, "interesting," "rewarding," had been determined already, and the world of metallurgy and a life spent calculating the profit potential in electroplating Bakelite seemed utterly bizarre to him.[2]

Feynman was an American; Ernest Rutherford, first geographer of the atom, was a New Zealander; Enrico Fermi, earliest explorer of uranium's disintegration, was an Italian. These were individuals united not by physical proximity but rather by ties that connected them in subcommunities and kept these subcommunities in contact with one another, enabling the chain reaction of ideas and experiments that comprised what is, after the fact, described by popular commentators as "scientific progress," but might more accurately be termed the cultural geography of pure science.[3]

Central to the beliefs of those within this scientific culture was the notion that information should be transmitted freely and without mediation. This axiom sped the process of scientific activity; it also placed the culture of science above all other allegiances for its members. Science transcended national obligation, religious affiliation, political beliefs—for none of these could interfere with the transmission of one's discoveries or theories. Without this openness and freedom of information, the scientific process must necessarily slow to a crawl, for so much of it depended on unplanned connection between otherwise unlikely participants across national and disciplinary boundaries, across gulfs of age, protocol, and professional standing rarely imaginable in other realms, like business or the military. As Robert Oppenheimer regretfully reported in his farewell speech to the scientists at Los Alamos in November 1945, "secrecy strikes at the very root of what science is and what it is for."[4]

The physicist Otto Frisch's tale of the discovery of nuclear fission typifies the way the community of physicists operated before the imposition of government organization and control. The story involved physicists from Austria, Germany, Denmark, Great Britain, Russia, and America, linked by kinship, mentor-student relationships, simple physical proximity, organized university research teams, friendship, and casual contact. Frisch was in Denmark working with a constellation of scientists including Niels Bohr. Arriving in Sweden to visit his aunt, Lise Meitner, for a holiday, he was just in time to listen to a letter she'd received from her German research team concerning the strange behavior of certain substances. (Meitner read it to him while he was cross-country skiing, as she trudged along beside him.) From his own research work with Bohr, Frisch was able to suggest that the cause of these phenomena might be the disintegration of uranium nuclei. Calculating quickly on scraps of paper while still in the snowy woods, he and Meitner applied Einstein's famous $E = mc^2$ (which Meitner had first heard from Einstein himself during a colloquium in Berlin more than a decade before) to determine that the hypothesis was feasible.[5]

Two days later, Frisch took the idea to Bohr, who told him to coauthor a paper on the discovery immediately. Frisch and Meitner worked out the paper by telephone between Copenhagen and Stockholm; Frisch coined the term "nuclear fission" upon the advice of an American biologist he ran into, and the paper was printed in the British journal *Nature.* Even before the article appeared, American physicists confirmed the conclusions, having learned of the idea in part from reading the early experimental data that had impelled Meitner and Frisch and in part from hearsay through Bohr's son, to whom Frisch had "casually talked" of his work. But Frisch pointed out that "in all this excitement we had missed the most important point: the chain reaction." Frisch's conversations in Copenhagen after the fact drove his Danish colleague Christian Moller to propose that concept. But Bohr then added the hypothesis that there could be no uncontrolled chain reaction, thereby temporarily scotching the notion of an atomic explosion; his eminent stature held sway, delaying what would later prove to be the basic argument making possible the atomic bomb.[6]

In the telling, the process of discovery seems almost chaotic. But the entire operation followed the dictates of pure science in its prewar state. Official and formal chains of communication vied with hearsay and conversation to move information across great distances and to connect otherwise disparate investigators and teams. Loyalty lay with the discipline of scientific questioning itself, and with those who served it most passionately and well. Matters of pragmatics, of usefulness or applicability, entered rarely if at all into the calculus that drove all these figures to make their contributions.

This moment in the history of pure physics, with its metaphysical geography, its radical democratic social system, its complete aversion to secrecy, and its rejection of practical goals in favor of a more exciting and more surprising process of discovery, was about to end. The war caused that signal change in the world of the pure scientists. The arrival of the Nazis in power increasingly threatened the university as a center for intellectual activity while destroying the information systems that held utopian science together. But the assault was especially vicious as it applied to scientists, and physicists particularly. As the totalitarian regimes of Europe geared up for war, they concurrently began to direct their scientific enterprises away from theory and toward the eminently practical questions of weaponry production and industrial efficiency.[7]

By the mid-thirties, wholesale dismissal of scientists and intellectuals from the universities had given way to even more fearful conditions. Whether scientists or stonemasons, Jews were disappearing from their homes and businesses, many killed or sent to the concentration camps. As early as the summer of 1933, an American scientist reported that even the protected were terrified: "In Munich," he wrote in a letter home, "everyone says not to speak too loudly or one will land in Dachau."[8]

The conditions under which the curious utopia of pure science had come to flourish quickly disappeared. Appointments at institutions rapidly became political; the direction of one's research was no longer determined by curiosity or its results judged by internal criteria of the discipline. Military needs dictated the status of research. Political bureaucracies ordered research in certain directions, with set goals in mind. Communication with other scientists was proscribed. Seminars and symposia were canceled or their topics redirected. Borders between countries closed. To escape the new conditions, to rediscover their utopia, many of the Europeans came to America.[9]

Pure science and America seemed at first a perfect fit. As Daniel Boorstin has described it, America in the twentieth century was a place of "everywhere communities" that "floated over time and space" and "could include anyone without his effort and sometimes without his knowing. Men were divided not by their regions or their roots, but by objects and notions that might be anywhere and could be everywhere." This description corresponds closely to the metaphysical geography of science, and not by coincidence, for the forces that impelled modernist science into its new geography also facilitated the creation of twentieth-century American culture, sprawled across great distances and numerous geographical and political boundaries, linked in part by the same technological and cybernetic systems that had held the scientific community together.[10]

This America of everywhere communities was more a goal than a reality for immigrants arriving on its shores with few words, little money, and limited experience in the gestures of everyday community life. Scattered across the continent—from Cal Tech and Berkeley, and eastward to the University of Illinois, the University of Chicago, the University of Rochester, MIT, and Princeton—without citizenship, hampered by differences of language and culture, abashed by the strange ways of their new land, the emigrés sought to maintain their connections with each other. Soon, as Charles Weiner has written, they strove to make America "a new site for the traveling seminar . . . on an expanded scale."[11]

The transition was not an easy one. The Fermis, Enrico, Laura, and their children, came to know well the alienness of this new place. They started in New York City but found themselves uprooted again and again, struggling to adjust to the vast continental sweep of their new country. Later, Laura Fermi would write of traveling "across the immense plains of the Middle West, plowed and harvested at night by gremlins, for in the daytime no soul is ever to be seen," and feeling "the impact of emptiness." Truly these were new spaces, different from the physical geography of prewar Europe, and soon to differ so drastically from the metaphysical geography of prewar science. Soon the Fermis would be on their way to a new and signally different scientific utopia, one born in desperation and not in hope, organized from without rather than within, and directed toward a single unalterable goal—not the creation of ideas but the destruction of things.[12]

MAPS OF POWER

In the winter of 1939/40, the Roosevelt administration made its decision to support high-level research into the explosive potential of atomic reactions. The effect was to draw the members of the scientific community into a new set of relations with government, industry, and each other.

To do this, the administration proposed to create formal institutions and to organize them into a hierarchical model that was the very antithesis of that militant democracy the scientist and philosopher Michael Polanyi had described as the foundation of "the authority of scientific opinion . . . essentially mutual . . . established *between* scientists, not *above* them." But this transformation was not cataclysmic; it was subtle.[13]

Central to the reorganization was the development of a string of administrative entities, some of them built one upon another, some simply replacing others that were only weeks or months old. At the earliest stages, the process offered an aura of empowerment to the scientific community, as it brought scientists into these new planning organizations, sitting side-by-side with high government and military officials.

Such a picture was deceptive from the beginning. First formed was the Uranium Committee, which promised parity among scientists, military officers, government specialists in engineering and weapons production. After humiliating dealings between the scientists and others on the committee, this program found itself subsumed within a new military-government bureaucracy just coming into existence. This National Defense Research Committee, or NDRC, was designed solely to marshal scientific talent in the production of weapons. Its authority was downward rather than upward—it towered over the scientists but was itself only an advisory subcommittee of the Advisory Commission of the Council of Defense. In the name of efficiency, the NDRC demoted the government's scientific institutes, drew the private and university scientists and their institutions under the wing of military-government forces, and began to enfold the entire enterprise into a complex hierarchical model, with the scientists as employees. With the NDRC program in place, scientific endeavor answered to a new military-government bureaucracy, and a technology of results replaced a science of unrestricted discovery.[14]

Central to the NDRC was its organization of the scientific establishment around a code of military secrecy drawn from army methods. Suddenly, scientific information and discovery were rationed materials, owned by the NDRC, restricted in distribution, and regulated on a "need to know" basis with need determined by military goals rather than research possibilities. Once the research-and-development contract was signed, the scientists working under the signatory institution received their orders from above. They transmitted the results of their activities to their superiors alone and, through them, upward along a chain of command that led from the quasiscientific NDRC to its military contacts.[15]

By the fall of 1940, the NDRC had effectively taken over the world of experimental atomic physics in America and had drawn a significant number of other scientific subcultures under its arm—and it was money that made it possible. In a matter of months, Columbia, Harvard, Princeton, Cornell, Johns Hopkins, the University of Minnesota, Berkeley, the University of Chicago, and a number of others were under contract—in fact, the list included virtually every academic institution that would later prove crucial to the Manhattan Project. The NDRC had tapped industrial and government institutions as well—Standard Oil's Development Company, the National Bureau of Standards, the Department of Agriculture.[16]

This stage quickly gave way to others as the atomic research program constructed supervisory agencies, administrative agencies, "advisory" and "decision-making" bodies both above and below. By mid-July 1941, the distinction between research-and-development and production had been further clarified, and actual production had moved under the control of the military. Within months, the NDRC had disappeared from the increasingly complex web of advisory committees and decisive bodies, replaced by the Office of Scientific Research and Development (OSRD), and the scientists had been placed under a new system of "program chiefs" with specific goals to achieve.[17]

By that time, the atomic-bomb project had been transformed from a small cadre of theoretical physicists spread across the continent to a highly complex, vertically structured bureaucracy under the aegis of the military. To see the significance of this shift, we might imagine how a single idea might advance from a scientific laboratory to the point of actual production—how an equation might become a factory for the final separation of plutonium. The concept would have to pass upward from the individual scientists to their laboratory director, the person actually under contract to the OSRD or its predecessor, the NDRC. The lab director would then transfer the idea to his or her superior, one of the three scientists serving as program chiefs. From the program chief, the equation would then enter a miasma of advisory, policy, and production committees. The concept might go before the Academy Committee, the S-1 Committee (for now the program was designated S-1), or the Planning Board. Alternatively, it might be sent over to one of the army and navy representatives who were not exactly *on* these committees but performed "a liaison function," in the words of the official army historian. It might require the concurrence of an official (but never-named) committee whose membership combined high government planners, military men, and the program chiefs. It might go to the Top Policy Group, consisting of the NDRC head, Vannevar Bush, Vice-President Henry A. Wallace, and Secretary of War Henry L. Stimson, in order to gain legitimacy before Bush took it up to Roosevelt. At some point, the still-amorphous production division of the military would have to be interjected into this process.[18]

It was not the desire for rapid deployment of information and quick conversion of theory into weaponry that dictated the reorganization of the program. A more fruitful way of understanding this reconfiguration might be to learn who it introduced into the program—what institutions and individuals—and how it arrayed them within the bureaucratic structure. That is to say, one might conceive of this reorganization as a conversion of the program from an information system to a system of power, and the resulting organizational maps not primarily as cybernetic maps, but first and foremost as maps of power.

Under these terms, the 1941 restructuring makes more sense. As a means of allocating power among competing interest groups, it accomplished a number of goals. It moved the scientists who had introduced the entire idea from the center to the periphery, without advertising the shift. It did this by dividing the scientists into figureheads ("advisory" members of the Academy Committee, principally); bureaucratic and managerial figures (the three program chiefs, but also the contract-signing heads of every laboratory and university department that went to work under the contracts of 1941 and early 1942); and finally, industrial workers, "employees of a contractor," in the words of Bush's chief deputy, James B. Conant—production-line laborers and wage-earners. Making the beginnings of an industrial-factory model, the reorganization concurrently introduced into the program central players in American corporate society.[19]

Consider the membership of the Planning Board, the group responsible for organizing the production system and determining who would run the enterprise when it shifted from theory to industrial manufacturing. Head of the board was Eger V. Murphree, a vice-president of Standard Oil's research-and-development corporation. He presided over individuals representing the corporations central to the manufacturing stage. Percival Keith was a vice-president of the Kellogg Company, the corporation that (under a wholly owned subsidiary, Kellex) would soon take responsibility for devising a gaseous diffusion system, one of the three uranium-enrichment production processes at Oak Ridge. George O. Curme served as the high-level representative for Union Carbide, whose Carbide and Carbon Chemicals Corporation (C&CCC) would play an equally essential role at Oak Ridge, holding the contract for K-25, the code name for Kellex's production system. L. Warrington Chubb was the director of Westinghouse Research, whose parent company would eventually be deeply immersed in the Y-12 plant at Oak Ridge—the plant that took the research cyclotron of a California physicist, Ernest O. Lawrence, and turned it into a giant enriched-uranium production facility. These men were brought together to recommend contracts to Vannevar Bush on these two processes, and quite naturally these corporate representatives recommended their own companies. They were accepted as prime contractors for the nascent production phase of the atomic enterprise.[20]

At one level, the Planning Board's role was to enlist the expertise of the most technologically advanced corporations in America, in particular those whose work most closely paralleled the processes that would be needed on the program. In this it served not only by attracting corporate representatives into its own ranks, but also by recruiting affiliated corporations through its informal network of fellow alumni of engineering schools, fellow directors on other corporations, and the like. Westinghouse, for example, had devised a process for manufacturing uranium metal; though its method was incapable of producing on the scale required for the program, Westinghouse employees knew of other techniques and other companies, such as Metal Hydrides, Incorporated, of Beverly, Massachusetts, which eventually took over much of the uranium-refinement work, by installing its process at a Westinghouse plant in Bloom-field, Indiana.[21]

The apparent disorganization of the new organizational map emanated from a deeper source; behind the committees and groups with their changing names, acronyms, and memberships, a shift in power was taking place. The scientists were losing their way, and the military technocracy was gaining precedence. As the administrator James Conant pointed out, this shift made the scientists employees and paved the way for their eventual militarization. More broadly, it introduced an interim stage between civilian and military control of the entire project; it hypothesized a moment when the military would own the program and would organize it as a mirror of the corporations whose representatives staffed the Planning Board and would serve as principal contractors for the program—with a chief operating officer (now Bush, soon to be Gen. Leslie R. Groves), an elaborate managerial hierarchy, and a research-and-development division prone to the pressures of production but isolated from actual decision making.

By January 1942, it was clear that the metaphysical geography of pure science, so successful before the war, was no longer appropriate to the new goals and constraints of the wartime program. As things stood at that transitional moment, scientific work on the project was scattered and contradictory in its organization—hampered by primitive security, by a contract system that dispersed work to various research areas, and by the fact that the most important scientists were not located at one or even a few institutions.[22]

The very division into "programs" with "program chiefs" represented a halfhearted transition from scientific organization to the organization typical of an industrial research-and-development program. Three men presided over polyglot programs. Arthur Holly Compton headed the University of Chicago team, clearly defined by location, yet covering such disparate areas as chain reaction physics and plutonium production. But Compton's team didn't really have responsibility for plutonium production—only as it might be achieved through uranium fission in an atomic pile. Ernest Lawrence and his group were responsible for experimental work with plutonium—it was a side job after his principal interest, electromagnetic isotope separation using the cyclotron. Harold Urey was to run the diffusion and centrifuge programs to separate isotopes—to get enriched uranium for use in the bomb itself, and also to provide the raw material for plutonium—but his team was also to work on heavy water production.[23]

The accomplishment of tasks divided among these three scientific groups was rendered even more difficult because portions of each task were being performed at a wide variety of institutions strewn across the country. In the old days of free scientific inquiry, this would have caused no problem. But the codes of military secrecy and security appropriated by the NDRC and then taken over by the OSRD meant that the open-ended broadcasting of ideas, theories, and experiment results, their publication in widely read journals, and the holding of informal symposia for discussion all became not simply impractical but treasonous. Scientists who might wish to move from site to site, drawing together the strands of work and serving as roving mailboxes, now found that travel required formal requests that first had to filter up the hierarchy, then investigations (by security officials), which might easily be lost in the confusion of responsibilities, and then elaborate precautions if one were lucky enough to go—proscriptions against speech, areas of discussion forbidden, utterly contradicting the purpose of the "traveling seminar." Young, promising scientists found themselves isolated from their colleagues under the new circumstances—out of "the loop" of information, falling behind in some areas, unable to communicate their discoveries in others. This could no longer be allowed; the loose individuation of scientific inquiry would have to be strictly centralized.[24]

The idea of consolidating workers on various tasks in specific locations began to surface at a number of bureaucratic levels. The scientists were among the first to be brought together—first at the Metallurgical Laboratory (the Met Lab) at the University of Chicago, and then at a secret site in New Mexico. The decision had profound though often hidden consequences. It was the death-knell for the utopian world of pure science that had first brought the atomic idea into being. It moved scientific activity further into the industrial R&D model. It required a significant number of scientists to give up their labs and their academic positions—some temporarily, some for the duration of the war, some permanently—and join the team under circumstances that pressured them to form a pecking order or have it imposed upon them.

In the upper echelons of the new bureaucracy, a consensus formed that physical sites were necessary, and that they would have to be organized under the rubric of a confident and unambiguous power structure, presided over by the military, operated by the corporate sphere, and coordinated by the contract system. As the Met Lab locked itself off from the rest of the University of Chicago, so also the soon-to-be-physicalized environs of manufacturing would also need to be isolated and controlled. But initially the process of converting from the hypothetical to the concrete was haphazard.

COLONIALISM

In the summer of 1942, the army assumed control over the project, and the rush to consolidate its elements under a production-line model intensified. The spring months of that year had brought a site for most of the production facilities, and a new player in the game—the military engineering firm of Stone and Webster, a longtime favorite of the Army Corps of Engineers. But with Clinton, Tennessee, designated as the appropriate locale for the production work, and with the planning divisions ready to let the contracts to begin things, there had come a curious lull. Something within this complex new bureaucracy seemed to impede action rather than impel it.

Frustration drove the OSRD representatives to the point of proposing military takeover of the program. On June 13, 1942, Bush sent up the report for approval; he recommended that the separation between science and manufacturing be made complete—$31 million would be transferred to OSRD for R&D, while the army would name an officer from the Corps of Engineers to take over the entire process of construction, including the $85 million in contracts that would go into effect on July 1.

The first district engineer for the atomic program was Col. James C. Marshall. A West Point graduate in his early forties, he had been district engineer for the Syracuse Engineering District. He had been responsible for a number of war projects and had done a credible job. But he was not a Washingtonian, or a gifted thinker. He had little or no understanding of physics; on the night of his appointment, he later confessed, he was left "puzzling over the contents" of the S-1 folder. "I spent the night without sleep," he reported; "I had never heard of atomic fission."[25]

Marshall was a manager, and the S-1 Project was a promotion for him. His appointment tucked the S-1 program firmly under the wing of the Corps of Engineers, diminishing the potential disruptions of a completely new system of weaponry and a command line that ran directly from the president but circumvented most of the proper channels. The most straightforward symbol of this process was a June 29 contract with Stone and Webster "to do all the work," in the words of Marshall's assistant, Col. K. D. Nichols.[26]

This was only the first of many decisions that would link the District and the Stone and Webster Corporation. But Colonel Marshall was not, finally, the person to preside over this relationship. While his West Point training was appropriate, his history in the hinterlands of the Syracuse District and his systematic, cautious, bureaucratic style were not. By early fall 1942, Marshall, deemed ineffectual at this sort of organization, was superseded by General Groves, a hard-line career military officer, head of military construction, and possibly the most powerful man in the Corps of Engineers. Within a week, Groves had ordered the Corps of Engineers to acquire the Tennessee site. A month later, he had authorized construction contracts for the plants that would dominate the atomic program, and had turned to his list of "proven friends" for subcontractors to do the work. Stone and Webster was at the top, and Groves gave the firm something approaching an open contract to construct the Oak Ridge facility.

The decision to issue Stone and Webster a blank-check contract signaled the direction in which the army as a whole was moving as it took over the project—toward the involvement of giant conglomerates in as-yet-unknown arrangements, and toward the emulation of the "holding company" structure that characterized those very conglomerates. In this, Marshall's new District was extending the metamorphosis of the Army Corps of Engineers that had begun between the wars, from an engineering to a supervisory bureaucracy whose primary function (and source of power) lay in subcontracting projects out to private corporations.

The corps had long used the technique of subcontracting to resolve disputes among the military, governmental, and civilian arenas. From its inception in the Revolutionary era as the professional wing of the American Army, the corps had traditionally seen itself as an epic-scaled, government-funded construction company. Under James Monroe's Directorate of Civil Works of 1824, it had assumed the task of waterway improvement and under that mandate opened the Mississippi and its major tributaries to riverboat traffic by midcentury. Even that early, the corps had served as an agency with a charge to move beyond the purely military and into the place where public and private intersected. It was the corps, after all, that made surveys for canals and railroads during the first half of the century's expansion boom. After the Civil War, it moved into flood control, another place where national and local governments, private-enterprise capitalism, and individual rights became confused. All the way into the twentieth century it had flourished by converting private desire into public programs without seeming to compete with private enterprise. Massive construction projects employed thousands of workers and generated economic booms in the regions where they were located; "multiple-purpose" reservoirs promised cheap power to their surrounding areas, offered the possibility of a burgeoning tourist industry, and represented highly visible testaments to the nitty-gritty abilities of representatives and senators to get more for their districts and their states. Since the mid-thirties, at least, the effects of these traditions were manifold. There were huge budgets, huge projects, and a concomitantly huge bureaucracy. Once created, however, such a bureaucracy never willingly shrinks; instead, it becomes the impetus to further projects. This was the case with the corps.[27]

At the same time, continual access to the central nodes of political power in America refined the Corps of Engineers, transforming it from a military organization into something more complex. While its administration bulged with engineering graduates of West Point, these officers looked to the outside world, to the realms of political power on the one hand and corporate power on the other. For the corps could not possibly do everything itself. Machinery had to be purchased, and so did concrete. Workers had to be hired, and once hired, administered. In short, subcontractors, small and large, became the closest tie of most corps directors.

This shift from construction to management continued during the interwar years, for it served admirably as a means of fighting off attacks from all sides. Scandals in the military construction programs of World War I brought moves within the army to have most military construction in the United States delegated to the Quartermaster Corps. At the same time, forces later arrayed on both sides of Roosevelt's New Deal agitated for a public works agency that would take over the activities of the corps, and enfold them, along with all other government building programs, in a "corruption-proof" administration. Private trade groups, notably the Associated General Contractors, took advantage of the resurgence of laissez-faire ideology between the wars to press for the diminution of corps activities on the grounds they took work away from private enterprise and led to creeping socialism.[28]

To counter all these attacks, the Corps of Engineers reinvented itself as a managerial enterprise. Rather than taking government money and using it to undertake projects, the corps became the contractor and supervisory agency for enormous public-works activities. In this way, it gained powerful allies in the free-enterprise world—allies who supported corps activities and saw the corps as a force for continuity and stability in the face of often chaotic government policy changes. In return, the corps built up its own list of favored contractors, contractors with "proven track records," corporations with ex-corps engineers on their payrolls and West Point graduates on their engineering staffs. Corps and corporation were bonded as well by mutual aid organizations that sometimes resembled secret societies. The most influential was the Rivers and Harbors Congress, a lobbying organization that drew Corps of Engineers officials into communion with contractors and their suppliers, representatives of other water-resource lobbies, utilities, large-scale agricultural interests, and local and state government agencies and officials—all under one rubric, with mutual self-protection as the most powerful motive.[29]

The corps had perfected its policy on the projects for immense dams that it built, in competition with the Federal Bureau of Reclamation, throughout the American West. But the World War II environment drove the corps and its corporations into a new frenzy of activity. Taxing the corps to its utmost, this period virtually guaranteed that corps officials, Gen. Leslie R. Groves most of all, would turn to their experienced cohorts to build what the army needed.

With Groves now heading the project, Stone and Webster again appeared on the contracts roster that filled a rapidly fattening file on Groves's desk. Other corporate presences were similarly represented: Westinghouse, Allis-Chalmers, the Kodak affiliate Tennessee Eastman. By the end of the year, Groves had signed off on contracts with Kellex, Union Carbide's C&CCC subsidiary, Bakelite, Western Electric, Bell Labs, the J. A. Jones Construction Company, Chrysler Corporation, and a number of other major American companies.

The result was the creation of an elaborate web of interconnected corporations, contracts, projects, and subprojects, all presided over by a military bureaucracy that mixed a rigid organizational system with a peculiarly indeterminate system of command. Groves courted this position of indeterminacy—for himself, and for his program. Under it, he was beholden to no one except the president, for no one could determine whether or not the general had the right to take over whatever territory he deemed necessary. Groves was able to remain in this position in part because of the sophisticated corporate structures of the principal contractors whom he hired to run the various arms of the program. "Everything we wanted, we got," Groves told an interviewer much later, and he credited this success to the "very limited organization" that he set up to intervene between the corporate contractors, the army, and the scientific community responsible for devising a system that the contractors could translate into physical weaponry.[30]

Groves's ascendance, his early success at forging a cooperative venture among government, military, and corporate entities, signaled a broader campaign of expansion and control, into labor relations, into social relations, even into language. This last area is perhaps the most surprising and significant example of the District's imperial tendencies. One of its earliest manifestations was the naming of the program.

The program began under the sort of title appropriate to military projects in the past. While still head of the project, Colonel Marshall had taken the recommendation of his superior officers, Generals Reybold, Somervell, and Styer, and named his command the Department of Substitute Metals (DSM) District. Groves found this unacceptable. For him, the naming of things had immense importance; he saw the name as equivalent to a public announcement. Of Marshall's DSM District, Groves later reported that he "objected to this term" because he felt "it would arouse the curiosity of all who heard it."[31]

Groves's argument was based upon a certain brilliant logic, one that would characterize his style as czar of the program throughout its history. For him, the single most important concern lay with "security" (Groves's term subsuming secrecy and control of information), and he envisioned language as a potent weapon for duplicity. Groves wished to devise a name that applied a language of normalcy to shield the project from sight, and thereby confuse the enemy. He insisted that the name duplicate the traditional structure of the Army Corps of Engineers—the atomic-weapons program should truly mimic an engineer district. This would account for its massive bureaucracy, for its autonomous relation with other army divisions and with the corps's own superstructure, for the size of its expenditures, and for its use of diverse scientific talent. Presiding over a district, the head of the program would be a district engineer, and he could then set up other, smaller false-programs, under which he could shuffle the work of the program to make the actual chain of events within the project invisible.[32]

But the project *was,* in fact, signally different from any actual engineer district in one significant way—geography. Every other district served a specific region and was named after the principal city or geographical feature; this new district would be exactly opposite—its functions would be scattered among sites strewn across the country. Its unity would be bureaucratic, not geographical. But this was precisely the motivation behind giving the region a geographical name—Groves believed a new district could give the illusion of geographic identity to belie its true nature as a metaphysical entity.

The principal difficulty lay with the actual name to be chosen. Groves and Marshall toyed with the idea of using "Knoxville" but discarded the notion on the grounds it would draw attention to the huge new Tennessee factory site that ran from Clinton to Black Oak Ridge. "You should get a name for it that people will just gloss over," Groves remembered telling Marshall.[33]

So they decided on "Manhattan." It was consistent with Marshall's current mailing address, and, surprisingly, that name had never been used for a project before. Its addition to the roster would seem logical, not gratuitous. And then there were the intangible benefits the name offered. In its own way, this cover location *symbolized* the nature of the project—its polyglot population, its community of intellectuals, emigrés, non-English-speakers, and Jews, its cosmopolitanism and modernity. If these affinities attracted Groves, they would also lend logic to the program's name; through it one could rationalize paychecks sent to people with names like Feynman and Farmer, Oppenheimer and Rabi, orders concerning metal fabrication, acquisition of raw ores, the use of prodigious amounts of concrete, the necessity for tens of thousands of new units of housing.

The name change symbolized as well Groves's larger program of duplicity: to hide the project in plain sight, to recast necessary but unsavory violations of law, logic, and custom by setting them within a new language-environment. It also symbolized the way in which the District would appropriate structures and strategies from a wide variety of sources, transforming them at the same time, so that they never remained as they once were.

So it was the bureaucratic organization of the Army Corps of Engineers, and the cybernetic organization of the prewar scientific community, drawn together, melded alchemically, that made the new organizational structure of the Manhattan Engineer District (MED). For advice in maneuvering along this recent and unstable terrain, the members of this new community would have to turn to Groves and, in turning to him, would find it necessary to sacrifice much in return.

This would never be a circumstance to which the scientists would gracefully bow. But Groves's appointment, and the peculiarity of his relation to the previous bureaucracies of the Corps of Engineers on the one hand and the program itself on the other, made it unlikely they would win if they battled him directly. It also made it extremely difficult for them to find ways around him within the peculiar geography of power he had created.

The army's official historians summed up this condition well: "Just as MED was unique as an Engineer district without territorial limits," they noted, "so General Groves was unique as an Army officer without clear-cut status in the chain of command." Groves effectively wrote his own official orders; they, like the Manhattan

District's name, used apparently frank and straightforward language to mask the true condition of things. Groves described the orders as deliberate "eyewash"— they said nothing of what he was to do, or to whom, or where. Invisible but omnipotent, General Groves directed a metaphysical district whose power lay in its ability to disguise.[34]

For the first year of his tenure, Groves further obscured this shadowy position by retaining Marshall as acting engineer, and hiding himself behind the official structures of the engineer's office. By year's end, however, Groves had determined that the masquerade was sufficiently established to eliminate Marshall and replace him with a district engineer, Col. K. D. Nichols, who could serve as his assistant rather than his double.[35]

Groves had built a camouflaged bureaucratic fortress, and this insulation meant that power, information, and control moved in one direction only. Such a position, galling enough for military officers like Marshall and Nichols, who were presumably trained to accept a militaristic code of obedience, was inconceivable to the scientists, recent arrivals from a utopia where all discourse was open and the organizational map utterly flat. Theirs had been an iconoclastic democracy; Groves had instituted something closer to a totalitarian regime.

This is not to say that the scientists didn't resist their change in status. As early as April 1940, central figures in the scientific community had argued that they should control the engineering and manufacturing aspects of the program. Einstein himself had urged the case in a letter (sent on April 25, 1940) to Lyman Briggs of the National Bureau of Standards, intending to add weight to the position of the scientists Wigner, Sachs, Fermi, and Szilard when they met with Briggs. The meeting was fruitless; the scientists were already superseded.[36]

After that, resistance centered in Chicago, at the Met Lab, where the first atomic pile would be built and most of the theoretical implications of the atomic bomb first worked out. As the Planning Board took over in 1941 and corporations increasingly controlled the programs, the scientists' hope of a democratically administered weapons program faded, and they saw, with greater clarity than ever before, the destiny of the project that had once been theirs. "The troubles . . . arise out of the fact that the work is organized along somewhat authoritative rather than democratic lines," wrote Leo Szilard in a September 1942 memo. Military compartmentalization had eroded the open architecture of the scientific community, isolating scientists from one another and destroying the communitarian zeal that had driven the program from the start.[37]

At this early stage of the project, the term *compartmentalization* referred only to a military strategy for preventing underlings from putting together enough information to guess the outlines of the program, by forbidding them to talk to any but their immediate inferiors and superiors along a clearly delineated chain of command.

For Szilard, compartmentalization—particularly as it was practiced at the Met Lab— was already redefining the entire scientific enterprise. He ended his memo with a clarion call, clearsighted and typically tragic in its vision. "A stage has been reached," he wrote, "where it becomes clear that we have to choose between two alternatives." One was to accept this new state of affairs, relieved that responsibility now lay far from them. The lab would become a model of an acquiescent technocracy; there, the scientists can lead a very pleasant life while we do our duty. We live in a pleasant part of a pleasant city, in the pleasant company of each other, and have in Dr. Compton the most pleasant "boss" we could wish to have. There is every reason why we should be happy and since there is a war on, we are even willing to work overtime.

   Alternatively, we may take the stand that those who have originated the work on this terrible weapon and those who have materially contributed to its development have, before God and the World, the duty to see to it that it should be ready to be used at the proper time and in the proper way.[38]

Szilard's manifesto differentiated the terms beautifully: between a structure in which the scientists served as employees, took orders, and did their jobs, freed of responsibility and equally free of opportunity; and one in which responsibility and control rested fully on their shoulders.

His argument was almost certainly influenced by the appearance at the Chicago lab that same month of a team of Stone and Webster engineers. The physicist Leona Marshall Libby was there when they arrived, and she recorded the reactions of her colleagues. At a meeting to describe the plutonium production program, for which S&W had begun to produce factory blueprints, Libby reported that "the scientists sat deadly still with curled lips. The briefer was ignorant; he enraged and frightened everyone."[39]

Indeed, Szilard was way too late in sounding his alarum; he wrote his assessment three days after the District had taken its decisive turn from democracy to authoritarianism. But the new codes of secrecy and bureaucratic obfuscation had already isolated him and his group. He did not yet know that Groves had been appointed head of the District and given a mandate to rule virtually without restraint.[40]

Two weeks after Szilard wrote his letter, Groves was at the Met Lab to determine just how to quell this insurrection and impose "discipline," as he called it, on the scientists. Listening to his new charges detail their proposals for a District based on the model of prewar scientific culture, Groves determined that they were "inflexible," and "their ideas were unacceptable." Offended by "the absurdity of such a proposal," convinced—as he told Compton—that "you [scientists] don't know how to take orders and give orders," Groves decided to destroy the scientists' movement.[41]

But he still needed them, and their "inflexibility" suggested they might resign rather than stay on as his underlings. Within days he had determined that the solution lay with splitting the dispute into two portions and presenting two solutions. On the one hand, he would ruthlessly suppress Szilard's call for a return to the old system of scientific control. On the other, he would resolve the issue of the incompetence of Stone and Webster by hiring a new and far more sophisticated industrial-technological corporation: Du Pont.[42]

Arranging matters this way, Groves sought to garner Compton's support, cut the legs off Szilard, Fermi, and the younger scientists, and remake the Chicago Met Lab into a "pleasant" corporate-industrial environment based upon (in Compton's words) "the tradition in American large-scale industry that research, development, and production shall be carried on by separate departments," with each "considered a specialized art of its own."[43]

Groves was not pulling Du Pont's name from the air. Like Stone and Webster, Du Pont was a corporation Groves knew well from his previous position supervising military construction on a national scale. While it was largely without experience in physics and particularly blank on atomic physics, Du Pont had built and run a number of "smokeless powder" explosives factories for the military, had sold nylon for parachutes, and had signed onto a long string of contracts for materials, for services, and for consultation. Most important, from Groves's point of view, Du Pont was highly experienced in bringing scientists under the wing of a highly structured organizational map, feeding them tasks, and then applying those tasks to its own ends. And its performance record was close to perfect.

Du Pont had its own reasons for wanting in on the program. The company was a legend among American defense industries, and the legend was not salutary. During World War I, Du Pont had profited handsomely from supplying both sides of the conflict, and the interwar years had brought a backlash against the corporation's alleged profit-mongering, its aggressively prowar posture, and its funding of saber-rattling organizations. Du Pont's hostility to progressive and New Deal politics attracted congressional scrutiny and spectacular headlines, and won the company a new moniker as "merchant of death." With a return to war came a huge increase in Du Pont's size and profits, as demand for its "smokeless powder" and many other products for the waging of war skyrocketed. But the corporation once again gained public notoriety.[44]

Extraordinary expansion generated a series of conflicts within the corporate structure of Du Pont. On one side lay the argument to use the war and its attendant boom as the opportunity for a more conservative development program. Why risk matters by moving into new areas? But other forces argued strongly for exploiting this sheltered period to move aggressively. The March 25, 1935, excess-profits tax in effect made R&D an investment that cost the corporation only thirty-eight cents on the dollar spent; the postwar years could see a new Du Pont poised for expansion in unexplored areas of technological production, if the wartime years were properly invested in preparing for that postwar consumer utopia.[45]

Equally basic was the issue of expanding munitions and war-related sales and their effects on the company's already tarnished image. One side, represented by Du Pont's longtime president, Lammot du Pont, urged the company full-speed ahead in war-materiel production while "educating the public in the need for free enterprise," in Du Pont's own words. The other side pointed to the huge hazards threatened by new weapons production, and the public-relations debacle that might ensue.[46]

This split reflected a deep internal division. Lammot du Pont's ringing call for profiteering (he pronounced the war "a seller's market" in one speech) had the force of the family behind it. But his stridency was muted by a new generation of leaders who had begun to take over the company reins between 1940 and 1942, a group headed by men like Walter S. Carpenter Jr., Du Pont's new president, and Crawford Greenewalt, a rising star in the corporation. These men were more circumspect in their statements, and more clearly a part of the corporate environment of the times. Their goal was to find the means to make the most of government work while remaining independent enough to continue consumer and other nonmilitary work. It was to this new breed of corporate executives that Groves turned late in October 1942 to propose his plan that the Du Pont Company take over the plutonium project.[47]

Greenewalt's meditations on the plutonium program and those of other Du Pont executives suggest a keen awareness of the potential benefits and disabilities of involvement in the program. On the side of benefits, the program offered the company workforce protection from the decimations of the draft; the chance for large-scale expansion of the corporation at a time when labor markets were shrinking; and insulation from the severe constriction brought to nonmilitary markets by rationing and shortages of materials and cash.

Overshadowing these considerable advantages was the single most tempting possibility, one that Greenewalt witnessed on December 2, 1942, as Enrico Fermi christened the world's first atomic pile, demonstrating his incubator for the creation of a new element, and revealing a radical new source of power at the same time. Groves was offering Du Pont near-exclusive access to this new world; Fermi was already talking to everyone he could about its potential as a new energy-generating system and its promise of other, as yet unknown, commercial applications. By February 1943, Du Pont representatives were debating how to exploit their connection with the Met Lab; Greenewalt argued that the important issue was to prepare Du Pont scientists to dominate the postwar atomic age, and the "best way to educate men now was to insert them into the Chicago program for training." Within a month, Du Pont's chemical department began to move wholesale to the plutonium program.[48]

But there were distinct disadvantages as well. One to which Du Pont executives were most sensitive was the matter of image. What good would it do to come out of the war the leader in atomics, if government and civilian disgust with the corporation hamstrung postwar projects? There was the even more troubling question of the real dangers of this unproven technology, and the possibility of immense liability problems should a plant explode or should radiation turn out to be even more toxic than was already believed.[49]

For these and other reasons, the negotiations with the government were delicate. Du Pont resolved the issues with an extraordinary document, a contract signed in late December. First, the contract stipulated that the corporation would take only a token fixed fee of one dollar. This settled the question of image. Now Du Pont could present itself as the opposite of a merchant of death; it could appear after the war as a thoroughly unselfish and patriotic force for good, while still leaving open all the avenues for self-protection and expansion. In addition, Du Pont made an astonishing demand of the government: that the United States, and not the corporation, take on all liability of the program, regardless of whose actions might have resulted in the liability.[50]

Groves and the various committees and arms of the sprawling administrative system surrounding him were now boxed in. They had made the commitment, had shown Du Pont executives and scientists everything; they needed the corporation to agree, and agree quickly. At a meeting of the Military Policy Committee on December 15, 1942, the corporation received all it demanded, and more. The minutes recorded an unprecedented agreement: "That in view of the unusual and unpredictable hazards in carrying out the work under this project," the government would "hold the Contractor harmless" in all regards, and would take on all liability, all responsibility for litigation and defense, and all costs that might result from harm done by the program.[51]

The significance of this decision is difficult to overstate. It indicated that Du Pont and the MED both believed the program to be wildly risky, that seemingly minor and unintended consequences might prove catastrophic, that the liabilities could be astronomical. Du Pont went even further, demanding that President Roosevelt himself sign a complete waiver of responsibility. The corporation thus revealed that it believed the risks so enormous that it could not trust the government to stand by its agreements without the explicit backing of the chief executive.

Groves and his people were already on an irreversible course. Within two weeks, they had given Du Pont its waiver, and Du Pont in turn had signed a letter of intent to oversee the entire production program. On January 1, 1942, the Met Lab became something close to a regional subsidiary of Du Pont—a training ground for its scientists in the new and potentially lucrative world of atomics, a recruiting ground for experienced physicists, a symbol of Du Pont's commitment to basic science and to the war effort, to be used whenever the corporation needed to represent itself to the scientific community as it sought new converts and new recruits.[52]

While the Met Lab scientists would continue to harbor deep suspicions of the corporation, they would never again have the opportunity to move back into the center of the Manhattan Project. The lines of communication between politicians and scientists, lines that had led to the project in the first place, were now interdicted by the Du Pont corporation and by Groves's military security organization. The Met Lab scientists were employees now, and employees in a wartime industry—forbidden to unionize, forbidden even to discuss "sensitive" matters without guards present in the rooms and without finding themselves accused of treason and threatened with punitive military conscription. The Manhattan Project had taken a fateful turn.[53]

CONSOLIDATION

With the appearance of Du Pont on the map of the Manhattan Engineer District, the process of incorporation entered its final phase. The model had been set forth, but it had not yet been fully implemented. Now was the time to embody the new structure in physical spaces.

Groves had committed the scientists to a compartmentalized organizational structure, scattered among many universities and labs, but everyone concerned had learned quickly that they couldn't work that way. Not for nothing had the prewar scientific culture been so radically open and democratic. With information scattered and individual scientists forbidden to talk across those spaces, crucial work was grinding to a halt.[54]

What was needed was a central location where the vast majority of R&D work could take place, supervised by "bosses" like Compton who were fully committed to the industrial model. But the scientists were still struggling to run the program on the model of the "traveling seminar," with its openness, freedom, and emphasis on curiosity and intellectual commitment. Though they remained, formally, research physicists within academic settings, the Met Lab people and their subgroups throughout the country had begun (despite themselves) to resemble the chemists at Du Pont. General Groves described this transitional moment with the brutal condescension typical of his relations with that scientific culture: this was the point just "before our scientific people came to realize that we were playing for blue chips and that they had to produce"—produce to *his* command, and not to the dictates of the scientific "problem."[55]

Impelled by the demands of Groves and his underlings, Oppenheimer and the scientist John Manley sought to reorganize the research enterprise. They—and the scientific community they represented—did not yet know how active a role Groves would take in reshaping their activity, nor how alien his system of control would be to their own familiar models. Their proposal was primitive and, significantly, centered on geographical solutions to the problems they had encountered. Their plan was to replace the invisible colleges of pure science with an ersatz approximation of a university environment, an ivory tower within which those scientists best able to push the project along could work closely, sharing a common purpose, isolated from distraction. With security systems externalized, in the form of perimeter guards and protected gates, more complete background checks, and rigorous exclusion of all but the most unimpeachable, compartmentalization could then be relaxed, and the scientists could return to their arguments and open transmission of ideas.

In one sense, the Oppenheimer plan represented an exercise in atavism, a move away from the sophisticated anarcho-syndicalism of modernist science, back to the cloistered model of the medieval university. And Oppenheimer's analogies for his new community corresponded to this romantically regressive impulse—"shangri-la," he called it, and "a monk's colony." Yet in another way, this was the first stage in the application of the managerial models of corporate capitalism to an area heretofore aloof from its influences. Describing it later, Manley, who took part, called the plan a matter of "consolidation," and it was. The new model derived less from the physics departments of European universities than from the few places in America where "practical physics" was institutionalized—places like the Bausch and Lomb Company, where research in light was translated into optical products, and the Bell Labs in New Jersey, the most prestigious of them all. What seemed to offer compensation was the promise of a return to openness within the walls—a promise that was never to be fulfilled.

Oppenheimer and Manley's decision to approach Groves with this proposal conceded the new conditions under which the program would operate. It represented a giant leap away from the world of pure science and into the domain of instrumentality. It moved their enterprise from the realm of the transgeographical, from the "everywhere communities" that represented the clearest defining characteristic of modernist science, and into the physical. It crammed a discursive space into a geographical place.

Manley reported on the general's reaction: "Groves saw the logic right away, not only from the technical point of view, but . . . from the security point of view. If he could coop these people up on one place, it would be a lot easier to control their talking."[56]

Early in October 1942, Oppenheimer and Groves met in Berkeley, and Oppenheimer wrote to Manley afterward that "some far reaching geographical change in plans seems to be in the cards and I do not know to what extent this will bring jurisdictional changes with it." Oppenheimer was probably referring to his own role in this new environment. Someone would have to accept the position that had lain with Compton at the Met Lab. Oppenheimer became that person—the head of R&D, and the man responsible for translating Groves's commands into some language his community could accept. Oppenheimer was a wordsmith; he would have need of his fluency over the next years.[57]

The location of this new facility fell to Major Dudley, an Army Corps of Engineers officer and one of District Engineer Marshall's assistants. Oppenheimer, Groves, and the Military Policy Committee had come up with basic site criteria. The location would have to support a total population of 265; it would have to be west of the Mississippi and inland a minimum of two hundred miles from the Pacific; it would have to have some rudimentary facilities, in order for construction work to begin unimpeded. "Isolated yet accessible"—that was the phrase. Its geographic requirements were quite precise: it would have to be a natural bowl, with hills close by to provide the means for guarding the site from above.[58]

Now that the program was firmly under the thumb of the Corps of Engineers, Dudley was comfortable with exploiting corps resources, tangible and intangible. He could draw upon site maps and topographical surveys, and he could call upon experts in each relevant engineer district; moreover, he could do this without revealing his purpose. "This Corps system is very helpful," he reported; "you can go into a strange office, meet people you have never seen before, and you do not have to negotiate a contract or a purchase order for them to work with you. You can get someone who knows the region thoroughly, who is accustomed to talking in the same terms you use, and who does not insist on asking a lot of unnecessary questions."[59]

By the first week of November, Dudley was done. He and Groves met with Oppenheimer in Berkeley, and Oppenheimer wrote to Manley that "the question of site is well along toward settlement. It is a lovely spot and in every way satisfactory, and the only points which now have to be settled are whether the human and legal aspects of the necessary evacuations make insuperable difficulties. Ed. [McMillan] and I plan to go down and have a look next week, and will probably spend a few days there getting some of the important questions settled. I know that you will be very pleased with the site if we can really get this one."[60]

Dudley had come up with a limited number of choices; he had weighted his report in favor of a New Mexico site at Jemez Springs. The site visit was scheduled for November 16; Oppenheimer, his California scientific colleague McMillan, and Dudley arrived first, and Oppenheimer immediately rejected the place. Surprisingly, Groves concurred—it was, to his mind, just too primitive to be convertible into an efficient plant location. As McMillan remembered it later, "Oppenheimer then proposed the Los Alamos Ranch School nearby; we all got into cars, we didn't ride horses as some people have said, (that's too far) and we went up to Los Alamos Ranch School."[61]

"I remember arriving there," McMillan recalled. "There was a slight snow falling; it was just a tiny, drizzly type of snow. It was cold and there were the boys and their masters out on the playing fields in shorts. I remarked that they really believed in hardening up the youth."[62]

The paramilitary discipline, the enforced hardship, and the relentless masculinity of the school must have aroused deep memories in Groves. He himself had suffered from "weakness" in a family of the chronically ill ruled by a domineering father who made his son strive to overcome his failings and work as well to support the family—

at menial and demeaning labor as a porter and a fruitpicker. Here, too, was the exact replication of his mental image of the scientific community—not "mothers facing the need to surrender control of their children as they grow up" (that was Nichols's analogy) but rather spoiled, wild children needing just the sort of rigid, systematic discipline and exposure to suffering that he had experienced, and which he now saw arrayed before him. "As soon as Groves saw it," McMillan recalled, "he said, in effect, 'This is the place.'"[63]

The decision to build at Los Alamos was almost exactly concurrent with the first stages in the creation of the Clinton Engineer Works along Black Oak Ridge in Tennessee—a manufacturing facility where enriched uranium would be produced for use in the uranium bomb, and where a pilot plutonium-producing pile would be set up under Du Pont. It anticipated by only two months the creation of a third site, where the entire plutonium program would be established, including huge atomic piles and even larger chemical separation plants where the plutonium would be extracted from contaminants and rendered pure.

In all three sites, strange contradictions came to the surface, contradictions in particular between geography and ideology. The military model for the programs tended to follow the fortress philosophy: to consolidate all activities in a minimal space, and to surround that space with protective perimeter walls that could hide military activity and provide an elevation upon which guards could reconnoitre both without and within.

General Groves had more than a little experience with this program; he had supervised the construction of the army's largest and most visible fortress: the Pentagon. Original requirements for the new scientific site had sought to duplicate the fortress in a natural locale; the mesa at Los Alamos didn't fit this model. Similarly with the Clinton site; there Groves and his planners had anticipated packing all the production factories within one perimeter wall. But Du Pont had insisted on a separate locale for the plutonium production facilities and had won the day.

Du Pont's reasoning was impeccable. Greenewalt and his engineers knew high explosives and explosives factories; they knew chemical factories and their risks. Their insistence on a liability waiver indicated that they knew something few others had as yet faced: the tremendous destructive potential of atomic explosions, and the risk of accident attendant upon an enterprise as speculative as this one. Du Pont wanted out of the Clinton site. The Military Policy Committee concurred. In a meeting on December 20, 1943, the committee reported that "a new plant site will have to be selected in an isolated area, but near power and water."[64]

Groves recruited Col. Franklin T. Matthias, a civilian engineer in the Army Reserves who had been called to active duty for the wartime effort, to represent the army in the site selection process. A meeting of Matthias with Du Pont's Gilbert P. Church, and Albert Hall on December 14, 1942, set the criteria; Du Pont wanted the place in the great West, preferably the Pacific Northwest. After a whirlwind tour of sites as far south as Los Angeles, the team chose the desert regions of central Washington, on the power grid that connected the Bonneville and Grand Coulee Dams.[65]

Just who reconciled the site and the site criteria, and how, remains unclear—in fact, it is uncertain whether the criteria came before the fact or after. Certainly they were precise, and almost exactly fitted to the Hanford location. The site would be a rectangle of something more than two thousand square miles, and without major railroad or highway routes that would have to be closed or rerouted. Inside this "reservation" would be an inner reserve of seven hundred square miles; within *that* would be a doubly guarded inner sanctum of about two hundred square miles. This bullseye arrangement would provide escalating security precautions as one moved closer to the epicenter; it would also define the production program by separating the manufacturing zone—the workplace, the space of production—from all others.[66]

Du Pont's site manager, Church, and its executive, Crawford Greenewalt, were well aware of the strange nature of the hazards on their new project. Groves had been set back on his heels by the Met Lab's inability to estimate how much plutonium it would need closer than a factor of ten; similar wild variations existed concerning the potential explosiveness of the materials with which Du Pont employees would be working, and the nature of its "criticality"—that is, what it would take to spontaneously generate an atomic reaction. Already, however, the scientists had communicated to Du Pont and the army the distinct possibility of "explosions of catastrophic proportions and the possibility of releasing to the atmosphere intensely radioactive gases."[67]

The scientists wanted to continue the combination of theoretical discussion and experimentation to resolve these essential questions—not to move until the scientific dangers were clear and their prevention determined. But this was no longer possible. The army ran the project now, and a new conception of time had been introduced. Groves later recalled that "we could not afford to spend time on the research and study that would have been necessary to make certain that the operation of the full-scale plutonium installation . . . would be safe." Setting site safety criteria at this stage was whistling in the dark; one either halted everything until the issue could be resolved satisfactorily, or made arbitrary decisions based upon intuition and superstition. Church, Hall, and Matthias resolved that they would widely separate the various aspects of the production process—the piles, the chemical separation plants, the fabrication laboratories. In this way, the planners hoped "that accidents in any one area should not affect the operation of the remaining units." Completing the site, the District would build an "employees' village." "The prevailing wind direction and velocity were factors that would contribute to the location of the various manufacturing areas relative to workers' housing." Unfortunately, it was doubtful that the site selection team would be able to make the necessary calculations before deciding on a site.[68]

Distance would afford protection, but what constituted sufficient distance? Without any clear answer, the site selection group guessed. What they wanted was a huge empty space, a wasteland, already coursed through by immense natural power—water power, twenty-five thousand gallons every minute—and equally enormous manmade power, one hundred thousand kilowatts. Just as the site at Los Alamos high on a mesa was fitting to a city upon a hill, the new project would be built on a landscape appropriate to it, a space of emptiness, power, and vast potential.

On January 16, 1943, General Groves arrived at the Columbia River site to look it over, and stopped in the town of Hanford to buy some crackers for his lunch. By now the site was determined; he was there to confirm the choice. He looked over the region; "the total population was small and most of the farms did not appear to be of any great value," he recalled later. What impressed him was the proximity of the power grid, the composition of the soil ("ideal for heavy construction"), the "abundance of very pure and quite cold water," and the distance of the nearest community—Pasco—so that "if an unforeseen disaster should occur, we would be able to evacuate the inhabitants by truck." Three weeks later, this—the last site—had been formally condemned.[69]

The Secretary of War's directive for Hanford completed the incorporation of the Manhattan Engineer District. It was an incorporation comprised of opposite movements. One led away from physicality, into the appropriation of one metaphysical geography and its enfolding into another, "a new engineer district, without territorial limits, to be known as the Manhattan District," in the words of General Reybold's general order of origination. This new entity would have its own maps—maps of responsibility and power, organizational maps of increasing complexity designed to trace the lineage of orders and enable a vigilant troubleshooter to determine leakage of power and of information on this metaphysical landscape.[70]

The other vector led into the corporeal, into particulars of dirt and wind, roads and houses, equipment and factory noises. This movement, too, involved the taking of spaces to a new end. Now the representatives of that first geography of power had determined the locale for those spaces. To *take* them, however, required uprooting everything already imbedded in these spaces. This necessitated a legal maneuver known as *condemnation:* the usurpation of legal ownership of lands and buildings, water rights and graveyards, by government entity through decree of eminent domain. Only then could the Manhattan District begin the process of embodying its fugitive structures in tangible form and realizing its right-by-decree to take dominion "without territorial limits."

On August 11, 1943, the House Military Affairs Subcommittee held an open investigative meeting at Clinton, Tennessee, site of the new Clinton Engineer Works. Representative Clifford Davis of Memphis, Tennessee, presided; Representatives Dewey Short from Missouri and John Sparkman from Alabama, both members of the subcommittee, were there, and John Jennings Jr., not a member of the subcommittee but the Representative for the area within which the Clinton Engineer Works had been carved, also attended.[1]

The subcommittee hearing was unusual. District and army had worked to prevent it, but this was an election year; the chairman of the Military Affairs Subcommittee was from Tennessee, and Jennings was one of the House's more colorful representatives. He had received letters from his constituents, letters that intimated fraud, strong-arm tactics, and other crimes against the common farmers who had once owned and worked this land. He had approached the authorities and they had rebuffed him.[2]

CONDEMNATION 3

The meeting opened explosively. The first witness was a Judge Cowder, a county judge for Anderson County, and himself the owner of four tracts of condemned land. His testimony described government activities that suggested incompetence, insensitivity, even outright falsehood and threats. Cowder went on to paint a picture of covert government agents sneaking around the countryside, forcing landowners off their properties and into financial difficulties with their heavy-handed, inept maneuvers.

Cowder's testimony set the tone. For the rest of the day, landowners presented themselves before the subcommittee to describe their own experiences. They reported army appraisals that were wildly below market value, and they produced independent appraisals to support their contentions. Witness after witness spoke of conflicting, ambiguous, threatening, or outright duplicitous statements on the part of government representatives, and a near-complete inability to determine where or to whom to turn for accurate information. They reported broken promises of immediate money if they signed, and threats that if they did not sign immediately, they could lose everything. They told of huge losses necessitated by the short time allowed them to liquidate their assets and get off the property. They spoke of timber on the property that had sold for more than the army's appraisal for the entire tract; of properties on which other sales offers were pending at far higher rates.[3]

The entire event was highly theatrical. One landowner, O. B. Anderson, sent his daughter to represent him, and her testimony caused Representative Short to declare that "he believed it wise for the committee to recommend that the Government representatives take a course in human relations." Local protesters produced an "expert appraiser," Lee Shaw, who reported that government offers were "on average . . . 45 percent low." Local government agents like M. N. Manley, the assistant county agent, were equally compelling adversaries of the officials produced by the District. Manley was known and liked by most members of the community, not least because, when the District refused to assist in relocation, he had made it his business to help families in their search for replacement properties. He reported that "the offers by the Government were insufficient to purchase similar property," an argument crucial to countering land office appraisers who had argued that their assessments were accurately based upon "comparable sales" in the region. "A very old colored woman" named Dicie Griffith caused a sensation when she testified that after her property was appraised at $75, a government representative came to her and offered her $300; when she refused to take it, the agent then signed her name to the form.[4]

Members of the committee encouraged the general atmosphere of melodrama, calling landowners in the audience to rise from their seats and confront their government adversaries with their accusations. One resulting exchange between a District negotiator and Mrs. Frances Leath Copeland became so acrimonious that the committee decided to strike the entire testimony from the record. Representative Jennings contributed to the histrionic air by declaring at one point that "it is hoped these men who have been mistreating these people will repent in the sight of God and man." Representative Short told the District's chief appraiser that he needed "a police force in order to keep your appraisers in order."[5]

In part this general atmosphere reflected the larger court of public opinion to whom the witnesses were appealing. By this time, many of these landowners had begun legal proceedings against the District. Lawyers and landowners alike understood that, when it came to settling court cases, local opinion would have a significant impact on the outcome. And Jennings's experience as a politician helped the District's opponents generate a compelling picture. The *Knoxville Journal* quoted Jennings's statement that a thousand farmers were in a "desperate plight due to undervaluation; delayed payment of money and eviction from their homes." Jennings's self-image as a committed public servant striving to protect his constituents against an unfeeling bureaucracy won central place in newspaper reports.[6]

Jennings's picture prevailed against the weak and self-righteous responses of District representatives not least because he knew on what turf the battle was being fought. Fred Morgan, land acquisition head, made asides in his report on the committee hearing that suggest the District was busy constructing an internal defense rather than preparing to redress grievances or striving to improve the image of the District locally or nationally. Morgan defended the District's policies without seeming to understand the circumstances under which the entire process of condemnation now stood: as a contest between a military bureaucracy and a collection of local citizens for control over the picture that would be drawn of the entire process. Probably coached by their lawyers, the landowners had succeeded in painting an epic canvas of a vast, unsympathetic, even tyrannical government victimizing helpless farmers.

This single political event represented the multitude of arenas within which the District was being shaped in its first year of life. On the most literal level was the physical space itself. The District's program entailed appropriating a large number of small holdings of marginal agricultural or commercial value and consolidating these tracts into a coherent space defined by clearly delineated boundaries. As the District's defendants would have it, this was the sum total of things.

But circle surrounded circle: the political sphere, where men like Jennings and Short staked their reputations on the pictures they drew of righteousness and wicked iniquity; the social, where the farmers themselves confronted wrenching losses of identity and fought back by drawing on their everyday alliances; the cultural, where myths of virtuous farmers and pettifogging bureaucrats contested with pictures of lonely soldiers and steely military leaders.

The high drama played out in the subcommittee's makeshift hearing room in what had once been Clinton, Tennessee, had a clear narrative to it. America's symbolic citizens, small independent farmers with deep ties to the land and to their communities, were being trampled by an authoritarian government bureaucracy whose excesses and incompetencies threatened not only the individuals involved, but the entire American democratic process.

But the District had final say in the process, for it was the District that finally controlled the avenues and agencies by which local issues expanded into national significance. With its influence over newspaper chains and press syndicates, with its power to silence elected officials, the District could effectively sever the link between local and national significance. So the subcommittee's story of the District's authoritarian regime remained a local story. At regional meetings, Representative Jennings might rail at the injustices of the War Department, might produce copies of his voluminous correspondence with its representatives, might, in other words, portray himself as the defender of the small American against the incursions of an unfeeling government. But his protests never fully made it into the public arena of congressional debate, or into the major newspapers and their affiliates. The legal condemnation cases that did benefit from the subcommittee hearings of August 1943 reached their conclusions long after the District had taken over the lands themselves, torn down the farmhouses and barns and pigpens and tenant houses, built the factories and barracks and administration buildings, and the streets that linked them. Even with these cases, then, the District could claim victory over its adversaries.

Yet this brief overview, with the conclusions foregone, cannot be complete. It does not detail the conflicts and paradoxes within the records, the twists of logic, the confusions of chronology and interpretation as one site became three, as the District showed its power, and as landowners and residents interposed themselves to resist. And it does not contain the call-and-response as residents became more and more adept, and District officials more and more impatient and intolerant.

In the end, the conflict over land ownership strengthened the District and extended its domain as a colonizer of spaces and cultures. Yet those who resisted the will of the District grew stronger as well, even as the conflicts shifted from open courts of law and public opinion to the more veiled and perhaps more influential realms of hearts and minds.

Condemnation was the District's first large-scale foray into the American landscape. Nothing within the District's own history had prepared it for this. Probably the largest single group of people from whom District officials had attempted to obtain anything had been the Met Lab, a tiny group of scientists already apprised of the District's mission and in agreement over its importance. This year would bring District officials into close contact with illiterates and lawyers, wealthy landowners and dirt-poor ex-slaves. By the nature of the project and the inclination of the District itself, the process would have to be cloaked in secrecy, even duplicity. And at all three sites, District officials were outsiders in regions that did not welcome outsiders easily.

The District *did* have a fund of experience with land acquisition by condemnation and an established bureaucracy within the Corps of Engineers whose sole function lay with appropriating land rapidly and at barest cost. This was the Land Acquisition Section of the corps, a formal division of the Real Estate Branch of the army's Quartermaster Corps and thereby an affiliate of the Corps of Engineers.

From first to last, land acquisition was a convoluted process. From "Preliminary Site Report" through negotiation to "final taking," the District wended its way through a labyrinth of some eleven separate stages, involving reams of reports and memos, and signatures by men and women ranging from local "land walkers" upward to the Secretary of War. The goal was to acquire the land cheaply, expeditiously, without protest or opposition.[7]

But the District's official procedure was the legalistic side of a far more informal and surreptitious program, already completed before the first legal briefs were filed. Indeed, long before the appraisers went out to inspect each site, the District knew what it would spend on land; long before the legal documents requesting the right to condemn property had been filed, the District knew when it would have the land for its own uses.[8]

The Tennessee site, designated alternately the Clinton Engineer Works and the Kingston Demolition Range, was the first space to be taken. (District land officials used the name to their advantage; Nancy May, holder of tract H-714, reported to Jennings's subcommittee in August 1943 that "one of the men told her she must move or bombs would be dropped in that vicinity.")[9]

The Real Estate Branch's procedures for appraisal were relatively straightforward. Appraisers were to visit the property, walking the parcel with the landowner, and marking down all relevant information concerning the land, its uses, crops and timber, all buildings, and whatever other information might bear on the value of the piece of land, including its accessibility, the presence of water and utilities, and the like. Appraisers were to photograph each building from at least two sides, and were to include the photographs in their reports. All the material was then entered on forms provided by the land office, which left spaces for the tract number; the name of the owner; valuation of improvements; replacement less depreciation basis; type of building and its size, construction type, roof type, foundation type, condition, value, and salvage value. Land office appraisers then sought "comparables"—property already sold, preferably recently—from which they made their final appraisal of the fair market value of the lands. Then the next echelon of officials came in to negotiate the final price and cut the deal with landowners.[10]

To get an idea of what the land was like, we can turn from the appraisals and the farmers' reports to the photographs appraisers made for the file. They provide an archive of evidence describing the lay of the land. These tracts ranged from rough upland ridge properties with scavenged-lumber outbuildings and log dwellings to very extensive river-bottom properties lush from the happy coincidence of water and fertile soil, and containing upward of thirty structures. Most tracts were in between—the middling parcel had a dwelling in fair-to-good condition (by the appraiser's assessment), a smokehouse, barn, henhouse, garage, and privy. Few of these had "utilities"—electricity or running water within the residences. Many of the larger ones had their own tenant houses on the property itself. The land parcels tended to be overgrown with trees; most were fenced with barbed wire. Houses were typically 1½-story, five- or six-room structures, with open porches on one or two sides. Most were rectangular or L-shaped. Judging from the photographs, most look to have been twenty-five to one hundred years old, and the appraisal forms bear this out, with dates of building that ranged back to the nineteenth century but in many cases were as recent as the late 1920s. Most were weatherbeaten, in need of paint. The driveways and roads were dirt. Children and women went barefoot; so also did many of the men. In the photographs, however, no one seems particularly to notice if they are poor or rich; they may be prepared for the photograph or casual before the lens.

The photographs required by the Land Acquisitions Section represent a compelling archive, one that lies almost entirely outside the contest between residents and the District. Nearly universally, the appraisers were inept photographers; they found it impossible to manipulate the medium to their advantage. Indeed, to do so seems never to have occurred to them. They were believers in the power of words—adjectives and adverbs appended to nouns laden with connotation. Words were written later, in the office or at home, as explanations and justifications for the assessments they accompanied. By contrast, the photographs were hastily made, carelessly framed: necessary but ineffective adjuncts to the reporting process. In a few cases, the act of photography served to provide an illusion of trust and value between appraiser and farmer; to photograph the farm, the appraiser might pose farmer and children, giving the impression that the result was a memento and not a bit of statistics.[11]

One of the most poignant of these photographs accompanies appraisal A-1-1, for the farm of W. B. Thacker (fig. 6). It is a picture of the Thacker farmhouse. In front of the house is a well-maintained late-model car, parked at the end of the driveway nearest the house. In front of the car stands a boy, perhaps twelve years old, in overalls and bare feet. He poses formally for the camera, his arms in front of him, his back straight, his eyes staring, above the lens, into the eyes of the photographer, giving his gaze the faraway look of a resolute dreamer. We can't know just why this picture was made, but we can speculate: that the photographer asked the boy to stand there, in order that he might have a guide to the scale of the building and the distance of the driveway; or that the boy asked to be included in the picture, saw it as an opportunity to have a picture of himself, his family's farmhouse, the car. In either case, the boy has been deceived. The photograph will never be returned to him; he is not to be memorialized in his pride of place, but to be evicted from that place.

The Thackers' property was one of the more highly appraised sites. Its farmhouse, a five-room, two-story frame building with a board-and-metal roof and a rock-post foundation, in fair condition, was appraised at $800; the other eleven structures, including a granary, a garage, a shop, a sawmill shed, and a hog house, all listed in poor condition, gave a total appraisal of $1,377, and a salvage of $125 (fig. 7).

This is not the only photograph where the resident is included along with the real property—there are many. Carl McKeehan stands in front of his house ("A-36-1, frame, 26 x 30, metal and board roof, rock pillar foundation, condition: poor, value 150"; the whole property valued at $220). The negative is indistinct; is he holding a gun in his

A-1-1

FIG. 6 Appraisal Report and Supplement, Tract A-1–1, Oak Ridge. Courtesy National Archives.

hand? A stick? Two men stand by the garage at James Comer's lot, tract A-39, total value $1,165; one appears old and stooped. The view of Comer's house shows him standing to the right, almost excised by the framing edge. In others, men in jeans or overalls stand in the dirt paths between buildings, or in the shadows of the open-sided hay barns or spring houses.

The dry, precise words of the appraisals rasp against the rich uncontrolled suggestiveness of the photographs, in which all that is certain and determinate is retained by the now-lost world of light and wind, of slow accents and long pauses, leaving only meditation for the photograph, which has stripped off a meniscus-thin wafer of sensual practice and stretched it between the waffled edges of a drugstore-developed 2¾ x 3¾ inch print:

> A-12 E. E. Hagler 4000: 2 story 8 rm dwelling 22 x 30 x 18 with 18 x 20 ell, frame with metal and board roof and brick/concrete foundation in fair condition; smoke house; garage; garage; poultry house; breeder; poultry house; poultry house; poultry house; tenant house; poultry house; smoke house 12 x 14 x 12; spring house; poultry house; poultry house; spring house; barn 30 x 34; old tenant house; tenant house; smoke house; spring house; crib & shed; barn 26 x 40; privy; old store; old shop. no conditions above fair except crib and shed, breeder, and lower barn. 26 buildings on property.[12]

In the photographs, the farmers appear proud, or at least comfortable and at home; the children are shambling but solemnly at ease with what is and will be their patrimony. In the text of the appraisals, however, the land is unattractive, the properties decayed and rarely valuable.[13]

Simply to look at the formal descriptions of condition is to see how universally the Land Acquisition Section held to a standard of value to which nearly all of these farms and village houses could never conform. Of a sample of eighty-six parcels, only five were rated positively ("good" or "desirable"); the rest went unrated or received ratings of "poor" or "very poor," "fair," "unattractive," "inconvenient," "ordinary," or "very ordinary." As a consequence, the appraisals priced the land low. Just how low would be a matter of controversy for considerable time.

Condemnation

53

The notices of condemnation for the Clinton, Tennessee, site of the Manhattan Engineer District went out beginning on October 7, 1942—in the mail, delivered by messengers, and, when residents were absent, tacked to the front door or to a nearby

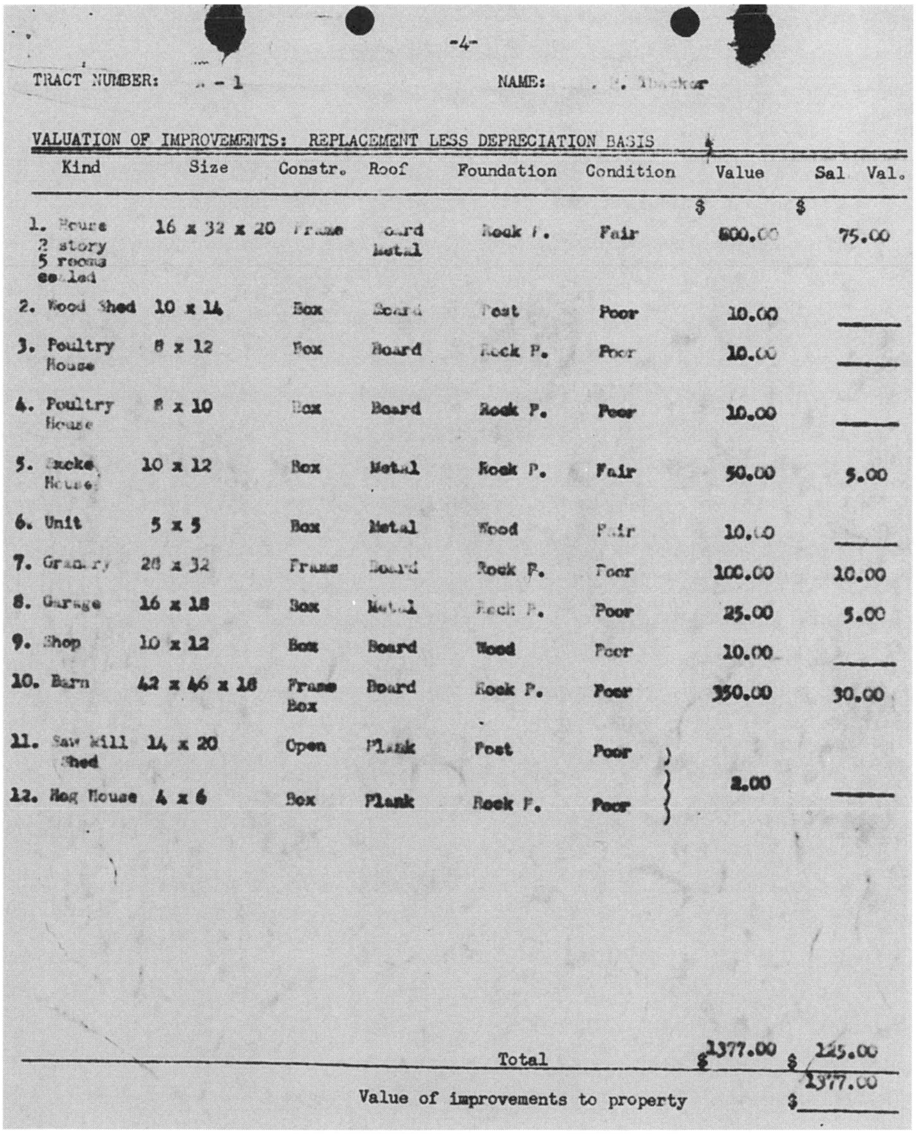

-4-

TRACT NUMBER: . - 1   NAME: . Th cker

VALUATION OF IMPROVEMENTS: REPLACEMENT LESS DEPRECIATION BASIS

Kind	Size	Constr.	Roof	Foundation	Condition	Value	Sal. Val.
						$	$
1. House 2 story 5 rooms ee led	16 x 32 x 20	Frame	ourd Metal	Rock F.	Fair	500.00	75.00
2. Wood Shed	10 x 14	Box	Board	Post	Poor	10.00	——
3. Poultry House	8 x 12	Box	Board	Rock P.	Poor	10.00	——
4. Poultry House	8 x 10	Box	Board	Rock P.	Poor	10.00	——
5. Smoke House	10 x 12	Box	Metal	Rock P.	Fair	50.00	5.00
6. Unit	5 x 5	Box	Metal	Wood	Fair	10.00	——
7. Granary	28 x 32	Frame	Board	Rock F.	Poor	100.00	10.00
8. Garage	16 x 18	Box	Metal	Rock P.	Poor	25.00	5.00
9. Shop	10 x 12	Box	Board	Wood	Poor	10.00	——
10. Barn	42 x 46 x 18	Frame Box	Board	Rock P.	Poor	350.00	30.00
11. Saw Mill Shed	14 x 20	Open	Plank	Post	Poor	}	——
12. Hog House	4 x 6	Box	Plank	Rock F.	Poor	} 2.00	——

Total $ 1377.00 $ 125.00
                                                          1377.00
Value of improvements to property $ _____

FIG. 7 Appraisal Report and Supplement, Tract A-1–1, Oak Ridge. Courtesy National Archives.

tree. The papers gave orders to residents to vacate the premises, in as little as two weeks, leaving everything but their personal effects. Immediately on their heels came the negotiators. They were there to make a formal cash offer to the owner and get a signed agreement, known as a "stipulation," to the amount set forth in the condemnation procedures.[14]

This was the first notification most owners received telling what the District was offering for their land. Negotiators had an arsenal of tactics at their disposal, and they used it. Many residents, knowing how little time they had before eviction, became distraught and preoccupied with figuring out how they would continue to live. Negotiators could play on this; they could promise immediate payment and threaten lengthy delays, and few landowners knew how accurate these promises and threats might be. Mr. J. W. Hackworth reported at the August investigative session that the negotiator told him to sign the stipulation or "he might never be paid." An unnamed owner called the process "black-jack bargaining." Another reported that the government representatives "weren't negotiators. They were persuaders. They had no powers to negotiate; only to talk the owner into accepting the price set by the appraiser." The routine argument of the negotiators was to say that if matters went to condemnation court, "they would not be settled for years and that the owners would not get as much money," in the words of another farmer.[15]

With immediate condemnation and eviction as weapons, the negotiators persuaded 506 of the 806 Tennessee landowners to settle on the spot, and the newspapers quickly published the amounts. Land prices in the immediate region skyrocketed overnight. Owners who were holding out soon saw the error of their ways; if they didn't get cash quickly, they'd be completely frozen out of the market for new lands. Another 151 of the holdouts went back to the negotiators and accepted the offers, at average increases of 33 percent. They had won more money, but it was already worth far less to them in an inflating market.

Most of these farmers found they were evicted not just from their lands, but from the region itself. Within days after the newspapers released the reports, available land disappeared from the real estate rolls. Residents began to pack and go. But the District offered no moving money, and for many, the money from their land sales was held up in title searches or bureaucratic snafus. The District showed some pity; it made a few exceptions to those who were penniless and had no place to go, allowing them to stay on as squatters until their money came through.[16]

For those shocked into inaction, the Land Acquisition Section had a reminder form, called a "Request to Vacate." Parlee Raby received his sometime after November 16, 1942, though the date given on the front of the document was five days earlier:[17]

> From: War Department
> Corps of Engineers
> Kingston Demolition Range
> Land Acquisition Section
> Harriman, Tennessee
>
> The War Department intends to take possession of your farm December 1 1942. It will be necessary for you to move, not later than that date.

In order to pay you quickly, the money for your property will be placed into the United States Court of Knoxville, Tennessee.

The Court will permit you to withdraw a substantial part of this money without waiting. This may be done without impairing your right to contest the value fixed on your property by the War Department.

It is expected that your money will be put in court within ten days, and as soon as you are notified, it is suggested you get in touch with the United States Attorney to find how much can be drawn.

You [*sic*] fullest cooperation will be a material aid to the War Department.

Very truly yours,
Fred Morgan
Project Manager[18]

For an educated American, this seems now and doubtless seemed then a clear statement, direct and forthright. But to the farmers, whom the District had described as "unskilled in the mechanical trades," many of them marginally literate and certainly unschooled in the niceties of the federal court system, it might as well have been written in German. For M. J. Atchley, whose farm was "located back on the mail route . . . away back and very inconvenient," or for Joseph O. L. Wilkerson, whose farm was located "approximately one mile . . . on a narrow rough road" from the RFD route, to "get in touch with the United States Attorney to find how much can be drawn" was nearly an impossibility.[19]

The relationship between access to cash and right to appeal was confusing not only to illiterate or uneducated hillbilly farmers. Even Lawrence S. Hitchcock, once headmaster of the Los Alamos School on the New Mexico site, and now a colonel in the army, found it necessary to get legal advice on the point before he would authorize withdrawals of money from the account deposited for the school. And his lawyers saw fit to remind him of a danger that now existed as a result of "innovations" in the wartime condemnation procedures: "formerly the price offered by the Government was considered to be the absolute floor and . . . the negotiations can only result in the rising of that figure or leaving it as originally offered. Recent decision of the Supreme Court, however, has decided that if the jury considers the Government offer too high, they may set a lower figure and the original owners would have to refund down to that. . . . however . . . this is not very likely to happen as the jury are more apt to raise the figure than to lower."[20]

The legal case mentioned by the lawyers was almost certainly one of those argued by a government lawyer, Norman Littell, early in the war. This series of cases had succeeded in establishing the right of the army to refuse to take into account the cost of replacement lands, or to calculate the extent that land inflation resulting from the army's actions might have on the value of condemned property. Can there be any doubt what a powerful weapon this decision became in the hands of District negotiators as they dealt with the far less savvy tract holders at the Tennessee and Washington sites?

Parlee Raby had a little less than two weeks to get off his property. And the earliest he could receive his money was ten days after the date on the front of his notice—

November 11, 1942. If all went well, he would then have four days to find the correct court and the correct office of that court, fill out and file the necessary forms, and then turn the District's money, or whatever "substantial portion" of it the court could be persuaded to release, into a new farm, onto which he might move by December 1, 1942.

Perhaps he was one of the high percentage of condemnees who had settled in the region after having been evicted from the richer bottomlands flooded by the TVA in the thirties. A few had already been evicted twice: once from the region of the Great Smokies National Park, during the twenties, and then by the TVA. As District historians admitted in 1946, these constant moves forced the affected residents to sell "a majority of their personal effects at a loss," in order to garner the cash to move at all. Not that moving was easy even with cash and a destination. District officials reported a "lack of moving facilities" in the region.[21]

The fact was that truckers all over the region were swamped, less by the eight hundred families leaving than by the thousands of families that had already begun to move into the area with the first tentative rumors of a huge new construction program to begin around the first of the year 1943. The war had begun to turn bust into boom, but not in the South, nor in many other pockets of America where unemployed workers desperately sought steady work. When the Kingston Demolition Range reached public ear, the news sparked a mass migration into the area. Condemnees fought with immigrants for land, for trucks, for jobs, shelter, food. All prices skyrocketed. In the confusion, most of the evictees lost their identities as residents of the region, as proud landowners and farmers. Some of them simply disappeared off the rosters; they surfaced (when they did) as far away as Chicago. Others huddled in the nearby towns, moved in with relatives, or lived in their cars, surviving on their condemnation money until the Manhattan Engineer District began to hire. Of the original owners, 60 percent ended up as tenant-workers on the lands that had been theirs. In their own eyes, *they* were the condemned.[22]

But their story is told in the records, and their rights (however abrogated) remained part of the system of laws and customs that characterized American culture. There was another group of people who had disappeared long before this stage in the process, a group that might be said never to have appeared. This was the substantial population of sharecroppers or "tenant farmers," many of them "colored people" or, more formally, "Negroes" (to use the parlance of the time), all of them propertyless, powerless, and voiceless. The District never admitted their existence. In formal assessments of the numbers of people in the area, it took the number of land parcels and multiplied by the average family size, then added on a few. With just over eight hundred parcels, it estimated a thousand families and three thousand people.

The land appraisal forms tell a very different story. They record farm after farm as having "tenant cabins" or "tenant houses" on them. For example, parcel A-12, belonging to E. E. Hagler, had a "dwelling house"; it also had three "tenant houses" listed on the appraisal form. Even that number may not reflect the true number of tenants, for Hagler's property had no less than seven poultry houses, suggesting that perhaps more families lived on the land, farming "on shares" or simply paying rent for housing the appraiser failed to take into account or miscategorized. The number of sharecroppers is never estimated, except in Orrin Thacker's original "gross appraisal." There he reported that "from 60–70 percent of the farms are owner operated." By this estimate, the District failed to take into account somewhere between 1,300 and 2,000 people; given how easily people disappeared up the hollows and along the ridges, the number might have gone as high as three thousand, half of them children. We see them in the photographs of the sites, often; they are found in the fields or playing in the dirt front yards of the "tenant houses" or walking along the paths and roads that crisscrossed so many of the parcels. They, and their parents, received nothing from the District, not even recognition. If we imagine a landowner having not only to contest the appraisal, deal with his or her own eviction, and master the complexities of the process, but also to inform the tenants of the necessity for them to leave, we can expect that these tenants had just days between the shock of notice and the reality of eviction. And then they disappeared.[23]

At about the same time that it took its lands in Tennessee, the District reached for the Los Alamos mesa in New Mexico. But that process was a more sedate and civilized affair, a matter primarily between gentlemen, fellow officers, lawyers. This is not to say that dispossession was any the less violent, or the losses any less extreme.

In retrospect, officials of the Los Alamos Ranch School recognized that the first hint of interest in a separate scientific site came long before it was admitted in the official records of the District. At the time, the notification that the school was to be closed, its lands and buildings condemned, and an unexplained secret army facility built in its place came as a bitter blow, particularly to the faculty and staff who had been with the school since its inception and who had assumed their lives would always be bound up with its insular culture and spectacular landscape.[24]

A. J. Connell and Fermor S. Church, the school's acting headmaster, were at a loss as to how to respond. As a delaying tactic, they insisted that only a letter from Secretary of War Stimson himself would persuade them of the inevitability of the process. Dudley promised the letter, and by the first of December Stimson had sent it out.[25]

School officials sought to postpone the condemnation, but Stimson's notice to the school revealed how deadly earnest the government was—Stimson insisted that school officials simply walk away from the property, and in the process "refrain from making the reasons for the closing of the school known to the public at large."[26]

The District took official possession on February 7, 1943. By that time, formal condemnation had passed into the courts; the District had a detailed inventory of everything held by the Ranch School, including garbage pails, sugar bowls, pie plates, mustard jars, cots, and candle holders. And here the signal advantage to the army of taking the school becomes clearer. Not only did the District receive an isolated tract of land; it also acquired all the trappings necessary to move immediately into Oppenheimer's "shangri-la." After all, Oppenheimer's original estimate, set out in the early site requirements, was for a community of 265—he believed that six scientists, "assisted by some engineers, technicians, and draftsmen, could do the job quite rapidly and effectively." With its fifty-plus buildings, working farm, and self-sufficient water and power systems, the Ranch School would (Oppenheimer assumed) be in move-in condition the instant its students and staff could be moved out.

But once Oppenheimer's utopia became Groves's property, its size and character changed dramatically. As early as November, army officials had issued a revised estimate, setting the population at six hundred, a result of Groves's skepticism concerning the ability of the scientists to work without an administrative infrastructure, and of his insistence that a large military force be stationed there as a security detail. That this expansion instantly converted many of the advantages of the site into liabilities could not be factored into the equation of District acquisition. The site had been chosen; now it would have to be modified until it was functional.[27]

The final weeks at the Los Alamos Ranch School were hard ones for those whose lives had been bound up with its combination of bracing scenery and manly rest-cure. By mid-December the road up to the mesa was a mess, destroyed by the gigantic trucks, bulldozers, ditch-digging machines, and other earth-moving equipment that lumbered up onto the mesa to begin the process of destroying what the army had bought. The noise was deafening. School officials watched precious stands of trees, idyllic pastoral spots, and athletic training fields ripped up and destroyed under the imprimatur of the Corps of Engineers. Hitchcock returned from Washington to help in the work of packing books, records, and files and whatever materials were left unclaimed by the District. For many of the longest-tenured school people, it was more than they could bear.[28]

School officials had the change of ownership flaunted in their faces; expecting a forthright negotiation among patriotic equals, they found themselves summarily treated. Hitchcock sent to his Los Alamos colleagues the names of the right men to contact in the Real Estate Branch and the Department of Justice. Meetings in Washington and Santa Fe had an informal, man-to-man feel to them, as both Hitchcock and Connell reiterated in their letters back and forth. Connell described one of these meetings in a letter to Hitchcock: "The whole dicker smacks to me of a horse trade. Perhaps if someone had passed around a bottle we might have reached some conclusion. Sorry I was not on hand to suggest it. As it is we now must sit back and await the second coming." Yet the result was anything but friendly—long after the District and school agreed to a sum in excess of the original amount deposited with the orders of possession, school officials were still waiting for their money.[29]

Much of the difficulty during the negotiation lay in understanding just what each side's figures represented, and especially the definition of "goodwill." For the army, the school's value was limited to the tangible property it acquired—the land, but also the plates, the pots and pans, the 46 bunk beds, the 60 head of horses and 50 saddles, the 121 bales of hay and 800 cords of firewood, and all the rest of the physical objects, small and large, treasured and matter-of-fact, that had made possible the school's existence for more than twenty years. As Connell wrote during the last stages of negotiation, "the great difficulty as I see it is the failure to recognize intangible values. . . . Of course a school has values with which they are utterly unacquainted, and, possibly, by their Department unrecognized." It would take another month for Connell to accept that these "values" were lost.[30]

On the District's side, however, there was no apparent confusion that this was a cash matter demanding the most ruthless of bargaining—so ruthless, in fact, that the case ended up in court, and the presiding judge called on the District to pay special interest based on its recalcitrance—a sum still unpaid when headmaster Connell died on February 11, 1944. Connell's final wish had been to be buried at the ranch, but the District refused.[31]

Connell's end, and the payment of the disputed interest sometime later in 1944, put the period on the condemnation of the Los Alamos Ranch School. But there is still the matter of the other residents of the mesa—the small ranchers, nearly all Hispano sheep-herders, who had taken up lands or grazing rights on the mesa—who had to be divested of their properties. In the case of the only other large private landholder, the Anchor Ranch, the Real Estate Branch reached a settlement of $25,000 without significant controversy. The Ranch School's lawyer had apparently been in touch with the Anchor Ranch owners when he reported to Connell that the appraiser had "been very fair with the stock men on their lands taken." The other owners in the area did not all agree with this reading of the situation. Elfego Gomez (120 acres), Ernesto Montoyo (160 acres), and Adolpho Montoyo (acreage unknown) appeared in the District's history as "the principal objectors to the amount offered," suggesting they spearheaded a campaign of protest. Their objections, while unsuccessful, aren't surprising. The small landowners held more than two-thirds of the privately owned land (and probably a similar proportion of the grazing rights), but they received less than an eighth of the money.[32]

Enrique Montoyo owned 222.5 acres and farmed another eight acres within national forest land under a special permit from the Forestry Service. His ownership of grazing permits is unrecorded but may well have been substantial. Bernie White's appraisal reported that all the federal land was held under grazing permits, and the War Department's site report set that land at 50,400 acres. The "small" landowners held plots ranging in size from ten to over two hundred acres, and equivalent grazing permits. There was a reservoir built by a man named James Loomis and deeded to A. M. Ross. There were the timber rights as well. Payment for all of this would have to come out of slightly more than $47,000, the amount remaining of the District's acquisition funds for the site.[33]

Searching for the addresses of these owners proved troublesome to the Real Estate Branch. For one thing, they had some difficulty spelling the names of the Hispano landowners. Even at the end of the process, some names remained incorrect or misspelled. So also with the legal addresses of these people. Although three separate lists of "purported owners" were made, some of the names had no addresses whatsoever, beyond "Santa Fe, New Mexico." These were not people the District took seriously. They had no power within its terms, and their lands were more easily taken if they remained anonymous.[34]

Yet behind the lists of names and addresses lie the traces of ancient and complex Hispano and Pueblo Indian kinship systems. Nearly all the known landowners were strung along Route 1 between Los Alamos and Santa Fe. Between the time of White's initial appraisal and the final disposition of the condemnation, some of these men and women had died and their holdings reverted to their kin, many of whom were already named on the address lists. Seven Roybals appear on the rosters, none at the same address. Four of the owners, all with different last names, shared rural delivery post box 144 on Route 1. Together, these smallholders represented large, often ancient dynastic landholders, hanging on to the last portions of once-giant estates, land grants, and tribal territories.

Whatever objections these representatives of ancient land claims might have had to the loss of their claims on the mesa, they were inconsequential to the District and the Real Estate Branch. Condemnation had already assured the outcome. The Ranch School's lawyer had his ear to the ground; he reported that the principal appraiser, Crowley, had treated the larger grazers and the timber harvesters "fairly." Likewise, the Anchor Ranch and the Ranch School, both temporary usurpers of Spanish land grants and Indian tribal homesteads, were judiciously rewarded for giving up their claims. But those who held the oldest title to the region, those whose families had resided on the land grants for centuries, were the easiest to uproot. No protracted legal negotiations, no manly talks among fellow representatives of the army, no "horse trade" sealed by "passing around the bottle." In gathering up the land, the timber rights, the grazing rights of the "small landowners," District officials reported, "no special problems were encountered."[35]

The circumstances at Clinton, Tennessee, not those at Los Alamos, provided the prototype for procedures at the Hanford Engineer Works in Washington. For all intents and purposes, the Tennessee site had been cleared by the beginning of March 1943, the point at which the notices to vacate began appearing in Hanford, White Bluffs, and surrounding areas within the curve of the Columbia River. "Gross appraisal" of the Hanford site had begun in early January 1943; Undersecretary of War Robert P. Patterson signed the authorizing directive for land acquisition on February 8; Lewis B. Schwellenbach, a federal judge, issued an order of possession on February 23; and on March 6, the vast majority of residents received their notices that they had between two weeks and three months to evacuate. These notices predated appraisals in most cases.

But here, as in Tennessee, there were two pictures of the process. One belonged to the District, the other to the residents. Not just the vantage point but the object of view differed. The District and its officials, Colonel Matthias the most prominent and influential among them, saw the process in the context of military inevitability. To them the imagined ideal was an orderly and vast industrial-military enterprise stretching across land that was, by District estimates, 88.2 percent "inferior grazing land"— scrubland and scabland, spotted with sagebrush and effectively desert. They viewed the river region as a minor part of the land, necessary for water intake and outflow from the various atomic and chemical plants, desirable as a site for a small "village" of "operators" and their families.

For the people of Hanford, Richland, White Bluffs, and the surrounding countryside, the ideal was located in both past and future: in a mythic idyll when water was plentiful and fruit prices were high, when families were unstressed and children played in the fields and swam in the irrigation ditches; and in a future in which rising wartime prices and other events would bring that perfect balance of progress and a return to an ideal past. Like the Clinton residents, these men, women, and children had no future outside of the land they owned or farmed or served. To lose that land would be to lose themselves.

The crux of this engagement between two cultures, so foreign to one another, lay in valuation. The District had to get its land quickly and cheaply; the dominant image of vast stretches of desert of little or no utility colored every aspect of the land acquisition process. By the District's lights, it was only continuing the process of land consolidation that characterized the region's history. The federal government already owned 16.5 percent of the land; the state, 10.6 percent; local counties, 9.6 percent; primary railroad lines, another 10.7 percent. Their enterprise consolidated an untidy agglomeration of landholders, making order out of disarray, finding use for the useless.

But for the residents, valuation of the land was also, in some fundamental way, a valuation of themselves. To read the newspaper reports, the accounts of protest meetings surreptitiously recorded by District officers, the letters of protest, and even the reminiscences collected decades later is to recognize how deeply individuals and families had bound up their identities in the lands they held, the lands they stared across, and the lands they imagined to be theirs. And who can be surprised? Every aspect entailed in the original marketing of those lands was bound up with the mythological American linkage of citizen and land—from the first sales brochures of the Hanford Irrigation Company through the wording of the state of Washington's land-settlement bills, to the pictures chromolithographed on paper and stapled or glued to the crates of fruit harvested on the lands and shipped across the country. To move onto these lands, to hold to them, often for a generation or two, was to commit oneself to the promise of what Woody Guthrie, writing after he saw the region while traveling for the Bonneville Power Administration, called "green pastures of plenty, from dry desert sand."[36]

We have two quite different narratives at work in the condemnation process. One is a narrative of events, a historical narrative. The other is a narrative of myth, a procession of pictures drawn and stories believed by both sides. It is not that the historical circumstances served as the ground for the generation and transformation of myths. Sometimes it is the opposite—sometimes the beliefs carried into the narrative to catalyze the events that formed the historical process.

At Hanford, the procedures entailed in land acquisition were similar to those at Clinton—if anything, they were more draconian. For example: while some residents had only two weeks to get out, the earliest checks took three months to be issued, leaving some residents with months during which they had no cash, no livelihood, and no place to live. The possibility of finding available land even slightly comparable to that lost to the District was even more remote here than in Tennessee, given the limited zone of irrigation on either side of the Columbia, the small number of working irrigation districts from which one might draw water, and the tremendous expense of laying pipe and developing irrigable land. While theirs was agricultural land, farmers were cultivating specialty crops, orchards and fruit-bearing plants that required significant preparation—sometimes years of it—before yields could be harvested.[37]

As in Tennessee, the appraisers had a mandate to keep costs low, which provided further pressure on land values. Though they were familiar with the state, few appraisers knew this region and its climatological and agricultural oddities. They came from the Federal Land Bank, and most of them had home addresses in and around the Seattle and Portland areas.[38]

Arriving on individual parcels with forms in hand, appraisers were often shocked by what they found. The farms were mostly small—ten to forty acres in size—and so were the houses. The outbuildings were rough, frequently constructed of scavenged timbers and slats acquired from abandoned farms. A few trees surrounded the houses. They were usually young-growth, stunted specimens, planted some twenty years before. Outside of these, there was little in the way of foliage. The grounds were often strewn with debris, the trees leafless and the yards unkempt.[39]

For appraisers used to the fertile lands of the Willamette Valley and regions served by the water-rich storms of the Pacific, these farms must have seemed unbearably bleak. Unless appraisers were familiar with the economy and the milieu of irrigation farming in the West, they could not have understood how important these factors were to the ecology of the region. Trees that didn't bear fruit were few because trees drew precious irrigation water; they were useful as windbreaks and shade providers around the house, but no more. As a result, lumber was scarce and expensive, and reusing scavenged lumber was the norm. Even today one can stand in the midst of the Hanford reservation and look in all four directions without seeing a single tree.

The orchards and fields as well were unlike what most midwestern or Pacific coastline farmers would have found familiar. Irrigation properties were labor and cash intensive. Unless the crops offered evident value for the expenditure, it was smarter to leave the land untended and await another year. The fruit trees were low and small; this protected them from windstorms and made harvesting easier, while contributing to the yield. Apple and other fruit orchardists prune ruthlessly, so that only fruit-bearing branches remain, making the tree more efficient and cutting down on irrigation costs; the result is not what tourists would consider an attractive tree. Asparagus, mint, grapes, and melons are also eccentric-looking crops; they provide extremely high-value yields but do not grow tall and green. Yet these were the principal crops of the area.[40]

These seeming oddities were the result of the irrigation ecology of the region. And the irrigation facilities themselves were difficult to assess without extensive experience in this sort of environment. The two incorporated irrigation districts, Richland and Priest Rapids, were relatively modern and well repaired, thanks in part to the sale of electricity from the power system. But the districts brought water only to the edges of land plots; from there, farmers and orchardists were responsible for getting the water into their land. The result was often a hodgepodge of open ditches, lined canals, wooden channels, open and closed pipe, some in good repair, some in ruins, most somewhere in between. As water costs went down, keeping ditches and channels in good repair became less crucial; when those channels went through other irrigable regions, allowing leakage was a way of servicing two areas of one's tract at once.

All of this assumed that the tracts were in fact occupied and in operation as orchards or farms. Many were occupied but the lands uncultivated; many were unused, their owners living on residential tracts in town or on other tracts they were operating. Few of the owners considered these properties abandoned, however; for most, they were temporarily uncultivated, awaiting the return of family members from the front or the shipyards, or the availability of contract labor, or simply a further rise in the profit margins of the particular crops. Some residents had bought tracts as investments, planning to expand their holdings into these areas but not yet having done so.[41]

There was also the matter of the season of appraisal. It was winter when the appraisers arrived, and winter in Hanford is a bleak season at best. Appraisal photographs show this well. Wintertime temperatures could plummet to twenty below zero; the winds howled across the empty land, shaking off the last leaves and whirling them into grim piles in the lee of buildings. Everything looked emptier and more desolate in the winter. With the growing season over, many farmers and orchardists left their tracts to move into town. The war had generated a boom in shipbuilding and other defense industries, and Seattle and coastal towns offered the lure of employment in lucrative trades. Appraisers arrived at some farms to find their owners gone for the season, due back in March or April. The Kennewick *Courier-Reporter* on March 18, 1943, detailed the story of Herb Morey and his family, who had left the area after the crops were in the previous fall and moved to the shipyards on the coast to work in defense industries. They returned in the second week of March to prepare the lands and found their farms lost to them, property of the Hanford Engineer Works of the Manhattan Engineer District, Army Corps of Engineers.[42]

No one was at the Morey family home to report to the appraiser that the homestead was occupied, a working farm, or to provide information vital to the appraisal process. Appraisers need the help of landowners in making their assessments, even when they are familiar with the region. Certain spaces on the Hanford appraisal forms often went unfilled, and not only because residents were unavailable to provide the information. Comparable properties were difficult to come by; so was information on crop yields, on when the land had been acquired and for how much, or on the irrigation rights attendant upon ownership. The appraisal forms are often ambiguous at best.[43]

But the appraisal amounts themselves weren't ambiguous at all. They were low—much below what even the most pessimistic residents had expected. The appraisers seem to have worked quite deliberately to force prices down—choosing unreasonable "comparables" upon which to base their assessments, choosing transactions made during the height of the Depression, rather than sales figures that reflected the wartime run-up in land prices. In addition, appraisers were instructed not to include crop values in their assessments, even though the timeline for condemnation assured that crops, too, would end up in the District's hands.

The Federal Land Bank drew its land pool from tracts sold over the past few years. Few of these were in good shape when sold; most had been abandoned. Until a group of Mormons arrived in the late 1930s and early 1940s to form a colony of sorts, it had been hard to persuade buyers to move into the area, given the demands of working that region and the expertise necessary to do it well. The Mormons had come, in fact, because of the bargain rates on the parcels they bought. Their renovation of these properties and the profitability they garnered from them spoke well of the prospects for the region; but the low sale prices they had paid served as a source for "comparables" and allowed the Land Acquisitions Branch to demand lower possible appraisals and sharp bargaining on the part of negotiators.

This explains why appraisals were so low—and we can say with assurance that the appraisals were low. Appraisers rarely used comparable-worth sales as their basis for assessing value. They often reported on the forms that the farms under consideration were in better condition than the comparable tracts listed—yet they routinely offered half the comparable worth or, if there were multiple tracts offered as "comparables," they routinely based their claims on the most run-down and valueless tracts. In some cases, land values were less than purchase prices fifteen years before, reflecting the widespread Depression-era deflation in land-values. By judiciously choosing those tracts sold in the depths of the Depression, the District avoided accounting for the run-up in prices that had occurred in the wartime years.

Because the appraisers arrived when the lands were fallow, they were instructed not to include any crop values in their assessments. But in a significant number of cases, the District did not take possession of the land until as late as August of that year. In addition, many of the crops were untraditional—one did not plant the seed in spring and harvest in fall. With apples and cherries, for example, much of the work preparing for the next year's harvest was concentrated in fall. Landowners caught in these circumstances gave up half their annual earnings; in the case of crops that were prepared but never harvested, an entire year's income could be uncompensated.[44]

The story of condemnation at Hanford bears a disheartening resemblance to the case of Clinton, Tennessee. What differed at this early stage was the District's approach to the situation. With a longer timeline between site selection and necessary occupation, District officials believed that they could smooth relations with members of the outer community by persuading them of the rightness of the District's position and the inevitability of its incursion. But this assumption did not take into account the vast gap between the pictures of the District and the residents, the extremity of the Land Acquisition Section's penuriousness, and the depth of the residents' identity with their land.

Colonel Franklin T. Matthias, designated head of the Hanford project, arrived early on the site. His plan was, apparently, to use his presence to persuade locals to accept the inevitability of the process, and to work wherever possible as a conciliator rather than an adversary. But Matthias was up against more than just low appraisals by appraisers unfamiliar with the region and its agricultural particularities. The District lands encompassed more than individual farms, orchards, residences; they also subsumed a wide variety of other types of property. There were, in fact, twenty-three different contingencies the condemnation procedure had to cover, and District historians in 1946 neatly mapped them out: they included pumping stations, irrigation pumps, an electrical switching station and the electrical power lines that transported dam-generated electricity into the power grid, private and public telephone lines, roads, schools, railroads, ferries, mineral deposits and the rights to those deposits, cemeteries, islands, the municipal water plant for Hanford, Indian fishing rights, water taxes and liens, and the Priest Rapids and Richland Irrigation Districts themselves.[45]

The District's forces arrived at the site from Washington on March 24. The delegation included General Groves, Mr. Connelly and Mr. Farrell of the Department of Agriculture, Colonel John J. O'Brien, head of the army's Real Estate Branch, and Matthias himself.[46]

Anticipating a quick cave-in by locals, Matthias had arranged a meeting with farmers at Richland for the next day. The idea was to explain the inevitability of the army's incursion, call upon patriotic ideals, and get the farmers reconciled to the process. To do this, Matthias and Groves brought to the meeting a man whom Matthias inadvertently called one of his "Real Estate people"—George Farrell of the Department of Agriculture. Farrell's role was to make clear the inevitability of the process, the unanimity of government support for the project, and the futility of resistance. At a meeting with farmers and residents, Farrell and the others told the landowners

Invention

64

they had only one chance to get an offer; turn it down, and they would have only the option of a lawsuit that "will cost you plenty," as R. S. Reierson, an irrigation district officer, recollected Farrell's words. Once condemned, landowners had no choice but to get off the land. If they refused, Farrell said, "we have a way of convincing people. Somewhere else where the government acquired land, a person refused to move. A caterpillar was brought to his home and started to move in on a corner. He decided he'd better move out then."[47]

Two weeks later, Matthias reported to General Groves that "the Richland farmers were quiet." But trouble was brewing. For decades, the difficulties and hardships of the region had worked to knit together individuals and families. Now the community fought to protect itself and its members. Reierson and the other area leaders moved aggressively on a number of fronts. They enlisted the power of the Grange, the national farmers' union, to plead their case in Washington. They got President Roosevelt's attention by arguing that the condemnations were removing crucially needed farmlands from the domestic pool; within days, Roosevelt ordered an investigation.[48]

Back at the site, the irrigation districts began to use their clout to fight the process. Calling in outside appraisers to provide alternative assessments of irrigated lands and equipment, the districts wrote to their farmers warning them not to sign the army's options form, as it contained a subtle clause giving the army ownership over the farmer's portion of irrigation district assets.[49]

The combination of pressures pushed Matthias to urge the Land Acquisition Section people to "use a little more tact and judgment in dealing with the owners." This, he hoped, would lower the level of antagonism between Manhattan District officials and residents. But squeezed between the steadily increasing local resistance and the continuation of presidential scrutiny, Matthias himself began to harden. By the end of April, matters had taken what seemed to Matthias an ominous turn: a Yakima attorney named Lloyd Wiehl arrived at a meeting between the county prosecuting attorney and Matthias, and signaled that he was prepared to represent any and all residents in a public legal dispute that was sure to cost the District plenty in time, money, and secrecy.[50]

Wiehl's appearance on the scene combined with the aggressive defiance on the part of the irrigation districts marked a new period of resistance. The irrigation district's appraisals of land came back; they were far higher than the army's appraisers' estimates. That the army still considered the appraisals to be a closed book only confirmed the extent of the outrage and the possibility that an organized campaign would result in real gains, as residents saw it. With savvy legal minds and experienced institutions ranged against them, with the president himself urging that they move to a more docile site, the District's officers prepared for a difficult battle.

To resist the District required more than a vague sense that the land condemnation was unfair. The Real Estate Branch represented the Manhattan Engineer District; the District represented the army; the army represented a nation at war, a nation whose officials had determined that sacrifices on the part of individuals, be they drafted soldiers or evicted landowners, formed a necessary and inevitable part of the campaign against a known evil. To fight back required that one make a moral stand of one sort or another. The unearthing of injustice was not enough; injustice was part of the equation of wartime, one of the sacrifices made by a nation and a culture at war. To set one's personal rights against the needs of a nation at war was—within the discourse of war, at least—an act of selfishness.

Much of the propaganda of the early wartime years was aimed at fostering that notion: setting self second to state; elevating loss and affliction, remaking them into the concepts of "sacrifice" and "hardship," where they became measures of patriotism; reorienting American values so that patriotism rose to the top of the hierarchy.

One of the Clinton evacuees recollected his experience with the army. Recorded after the war, his reminiscence provides a telling composite of the pressures and conflicts present at the moment of loss:

> I was born in the house my grandfather built back in 1846. . . . All the folks in these parts were farmers. They worked the year round and minded their own business, peaceful folks living a simple life. . . . We didn't pay much attention to the outside world and they didn't bother with us. That was up to 1942 anyway, when one day a man came to our house and said he was from the Government. "We're going to buy up your land," he said to me. "All of it?" I asked. "Yes, sir," he said, "we're going to buy all the land in this section. Everyone has to go."
>   Well, I went outside the house with the visitor and looked around me . . . up at the green hills my grandfather had come across 100 years earlier, and I looked at the farm I'd worked for half a century. I asked the visitor what the Government was going to do and he said he didn't rightfully know, but it was for winning the war. I had three sons in service—two overseas—and I figured if giving up my home and my land would help bring them home sooner, I'd be happy to do it.[51]

This unnamed farmer's report is chock-full of symbols appropriate to the wartime moment—farmers with roots generations deep, tilling the soil and minding their own business, "the green hills," and a man "from the Government," who threatens that life but who represents the interests of "three sons in service." These pentimenti of years contain the traces of that particular farmer's very real dilemma: his attempt to reconcile a self-definition bound up in his land and its national symbolism, with a call that he give over this land to the nation and bring his own boys home sooner.

The outcome in this case fit the government's ideal. This farmer made the correct decision, sacrificing his farm for his country. A District propagandist, George O. Robinson, told this story probably in late 1945 or 1946 and thereby memorialized the man. Not so the others who fought army incursion—they and their heroics do not appear in books like Robinson's *Oak Ridge Story.* To resist was an act of futility, setting oneself against the vast forces of a preeminent modern nation united in its goals and convictions. But the record suggests that resistance was not in fact futile; that even within the government could be found allies and dissenters.

First, however, there had to be a social system already in place from which resistance could spring. At Hanford, the arrival of a champion gives a deceptive cast to the opposition. But Lloyd Wiehl was not a Lone Ranger. He was instead an integral part of the local network the District sought to usurp. He was a local boy; his father had operated the rough flatboat that served as a ferry across the Columbia, and Wiehl had grown up on one of the irrigation farms. He had emigrated to Yakima to practice law because that was the nearest town large enough to sustain a practice. His return to defend his neighbors might be seen as a repayment of a tithe of his birthright; it was also a shrewd financial move, made possible by Wiehl's particular combination of legal expertise and local knowledge.

Wiehl was one prong of the Hanford resistance. The irrigation districts and power cooperatives represented another. Together, these opponents promised a tenacious battle. By August 1943, the army had decided the process wasn't worth it; Groves and Matthias, among others, had decided to close off negotiations and move the issue to the courts.[52]

But there was a complicating factor here. On June 18, 1943, with less than two weeks before evacuation day, Matthias reported that "only 19 checks had been delivered to land owners out of something over 2,000 transactions which had been completed." Evacuees couldn't buy new lands; they couldn't pay for moving expenses. Wiehl's client list was expanding and the atmosphere of confrontation grew more heated day by day. Farmers began to invade the site wholesale, bringing hired hands and commercial fruit pickers, and they were "picking all fruit, including green immature apricots," to the horror of Matthias and his assistants. Investigating the situation, Matthias discovered that the Real Estate Branch's people had failed to institute legal evacuation proceedings, nor were they "serving notices that possession would be taken on July 7, and that no fruit would be permitted to be moved out after noon today. . . . It is, therefore, not possible to legally prevent the picking of fruit." Ready to begin clearing the land, Matthias envisioned a complete breakdown of security procedures, with farmers and their hired hands roving the land with impunity.[53]

Though he had no legal backing, Matthias decided to take action. Writing in the dry legalese that would become the *lingua franca* of the District over the following years, Matthias reported that "instructions were issued to the guard patrol to stop pickers from coming in and to hold fruit headed out of Area 'A.'" At the same time, he instructed the Real Estate Branch to issue orders of possession and "report immediately if any persons refuse to accept the notice of possession," so that the refusal could be presented to the court as justification "to expedite a court order forcing removal of these people." Within a matter of days, the guard patrol was forcibly taking people off the site. Still the land payments remained unmade.[54]

Matthias's hardened tactic failed to work as planned. The colonel had envisioned a surgical clearing of the lands, with disputes to be resolved in the courtroom of Lewis Schwellenbach, the presiding federal judge. But he had not calculated on residents' resilience nor on the site's own recalcitrance. The stretches of land were vast; the District had no outpost on the land and had to resort to roving patrols that were understaffed and unfamiliar with the geography. Some ex-landowners never did get evicted; others returned to their farms and houses as quickly as they were taken off; still others roamed back and forth over the boundaries, tending their crops and orchards. For many, the promised payments to which they were entitled had yet to be sent out, and they apparently believed that the withholding of payments had a direct relation to their disputes of the appraisals. When guards or officials confronted them, many of the residents exploited the utter confusion of law and the byzantine interconnection of army and government officials and offices operating on the site, to argue that they had rights to be where they were. By the end of August, Du Pont had its own project manager on site; he reported to Matthias that "there were a number of people living in the 'A' area who still owned their property and could pick their fruit." Matthias had to remind Du Pont's Mr. Church that the main area had long been "taken over by the Government."[55]

In the courts themselves, matters were not much better. Sometime in late August, Judge Schwellenbach issued a court order preventing the District from condemning the land of a Mr. Bruggeman before November 15. This was a serious blow to the District's representatives, who had been assuming that the judiciary would stand squarely behind them. If the judge could stop one condemnation, he could stop others; meanwhile, even one stayed condemnation prevented the District from beginning work with a blank canvas.[56]

Over the next months, and as the months stretched into years, the District continued to apply a combination of threats, intimidation, thinly disguised bribery, appeals to patriotism, and offers of conciliation in an attempt to turn matters its way. Conflicts with Schwellenbach grew more and more confrontational, spilling over to affect other judges considering the cases. At more than one point, District officials violated fundamental legal rights of the landowners by holding private discussions with the judges without opposing counsel present. The outcomes of conflicts between the army and the Justice Department's Lands Division, the latter led by its firebrand liberal head, Norman Littell, once the darling of the army but now an expendable figure, signaled the District's steadily strengthening presence within the governmental landscape of wartime; the results of these conflicts left landowners still further disenfranchised. Representatives of the Security Section of the MED appeared on farms, in courtrooms, even in judge's chambers, adding their own weight to the dispute.[57]

Yet these steadily escalating attacks on the basic rights of citizens and institutions, made in the name of wartime expediency, failed in all three of their ostensible aims— failed to expedite land acquisition by enabling quick, extralegal condemnation; failed to save the District money by limiting land costs to something far below their current values; and failed to keep the process secret. When, finally, the contested land suits went to trial, the District's heavy-handed tactics backfired—landowners began to win huge settlements, in part because delaying tactics employed by the District enabled a couple of good harvests and the general wartime run-up in land values to increase significantly the assessments of the now-lost property. Meanwhile, the large-scale acquisition of lands in an otherwise unnoticed part of the country now had been subjected to the glare of publicity, from Washington politicians and from the press. In the first court case, Senator Harry Truman's Senate Military Affairs Subcommittee turned its attention to the scandal, forcing Secretary of War Stimson to go to Truman personally and promise to stake his own reputation on the Hanford project—a decision that would have significant effects on the project's future.[58]

By this time, however, newspapers had long been collecting data on the Hanford site, and on December 17, 1944, the *Seattle Times* ran the first of what it declared would be a series of articles on the process of land acquisition in the area. The article revealed nothing that was not general knowledge in the region, but it did point out that earlier victims of the condemnation process could appeal their dispensations, and thereby awakened local interest in reopening a number of cases. Matthias complained in his diary that publicizing this option "will probably be expensive and cause considerable trouble" as others who had settled for small claims came to realize that they had continued recourse in the courts.[59]

Matthias decided to stop the *Times* from publishing any more articles in its promised series. He set a representative, Lieutenant Cydell, on the editors, exacting from them a tentative agreement that they would not publish anything further. But the paper's managing editor, a man known only as McGrath, objected to this and took his objection to Matthias as a First Amendment matter.

On December 18, Matthias called McGrath and accused him of violating agreements with the War Department and with the Bureau of Censorship. McGrath violently objected but Matthias insisted that even if all the facts had already been published and were well known, they could not be published without previous approval by the District. Under heavy pressure, confronted by subtle threats to his paper and his livelihood, McGrath caved in. The final solution was a series of articles "edited jointly by Lt. Cydell and their man," as Matthias phrased it. Matthias and Groves agreed that the District would work more assiduously to keep the press from introducing even the least of comments on the site.[60]

The entire legal process, from the first meeting with Schwellenbach in the summer of 1943 to this moment, reflected a larger procedure by which the military sought to encroach upon, and declare its own, territory to which it was justified only by the broadest interpretations of law. In this, the legal issues reflected in metaphysical and philosophical terms what had occurred at the site itself. In the name of wartime imperative, the District had taken the land, had kept for itself what was useful to it, and had bulldozed the rest or left it to fall into decay. In the process, it had created a complex new superentity that subsumed the traditions of peacetime democratic institutions.

In some ways, the Hanford landowners fared better than the institutions that intervened on their behalf. Many of them did, finally, receive recompense for the lands they had lost. For those who set themselves against the District and the army, risking the threats of army representatives and the accusations of unpatriotic, even treasonous behavior, the rewards came in settlements far above those set by the original appraisers. But the dispositions were slow; many dragged out until after the war had ended. By then, these citizens had come to see themselves as subtly isolated from the mainstream of wartime American life. Ostracized by the District, evicted from their sense of place, redefined as selfish, unpatriotic outsiders, intimidated, forced into the position of legal opponents to the American army, these men and women ended up marginal Americans, examples to the larger American community of the consequences of dissent and resistance to the will of this vast military-bureaucratic force that was building, literally and figuratively, across the American landscape.

The chronology of condemnation is a peculiar one. Time folds upon itself; it does not move along the straight line of narrative. The condemnation program was still incomplete when Nagasaki lay in ruins. It was a matter of law, a place where land became an abstraction and the battle lay with the formula for converting that abstraction into the abstraction of money. The land itself, the physical land, had been large-ly emptied of residents by the end of summer 1943. At each of the sites, construction had begun, on contested and uncontested land alike, according to the dictates of planners and designers, engineers and architects.

At each site, fences were among the very earliest physical embodiments of the District. Where and how to build them; how to patrol the lines they demarcated between what was the District and what was not: these issues moved through the District's hierarchy even before the sites had been chosen. For they decided how the District would make tangible what condemnation had already declared in language. The District had made three reservations; within their boundaries, it reserved not just land but every aspect of social and cultural life, hypothetically immune from local, state, and federal laws, subject only to the regulations of military culture.

Though formal eviction at the sites was completed by the end of August 1943, the farmhouses and homes at all three sites did not all fall vacant. Some were occupied by the guards assigned to walk the perimeters, others went to roving firemen. Others became the homes of officers in the District; older structures, often built to last for generations and house the builder's family, these were highly desirable residences.[61]

But some of these houses remained the homes of those who had occupied them before the District appeared at the site. These residents were lucky; they had managed to reach the ear of those officials who had control over the details of life at the sites, and they received permission to stay, if only for a little while, on the lands that had been theirs. Yet these people remained under new conditions. They were no longer owners; their ties were not to the communities that had once existed and in whose fabric they had found the order of their lives. They were now citizens of the Manhattan Engineer District, subject to its laws and imperatives.

What these were, they did not yet fully know. They had bargained for inclusion in a culture still being invented, whose meanings and manifestos were still being constructed. As the District began to build on possessed property, making houses and factories, prisons and barracks and streets and all the other materialities necessary to the proper running of complex social systems, it also began to build—sometimes by conscious plan, more often by habit and accident and accretion—the systems to which these new residents would discover themselves subject. Condemned as one sort of American, they would now be constructed as another.

In the winter of 1942/43, construction began on all three Manhattan Project sites. It never did end. Long after the explosions at Alamogordo, at Hiroshima and at Nagasaki, even after the Atomic Energy Commission vaporized Elugelab Atoll with the first hydrogen superbomb, bulldozers continued to grade raw land at Los Alamos, Oak Ridge, and Hanford, pushing at the boundaries in relentless acquisitiveness, modifying undeveloped and developed lands alike, constantly reconstructing spaces and—by extension—the meanings and messages that underlay their physical presence.

Construction was a stage—not a stage in time, but a stage in conception, and also a theatrical stage upon which certain dramatic tensions came forward and were resolved. At each of the sites, and at the smaller District facilities scattered across America, the drama followed a common narrative. Out of some environment older, more stable, and, to newcomers, more natural, the District arrived to set up its boundaries: imaginary lines, social distinctions, real fences. Within these borders it defined an army reservation, immune from the laws of nation, state, county, municipality—designed to transcend environmental, cultural, and social regulations, to hew, instead, to the laws of military expediency.

And then the building began. Ruth Marshak arrived at Los Alamos that winter with her physicist husband as part of the second wave of scientific immigrants to the mesa. She was not sure what her destination was to be, but the trip up from Santa Fe had thrilled her. "As we neared the top of the mesa, the view was breathtaking. Behind us lay the Sangre de Cristo Mountains, at sunset bathed in changing waves of color—scarlets and lavenders. Below was the desert with its flatness broken by majestic palisades that seemed like the ruined cathedrals and palaces of some old, great, vanished race. Ahead was Los Alamos, and beyond the flat plateau on which it sat was its backdrop, the Jemez Mountain Range."[1]

CONSTRUCTION 4

Turning the corner, into the site, set the contrast between a vast magnificent natural environment and a far different human one. Los Alamos was "an island in the sky," Marshak recalled in 1946, but it was not an idyllic one. "My first impression was discouraging," she remembered. "The rickety houses looked like the tenements of a metropolitan slum area; washing hung everywhere, and the garbage cans were overflowing. Dust rose in great clouds around our car. . . . Locating any place on the mesa was difficult; the sprawling town had grown rapidly and haphazardly, without order or plan."[2]

Eleanor Jette arrived in January 1944. Here was the way she first saw it:

> We stopped at the first guard house about half an hour after we crossed the Rio Grande. It stood just east of the fence which was a seven-foot chain link affair with three strands of barbed wire at the top of it. It was liberally festooned with signs which read:
>
> U.S. Government Property
> DANGER! *PELIGRO!*
> *Keep out*

The MPs in battle helmets who manned the guardhouse were a formidable looking bunch of young men. They inspected our passes and recorded their numbers. . . .

After we left the gate, the road wound through thickets of piñon and juniper for a couple of miles. The sun sank behind the Jemez Mountains. The umbrella of black smoke ahead marked the town site. As we approached it, the thickets gave way to an open field. Green construction workers' huts stood disconsolately on the right. There was a barracks area on the left. The whole scene was as raw as a new scar. . . . The fresh snow was covered with soot. . . . The apartment buildings looked like hell. The green barracks-type structures sat jauntily in a sea of mud.[3]

Many (though not all) new immigrants made the mistake of thinking as Marshak did, that the site that greeted them had grown up "without order or plan." Jette knew otherwise. Her reminiscence described more than just a haphazard agglomeration of buildings strewn across a "sea of mud." The site *began* with "the first guard house," the "seven-foot chain link affair with three strands of barbed wire" that was the perimeter fence, the threatening signs phrased in the imperative, the guards with their "bulldog faces," the ritual of being inspected, of having one's credentials checked before being allowed to pass inside.[4]

Once within, escape was difficult. "It's true the women lived behind barb wire, and we tried to control access," Colonel Matthias, director of the Hanford site, recalled unapologetically. At Los Alamos, Bernice Brode recalled, the scientist Hans Staub raised the basic question: "Are those big tough MPs, with their guns, here to keep us in, or to keep the rest of the world out? There is an important distinction here and before I leave this place, I want to know the answer."[5]

Here was another construction of the sites, as zones of force; their miserable living conditions, and the violence done to nature and tradition, were extensions of the priorities imbedded within District regulations. Many beside Hans Staub saw the sites as prisons and forced-labor camps. Others conceived them in broader terms: as places where the imperatives of machines and systems held sway, and the needs and desires of people were supplanted and suppressed. Laura Fermi was one who linked environment and ideology. She understood (after the fact, at least) that this quality of temporariness was permanent: here would be, for as long as she would live there (and in fact much longer), a landscape of "construction materials and felled trees . . . piled along the sides of rutted roads, where bulldozers, cranes, and trucks sped blindly away as if they were masters of the place."[6]

But most District officers and administrators would have disagreed violently with this picture. For them, the sites were quite simply the best that could be managed given the urgencies of wartime, the economies of a nation with its priorities set on eliminating tyranny from the globe, the compromises and consequences of the half-conceived nature of the atomic bomb program itself, in which the necessity for starting construction occurred against the backdrop of a still-dim understanding of the ways to turn abstract theoretical physics into concrete, working weaponry.

In either case, what seemed lack of order to Eleanor Jette was something else—adherence to a system of order somehow alien to her experience as an American. At Los Alamos, at Hanford, at Oak Ridge, the Manhattan Engineer District was constructing not towns (as Marshak thought) or communities, or even (the District's own term) "facilities." It was assembling the pieces of a new social whole, using laws, beliefs, customs, and myths signally different from those that underlay prewar America, or even wartime life outside the fences of the reservations. Imbedded in the details of housing plans, in the width of streets and their arrangement across the landscapes of the District, in the instructions that came to those soon to arrive and those already there, in a deep webbing of decisions, orders, plans, reports, memoranda, and enactments: the Manhattan Engineer District invented itself as a new form of American culture.

Some of this came about blindly, unconsciously. But not all of it. Besides the military planners and the polyglot residents, there was a third influence: the planners and architects who supervised work at Hanford and Oak Ridge. They had their own vision of the construction process, one that set a new ideal of rationality and conscious attention to the possibility of a new urban modernity. For them, each site, each town plan, each housing program afforded the opportunity to make a new American community, formed the motivation for the planning of something approaching a utopia, and provided the battleground for a war (as they pictured it) between humane planners and officious, mendacious, obstructive bureaucrats and army flack-catchers. For men like Nat Owings of the well-connected architectural firm of Skidmore, Owings, and Merrill, or G. Albin Pehrson of Spokane, architect of Richland, Washington, each space became the site of conflict between the high aims of American utopian city planning and the petty forces of laissez-faire or something worse.

But even this picture of influences oversimplifies. The planners themselves were divided in their perspectives, and so were the residents, and even the military administrators. What is significant here is not the number of different visions at odds with each other, but rather the fact that so many of these factions engaged so deeply in the battles for identities and mythologies that could inform the higher and lower life within the boundaries. Everyone agreed that these spaces were significant, that what was to be built within them was important. Everyone agreed that symbols mattered, and that these spaces were—and would be—vital American symbols.

And so the construction process became a contest among pictures or, more interestingly still, a contest to invent and apply quite different pictures of what an American community, conceived in wartime, hobbled by haste and economies and limited understanding of the extent of the final reality, might aspire to be. And from those intentions came, almost inevitably, the beginnings of postwar plans that would infuse not just city planning, but relationships among government, corporation, and labor, and even broader notions about what might represent permissible areas for incursion into personal, social, and cultural life, and what sacrifices might be demanded as the price of loyalty in a world of fear.

Most American communities don't begin with plans or programs. They start, perhaps, as ideas—some explorer or settler sees a confluence of geographical details and imagines a town there. But even then, the community begins with a house, a collection of dwellings, a roadside store or a rough plank wharf jutting out into the river, the lake, the bay. Settlers write back; their families or friends or neighbors, reading the account of this new place, decide to make the journey. Or the process occurs more randomly still; emigrants bound elsewhere run out of food or money or wheels or patience, and stop here. Eventually the assembly begins to develop a momentum of its own. After a time, people notice that they are in a *place.* They may even recognize the need for planning, intervention, giving order to the growth that now infuses their environment. Perhaps they name it. Some call it home.

This was not the pattern of the atomic spaces—at least, not on the surface. They came from the mold of utopian planned communities, communities built from a box, built to a pattern, built to embody and to promote some larger goal. They had their precedents in the American past: Puritan cities on their hills, Mormon beehive communities, railroad towns built to accord with the lithographic images of places allegedly thriving but actually empty as the plains they hope eventually to occupy.

Los Alamos was the first, and originally the simplest, of the three sites, from the standpoint of planning. There the District applied standard organizational strategies, in a program that reflected a general conception of the site as a military installation rather than a town. General Groves may not have gotten his way in militarizing the personnel of the site, but the environment within which they would work would be military with a vengeance: military-designed, military-built, as quickly, and violently, and cheaply as could possibly be.

On November 30, 1942, Groves sent a memorandum to the district engineer of the Albuquerque Engineer District, authorizing him "to proceed immediately with the construction described herein at Los Alamos, New Mexico." No site plan accompanied the letter of instruction. Buildings were described by size and by Corps of Engineers plan number. The administration building was to be built from plan T.O. 700-5820, the enlisted men's lavatory from T.O. 700-6605. Housing apartments for scientists were listed by number of rooms, number of units required. Translation into physical space needed not be spelled out. Albuquerque District would know how to do it. The district office would bid it out to a trusted subcontractor, specifying the maximum cost per unit the Corps of Engineers would allow. And the rest would be a matter for the contractor's discretion.[7]

For security reasons, the MED insisted that the Los Alamos site be defined as a set of concentric fenced areas. The outer fence separated the site from all else. A few feet within this outer fence was a second; the two formed a dry moat into which perimeter guards could shoot with impunity. Behind the guards was the high-security work zone, called the Tech Area, further fenced off, guarded, and closed to outsiders without high-security clearances. Beyond that rudimentary rings-within-rings structure, the rest of the site grew, a hodgepodge of haphazardly organized facilities: apartment houses, barracks, PXs, original Ranch School structures, recreational buildings, and all the rest of the required elements for an army post.[8]

This jumbled environment was not the outcome the District's planners expected. When Groves had supervised construction of the Pentagon and overseen the construction division of the Corps, nothing he'd built had approached the disorder of Site Y. Los Alamos should have been an army post—an orderly grid upon which were set neatly rectilinear boxes of housing, administration, and the like, each building type set in its proper place. Both the original plan and the organizational ethos behind it were overwhelmed from the first, however, by the frenetic expansion that characterized the site throughout the war. Other elements conspired with this relentless, explosive spread in scale and demands. The army was used to building on flat, largely empty sites suited to the bulldozer techniques appropriate to rectilinear plans. The irregularity of the terrain, the variety of soil types, the presence of whole forests, the difficulty of getting construction equipment up the mesa road, all made the building program impossible to execute as proposed.

Another element contributed to the rapid dissolution of any order on the site: the fundamental incompatibility of Groves's and Oppenheimer's ideals, and the District's failure to negotiate a compromise. Groves's desires were easy to set forth—they were normal within the culture of the military. On December 2, 1942, for example, Colonel Matthias, then Groves's assistant and soon to be commander of the Hanford site, wrote to Albuquerque District officials, reminding them that "particular attention be directed towards the omission of all non-essential features and 'trimmings' from the construction authorized." He had no need to say more; Groves was a legend in the corps, and his definition of "trimmings" was well known.[9]

Oppenheimer's concerns were more difficult to accommodate, in part because they represented a philosophy alien to the military: of attraction and persuasion rather than coercion. Groves had hoped to solve the problem of drawing scientists to Los Alamos by militarizing the site and drafting the specific scientists Oppenheimer designated as necessary. This would never have worked, not just from a philosophical standpoint, but from the more practical one that many of these scientists were undraftable aliens, already at work in high-priority military projects, and the like. Oppenheimer's plan was to attract his cadre by declaring high military necessity, by offering exciting scientific research in something resembling the prewar utopia of the international scientific community, and by promising a living situation that was at least adequate.[10]

The idea that one might make housing and living facilities part of the package to attract residents was unusual enough for the District, especially Groves. Yet Oppenheimer was apparently able to prevail in some of the most basic areas. The original plan had been typical of an army base in its relentless application of the grid, no matter how inappropriate to the mesa's topography or the desires of those who would live and work there. Oppenheimer had insisted to Groves that the streets should follow the natural topography wherever possible, and he had prevailed at this earliest stage of building (it was about the only time). Similarly with the apartments themselves; Oppenheimer was the one who called for hardwood floors and fireplaces in the apartments, while it was the District that insisted on soft-coal-burning "Black Beauty" cooking stoves, which emitted choking clouds of black smoke, were virtually impossible to regulate, and tended to explode.[11]

The conflicts between these two mindsets resulted in a cityscape composed principally of the worst of both. From Groves's standpoint, the ugliness and failures of livability that resulted could be traced to the impossible demands of Oppenheimer and his clientele. But the record suggests the primary culprit was the District, with its more basic decisions to place speed far ahead of any other priority, to build first using the flimsiest of projections, and to decide later what would be done with the buildings.[12]

The results were often comical. John Manley, the scientist whom Oppenheimer delegated as liaison with Stone and Webster, spec'd a building to hold the atomic accelerators and the Van de Graaff generators. The generators were incredibly heavy and needed true stability and a strong foundation; the accelerator was vertical and required a basement—"so we'd specified that a basement be excavated for that machine and there must be a good foundation under the Van de Graaff accelerators. Cost and construction time could obviously be saved if they selected the terrain properly," Manley later reported. Arriving at Los Alamos, the scientist recalled, "of course the first thing I wanted to see was the building that I'd specified be oriented properly back in Boston. There were enough jokes about the way of the Army so you can guess what I saw. The basement for the Illinois [accelerator] had been dug out of solid rock and that rock debris taken over to the other end of the building and used for fill under the Van de Graaffs, where there was supposed to be a good foundation. This was my introduction to the Army Engineers."[13]

Construction carried its own destruction; the road up from the valley exemplified that maxim. Part of the attraction of the Los Alamos site had been its near-complete isolation from the rest of the world. When the plan was for a cadre of one hundred scientists, armed primarily with blackboards, chalk, paper, and pencil, the steeply forbidding road, with its switchbacks and boulder-strewn dirt surface, had the dual attraction of deterring visitors and discouraging escape. But as the population increased in great leaps, the road decayed rapidly. First the District paved it, hastily, on frozen winter earth. Quickly the new surface disintegrated. Repaving wasn't enough; the road would have to be entirely rebuilt, made wider and stronger, the slopes above it reworked to prevent further landslides and boulder storms. Bringing in sophisticated roadbuilding equipment to do this project, however, further blew the security cover of the site, drawing attention to the scale of the programs within the fence. The roadbuilders had to be fed and housed and paid, and the specifications for the new road drawn by Stone and Webster and approved by the District's engineers, necessitating a further blizzard of memos and papers. So the physical site had to be adjusted to account for these new needs, and expansion bred its own further expansion, all of it beyond the scope of original plans.[14]

For the residents, the true test of the District was found in the housing. The M. M. Sundt Construction Company, hired in December 1942 as the principal contractor during the initial stage of construction, built the first installment of residences. (District security officials liked Sundt because it was a comprehensive corporation, with its own trucks and truckers, plumbers, electricians, and painters—less to control.) Sundt built the first set of tech buildings—J, M, S, T, U, V, W, X, Y, and Z, and boiler house 2—as well as the first batch of housing, all on the basis of the first plan for the community, which envisioned a total population of 265.

From the beginning, Sundt's work separated the housing by class. The most prestigious residents found themselves assigned to the converted Ranch School buildings—lovely if a bit primitive. Then came the first new housing: the so-called Sundt apartments. These were one-bedroom duplexes; four-room apartments in two-story fourplexes; and efficiencies, two-, and three-bedroom apartments in larger two-story buildings. They grew uglier on the outside and more crowded on the inside as the size of the buildings increased. The nicest was the Sundt duplex (fig. 8), which had fireplaces, hardwood floors, good-sized windows, and a habitable kitchen; the two-bedroom Sundt apartments were similar. In both cases, the bedrooms were tiny, but each room had fairly large windows

SECRET

FIG. 8 Sundt duplex living room, Los Alamos. Manhattan District History, courtesy National Archives.

to relieve the claustrophobia. The dormitories, built to house single scientists and civilian personnel, were the least habitable. The elite scientific personnel had the Sundt houses and apartments. Construction workers, support personnel, and "tradesmen" as well as other "low-salary employees" lived in "hutments" (16 x 16' primitive huts—the prefabricated semicircular tubes of plywood, corrugated metal, and Celotex known to and reviled by every GI as Quonset huts) and "dormitories of cheaper construction," as the District historian, Edith C. Truslow, described them in 1946.[15]

Sundt's first-stage family housing accounted for only 332 families, however. Over the next months and years, that population grew and grew, and Sundt raced to keep up with the demand. The result was a steady subtraction in amenities, especially in the larger buildings. Clapboard siding went by the wayside; in its place was the ubiquitous tarpaper-covered plywood. What rudimentary site preparation and preservation had been extracted from the construction personnel by irate residents now melted away. If the houses and apartment buildings sank into seas of mud in the winter, they periodically disappeared behind "clouds of dust" in the summer, as residents forlornly reported.[16]

But the expanded Sundt contract work, completed in November 1943, proved hopelessly insufficient. In the following January, a new stage of housing construction signaled a further step in the transformation of housing type from permanent to impermanent. The Albuquerque Engineer District, which had been responsible for the letting of contracts on the Los Alamos site, hired J. E. Morgan and Sons, of El Paso, to assemble prefab structures in one-, two-, and three-bedroom duplexes, using kits constructed by the Houston Ready-Cut House Company.[17]

The resulting buildings were squalid. Residents and newcomers lived in fear of assignment to "Morganville," the civilians' ironic variation on "Hooverville," as Depression-era shantytowns had been known. Ruth Marshak's description of her apartment echoed those of most equally dismayed residents. "Our tiny half of the duplex in Morganville was scarcely adequate for even a family of two," she wrote, shortly after the war. "We had a bedroom, a small living room, a minute kitchen, and a bathroom with a shower but no tub. There were no trees in our section of the mesa, and the unpaved roads were muddy during wet seasons and dusty during dry ones."[18]

Despite this, Morganville's status rose considerably once the next stage of construction began. Now it was the Robert E. McKee Company of El Paso, one of the largest construction companies in the country, that contracted to assemble one hundred more prefab units, even less commodious or "permanent" than the earlier ones. Flat-roofed, with paper-thin walls, set up on blocks, these were closer to trailers without wheels than to houses. Finally, in a last, desperate push for housing, the administration brought in 107 "Hanford" or "Pasco" houses—prefabs designed to alleviate shortages of housing at Pasco, Washington, where workers had overwhelmed the local housing market, and built as well in Richland. Trailers, too, dotted the landscape.[19]

Oppenheimer understood the effects of these conditions on his crew. In late September 1944, he had one of his assistants write a detailed memo concerning the problems of housing at the Los Alamos site. "Everyone understands that no attempt has been made or could be made to match the housing to which they had been accustomed, but . . . certain poor housing conditions which the people here believe could have been bettered, and should have been bettered in any new housing construction[,]" had instead grown worse, despite their pointed complaints. The effect, Oppenheimer argued, was a loss of faith not simply in the housing arm of the District, but in the entire District hierarchy. These residents were intelligent people, and they had been asked to relinquish their independence of mind to a higher authority. Now everyday matters made them less and less sure of their bargain, more and more suspicious of the authority to whom they had deferred. If, as the scientist Emilio Segrè pointed out in a letter to a Major McGavock, the District was incapable of keeping the heat in an apartment from shooting up and down between 55 and 81 degrees, even when all the windows were alternately shut and opened, and if the District ignored the health and welfare of its most important workers, and on top of it all continued to build the failures of old design into new housing, how could one believe they would act more responsibly with superweapons and their deployment? And when District officials responded by denying the problem, and at the same time promising to fix it, all without final effect, what good faith could remain?[20]

This was to be the formula for planning at Los Alamos to the end: military programs resisted and modified wherever possible by the scientific personnel, overwhelmed by the constant and largely uncontrolled expansion in personnel and programs, barely visible under the chaos of an administrative structure whose focus rapidly turned from physical organization to the organization of thought, from orderly spaces to obedient minds.

Los Alamos was a military site disintegrated by civilian demands inadequately addressed. Oak Ridge was its opposite: a civilian town occupied and transformed by military-industrial planners.

We see this in the simplest and most basic of details. Los Alamos was built by the Corps of Engineers—by its Albuquerque Division—in typical corps fashion. At Oak Ridge, the Manhattan District chose to move to a significant variation of its usual procedure. Rather than designing the site, the city, and the buildings through stock plans and the discretion of subcontractors, the District brought in professionals to orchestrate a symphonic arrangement of elements and avoid the sort of disaster that was brewing at Los Alamos.

The prime instigator of this decision was Col. James C. Marshall, once head of the entire Manhattan Project, now district engineer for the Manhattan Engineer District, a position of considerable ambiguity considering that the real power lay with General Groves, and that relations between the two men were strained. But Marshall took seriously his role as a planner and administrator of the physical aspects of the District. Los Alamos was off-limits to him; it was Groves's peculiar obsession. Hanford was soon to be overseen by Groves's close associate and assistant, Colonel Matthias. Oak Ridge became Marshall's site. He had helped to scout the location; he had met with Stone and Webster as early as June 1942 to discuss the outlines of the town; he had resisted from the first Groves's call for inadequate facilities when Groves was still running army construction. As district engineer, Marshall took Oak Ridge as his head-quarters. There he lavished his particular brand of care, his concern for the living experiences of those under his command, his deliberate, often plodding style.

From the first, Groves's decision to turn overall planning for the District over to Stone and Webster constrained Marshall. But even the earliest specifications given to the engineering firm reflected a different model than the traditional army-base specification list exemplified at Los Alamos. At Oak Ridge, Stone and Webster was to be a town planning firm, not an engineering corporation. Marshall understood early on that, as he wrote in his diary in 1942, "primitive housing could not be expected to meet family requirements of the class of personnel to be employed on this particular project." He was even able, over time, to gain Groves's grudging acquiescence to this shift from coercion to attraction.[21]

But Stone and Webster never mastered the difference. Long before they had developed a town plan, the engineers sent in heavy equipment to bulldoze and grade the site, removing such "obstructions" as trees, vegetation, housing, and the like, and doing their best to convert the topography from hillside to plain. By the time the firm submitted its general plan, at a meeting on October 26, 1942, the site was devastated, with much of the topsoil removed and the subsoil already eroding into miniature canyons. Natural drainage systems filled in even as a new drainage system had been started, and the general roadway plan was already staked out, marching up and down the hills.[22]

But the outcome of this conflict of ideals was by no means inevitable. That was clear from the interplay of forces at the October meeting that brought together all the principals of the District—Groves, Marshall, Col. K. D. Nichols, the eventual replacement for Marshall as district engineer, and also Wilbur Kelley, one of the most experienced planner-engineers in the Corps of Engineers. This meeting was the first major presentation by A. C. Klein, Stone and Webster's town designer and "project engineer" for the site plan for the town of Oak Ridge—the "administration, laboratory and housing layout." It should have been a ceremonial occasion; it was not.[23]

We can reconstruct some of the controversy surrounding the original Stone and Webster plan by imagining Klein's presentation as he unrolled the plans and tacked them up at the October 26 meeting. Houses would dominate the cityscape. The bulk of the village would consist of single-family houses of five types: twenty-five $3,500 two-bedroom houses; fifty $4,500 two-bedroom deluxe houses; fifty $6,000 three-bedroom houses; and ten each of two types of $7,500, two-story, three-bedroom houses—the 7500A and the 7500B. Lots would be 80 x 100'. Roads would have a forty-foot right-of-way, eighteen-foot paving, and sidewalks on one side. Garages would be grouped, four cars to a garage.[24]

Within the slender rectangle of the site, Stone and Webster had planned to include most of the elements of a prosperous midsize town. Athletic facilities were to be clustered in a single 1,000 x 500' space, excluding tennis courts, which were to be scattered amidst the housing. A single recreation building would include a lounge, a gym with stage, bowling alleys, a library, and high-school classrooms. Commercial buildings were to be located in a "store center." The city would have a cafeteria and a restaurant, separated but sharing a kitchen. For authorized visitors, a guest house was to be constructed. A hospital would be located near town. A separate "negro town" was planned. Perhaps most important, town management would be under government control. With the plans and other visual aids out in front of the assembled District officials at the October meeting, Klein learned new lessons in the dangers of dealing with Groves. Klein had attempted to lay out the virtues of his team's plan but found himself constantly interrupted by the general. Over the next few minutes, Groves proceeded to set down new assumptions—some picayune, some far-reaching: "General Groves says no scattered toilet facilities and no tubs." "General Groves says figures on married couples are low. . . . What will initial construction program be? (General Groves)."[25]

With the large plans in front of the group, Groves then took over the meeting. Groves assailed the plans with his scattershot critique and ordered changes largely without pattern. By the end of the meeting, Stone and Webster's design was a shambles. The designers had made their plan with too little information available, with guidelines too broad, and without a true understanding of Groves's peculiar temper. Groves's questions overwhelmed them; rather than offering rationales to defend their plans, Klein and the other Stone and Webster representatives were reduced to silence. The meeting ended with a barrage of orders from Groves, from which the Stone and Webster team would presumably modify its program.

Marshall and Kelley were also horrified by the overall plan, but for reasons very different from those of Groves. Marshall had already traveled to a number of other installations with extensive civilian populations, notably one at Ocala, Florida, where he had seen housing and town-site plans enacted in such a way that the overall landscape remained largely unaffected. There, the building programs had left native trees and flora on the house plots, subduing the rawness of the new town and deemphasizing the dull sameness of building types. The result had been, to his mind, a solid combination of army efficiency and civilian livability.

But Marshall had an even more immediate precedent to which he might compare Stone and Webster's plans: the TVA's Norris Village, located just a few miles north of the Oak Ridge site. There, too, big government served as planner and expediter of an

entirely new community. Housing relocated farmer-pioneers in a newly planned sym-
biosis with the economic and technological avant-garde, a community in which crafts-
men labored in decentralized small factories and farmed the plots surrounding their
homes. Norris's designers had been among the most innovative and well-educated
architect-planners in the nation, and they had drawn from the vast literature on new
towns in Europe and America, from Radburn in America to Hampstead Garden in
England. In addition, they were informed by a deeply nostalgic respect for the folkways of the rural America they believed would have to be rejuvenated and rechan-
neled if the nation was to survive. Their plan—to set up a village full of the cues of
past pioneer virtues, housing residents who would labor in the new ultramodern factories drawn to the TVA by cheap electrical power—had attractive implications for
Marshall's ideal Manhattan District.[26]

Norris's design particulars also offered valuable precedent. There, as at Ocala, designers and builders had worked to retain the native landscape, had combined pic-
turesqueness with innovation. In the housing itself, Norris's planners had worked
brilliantly to intermesh technological forwardness with an architecture of nostalgia
and human scale. Some houses used irregular shake siding; others were built of cinderblock, whitewashed to resemble stucco and set within cul-de-sacs that paid hom-
age to both the English village and the New England town. But the houses were efficient and extremely cheap—the cinderblock houses cost only two thousand dollars
each in 1936.

Remembering Ocala, walking through Norris, Marshall could see that this plan of
Stone and Webster's was not going to work. With Groves's wide-ranging objections
as the excuse, Marshall set Kelley to work critiquing the plan.

Stone and Webster worked hard to satisfy the demands coming from both sides of
the District. By December, S&W's Klein understood that there was trouble. He had
called Marshall on December 17 to straighten matters out, and more generally to reassure the colonel that his division could get things done. At that point Marshall told
him directly that he didn't like the plan or its components. Marshall was evidently
thinking of Norris as he spoke to Klein; every one of his comments invoked the utopian TVA village's most notable qualities. Klein promised to listen to Marshall's idea,
and S&W began rather frantically to modify its plan.[27]

But it was too late. Rather than waiting, Marshall and one of his assistants had
turned first to the John B. Pierce Foundation, and then to its commercial affiliate,
Skidmore, Owings, and Merrill. Marshall and his men knew of the foundation because Pierce had developed a low-cost modular housing type, using building materials it had developed with the Celotex corporation, particularly a light, weatherproof,
prefab paneling material called Cemestoboard. Already Pierce had used its plan to
build housing for the Glenn Martin Bomber Plant in Baltimore and dormitories in
regions surrounding Washington, as well as other government agencies in different
parts of the country. The District liked Pierce's modular housing because it was efficient, rapidly built, and cheap. The foundation's approach seemed ideal for Oak Ridge,
and so Marshall went to it with his problem. Pierce's head, Joseph O'Brien, suggested
bringing in SOM.[28]

At a meeting January 29, 1943, in the offices of the Pierce Foundation that brought
together O'Brien, Louis Skidmore himself, and Captain Bloch and Lieutenant Moore

of the Manhattan District, the Pierce/SOM consortium made a staggering offer. O'Brien and Skidmore told the District representatives that "in a matter of two weeks they could present complete plans and specifications, a site layout including stores, dormitories, recreational facilities, hospital, etc., and cost estimates based on any size town we wished to specify." And "it was suggested by Mr. O'Brien that their plans could be used as an alternate in the bidding of this work."[29]

Pierce and the architects of SOM made good their promise. On February 10, Nichols sent out a formal letter taking Stone and Webster off the townsite program. There, he detailed the new arrangement: Pierce Foundation would do all design work; S&W would let the contracts and supervise construction, design and build the water, sewage, power, and telephone systems, roads, and drainage, according to the Pierce/SOM layouts.[30]

Stone and Webster came out of the controversy in excellent shape. Marshall's evident hostility to its program, and his suspicion of the firm's abilities, mattered little—Groves was the figure who held the purse strings. And the engineering firm, not Pierce or SOM, retained control over the all-important patronage matters—the subcontractors, the letting of contracts, the hiring of workers.

Progress from that point was rapid, even by wartime standards. Maj. Warren George reported to the Manhattan District office on March 17 that Pierce had already done the entire site plan, including plans for 425 individual buildings, which Stone and Webster had then transferred to the site itself. Three hundred houses were staked out; 75 percent of the roads had been cleared and most of them graded. Construction had begun.[31]

Skidmore and Pierce offered the District a brilliant amalgam of forward-looking and deeply conservative themes. Pierce epitomized the technological innovations that had emerged from a generation of faith that technological progress would serve as the springboard to a bold new world. Pierce's original Depression-era cemesto home project had combined European and American utopian housing schemes of the previous decades. Rapidly made, easy to transport, built on uniform proportions, the cemesto unit extended assembly-line techniques from the factory to the home building site itself. The units, quickly fastened together and laid on a concrete foundation, promised mass housing for the proletariat.

Unfortunately, as Nat Owings dryly noted, America had no proletariat, even in the depths of the Depression. What it had was an aspiring bourgeoisie (to use the European term). Most of the American working class envisioned itself as eminently middle-class and wanted "a village of brick or stone houses," untouched by "the intrusion of paper-thin, painted panel houses—usually with flat roofs"; these obtrusively modern designs "downgraded the surrounding property." The cemesto home plans put SOM on the cover of *Better Homes and Gardens*, but even this coup failed to translate into mass sales.[32]

It took the war to reinvigorate the prefabricated, factory-built house. The Pierce-SOM designs were marvelous—cheap enough to satisfy Groves's demands for housing costs that conformed to military budgets, and appropriate to an invented city, where they had no conventional houses against which to compete. Their modular nature meant that Celotex, the production company, could ship wall units almost indiscriminately; these could be stored in warehouses or under tarps until needed, and used with equal ease in a number of different housing types. Not just houses, but schools, shops, and supermarkets could all be assembled by applying variations of the basic modular unit and its supporting skeleton.

The smallest houses were the two-bedroom "Type 'A'" units (fig. 9). Boxy and simple, these were tiny by prewar standards, but they pointed toward the postwar mass-production communities like Levittown, Long Island, America's prototype postwar bedroom suburb. The "B" added another module to the format, turning a box into a rectangle. The "C" unit extended the rectangle into an "L"; "D" stuck an "A" unit onto a "B" unit in a near-perfect prototype of the postwar "ranch house." The "E" fourplex (fig. 10) looked like a mock-Colonial with two wings. The "F," most luxurious of all the single-family units, was an expanded version of the "C" house. In this first major stage, completed as of September 1944, 700 "A" two-bedroom houses, 800 "B" two-bedroom houses, 400 "C" three-bedroom and 447 "D" three-bedroom houses, and 53 "F" three-bedroom houses were scheduled to be built, as were 150 fourplexes.[33]

In building materials, and in construction techniques, the houses were brilliantly innovative. In the overall site planning, and in the symbolic details of the individual houses, the program was deeply conservative. No matter how small, all of the houses had porches and fireplaces. While the porches might have been considered appropriate concessions to the Tennessee climate, the fireplaces were not—they were never meant to provide heat, only ambience. And the porches were in actuality architect's sham; they made the blueprints look spacious, finished, and civilized, when in reality they were nothing more than large covered entryways, unscreened and useless to residents except as storage for gardening tools and wet-weather footwear, or as a place where they could stop and scrape the ubiquitous mud off their boots.

The building plans of these houses reveal much, not only about the Pierce-SOM ideals, but about the District's social planning as well. The development of two different two-bedroom houses, and three different three-bedroom plans, separated residents of this new town in a way entirely absent from the Los Alamos program. Whereas at the scientists' community one's apartment depended upon the size of one's family, the time of one's arrival, and the random vicissitudes of military paperwork, at Oak Ridge, the District and its planners offered very different levels of luxury and space, making housing a means of attracting and rewarding residents.

Nat Owings recounted the thinking behind the firm's program with eloquence and wit when, thirty years later, he wrote of Oak Ridge in his memoirs. "We adopted the same general policy of secrecy for our specialty as that we met with in the Army Corps of Engineers in their dealings with their secret projects. We discussed mystically new concepts involving the theory of interdependent settlements. We would have submitted to torture rather than admit that all we wanted was a series of homely little American villages tied together with a road to take care of the long-distance traffic and permit the men to be on time to work."[34]

Conceiving Oak Ridge not as a city but as "a growing small town" moved it from the world of urbanity, civilization, and corruption to the core of American virtue— the mythic American town, populated by good neighbors. Owings tapped into this symbolic core when he declared America to be, "in effect, a nation of villages; therefore, why not start at Oak Ridge with a healthy natural unit, the village? This we did."[35]

With this, SOM designers rejected the modernist city-building tradition, the tra-

FIG. 9 Plan for House "A," Oak Ridge. Skidmore, Owings, and Merrill. Courtesy National Archives.

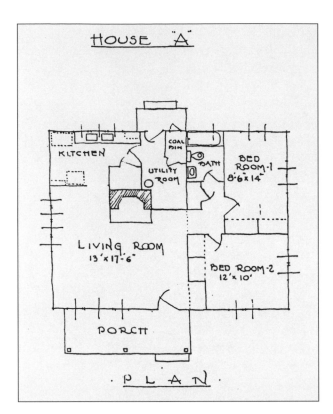

HOUSE "A"

KITCHEN

COAL BIN

BATH

UTILITY ROOM

BED ROOM·1
8'·6"x 14'

LIVING ROOM
13'x 17'·6"

BED ROOM·2
12'x 10'

PORCH

· P L A N ·

FIG. 10 *Apartment Building, 214 W. Tennessee Ave.,* Oak Ridge. Photo by James E. Westcott. Oak Ridge Operations Office, Department of Energy.

dition that had spawned not only Corbusier, Mies van der Rohe, and Walter Gropius, but also hundreds of aspiring American modernist architects and city planners. Instead, conservative "safety devices"—Owings's term—dominated the Oak Ridge city plan.

Already implicit in the District's requirements for the town was the first law of mythic village life: separate work from living. The other prerequisites were more peculiar to SOM. First, use the radical innovations of Pierce's modular construction to design houses that satisfied the desire of conservative corporate managers for the trappings of traditional American houses: porches, fireplaces, sleeping quarters relegated to separate wings. Then cluster the housing in the "village" so that, from the outside, the different types didn't clash unduly. Keep the individual villages small; this prevented the sort of anonymity and heterogeneity of the modern city. (SOM's villages were each comprised of about 1,500 families, in a combination of single-family and multiunit dwellings.) Reject the grid or any layout that might open the residential areas to mixed-use development or to the emergence of high-traffic streets. Instead, build in "clusters" radiating off the Oak Ridge Turnpike, so that expansion could involve adding clusters rather than increasing the density of existing living areas. Keep commercial and business sections to a bare minimum; focus the administrative, service, and commercial functions in a centralized area immediately off the turnpike.

All of these imperatives ensured a conservative, intimate, inward-directed social structure drawn from the nineteenth-century American farming village seen in its most sympathetic light, as a place of common feeling and shared values, rather than as a petty, coercive, smothering place. Consider Owings's mood as he wandered through the now-vacant farming lands that were the raw material for his firm: "Throughout that rugged, heavily wooded country, I was often struck by the nostalgic charm of quaint little cemeteries . . . tottering cabins, tumble-down barns, patches of tobacco and sugar cane, which we viewed as we tramped along narrow, rutted roads in pastoral scenes. In theory this terrain offered the perfect opportunity: a kind of clean, uncluttered, uncommitted area with nothing to stand in the way of an ideal plan." Owings's allegiances were to the ideas of American rural and village life, likable as long as they conformed to the picturesque idylls of a Currier and Ives chromolithograph. Tramping about the countryside, he watched it become instantly picturesque, full of "nostalgic charm"—representative of a past that should never be reclaimed, but could be modified, modernized, and adapted.[36]

This was the brilliance of SOM's entire Oak Ridge program: its combination of conservation and innovation, its melding of the mythic qualities of past American utopias with the modern vision of centralization and government management. At the heart of this synergistic alchemy was the planners' conception of a community imbedded within and deeply respectful of nature—or, more appropriately, Nature. For all its modernity of technology and its application of an industrially streamlined assembly-line construction program, the plan harked back to the American romantic conceptions of the place of man in nature—conceptions found in Thoreau but applied to town and city planning by Andrew Jackson Downing and Frederick Law Olmsted and their inheritors, writing about the blight of large cities, and constructing suburban communities like Riverside—and, of course, the more proximate Norris Village.

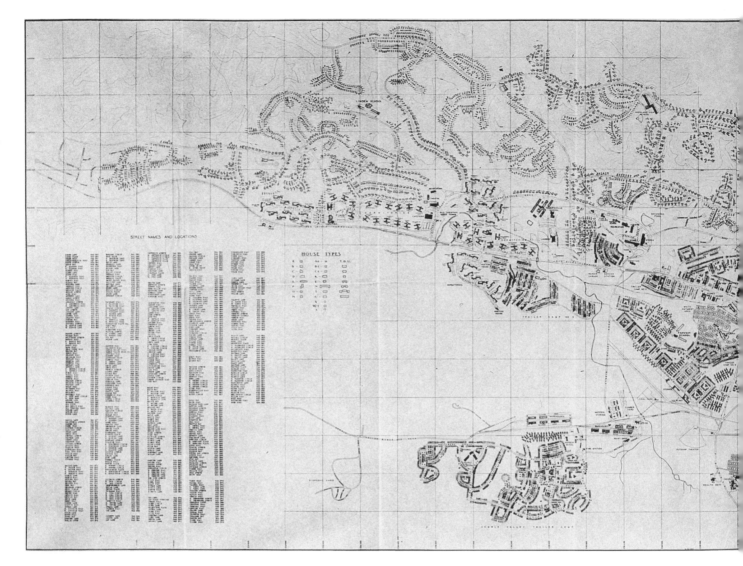

STREET NAMES AND LOCATIONS

HOUSE TYPES

FIG. 11 *Town of Oak Ridge— Tennessee. Manhattan District— Corps of Engineers.* Skidmore, Owings, and Merrill. Manhattan District History, courtesy National Archives.

This adaptation to nature infused every aspect of the plan, from the largest elements like the siting of the individual clusters or "villages," to the question of the orientation of individual houses and their relation to the other elements of their plots of land and the surroundings, both built and natural. Whereas the Stone and Webster program had strong echoes of the military barracks town in its street layouts, SOM planners designed their streets to conform to the contours of the landscape itself. Houses nestled in the hillsides, their relation to one another and to the landscape dictated by curvilinear streets that circled back on one another or on themselves. Rather than setting houses of one type all together, the planners interspersed different classes of house one with the other and set them at different angles to the street in order to make them seem more varied than they were. This concept of organicity came straightforwardly from parks and street plans of the picturesque era in landscape design, and its function was similar: to counter the uniformity and homogeneity of modernized urban life with as much variety and surprise as possible.

Individual houses, too, were sited to emphasize the planners' ideals of an integration of people and nature. "Houses were to be oriented for sun and prevailing winds,"

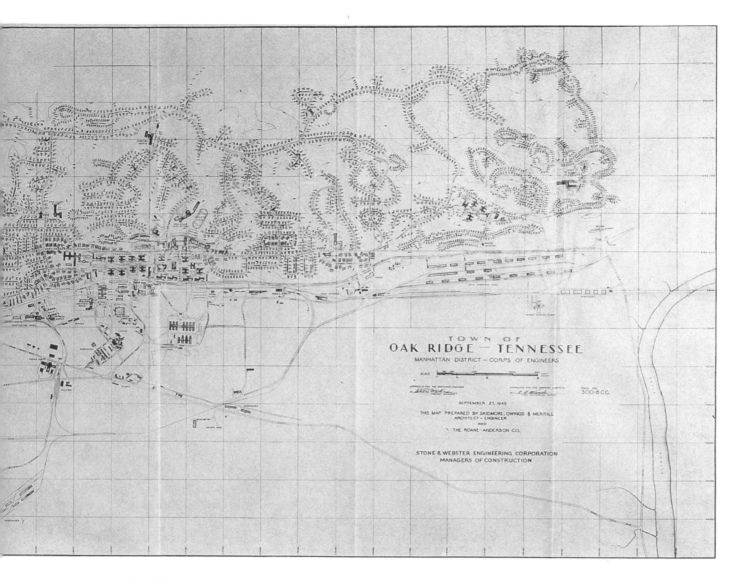

TOWN OF
OAK RIDGE — TENNESSEE

MANHATTAN DISTRICT — CORPS OF ENGINEERS

SEPTEMBER 27, 1945

THIS MAP PREPARED BY SKIDMORE, OWINGS & MERRILL
ARCHITECT - ENGINEER
AND
THE ROANE - ANDERSON CO.

STONE & WEBSTER ENGINEERING CORPORATION
MANAGERS OF CONSTRUCTION

Owings recalled, "ample land provided so that the grass and the trees and the flowers might grow. . . . On the opposite side of our houses were the living rooms and recreation areas, facing either a field or a park or an individual garden."[37]

Most of the technical matters of city planning disappeared from sight in the blueprints; that was an indication of the brilliance of the design team. Seen in plan (fig. 11), the Pierce-SOM townsite was remarkably picturesque. Owings rather cynically described the process: "All we had to do, apparently, was turn out a quaint little Cape Cod village with just the right amount of California mission style, then beat well for ten minutes and season to taste with a touch of the great Northwest."[38] But the site plan—with its lanes and cul-de-sacs, its apparent respect for the topographical features of the Tennessee hills—looked more than anything else like America's first planned picturesque suburbs from the turn of the century.

But this quality, so evident in the feet-long town-plan blueprints, disappears when we look at the photographs of the site (figs. 12, 13). What they show is a more harshly unrelieved landscape of conformity: houses, lined up in even rows along the ridges, on muddy sites stripped of vegetation by District graders and marked by rivulets of

FIG. 12 *Housing for Employees, Oak Ridge, Tennessee,* 1944. Photo by Hedrich-Blessing. Chicago Historical Society, ICHI-HB-08014–J.

FIG. 13 *Hillside Road, Oak Ridge.* Photo by James E. Westcott. U.S. Corps of Engineers, Manhattan Engineer District, Oak Ridge, Tennessee.

erosion. In these pictures, the architects' struggle to integrate and differentiate seems to have failed. The different classes of house—"A," "C," "E," and "F"—look drably uniform in style, their kinship accentuated by the view of their essentially similar rear "porches" with horizontal protective slats repeated house by house. And the curved street plans, so pleasingly irregular in form on the blueprint, have been replaced by the regularity of arrangement on the hillsides themselves—they are layered, one above the other, in even stripes.

These photographs in the final reports were to have been the triumphant conclusion of the planning process. SOM had the opportunity to use the District's own photographic corps, headed by Ed Westcott, to build an archive of images for its file, and indeed, it made full use of Westcott's team. But for the formal reports themselves, and for its own internal files, SOM chose to turn to the Chicago architectural photography firm of Hedrich-Blessing. Westcott did solid, professional work—we have seen the results in the housing illustrations. He understood that the photographs should show the houses in the most finished and understated way possible. Hedrich-Blessing, however, was the preeminent professional architectural photography firm in the nation. Commissioning the firm meant getting not just pictures but dramatic incarnations of the buildings. Hedrich-Blessing photographs required no apology

FIG. 14 *Post Office for Employees, Oak Ridge,* 1944. Photo by Hedrich-Blessing. Chicago Historical Society, ICHi-HB-08014-W2.

when sent to the *Architectural Digest* or the *Forum;* viewers understood that they marked the architect's pride in design and execution (fig. 14).[39]

These photographs convey an ironic sense never meant in 1944, but hard to resist today. For these buildings were to have housed an ideal community, in which, perhaps, the ideal population would have acted with about as much self-consciousness as did the models brought in by the photographer and stiffly posed for the big architectural view camera's seconds-long exposures. A tourist with a small hand camera would not have recorded such scenes once the houses were occupied and the schools populated. *Those* pictures might have recorded the chaos of classrooms crowded to three and four times their capacities; school grounds churned back up into alternating cycles of mud and dust; houses stained by leakage and flooding and the hands of children and adults leaning against their walls to take off clay-soaked shoes. But no tourists were allowed within the fences of Oak Ridge, and hand cameras were forbidden as well. So the picture of the site provided by Hedrich-Blessing served the fantasies of its architects well, providing the best available composite of what their utopia might have been like if only it had not been overrun by the forces of expansion.

So also with the pamphlets for "Prospective Residents" that the District began to produce in the early spring of 1943. These, too, offered orderly lists of the features immigrants to Oak Ridge could expect, noting that "all houses are equipped with garbage cans"; "attractive color schemes have been used in the interiors and trim and roofing colors are varied in arrangement"; "Separate living quarters in the area will be available for colored maids at a cost of $15.00 per month for single rooms and $10.00

per month each for those occupying double rooms"; or "Normal movement throughout the townsite area is permitted."[40]

In the calm promissory prose of the housing brochures and the overdetermined rationality of the photographs, Oak Ridge's communities began to resemble the manufacturing zones their residents would service. These factories were the engines that drove the housing program and its constant expansion, eventually causing the explosion of plans into seat-of-the-pants building and rebuilding.

Four processes in four production complexes comprised the manufacturing facilities of the Clinton Engineer Works. Three were designed to produce enriched uranium using competing techniques; the fourth was a pilot plant for the Hanford plutonium-production facility, an atomic pile midway between the tiny rudimentary demonstration pile built under the squash courts at the University of Chicago in December 1942 and the full-scale piles at Hanford.

By unanimous agreement, corps and corporation decided that all four facilities had to be isolated from the housing zones. No one could yet determine the potential for catastrophic accident in each manufacturing process. The precedents from the chemical manufacturing industry suggested such accidents might well occur (and some did, though by sheer luck none of them resulted in the sort of disaster that might well have eradicated the entire Manhattan program).

Engineers and planners had little upon which to base their calculations of appropriate settings for the plants from a safety standpoint. Members of the scientific community might have provided approximations but Groves and his cohorts had begun calling them "crackpots" early on, and the position had hardened. The technological processes themselves were incomprehensible to all but a few engineers, whose attention was directed not to safety but to expeditiousness. As a result, the siting decisions seem to have been made intuitively. Y-12, the electromagnetic separations program, was built on a variation of the "calutron," the Berkeley physicist Lawrence's modification of the cyclotron "atom splitter." It had precedent, in railroads and test tracks, and in guns and ultracentrifuges. K-25, the gaseous diffusion process, looked far more dangerous and uncontrolled, with its vertical "cascades" and as-yet-undetermined "barriers." The "piles" of X-10 seemed equally unpredictable.

Y-12 was not far from the original housing community, just over the ridge from Gamble Valley, where the huge sprawl of a trailer park soon grew up. As far as the engineers could determine, the two ridges that rimmed Gamble Valley would (they hoped) contain any potential explosion. K-25 ended up as far from the village as possible, on a site appropriate to fear but probably wrongheaded from technical and engineering standpoints. S-50, a slapdash affair meant to intervene between the production vacuums of the other two processes, was clustered next to K-25. X-10 was set nearly as far away—but, like Y-12, at a distance from the other plants, so a disaster at one might not affect the entire program.[41]

In manufacturing, as in housing, inside and outside seemed utterly opposed to each other. Inside the plants, unimaginable new processes were at work—processes, in some cases, still not invented as the facilities neared physical completion. But on the outside, all was order and normalcy. Each manufacturing plant came to resemble a prototype in the industrial world. Y-12 (fig. 15), the electromagnetic plant, resembled nothing so much as a standard chemical synthesis plant of the sort that filled the landscape of Port

Arthur, Texas, or stretched upriver from New Orleans for close to a hundred miles. Flat-roofed concrete-and-brick structures with standard factory windows alternated with lower wooden buildings with angled roofs; the streets connecting them were overarched by layers of pipework and electrical wiring. Vertical smokestacks spewed black smoke; the gaseous diffusion plant could have easily been mistaken for an auto factory, with its long, low buildings cut in their flat tops by unidentifiable facilities—for air conditioning, perhaps, or air filtration; K-25 looked like a small steel mill.

In all of these, the manufacturing facilities mimicked older industrial plants because that was the precedent both Stone and Webster and the subcontracting corporations understood. There was no need for a new architecture to match the new processes, because these were not structures meant for display, literally or symbolically. Yet the final designs were not dictated by the internal function either; rather, they reflected a desire on the part of their makers to make something comfortingly familiar, something that could be constructed off the shelf with a minimum of fundamental rethinking.

Between labor and living were the netherzones; the roads and transportation systems, the "clock alleys" where workers punched in, and the commissaries and first-aid stations and the rest. In these, too, the District, the supervising engineers, and the subcontracting corporations depended upon what they already knew. "Clock alleys" would be located at the boundary line of the village itself. Workers would congregate outside the gates, just as they might have at a steel mill in Gary, Indiana, or South Chicago, Illinois. Once punched in, they would proceed by bus to their workplace. And Negro workers (the District's term) would have a separate clock alley, sequestered from the place where white workers would congregate. Labor would be segregated.[42]

This was the unspoken agreement between the District and its corporate subcontractors: not to make a new workplace and a new conception of work to match the invented nature of the manufacturing processes inside the giant factories, but rather to clothe the new in the rituals and symbols of an older industrialism with which they were all familiar. And despite the high rhetoric of the Pierce Foundation and SOM,

Invention

92

FIG. 15 *Panoramic View of Y-12.* Photo by James E. Westcott or assistant. Manhattan District History, courtesy National Archives.

the housing plans, too, fit neatly into this unfolding program. All over Oak Ridge the compact came into force, informing the architecture, the social control mechanisms, even the imported folkways the District hoped would serve to tame the potentially uncontrollable forces brought into critical proximity at this site.

Los Alamos was originally conceived as a military installation built by military contractors to military specifications. Oak Ridge was to have been a planned community, a new town to rival the best of government-planned American utopias of the 1930s.

Hanford Engineer Works, however, was always a schizoid site. It was to consist of three fundamental elements. The largest was to be a vast manufacturing zone in which giant, blocks-long concrete monoliths, nicknamed "Canyons" and "Piles," were scattered across the desert, linked together by shiny rail spurs that would carry the furiously toxic products of each stage of plutonium production onward to the next stage, with a minimum of human contact and human danger. Far from these plants, with their high smokestacks spewing out substances never before imagined, would be two communities as unlike each other as they were unlike the huge inhuman production zone. One, Hanford Village, was to be a temporary construction town, built like a traditional military cantonment, on the hard grid of the military base, a modern incarnation of the Western forts of the 1870s, and infinitely expandable. The other, Richland Village, was to be an "operator village" similar to the one at Oak Ridge, modeled not on the TVA towns, however, but upon the Du Pont company towns that the corporation's design division had built in the past.

This division of elements incompletely resembled a Brobdingnagian assembly line. Early on, during the site selection process, scientists from the Met Lab and engineers from Du Pont agreed that the unpredictable nature of the process was such that the best plan would be to create duplicates of each of the stages and separate the manufacturing steps one from the other by a "safe distance." That way a disaster in any one of the stages—an atomic meltdown, for example, or a catastrophic spill—would not scotch the entire plutonium program.[43]

The choice of a vast desert site (fig. 16) expedited this line of thinking: a topography marked by sublime distances and isolated from population centers. Having so much naked space with which to work, designers could treat the site as something close to a game board, pushing hypothetical locations around the map with an insouciance forbidden them at Oak Ridge.

But where to house the people? The original specifications had called for a minimum distance of ten miles between the manufacturing components and worker living areas; this was the scientists' rough guess of the least distance that could afford a buffer zone for the unpredictable dangers of this still uninvented process. The three original towns—Hanford, White Bluffs, and Richland—offered water, sewage, and utilities, saving both money and time; they were also located on ideal townsite topography. But the atomic piles had to be located on or very near the Columbia River, for they would be cooled by the directing of river water into the piles and back out again. Locating the piles at the far north and west of the reservation's stretch of the Columbia still placed them on or very near White Bluffs, and only six miles from Hanford. Even then, workers would have to be moved as much as twenty miles to the farthest construction projects. Establishing the worker housing at Richland, however, provided safety but made travel distances even greater—as much as thirty miles, too far, the military argued, for construction crews to travel back and forth and still get in a ten-to-fourteen-hour workday.[44]

Balancing all these priorities required compromises. The final resolution was elegant. First, separate workers into two classes: construction laborers and manager-operators. Laborers could be defined as transient; in this way, their facilities could be rough and temporary and the argument made that they would, after all, be gone by startup. Since they *were* temporary, their camps could be located close to the construction sites. The operator village, on the other hand, could be sited much further away. Build a temporary construction camp at Hanford, six miles from the nearest pile, and build the operator village at Richland, far down the Columbia.[45]

With the site-selection criteria before them, Colonel Matthias and Du Pont's Gilbert Church met in Wilmington on March 2, 1943, and inked in the basic outlines of the Hanford Engineer Works. The Hanford Camp would consist of traditional military plans for barracks, huge eating halls, and a trailer camp to house the nomadic communities of defense construction workers who would arrive from other just-finished military projects, from Alaska to Texas. Construction crews would begin moving in as soon as plans were approved, hopefully within a month. Those in the first wave would live in whatever was available; boarding in private homes, sleeping

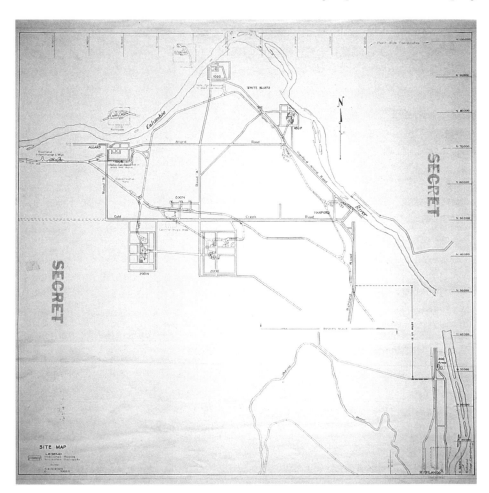

FIG. 16 *Site Map, Hanford Engineer Works.* Manhattan District History, courtesy National Archives.

in cots and on the floors of the old Hanford Grange Hall and the Hanford High School auditorium. Workers who brought their own tents or trailers were to be directed to a shaded area that would later become the site of the first organized trailer camp. These earliest arrivals would be set to work building the barracks and mess halls that would then house the next waves of workers arriving. These, too, would work on their own housing, living, and recreational facilities. At a certain point, construction of the Hanford Camp would reach sufficient size that a steadily increasing number of construction workers could be deflected into construction of the "operator village" at Richland and the manufacturing facilities themselves.[46]

In their meeting, Matthias and Church also came to an agreement on a fundamental philosophy to define the Richland community. "The village is to provide family housing only to those who must be kept under control for security reasons," Matthias wrote after the meeting. Everyone else would be kept offsite, to blend into the surrounding communities of Prosser, Kennewick, even Walla Walla. "Service buildings and commercial facilities," as well, were "to be kept to a minimum, utilizing what is available in adjacent towns to the maximum, and utilizing existing buildings in Richland to the maximum."[47]

This plan would ensure that the so-called "operator village" would remain aloof from the rabble of the construction crews, and of the industrial workers as well. But this plan didn't just distinguish the population by class; it also distinguished by the consequences of class—the necessity of sequestering those sophisticates who understood even the rudiments of the program, "protecting" them from curiosity in one interpretation, silencing and supervising them in another.

At this same March 2 meeting, Du Pont requested formal permission to subcontract its architect-engineer functions for Richland, confirming a decision that had been reached previously. At the Washington site, Du Pont would be the client; a highly competent and sympathetic military officer, already comfortable with Du Pont's top site supervisors, would serve as buffer to Groves. Most important, every detail pointed to a more pragmatic, less visionary conception of the village itself. Rather than seeking out a nationally known architectural firm, as had Marshall, Matthias and Church sought a designer "familiar with local problems," to cite the wording of an early report. And the designer, Du Pont and Matthias agreed, would be judged by the criteria of pragmatism, adaptability, and experience.[48]

At four in the morning on March 2, 1943, a Colonel McAndrews of the corps's Washington headquarters awakened G. Albin Pehrson in Spokane with a phone call asking him to survey the site and bid on the project. McAndrews arranged for the architect to meet with a Du Pont representative to walk the site; Pehrson made his bid on March 12, and it was accepted, over several others, on March 16.[49]

Pehrson had the low bid, and he had the combination of vision and pragmatism necessary to mediate between Groves's spartan military vision and the conservative middle-class tastes of Du Pont's employees. He researched the area, determined the necessary elements to a town of the size—right down to the average number of beer halls and funeral parlors—and set to work in a makeshift facility in the Pasco High School, designing every building, every street, and every amenity, for a town that had now grown from 4,000 to 6,500 and would continue to expand throughout the design and construction progress.

Pehrson accepted the military demands on the site: speed, adaptability, efficiency, cheapness. But Pehrson's true client was the Du Pont corporation. "Du Pont . . . held the view that the comfort and the welfare of the workers were the criteria to be applied," Pehrson wrote, and his design sought to apply those criteria to make, not utopia, but "an exceptional war housing project . . . in . . . a setting at once beautiful and healthful."[50]

Du Pont desired a village in which it could sequester the most sensitive operator-employees, keeping them and their families isolated from life outside the reservation. To do so meant building housing that could be satisfactory to the differences of class, of education, of taste, that would characterize these occupants. Some would be upper-level executives for the corporation, others top engineers moved from comfortable lives in Wilmington and dropped for an indeterminate duration in a region not of their choosing. Drawing them out to the site, and keeping them, if not happy, at least satisfied, would be a crucial task of Pehrson's. But the town would house others, as well—lower-level industrial operatives assigned to the village because of the sensitivity of their work; military representatives, including a number of high-ranking officers, but also the minions of military security and even the perimeter guards. These people, less fastidious in their tastes (Du Pont presumed) and certainly less well heeled, would also need accommodations. Security risks imprisoned at a remote site, the residents at Richland would, Du Pont hoped, see themselves instead as lucky occupants of a community that combined the familiarity of the American "village" with the amenities of "a modern town," in Pehrson's words.[51]

Pehrson looked like a pragmatist, but he folded a powerful strain of utopianism into his practical designs. His completion report evidences this; it is full of meditations on the ideal democratic environment and defenses of his proposals couched in the language of the visionary urban designer. "The planners had a definitely democratic attitude in the planning of the houses," Pehrson wrote in his report: "Since the whole venture is a use of public monies, such an attitude is relevant to a high degree and should interest the public. . . . [Thus] the building types are . . . as similar . . . as could be planned so that no one might feel himself slighted in the quality of housing. The smallest house has a proportionate share of the things considered vital to good living."[52]

Behind this desire for a community embodying the democratic values for which the nation was fighting there was something more pragmatic, Pehrson noted,

> the necessity for maintaining a high morale among workers transplanted to what will probably seem a strange country. High morale cannot be achieved by crowding skilled and veteran workers into inadequate dwellings. Neither can it be predicated upon salary, position or caste distinction. No village can eliminate such distinctions entirely, for it is the American tradition to aspire . . . and where [the top] men locate will undoubtedly be considered favored territory; but in so far as the planners could arrange these matters, all types of houses [were] scattered throughout the project.[53]

Pehrson's plans thus intermingled a number of basic values. First was the democratic as Pehrson conceived it—his belief in an American community in which differences of class weren't permanent, but were, rather, surmountable disparities of achievement. Pehrson believed in an American democracy that could tolerate inter-mingled classes and occupations, because its members saw their place on that ladder to be temporary. In this, Pehrson echoed the program of SOM at Oak Ridge. His house plans, too, shared the Oak Ridge designers' desire to make every house type as suc-cessful as possible within its limits of economy and scale. The results, however, were far different than the Pierce-SOM plans.

Pehrson's criteria were ambitious. Each housing unit should provide as much pri-vacy as possible; duplexes like his "A" house should have a minimum of shared walls, and single-family dwellings should be sheltered by location on the lot and use of trees and shrubs. Houses should take climate and environment into account. "In a desert like country, this is an important comfort factor," Pehrson wrote, explaining his choice of a one-story duplex design to maximize cross-ventilation. "During the hottest weath-er there is usually a gentle wind from the west and southwest and, since the nights are reasonably cool, window ventilation is highly desirable." Pehrson wanted houses in which each room had good light and ventilation, and each looked out on at least two different outdoor scenes:

> In an area with considerable temperature extremes . . . the comfort of
> the worker has a marked effect upon his efficiency. Moreover, there
> would undoubtedly be a psychological hazard in a too-cramped plan.
> Although city dwellers are confined to narrow lots and restricted views,
> these are an accepted part of their environment. In the desert, where
> space is the key characteristic of the view, a cramped village of cramped
> houses would be out of character, a palpable and conscious discord.[54]

In this, as in each housing type, Pehrson looked to the psychological health of his residents, to define not only the spaces and elements within each house, but larger issues of aesthetics and relation to site and to the environment more generally. His duplex was "box-like," he admitted (fig. 17), but because only a few of these appeared in each block, "there is no effect of monotony." The smaller two-bedroom "B" duplex was "ranch-like," low to the ground, with the bedrooms at the outside to increase privacy. The "D" was a suburban Cape Cod with an "el" at the front and a dormer above the front picture window. The "E" was a single-story house built on a "T," while the F" was a single-family reduction of the "A" duplex, but with details added to dis-tinguish it. The "G" and "H" houses, likewise, were sufficiently distinctive from the others that they could be combined without setting a monotonous repetition of ele-ments or a sense of cookie-cutter planning.

But to compare any of these houses with a more consciously inventive housing type—even the flat-roofed TVA C-1 units brought into Richland during a later and more uncontrolled period of expansion—is to see nonetheless how conventional was Pehrson's design repertoire, and how much his designs prefigured the basic types found in nearly any suburban housing area to be built after the war. All were varia-tions on two prevalent housing fashions—the "Cape Cod" and the "ranch." All used the most acceptable and conservative of doors, windows, and trim—portals, lintels, and the like. This was surely what Pehrson meant when he admitted that his designs "may seem to offer nothing new or experimental in method or design." But this was

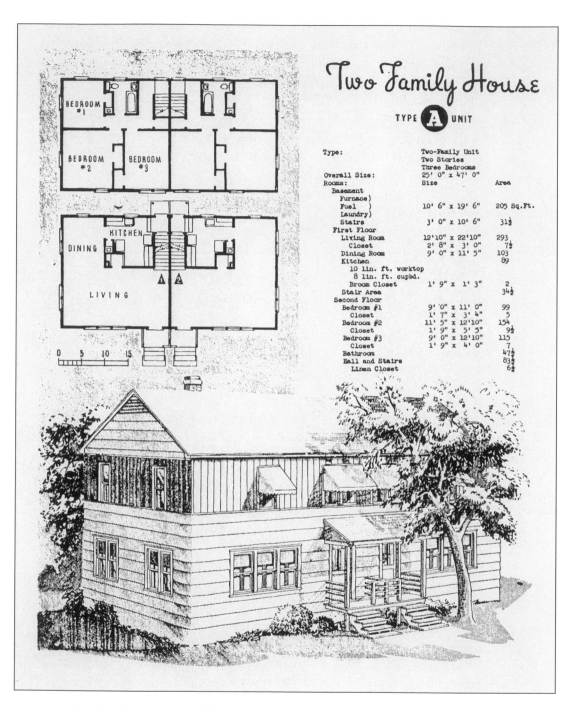

FIG. 17 *Two-Family House, Type "A" Unit.* Office of G. Albin Pehrson, Spokane. From Pehrson's *Report.* Hanford Science Center, Department of Energy.

a virtue not only because it enabled the District to use nearly any builder—Pehrson's rationale—but also because these designs were comforting, familiar, and desirable to those whom Pehrson sought to attract and satisfy.[55]

Still, Pehrson's larger philosophy—of creating varied housing, built to satisfy the needs of middle-class corporate managers yet to avoid incurring the wrath of cost-conscious army overseers, scattered across neighborhoods to prevent class separation, designed to adapt to climate and ecology, specified for rapid building using mass-production methods—was realized, at least in the first stage of planning and building. And for that stage, Pehrson's larger overall plan for the village won out as well. His plan was, in many ways, similar to that at Oak Ridge: cluster into one dense area the vast majority of commercial and service buildings in a central shopping and administrative area, making a true "downtown," like the downtowns in the idealized American town, and keep only neighborhood grocery, drug, and auto service facilities scattered within the housing. The pre-army Richland had a food store/post office, a pool hall, a drug store, a variety store, and a few other rudimentary stores. The new Richland required much more, and Pehrson designed everything from supermarkets to a bank, a beauty salon, a shoe repair shop, and a "milk depot." In the commercial and public buildings, as with the various housing types, Pehrson saw the opportunity to build anew the prototypical American town.[56]

But here even more than with the housing types, the architect came up against the force of Groves's vision of a different type of town. Perhaps the most symbolic manifestation of this was in the matter of plate glass facades. Groves was against them. They made the village too much a town and not enough a utilitarian, civilian equivalent of an army base. In commercial buildings, Groves wanted the few that were essential to resemble the army PX. "Show windows," as Pehrson called them, symbolized the sort of living inappropriate to a wartime setting—notions of "window shopping," of entering stores on impulse, of appealing to the spontaneous forces of desire, rather than providing the bare minimum of goods in an atmosphere reflecting the austerity of the war. Pehrson had an entirely different idea. He *wanted* "show windows" because "their elimination was considered too radical, as the public and the operator have definite ideas of what a commercial building should be." Once again, he was the defender of American values—free-market capitalism, now, rather than "democracy"—while Groves was the "radical."[57]

But Pehrson took too much credit, here as in the case of democratic housing. Actually a broad consortium of officials pressed these ideals upon the architect, or supported him when he presented them on his own. Even Colonel Matthias pushed for heterogeneous neighborhoods and urged a traditional commercial center. This broadly based support of a more conservative, more "American" community made possible the victories over Groves and his adherents.[58]

The final town plan was a compromise between these two visions. Groves's picture of a rudimentary urban center won out when he ordered that onsite housing units be kept to a minimum and that the National Housing Authority be required to build facilities in surrounding towns for the rest; it won when he forced Du Pont to accept scaled-down fixtures and amenities in the houses; it won when Groves personally lopped the greenhouse, the large men's clothing store, and even the funeral parlor off the plan, at a meeting on June 24, 1943. Pehrson and Du Pont won when they insisted that lot sizes be expanded, that more three- and four-bedroom units be built, and that the commercial center contain far more businesses than originally planned. Again and again, they urged their case that "it is essential to maintain the necessary number of qualified workers that good and adequately large housing units be built," and that equally attractive commercial facilities be supplied. And, as Pehrson himself predicted, the realities of an occupied town proved the architect right more often than Groves, and resulted in the reinstitution of facilities and housing types originally eliminated at Groves's orders.[59]

Yet the final plans were never realized; at Richland as at Oak Ridge, they were continually redefined by the process of compromise, negotiation, and underhanded tactics on both sides. Nonetheless, the city began to go up. In its broad outlines, it had many of the qualities found in the Oak Ridge plan. Many of its streets were curved and its housing areas defined by dead-end streets and cul-de-sacs, though to a far lesser extent than at the Tennessee site. With the Columbia River as its defining topographical feature and its single most attractive commodity, the Richland Village curved along the river's banks, with the first and the most exclusive neighborhoods set up on its bluffs. The central business district was served by a "shopping loop" off principal access streets. Buses would run from the Hanford workplace to the downtown, and from the downtown up into the housing clusters. Richland would look like, would *be* like, an ideal democratic town. Its whole-cloth invention, its innovations of construction and design, its attention to cost, all would make it a prototype for the new world that would appear after the war, when Depression-ravaged, war-postponed American dreams of universal access to village living would once again have the chance to be realized.

Richland was to be permanent, if not in its final execution, at least in the programs it was meant to express. Hanford Camp was to be its necessary opposite. Compare Pehrson's idealized site drawing of Richland, made in 1943 (fig. 18), with the map that went out to Hanford Camp residents at about the same time (fig. 19). Pehrson's artist made a perspectival bird's eye of the village, showing its proximity to the Columbia River, its asymmetrical, curvilinear design, its use of clusters. The unnamed military draftsman who made the orientation map of Hanford Camp produced a bare collection of rectangles that only emphasized the rigorous grid upon which the camp was built. Streets at Hanford had no names—they were "Avenue D" or "7th Street." Even the arrangement of buildings within each block never made it from camp to map.

The spartan minimalism of the map conformed to the camp it represented. Camp housing was, from the first, planned to be spartan and as efficient as possible. Originally assuming that half of the 28,000 planned workers would be "absorbed" by surrounding communities, District planners instructed Du Pont to build ten four-wing men's barracks and ten two-wing women's barracks, serviced by a central mess hall and a commissary. The barracks, multistory wood-frame buildings heated by fans blowing air across steam coils attached to a giant central steam plant, and cooled by "evaporators," housed white male workers two to a room, 191 men to a building. At a distance was a second barracks section for white women, who were housed in smaller, two-wing barracks.[60]

As the barracks went up, other facilities went up with them—first the mess halls, then the commissary building, then the smaller amenities, like barber shops and the

FIG. 18 *Site Diagram.* Office of G. Albin Pehrson, Spokane. From Pehrson's *Report.* Hanford Science Center, Department of Energy.

library. Once the first batch of barracks was built, the District moved more than eight hundred construction workers out of the large, wood-sided tents. Trailer camps, however, were another matter. These were essential, and they formed another enormous portion of the camp—originally 489 lots housing some 1,600 people in what the District called "a modern well-planned miniature city with all streets parallel to each other and perpendicular to the main avenues."[61]

The design of Hanford Camp included one more essential element—the "Negro Area." This was a separate zone, invisible on the maps unless one knew how to look for the proper combination of bowling alley, Valley Theater, recreation hall, mess halls, barracks, and hutments. For black workers and their families, the area was as distinct and as significant in its boundaries as was the camp itself. Built ostensibly at the request of representatives of the "Negro community," it satisfied Groves's desires for complete sequestering of all "colored" workers from their white counterparts, and, most especially, the separation of black males from white females.[62]

And the Negro Area underscored the fundamental law of the Hanford Camp: proper separation of each element into its proper and separate place, with the whole arranged to organize these parts as efficiently as possible. Just as the barracks were prefabricated from hundreds of separate elements cut and assembled at central facilities and shipped to the separate locations for final construction, so the camp itself was the communitarian equivalent, designed to keep men and women, white and non-

FIG. 19 Map of Hanford, Washington. From *Here's Hanford.* Hanford Science Center, Department of Energy.

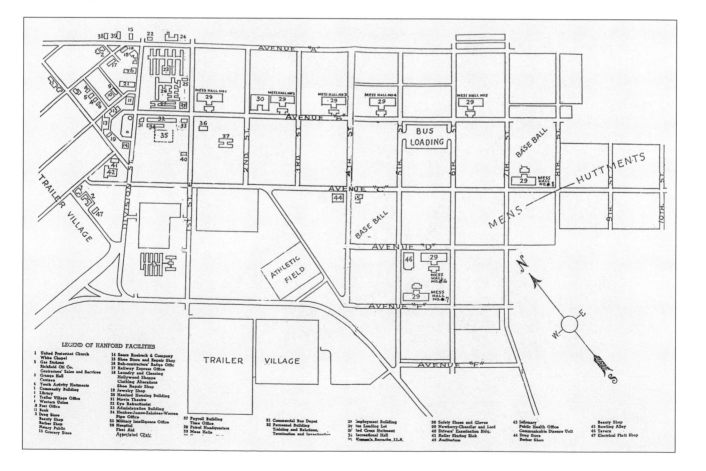

white, families and single employees, workers and managers, each in a separate zone, protected one from another, and distanced to prevent the spontaneous, uncontrolled creation of a critical mass of social energy.

Despite the supervision of one of the nation's most sophisticated governmental bureaucracies, despite the work of highly trained engineers experienced in military models of order and rectitude, despite site planning by some of the most prestigious corporations in the nation, the Manhattan Engineer District seems to have faltered, then collapsed, as it attempted to administer its mandate to create expeditiously a new manufacturing system and the culture necessary to sustain that system.

We can see this in the boundary between nature and culture, between the Hanford reservation and the surrounding land. Construction in the desert is a particularly delicate matter. The surface of the soil is extremely shallow; the slightest disturbance can have consequences far beyond the builder's expectations. Native plants that hold the soil in place are easily damaged; once removed, they rarely grow back at all. Because rainfall is rare and, when it comes, torrential, the topography has often had millennia to adapt to the circumstances.

The immediate effect of a massive construction program on a desert site that is also windblown and subject to violent extremes of temperature can be summed up in a single word: dust. Dust can be composed of microscopically fine particles of alluvial silt deposited on a riverbed long ago and dried to a rock-hard brick—until it's released by the bulldozers and road graders. It can also be closer to coarse sand, especially when the winds have been harsh for long enough, and when they continue to have enough velocity to lift the grainy silicates.

At Hanford, they had every kind of dust imaginable. Veterans of the Dust Bowl, arriving in Pasco on the night train, recognized the smell, the feel, immediately. Robley Johnson recalled the effect on the recruits: "A lot of them would get off the bus, stand around for a while, see a dust storm coming and get on the next bus back to Pasco. They never even stayed overnight, a lot of them." The local term for the dust at its worst was "termination wind." When the winds blew, workers left the site in droves, with or without certificates of availability.[63]

Shortly after war's end, while Manhattan Project engineers waited to see what would happen to the Richland site, Charlie Wende wrote the lyrics to a song commemorating the wind:

> I cleaned my house and garden
> and I was feeling gay;
> Then came that nasty wind and blew
> my garbage can away.
> Blow ye winds of Richland,
> Blow ye winds high-o,
> Blow ye winds of Richland,
> Blow, blow, blow.
> That fearful termination wind,
> can't stand it any more;

each time I sweep
the dust so deep
blows underneath my door.[64]

The effects of the construction program on the human society were violent enough, and the District paid close attention to them. Far more violent, however, were the effects on the larger desert ecology. Construction profoundly damaged the ecology of the region, not only within the bounds of the site, but far beyond. Later atrocities jolt us: radioactive iodine 131 emitted from the chemical separations stacks entered the food chain, killing cattle and the children who drank their milk; failing waste tanks leached toxic radioactive waste into the porous desert soil, then into the water table, and, finally, into the Columbia River. These facts have high shock value, because the ecological consequences affected people, many of them outside the zone of responsibility. But the most violent transformations of the landscape were the far more inadvertent consequences of intruding a population of some fifty-one thousand into a fragile desert ecosystem.[65]

The very scale of the Hanford site forces the eye to adjust to vast spaces and high walls, focusing on infinity rather than on the microcosmic zones where one might see the changes in root structure of plants, or the crushing out of spores and lichens. But that is where most of the effects took place.

With the lens set for a panoramic survey—most appropriate for documenting "planning"—Hanford was the most successful of the three sites. In aerial photographs of the system under construction and then in operation, and in movies made from surveillance planes by District security people, one can see how neatly Hanford worked out. Imagine a film (a composite) that begins at Hanford Camp early in the morning, showing workers streaming into the clock alley and buses full of shift workers moving in each direction along the long, straight roads that lead toward the worksites. The plane carrying the filmmaker swoops across from pile to chemical separation plant, following the rail lines along which will run the trains carrying "hot" plutonium slugs to be doused and stripped of useless contaminants. Then the camera follows the roadway back toward Richland, where—nestled in the curve of the Columbia that had once housed a small population of dreamy farmers—a new city has nearly finished taking shape. The gospel of efficiency has won out—everything will be completed in time, production will yield its fruits. Soon Colonel Matthias will be carrying the shipments of plutonium to Los Angeles, handing them to an agent taking them to Los Alamos, where they will be added to the other, more conventional components making up the bomb to be known as "Fat Man." If the pilot doesn't drop low enough to reveal the details of things, the narrative seems flawless and sensible.[66]

But the actual process of translating Pehrson's, Du Pont's, and Groves's plans for the two communities and the production area that together comprised the Hanford Engineer Works resembled more closely the out-takes from such a film—the fragments and dislocations the army's propaganda editor might have left on the floor.

Logically, everything should have worked out well. Hanford was a temporary camp; it would disappear when construction was done. Richland was a permanent village; it would be occupied as production came on line and operators were hired and managers emigrated from Wilmington and the countless other Du Pont facilities. But the

Hanford Camp ethos involved mutually contradictory hypotheses. One was that the camp, being temporary, could be allowed to grow as needed, could accommodate the "instant-city" qualities of other construction and mining camps in the Great West during the nineteenth and twentieth centuries, from the Union Pacific towns that came and went as the railroad passed them by, to the mining towns of Colorado, Montana, and the Dakotas, to the construction camps that grew around the vast New Deal dam-building projects of the thirties. This aspect of Hanford gave it "the atmosphere of a Wild West frontier town," in the words of the corps's official historians. Leona Marshall Libby, who traveled there regularly and was eventually stationed there as a resident physicist, confirmed this picture. "There was nothing to do after work except fight," she wrote, decades later, "with the result that occasionally bodies were found in garbage cans the next morning. . . . It was a tough town."[67]

Libby exaggerated—crime statistics reveal that murder was a relatively uncommon crime at Hanford. But she recorded the rumors and gossip that were rampant among Hanford Camp residents, and even more so among Richlanders who looked upon Hanford as the unruly opposite of their stable planned community. Murder may not have been prevalent, but the other qualities of the Wild West town were there in spades— transience, temporariness in everything, especially the physical environment, a constant sense of imminent, spontaneous change. Hanford was meant to house only half of the projected 28,000 workers—the rest were to live offsite, in Kennewick, Walla Walla, and Pasco. But these couldn't begin to absorb close to 15,000 workers and their families. And the influx was almost instantaneous, forcing Matthias and the town representatives of surrounding regions to scramble desperately and largely ineffectively to find money and authority to begin new housing projects. By July 1943, more than 10,000 workers had arrived, and many brought their families, swelling the population in the area by some 20,000-plus. While these workers hammered together barracks, hutments, and mess halls, they lived in tents scrounged by Matthias, in shacks they themselves built out of scrap lumber and used concrete forms, in vacant houses, in warehouses, in the grange hall. Women were allocated the auditorium and upper rooms of the old Hanford High School. There were few sanitary facilities. Experienced wartime construction workers who brought house trailers with them were allowed to set them up under the shade trees by the river. By default, that site eventually became Trailer Camp 1. At first there were no sewage facilities to service these. This area became a ramshackle, boisterous shantytown, lasting through the duration of the project.[68]

Against this spontaneous community, seen by some as dangerous and by others as a place of freedom and joy, is the other Hanford Camp, the one supervised by Groves, built by the military, completed in time for peak occupancy in 1944, ruled over by a combination of military regulation and corporate company-town paternalism. The Hanford town-planning program had obvious advantages over the planned communities of Richland and Oak Ridge. Built on a grid, upon a flat plain bounded by empty scrub, using standard-issue barracks, mess hall, bathhouse, and recreational facility plans drawn by engineers at Du Pont and at the Army Corps of Engineers, this city plan was almost infinitely expandable. Setting all workers two to a room and building the mess halls to service the same numbers of workers in equal proximity to their housing meant that no one could complain of inequitable treatment (unless you were black, and then, complaint was useless).

Building was to be as efficient as the design. Because the barracks and the later plywood hutments required a total of only four housing designs, lumber could be precut to a very limited number of sizes. District carpenters working at centralized locations assembled the barracks frameworks and then delivered them to the sites. Door and window frames, trusses, and most of the smaller aspects of building construction were likewise prefabricated on assembly lines. Separate assembly lines for plumbing, piping, electrical, and mechanical units provided the raw materials. Worker teams moved quickly from site to site, doing their predetermined jobs on each successive barracks.[69]

And *this* Hanford Camp could sell to workers in recruitment pamphlets. *Dear Anne* (aimed at potential female workers), *Here's Hanford,* and *Highlights of Hanford* all emphasized the predictability, the egalitarianism, and the reassuring safety of the Hanford Camp.

But arriving workers, at least during much of 1943, saw a picture that combined both elements—efficiency and disorder. Though worker population topped 10,000 by June, living facilities lagged far behind. Dormitory/barracks construction began January 21, with the first stage comprising 89 dorms housing 13,189 people. The first six were not occupied, however, until June 15. On April 14, Matthias reported in his diary that "the first meal in the Hanford Camp was served by the Commissary Company tonight." On April 23, Matthias managed to get 100 tents shipped from Seattle, with another 50 on order. May 6 brought what may have been the most important entry in Matthias's diary: "General Groves approved sale of beer at Hanford." On May 11, "2,380 employees at work." But only 700 of them were housed in the construction camp, and only 1,200 to 1,300 ate in the mess halls, and "no hot water is available in the construction camp."[70]

By the end of May, everyone involved agreed that things weren't going to work out as Groves and his planners had envisioned. A meeting Matthias held with Du Pont representatives in Seattle on May 18 was devoted to the new demographics and their implications. The camp would be far, far bigger than planned; although Matthias had been able to get some National Housing Authority commitments to build new housing in the nearby town of Kennewick, the offsite housing was never going to provide for half the population, as Groves had ordered. Moreover, the actual population was rising dramatically. And it was finally becoming clear that construction and operations would overlap. Even if the District allowed workers to remain at Hanford during and after startup, still there would have to be an adaptation of Richland to accommodate construction workers, if only for a period of months. And not only construction workers would swell Richland; Du Pont projected that the operations staff would be triple that upon which Pehrson and the Du Pont designers had based their plans for the two communities.[71]

As 10,000 construction workers became 30,000, and then 40,000, and then 47,000, the District's first impulse was to pack more workers into the barracks currently in place. But this damaged already strained recruiting efforts—no one wanted to move to the desert to be packed eight to a tiny room. Another solution lay with the trailer areas. Trailers were usually worker owned and therefore cheaper to add. But the District was always quietly opposed to trailers because they usually had families packed inside them. Families sapped a worker's willingness to work whenever ordered. Families introduced women to the site, in circumstances where they could not be controlled as they were in the barracks described in *Dear Anne*. Families introduced children, and children required schools and hospitals and nurseries and playgrounds. Trailers had 3.3 occupants per unit, a District census determined, and usually only one was working.[72]

But trailers also offered a pragmatic solution. Trailers could be purchased or borrowed from other government agencies, and family life did represent a reassuring antidote to the picture of a Wild West town of burly, drunken, dangerous men on a spree. With few options, Matthias embraced trailers, and they eventually formed a central part of the largest expansion programs. At peak occupancy in 1944, the trailer camps siphoned off something close to four thousand workers, nearly as many as occupied the white men's hutments that formed the second of the District's expansion strategies.[73]

Barracks structures demanded much wood in a treeless environment. More important, they had "practically no salvage value." By this time, in January 1944, both Du Pont and the District had begun to look with alarm at their soon-to-be-discarded town of more than forty thousand, and demountable structures, so successful at Oak Ridge in satisfying the calls of Groves for minimal cost, were very attractive. Prefabs, too, many of them modeled after the Oak Ridge houses, formed the third option—though they turned out to be far more trouble than they were worth.

These structures had none of the touches that made the barracks more than bearable. The hutments, at least, were air conditioned, but they were "heated" with central coal stoves, hardly appropriate to the worst of Hanford winters. The "demountables" resembled trailers, but without the connotations of adventure and travel, and without the family and community living typical of the trailer camps. In addition, the prefabs had a nasty reputation, especially among Richlanders, as harborers of the lower classes. All of these matters made them unattractive options for a bureaucracy desperate to attract and retain workers in a scarcity economy. By this time, however, the District had turned to other methods of drawing Richland workers to the site, and keeping them—satisfied or not.

From the air, however, the always-incomplete "completed" Hanford Camp of, say, early 1945 still retained its reassuring grid (fig. 20). Vast in extent, unobscured by trees or topographical features, the camp looked to be the model of efficiency, rationality, and order. And to its south, the idyllic managerial suburb of Richland was taking shape along the bluffs, where its cul-de-sacs and curved streets mirrored the curve of the Columbia and where every day the town expanded further, according to the mass-production techniques used at Hanford to produce houses and a community more generally designed to disguise regimentation and uniformity. At age eighty-two, in 1990, Robley Johnson remembered the momentum: "You'd go to work in the morning and there'd only be one house on the block, and you'd come home and there'd be two houses done and one studded up and one foundation and a couple of big holes in the ground at the end! Each house had a number like l-7120, and they'd cut everything for the house and mark all the studs and so on with the number; they'd build a complete house in a half-day."[74]

Meanwhile at Oak Ridge, the wild disparity between dream and manifestation, hidden in Los Alamos, suppressed at Hanford/Richland, came violently to the fore.

FIG. 20 Aerial view of Hanford Village and Columbia River, ca. 1945. Photo by Robley Johnson or assistant. Hanford Science Center, Department of Energy.

Skidmore, Owings, and Merrill never had the luxury of seeing the completion of their utopian plan for an American village housed in ultramodern mass-produced dwelling "units." On November 10, 1943, SOM and the District's office met and determined that the firm would have to develop a new, expanded city plan, to provide for a "final" village of 6,000 family dwelling units, men's dorms for 1,600, and women's dorms for 6,000. Though the production teams were completing cemesto houses at the rate of one every thirty minutes, seventeen houses a day, and "attempting to attain a higher average" (as Kelley wrote to one of Tennessee Eastman's more demanding managers), the needs were even greater. Already the firm had compromised on its lovely program of spring 1943, adding TVA housing types, army hutments, and more dormitories, and setting up a trailer camp.[75]

The sprawling Gamble Valley trailer camp that grew out of this sudden expansion represented a breakdown of planning that threatened worker safety. For Gamble Valley was the buffer between Oak Ridge and Y-12; it had been kept vacant thus far because it was the area military engineers and scientific planners expected would be most likely to be devastated in an atomic accident. Somehow the need for expanded housing overpainted the issue of village safety.[76]

This overtaxing expansion program of early 1943 was still not sufficient to satisfy the demand for housing and services. The original plan by the District, imbedded in S&W and SOM's town plans, had been to house a significant number of workers, particularly construction workers, offsite, in "nearby towns with adequate transportation." By September 1943 everyone knew it wouldn't work. In the words of W. E. Kelley, Tennessee Eastman Y-12 operations officer, "the housing situation is extremely acute and is becoming progressively worse . . . , having a very serious effect on employee relations and on the recruiting of new employees," making it "necessary to curtail the recruiting and training programs, which will of course result in curtailed production in the Y-12 project." Kelley was, in effect, threatening the District with a shutdown if it did not provide Tennessee Eastman with adequate onsite housing.[77]

Soon the other corporations had joined the chorus demanding more housing, and the frenetic pace increased further. Nat Owings recalled that phase: "Sixty-four-hour weeks were common enough. When a decision was made, the trap was sprung, the greyhounds unleashed. There was no time to correct errors or restudy anything. Once done, there was no alternative. Through heavy timber, rocks, thick underbrush, uphill and down, our boys would scramble along, staking out roads and sewers and water lines. The constructors followed closely behind, led by axmen, dynamiters and the great bulldozers."[78]

Owings vividly remembered not just the working conditions and the consequences; he also recalled the bureaucratic circumstances that amplified the discord and chaos, the immunity from responsibility, and the overall directive atmosphere that "goaded us on." The files bulged, then overflowed, with memos from offices and suboffices that appeared overnight, staffed with new workers.

This was the dramatic manifestation of another construction program within the District, perhaps more important than the physical program that was resulting in streets and houses: the construction of a bloated managerial bureaucracy of a scale that would have been inconceivable to the scientists who had originally approached Roosevelt with a possibility for a weapon. As the manufacturing programs themselves drew more and more heavily on the subcontracting corporations, like Kellex, Tennessee Eastman, and Du Pont, the District began adding layer after layer to its own managerial structure. With each addition came promotion for those who had been there from the start. The names of officials who signed off on requests in late 1942 remained on memos of increasing complexity and imperative tone over the next three years. The titles before their names, however, moved up the promotion ladder: lieutenants rose to lieutenant colonels, even colonels; and new lieutenants appeared to take their places at the bottom of the pyramid.

We can see this process vividly by imagining this bureaucracy as a topography like that of Hanford or Oak Ridge. For this imaginary topography of bureaucratic power, the District drew its own maps—organizational charts, District officials called them—that revealed even as they disguised this immense expansion in scale and complexity, an expansion that threatened, like the physical expansions at Oak Ridge, Los Alamos, and Hanford, to overwhelm planning and social structure and to engender chaos rather than efficiency.

Take the organizational charts for the District that map the program in April and August of 1943. Both are of roughly equal height and width. Both contain roughly seventy boxes. But the equivalence is deceptive. The first rises to President Roosevelt, and reaches down to the individual sites. The second covers only a comparatively small area. It also reflects a far greater geographical decentralization, including the small subsites, and draws into single units the organizational entities that were separated in the first plan.

The second chart hides a basic managerial reorganization in the District, in which each major site developed its own divisions of administration, operations, engineering, law, security, and military activity. Within each of these divisions, the District drew more and more army and civilian officials—public information officers, town administrators, undercover informants within the dormitories and hutments, legal representatives to work on a daily basis with claims against the District, doctors to treat illness, and medical researchers to experiment with radiation dosages and hazardous waste ingestion in hopes of avoiding the disasters attendant with large-scale, largely unregulated handling of radioactive materials, and of limiting the District's liability when accidents and injuries might occur.

We may quantify this change by saying that, between 1942 and 1945, the District rolls expanded from a few hundred to more than 120,000. But this, too, oversimplifies. For we must remember that the District added each official in order that he or she do some specified task deemed necessary by another official; and each addition required complex determinations by other officials both within the District and outside of it—arranging pay vouchers, reading and initialing memos, attending meetings called to bring the new worker up to speed. These tasks themselves complicated the working lives of every worker who lay below the new official, from subaltern to mailroom clerk. The addition of a single new officer—for example, the public relations officer George O. Robinson, who was appointed to the Clinton site in the summer of 1944—required security officials to run a clearance investigation. Then began the process of inserting this face into the network of the District as someone who could now be allowed inside the fence. Ed Westcott, District photographer, received a requisition order from the Security Division; he scheduled Robinson into the identification office, where a Westcott assistant took his picture and the machinery was cranked up to make a security pass and to add the picture to the security dossier. After all this, the new employee had to have an office, with furniture, an assistant (in Robinson's case, an army officer who had previously handled the District's public relations), and a house in which to live. Even a few days' work by someone like Robinson resulted in a blizzard of paper, a rash of transcontinental phone calls, cables to and from various District offices, reports that went up the ladder of command to the District Engineer and, if rejected, generated appeals and counterresponses, or, if accepted, required the work of new employees.[79]

Robinson was only one man; his instructions joined a rising chorus of imperatives that filled file after file, cabinet after cabinet, in the District's offices. And the paperwork, the burgeoning personnel, the added typewriters and mimeo machines and the desks to put them on, formed a vast unplanned segment in the continuing expansion of each site. To accommodate these augmentations, other offices had to be relocated; usually they, too, were expanding explosively, and the net effect was to require a hugely enlarged network of bureaucratic spaces—offices, buildings, and compounds. This expansion required an equivalent expansion in infrastructure, in communications equipment and telephone lines, in electrical generating plants and water tanks and sewage treatment facilities.

The District's own people formed but one part of the total population of the sites, especially Oak Ridge. Because Clinton became the headquarters of the District, corporate officials from all of the submanufacturing processes either located there or cycled through, and they required a managerial structure to do their bidding—secretaries, typists, engineers, inspectors, employment trainers, interviewers, and all the other positions implicit in a giant corporate enterprise closely resembling the chemical industry. Kellex alone eventually had 3,700 employees, scattered in the New York corporate headquarters and research laboratories, the Kellogg plant in Jersey City, and the Oak Ridge facility.[80]

The effects were not merely managerial. They were physical and social. The November 1944 modification in the Oak Ridge site plan represented more than simple expansion of the original program. It required added development of 2,000 TVA-type houses, 1,000 multiple-unit houses, 7 men's dormitories, and 22 women's dormitories. These had to be crammed somewhere, disrupting a site plan that was elegantly complete in March 1943 and already distended by the fall of that year. The TVA units, especially, gave an aura of decrepitude, perched as they were in oceans of mud that Owings described as "thick, sticky gumbo." Balanced on weird stiltlike foundations to keep them from simply washing away, they were nothing more than shacks with canvas roofs. Nothing could have been further from the original Pierce notion of radical housing for the masses, to be built with radically new technology to provide amenities unheard of at prices unimaginable before.

SOM's solution to the call for a new city was to build a series of slum "villages" separate from the original cemesto communities. Like most slums, these were placed along the main roadways, or grafted onto the backs of existing housing clusters down in the valley, notably the Negro Village that had long ago been redefined as an all-white "East Village" complex for less desirable workers.[81]

This increase in population taxed the fundamental notion of the SOM town plan— its separation of housing into "clusters" nestled in the hillsides, with minimal service facilities, linked together with roads that ran into the central avenues or turnpikes, which then provided transportation to the central service area, where shopping, administration, and all the other requirements of everyday living could be satisfied. Adding eight beauty parlors, for example, meant interspersing them in the housing areas, even as the central shopping area became overcrowded and long lines came to characterize the search for any commodity, from bread to flowers. The combination destroyed the philosophical basis of the original plan—its separation of housing and service, its protection of home as a place of renewal amidst nature and culture—and made a sham of the pragmatic solutions the arrangement had offered, in the form of a commercial area that could be easily serviced from the main road and the railway. Now trucks would have to bellow up onto the ridges and into the dwelling areas, after contributing their part to the gridlock that struck certain of the main streets connecting housing to commercial zones.

Expansion wreaked a different kind of havoc on the landscape elements. SOM had planned to intersperse its housing clusters in wildflower-filled fields and stands of native timber, visible through the picture windows of the utopian houses. Stone and Webster had allowed destructive grading, but SOM figured the fecund southern climate would quickly heal those scars. Instead, the exponential expansions in population and facilities filled in the empty areas with housing or service buildings, and the continuing process of bulldozing began to resemble strip mining. Erosion sent torrents of mud down from the ridges toward the lowlands. Construction vehicles caused the overloaded, underprepared roads to collapse. Residents attempting to drive their cars under such conditions often had simply to abandon them. Once John Merrill, the chief architect, turned up in the rain at a large meeting barefooted—"the mud had sucked off his boots," Owings recalled. In the rain, especially, the once-charming streets disintegrated, cars and trucks competed for traction, canvas roofs leaked, gas space heaters failed, and Oak Ridge became a slum.[82]

The social utopianism of the original SOM plan lay in ruins as well. Unlike the communistic egalitarianism of Los Alamos, SOM's housing program had started from the assumption that different types of managerial employees would garner different levels of spartan or luxurious housing. Various amenities had been designed into the different housing types, so that companies like Tennessee Eastman and Du Pont could promise their higher-level technocrats and managers something approaching the housing they would be leaving in Wilmington or Memphis. But SOM had interspersed the various housing types within the cemesto clusters. In this way, each neighborhood would include the various classes of workers and their families, their children building forts together in the woods, attending the local schools together, so that all were equal, if not in wage or status, at least in social possibility and future hope.

This quickly ended when slums housing more than six thousand people were interjected into the villages. Soon the cemesto houses became scarce and highly desirable commodities, and the contracting corporations vied with each other to garner empty ones for their employees. Once that happened, the cemesto communities, high up on the ridges, became exclusive enclaves; it was only a matter of time before they were renamed "Snob Nob," "Brass Hat Circle," and "Snob Hill."[83]

The effect of all this on SOM's plan for a community design that would attract middle-management technocrats and their families, and keep them on the site despite the hardships of wartime, was devastating. Absenteeism skyrocketed; employee turnover reached unprecedented proportions. But by this time, physical planning seemed the wrong place to effect changes. The picture drawn by the Pierce Foundation and endorsed by District Engineer Marshall—of a program that could apply the market pressures of a peacetime capitalist system, combining patriotism, steady work, good wages, and location in an idyllic environment where social differences could be recognized but might remain fluid—had been overdrawn by the circumstances of an increasingly hasty and vastly expanding managerial bureaucracy on the one side, and by the consequences of a scientific program that was now, finally, beginning to estimate the enormous consequences and costs of an atomic weaponry program.

This phenomenon repeated itself at each of the three sites. As plans became realities, and blueprints turned into communities, the messy stuff of American community life—everything from noisy town meetings at Los Alamos to strikes, rapes, and murders at Hanford and Oak Ridge—came increasingly to dominate the attention of District officials and occupants alike. Soon a new possibility began to present itself: the possibility that these communities would outgrow the District, and in so doing declare some form of independence from it.

Creating an efficient production process had from the first been the District's primary aim. Its goal was not justice within the borders or happiness for its wards, but the creation of weapons that would significantly affect the outcome of the war and, in the process, vindicate billions of dollars spent and massive resources deflected to a program of dubious usefulness. What planning had been introduced into each site's creation had always been pointedly in service to this final goal. But as vast, usually haphazard expansion everywhere in the District threatened something approaching social disorder, that theory—that a satisfactory environment would further the District's own goals—began to seem more and more questionable.

And so—at Oak Ridge, at Los Alamos, at Hanford and Richland—the District would increasingly turn to social and political coercion rather than environmental planning, using the arsenal of wartime regulations and the peculiarities of its super-secret status to construct a new social code based not on satisfaction and enthusiasm, but on obedience and submission. As the sites turned into communities rather than simply production facilities, the District's attention shifted to changing the way its residents imagined their lives.

This concern over the pictures drawn by people, and the palpable effects of those pictures, was in the end a part of the entire construction process and the struggle of the District to remain on top of that process. Now, however, figures like Matthias, Nichols, and (though with less consciousness) Groves sought to control the meanings that could be placed on things. From new rooms to newsrooms, the shift was to exploring, developing, and controlling the modes of persuasion necessary to gather, retain, and efficiently employ over one hundred thousand people on the sites. And the District began, if only tentatively at first, to consider the interpretations that would develop after the war among the rest of America's citizens, and the citizens of the world as well. What was needed was an overriding picture, bigger, bolder, more spectacularly colored, overpainting all the others and filling the sight of resident and citizen alike. This became the task of a philosophy, already prevalent in the workplace, quickly expanding outward into the rest of the District's zone of force, known enigmatically as "compartmentalization."

File 601 of the Manhattan District files contains the case of Tennessee farmer Sherman F. Owen and his request, in January of 1943, for an easement across a portion of the Clinton Engineer Works. Ostensibly the case concerned a peculiar problem of boundaries. Owen's own letters and petitions have been lost. What remains are two letters from within the closed confines of the District's administration. Through them, we can approximate the circumstances of his plight and gain a picture of the ideological core of the Manhattan Engineer District.[1]

COMPARTMENTALIZATION 5

Sherman Owen's farm had occupied a portion of rich bottomland along the western shore of the Clinch River in what would end up as the Oak Ridge, land that he farmed, used for pasturage, and harvested for hay. In fact, his was among the richest farms to be condemned—it contained sixteen structures and was valued at $4,750. His land had been expropriated, along with the rest of the Clinton Engineer Works, in the fall of 1942. But the officials of the Real Estate Office had not taken all of Owen's farm. In order to keep expenditures down, Land Acquisition Section experts had left the islands in the middle of the Clinch in private hands. At least two of these islands were parts of farms to the west of the river, farms now owned by the District. Mr. Owen's island was one of these.

Owen's island was large and relatively high, rich in nutrients, well watered, located close to the riverbank—the east bank, now the property of the Manhattan Engineer District. It had formed a significant portion of Owen's farm. Before the District's arrival, he had found it a simple matter to "travel through the shallow water with a team and farm implements" to plant, cultivate, and harvest on the island. Now, however, the District had left him with no access to the fields.

Owen wanted the District to grant him an easement so that he could cross the Clinch onto District lands, drive his farm equipment to the ford, and cross over to his island as he always had. Barring that, he wanted the District to buy the island outright, rather than leave him with a useless portion of a once-prosperous farm.

His request arrived on the desk of Fred Morgan, an administrator for the Clinton Engineer Works. But Morgan was a civilian. His responsibilities lay with administering the development of the site—with organizing and keeping tabs on the multitude of projects simultaneously gearing up to transform the site into a model industrial community. He had no power to divert funds to purchase Owen's island. Nor did he have the authority to make an exception to the District's rules that no one from outside the District could enter its lands. He was the visible representative of the District to the surrounding population, and as a civilian, he had allegiance to both the District and the larger American community. So he took it upon himself to pay attention to Owen's claim, and to expand it to include the case of a second farmer, B. F. Waller, who was in the same circumstance with his Waller Island.[2]

Morgan's recourse was to write Lt. Col. Warren George of the Army Corps of Engineers. George was head of Clinton's Construction Division. His responsibility lay with overseeing the building of the three principal production facilities on the site—

Y-12, the electromagnetic U-235 extraction process; K-25, the gaseous diffusion extraction process; and X-10, the pilot atomic reactor pile for plutonium production, from which the plans for the giant piles at Hanford would be made. He was also one of the District's procurement specialists.

Actually, George was not the appropriate figure to resolve the problem. There was none. Owen's problem concerned land acquisition, which lay under the purview of the Real Estate Branch of the Army Corps of Engineers, separate from the Manhattan Engineer District, but subcontracted by the District to oversee its land acquisitions. Once land was acquired, further acquisition was a matter for the Procurement Division. Procurement was a staff unit, part of the Administrative Division—probably Procurement and Contracts, although it might have been a part of Property or even Priority and Materials. The Construction Division was an operating unit of the Clinton Area of the District. Morgan wrote to George, however, because George was his immediate superior along the elaborate system of command; in addition, George had some influence with other areas within the District structure—he was the corps officer most directly in charge of day-to-day matters at that moment, the end of January 1943. Morgan apparently thought this was an open-and-shut case: Owen was right, he deserved redress, and George needed only to find the proper bureaucratic mechanism to do so.[3]

But George decided there was no need to determine a route through which an easement or purchase order might have to pass (perhaps his decision was influenced by a desire to avoid the "inefficiency" of finding such a path, committing himself to it, and then following it through). He saw a much more efficient option—do nothing at all. And he found precedent for the determination.

Two days after Morgan wrote to him, the colonel rendered his decision. Easement was out of the question, he wrote, because "as a general policy, this office is unwilling to grant any rights or interests to outside parties which would permit access into the Reservation by such parties." The phrase "as a general policy" signaled the official stance; each individual act was an act of policy, and general policy provided the framework for decisions. To grant Owen's request would violate both strictures.

George understood, however, that Morgan, and doubtless the farmers themselves, already knew of easements granted to the Tennessee Valley Authority and the Southern Bell Telephone Company; he papered over this awkwardness with the argument that "in those two instances this office will demand rigid adherence to our identification requirements"—as if two farmers might be harder to identify than the cadre of repair and maintenance workers both organizations would bring across the boundary.[4]

Purchase was impossible. Despite the poisonous relations engendered by the land acquisition scandals, George did not agree with Morgan's civilian sensibility and sympathies, that it might be more efficient and more politic to buy the lands outright; after all, "insofar as this office is concerned, the possession of Jones and Waller Islands is not essential to the project."[5]

George did not close the door entirely. To do so would have made him solely accountable for the decision; should it later turn out to be a suspect one, he would be visible as the responsible party. So he ended his letter with a caveat. If, "by obstructing the present owners' only means of access to the islands, it is necessary to pay damages equal to the value of the islands, this office sees no objection to including the islands in the Reservation boundary limits." But that was precisely what Owen had argued in his appeal to Morgan, and Morgan had then passed on in his letter to George. Just how the farmers were to prove their case more fully, or—more to the point—to whom, Lieutenant Colonel George did not detail.

The case of Sherman Owen's island might lie more neatly as a coda to the process of condemnation. But its every aspect is shot through with the system of bureaucratic control that defined the District's public program and its unspoken philosophy. For the isolation of Owen's island into a geographical never-never land was typical of the goal and the technique embodied in the concept of compartmentalization. To separate the District from its geographical, social, and political surroundings; to divide the District's own tasks into small units of interchangeable size and influence; to set these boxes of authority in a vast pyramid; to forbid communication across branches and thereby direct all information upward to the centralized hierarchy and all power downward from that same elite: all these elements were fundamental to the ethos of compartmentalization and contributed to the outcome of Owen's small appeal. Owen and his problem lay outside the logic of the District, and that logic could not be modified to accommodate him.

HISTORY

In most of the production facilities, at Hanford and Oak Ridge both, the District and its corporate contractors had determined that the ideal line worker was to be a young woman, preferably just out of high school, certainly no more highly educated than that. Many of these women were imported from the surrounding areas. Training consisted of teaching only the skills, acts, and movements essential to the specific job each worker was to do.[6]

One of these workers was Yvette Berry. She had come from Minnesota to work as part of the construction program. She was better educated than the recruiter might have wished—she'd had chemistry and physics, and a college math class. The recruiter told her she needed no experience; "I would be trained as I worked. I was not to learn any more from him," she recalled in the fifties. The first day after she completed a rudimentary training program, she took a bus out to the production facility, to Chemical Separation. She did not know what the factory was—she saw "lots of overhead pipes—a tall stack and some shorter ones. . . . I walked into a guard house where identification was again checked and I was handed a metal-framed badge, complete with photo, and two 'pencils' that looked more like fountain pens to me." They were, in actuality, radiation dosimeters. "The cement block-like buildings were there and each of these buildings was fenced in with another guard house to go through. You went where you were scheduled to go and nowhere else. . . .

"The heavy door closed behind me. I was in. Without windows to count I do not know how many levels there were. In the women's locker room I was assigned a locker and given a pair of white coveralls and canvas shoe covers." The women coming off the previous shift were forbidden to speak to her. "I entered the laboratory . . . I felt encased in cement."[7]

In a white room without windows, dressed in a white suit, instructed that she must remain silent, Berry went through only the rote motions she had been trained to do for her set task. "I remembered that first day when I saw a girl scrubbing one particular area on the floor. It looked so clean I wondered why she didn't go on to another part of the floor—but no, she stayed in that one spot, over and over. I was sure either she or I was ready for a mental hospital."[8]

This was compartmentalization, the District's system for assuring security in the production system. Its model was straightforward, simple, elegant. Two workers stand at a laboratory table. They may not speak to each other; only to their immediate superiors. These superiors may only speak to their superiors, who may only speak to theirs, and so on up the line, until finally the two superiors turn out to be the same person. In this way, information passes only vertically, up the command hierarchy. It cannot pass horizontally among workers of similar rank, nor can it pass across the barriers of organizational bureaucracy. The physicist Leona Marshall Libby recalled it as a matter of language: "you can talk with those just above you or below you, but you must not talk between the lines—that is, technical should not talk with operations except at the top layer." Nor could a scientist in Los Alamos communicate directly with a counterpart at Hanford or Oak Ridge or the University of Chicago, without explicit policy intervention from the top.[9]

Compartmentalization had a simple security goal, and it is illustrated in Yvette Berry's story. Like the policy of isolating shipments of highly radioactive "product" to prevent an explosive critical mass from developing, the isolation of intellectual and human elements one from another would prevent any individual or group from gathering enough information to form a picture of what exactly the District was doing. The program was the same whether one was a high-level physicist or a common laborer (though the punishments for infractions differed). Leona Libby, one of the senior physicists at Hanford, found herself "in hot water . . . for not realizing that this protocol existed. . . . It was a new experience to be required to remain aware of who should speak with whom." For construction workers or production-line employees like Yvette Berry, the punishment was more severe than simply "hot water"—it meant investigation, then termination, eviction from the site, and imprisonment if the violation was deemed sufficiently severe.[10]

Compartmentalization began as a security procedure borrowed by the Army Corps of Engineers from other army programs. Simple and straightforward, its procedure of disintegrating information to make it incomprehensible to all but the authorized had consequences far beyond the prevention of espionage. As the District grew in power and scale, compartmentalization became a means to consolidate power at the top of the pyramid. It turned the scientist's utopia, where knowledge was power, into a perverse caricature, where absence from the centers of power meant exile to ignorance, and ensured further powerlessness. This was part of the reason General Groves embraced the policy so early, and so expansively—it was a means to redesignate scientists and engineers as workers, equivalently obligated to management. "Adherence to this rule," Groves wrote, "not only provided an adequate measure of security, but it greatly improved over-all efficiency by making our people stick to their knitting. And it made quite clear to all concerned that the project existed to produce a specific end product—not to enable individuals to satisfy their curiosity and to increase their scientific knowledge." Speaking at the Oppenheimer hearings after the war, he was equally direct: the compartmentalization of information made sure the scientists weren't "frittering from one thing to another."[11]

As Groves expanded the program over the next years, compartmentalization took on a larger meaning to match its larger scope of influence. It ensured the continued consolidation of power in an upward direction along a steadily enlarging bureaucratic pyramid that found its icon in the organizational charts that obsessed District officials and that mutated almost daily.

And yet in fact Groves did not appear on the bureaucratic maps of power, no matter how vast or complex they became over the years of the District's history. At the top was always the district engineer—first Marshall, then Nichols. Groves himself existed immaterially, at once everywhere and nowhere.

The organizational charts described the way information and power traveled upward and inward toward the vanishing point that was Groves. But it was in the nature of the system of compartmentalization that few saw those charts or understood their significance. The program inscribed itself across the social landscape in myriad ways, taking physical form in everything from the arrangement of fences to the layout of control rooms. In everything the District built was imbedded the philosophy that those who lived and worked there should be utterly alienated from their work, ignorant of its significance, yet willing and efficient, perfect machines, in all that they did.

For the resident-workers on the Manhattan Engineer District, the effect of this structural disintegration of meaning, and consolidation of power, was both subtle and pervasive. Consider that most common and inoffensive of landmarks, the municipal water tower. The 300 Area at Hanford, known as the Metal Fabrication and Testing Area, had a large wood-and-metal water tower that rose above the desert and the squat mass-production buildings of the area, opposite a high smokestack. Black and plain, it faced southward, aimed toward Richland and the entrance to the reservation. On its south side was written, in bold capital letters, the fundamental law of the Manhattan Engineer District: "SILENCE MEANS SECURITY."[12]

That water tower is a model for many more pervasive, and less obvious, tools of the District. Adapting an everyday object, the District replaced common uses with new ones. In most American towns, the civic water tower was emblazoned with the name of the town, and perhaps its local mascot; sometimes, as here, with the town's motto. Yet the Hanford water tower was the highest object in a flat landscape where (when the dust didn't blow) the dry air was clear and visibility superb. Far from the 300 Area, probably as far away as the entrance to the reservation, workers might see that sign. Even further away, one might see the water tower itself, rising above the scabland; after a few days, everyone knew what it said. Its message floated above the drably utilitarian buildings of 300 Area, barely noticed, fading into the background noise of the site, yet never bereft of its power.

Information from below; orders from above.

PERIMETERS

The District's ideals of regulation, order, and efficiency weren't conveyed just in organizational charts or slogans. They found their power as they were imbedded in every aspect of the physical spaces themselves.

In an ideal chronology envisioned by the District, the process of imposing those ideals might have gone like this: isolation of the sites; elimination of all that was not immediately useful; development and implementation of an "infrastructure," completed by building an efficient system of production and an equivalent living environment for workers—both of them designed to minimize diffusion of information and knowledge, expense expended on human needs, and loss of control by the supervising authorities. This would then culminate in a rapid solution of theoretical and engineering problems, and production of the promised weapons.

Isolating the huge sites was the District's first goal. Early, officials toyed with two very different plans of approach. One looked like a traditional high-security wartime factory, to which workers would stream from outside communities, work in silence under close surveillance, then leave for home. This was the original plan for Oak Ridge.

The other looked like a prison. No information about the internal workings inside the perimeter of silence could pass forth, because no outsider would enter, and no insider leave. This plan required the site to be self-sufficient. Once within, workers would not be free to leave, nor could they complain to other or higher authorities. Conditions could be spartan, authority severe, work arduous, punishment harsh. The result would be a site completely invisible from the outside. This was the original plan for Los Alamos as the District conceived it.

Over time, both ideal plans turned out to be unsatisfactory. Workers commuting to the production facilities based upon the factory model also commuted from them, and when they crossed the perimeters, it was hard to control their speech—even under the wartime circumstances of a populace highly conscious of military security and a national security program that had gone a long way toward sacrificing free speech and association rights in the name of patriotism.

On the scientists' site, the image of Oppenheimer's "shangri-la" belied the reality. Never a Tibetan monks' colony, Los Alamos required all sorts of supplies and services that breached the high wall of secrecy, leaving a space for information to escape. Trucks trundled in and out, bringing vegetables and cyclotrons; finished goods, ideas, secret-mission envoys all drove out. The road from shangri-la to Santa Fe was open and the community curious. Everybody knew something big was up.

There was also the matter of recruiting at both types of site. Few go willingly into a situation completely blank to them. Groves wanted to solve this problem in the military way: by conscription. But one cannot draft those who are not citizens, those who are old, infirm, or otherwise unfitted for the military—not easily, at least, and not without drawing attention to oneself, if those whom one drafts happen to be vocal, prestigious, and articulate. The scientists needed for Los Alamos were all those things.

At the production sites, taking a laissez-faire approach to the problems entailed adding thousands of people to sparsely populated, insular regions, and promised a recruiting disaster. The original proposal for Hanford conceived that fourteen thousand workers and their families (perhaps as many as thirty thousand people) "could be absorbed into communities adjacent to the Project," in the words of the District historian, writing in 1946. But none of the areas surrounding the sites had an infrastructure capable of handling influxes of workers who could, in a season or even a month, double the population of a town. To build housing would require complex cooperative relations with the MED in order to garner the war priorities that would ensure supplies of scarce building materials.[13]

A quick glance at the geography surrounding Hanford is enough to bring home just how ill-considered was this policy. Within twenty miles of the site, there were only two communities—Richland, which had already been appropriated for the operator village and was off-limits to construction workers, and Connell, population 850. Pasco (population 8,500) and Kennewick (1,918) were 36 miles away or more; Prosser (population 2,250), Grandview (1,876), and Sunnyside (3,500) were all between 36 and 44 miles away. The only substantial town at all was Yakima, population 28,840, 62 miles distant. What the plan envisioned, in other words, was to more than double the population of the surrounding area, leaving it to workers to figure out how to add close to two hours' average commute to a 58-hour workweek. Gas rationing alone made the prospect arithmetically impossible, even if workers traveled five to a car.[14]

Nor were surrounding regions likely to look favorably on the type of population promised by the District's plans. Highly transient male workers, isolated from their families or without families at all, many of them urban industrial workers with big-city urban ethnic backgrounds, and some of them black or Hispano: for most rural communities, these were dark and threatening incarnations of disorder. Workers with families, wartime gypsies carrying trailers from worksite to worksite every few months, were almost equally unwelcome. A newly opened construction site that drew these gypsies could in one season triple the school-age population, without bringing in a penny of new tax money. Politicians in towns like Prosser, Washington, and Clinton, Tennessee, violently resisted the District's plans to house workers offsite.[15]

That assumed, of course, that workers were eager to go to the site in the first place. In a wartime economy, highly skilled workers were in high demand and could afford to be picky. Worksites without adequate housing or living amenities and little else to offer but patriotic assurances weren't likely to be high on the list.[16]

District planners, especially those involved in labor recruiting, rapidly recognized the inevitable and scrapped their plans for production sites devoid of living spaces. But Groves and many of his subordinates clung stubbornly to the ideal of cheap and simple worksites. The Corps of Engineers knew how to contract with corporations to build and manage factories. And the expenses, the calls for scarce wartime manpower and materiel, would be far easier to justify if they went exclusively for manufacturing facilities.

The result of this tension between desire and pragmatism wasn't a carefully conceived compromise between the two site types. Rather it was ad hoc decisionmaking at the microscopic level of hasty meetings and battles between subcontractors and District supervisors, never resolved because, for most of the project's duration, every day brought new demands for expansion in workplace, in materiel, in labor, and in living quarters. What emerged wasn't really a process so much as a set of abrupt gyrations from one criterion to another. Security, frugality, efficiency, haste, attractiveness: a week might see each of these given top priority and then dumped when a crisis in some other area brought its needs to the fore.

This was the case with the designation of Clinton as an "exclusionary zone." Such a declaration came from the War Department, and it meant that the military declared preemptive and absolute control over who and what could enter the region, and warned of its plans to fence, guard, and enforce its perimeters. The declaration made absolute the military's freedom from local, state, and even federal laws, and made official the District's usurpation of the rights of residents within its boundaries to engage in representative government—to vote, to form and participate in local governments, to voice their complaints and desires to elected officials.[17]

This at least was the program set forth by the District's planners. It was dependent upon the accession of the state of Tennessee to the right of the federal government to make the Clinton Engineer Works a federal "reservation"—reserved, that is, from the local and state systems of government. District officials were able to get Roosevelt's Public Proclamation Number Two in late February 1943. By that time, they had already condemned the lands and begun construction. Sometime in July of that year, someone, probably Colonel Marshall, who was then district engineer, apparently read the proclamation and saw that it required public posting and official notification of the relevant state and local authorities. Orders descended, from Marshall's office to the commanding officer at Clinton, Maj. Thomas Crenshaw. Capt. George B. Leonard from the security office received the orders to travel to the state capital and notify the proper officials. To be on the safe side, Leonard insisted on presenting the document directly to Governor Prentiss Cooper. This was Cooper's first official notice that his state was now host to a giant military project, and one about which he could receive not a whit of information. He lost his temper, declared that the project had stolen land from his farmers, stolen roads and bridges from his municipalities and from the state, all for "an experiment in socialism," as he characterized it to Leonard. He then refused to accept the proclamation, tore it up, and ordered Leonard out of his sight.[18]

This was not an easy controversy to resolve. In the end, Groves himself went hat in hand to Cooper to craft a proposal that he hoped would placate the governor; it involved specific promises for federal government financing of "improvements" to the road systems in return for state cooperation. As befitted his invisible presence, Groves then returned to Washington, leaving it to his assistant, the "official" district engineer, Nichols, to represent the program.[19]

Nichols's strategy was typical of the way the District engaged with officials whom they could not easily control. Nichols behaved with great deference, brought Cooper to the site, plied him with bourbon, and invited him to become an actor in a carefully scripted drama of patriotism, danger, and secrecy. He allowed Cooper to see the outsides of everything, treated him as a major player, but at the same time stressed the necessity of utter secrecy. Persuading Cooper to a promise of silence concerning what he had seen made him one of the players in this drama; the fact that there were further secrets to which even he could not be privy only made the importance of the project itself more impressive. Cooper left having conceded all that the District desired, and having received in return promises tangible and intangible.[20]

As Nichols himself later reported, "the way we had handled Governor Cooper's visit became our standard operating procedure," and it applied not only to the Tennessee site. At Hanford, Matthias was early able to garner support from elected federal and state officials by making timely calls upon them, at their convenience, by entwining them in the intrigue of the program, and by then gathering commitments of support as a result. Matthias applied a similar strategy to the most important newspapers in the state; he approached their editors and publishers, and from them received assurances that they would supervise all reporting on issues related to the site and alert the colonel to any plans to publicize matters related to the project. Where necessary, Groves even involved himself in this process of connecting high government officials with high District officials and garnering their allegiance to a program whose benefits to their constituents were marginal at best.[21]

One aspect of this strategy was its reorientation of focus from the local and state level to the national and international. Seen another way, however, it was a process of refocusing sight from the physical to the bureaucratic, of reminding these elected officials of their allegiance to the realm of government and its attendant culture. For this reason, the campaign worked best on officials, such as Senator Holmes of Washington, who were longtime members of the Washington-based cohort, and it worked less well with political figures who were committed, whether by relative inexperience in the Washington bureaucracy or by their self-declared populism, to the welfare of their electorate—as was the case with Washington's Warren Magnuson and Tennessee's John Jennings.

The more imbedded in the local, the more difficult to persuade: that became the District's rule of thumb, garnered from experience at each of the sites. Outside officials who operated closer to the ground were far more aware of the effects on local tax bases (*their* tax bases) that expropriation of vast stretches of land would have, and aware as well of the expensive demands on housing, educational, and welfare programs that would result from the influx of workers and temporary residents. Promises of employment and a revitalized regional economy didn't necessarily compensate, especially when wartime shortages and full employment had already made themselves felt.

Roads were one place where this conflict between District bureaucracy and local authority came to a head. Both the production sites had been chosen in part because of their ideal transportation connections. Hanford had a railroad spur line running into it, and two major highways, one of them the old Washington 11-A—a principal connection between Yakima and the entire southwestern portion of Washington state. At the Tennessee site, state highway 61 (now called the Oak Ridge Highway) ran directly down the center of the site; in addition, bridges across the Clinch River connected southern and western communities with roads and markets to the north and east.[22]

Taking these roads out of circulation wreaked havoc with local folkways and local economies. Farmers could no longer truck their goods to market, without resorting to circuitous detours along roads that were often far less well maintained. Entire communities—Clinton, Harriman, and Oliver Springs in Tennessee, and Benton City, Vernita, and Richland in Washington—were instantly disconnected from each other. The District's strategy—to keep high officials (governors, senators, congressmen) informed and enthusiastic, while ignoring the more immediate calls of local officials, set a precedent that would prevail throughout the District.

But the District rarely won its case without losing on other fronts. At Clinton, the condemnation of roads leading to two principal bridges left municipalities paying on bonds for amenities they could no longer use; the sheer absurdity of it sparked a brilliant campaign of bureaucratic guerrilla warfare on the part of local officials. Eventually, the District found it necessary to concede the point and compromise. But by that time any chance at conciliatory and amicable relations dimmed, and area residents came more completely to view the site as enemy rather than friend. At Hanford, too, local officials fought for their communities, lost, and came to dislike and mistrust the District as a result.[23]

The District wasn't eager to generate alliances at this local level. Its attention was on the biggest players, in particular the federal agencies that controlled water and power—like the TVA at Oak Ridge, or, at Hanford, the Bonneville Power Authority, controller of the Columbia River's huge power-producing dam, and the Federal Bureau of Reclamation's Columbia Basin Irrigation Project.[24]

At the Hanford site, the District joined the consortium of big interests carving up the water and land resources of the region. Because of its access to the seats of power in Washington, the District could give or withhold vital resources to local agencies and municipalities—rail for branch lines and sidings, asphalt for roads, wire and capacitors for the electrical grid. The effect was to force local and state officials into the District's fold. By late 1943, Hanford's region had been fully carved into a collection of fiefdoms "owned" by giant federal superagencies—some controlling water, some power, some roads, some irrigation—with the District serving as both broker and beneficiary.[25]

As of early 1944, Hanford's Colonel Matthias was busy building other collaborations. In February, he held a meeting with heads of the Federal Works Administration, the Farm Security Administration, the Federal Housing Administration, the NHA, the Public Health office, the FPHA, the War Food Administration, the Office of Price Administration, the Office of Civilian Requirements, the Solid Fuels Administration, the Petroleum Administration, the ODT, the WPHG, the War Manpower Commission, the War Labor Board, and the Urgency Committee—virtually every federal agency having remotely to do with the needs and effects of the MED. Matthias presented these bureau heads with a proposal to create a federation of bureaucratic corporations, based on an assumption of mutual need and mutual value; in this way, the government agencies could work sympathetically and efficiently, while at the same time, no release of classified information would be required of the Project, on the assumption that all actions by the Project were necessary and right. Thus there would be no justifications, no investigations, no demands for statistics or reports, no calls for information except where necessary to expedite Project requests, and no complaints when requests of any sort might be denied unequivocally by the Project.[26]

Matthias's success at that meeting signaled Hanford's integration with transregional superpowers and its break with regional entities. This process had its counterpart at the Clinton site. There, too, a huge and highly organized federal project created by the New Deal lent its bureaucracy and clout to the District. The Federal Housing Administration and the Federal Public Housing Authority provided housing plans and subsidies for offsite housing in surrounding Tennessee communities and brought trailers down from as far away as New York; the Federal Works Administration oversaw operation of new schools; and the state of Tennessee itself, under the prodding of the newly converted Governor Cooper, committed itself to providing access roads, school planning, law enforcement, and a host of other ancillary services.[27]

District officials regularly chose to forge their alliances with these national bureaucracies (replicas of their own program) rather than with local officials and local residents. They believed that this enfolding of the local into the national would benefit everyone, even if it meant the end of local autonomy and the sacrifice of local power to the national good.

To some extent, they were right. Over time, many of the local needs and demands would be resolved, through the techniques that were most attractive to the District's bureaucracy and most in concert with the internal structure and the systems of belief inherent to it. By the fall of 1944, for example, the regions surrounding the production sites at Hanford and Clinton found themselves immersed in federal programs, promises, and obligations. Schools were being constructed with 50 percent federal aid under the Lanham Act, which provided for schooling of military brats in civilian districts. A variety of federal agencies granted seed money and subsidies for new housing construction to be occupied by site workers or by those displaced by the quantum leaps in population throughout the areas. The Federal Works Administration was funding new town, county, and state agencies (like Knoxville's Recreation and Park Board, the city's first bureaucracy for recreation), and these in turn were drawing money from local coffers. Health centers, hospitals, sewer systems, water treatment plants, day-care centers: all of these came into being under the pressure of these chaotic influxes of outsiders, the expectations of federal agencies, and the promise of federal matching money.[28]

By October 1944, in fact, the regional officials who had fought so hard against the incursion of big government now found themselves emboldened into an era of unprecedented governmental activism. The town of Clinton had a new housing subdivision, paid for by Federal Housing Administration funds, and had begun planning new access streets to encourage even more development. More significant, the town, once a tiny hamlet virtually without government at all, was debating a proposed "complete rehabilitation of the street system . . . as a postwar plan" and looking toward a time when local, state, and federal governments would cooperate to create a new park system and an equivalent recreational agency. The days of small-town informal government had been replaced by a new allegiance to the concepts of the welfare state.[29]

And so the District's presence, which earlier had awakened opposition to hegemonic power and the intrusive state, became, increasingly, a model for new government and a new social compact within the surrounding countryside. The District intervened in the lives of its people in an unprecedented fashion. The life of the surrounding region could never again take as its norm the pre-District rural intimacy of towns like Connell, Washington, population 850, or Kingston, Tennessee, population 800. These surrounding communities had responded to the District, had replicated the District, and now depended upon the District for their new "normalcy."

This was the pattern at the industrial sites of Oak Ridge and Hanford. At Los Alamos, matters traveled toward a similar end along a different path. Los Alamos had begun its life aspiring to be completely invisible. For the District, for Groves most of all, Site Y was to have been first and always a place of austerity and discipline, utterly isolated from dangerous influences and prying eyes. With most of its population imported from outside, many under assumed names, all under assumed addresses and false credentials, and with the location truly isolated from other communities, both geographically and topographically, Los Alamos seemed to live up to the District's original plan.

To further this end, Oppenheimer issued a series of "notes on security" at intervals during the life of the project. Basic to each was the order that the District's compartmentalization policy must "involve essentially breaking the social relationships between the personnel employed at Los Alamos and people not so employed." In the May 22, 1943, version, he reminded residents "it is important that our personnel should maintain no social relations with people in the neighboring communities." No visits, no visitors: that was the law.[30]

"The shadow of Security lay everywhere," recalled Jane Wilson shortly after the war. "Once, by chance, I met an acquaintance from my college days on the streets of Santa Fe," she reported.

> It had been more than a year since I had talked to anyone I knew other than the people who lived on the Hill. It was wonderfully exhilarating to see someone from the outside world. . . . But even this encounter was against the rules. . . . I was numb with embarrassment. . . . A moment's slip and I . . . felt that I would find myself hurtling into the gaping entrance to hell. It was a relief to say goodbye. Then, like a child confessing that she has been naughty, I reported my social engagement to the Security Officer. Living at Los Alamos was something like living in jail.[31]

Of course, this enforced invisibility failed. Eleanor Jette's aunt knew where her niece was going even before Eleanor knew—she worked for Mountain Bell in Denver and had learned of the site's location because of the routine arrangements necessary to get phone lines up and running. Many of her colleagues knew as well. Ruth Marshak recalled stopping for gas somewhere in Colorado, where the station attendant noticed her overloaded car and east-coast plates. He told her and her husband that they were going to "that secret project," in his words. As Marshak reported in 1946, "He needed no encouragement to launch into a detailed and accurate description of our new home." Probably the most blatant security failure was an article on the site that appeared in the Cleveland *Plain Dealer* in mid-1943, complete with a cartoon rendering of the entry gate with its perimeter guards caricatured as bulldogs in uniform. The piece went out on the wires, and was picked up by the Santa Fe *New Mexican.* Although, as Eleanor Jette recalled, "the security boys hit the ceiling" and "landed hard on both [newspapers]," the news was definitely out.[32]

At the production sites, Hanford and Oak Ridge, Security sought to prevent unauthorized people from getting inside. Los Alamos strove to *keep* everything in. Security's attention went to prevent escape: of information, of personnel, of unauthorized activity.[33]

The boundaries beyond which one was forbidden to wander were demarcated in a rough quadrangle formed by Albuquerque, Las Vegas, Taos, and Cuba, New Mexico. Residents not authorized to bring their families (and this constituted all military personnel, as well as some others) found that the District forbade them to have their families closer than a hundred miles from the site, in order to discourage commuting from home to work. (As did Clint Gass, many found that Albuquerque was just 105 miles offsite, and set up their families there, commuting home on weekends, hitchhiking or sharing rides.) Originally, only Oppenheimer could designate visitors to the site. That authority lasted slightly more than three months; on May 8, 1943, the District announced that Groves alone now held that power.[34]

To leave the site, even for an hour, wasn't easy. Residents had to show their passes at the entry gate; they had to register their travel plans with the central office; if they went to Santa Fe, they surrendered their passes at the District's Santa Fe office at 109 East Palace and received their return passes there when they were done for the day.[35]

Most of Security's attention turned to preventing unauthorized escape from the site. (Both Klaus Fuchs and Sergeant David Greenglass, the two alleged spies at Los Alamos, moved to their assignations under fully authorized circumstances.) The precautions against *incursion* were surprisingly lax, and remained so throughout the war. A security report made to Oppenheimer in October 1943 decried the looseness at the perimeter. "The post is easily entered by unauthorized persons," it said, "and daily hundreds of 'transient' workers enter who have no real connection with the technical work."[36]

Lois Bradbury, wife of the physicist and navy man Norris Bradbury, described these "transients" as they paraded past her window each day, in a not-yet-censored draft of a letter to her parents in 1944: "Yesterday morning as I was hanging out my dish towel, I saw passing below me eight soldiers on horseback talking 'Army,' a bunch of Indian women, imported to help the mammas, talking 'Indian,' some Mexicans talking Spanish. . . . Cowboys are all over the place too. The procession passing below our windows to work each morning is fantastic."[37]

All these people were necessary; the problem was, they were also contributors to a general chaos of coming and going, of passage from inside to outside. As the security report told it, "It has been actually demonstrated (by members of this committee) that a person without any kind of a badge or pass can easily come from outside Los Alamos not only into the post but into the technical area itself."[38]

The most dramatic of the violators was in fact a legal resident. He was Richard Feynman, at the time a junior scientific minion, a graduate student recruited by his mentor:

> One day I discovered that the workmen who lived further out and wanted to come in were too lazy to go around through the gate, and so they had cut themselves a hole in the fence. So I went out the gate [which meant checking out with the security officers there], went over to the hole and came in, went out again, and so on until the sergeant at the gate begins to wonder what's happening. How come this guy is always going out and never coming in? And of course, his natural reaction was to call the lieutenant and try to put me in jail for doing this.[39]

The security program couldn't close or even control the perimeters, but it did make life for residents increasingly frustrating and difficult. Phyllis K. Fisher was one of the young women who came with their scientist husbands and their infant children to make a new life in the west. One day soon after her arrival, she had to leave to take her dog, Fawn, to the vet. Here is her description of the gate, drawn from a letter to her parents (the version before its evisceration by the censors):

> Now, listen to this very carefully and try to understand. I can't. We have a gate here that isn't a gate at all. It consists of a guardhouse and an unfriendly signpost surrounded by sentries. Regulations governing passage of said "gate" top any screwy regulations of any Army post anywhere. It

seems that you can *drive* past it in an automobile without showing a pass, but you can't *walk* past it. Pedestrians must show passes. No exceptions.

I drove past the gate (to the vet's) with Fawn and, naturally, wasn't stopped. The veterinary hospital is only about 100 yards beyond and is visible from the gate. After our visit with the vet, I rushed out with my shivering dog, climbed into the car to start back, and—you guessed it— the car wouldn't start. By this time, it was snowing. I began to run as best I could, with Fawn held securely inside my coat. Of course, I was promptly stopped at the gate. I had no pass! I explained. . . . None of which made any difference. Only one word seemed to have meaning, the word "regulations.". . . . They could see my car standing there, but that didn't make any difference. . . .

Then through the gloom and the swirling snow, there appeared a jeep, with driver, of course. . . . Right in front of the MPs, I asked the stranger for a lift. He agreed. I climbed into the jeep and in we went with full permission of the guards at the gate![40]

The failures of security guards to control the perimeters suggested that the District couldn't understand what it had made. District planners and administrators grossly overestimated the power of geography to conceal or disguise. Yet because none of the sites could become truly self-sufficient, they grew increasingly dependent upon their surroundings. And their mere presence affected their surroundings in profound ways, creating a transformed sense of what communities and regions could be, even as the spaces themselves were irrevocably changed. It might be as simple and as destructive as Los Alamos residents' blithe violation of government laws and basic respect when they went on Sunday incursions into the surrounding hills, pawing through aboriginal sites for potsherds and mementos. Or it might be as complex as the gift of a new irrigation and road system at Hanford, the undramatic consequence of which was to create a new community of farmers now dependent upon the network of government agencies and services the District had engaged in its efforts to correct the effects of its own incursion.

MAPS

At Oak Ridge, the fences went up first. Most of the barbed wire was scavenged off the various farms that comprised the bulk of the area before condemnation. One District official, Robert Blair, ordered that "the field forces at the Tennessee site construct and erect signs approximately two feet by one and one-half feet containing the words 'Military Reservation No Trespassing.'" As Blair told Stone and Webster, "These signs should be installed at intervals of approximately six hundred feet around the line reservation boundary." These were supplemented by at least five lookout and observation towers, called "copper towers" in the requisitions, which stood high above the fencing. In addition to these features, the individual plants would receive more elaborate fences—chain link eight feet high, with a foot of barbed wire at the top.[41]

The perimeter fence at Los Alamos combined a seven-foot-high chain-link base with an upper fence comprised of interlocking strands of barbed wire—three of them.

High guardhouses rose above this outer fence, and from them the military police detachments sent out their perimeter patrols, on foot or on horseback. Other patrols manned the hills surrounding the site. Visitors arriving at the location had to stop at the gate house, to have their credentials inspected.

Inside the outer fence at Los Alamos was a second barrier, separating city from wilderness. The Tech Area got a third fence, separating work from living. You might easily sneak through the outer fence simply by observing the guard schedule, but few entered Tech without total scrutiny and the most impeccable of credentials (especially after the release of the Security Committee's report to Oppenheimer). At the least, you held a badge: white gave you extensive access; blue limited you to the single small compartment of your work. Badges made the inner workplace an elite zone, occupied by the cadre of scientific personnel who had been brought to the site for their expertise, and supplemented by the technical forces—the military engineers of the Special Engineer Detachment (the SED), and the lowest-level employees, the secretaries, typists, and "computers" (adding-machine operators), consisting largely of the wives of scientists, who were hired on part-time and isolated from the real work.[42]

At Hanford, the question of fencing was more complex. Because the outer perimeter was so enormous, simply constructing a government-issue fence like the one at Los Alamos would never be sufficient. Colonel Matthias discovered this early on, when the Hanford and White Bluffs farmers and ranchers came back to harvest their orchards. Old-time residents had no qualms about climbing barbed wire—climbing, or using their orchard ladders, or simply cutting the wire with pliers. Assigning perimeter guards to such an area was prohibitively wasteful. In addition, the Du Pont corporation representatives resisted the tighter security measures Groves and Matthias envisioned as necessary.[43]

Matthias solved the problem by adapting the Los Alamos fences-within-fences plan, so that each "area" had its own fencing, guardhouses, and guards. More interesting, Matthias applied the innovations of modern wartime technology to the immense reaches of the West; as early as August 1943, he was working on a plan that used aerial surveillance employing small planes that droned across the great stretches of Hanford reservation, divvying up the space into quadrants and subquadrants and sub-subquadrants.[44]

This plan was uniquely appropriate to the Hanford site, with its flat desert topography broken by a few rises featureless enough that a single person stood out glaringly in the daylight. Enrico Fermi and Leona Libby found out just how efficient this technique was, and how pitiless, when they decided one day to take their lunches outside and explore the topography a bit:

> After some desultory wandering, Enrico selected a giant sage bush under which to have lunch. We sat down and were making guesses as to how long ago the Columbia River had flooded the desert, dropping out the bits and pieces of sedimentary rock that was intermixed with sand (this was before the invention of radiocarbon dating) when we noticed a small airplane circling overhead, around and around. We gave it little thought and after a while, it went away. Next we noticed a man in the distance, carrying a revolver pointed toward the ground, head bent, looking down and walking slowly and methodically in an apparently random way. No-

body was in the desert except him and us. We kept on talking, eating our sandwiches, when suddenly the man came around the next bush, pointed the gun at us, and told us to put up our hands. Fermi put up his sandwich and I put up my apple. . . . The man said we were to walk back to the 300 area which we did. He had been walking aimlessly because he had been following our aimless footprints, having been put onto our track by the spotter airplane.[45]

The problem with aerial surveillance was telling official planes from enemy planes. As Matthias's diary reveals, the general military paranoia over invasive surveillance planes, pilotless "drones," and even observation balloons took its toll in the vertical fencing of the Hanford site. Navy pilots training at Pasco might accidentally stray over the site; clouds, children's balloons, heat mirages, and even the District's own military surveillance planes all at one time or another caused the District to go onto invasion alert.

Fencing of one sort or another set the boundaries within which the District's transformations would take place. Inside those boundaries, however, nearly every aspect of the construction process served to compartmentalize—to separate *this* land from *that,* human environments from natural ones.

These invisible vectors of contact between labor and living, and among the various aspects of the production process, revealed the District's roots in the mass-production industrial process, albeit a vastly expanded version. To look down from above (as Groves did, on his periodic airplane tours) was to see an orderly set of interconnections between the various tasks of each site. Top-rank officers or highly important civilian representatives carrying sensitive information arrived by plane at the newly built or modified airports on the sites. Workers moved from outside life to work and from job to job along roads controlled by the District—either directly, within the site, or through the alliances founded with other superagencies, outside the boundaries. In the most sensitive areas, buses—some of them owned and managed by the District, others owned by the District but farmed out to private companies—provided transportation to workers within the security zones. Goods entered by truck, checked in at gates, off-loaded at specified warehouses. Or they came in by rail, the boxcars and flatbeds on which they rode uncoupled at sidings and then collected by District rail services, to be run to factories or warehouses along the interior rail lines taken over by the District, or along new lines constructed to run between one facility and another.

What looked efficient from above was often far different when encountered below. District pamphlets and internal descriptions painted a rosy picture of transportation over interstices on the Hanford and Oak Ridge production works. But this often meant something far different for workers at ground-level. Bus transportation for workers turned out to entail "long open buses towed by a truck," as one resident, Harry Petcher, recalled more than forty years later. And the drive: "Let me tell you, we ate more sand in the 40 miles to Hanford; it was endless." Crowds waited in the heat or the cold for transportation to their factory assignments or to the construction sites on which they were working. At night, it was worse: they waited longer, and they shared the bus with workers returning to their barracks from the beer halls, loud, drunken, spoiling for a fight.[46]

Long, straight stretches of roadway, gleaming vectors of track converging at the horizon, power lines running across the site, often at diagonals to the road or rail lines: these networks connected the isolate elements of the Hanford site. The connections were successful when they hewed closely to their conception in the mass-production ethos. When they attempted to move people instead of materials, they fell sharply from their ideal.[47]

FACTORIES

The production facilities were massive even by the standards of wartime defense plants. At Oak Ridge, they nestled in the valleys, usually surrounded by a buffer of bare earth. Parking lots filled with workers' cars punctuated the muddy surroundings. The buildings resembled their prototypes in other industrial production systems—they were simple rectangles, often the size of multiple city blocks, connected by mazes of piping and electrical lines to the smaller support buildings that often crouched, rather haphazardly, around them, stuck in corners or at odd spots on the rectilinear grid. Y-12, the electromagnetic uranium separation plant at Oak Ridge, consisted of shops, a power substation, a series of process buildings in two clusters, and two large factory-like structures at the edge; these were the Alpha II buildings. On one side, a large parking lot abutted the roadway (at its peak, Y-12 employed close to twenty-five thousand workers), and beyond the road, a hillside entirely denuded of vegetation was first decorated with construction refuse; eventually rains and erosion left tires, pipes, and abandoned pieces of equipment peeping over a plain of clay inhospitable to even the most hardy of southern plant forms.[48]

New workers entering these factories found them to be confusing and sometimes terrifying warrens of piping, walls of analog dials, valves, and knobs, marked with Bakelite labels in the arcane language of the engineer. The electromagnetic plant alone used close to 250,000 valves to control the materials coursing through 1,175 miles of piping. Engineers and industrial production workers found the environs familiar, yet eerily strange. At Y-12, operators in the control rooms sat on high stools at six-foot intervals. Six days a week, usually ten hours a day, they stared intently at rows of dials that represented (though the operators were not allowed to understand this) the activities within the giant oval "racetracks" where uranium atoms accelerated until the centrifugal force pushed the heavier elemental uranium needed for weapons out into collection areas. When District historians archived a photograph of the operations room, they added a caption: "This view shows the cubicles in the control room with the attentive operators at work. Note books required for necessary records. Phones on cubicles are for communication with the track and vacuum operators." No windows punctured the walls in the control room. It was lit with overhead banks of lights; at each end, on the wall, a large electrical bell was mounted. The official record offers no insight as to how plant managers dealt with bathroom breaks—whether spare "girls" waited to take over temporarily vacated positions, or managers took the line, or operators at adjoining cubicles took both areas for a time. All cubicles were identical.[49]

The sterility and order implicit in photographs of the factories belied their dangers—many of them dangers that would have been similar to those at plants of equal complexity in a number of other areas, particularly chemical materials production. But no other industrial process ever imagined was as complex or depended on tolerances as critical as those of the MED. Officially, Y-12 reported only eight fatalities: five electrocutions, one man gassed, one burned to death, and the last killed after falling into the machinery. But the reporting system parceled out deaths and injuries among contractors, subcontractors, and the MED itself, and the records are incomplete, some still classified. Added up, these present a different statistical picture. Within the plant, danger seemed defined by one's work. The high-school-graduate female "operators" for Tennessee Eastman, who read dials, were safest. Workers involved in the installation of the highly complex maze of electrical, mechanical, and chemical machinery were most at risk. If one worked in the production area itself after the racetracks began running, the danger was intense, invisible, unknown. When Y-12 was fully operational, Tennessee Eastman's occupational medicine division treated an average of 150 cases of occupational injury or occupational illness every day.[50]

Some factories were more dangerous than others, and the dangers more unusual. Outside of work in the areas where daily contact with radioactive elements was common, work in the gaseous diffusion plant (K-25) at Oak Ridge afforded the risk of contact with some of the most corrosive and dangerous of industrial substances—fluorine and the gases associated with fluorine—principally, hydrogen fluoride and uranium hexafluoride. These were deadly if inhaled or even if touched. The electromagnetic (Y-12) process potentially exposed the worker to phosgene, a World War I poison gas that, District medical division officials reported, "produces a devastating effect on lung tissue." Carbon monoxide, fluorocarbons, tricholoethylene, beryllium, cadmium, and nickel all were part of the various processes, and all exacted their tolls on workers. Medical problems from these weren't the District's immediate responsibility; the subcontractors treated and reported them. As a result, statistics are difficult to garner.[51]

The racetracks—the electromagnetic variants of the cyclotron—dominated the Y-12 plant. Liquid Thermal Diffusion—K-27—was a plant filled with giant "racks" containing columns, each 48 feet high, a total of more than 2,000 of them, topped by elaborate refrigeration coils, marked by complex mazes of pipes and valves. But that wasn't where workers spent their time; they were in the eleven control rooms and the eleven transfer rooms that ran along one 522-foot-long side of the black, 75-foot-high process building. There the dials provided clues to the hidden uranium enrichment process that went on behind the concrete walls.[52]

What most of the factories shared was a topographic separation of operators from that which they operated—necessitated by the extreme hazards entailed in the system, but also by the strategy of compartmentalization, which prevented workers from knowing what they were doing. Within these walls, manufacturing occurred in a "black box."

At Hanford, the factories stood in the desert spaces like giant megaliths. Workers called the chemical separations plants "canyons" (because, during construction, the excavation made at the center to accommodate the furiously toxic processes gave the unfinished, high-walled facilities the look of manmade tourist attractions) and "Queen Marys" (fig. 21). And in the empty reaches of the Hanford landscape, they did look like ships. Separation Building 221-T covered 66,319 square feet of desert. Its window-

FIG. 21 Aerial view of Hanford facilities, including Queen Mary. Photo by Robley Johnson or assistant. Richland Operations, Department of Energy.

less outer walls, made of unpainted reinforced concrete marked by the barely discernible pattern of the plywood forms that had once encased it, rose 80 feet straight up, the facades broken only by periodic extrusions (ten to a side) for stairways, themselves windowless. Set diagonal to the grid of service roads, the chemical separation plants were the most intimidating of all Hanford's facilities. By comparison, the atomic piles were boxy concrete shells with three-tiered roofs.

Inside, the Hanford plants were brutal extensions of the industrial processes that had preceded them. The chemical separation plants were warrens of piping and, deep in their centers, sealed "cells" within which the separation of pure plutonium from the dross took place entirely by remote control. Surrounding these cells were thick walls of concrete, and behind them, corridors and stairways along which "operators" traveled to the rooms where the operations were run through mechanical arms and monitored by primitive television—the first-ever closed-circuit surveillance cameras. Leona Marshall Libby went with Enrico Fermi into one of the "canyons" just before startup in 1944, to trace the relation of reality to blueprint, and to look for dangerous errors: "We went along the empty and echoing balconies of the canyon, checking pipes and valves, going step by step through the process as yet tested only in pilot-plant stage; how does this effluent get removed, how is that precipitate carried into the next cell, and so on. We found only one mistake; it had already been discovered a day or so before by an independent checking team. It was a pipe that had been blocked off in a maze of pipes."[53]

To a more extreme degree than did their counterparts at Oak Ridge, the chemical separations facilities in the 200 Areas compartmentalized the process, and located each element in a separate building. Chemical separation had six processes: slug dissolving; extraction by precipitation using bismuth phosphate carrier; decontamination (actually a series of stages that brought radiation emission to a point where the District believed it was possible to process the material without "massive shielding"); concentration; isolation; and disposal of wastes—gases, liquids, and solids. The first three stages occurred in the "canyon" buildings, where the processes took place underground. Then the material was moved to the Concentration Building, which itself had six separate cells. After concentration was completed, the material—originally a ton of uranium slugs, now a tank containing eight gallons of sludge weighing seventy-nine pounds—moved to the Isolation Building, where final preparation took place, and the plutonium metal was stored until transferred to the Magazine Storage Building.[54]

On maps and charts, even in descriptions, the process seems orderly and efficient. Uranium went to Oak Ridge. There it was converted (by the electromagnetic process, by gaseous diffusion, by thermal diffusion) into enriched uranium. Some of this went to Los Alamos for use in production of the uranium bomb. Some of it went to Hanford, where the atomic reactor piles turned it into a combination of radioactive products, including, in trace amounts, plutonium. Chemical separations plants purified the plutonium, which then moved by convoy to Los Alamos to be fabricated into the plutonium bomb. Raw material in, finished technologically advanced product out.

On the ground, or under it, different realities intruded. Perhaps the most glaring example yet to come to light concerned waste treatment at Hanford, where the maps and plans depicting materials moving in rational fashion from danger to inoffensiveness overlaid a far more chaotic and haphazardly implemented set of programs.

Though the production program rarely mentioned it, many portions of the Hanford plutonium production process yielded highly toxic and radioactive waste. The piles themselves were culprits in at least two areas, both involving Columbia River water, which cooled the reactor cores, and provided pools into which the actual uranium-plutonium "slugs" dropped out the back of the piles and where they remained until they released sufficient short-decay radiation that they could be moved. Both forms of water were too "hot" and full of known toxic materials to simply dump back into the Columbia. So District engineers devised a "flow-circuit" to move the water from the Columbia through the piles and then back to the river.

As it appeared on District charts (fig. 22), the flow circuit appeared efficient and logical. But a closer look reveals that virtually all the District's attention lay with the stages from river to pile—where, in other words, the quality of the water reflected on the industrial output of "product," to use one of the District's code words for plutonium. In that half of the circuit, thirteen stages moved the water from the river, held

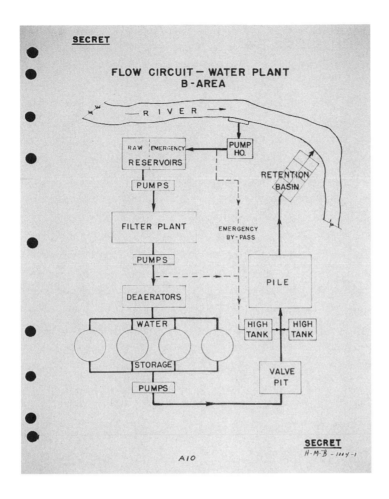

FIG. 22 Flow circuit—Water Plant B-Area. Manhattan District History, courtesy National Archives.

it in reservoirs, filtered, demineralized, deaerated, cooled, and refined the water so that it might enter the pile. Afterward, however, it was simply pumped into a 7,200,000-gallon retention basin, where it sat while the radioactive materials with the shortest half-lives emitted their radiation until the District determined it was practicable to pump it back into the Columbia.[55]

Determining the standards for water safety required balancing expediency and haste against scientific knowledge and commitment to health standards. But the District had no real knowledge as to what constituted safe or unsafe dilutions of the particular toxic materials involved or of the short- and long-term effects of radioactivity on humans, on animals, on ecosystems. Some of this information could be garnered from existing scientific studies—particularly when the effluents were heavy metals like lead and arsenic. But the knowledge concerning the behavior and effects of uranium and other radioactive substances was minimal at best. Most of it had come out of the radium-dial disasters of the twenties and thirties and for the most part pertained to the question of what constituted a safe exposure dose by workers. The medical and scientific literature on long-term and low-dose effects was negligible at best, and the tracing of effects along the ecological chain was equally paltry. Then there was the matter of time. Sophisticated scientific studies of the questions aroused by the District's production program were not only complex. They required years to complete.[56]

Concerning medical hazards to workers on the sites themselves, the District had early developed a bureaucratic system and a set of standards, however halfhearted. These were areas relating directly to production and to the mandate of the MED. But radioactive wastes inched their ways off the sites and onto the perimeters, and from there were taken, by the waters of the Columbia or the prevailing winds above the site, far beyond the District's sight. In this area, District officials found few precedents within the military culture from which they came; the military reservation was already notorious as a bad neighbor, immune from the most basic state and local laws concerning hygiene and waste disposal, even when that waste was nothing more than human garbage. And so the question of what to do went up to the invisible office of General Groves, and from him traced its way back down the pyramid.

Groves, Matthias, and the various heads of various District subareas had a range of options. They could engage a program of rigorous investigation into the dangers of radioactive waste, to human life, immediate and long term, and to aquatic life and the ecosystem more generally. From this they could then determine what would be necessary to treat the water, and at the least how long it would have to be stored before returning to the Columbia. If the investigation process took longer than the interval before startup, production would have to wait. Should the recommendations call for substantial changes in the program, production would have to be delayed until these could be instituted. If the scientific research did not result in clear-cut guidelines, or revealed that decontamination was beyond current technological abilities, the plutonium production program would have to be shut down, and one whole area of weapons production would come to an end. Barring that, the District would have to accept responsibility for compromises—for decisions concerning how much and how long-term the danger to human occupation of the surrounding regions was allowable, and just how much damage to the Columbia River ecosystem could be tolerated in the name of war.

Or it could do nothing. Everything within the District's culture pointed to the last course. The mandate for the District was to build weaponry, and to do it quickly. It had made a decision to pursue both the enriched-uranium and the plutonium-fuel bomb design. It had devoted huge amounts of resources to the conversion of an idea into an engineering system and then into a manufacturing system. At the same time, there was no evidence that scientific study could quickly determine the nature and extent of the risks—or if it ever could. Meanwhile, the plutonium production facilities would have either to lie idle or go into production until the retention basins filled up with irradiated water, and then stop.

On the issue of water contamination, the District moved in two directions at once. On one side, it continued construction with all dispatch, building its retention basins and moving ahead with production plans. The priority was clear: delay or cancellation of the program was unthinkable. At the same time, it moved, at Groves's urging, to do its best to prevent significant fish damage and to provide the appearance at least of scientific programs to understand and limit contamination in general and damage to the salmon crop especially. In this way Groves and the other officials of the District believed they could mollify the influential salmon lobby and provide the basis for a legalistic defense.

But the programs to investigate radiation effects on fish were prototypical of the District's more general medical and medico-legal investigations. They were small pilot programs, unlikely to provide evidence that might threaten District operations until long after production was underway and—with luck—the war over.[57]

Judged even by the standards of the wartime 1940s, the District's scientific program was incomplete, the resulting rearrangements in the production process hasty and ill-considered, and the results unhappy. The atomic pile wastewater was far from benign—the District reported in 1946 that it developed such toxicity that it had to be injected with "a lime slurry . . . to prevent corrosion of the concrete sewer lines" leading to the retention basin. Later studies confirmed that, undiluted, the water emitted into the river had immediate, highly toxic effects on infant salmon and "was occasionally quickly lethal." And it appears that none of the studies considered issues of genetic mutation of the fish stock or long-term effects—for the studies were too short-lived. Nor, it seems, did anyone consider with scientific sophistication the effect on people eating the fish. The concern seems instead to have lain with preventing massive fish kills that would do untold damage to the District's public relations.[58]

Both Fred Foster and Dr. Lauren Donaldson, the icthyologists who studied the Hanford fish contamination issue, stood by the program for decades afterward. Both believed that the damage to the ecology (human and natural) surrounding the Hanford atomic plants was minimal. Foster reported to Washington state's Ecological Commission in 1970 that "the radiation doses received by the public have been well within the guidelines and that no discernible radiation or thermal effects have occurred to the valuable populations of fish and wildlife." His argument has been largely discredited by the more recent investigations of the Hanford Dose Reconstruction Project, which is even now struggling to ascertain the extent of the damage most especially to the tribal traditionalists who saw their fishing grounds as sacred and continued to harvest and eat the salmon of the Columbia for decades after the Hanford production programs began pouring their lethal mix into the waters of the river.[59]

Even without benefit of hindsight, the record suggests that the District set a clear course. Nothing could be allowed to slow appreciably the production of plutonium or add substantially to its costs. After these requirements had been met, study of the problems of radiation and toxicity, and modifications to the production line to diminish these problems, could be considered.

This order of priorities runs exactly counter to the after-the-fact account that Groves produced for his autobiographical apologia, *Now It Can Be Told,* in 1962. There he wrote that "all design was governed by three rules: 1, safety first against both known and unknown hazards; 2, certainty of operation—every possible chance of failure was guarded against; and 3, the utmost saving of time in achieving full production." But the facts prove Groves the liar. The first priority lay with production, then with prevention of liability or bad publicity, and last of all with health or safety. As District officials wrote in 1946 of Donaldson's studies, "insufficient time has elapsed to form any conclusions from this study"; Foster's onsite studies began only in June 1945, after the production system had been in full-scale operation for six months and had produced much or all of the plutonium necessary to end the war; and Matthias commented concerning fears of possible liability and of "claimed serious exposure" and the possibility that the Du Pont affiliates would "be accused of being biased in their findings" if they were seen as connected to the fish studies. According to Matthias's diary, he made the latter statement on March 6, 1945, when he urged District Engineer Nichols to assign the "fish tank" programs to someone outside Du Pont, "on the basis that this would put the experimental work in a much stronger position than would be the case if the Company officials handled it, as they could possibly be accused of being biased in their findings." Assuming that Matthias believed that Du Pont would not actually falsify or modify experimental results, his diary entry can only refer to a concern with the public relations value of these reports, and their value as means of countering liability suits. This last issue—of devising means of defending the District against possible liability—is a thread in the diary; it is found also, for example, in an entry for February 28, 1945, concerning airborne emissions.[60]

Colonel Matthias came to see the studies—Donaldson's especially—in a far different light than the scientific and medical. Writing to Groves in the cold-war climate of 1960, Matthias told his commanding officer he considered the proposal for a fish study "a really brilliant tactical move. I am convinced that we would have had a very bad time with the fish people after August, 1945, if we had not been able to demonstrate so conclusively that we had considered the salmon problem a serious one and had produced much evidence to show the effects were not serious."[61]

Groves later reported that he had early been warned of the public-relations dangers of interfering in the fish environment of the Columbia—he recalled a fish specialist from the Bonneville Dam telling him that "you will incur the everlasting enmity of the entire Northwest if you harm a single scale on a single salmon." But the hot water from the piles was not the principal threat to the health and safety of workers, residents, and the ecology of the region. The real problem area of production was the chemical separation process, located in the "canyons" at 200 West and 200 East. Dissolving the slugs in nitric acid, "washing" them in various materials to remove "impurities," concentrating the resulting material—all of this produced wastes of a toxicity never before created or even conceived by mankind. Most of this came in the form of liquids containing the raw material, including uranium itself, that had once been included in the "slugs" that went into the atomic piles containing enriched uranium and were pushed out the back into the holding pools having transmuted some of that uranium into plutonium. The chemical separation plants removed with great care the pure metal from the dross. But the resulting waste was immensely toxic, and only time—tens of thousands of years, in the case of plutonium—could relieve the dangers to all forms of life presented by this toxic "soup"—time, or complex and expensive processes only dimly projected by the District's officials.

District officials responsible for long-term planning never even considered radioactive waste treatment. This was the recollection of Du Pont's Raymond P. Genereaux, who designed the chemical separation plants, using pilot programs run by Glenn Seaborg at the University of Chicago's Met Lab. At the design stages, Genereaux reported some forty years later, he and other engineers planned to build a separate "waste concentration facility" that would reduce the volume of waste. The facility wouldn't decrease toxicity, but it would shrink the volume of waste, making it "significantly small enough to encapsulate in some way and then bury it somehow." Just how or where it would be buried never really came up.[62]

Genereaux's somewhat nebulous plan for concentrated waste disposal never made it past the stage of pipe dream. "The urgency of getting the plutonium meant we had to put that idea aside," he recalled. Instead, the District decided to compartmentalize the materials according to estimated toxicity. Some of the less toxic materials would be piped to "cribs" and then "jetted" into the ground beneath, to percolate through the soil and eventually dilute themselves with groundwater and then leach into the Columbia River. (Behind this was a rather hazily conceptualized notion that some of these unstable radioactive substances would chemically bond with the soil, forming less toxic and radioactive materials.) Much of the waste material was far too "hot" for that, even by the standards of a weapons production facility in 1943. Writing immediately after the war, an unnamed MED official described the reasoning: "Large volumes of liquids are accumulated which, because of the value or health hazard of the constituents, cannot be disposed of by ordinary means." The most valuable was uranium itself, which the District determined should be "stored for future recovery and re-use." At the time there was no technology, existing or hypothesized, for doing this. One had to have faith.[63]

But the uranium was rarely alone. Instead it was mixed in with other materials— "radioactive fission by-product elements . . . so long-lived and so hazardous that disposal into the sandy soil of Hanford, or into the Columbia River, is impracticable because of its possible effect on water supply and fishing industries," as one MED official put it. This chemically complex "soup" came from various buildings in varying concentrations; most of it came from the chemical separations areas. Each half-pound of plutonium generated about fifteen thousand gallons of the liquid. A complex system of pipes and pumps moved it onto the "241 tank farms." These bore no resemblance to farms, except insofar as the liquid was planted underground because the radiation was so furious that it required a thick wall of dirt atop the tanks to enable the substance to be stored at all.[64]

The tanks themselves were single-walled steel vessels, each holding approximately 560,000 gallons. The tanks were actually composed of three "boxes," one above the other, in a "cascade" arrangement, whereby the top box contained the most radioactivity, and lesser wastes overflowed into the lower "boxes." The contents of these top boxes were so highly radioactive that they boiled, and the boxes had to be equipped with condensers so they would not "boil dry." Such an event would have been disastrous, for any number of reasons—the most dramatic being the possibility that the concentration of the dried materials would be sufficient for the contents to "go critical," or that the tanks might develop crusted coatings (as occurs in an old paint can, for example) beneath which volatile hydrogen gases would accumulate, only to explode, spewing radioactive waste across eastern Washington and Oregon and western Idaho. Or the gases might simply vent to the outside atmosphere, distributing radioactivity to the surroundings and introducing it into the food chain. (At Hanford today, all three of these remain active possibilities.)[65]

On an engineering blueprint, the tank-farm system was a marvel. The interconnections were so complex that each of the boxes could be "cross-fed, emptied or filled one from the other," in the words of the District's postwar report. Because each tank was to be subjected to the extremes of wastes so toxic they could eat concrete and so radioactive they could eventually turn metals brittle, the District paid special attention to the weld joints, the points at which collapse was most likely. Each weld joint was to be individually X-rayed to be sure of its integrity.[66]

The care lavished on planning for these waste-tank farms reflected one of the fundamental Catch-22s of the Manhattan District. The ideology of technological progress upon which the District based its programs posed a rosy future in which engineers and scientists would render neutral, or reclaim to benevolent use, the toxins of atomic bomb production. This had been an assumption from the beginning. (A District report phrased it this way: the wastes "are placed in large . . . underground storage tanks which will permit appropriate action to be taken at a later date.") But as planning turned to production and the District measured its existence in years rather than weeks or months, this mirage of "appropriate action" seemed to have receded further and further. Writing in 1946, District officials confessed that the materials "cannot be disposed of by ordinary means." (By the 1950s, this became mere rhetoric, while within the world of classified research and planning, atomic engineers and bureaucrats focused on dilution of the wastes by land, air, and water, rather than hoping for some better solution.)[67]

The waste-storage tanks thus took on a complex life. Since they were stopgaps, planning their scope and their permanence put engineers in an impossible situation. To propose sophisticated double-walled construction design for the tanks was to admit to doubts about the ideal of technological progress upon which the entire District built its program. But to build cheap temporary tanks was potentially to endanger the lives of workers, residents, and citizens throughout the Columbia River aquifer, from nearby Pasco's municipal water supply to the food shellfish of the Pacific shoreline.[68]

If this posed a moral dilemma for engineers and planners, it provided an opportunity for District bureaucrats. Building the tanks while reiterating the inevitability of a true solution to atomic waste hazards allowed the District to go on with the plutonium production facility. At the same time, the temporariness of the solution enabled District officials to justify failure as success. If the tanks couldn't be made safe over the long term—well, then, it wasn't so important. After all, the tanks would soon be pumped out and their contents rendered benign by processes not yet perfected but sure to issue from the legions of atomic scientist-technologists even now at work. In this, the tanks rendered visible one of the basic unspoken axioms of the Manhattan Engineer District: one could go ahead with nearly any line of activity, trusting one's mistakes to be rectified by progress.

Early on there were troubling presages of what was to come. One of these concerned the integrity of the tanks themselves. Even if the future were to make the tanks obsolete, they had to last until progress caught up with them. The scientists and engineers responsible for the tank designs were none too comfortable with that future; hence their requirements that the tanks be built of "pre-stressed" metal and that all the weld joints be X-rayed.

X-raying joints was not a new technology, but it was a specialized one. Only a few companies had the expertise to build tanks to such high specifications. This was the argument of one of the leading specialists in such construction, the Preload Company. In January 1944, Preload sent representatives to call upon Colonel Matthias to "see if they could take over design and construction of the pre-stressed tanks to be used in the 200 area." Preload maintained that it was far more experienced and efficient than the current 200-Area contractor, Morrison-Knudsen. Let the principal contractor do all the other work, Preload proposed, but leave the crucial task of making high-integrity tanks to an expert company.[69]

Preload's proposal thrust Matthias and the District into another Catch-22. To admit to concerns about Morrison-Knudsen after having contracted with the company was out of the question. It cast doubts on the omniscience of the District—especially since Morrison-Knudsen was a major player in the Corps of Engineers subcontractor list. Yet if Preload turned out to be right, and M-K turned out to be incompetent to do the welding, matters might be even worse. But District culture prevailed: Matthias turned Preload down.

Unfortunately for the District and the residents (present and future) of the region, Preload was right about Morrison-Knudsen. The firm was not adept at the tank construction. Three months to the day after Preload came to speak to him, Matthias reported the results of an inspection of the tanks. "Considerable difficulties have been encountered with the welding on these tanks," he wrote in his diary, and the botched job "has left the bottoms in a rough and deformed condition." Matthias's response was to work within the parameters of military contracting. He wrote that "the company is working in a well-organized way and it appears that most of their difficulties have been or will be, corrected in the near future." Matthias did nothing. Indeed, Matthias wasn't particularly worried about the integrity of the tanks; he was more concerned that Morrison-Knudsen wouldn't be done with the job in time, so that the uncompleted tank farms might hold up production. On that score, he wrote, "there appears no reason to believe that they will not get their work done within the time limit as now set out in their agreement."[70]

Even if M-K couldn't do the work, the X-ray inspection program was supposed to assure that the tank welds wouldn't fail. But this did not turn out to be true. Nearly two months later, Morrison-Knudsen had still failed to resolve the problems with the tanks. In fact, the X-ray inspection was revealing a significant number of failures, forcing continued rewelding of joints, with worrisome slow-downs as a result.[71]

In District terms, the threat to scheduling rendered the problem a crisis. Though the information is ambiguous, what appears to have happened is this: Morrison-Knudsen was building the tanks, only to have them flunk the X-ray test. This required that the tanks be rewelded. These new welds were then retested. But since the same welders, using the same tools and techniques, were doing the rewelding, an equal percentage of the rewelds failed. These rewelds then had to be welded again, and an equivalent number of these, too, failed.

At this point, Matthias could have had Preload take over this portion of the contract. Or he could have told Morrison-Knudsen to hire Preload, or some other firm that specialized in such work. Or he could have ordered Morrison-Knudsen to continue rewelding until the tanks all passed.

He did none of these. Instead, he lowered the specifications for the X-ray testing of weld joints. "After considerable discussions" with Morrison-Knudsen, "and after an actual check of the weld joint on the steel tank for the 200 area," he reported, "it was determined that the X-Ray inspection was too rigorous. Arrangements have been made to change inspection standards to permit proper interpretation of results. This will permit Morrison-Knudsen to go ahead with construction and should reduce the rewelding."[72]

This bureaucratic sleight-of-hand made the problem disappear. After all, the tanks were "temporary," meant to last only "until such time as proper disposal of the wastes could be made," to quote District officials. The tanks, of course, were as dangerously ill-made as ever; only the safety program was gutted. Inspectors had been told that rigorous inspection was not "proper." Moreover, Matthias justified his action on the basis of "an actual check of the weld joint on the steel tank." Of course, the X-ray inspections had been instituted precisely because simple visual or conventional checks of the joints could not provide the necessary accuracy. But Matthias had spoken.[73]

Even this lowering of standards was not enough for Morrison-Knudsen. Three months later, in late August 1944, Matthias had another visit from representatives of the company: "Mr. Dunn and Mr. Levinten of Morrison-Knudson Company were in concerning the tank job," he wrote in his daily log. "They feel that they are now being inspected too rigorously by the X-Ray Department and the X-Ray people are holding them up in their work." By this time, company representatives had developed an understanding of what worked within the District culture. They framed the company's failure to meet the already downgraded welding standards by accusing the X-ray process of delaying the entire program. Whether they were able to sway Matthias this time, the colonel did not say.[74]

Then in early September, as deadlines began to loom, Matthias met again with representatives of Morrison-Knudsen. He reported that the representatives had come in "to pay a courtesy call," but the real subject continued to be the issue of the weld joints, and the effect of the X-ray specifications on what they termed "work progress." "I agreed that we would continue to check the inspection and do what we could to coordinate this work to expedite the X-Ray inspection to prevent delay on the completion of the tanks," Matthias wrote in his log.[75]

Though Matthias was steelier in responding to what seems a transparent attempt to further sandbag the inspection program, his attention remained focused firmly on the question of getting the tanks done on time; the issue of their ultimate integrity never came up in his entry.

As it turned out, the tanks were completed in time to accept their load. But not just the X-ray program had to be gutted to make this so. Matthias and other District bureaucrats also had to respecify the wall materials, permitting lower-grade forms of steel. Then, when stainless steel piping grew hard to get, they switched to cast iron, though the scientists warned this would set up a chemical reaction that would speed the corrosion and failure of the points where pipes and tanks came together. And the weld joints *did* fail under the combination of highly toxic and corrosive contents and constant bombardment by radioactive particles emitted by the soup. Because these tanks were single walled (later tanks were double walled, so the failure of one wall did not immediately breach the integrity of the tank itself), their contents leached into the soil beneath them.

There they joined materials the District had been releasing directly into the soil— the waste that was considered benign enough (or valueless enough to the District) that it could be allowed to leach into the soil from holding "cribs." This process was always problematic, however. It proposed that soil materials would bond with the radioactive materials and neutralize them, and that the materials would remain in highly defined areas above the water table. In other words, it proposed that Hanford was not the desert site it was, that its soil was not an incredibly thirsty mix of rock and sand. As early as the end of February 1943, the District had commissioned the

Seattle District of the Corps of Engineers to do geological testing of the area. These drill holes had reached down about 450 feet and had not encountered rock. This suggested that the earth had no natural barriers to prevent the mixing of groundwater and wastewater. Rainwater that soaked into the ground would pick up and carry the toxic wastes into the subterranean aquifers from which local wells drew their water. Eventually the contaminated water would reach the Columbia River. The core sample results suggested that releasing materials into the soil was extremely chancy—in the long term. In the short term, and this was the term under which the District was now operating full-bore, the dangers were negligible.[76]

Nonetheless, the waste-tank system did cause some problems after coming into service and before the end of 1946. One of the most revealing of these concerned a separate set of tanks located outside the Concentration Building. These waste-settling tanks began filling up with what District officials later called "sludge," as the heavy, more toxic materials sank to the bottom. The District attempted to pump the sludge from these tanks to the 241 tank farms, so that the Concentration Building would continue to have its own tanks available. But the process failed—apparently the sludge was too thick to pass through the pumps and pipes.[77]

With the tanks full, either production would have to be stopped or some other destination would have to be found for the concentration wastes. And so the District began piping these wastes directly to the 200-Area (Chemical Separation), bypassing the waste-settling tanks, and storing them in the 200-Area tank farm. Meanwhile, Du Pont began to construct "crib trenches" that it would use to release the least-offensive effluent directly into the soil. By the end of 1946, this program of "jetting" wastes "through cribs into the ground" was so successful that the District was considering doing the same with so-called "second cycle wastes" from the chemical separation areas. Faced with adding new tank farms at regular intervals to hold the steady flow of effluent (already, General Electric, the new contractor at Hanford, was calling for bids to build a new set of such farms), pumping the wastes out of the tanks and into the earth seemed a highly cost-effective expedient. District officials reported that, as of December 31, 1946, the expansion proposal was under consideration, and plans were underway to drill a series of test wells, "in order to follow the floor of activity and thus to determine the feasibility of continued flow of wastes into the ground."[78]

The District's waste dilemmas clarified the way the culture of haste and the general military operating style served to press long-term problems out to the area of peripheral vision, and then out of sight altogether. The District resolved part of the difficulty it encountered with liquid wastes by rendering the problem invisible. When the District's chosen contractor could not produce proper weld joints, Colonel Matthias had redefined the meaning of the word "proper." Contractors, observing this weakness in the wall of rectitude that the District erected around itself, quickly moved to exploit the opportunity. The weld joints that resulted, and the single-walled tanks that they held together (however tenuously), eventually ended up underground. When the effluents the tanks were meant to store began to fill up, or to behave unpredictably, the temptation was to jet the offending material directly into the soil. There, too, it would be invisible.

The release of radioactive wastes into the surrounding water table was not limited to the Hanford Engineer Works and the Columbia River. In June 1944, evidence surfaced of potentially dangerous radioactivity in the mud and water at White Oak Creek and White Oak Lake in Tennessee. District officials gave the Medical Section the responsibility for determining the danger involved. Over the summer and fall, Medical Section personnel tested the water and mud radioactivity, analyzing the amount of "active material present in five fish and one crayfish." (Any statistician would laugh at the notion of drawing conclusions from a sample this tiny, haphazard, and expeditious.) In late October, Dr. Stafford Warren reported to the district engineer that the dangers to fish, to workers on the river or lake banks, to people drinking the water and eating the fish ranged from "minimal" to "exceedingly remote." But the discovery of this effluent and its radioactivity motivated the Medical Section to propose a program of "careful surveys at regular intervals" and plans for "necessary safeguards and measures." The source of White Oak's radioactivity remains unknown. Nowhere in the declassified record was it suggested that the District might halt the process that resulted in these materials and their discharge into open streams and lakes.[79]

Tracing the paths of liquid waste was relatively easy. Tracing gases was more difficult. From the first, the Met Lab at the University of Chicago had recognized that there would be highly toxic gases released by the chemical separation process. Designers had responded by planning a program to do what most industrial factories did with their toxic gaseous byproducts—vent them to the atmosphere, where, it was presumed, they would mix with the outer air and be diluted into insignificance. To this end, the District designed the Stack and Ventilation Building (291), "for disposing of gaseous radioactive products into the atmosphere." This building would use a two-hundred-foot smokestack to get the gases high enough that they wouldn't simply descend back to the earth undiluted, endangering workers, residents, and the ecology of the region.[80]

But the extremely toxic nature of these particular gases impressed District officials and Met Lab scientists alike. As early as May 1943, the Met Lab held a meeting to discuss the best way to determine the contents of gaseous wastes and their behavior and to seek ways of limiting them or making them less threatening to human life. At about the same time, the District engaged Philip Church, a meteorologist from the University of Washington, to make a preliminary study of the winds in the area. He was hired at the urging of the newly active Medical Division, which saw ingestion from airborne emissions to be the most likely of all the contamination paths for those not directly at work in the chemical separations facilities. Then, as construction on the plants began in the fall of 1943, the meteorological team arrived to run dispersal tests using army smoke generators to put an oil-fog mixture into the air.[81]

The conclusions from their tests were quickly clear: under "unstable" conditions, emissions were "brought to the ground by down-drafts . . . and some reached the ground within a few feet of the stacks. . . . dilution of as little as 200:1 occurs rather frequently within 500 feet from the stack." The mixing under unstable conditions "does not take place uniformly."[82]

To provide graphic evidence of the effects, Du Pont instructed Robley Johnson to have the tests photographed using time-lapse photography. Between March and October 1944, Johnson's Photography Division made an extensive and sophisticated set of photographs documenting emissions from the high stack at the chemical separation plant. These included aerial views in which the elevation, the time, and the direction of camera were all recorded on the prints (figs. 23, 24). In addition, Johnson's

Invention

144

OPPOSITE:

FIG. 23 Aerial photograph, oil smoke experiment, Hanford, 9:26 A.M. Photo by Robley Johnson or assistant. Richland Operations, Department of Energy.

FIG. 24 Aerial photograph, oil smoke experiment, Hanford, 9:29 A.M. Photo by Robley Johnson or assistant. Richland Operations, Department of Energy.

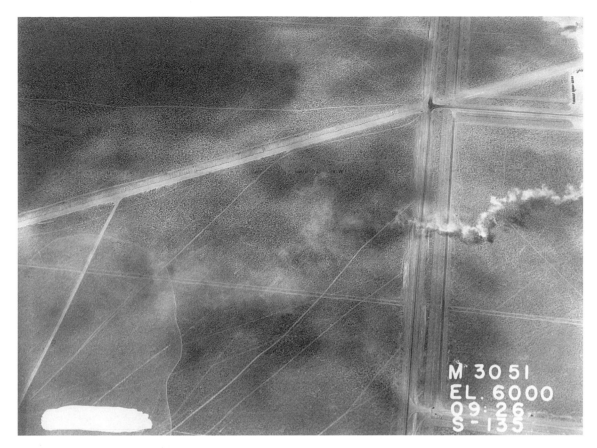

M 3051
EL. 6000
09:26
S-135

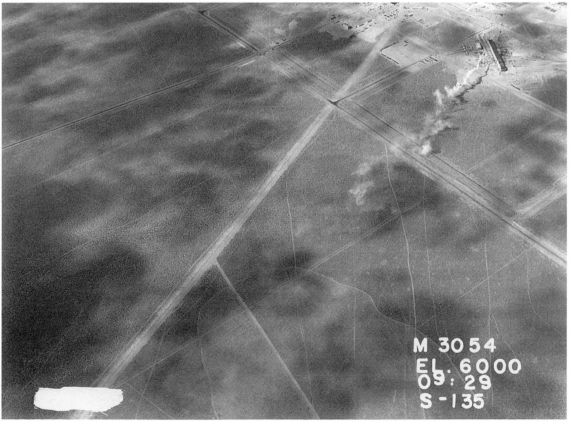

M 3054
EL. 6000
09:29
S-135

division made a set of prints from ground level, again with the time stamped on each print. In both cases, the photographs were made at between one- and ten-minute intervals. They clearly showed the smoke dipping to ground level while still highly concentrated, perhaps half a mile to a mile from the stack. A later set of pictures, made by Robley Johnson on December 8, showed all the details of the meteorological station built to monitor winds and emissions.[83]

Looking at these photographs today, armed with knowledge of what they presaged, is a complex experience. In some of these pictures, made at ground level, the smoke is as tight as a cyclone imagined by a child, as it shoots downward to the ground (fig. 25). Seen from above when conditions were calm, it casts a firm, clear shadow over the buildings, roads, and desert beneath it, for as far as the camera can see. In other views, it is a diffuse, cirruslike formation; in still others it fans out from the stack directly toward the plane from which the cameraman made his pictures, looking like the smoke from a damaged bomber going down into the sea in a war picture. In some, it curls toward Yakima, toward Richland, Kennewick, and Pasco, toward Spokane, toward Pendleton, Oregon. In the immense scale of the desert below, in the clarity of morning desert light, in the transparent air of an utterly unpolluted region, the plume sometimes seems to stretch, undiluted, to Canada, to Idaho, to the Pacific. The pictures are lovely.

Over the five months from October 1943 until the end of March 1944, the meteorological team determined scientifically what the photographs illustrated graphically: that highly toxic emissions would hit the ground in all directions from the stack, often within populated areas, and that both dilution and direction could not be predicted under the unstable meteorological conditions that often prevailed in the area. Stable conditions brought a new set of problems, the researchers noted in their March report—"mixing is greatly reduced from that under unstable conditions; the ratio is about 1 to 8." Emissions on summer nights allowed dilution to occur over the longer distances that the smoke traveled before reaching the ground. A mile and a half from the site, dilution had reached 1,300:1. But under these conditions, the emissions moved in one prevailing direction—southeast. Southeast of the plant were Richland, Pasco, and Walla Walla. As long as dilution continued at a steady rate, the meteorologists believed the dangers to be slight. But their measurements were limited to the areas immediately surrounding the stacks, and their samplings were too small to be statistically significant. The basic elements affecting emissions dilution—temperature of the emissions versus temperature of the outside air; wind velocity and direction; inversion, which tended to keep the emissions up—these they understood. The interactions of these elements, however, seemed effectively unpredictable.[84]

In late February, the difficulty with prognostication drove Philip Church, the meteorologist, to tell Colonel Matthias that "he did not know, and apparently no one else knows, what opportunities there will be to control the discharge from the 200 Area stacks." Church wanted Matthias's approval for a program of expanded meteorological studies, "with specific emphasis on the need for continued information throughout operations to determine at all times what danger points might exist." Matthias proposed that Du Pont determine whether it was "possible to hold the discharge from the stacks through a fairly long period and blow it out when weather conditions were favorable to diffusion." If that was the case, then the District would have to construct

M 6557
10:43

FIG. 25 Ground-level photograph, oil smoke experiment, Hanford, 10:43 A.M. Photo by Robley Johnson or assistant. Richland Operations, Department of Energy.

a network of monitoring towers surrounding the stacks, from which they could determine the optimum moment for discharge. If the discharge wasn't controllable, then "there was no point in attempting to maintain complete and current information on conditions in the upper strata," and researchers should instead look for predictable patterns of intensity, which "might result in danger points."[85]

It was this last program upon which Du Pont and the District then focused their attention. They built a high tower from which they could make meteorological readings. And the plan was to run the chemical separation plants only when conditions were most conducive to safe discharge. By March 1944, Church was assuring Matthias "that the picture of meteorological conditions is beginning to assume some shape and that with continuing work it will be possible to develop a pattern to fairly accurately forecast the point or points at which serious concentrations of discharged gas might reach the ground."[86]

On January 17, 1945, the Chemical Separation Division began its first processing run. Immediately the emissions controls proved inadequate. Because of the use of hydrogen peroxide in a pre-reducing step, this first run generated significant "health-hazard" bubbling of the solution, and allowed "a hazardous quantity of product [i.e., plutonium itself] to escape via the vents into the exhaust air filters."[87]

"The ventilation equipment provided by Construction included only a single exhaust fan to draw air from the process and other 'hot' hoods and through the filters before exhausting to the atmosphere via a 50 foot stack on top of the building," reported District scientists. Plutonium, relatively low in radioactivity when handled, is fiendishly toxic when ingested—eaten or breathed. And it was almost certainly falling, in relatively dense concentrations, in the area immediately surrounding the plant—especially since this part of the process vented to a separate little fifty-foot stack.

District officials were thrown into a major crisis, with only three possible options. They could turn off the ventilation system and poison the workers inside the plant when the plutonium spilled off the production line. This was inefficient, because these were highly trained workers, and their deaths would mean slowdown or halt of the program while new workers were trained. (Compartmentalization aside, there was always the danger that the deaths of these workers would become known, making it hard to find volunteers to replace them.) In another scenario, officials could close down the chemical separations plant entirely and try to develop some alternative design for the line and its ventilation. This, too, would stop production for an indefinite time. Or they could ignore the problem and continue the production runs as originally planned. This would mean that, once chemical separation started up, plutonium wastes would exhaust to the atmosphere continuously for the duration of the chemical separations run. This first run was typical of the early ones; it began on January 17, 1945, at 9:15 A.M. and ended almost three days later, on January 20 at about 4:00 in the morning.[88]

From January until April, Du Pont and Met Lab scientists and engineers looked for a way to resolve the problem. But the District imperative could not allow the postponing of chemical separations production until a solution could be worked out. And so the "pre-reduction step" continued unaltered, and so did the emission of "product" up through the primitive venting system, through the fifty-foot stack, and into the air.

Meanwhile, there was the problem of the wastes from the tall stack. Leona Marshall Libby later described the sight of the chemical separation plants in operation:

> When the Queen Marys began to function, dissolving the irradiated slugs in concentrated nitric acid, great plumes of brown fumes blossomed above the concrete canyons, climbed thousands of feet into the air, and drifted sideways as they cooled, blown by winds aloft. The brown color was, in part, caused by the gaseous effluent dinitrogen tetroxide, a common component of big-city smog, but also by iodine vapor, which the slugs contained as a product of fission of irradiated uranium metal and which was released as the metal slugs dissolved in the concentrated acid bath. The plumes cooled and descended on the desert where the iodine vapor stuck to the artemisia leaves; these leaves were eaten by the rabbits, which in turn were eaten by the coyotes.[89]

Libby's description, written some thirty years after the fact, remains compellingly visual. And it describes the chain of effects that began with the chemical separations run and ended imbedded in the ecosystem. The chain *she* described was a convenient one for MED monitors. Because the chain ended with the coyotes, which are highly territorial creatures, it was possible for monitors to determine the distribution of radioactive iodine in the landscape. Libby recalled it: "The Army guards of the huge reservation, with nothing else in particular to do, were asked by the medical staff to procure some coyotes at regular intervals, and so they drove around in jeeps over the desert floor, bucking across arroyos and gravel residues of ancient high water, shooting a monthly quota of coyotes. From the carcasses, the increasing radioactive iodine content of the coyotes' thyroids was regularly monitored. All this was long after start up of course."[90]

The results of studies of the surrounding areas first came forth sometime in 1945, and they were not encouraging—iodine 131 was appearing in the ecosystem as far as eighty miles from the site—not the stack, the site. Once the war was over, District officials approved a simple procedural change, known all along, that cut the iodine 131 emissions considerably—the slugs were allowed to stay in storage while the short-half-life iodine decayed to a far safer level. But until war's end, District officials refused to add that extra few days to the production cycle.[91]

Iodine 131 is a peculiar product. It does not appear in nature without the help of people. Its half-life is only eight days; holding the material before separations, or filtering the iodine out and holding it separately, turns it into a nearly harmless substance. But it *is* iodine. In coyotes, it concentrates in the thyroid; so also in humans. To the east and southeast of the Hanford Engineer Works, iodine 131 drifted onto the grasses and sagebrush and artemisia. All these were eaten by dairy cattle—some of them family cows, some herds belonging to two or three large dairy cooperatives. Consumed by cows, the iodine 131 concentrates in the milk. When that milk is not sufficiently diluted, it retains its toxicity. Drunk by babies or children, it deposits in the thyroid glands. In the thyroid glands, it causes cancer, and it has been implicated in a host of other debilitating illnesses.[92]

For Met Lab scientists, and particularly for those who had come into the project from work with radioactive isotopes, byproduct emissions were a very real and often terrifying prospect. These were men and women only one generation removed from the first experimenters with radioactivity. They had known colleagues—some of them teachers and mentors—who had died as a result of their contacts with the materials of their studies. The potential of the process and its materials to wound or sicken workers who had no idea what was entailed in their work recapitulated that experience and gave real urgency to their quest to determine the safest way of handling the program. The military directors of the District, however, operated from an entirely different point of view. They were used to casualties—injury and death was inevitable to the achievement of a military goal. Of course the ideal was to achieve the goal with minimal casualties, but in total war, death and injury went with the territory. To them, the scientists' desire for "the elimination of health hazards" (to quote one of the medical team members) was admirable but not essential. What was essential was the production of an atomic weapon in time to be used before the war was over.

Outside the factories, where the closed confines of walls and ceilings gave way to the infinitude of sky and air and water, the possibility of waging an effective safety campaign diminished toward the vanishing point. The very ephemerality of the effects wrought by liquid and atmospheric wastes mitigated against their being taken as seriously as definable effects that might slow production by taking critically needed workers off the lines. Indeed, it was not until the mid-fifties that the complex and dangerous chain from chemical separation to the thyroid, brain, and other cancers of children and adults came to scientific attention. And the other discovery—that microdosages had far greater effects over far longer (even intergenerational) time spans—was a matter of controversy all the way into the early 1990s.

Yet this cannot absolve the District of responsibility. While medical and scientific knowledge did not pinpoint the systematic process by which radioactivity might convert to injury, a significant collection of declassified documents reveals that District officials believed the dangers to be very real. These people recognized the strong possibility that airborne as well as waterborne effluent could carry life-threatening implications, for District residents and locals alike. But this perception of danger alternately grew and shrank in the vision of District officers and bureaucrats, depending on the strength of the awareness that such danger might slow production or make it more expensive. In the end, production won over safety and, as Yvette Berry, the chemical separation worker, recalled it, "the yellow stack would sometimes belch yellow fumes into the darkness of the night."[93]

LIVING QUARTERS

The District constructed areas for living that were sequestered by distance and other barriers from the production facilities. These residential developments, too, were the products of the District's ethos of compartmentalization, and they transmitted that philosophy to workers and residents in ways both subtle and direct.

Virtually every housing type, from the highly planned Richland Cape Cods, through the cemestos at Oak Ridge, past the TVA prefabs, and down to the canvas-roofed demountables, was based upon mass production. Some were assembled offsite and shipped to the sites. Some were brought in pieces and assembled onsite. The most traditional housing types were built using the methods that would later be claimed as invented at postwar subdivisions like Levittown: teams of workers, each with a single ordained job, would pass from house to house, so that whole blocks went from foundation hole to lived-in house in the space of a day.[94]

At each site, housing compartmentalized residents and their societies. One of the ways was by class. At first, as we have seen, this was not to have been so, at least not in Richland and Oak Ridge. But the living result of plans by SOM and Pehrson separated workers by class in a number of ways. Most obvious was the difference between managerial neighborhoods, carefully conceived from the outset, lavished with attention by architects and planners, built with some care and money on the bluff above the Columbia or on the crests of Oak Ridge, and assigned to the top echelons, and the far more haphazard, temporary, cheap, and dangerously sited neighborhoods designated for maintenance, service, and construction workers.[95]

At Los Alamos, rent was a fixed percentage of salary. Supposedly this meant that everyone had an equal shot at the nicest residences. But in truth, houses were status symbols, and the most desirable workers eventually received the best housing, even if they had to fight, and wait, to get it. At Los Alamos, addresses on "Bathtub Row" (the original Ranch School houses, rich in ambiance and equipped with bathtubs and other amenities) were reserved for the earliest, and most prestigious, of scientists and administrators. Generally, the longer you were there, the more important was your work, and the higher your status, all of which translated into the greatest likelihood of receiving a desirable housing allocation. SED workers, like the unmarried scientists, were quartered in traditional army barracks. The SED barracks were further from the life of the community and were subject to military supervision. At the bottom were the soldiers themselves—for them, Los Alamos was just another primitive and isolated barracks town.

So also with furniture. At Los Alamos, Richland, and Oak Ridge, District recruiters and the orientation materials produced by publicity officers encouraged the elite workers to bring their own furniture—in some cases, moving expenses were paid by the District. Almost any furniture one already owned was superior to the government issue. Richland's houses were furnished like any middle-class house—the living rooms got rug, desk, couch, "occasional table and mirror," platform rocker, easy chair, floor lamp and three table lamps; the dining room was equipped with a dining room table, six chairs, a cupboard, and a rug; the bedrooms got beds, bureaus, night tables, lamps, and throw rugs. Workers at Hanford Camp got a bunk and a desk if they were lucky, a bunk and a locker if not. For them, army barracks buildings were the best they could hope for—better than, say, "hutments" or tents. In the barracks, each room was designated to receive "2–30" steel cots each with felt-pad mattress, two straight-back chairs, one 30" writing table, one 30" 4-drawer type chest, and two built-in closets."[96]

After houses came apartments; after apartments, barracks. Hutments were the next step down: more crowded and more primitive. They were worst at Oak Ridge, and worst of all for male black workers. Workers assigned to the hutments at Oak Ridge each had a bed built onto a wooden box where they were to lock their belongings. The boxes were easy to jimmy; thefts were common. With five white men in each hutment, no provisions for ventilation, shutters instead of windows, and a single coal stove in the center for winter heat, these hutments resembled prisoners' quarters. When Matthias made an inspection tour to the Clinton Works in May 1943, he called the hutments "light and airy" but noted with some puzzlement that "the laborers do not particularly like living in the camp."[97]

At all three sites, eating and its rituals separated the population into readily identifiable classes. Scientists and managers able to get their families onsite got houses with kitchens; maids were offered as a perquisite to certain families. Scientists at Los Alamos could eat at the restaurantlike lodge where the food was adequate and the ambiance was that of a nice restaurant in, say, Berkeley, California. The other sites had similar settings for managers and high-level officials.

Everyone else ate in commissaries. Hanford Camp's arrangements for eating were assembly-line efficient, typical for construction camps. "You won't find any fancy cooking here, but it's good, wholesome food for hearty men," *Highlights of Hanford* told potential recruits. "You'll eat in a Mess Hall, family style, and you'll always get plenty to eat." At Hanford, the Olympic Commissary Company served 20,950,181 meals, plus 3,088,480 box lunches, and advertised their mass-production cooking processes. Nearly every reminiscence of Hanford reiterated the working-class atmosphere of the mess halls, with their prodigious eating contests, their unceasing din, their emphasis on fast delivery and fast eating. Even the terms applied to the meals were working-class terms: Breakfast, dinner, supper. Workers ate. Managers dined.[98]

Compartmentalization into classes occurred, in these and many other areas, by indirection. Take the question of toilets and bathrooms, perquisites of civilization. Those people granted houses, duplexes, and apartments had private toilets and, at least, shower facilities. As Bathtub Row at Los Alamos demonstrated, there was an echelon above privacy—to rest supine, in a private room, in hot water, was the ultimate status symbol. Those whites granted leave to live in trailer camps had private toilets and, depending on the model of trailer, primitive shower facilities. Otherwise they showered in communal bathhouses. Those assigned to hutments and barracks did their duties in public toilets and showered in common bathhouses that were assigned to clusters of hutments or barracks.

At one level, the District's decision (impelled by Groves's philosophy) to build deliberately inadequate facilities at Hanford/Richland and Oak Ridge ignited conflict over status and hypersensitized residents to their own place on the ladder. Because there were never enough houses, stores, barber shops, or funeral homes, competition for what goods and services there were became increasingly fierce, and haphazard supplemental facilities were inevitably less desirable. With the "adequate" family houses at Oak Ridge filled by 1944, companies fought each other over the allocation of housing for their engineers. And the engineers themselves made their decisions to stay or leave based not upon their patriotism or the importance of their work, but upon their understanding that status was disbursed through housing assignments, and their perception that their own place on the ladder was high or low.[99]

Compartmentalization permeated and defined every aspect of the atomic spaces. It declared hegemony over the domain of time as well. Daily life began in the construction and worker areas with sirens that rang the awake call; sirens rang out throughout Los Alamos, and in the Hanford Camp, to summon workers to their work (fig. 26). Buses left from the clock alleys to take workers to the Hanford construction sites (fig. 27); workers late to the factories at Oak Ridge or Hanford were disciplined. Recreation, too, was disciplined and ordered from above. Buses took residents from

D 1966

FIG. 26 Waiting in line at Clock Alley to enter the workplace, winter morning. Photo by Robley Johnson or assistant. Richland Operations, Department of Energy.

Los Alamos to Santa Fe, from Hanford Camp to Pasco and Kennewick, from sleeping quarters to movie houses and bowling alleys—and to taverns. Meals were served at certain hours only. Portable "banks" came in to cash checks at set hours. Women and men, "Negroes" or "coloreds" and whites, children and adults, servants and rulers: all obeyed different schedules. And in each of these meterings of daily life, the District enforced its control over the behavior of its citizens, declared its precedence over their economic lives, their emotional lives, even their bodies.

At the absolute core of the District was the policy of compartmentalization, and from this ideological core emanated the pervasive atmosphere in which everyone lived their lives. Its doctrines—of secrecy, disenfranchisement, control, obedience, limitation—permeated the high ideals district officers presented to their minions, and underlay the most mundane matters of toilets and telephones. Under ideal circumstances (ideal, that is, by District standards), regulation and compartmentalization should have forced a complete reorganization of life within the boundaries of the sites, creating a culture far different from that which had preceded it, or which lay outside its boundaries. But the District, as a bureaucratic entity, as an ideology, had to implement itself in the physical, the historical, and the cultural worlds that surrounded it in space and time. In some cases, this translation from ideal to action came up against flashpoints, places where the plans could not help but go awry. Negroes, Mexicans,

FIG. 27 Buses at Gondola Yard, from *Highlights of Hanford.* Photo by Robley Johnson. Private Collection.

and Indians: how were they to be managed in a system invented by white people to control the behavior of white people, placed upon locations already troubled by racial conflict? Women and children: how could the District, near-universally male and adult, account for their unmanly and unexpected countervailing identities, societies, cultures? How could the doctrine of obedience be forced upon the nonconscripted bodies? How to control desire, procreation, infection, illness, death? These were the questions the District confronted again and again at each site: disruptions to the ideology, to the system.

OCCUPATIONS

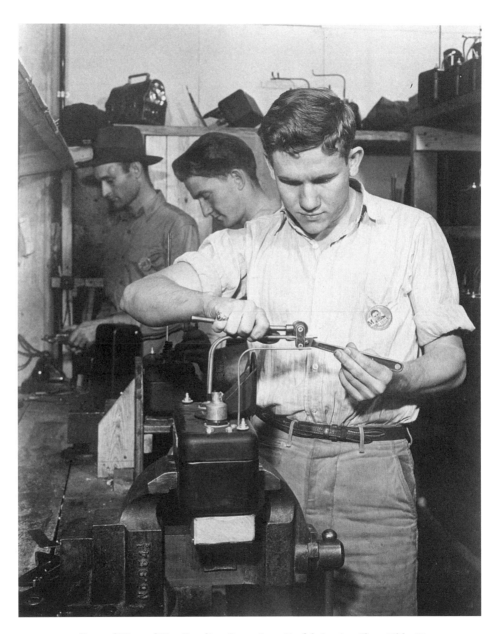

FIG. 28 *General View of Pipe Bending Operations, Prefabrication Shop, Bldg. K-300.*
Photo by James E. Westcott. U.S. Corps of Engineers, Oak Ridge, Tennessee.

FIG. 29 *K-25 Gaseous Diffusion Cell.* Photo by James E. Westcott. U.S. Corps of Engineers, Oak Ridge, Tennessee.

The founders of the Manhattan Engineer District had imagined ideal sites, perfectly isolated, and ideal occupants—completely accepting of District ideology and mandates.

Once the sites had been occupied, the District found its attention increasingly focused on the problems of finding, transporting, and managing its small army of people. From the beginning, two countervailing concepts were at work. The District's first engineer, Colonel Marshall, had imagined that the goals of the District could be better attained by voluntary commitment than by the force of orders and the threat of pain. General Groves's utopia was a military one: spartan efficiency facilitated by obedience; obedience engendered by the force of authority and the withdrawal of power, autonomy, even identity from the bottom of the organizational pyramid.

In the rush of events, in the crush of bodies and the clash of languages and the mix of desires that defined the reality of new communities made too quickly with too little knowledge, a different set of conditions emerged, an uneasy intersection of civilian and military, of Marshall and Groves. At each of the MED sites, people came with their own allegiances, and they did not give them up willingly. Though the sites might be fenced and isolated from their surroundings, entry and exit strictly monitored, still every resident inflected life and work on the District sites with myths and values from outside. How to control these incursions—how to eradicate them, where possible, how to limit their growth, to adapt them, to manage them where necessary—became the task of the District.

With labor—hiring workers, defining work, and organizing the working environment—the District faced one type of problem: to exploit and modify traditional labor-management structures in ways that would fit its specific needs, desires, and resources. Here the District was able to appropriate New Deal strategies to distinctly different ends, melding them with wartime restrictions and regulations and its own military philosophy. The result was a fundamental realignment of forces within the world of labor, and it would have profound implications for the postwar, cold-war world already being envisioned by District officials.

With the question of race, the District confronted an even more complex and demanding challenge. Though its officials might have wished to, they were forbidden by circumstances and by presidential decree to isolate their sites by race as they had striven to do by geography and culture. To bring races and ethnic groups together on the sites meant recapitulating the heritage of racial and ethnic conflict in America. Of all the preexisting identities brought to the forced spaces of the District, racial identity seemed at times the most basic, and potentially the most poisonous. If the District could solve even some of the attendant problems, it could serve as a beacon for postwar America. If it could not, it risked a scenario in which race undermined the fundamental District values of obedience and efficiency and subverted the end goal of weapons production.

Less threatening but even more nettlesome was the question of women. As did blacks, women imperiled the homogeneous foundation of the District. But whereas most black men came on the District with the same desires as their counterparts—for jobs, for money, for a sense of contribution to the war effort—women brought with them values that were often antithetical to those of the District.

And then there was the question of bodies, those universal individualities. The

District imagined workers immune to appetites and injuries, to the everyday consequences of everyday life, and to the extraordinary and often unknowable conditions of the atomic world just coming into being. How to manage the unsettling spontaneity of bodies, and what value to place on them, became in the end a recapitulation of larger conflicts over values that underlay the District's conversion of plan into actuality. And when those bodies were injured by the secret core of the District's mission—by radiation accidents and stray atomic particles, by ingestion of plutonium or dusting with uranium—District policies took a dark turn.

Seen from a distance—from Washington, D.C., say—all these represented disruptions to the ideal. But their management, however haphazard or spontaneous, reflected back the District's underlying values. At the same time, the effects of disruption, its containment and its management, further transformed the District itself, resonating from the smallest details to the largest picture.

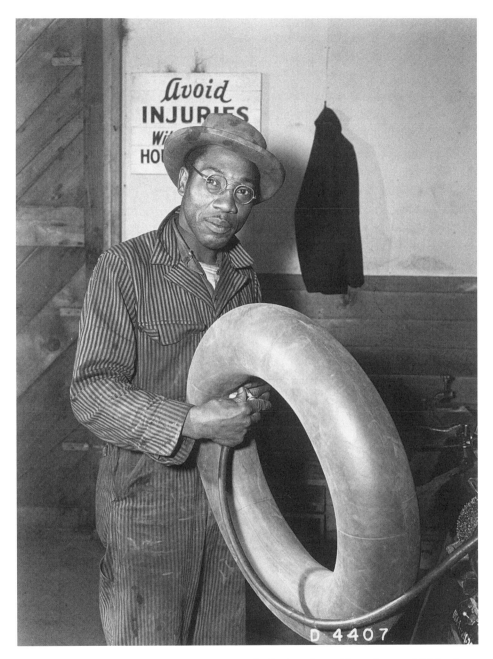

FIG. 30 Unidentified "Negro" Worker, Hanford. Photo by Robley Johnson. Richland Operations, Department of Energy.

The Manhattan Engineer District needed workers. At its peak, in the late spring of 1944, it needed over 150,000 of them—88,000 construction laborers, 68,000 operations and research personnel, the rest managers, military men and women, contract laborers—about $\frac{1}{10}$ of the idle labor force that year, approximately $\frac{1}{300}$ of the nonfarm workforce, about the size of the Allied D-Day invasion force or the army contingent that began the battle at Okinawa, and just under $\frac{1}{100}$ of the entire wartime armed forces that year.[1]

It needed those workers on supersecret sites, isolated from the rest of the world, working on projects most would never understand, under conditions often arduous, sometimes dangerous, even deadly. And it needed them during a nationwide labor crisis brought on by the demands of wartime.

WORKERS   6

These were the men and women who built the project—poured the hundreds of miles of concrete that filled the plywood forms needed to make the canyons and Queen Marys at Hanford, laid the roads that crisscrossed the areas, unloaded the prefab houses and then assembled them, bolted together the metal Quonset huts. These men and women were also the operators, who sat in cubicles in control rooms of the uranium enrichment factories at Oak Ridge and the chemical separation plants at Hanford. They milled uranium and fabricated triggers. Some of the work was primitive, some highly sophisticated. They did it all without the least understanding of what they were making, or why. Theirs was truly labor alienated from its product.

Because of its commitment to secrecy, the District sought an unprecedented measure of control over every aspect of its workers' lives—sought to make these workers into something close to machines. But whereas most employers were constrained by economic laws of labor supply and demand, by government regulations, and by the rights of individuals in a democracy, the District was a military entity with the power to enfold its corporate contractors and their workers under its particular exemptions and its peculiar culture.

When General Groves first assumed control over the Manhattan District, he revealed that difference decisively, by urging the complete militarization of the program. Had such a program been possible, it would have meant the end to a labor "problem," replacing recruitment with conscription and relieving the District's need for programs to render life within the sites minimally attractive.

With the District's particular requirements, militarization would have been particularly appropriate. When you believe you must maintain absolute secrecy, regulate the comings and goings of every individual, refuse entry to casual and even official visitors, dole out information only under absolute necessity, and spend immense sums of government funds without revealing the purpose, isolating an entire program from the regulations of a democracy doesn't seem like the best way—it seems the only way. Then, too, most military conscripts accept that life in the army must be fundamentally different. Grumbling, they accept spartan conditions and high regimentation as necessary, particularly during wartime, and they believe themselves compensated by their place in the final victory.

For America lying outside the perimeters, there were other advantages to Groves's proposal. What occurs on a military base is rarely imagined to affect the underlying laws and beliefs outside its boundaries. When the war is over, rights usurped by the crisis will be restored, the power of the military will shrink again. The distinct borders, both physical and philosophical, between military and civilian worlds allow freedom to coerce within the boundaries, freedom from coercion outside them.

But Groves lost his bid, and so the line between the District and its surroundings blurred, as the planners and managers within the fences attempted to find a compromise between two antithetical cultures: the military culture of sacrifice and coercion, and the democratic culture of self-interest and negotiation. Yet Groves and his men never abandoned their yearning for a perfect labor force.

Seeking workers, the District tapped into the civilian labor market. There it joined a complex and evolving environment, in which unions, employer associations, government bureaucracies, corporations, politicians, and individual workers contested for the future of American working life, at a particularly volatile moment. The Depression had brought a significant shift in labor-capital power relations. Labor union centralization and consolidation, bolstered by the passage of important legislation protecting rights to organize and bargain collectively, had shifted the atmosphere from that of the laissez-faire, management-dominated twenties. Labor unions grew in strength, while many "enlightened" corporations sought to take advantage of the circumstances to develop a new, more cooperative working environment, in which strikes and labor dissension were forbidden or limited by regulation and by contract, and the newly empowered unions took on many of the regulatory and peacekeeping roles that corporations had sought in founding their own "company unions."[2]

But resistance to these new relationships was also extremely powerful, especially after the Supreme Court supported the Wagner Act's labor-management provisions in 1937, including the effective banning of "company unions"; the rights of unions to organize, to serve as bargaining agents, and to demand collective-bargaining agreements; and the power of government to intervene to ensure a more harmonious and efficient labor-management relationship. Corporate organizations like the National Association of Manufacturers, the Special Conference Committee, and the American Liberty League pressed for a strident antiunion policy and exploited the return of bad times during 1938 and 1939 and the resurgence of conservative politics after the elections of 1938 to promote their agendas.[3]

Perhaps most important of all the innovations of the thirties was the new relationship within the labor marketplace proposed for government. The Wagner Act, in particular, had imagined a new government bureaucracy to mediate between the weak and the strong, to encourage cooperation and efficiency, and to enforce harmony where necessary. Beyond the specifics of the Wagner Act lay its underlying picture of a cooperative relationship among the three dominant forces in American capitalism—corporate management, labor unions, and government bureaucracies—in which a new cadre of labor leaders and a newly professionalized class of industrial relations experts came to the table committed to a strife-free, efficient, and prosperous workplace. When the Supreme Court endorsed the Wagner Act in 1937, its National Labor

Relations Board (NLRB) became a potentially powerful force in this new vision of cooperative American capitalism.[4]

By war's beginning, this new ideal had resulted in significant changes within the unions, the corporations, and the government itself. In the world of capital and corporate management there continued to rage a debate between those advocating a policy emphasizing cooperation and cooptation and those seeking a return to management control over the workplace. Government agencies devoted to investigating, mediating, and regulating labor-management disputes had become more permanent and more conservative. On the side of labor, there was a shift toward larger, more centralized, and more bureaucratized national unions, and a change in emphasis toward a goal of bureaucratic self-perpetuation over the rights of individuals and the power of the usually more strident and radical locals.[5]

This shift within the ranks of labor was not by any means complete as the war began. Seeking a more radical unionism and resisting the centralization of labor union power in the hands of the "national officers," "brotherhoods," or "internationals" (as they were often called), locals engaged in wildcat strikes and work stoppages and resisted nationally negotiated contracts. With these acts, the locals presented a warning for all three players at the big table. As the war's prosperity and full employment brought a new era of American labor-management relations, the locals and their resistant acts quickened the momentum toward a more fully cooperative wartime labor policy.

The effect of all this on the inflaming wartime economy and the shrinking labor pool was primarily to press all three principal parties toward a general goal of enlightened cooperation within a labor marketplace regulated by government bureaucracies like the National War Labor Board (NWLB), the War Manpower Commission (WMC), and a veritable alphabet soup of commissions, agencies, and organizations. Yet behind this seeming harmony and cooperation, deep ambiguities remained; all those at the table saw the war as an opportunity to push things their way, and each feared the incursions of the others. This was the uneasy environment into which the District ventured.[6]

Once the army took over the Manhattan Project in June 1942, and as Groves increasingly assumed responsibility and power in the summer and fall of that year, something of the complicated and critical demands of the labor market began to come clear. Almost immediately, District officials discovered themselves in a cutthroat competition with other wartime industries, with the military draft, with competing bureaucracies seeking to gain and hold workers. From that point until District labor demand peaked at 125,000 two years later, finding and keeping workers became not a smooth campaign but a frantic and often disorganized attempt to overcome that early inertia and devise a coherent program of labor relations.[7]

The difficulties were numerous. District officials began by underestimating not only their own needs, but the suddenness, extent, and longevity of the national labor shortage that came with wholesale commitment to the war effort. Even worse was the competition for the particular types of workers the District needed in extraordinary numbers. And then there was the matter of the draft. Pearl Harbor and the declaration of global war with multiple enemies brought a wave of military volunteers; the passage of the Selective Service Act in 1940 had provided the basis for a rapid and efficient transfer of white men out of the labor pool and into military life. So the District began its construction just when the labor pool began a cataclysmic vanishing act.

To get its workers, District labor officials had to thread their way through a tortuous maze of bureaucracies and regulations designed to regulate this scarcity of workers and apportion workers according to the wartime need. Central to this bureaucracy was the War Manpower Commission, which carved the nation up into regional fiefdoms within which new programs competed for labor with established employers—Hanford with the Seattle and northwest coast shipyards, the Aluminum Company of America (ALCOA), and Boeing Aircraft, to cite one remarkable example. But the WMC was only one obstruction. Even as late as mid-1943, labor recruitment passed through often-competing bureaucracies—the United States Employment Service, the War Manpower Commission, the Labor Section of the War Department, the War Labor Board, and the War Production Board (WPB), to name only some of the more prominent.[8]

The very nature of the recruiting system worked against the MED. Hanford's situation was the worst; at one point, its competitors sought simply to close it down as a costly and unnecessary drain on regional labor resources. But Hanford's labor problems applied to Clinton as well—and even, in a modified version, to Los Alamos. In all three cases, recruiters had to cope with a complex policy of regional labor zones, within which recruiting occurred in WMC-mandated U.S. Employment Service (USES) offices. And the District didn't do its own recruiting. At first it religiously followed its philosophy of subcontracting everything out to corporations; the companies and not the MED were to be responsible for getting their own materials and their own workers. This meant that companies within the sites regularly found themselves competing not only against other defense industries, but against other MED contractors, often fighting over the same few workers.

This formula wreaked failure from the first big push to get construction workers, in the spring of 1943. At the industrial sites, recruiters found themselves hampered by the very limited picture they could draw of the work, the area, and the living conditions. Secrecy prevented them from saying much about the work itself—only that it was a "vital war-related project." Workers could choose to build bombers in Seattle, or battleships to replace those demolished at Pearl Harbor—or they could choose this unspecified project. To describe the sites themselves was to court failure. After all, both had been chosen for virtues (invisibility, inaccessibility) that made them unattractive workplaces. Hanford competed with Seattle and the seacoast and lost. Oak Ridge was somewhat less isolated, but it fought for workers in a region notorious for the unwillingness of residents to move even if moving offered them substantial opportunities.

And then there was the matter of living conditions at the sites. At first, recruiters couldn't even describe the housing—there wasn't any. At Hanford, workers were living in tents with primitive sanitary conditions or none at all, while they began to build the barracks and eating halls and outhouses that they would eventually occupy. Oak Ridge workers were supposed to be housed in surrounding communities—communities with populations, for the most part, of less than five hundred, located along winding primitive roads at some distance from the site—and the District had no real program for finding worker housing in those outlying areas.

By mid-spring of 1943, District officials recognized that the recruiting program wasn't going to work. Typically, it was Groves who stepped in to take over. He began by hounding WMC representatives and War Department officials, all the way up to the Secretary of War, to exempt the District in important ways from the national labor program. By the summer, Groves had won his first concessions from the manpower bureaucracy and was on his way to devising his own labor control program.

The first exemption seemed the most promising: the WMC agreed to let District recruiters go national in their search for workers. That set the District at odds with just about every private industry in the country. Local employers hated the competition implicit in the MED's national labor recruitment program, and so did the local unions, which had working relationships with local employers. On top of it, workers themselves boycotted the USES programs. And so the MED's national campaign failed most noticeably in regions with a strong sense of place, with deeply rooted communities, with communities where workers and their families had been members sometimes for generations, and where, often, recruiters for the USES and workers shared community ties. The MED just couldn't compete; by the end of September 1943, Matthias reported that Hanford was getting only half its allocation of workers.[9]

Groves then directed a second strategy to resolving this problem. Apparently Groves spoke directly to Acting Secretary of War Robert Patterson concerning the WMC's foot-dragging; Patterson's directive was unequivocal. He ordered "that in each local United States Employment Service office where recruitment is undertaken, workers must not be offered any other employment until after they have been rejected for employment on these projects [at Hanford and Clinton]."[10]

This policy had far-reaching implications. It meant everyone applying for war work went through the MED recruitment process. It meant everyone who did not explicitly reject all the District's offers (and they could be multiple, if a number of contractors needed the same type of worker) waited without work until their security clearances were approved or rejected. Perhaps more important, it involved the government in a policy of deliberate duplicity; Groves and Patterson designed the strategy to give job applicants the impression that they could work for the District or not work at all. And the plan quickly developed more draconian features. By early July, the WMC had agreed that it simply wouldn't allow workers needed by the District to take non-MED work anywhere in the nation where there was spare labor.[11]

By November, this policy was drawing carpenters and laborers from all over the United States to the Hanford project, as Du Pont recruiters worked out recruiting scripts that they distributed to USES interviewers, with instructions that any applicants in those needed trade categories were to be shunted directly to "central collection points" from which Du Pont recruiters would send them by rail to Pasco and thence to Hanford. Only after workers had gone to these "collection points" and actively refused Du Pont offers were they to be sent back to their home hiring halls and allowed to see other opportunities.[12]

But even programs like this, worked out at meetings in Washington with representatives from all affected agencies, weren't sufficient to significantly improve recruitment. Like so much else in the history of the District, proposals deemed ideal up above disintegrated under resistance from below. Local USES offices became the sites of something approaching guerrilla warfare, with local industries subterfuging the national directives in order to keep their conduits to local labor. And where national pressure required the agencies to follow Groves's policy nonetheless, there were more subtle ways to undercut him. It took only a slight shift of wording, a glance or wink on the part of a USES official to undercut the directive, so that workers who simply refused the assignment outright could be quickly shifted to local work.[13]

Throughout the summer and fall, the District fought to overcome this sabotage, lobbying the secretary of war, jawboning Paul McNutt, head of the WMC, and protesting to local offices. It was hard going, and successes were limited. Looking to hire tens of thousands of workers, the District found it was getting only hundreds.[14]

By the late fall, local site administrators, both District officials and contractors, found themselves drawn more deeply into the recruitment race in order to fulfill their commitments and contracts. At Hanford, Colonel Matthias persuaded the army to cover "travel and expenses" for recruited workers to move from their homes to the site, "on the ground that it was almost impossible to recruit this class of personnel under present conditions." Contractors and local recruiters, too, began to find the right techniques to overcome local resistance and get their quotas. Recruiters began to boycott the prescribed recruitment centers, going instead where workers had just been let go. In October 1943, recruiters from Hanford raced to ride the boats filled with workers coming home after work on the Alaska-Canada Highway closed down for the winter months. Recruiters began to haunt defense plants where WMC and industry informants told them cutbacks were about to take place. The biggest corporations (including Du Pont) began actively transferring their own workers from other contracts to Manhattan District work.[15]

Still the jobs went begging. And so the District's labor specialists began to float another idea. At a meeting in early September, Hanford's Colonel Matthias and the Clinton site's labor specialist, Lt. (jg) John J. Flaherty, worked out a new and far more aggressive plan, one that called upon the *unions* to accept responsibility for providing a quota of workers each month. With the war as justification, and with patriotism as the goad, the District was effectively asking that the national offices of the largest unions became management entities—labor recruiters and suppliers, smoothly expediting labor flow.[16]

Such a process could not have been imagined without the increasingly powerful presence of the national labor union bureaucracies to provide the muscle. "Internationals," the District officials called these rising forces in American capitalism, taking up the parlance of the day. These were the occupation-based union organizations, many of which were clustered loosely into the AFL or the CIO. Their headquarters were usually located in New York or Washington; most had grown up during the bad years of the Depression as hard times for labor called increasingly for a concerted, cooperative approach to wages and contracts on the part of widely scattered "locals." Alone, the locals had little power against their opponents, but united, they could garner the clout to oppose international corporations and centralized manufacturing and industrial concerns. Over the wartime years, these Internationals would consolidate their power within the labor movement by their presence at the tables of the major agencies conducting labor and production policies (the WMC, the WPB, and the rest)—but they would find that seat a perilous one. With the District it would be no different.[17]

The District's call for union recruiting pressed the union movement further toward centralization. This was not accidental; witness the District's strategy for implementing the union recruiting procedure. As Matthias and Flaherty worked it out, the idea was to approach the Internationals from two directions—through the military bureaucracy, and through corporate labor negotiators—inviting them to join a developing consortium of labor-management forces which included the WMC and the Labor Relations Board as well as the corporations, the military, and the District.[18]

This early plan altered the interrelations within American capitalism in what was still a relatively conservative way. Flaherty's plan continued to replicate the New Deal vision, whereby government agencies (the WMC, the Labor Relations Board) intervened between the hostile forces of labor and management, protecting the weakest force—the worker—from the depredations of the stronger, while encouraging cooperative commonality.

But already this liberal vision of the power relations among the three great forces of American capitalism was waning. Flaherty's plan accepted that the Internationals had come into being to equalize the forces of labor and capital. He and Matthias recognized implicitly that the wartime environment was bringing about a newly shifted role for government—from protector of the weak to facilitator of the deal, as a bureaucracy among bureaucracies.[19]

Then in October, the balance of powers shifted decisively: Colonel Matthias at Hanford finally lost all patience with the War Manpower Commission and decided to push Flaherty's proposal one step further. "It appears that we may have to resort to recruiting direct from the Unions without regard for WMC," he wrote in his diary. Matthias's entry marked the District's unfolding decision to build an alternative culture, not just on its sites, but in the metaphysical spaces of its bureaucracy and, now, in the larger realm of political economy that was being worked out on a day-by-day basis under the aegis of the Manhattan District. Flaherty's plan had been evolutionary. It took the channels of wartime American culture and bent them to the District's ends. Matthias's proposal was to scrap this complex web of institutions and relationships and deal directly with the principals.[20]

Such a revolutionary sea-change could not have occurred even six months earlier—not with labor-hating Groves directing matters from above, and not without a settled working relationship between the MED and the unions whose ranks comprised its most vitally needed skilled workers: electricians, pipe fitters, machinists, and the like. But Matthias had been meeting with union representatives, and so had others throughout the District. From those meetings had come a glimmer of an idea about a new political economy reflective of the District's larger philosophy of management from above.

Already the disruptive, difficult-to-control labor locals had begun to rankle Matthias. Locals were small; they were built from below; their officers were laborers too, or they were barely removed from the workplace. Locals responded to the complaints of workers about the small, essential issues of workplace safety, of unfair discrimination, of overtime given or taken away. Internationals dealt with the big contract negotiations, with wage scales, with civilized negotiations in which everyone wore a coat and tie. Local disputes occurred on the sites, and the local official was right there because he (or, rarely, she) usually worked onsite. Internationals called for strikes over wages, health benefits, and pension funds; locals might stage wildcat walkouts over the quality of the food or the lack of ice water on a dangerously hot day.[21]

Matthias disliked the locals. His diary is laced with reports of their threats to efficiency, with complaints about their intransigence, their fundamental radicalism, their power to make matters difficult, their microscopic focus. But he, like his mentor Groves, understood the Internationals to be different animals—bureaucracies like the District, staffed by managers like himself.

The District approached and won over its corps of Internationals in part by offering these unions and their officers a picture of themselves as civilian wartime heroes. (And if they opposed the bargain, the District had another picture prepared—an image of organized labor as a nest of slackers, obstructionists or, worst of all, subversives and Communists.) District officials had secrecy to spice the pot; they could speak darkly of the project; they could offer participating union officials membership in an exclusive club. And they had something more lucrative and appealing to the Internationals: the rights to organize on the sites, now, and after the war.

This was a real temptation. Already, over the past year, the unions had seen their control over wage rates and their rights to oppose management alarmingly limited. First the War Labor Board had taken over the job of setting wage rates when negotiations broke down; then in the spring and summer of 1943, Roosevelt widened the board's authority and effectively took wages off the table when negotiations between labor and management took place.[22]

Union rights on military sites (even when contractors ran the plants)were seemingly liberal, but that liberality was in appearance only. Early in the war, army and navy officials drew up a document that laid out the labor rights on military projects with civilian contracting firms. The government conceded to unions the right to collectively bargain, but held the right to accept or reject the results unilaterally. Unions could negotiate with the contracting firms; the power lay with the military supervisors of the projects. In addition, the army declared its right to fire any worker simply on suspicion of "subversive activity," and it reserved the right to consider the phrase as broadly as necessary.[23]

The confederations of Internationals—the AFL and the CIO—were labor's signatories to the agreement. Again it was an agreement based upon union willingness to forgo power in the present in return for a promise of power later, when the war was over. This "Statement of Labor Policy," signed in June 1942, set the precedent that Matthias applied in his recruiting proposal—a policy of cooperation among national union leaders, corporate contractors, and the army, with the army serving as facilitator and ombudsman. But it also placed those unions with a strong presence on the sites at an advantage, and it threatened them with the possibility of eviction from the sites if they failed to cooperate. And eviction from the sites meant losing postwar organizing rights, in vast new factories, and—more important—in a secret but clearly promising new industrial sector.[24]

On the Manhattan District, codas to the policy statement concerning secrecy, security, and "subversives" gave army officials vast powers over unions and restricted union rights concomitantly. On the District, unions couldn't appeal directly to the National Labor Relations Board in a public hearing—appeals went to the District itself, instead. Similarly with violations of the Fair Labor Standards Act—the District served as its enforcer, under the dubious argument that it was an unbiased third party positioned as arbitrator between labor and management.[25]

Big labor was clearly the weaker power on the sites, and District officials exploited the advantage in their quest "to recruit and maintain sufficient manpower for the rapid construction and efficient operation of its projects," to quote the District's classified records. Those labor organizations drawn most deeply into the net—the CIO, the Building and Construction Trades Department of the AFL, the International Brotherhood of Electrical Workers (the IBEW), the International Association of Plumbers and Pipe Fitters, to name a few—ended up furnishing most of the skilled workers on the sites.[26]

But the most startling innovation in labor recruitment came at the peak of construction. By the middle of 1944, as the big plants were nearing completion, the industrial sites needed electricians in particular. Again the District turned to the International for help. The result was the Brown-Patterson Agreement, worked out between the undersecretary of war and the president of the IBEW, which effectively drafted electrical workers, pulling them out of their jobs, shipping them to Hanford and Clinton, and keeping them there for a period of three months.[27]

Brown-Patterson represented perhaps the climax in direct regulatory reforms designed to give the District priority above all else. The agreement depended upon an alliance of institutions outside the District, with the District as final beneficiary—in this case, the Internationals, representing institutionalized labor, and the War Department, representing national government and the military. The agreement served as an important precedent, applied at both the other sites and then extended from electricians to workers in other shortage-plagued trades.[28]

All these programs sought to replace traditional supply-and-demand elements of labor recruiting with programs that turned the unions from champions of worker rights and freedoms to representatives and labor subcontractors of the District and its contractors. (In the case of Brown-Patterson, it was the union reps who provided the train ticket to Hanford or Oak Ridge.) In a sense, this net of programs was one part of a larger attempt to expand military culture beyond the sites and into the institutions of civilian life. But while these places succeeded at the institutional level, persuading the institutions and persuading the individuals were different things.[29]

So there were two directions to labor policy. One was toward increasingly coercive and authoritarian regulation, legacies of the old corporate-management hostility to labor, and the District officials' connection to the world of management and to corporate culture more generally. The other was toward a benevolent paternalism combined with a newly "enlightened" interest in forging cooperative agreements with unions.

As the District quickly learned, the most direct way to draw workers was to offer money. After an initial wrangle, District labor officials raised wage rates. But these were relatively small amounts; further raises galled Groves and ran up against the resistance of the wartime federal wage-control bureaucracies. Overtime was a better route: recruiters advertised that there was work and plenty of it; that overtime rates conformed to national labor laws; that good workers found plenty of overtime opportunities.

Overtime was particularly attractive to the District's ideal worker. He was a male, thirty-eight or older (to move him out of prime draft years), preferably with a solid draft deferment—a nonhandicapping physical problem (flat feet, sinus trouble) or, in the skilled trades, an "essential craft" deferment. Ideally, the worker was single, divorced, or already separated from his family—for example, working on another project, with family far away. "Defense gypsies," these men were called; they often traveled in groups, often with relatives—brothers, cousins—and sometimes carried their housing with them, in the form of trailers they towed from worksite to worksite. For them, the war defense industries offered the closest thing to a working man's get-rich-quick scheme. Defense gypsies cared about the workweek not because they wanted leisure time, but because the longer the workweek, the greater the bonus pay.[30]

"We worked overtime nearly all the time," Hanford's Leon Overstreet recalled forty years later. Overstreet came close to embodying the ideal worker. He was an Okie, but he came from a pipefitting job outside Kansas City. He'd heard about the Hanford recruiting program in the men's room of his old job, and he took his brother and some friends with him, so they could share the necessary rationing tickets for gas and tires. Like many early recruits, he'd thought Washington was all mountains and running streams—he'd never heard of the scablands in his geography classes. He came for the pay, and he stayed for the overtime.[31]

But Overstreet was unusual in other ways. He was a lucky catch—he jumped right into the boat. Once there, he couldn't quickly leave—he'd used up his gas rations getting to Hanford. And he was able to get his family out to nearby Prosser, so he commuted every day: he fit the original plan, under which the District built no housing and kept its workers offsite to save money and keep secrets. Once he'd settled, he wasn't likely to leave.

Potential recruits who came to USES job interviews weren't so easy to net. Recruiters needed incentives besides money, and this required the District to make concessions in housing and living arrangements. At Hanford, for example, recruits came in on the train, and at first they were required to pay their own fares. That way they had money invested and would think twice about leaving quickly. That was the District's philosophy. But as the labor problem became increasingly acute, recruiters persuaded the upper administration to a compromise: to offer an advance against wages that could be "worked off" with a good employment record. Beginning October 28, 1943, workers who stayed at Hanford for four months with less than four days of absence had their one-way travel costs forgiven; three more months meant return fare.[32]

The labor specialists also quickly came to realize the cost of workers who left. Training replacements took time; new trainees weren't as efficient or skilled; new arrivals cost dearly in services, from housing assignment to job training. Those were the tangibles. There were also the less immediately calculable costs to the security of the site. Each worker who left carried knowledge of the project out into the world; each new recruit punched another hole in the wall of secrecy with which the District tried to surround the sites.

And so the District began to change the picture it painted of the physical and social environment in an attempt to get the workers it needed and keep the workers it had. Working simultaneously from grassroots and from the highest echelons, the District began to remake itself as a benevolently paternalistic company town.

Most of the changes were small in cost but great in effect. Consider the worker arriving at Pasco, Washington, armed with a work assignment form and little else. He thought he was going to someplace called Hanford. But the schedule of the train put him in nearby Pasco in the dark, predawn hours, without transportation to the site or a place to eat or sleep. Many arrivals surveyed the primitive circumstances and got right back on the train, preferring to take their chances in Seattle. It was Groves who changed this. On July 21, 1943, he called Colonel Matthias to tell him that he'd been receiving reports that the arrangement gave recruits a window during which they might "become disgruntled and leave." Within two weeks, Matthias had marshalled resources from Du Pont and its subcontractors, from local and national government agencies, and from labor unions; now workers were fed, housed, and given a pep talk right off the train.[33]

The problem then shifted to the sites, ugly, half-built, overcrowded, and overburdened. Workers hemorrhaged out of the sites at a remarkable rate. Construction workers left Hanford at the rate of 20 percent a month; Clinton was barely lower at 17 percent a month. Operators, too, left at a far higher rate than at comparable plants outside the District.[34]

Not just quitters devastated the District's labor plans. Absentees—people staying home to care for a sick child, or sleeping off a drunk, or taking time off to visit family back home, or simply taking time off—overturned the carefully made plans concerning the number of workers needed, the number of houses needed to shelter them, the number of recreation halls and beer dives needed to entertain them.[35]

As the weekly worksheets from each subcontractor came in that spring of 1943, District officials wrestled with ways to stanch the flow. From the District hierarchy came one initiative, typically bureaucratic: the "exit interview" whereby all workers leaving the site found themselves subjected to an elaborate questionnaire and a personal interview with a District bureaucrat, all of which resulted in reams of paper and little improvement.[36]

Conceived by District officials far distant from the site, administered by bureaucrats who had little or no contact with the real life on the sites, the exit interview procedure represented everything that was wrong with the District's foray into paternalism. The checkoff list of reasons for leaving symbolized this distance from reality: in dry bureaucratese it asked about "recreational and social facilities" instead of "bars too crowded and dangerous"; "interest of work (e.g. monotony)," rather than "theft in the hutments," or "car got stuck in mud and was run over by bulldozer," or "no trees." Yet these were the realities residents remembered years, even decades, later.[37]

To redeem the program, Matthias and others set up their own alternative. There, open-ended interviews by company and District reps who really listened resulted in on-the-spot offers and promises. Unauthorized, but realistic, this program worked.[38]

Conflicts on the job weren't usually the reason people left. At Oak Ridge, especially, workers quit over the horrendous housing conditions, the bad food served in the cellblock atmosphere of most cafeterias, the chaos that substituted for everyday life off the worksite.[39]

To change these, contractors lobbied directly with local MED officers to develop alternatives that flouted District regulations but served the workers and the job. This was probably the most successful reform, because it created an alternative, site-based counterculture of administrators with an attitude both more pragmatic and more messianic—an alternative administration more likely to listen to, hear, and respond to the calls and complaints of workers.

The result of this growing web of conflict and attempted resolution was a double administration, one devoted to visible and public government by directive from a distance (physical, bureaucratic, ideological), the other to a more closely observed and pragmatic program, coercive in an indirect, even disguised, fashion.

The District might not be able to fix the cause of worker complaints; it was remarkably adept at punishing gripers who went outside the fence with their complaints. One man wrote his home-state senator, Democrat Homer Truett Bone, concerning the difficulty getting groceries, goods, and services at Hanford. The senator inquired into the matter. Within days, General Groves was on the phone to Matthias with the name of the offending employee. Response was swift. Matthias reported in his diary that "reply was prepared, and will be dispatched by teletype tomorrow morning." Senator Bone received his apologia; meanwhile the District's Military Intelligence team went off to interview the transgressing employee.[40]

Often the result of this conflict between punishment and accommodation was a rapid playing out of unhappy effects far different than those the District planned. Such was the case with the question of beer. Officially, District officials had planned to keep alcohol of all sorts off the sites on the grounds that it impeded worker efficiency and encouraged absenteeism. But Matthias among others reported to Groves that the lack of beer was one of the main reasons workers left the sites, and he began to lobby heavily for a change in the program to include construction of beer halls or saloons within certain of the recreational facilities.[41]

At the local level, Matthias had graphic evidence of the ill effects of the District's no-alcohol policy. He needed only to look at the fire reports for a one-month period in the late spring of 1943. On May 29, Barracks 3D was "completely gutted" by fire and a "Swede" named Carl Swanson, who had been allegedly drinking in Pasco with Cornelius Murray, his roommate, burned to death. Swanson told the doctor on his deathbed that he had been drinking for "several days." Murray had been trying to sober him up before he went back to work that night at the Olympic Commissary. At 2:30 A.M. on June 20, 1943, Joel Walker, a brickmason tender from Seattle on contract to Morris-Knudson, burned to death in the back seat of a car. The owner of the car, a brickmason named M. E. Wilson, had picked up five men in Pasco and brought them back to camp, after all had been drinking at Pasco. Walker had passed out; "he was left on the rear seat and covered with a blanket. Shortly afterwards the fire was discovered. . . . The automobile was a Studebaker carrying California license No. 8-Q-9417." On June 21, 1943, J. A. McGinnis "was drunk and smoking in his room while lying in bed," with predictable results. Uninjured, "McGinnis was apprehended and confined until he sobered up. The following morning he was discharged from the job."[42]

Matthias understood what was happening; workers forbidden to drink on the sites went offsite for uncontrolled binges. The isolated geography and the deliberately primitive roads into and out of the gates encouraged workers going offsite to stay drunk for the duration of their time off. Brawls and drunk-and-disorderly jailings in the surrounding towns skyrocketed. By the fall of 1943, the roadway from Pasco to Hanford was littered with wrecks. Those who made it back to Hanford burned down the barracks, died in their beds, stayed off work for days, fought with their barracks-mates—everything District officials feared most from workers on alcohol.[43]

Finally Groves himself intervened and decreed that the District would introduce a limited number of saloons at each site. But even this policy had unexpected consequences. The very notion of limited access only inflamed the competition, with workers lined up eight or more deep outside the tavern doors, especially after shift changes. Leona Marshall Libby, among others, reported that drinkers sold their barstools for premium sums to waiting workers, or simply drank until they fell off the stools, so as not to lose their places. DeWitt Bailey of Hanford later remembered the beer hall as "a fairly wild place. They used tear gas in there several times to quieten somebody."[44]

When Groves finally did accept the necessity of providing more humane living conditions, he did so grudgingly, and he spent significant time and attention explaining that he was not in fact offering luxury, but necessity. Summertime heat at Hanford sometimes struck 110 degrees (it was 105 in Pasco on the day Harry Petcher waited for the bus out to Hanford). Workers routinely collapsed from heat prostration until the District began providing ice water in sealed barrels (sealed, one worker remembered, after someone caught a fellow worker washing out his dentures in the water). Though the night-time temperatures were a bit better, the cooler evening air rarely penetrated the hotboxes of barracks and hutments, with their heat-absorbing tar roofs and their rectilinear layouts, too close together to allow a breeze to enter. Workers arriving in the summer tended not to last the week. Fights in the housing areas broke out nightly; heat ignited the tempers of workers already exhausted from the fifty-eight-hour workweek.[45]

Air conditioning was out of the question. Groves could not allow an extravagance of that sort. And so someone—probably Matthias—invented a face-saving solution. Hanford's was a desert heat, devoid of moisture. So the District installed ventilators that drew the interior air up through the ceiling and through "desert coolers" or "water chillers" on the roofs of dorms and hutments, where they cooled interior air by running it through primitive evaporators.

Groves never liked these boxes—they were highly visible, and they symbolized the victory of comfort over frugality. In a pair of memos to the deputy director of the Army Service Forces Production Division, however, the general found himself defending them, because "the use of these . . . 'desert coolers' has during the past summer resulted in a large reduction in terminations of workers."[46]

But Groves could never call them *air conditioners.* He could not, because the army did not requisition air conditioning for construction workers without terrific resistance; he *would* not, because he himself had all along opposed such frivolousness at his sites. So he called them "heating units" that worked secondarily as "desert coolers," shunning the term "air conditioning" completely.[47]

By mid-fall of 1943, labor was in such a crisis that even Groves became briefly converted to the cause of a newly humane workplace. Typically, he showed his concern with a flurry of dramatic phone calls to his subordinates. He told Hanford's Colonel Matthias to pass along to "Foremen, Craft Superintendents and others the importance of making what job adjustments are necessary to keep the employees reasonably well satisfied." Groves became equally obsessed with improvements off the worksite. On October 16, Matthias reported in his diary that Groves called again "requesting information as to when the Theater would be completed . . . and when we would be able to sell beer in the Recreation Building. He requested a specific report as to when the Theater will be completed."[48]

Groves intervened from above. Usually, humane changes came from the ad hoc decisions of local administrators. This is the system most graphically described in Colonel Matthias's daily diary. In this world, meetings were far more important than memos; and the meetings that occurred were rarely between managers at the same levels or within the same areas. Matthias might meet with Du Pont's Church, and if the issue was labor, one might find present a representative from the International Brotherhood of Electrical Workers or the laborers union, a couple of foremen from the site, and perhaps an official from the MED's labor division, located in Oak Ridge. If the matter was housing, such a meeting might include the president of a construction firm, a representative from Du Pont, a couple of MED people, and Matthias himself.

Bizarrely, General Groves came increasingly to seem an exile from his own bureaucracy, and a participant in the seat-of-pants commonwealth. Here he could most directly influence the day-by-day matters of the District, and he was most comfortable with its empirical nature, its focus on specific problems with specific solutions. Groves was an astute man; he was quick to understand that the elaborate bureaucracies he had worked to create were increasingly turning inward, feeding themselves rather than the actual work of the District. Indeed, it is tempting to say that Groves understood and feared that the District was redefining its end product: not an ultimate weapon, but an ultimate bureaucracy.

By the winter of 1943, it began to be clear that none of the various strategies for salvaging the labor situation was anywhere near sufficient to get the program on track. And so the directors began anew with draconian programs to enforce discipline upon the workforce. If workers could not be persuaded to remain on the sites, to work harder and longer, they would have to be coerced.

The simplest and most direct of these programs adapted traditional "free-enterprise" labor techniques from outside the District, often spiced with highly particular interpretations of wartime labor regulations. The single most successful of these involved the national program for labor retention known as the "statement of availability" or "certificate of availability" system. Under a new set of regulations, a worker who left one job, for whatever reason, had to receive an availability statement from the former employer before he or she could be hired at another job. Statements of availability were the means by which employers controlled their labor force, for the employer was under no obligation to provide such a document unless the worker was laid off due to lack of demand. To be fired, or to quit, meant no statement of availability; without one, a worker could not be hired for thirty days at first, then (as the labor crisis deepened) sixty days.[49]

The availability program was a godsend to desperate labor specialists in the District and its contractors. Workers could be recruited from "essential" jobs by promising automatic certificates of availability to anyone who came to the MED. Once they were there, the District had remarkable flexibility in determining who would and who would not actually be allowed a certificate. If, for example, a worker opted to leave on grounds that could be determined in the exit interview to have been justified, the interviewing official could direct the worker back to the site on another job, and threaten not to grant the certificate if he or she refused. And as a means of policing behavior on the job or off, the certificate program was ideal, for, as the District warned in a mass circular late in the war, "an employee who has deliberately provoked his discharge . . . is not entitled to a statement of availability."[50]

There was a procedure for appeal; the worker had the right of review by the USES, which was obligated to investigate the case. But this process might last weeks or months, a long time to be unemployed. And it was of no use if the worker had quit—regulations clearly stated that the USES was to deny the worker a statement of availability and "negotiate with the worker and the employer for the worker's return." If the worker was fired with cause, appeal was also useless. To be granted an appeal, you had to argue you'd been unjustly fired, and you had to prove it.

The way such a program might be exploited by the District can be seen in a memo Oak Ridge's Lt. Col. John S. Hodgson sent out concerning plans for a new "Campaign to Obtain Maximum Labor Efficiency—Field and Office, Clinton Engineer Works" on June 14, 1944. In an attempt to "institute more vigorous efforts to obtain maximum labor efficiency from contractors and operators" Hodgson proposed a publicity campaign directed to all personnel, "emphasizing (1) The continuing urgency of the program; (2) Appealing to their sense of patriotism; (3) Making clear that we now can afford to weed out inefficient personnel and that it is intended that such action will be taken." Among other things, Hodgson proposed to use the availability program to prevent the increasingly disturbing phenomenon of unregulated job hopping, something that had been made possible early on by the desperate shortage of workers. Hodgson warned that "personnel discharged for cause will not be permitted to work for any other organization on the area unless investigation reveals that discharge for cause was improper." Hodgson thus made clear the implications of the availability-statement weapon in the hands of the District; to be fired with cause was to lose all possibility of working on the site for the duration, and to lose all employment for the designated period of thirty or sixty days or possibly more.[51]

The statement of availability program worked best as a means of intimidation invoked in combination with other wartime labor policies. One involved the District's right to terminate any worker simply under suspicion of "subversion"—a term that could mean anything from spying, to labor agitation and union recruiting, to "seditious talk" as determined by informers. Even to be accused of any of these meant termination "with cause," and that meant unemployment for one or more months. To ensure that such workers were quickly identified and as quickly expelled, the District employed a larger and larger army of "informants," to infiltrate union locals and work areas, and, eventually, to live in the barracks, dormitories, and hutments, to keep an eye out for seditious individuals. Once ferreted out, they could be quickly dismissed and their plight as unemployables without availability statements held up as a warning to others in their union, work gang, or barracks.[52]

To be fired meant more than forced unemployment without a statement of availability. On the District, it meant immediate eviction from onsite housing, not just of yourself, but of your entire family. Within twenty-four hours of being fired, workers and their families found themselves and their belongings deposited (sometimes forcibly) outside the gates—and at Hanford, those gates were shacks in the midst of a treeless, windy desert, baking in summer sun, blowing with winter wind and snow, many miles from commercial bus or rail transportation. Children attending onsite schools lost their rights to schooling; spouses employed in subsidiary jobs might find themselves fired as well—if not, then the family was split asunder.[53]

There was also the matter of getting back home. Workers who had driven to the site had a distinct advantage here, for they could drive back out—assuming they had been lucky and prudent enough to collect the necessary gas and tire rations to make the trip. Workers who'd come by train had to find the return fare. Those who had accumulated credit toward District payment of their transportation expenses lost that credit if they quit or were fired. But the worst case involved those whose transportation to the site had been advanced by the District. If they left without permission, they owed the train fare, which could come out of their final paycheck if the District wished to extend its reach to the extreme.[54]

Even this technique didn't succeed in fully dissuading labor organizers or resolving labor problems. By early 1944, District officials were looking for further incentives to docility. Matthias hit on the idea of driving ex-employees right out of the region. At the same time, he began to beef up his staff of "intelligence agents." And District "public information officers" began to plant stories reminding workers that the District was ready to have dissidents fired and arrange to have them immediately drafted and shipped to the war front. As early as July 1943, District propaganda officers on the Hanford site warned in the Hanford house organ that "selective service officers in this state have announced that chronic absenteeism from war-plant jobs for which workmen have been deferred will make them subject to immediate reclassification. Such stern measures apparently have become necessary."[55]

But this seemed to workers just one among so many pieces of paper, instructing them in obedience, warning them of punishment. When the pipe fitters' union fought the District in the summer of 1944, Matthias and other District officials took the resistance as an affront, proof of the need for even more severe tactics. That case provided the excuse enabling District officials to introduce a new strategy: they began actually employing soldiers, temporarily transferred from the fierce fighting in the Pacific arena, as replacement workers. This, they believed, could provide graphic evidence of the alternatives to good behavior—and it did.[56]

In part this ratcheting up of labor militancy on one side and District authoritarianism on the other reflected fundamental shifts in labor relations that occurred in the middle of 1944. The great battle of industrial catch-up had been won, the Allied forces supplied, and the defense industries began to shorten shifts, lay off workers, and close plants. The result was a wave of panic among workers and an increase in available workers at the sites; but tied to this was an equivalent increase in labor militancy as union leaders and rank-and-file workers sought to preserve what they had won and prepare for a postwar American capitalism. Management, meanwhile, worried at the possibility of a union-directed socialism in which, in the words of one NLRB representative, everything went to labor except "the stockholder's last right—the ownership of the corporate stock." "Some limit has to be set," warned this industry voice.[57]

Industry and capital leaders yearned for the means to limit what one spokesman for management described as "absenteeism, tardiness, early wash-up, disinterest in application to the job, lessened pride of workmanship, insubordination, and just plain soldiering." The Manhattan District had those tools and, increasingly, sought and applied others.[58]

Individuals always seemed to be the District's bane; when it came to groups, organizations, or incorporations, men like Groves, Nichols, and Matthias stood on firmer ground. Seeking ways to regulate group activity on the job and off, District officials saw unions both as the means to greater control over workers and their work and as competitors for hegemony. As they had with recruitment, District officers looked to the International union headquarters as their allies onsite and off. Internationals could be used to direct the local officials; they could discipline rebellious locals, they could expel dissident local officials, and they could even take over a site from the locals if necessary.

At the top of the District hierarchies, offsite and on, officials treated the Internationals with public respect and private disgust and contempt. Interviewed decades after the war, Colonel Matthias retained that attitude:

I dealt with the unions, and Du Pont and I did a good job of batting problems back and forth and confusing the labor leaders. I did that also with the colonel in Washington, DC[,] who was head of labor relations. We kicked problems back and forth. I would say, that bastard in Washington doesn't know what he's doing. He would do the same thing, and blame me for all the problems. It worked great. We kept kicking them around until they disappeared.

We had a one-day work stoppage, by the pipefitters and plumbers. We didn't have much trouble. Joe Keenan, secretary-treasurer of the Building Trades Council, came out from Washington to help us when there were potential problems. He was a great help to us. When I talked to Keenan, I had to guard against making dirty cracks about unions. You got the feeling he was one of you.[59]

Matthias's recollection graphically connects the elements of the District's union strategy: deal with Internationals, using them to control the locals; call in their representatives from headquarters and treat them as if they were part of a management team and not the champions of workers against management; and then use the power, extent, and baffling nature of the project's management system to confuse opponents, stalling for time, scattering opposition, providing an impenetrable bank of bureaucratic fog between the "enemy" and its goal.

The District was a military reservation and an essential wartime industry, so its workers could not formally strike. Throughout the home front this restriction on strikes served to change the nature of labor disputes. In part this occurred because many of the industries targeted as essential to the war effort exploited the opportunity afforded by the no-strike clause to their advantage. Without strikes called from the national platform of a union's central administration, and with these International headquarters increasingly wooed by government and military alike, disputes typically took the form of wildcat strikes, sudden work stoppages, local slowdowns, or vocal disputes between local officials and management.[60]

District officials followed the lead of management throughout the home front by calling on the Internationals to exercise discipline over the unions and step in to prevent such disputes. Where the District deemed the response to be inadequate, it could threaten to dismiss recalcitrant unions and call for new representation—or even no representation at all.

Playing unions off against each other kept individual unions from becoming too powerful, and it limited cooperation among unions wherever possible. At Hanford, for example, as early as September 1943, District officials manipulated the wage scales of various crafts and professions to prevent individual unions from becoming more powerful and to encourage conflict and competition between unions, such as the mechanics and the machinists, which might with equal likelihood supervise the same workers.[61]

Using the Internationals to control the locals meant retraining some union officials so that their allegiance moved from the worker to the job. In one case at least, it required the direct intervention of a site commanding officer to do this. Dave Beck, the now-legendary Teamster's International vice president, would, after the war, become the embodiment of big-union corruption and viciousness, a national disgrace whom antilabor politicians could hold up when they sought a symbol of the depravity of unionism. Even during the war he was famous for his wholesale manipulations of the labor market to his own ends. When housing was tightest and times were most desperate at the Hanford site, Beck, who controlled the West Coast teamsters, began slowing up the transportation of prefab housing to Hanford. He was the beneficiary of the full District treatment. He received a visit from Colonel Matthias and a military intelligence officer. By the time they were done with him, he'd capitulated entirely, to the extent, even, of agreeing to allow the District to edit the teamster's newspaper. Matthias and Groves had found their ideal union leader—suspicious of locals, contemptuous of workers, corrupt and corruptible, hungry for power and obsequious toward those who had it. Matthias was, obviously, pleased. "I do not believe that there will be more difficulty from that Union as it appears that Mr. Beck rules the locals without question," he wrote, with evident satisfaction.[62]

The presence of military intelligence at the meeting with Beck reflected the surreptitious side of the District's struggle to retain control over the sites, their occupants, and the lives they led. Spies and "informants" riddled every part of the District's culture, and labor was not immune. In November 1943, "a confidential and reliable informant" reported union organizing activity to intelligence officials, who then called for the head of the Oak Ridge site to monitor "any rumors or other reports concerning this item." A handwritten note by an A. E. Kyle went to the District in July 1944, reporting a similar organizing Oak Ridge attempt; there was a flurry of activity between military intelligence and the FBI trying to determine whose informant he was. Informants infiltrated secret union meetings held offsite, including one concerning inadequate recreation, spoiled meat, timed restroom breaks, and other grievances. Similar programs were in place at Hanford, as well.[63]

In the case of the grievance meeting at Oak Ridge, District labor officials had good reason to be concerned, at least from their standpoint. Just a day before, two workers involved in a dispute had refused to reveal their badge numbers to authorities and ended up running; one was caught and taken to the stockade. The result was a spontaneous work stoppage, and a crowd of workers who had watched the incident organized a protest march, "but the men found that the guards had set up machine guns and had tear gas so the workers caused little disturbance."[64]

This incident brought into graphic relief the usually hidden threat of violence that lay underneath the District's show of accommodation and compromise, its rhetoric of cooperation and communality in the common goal of winning the war. This was the final extreme: armed conflict between angry protesters and authorities ready to unleash tear gas and machine-gun fire in order to "restore order."

How well did this entire net of laws, regulations, and threats work in inducing workers to remain on the site and to labor to the District's satisfaction? Certainly workers took the threats seriously. A rent increase in the barracks at Clinton due to take effect on March 1, 1944, brought a protest petition from a number of workers, arguing that workers on the site were effectively captive to the whims of site administrators. But the petition's tone was anything but militant; it ended not with a demand but a request: "that any man desiring a termination for this reason be given a clear release."[65]

This episode provides some sense of the way these programs worked: not in isolation, but as part of the elaborate culture of covert coercion in which the District became increasingly expert as the project continued, its scope expanded, and the District's bureaucracy exploded in size and power. Its goal—to intimidate workers and their leaders into silence and obedience—was reached not simply through deliberate acts and regulations, but through engendering a climate of fear, in which rumor and the symbolic scapegoat could serve as well as a ream of regulations. In this case, the District had the power to refuse statements of availability, to evict workers, even to charge selected residents whatever it wished for housing, to make life miserable by arousing resentment among other workers, residents, and the schoolmates of one's children. In fact the District could never truly force someone to stay on the job. Yet this was the impression these workers had—that the cumulative effects of District strategies had made them prisoners and their only resort was impotent supplication.

To understand the full flavor of this process, we may look to Hanford in 1944, and the cases of pipe fitters and electricians. These crafts were essential to both the Hanford and Oak Ridge projects. Every building in the factory areas employed miles and miles of pipe, laid out in tortuous mazes, in which precision was essential. Serpentine miles of wire accompanied the pipes, often in necessary but potentially catastrophic proximity to one another. Water to cool the atomic piles in which controlled nuclear reactions alchemized uranium to plutonium ran through pipes; chemical separation required the piping of the toxic materials from stage to stage. In both instances, once processing began, the pipe was effectively sealed off by a wall of toxicity and radioactive poison. Remember Leona Libby and Enrico Fermi, wandering through the separation plants, "along the empty and echoing balconies of the canyon, checking pipes and valves, going step by step through the process as yet tested only in pilot-plant stage," and finding "only one mistake . . . a pipe that had been blocked off in a maze of pipes." Libby described the plans from which she and Fermi worked as "plumbing diagrams," and yet "the plants . . . had to be provided with centrifuges and valves and other handling equipment, all of which were operated remotely from behind 7-foot-thick concrete walls, using periscopes and TV cameras to view work performed by remotely operated mechanical hands using various tools." Aluminum tubing, stainless steel pipes, cast-iron and copper and ceramic: all these required the expertise of pipe fitters before they could carry the process materials through the elaborate distillation and purification stages. These processes also required electrical power to run them and to control them—wiring between the machinery and the remote controls, the gauges and the monitors that provided contact, however attenuated, between the operator and the action (fig. 31).[66]

But pipe fitters and electricians were in high demand throughout the defense industrial sector. (At Oak Ridge, pipe fitters assembled equipment for the gaseous diffusion process and electricians drew together the distant parts of the various processes into orchestrated wholes. There, too, the district engineer reported desperate shortages of workers.) Skilled workers who came to Hanford found the work environment grueling and day-to-day operations dangerous in the extreme. As labor shortages had appeared, Du Pont, Matthias, and Groves had all reacted by attempting to squeeze more productivity out of those workers they had. The means reached downward to the most picayune attempts to extract a minute here, a minute there, in the hopes it would add up to real savings. Labor managers told Hanford workers that transportation from Hanford Camp to the worksite would no longer be considered part of the workday—workers would make the trip on District buses (often taking over an hour each way) on their own time. Workers were told that putting their tools and equipment away after work would now have to occur on their own time, but disarray in the tool areas would be a punishable offense. In order to save pipe-fitting labor, District and Du Pont labor specialists began to shift labor to other crafts, resulting often in a frustrating loss of efficiency as fitters waited for the riggers to show up to do something.

All this gained particular poignancy after an accident at Hanford in the early summer of 1944 in which seven workers died. It was a routine industrial accident: a tank, being moved into position for installation, dropped from the crane, crushing the workers underneath. Because some of those who died were pipe fitters, local union officials moved swiftly to press for changes in safety regulations. Rebuffed by the District, they attempted to appeal but lost again. Then, meeting with Matthias, they cut a devil's bargain that might exemplify the District's goal in regard to labor. Giving up their rights to have local representatives on site, they gained in return an agreement that the District itself would collect union dues from all appropriate workers and siphon the money to the International office.[67]

This conference represented the conclusion of the District's program to fundamentally modify labor relations at the Hanford site. It meant the evisceration of recalcitrant locals and their replacement by "members . . . of the grade of International Representatives." It signaled the basic deal, whereby the unions were granted a cooperative relation with management (to the extent, even, that management collected dues for the unions), in return for which they abandoned their role as spokesman for workers and antagonist to management. Prevented from holding grievance meetings or sending their business agents onto the site, representatives of the International instead found themselves holding "informational meetings" on the site—meetings concerning issues essential to management, not to labor.[68]

The strategy of labor relations worked out in the meetings of early June dominated relations thereafter. The rules were straightforward: do not intervene in labor disputes at the local level—bump them up to the International, and then work with representatives from that office; make all requests of the International, letting orders work

FIG. 31 *Pile Pressure Control Panel,* Hanford. Photo by Robley Johnson or assistant. Manhattan District History, courtesy National Archives.

downward through them. When a conflict arose between pipe fitters and riggers concerning who was supposed to transport pipe from one area to another, for example, Matthias issued instructions that Du Pont was to ignore the matter and let the army work directly with the International, thereby cutting out the local representatives. Matthias's description of the philosophy behind their decision was apt: "We do not feel there would be any difficulty if the headquarters of the unions would get together and make a decision."[69]

But this technique was not necessarily successful. Instead, it could serve as an inflammatory gesture. This is what occurred in another dispute with the local pipe fitters during that summer. On July 22, 1944, Matthias reported that "General Groves called concerning the report on the activity of the State A. F. of L. Convention in which they passed a resolution charging that union representatives were barred from this project, that men were being killed in accidents resulting from unsafe practices and that the Du Pont Company seemed to be using the military situation as a cloak for anti-labor activities." Groves's concern about the AFL meeting reflected the entire range of difficulties concerning labor on the project. Whereas Groves and the army considered themselves to be behaving in the best manner to engender efficient, rapid results, the labor representatives themselves saw it far differently.[70]

The entire handling of safety issues came to reflect the fundamental conflicts between the army's worldview and that of virtually every American institution outside the boundaries of the Manhattan Project. For Groves, Matthias, and the others, safety was a private, internal matter; they were responsible for safety, and they must be trusted to operate in everyone's best interests. They alone could balance the competing interests of the project, interests that set the safety of the workers, the rights of individuals, the values of surrounding communities, and even the basic values of a national culture against the necessities of war—the safety of millions of soldiers, the possible future of American values, even culture itself, threatened by totalitarian forces.

But the workers, and their union locals, saw matters in an entirely different way. Their working conditions were manifestly unsafe, and they were forbidden to investigate the dangers, to speak of the dangers, to strike or even threaten to strike over those dangers. It was *they* who called for congressional investigation, and it was that threat that resulted in Groves's action to improve safety procedures—though it was accompanied by heavy-handed arm-twisting on Groves's part to assure that the congressional investigation be halted before it began.[71]

Clearly the threat of a Congressional investigation lay not in the possibility that it would require new safety procedures on the part of Du Pont—Groves's order did as much. Nor was it simply a fear that the District's secret mission would be revealed. Rather such an investigation signaled a far deeper danger to the Manhattan Project— the danger that Congress might dismantle the complex hierarchy of power, the symbiotic relationship between power and secrecy, the compartmentalization of all activity on the project, and, most important, the isolation of the project. Groves and the rest of the District hierarchy agreed that congressional investigation would result in congressional intervention, and that secrecy calls alone would not be sufficient to prevent this.

Why, we may ask, did they believe this to be so? What the army feared—and perhaps understood, as well—was that congressional investigation would reveal how completely the project was at odds with the basic values of American democracy of its time, even with wartime patriotism and sacrifice taken into account. Everything about the project's relations with the outer world thus far, beginning with the condemnation of the sites and extending to the development of boundaries separating each of them from the surrounding communities, to the refusal to allow congressional investigators on the sites, to the controlling of press access, managing of information, and stifling of dissent: all these represented extremes of the MED's drift from democratic ideals to authoritarian "necessities." The army feared that allowing a congressional investigation of even so simple a matter as safety would result in revelations of just how closely the Manhattan Project had come to resemble its enemy, and how subtly, yet significantly, the enemy of the project had come to embrace not just the Nazis and the Japanese, but Americans as well.[72]

This was why, in case after case, congressional investigators found themselves rudely treated. At Hanford, congressmen stood fuming at the gates on more than one occasion; those who were allowed onsite entered under only the most restrictive of circumstances, and only after their power to damage the program had been unmistakably made clear. Matthias, Nichols, Groves, and others understood how threatening such intervention might be, and they risked a great deal in opposing congressional teams.[73]

In the end, the army's resolution of the larger and the smaller issues of labor and workers' rights served to shore up its position that it must serve as an authoritarian force in order to get the job done. While on the one hand the highest military powers twisted arms to silence the call for congressional investigation, those same forces were able to force the issue of labor conflict to an unhappy resolution.

This most devastating denouement concerned the pipe fitters, who were in such short supply, whose work was so essential to the plants at Hanford and so dangerous to themselves. There the District managed to stifle the locals, coopt the International, and thoroughly intimidate the individual workers, all of which provided what Matthias called "a wholesome influence" sure to "get a good deal more production per man in the future than we have in the past."[74]

The District's campaign was further strengthened at a meeting in late August, at which the WPB and the War Department acted as a team to strong-arm the Internationals. Undersecretary of War Patterson declared that carpenters, boilermakers, and machinists *could* take over nonskilled pipe-fitter work; that the army was itself going into competition with the pipe fitters' union by furloughing "150 to 200 steamfitters" from the army—"and these men will be used whether they are union members or not." This strong-arm tactic had its effect—it forced union officials to guarantee that "the union will make every effort to feed men to the project."[75]

By August 30, 1944, Patterson's intervention with the national union of pipe fitters had resulted in an extraordinary set of agreements at the local level, giving a number of other unions the right to work at traditional pipe-fitter tasks without transfer out of their regular unions. At the same time, the pipe fitters' union agreed to begin a newly aggressive recruitment campaign of its own, not least in order to provide its own members to do the work at Hanford.

And yet the entire campaign failed in one of its ultimate goals—to keep workers from striking. For while the International agreed to follow the District line to the letter, its representatives lost their credibility in the process, and the local representatives regained worker support. Suddenly there began to erupt a series of wildcat strikes and stoppages—activities that occurred despite the union agreements.

The top managers at the District did not hesitate in responding to this new threat by using even more draconian tactics. The District's first response was to call in the Internationals, using them to force acquiescence at the local level. On the site and at the workplace, the next stage involved isolating and harassing local strike leaders, evicting them from the site and threatening them if they returned. Matthias reported that "one of the agitators was found to be a man who had been referred here for work but had not started to work and he was removed from the project this afternoon. After the discussion with him it is felt that he will not be the cause of further trouble. Other agitators are being identified as fast as possible."[76]

The physicist R. R. Wilson clarified just what it meant to be "identified" and "removed from the project" when he recounted the way a District "labor relations expert" handled an organizer from the electrical workers' local. When Wilson reported that the man was onsite, the District officer suggested: "'Why don't you let me talk to him a bit.'. . . A few days later, still no report about the meeting. 'But what was the result of your discussion?' I asked. 'Doc,' he said, 'It's hardly worth mentioning. . . . I just beat the hell out of him. . . . so he went away.'"[77]

At the same time, District informants were pursuing a third strategy, intervening in union meetings and presenting themselves as representatives of workers, forming committees "organized . . . [to] develop grievances and . . . present the entire problem to Colonel Barker [of the Washington labor area] when he arrives next week."[78]

By September 1944, everyone at Hanford knew that soldiers were coming in to do the work of the resisting pipe fitters. Only a few days before, Matthias had arranged with Du Pont's Church to have the first shipment of furloughed soldiers brought to Walla Walla to receive their instructions. The deal was clear: "they will work for us as civilians," Matthias ordered, and "if their services are not satisfactory, return . . . to Walla Walla for reinduction. This will give adequate control. . . . Colonel Barker intends to be here to give them an indoctrination talk at Walla Walla before they begin to work. He wants me to be present at the first meeting; after that we will handle this indoctrination discussion."[79]

From the first, Matthias saw the soldier-scabs as examples and warnings to the men onsite, and he was clearly happy with this arrangement. The new men, relieved of the fear of assignment to the bloody battlegrounds of Europe and the Pacific, were, he reported, "very much interested and very enthusiastic and it is felt will work here and help the job materially. None of them wants to stay in the army." It was a perfect combination—men so grateful for mustering out that they would work enthusiastically and without question, knowing that disobedience would merit return to the front. And these men served as warnings and goads at once—they threatened existing pipe fitters with their most general fear (shortened working hours and thus smaller paychecks), while providing vocal examples of the dangers of being fired, losing the statement of availability, being drafted, and finally sent to the battlegrounds.

The worker-soldiers did their work, in all the ways Matthias hoped they would. By September 20, he reported that "the pipe fitters are now working much better than they have in the past many months." Reporting to General Groves on the twenty-first,

Matthias credited the soldiers with enabling contractors to use intimidation tactics much more effectively; the evisceration of the union grievance process, the threat of firing, and the reports of the pipe-fitting soldiers about life on the front had served as effective deterrents—all of these had "jolted the pipe fitters considerably and made them somewhat less independent" and Du Pont managers were now "vigorously firing anyone who is loafing or otherwise not producing."[80]

Though these labor retention programs may seem extreme, there was a further and perhaps final step in the District's march from democracy to authoritarianism: convict labor. But the Manhattan District applied a peculiarly American twist to this age-old tactic of totalitarian states at war: it introduced free enterprise. Rather than running the convicts itself, it contracted with a convict-labor corporation and sold the products of convict labor back into the prison system, in the form of canned goods to be used as part of the prison diet.

This experiment took place in Hanford's fruit orchards, in the summer of 1943, that first summer of eviction, when workers and ex-residents alike bedeviled District officials by poaching the fruit. By July, the plans had moved to the final stages of negotiation. Federal Prison Industries, Incorporated, a corporation using convicts from the McNeal Island penitentiary, would take over the entire agricultural area, pruning, weeding, maintaining, and guarding the crops, harvesting them, and then shipping them to the penitentiary, where they would be processed—the fruits canned and used in prison diet, and the surplus sold on the open market. Groves was enthusiastic; the program satisfied his needs for cost savings, for secrecy and control, and for a disciplined labor force.[81]

To run a prison camp by itself would have risked profound political damage. But this was the beauty of subcontracting out the convict labor. As a Prison Industries representative named Squier told Colonel Matthias in a meeting on June 10, 1943, "their experience has been that few, if any, prisoners escape from such a type of installation." Prison Industries officials knew just which workers to use on such an installation, and the best way to control them. By the end of the fall, the camp was a permanent fixture of the Hanford site. As the District's official historian reported in 1946, the camp worked especially well because Prison Industries staffed the camp with the very best of prisoners: three hundred special inmates, predominantly "conscientious objectors," who "were easy to handle in field operations" and less likely to escape.[82]

But there is another issue hidden beneath the memos and contracts; a question of what might be called the *relative humanity* of prisoners, laborers, managers, and military officials. By February, when the head of Prison Industries strove to extend his labor force with the introduction of other contract laborers, Matthias had set up a hierarchy of human value, which translated neatly into the geography of danger on the vast site. At the top was the category of normal outside workers, who had to stay off the radiation danger zone demarcated by District scientists and medical officials. Below them were women and children already onsite, who could work and play within this area but still sleep at a distance from the piles and plants. And then there were the convicts, who would do all the work in the areas dangerously close to the production facilities themselves. One need not be a social theorist to see that Matthias's list was a *sub rosa* ranking of the value of these groups to the District.[83]

Prison Industries was to serve the District well in another way. Agreements worked out in January 1945 provided the District with prison labor to dismantle the Hanford Camp after its evacuation in mid-February when the production facilities would reach production stage. This resolved a basic difficulty encountered by Matthias and Church. They were facing scheduling problems because they could not begin production while thousands of war workers lived in Hanford Camp, so close to the proximity of the atomic pile designated 100F. Letting prisoners do the dismantling meant that "civilian" lives would not be risked by requiring them to work at close proximity to both pile and chemical separations facilities. The result would be, in Matthias's words, "a very economical way to get labor done."[84]

The dismantling contract with Prison Industries was worked out in Washington at a meeting with Groves, Matthias, and representatives from the Federal Bureau of Prisons on February 17, 1945. There the District decided that they would modify the contract to sweeten it, "in view of the fact that the Prison Industries suffered a severe loss during the last season"—a bad harvest had minimized profits. And the group discussed the question of who would profit directly from the sale of processed fruit once the Prison's needs had been satisfied.[85]

The prisoners began demolition on May 21, 1945, while pile operations and chemical separation were in full swing. But this arrangement did not sit well with labor leaders in the surrounding communities. From June on, there were objections coming into the District concerning the use of nonunion labor on the site. Matthias explained more than once to labor union representatives that the combination of security and danger to workers in the area precluded traditional contract labor. But by the fall, the issue had reached the ears of Washington's Senator Mitchell and Representative Holmes, and Matthias met with them on October 9 to justify the situation. He "explained to them the basic purpose behind the dismantling of the camp by prisoners and explained the entire set-up of prisoners taking care of the orchard land and other agricultural land on the project. Both Senator Mitchell and Representative Holmes seemed to be satisfied with the explanation."[86]

But less than a month later, Matthias had to respond to a similar complaint from Senator Magnuson. And Groves himself finally decided that the dismantling contract with Prison Industries was more trouble than it was worth, ordering Matthias on October 31 "to stop the use of prisoners at the Hanford Camp for dismantling purposes."[87]

Still, Federal Prison Industries kept its convict laborers on the site through the new year. On December 6, 1946, six months after the end of the war, District and Federal Prison Industries officials met to work out arrangements so that dismantling could stop but other work would replace it "that would keep the Prison Industries' camp busy during their off agricultural period."[88]

The final episode in this saga may be the most bizarre. Writing in 1946, the District's official historian reported the end of the program. "Originally the FPI [Federal Prison Industries, Inc.] farmed approximately 1300–1500 acres," he reported, "but by 1946, this area had dropped to 800, from which excellent yields were obtained in fruit, produce, and hay, while fruit on the remaining portion of orchards inside Richland proper was sold to the village residents on a self-pick or picked basis." Despite the "excellent yields," however, Prison Industries closed down: "After the cessation of hostilities, the number of conscientious objectors decreased and it became difficult to supply the camp with inmates because of custodial problems presented by the more hardened type of offenders."[89]

Unspoken in this entire debate was the fate of the fruit and other crops themselves. After January 1945, the fields began to be dusted with a thin film of toxic and radioactive material (of which iodine 131 was only one component), precipitated from the clouds of emission spewing from the waste stacks of the Hanford Engineer Works. The materials that had leached from the leaking and overflowing toxic waste tanks filtered down to the water table and were taken up into the root structures of trees and crops alike. The fruit harvests went west to McNeal Island, where they served in part as food for prisoners, in part as the raw materials for the prison's lucrative food canning program. The canned and processed fruits, vegetables and herbs went out on Lend-Lease, to army and navy distribution centers, and onto the open market, where they fed a ration-hungry nation. The hay, harvested by conscientious objectors and (later) "the more hardened type of offenders," went to local dairy farmers, where the iodine 131 within the grasses moved into the milk and thence to the bottles of babies and the glasses of children and adults while the other precipitates, with their longer half-lives, were ingested as well.[90]

The poison, the secrecy, the hidden effects of this food program might serve as a metaphor for the larger effects of the District's labor policy, a policy capped by the contract with Federal Prison Industries. For this labor program, growing as it did out of the District's larger imperatives of efficiency at all costs, exploited the secret nature of the site, and the special rights of wartime, to devise a new calculus of labor relations. On District sites, workers were chattel to be brought in and kept on however possible. The welfare of workers was never a goal in its own right; rather it was a necessary evil to be attended to if required to attract workers or to keep them only when all other programs were insufficient.

Yet none of these programs of coercion was ever sufficient. Perhaps as a result of the resistance of American workers to the use of duplicity and force, perhaps simply as a result of the addictive quality of coercion on managers, military officers, and bureaucrats already predisposed to use force over negotiation, each strategy required a successor even more compulsory and compulsive, while each program itself compelled its own modification into more and more extreme forms.

Within the Manhattan District, as elsewhere within the war economy, workers meant white men first. But white men weren't enough. Black Americans, Mexican-Americans, Native Americans, women: all came to the District to further its work.

Even before the war, "Negroes" and "colored people" had formed a significant part of the workforce in the areas where hard labor at low wages was the norm—particularly in construction. The wartime draft exaggerated this condition. Because military officials feared an integrated military fighting force and could not easily figure out how to deal with black soldiers, the draft took a disproportionate number of white male workers, leaving the civilian workplace increasingly "colored" and female. If the District was to fulfill its mandate for rapid deployment of a new weapon, it would have to hire nonwhite workers.[1]

This was the case both before and after the charged circumstances that brought about President Roosevelt's Executive Order 8802, of June 25, 1941, which declared that "there shall be no discrimination in the employment of workers in defense industries or government." Roosevelt's order was his attempt to defuse an impending crisis in race relations precipitated by the March on Washington Committee, which had organized a massive mobilization of black Americans and their allies to call for an end to racial discrimination in the military and in defense industries alike.[2]

But presidential directives do not change a nation overnight, if ever. In the complex interweaving of social and cultural pressures that is reduced to the deceptive term "race relations," the Manhattan Engineer District acted out its central themes. The District did, over time, develop what might loosely be called a policy on race, though haphazardly and without much conscious planning. It is found not in any specific record but in a string of often-conflicting memos and orders, in records of official and unofficial meetings, and in the memories of workers. Had it been formulated as a policy it would have adhered, roughly, to the following six directives.

1. **Hire reluctantly.** Though presidential order, federal regulation, and strict necessity all required the hiring of "colored workers," the District did so only when it was absolutely necessary. Early on, Groves and other administrators and planners vacillated between using the military nature of the project to keep the District entirely white and exploiting the availability of black workers (particularly in the South) to expedite production, lower labor costs, and keep white workers on their toes.[3]

Expansion of the entire project quickly put an end to that tack. In addition, the subcontracting policy of the Corps of Engineers virtually guaranteed that part of the workforce would be black. Construction companies, especially, routinely employed black men to do certain tasks judged too dirty or disreputable for whites. Wartime wage stabilization froze those wage schedules, and scarce labor made it even less likely that white men would move into those jobs. Still, the District itself did little or nothing to encourage labor integration. As late as June 1943, when the federal government's Fair Employment Practices Commission (FEPC) began an investigation of racial discrimination by Du Pont at the Hanford site, there were no "colored men" on the plant site, according to Du Pont's monthly labor records.[4]

This investigation represented a watershed in American racial politics. Less than a month before, Roosevelt had emboldened the FEPC with a new leader, an increased budget, and independent status as an investigating organization. On top of that, he had given the FEPC the power to conduct public hearings on its antidiscrimination cases.[5]

The FEPC's investigation spurred action in two directions. The first was defensive and bureaucratic. The District was deeply committed to the status quo, and that meant racial segregation wherever possible. Instinctively, the District allied itself with the Du Pont corporation and against Roosevelt's FEPC. But the fact that the District had no housing for nonwhite workers left corps and corporation defenseless against FEPC charges; they could not argue that they were planning to "integrate" Negro workers with whites, since military policy was to keep races sequestered one from the other. And so groundbreaking began on a "Negro camp" shortly after the FEPC investigation began. Still, progress was suspiciously slow.[6]

The idea was to gradually introduce nonwhite workers—enough to satisfy the need for construction and unskilled laborers, enough to keep the FEPC at bay, but not so many as to disrupt matters. Behind this reluctance lay an understanding of the prejudices of the highly desirable class of laborers known as "boomers"—experienced, efficient defense workers who traveled from one crash defense construction program to another, looking for overtime, bringing their tools and their trailers, traveling in premade communities that required little supervision or costly support services. But "boomers" were predominantly lower-class southerners notorious for their hatred of Negroes and Mexicans. These were the men officials believed were most likely to protest, leave, or strike when they saw they would be working alongside Negroes.[7]

The District responded by developing a quota for colored workers, a number sufficient to satisfy investigators, keep the workforce up to size, and remind white workers of the potential pool of replacement workers should the urge to strike hit them, yet not so many as to foment racial conflict. At Hanford, that number began as roughly 10 percent of the construction workforce, and reached as high as 20 percent at the peak of construction. At Oak Ridge, it was *exactly* 10 percent of the labor population. There, reports and statistics indicate that the District set a quota, and that the subcontracting corporations maintained that quota to the man—in blatant violation of federal law.[8]

Some workers saw the connection to District policy, took the risk of retribution, and complained about the paucity of positions available to black workers. One of these was Carlton Smith, a Hanford worker. Smith had protested to Washington that there was "discrimination against negro workers at Hanford," first in construction (his may well have been the complaint that led to the FEPC's investigation) and later in operations. He wrote to Senator Harry Truman, whose committee was responsible for investigating such charges, and to the president himself.[9]

Smith's complaints set an investigation in motion; a query went out, and Matthias replied. "At the present time, there are only two colored workers on the operations payroll; both in the labor classifications"—that is to say, employed as janitors or the like. The colonel gave the usual reasons—"there have been very few applications from negroes and in several cases those who have applied have obtained other jobs before the process was completed out here." This was tacitly disingenuous. For years, the District had been beating the bushes for workers, threatening bureaucrats in various powerful federal agencies, supervising a small army of labor recruiters nationwide in order to gain the workers if needed. But that energy went toward recruiting white workers. Blacks had to apply; if they didn't, District officials blamed them for, in Matthias's words, "indifference and impatience."[10]

2. **Use colored workers only for low-skilled and low-paid work.** On the District, racial employment policy should have followed the national trend toward increasing participation of colored workers in the wartime workforce. As the war progressed, more and more black workers entered the labor force, and more and more of them moved into areas from which they had previously been interdicted—government work, skilled jobs, professions.[11]

On the national scene, this process occurred with what Negroes considered glacial reluctance. On the District, it never happened at all. The MED shunted nonwhite workers to traditionally lowest-status categories and kept them there by a number of creative strategies. Negro workers on the District were disproportionately hired as "helpers" to better-paying occupations. They were chauffeurs, but less commonly truck drivers; they were chauffeur's assistants, and very rarely mechanics; when they were cement finishers, subcontractors assigned them to roads and runways, rather than buildings—and they earned 47½¢ less per hour. In all of these areas two strategies coincided: keep Negro workers out of skilled areas; and redefine their worker classifications so they'd be paid less well and closed out of opportunities to rise in the job classification hierarchy.[12]

All this resulted, no doubt, from largely unconscious decisions made by recruiters, managers, and upper-level officials in the corporations and the District and exacerbated by a national trend in defense industries to keep colored workers out of the skilled trades. The AFL's member unions tended to be the more skilled unions, and the AFL had a whites-only policy. The District worked with AFL unions as part of its agreement with labor, which meant that no colored workers made it into the trades where AFL unions controlled the workforce—though that changed some as the war progressed and employers and unions alike faced increasing pressure to hire more broadly to overcome labor shortages. Nevertheless, on District sites, colored workers entered the ranks of the skilled professions only when they were necessary to administer to all-colored populations that white workers (nurses at Oak Ridge, for example) refused to serve. When they worked in the Operations Division at all, it was as janitors or clean-up men or bottle washers.[13]

3. **Observe the local status quo, as long as that status quo militates against integration and improved conditions for colored workers.** On August 18, 1943, Hanford's Colonel Matthias had one of his periodic peacekeeping meetings with Washington's Governor Langley. The two "discussed the general social problem with the project"; Langley was "concerned with . . . the social dislocation caused by a high concentration of work as it might affect the postwar position of the State. He hopes that arrangements can be made to return most of the construction workmen back to their original centers of activity, particularly the negroes. . . . I feel that Governor Langley is definitely one of our best friends."[14]

At both the industrial sites, the District used local law and local sentiment as the explanation for policies that compartmentalized work and living by race, and set nonwhite workers at the bottom. In Washington, D.C., this meant maintaining a general posture of racial suspicion, at least, and may well have dictated the District's *de facto* policy of dismissing colored—and especially black—workers as the labor crunch eased, and making certain those dismissed workers went away. Regional suspicion of nonwhite workers also pressured the District to keep its nonwhite workers onsite wherever possible, from the fear at least of damaging fragile relations with outside communities.[15]

In the state of Washington, outside pressure from surrounding communities influenced Hanford administrators in their decisions to build Negro housing, recreation facilities, and other amenities. At Oak Ridge, state Jim Crow laws served the purpose. Workers had to be rigidly separated by race, and all facilities had to conform to the Jim Crow laws. Black children were forbidden not only from white classrooms, but from entire schools. Indeed, most facilities had to be under separate roofs, in separate areas.

At Oak Ridge, however, the District required Negro workers to live offsite. This wasn't the original plan. Late in 1942, when he was still relatively new to absolute control over the District, Groves instructed the Oak Ridge site planners to satisfy local law by producing a classically separate-but-equal town for Negro workers, called, simply, "Negro Village."[16]

Groves's order specified that the Negro Village have the "same construction for same class of employee, black and white." But his instructions masked a more pervasive opposition to the idea of humane living quarters for Negroes. Beneath his command, subordinates made it clear, directly and by implication, that the ideal solution was a substandard and isolated shantytown for Negroes. For a while, the plans showed a truly separate-but-equal housing proposal. But it was so nice that planners transformed it into an extension of the whites-only housing area, and left the Negroes to shift for themselves. Negro Village became East Village.[17]

Apparently District officials understood that their decision might meet with some resistance, and they cast about for a rationale. The officer in charge of the building program, Lieutenant Colonel Crenshaw, tried to explain the failure as an outgrowth of the Negro nature. Negroes, he argued, didn't want the fancy houses SOM had designed for them—they liked the shacks and cabins to which they were accustomed, and they would feel obliged to live up to "standards" (his word) too high for them. Negroes—especially Negro women—also understood that their race just wasn't equipped for the discipline and rigor of life onsite, Crenshaw reported. A perfect explanation (countered by the facts, by surveys from Negro workers), it provided the rationale for giving East Village to the whites.[18]

Removing Negro Village from the Oak Ridge plans was an exhilaratingly efficient solution to the problem of setting up a site in compliance with Jim Crow. Apartheid in the workplace had been a part of the plan from the beginning; at Groves's urging, Stone and Webster had arranged for "Negroes to have [a] separate clock alley" so that they could punch in to work without encountering white workers. Groves had isolated the races even further—he had ordered the planners to provide a separate road, "from negro town to store center, fenced off from white village." On the worksites, blacks and whites would work in separate labor gangs, with separate foremen, under the authority of different unions, having moved to their worksites in separate buses or (later) separate areas of the same buses. Keeping Negro housing off the site saved considerable expense, avoided accusations by jealous white locals, unions, and workers, and kept the FEPC off the District's back, all at once.[19]

4. **Espouse separate but equal; create separately and unequally.** "The responsibility of the Office of the District Engineer . . . is not to promote social changes . . . but to see that the community is efficiently run and that everybody has a chance to live decently in it," wrote an Oak Ridge official late in 1944.[20]

The concept of decent living differed dramatically by race. As the fate of the Negro Village demonstrated, and as Crenshaw's bizarre rationale underscored, District officials argued that Negroes actually *wanted* substandard conditions. Sometimes, the "requests" for separated facilities, reported by District officers as coming from groups of Negro workers, occurred before there even *were* Negro workers on the sites—an act of extraordinary prescience. And once the District scotched the SOM Negro Village town plan, conditions for nonwhites at Oak Ridge and Hanford rapidly deteriorated. Having recently determined that expansion would require the use of the infamous "hutments" and some portable houses, District planners decided to designate these new and far less desirable dwellings to Negroes first. The substitute for the village was a planned ghetto, comprised of the lowest of all housing types, crammed together, separated from white areas, with a minimum of facilities, and with far more workers in each unit than for the same units in white areas.[21]

At Oak Ridge, both whites and blacks lived in "hutments." These were not the same structures the white workers at Hanford had—*those* were plywood Quonset huts, insulated, heated, even cooled with "desert chillers" in the summer, with separate rooms occupied by two workers, each room with a window. The Oak Ridge hutments were plywood cubes without interior walls; the upper half of each wall was "window"—but window without glass and usually without a screen, and "secured" with large, hinged, drop-down "shutters" that could only be pulled up out of the way, or locked down. In the summer, residents had a choice: they could leave the shutters up, affording some ventilation, but sacrificing all privacy and leaving the hutments wide open to mosquitoes and other insects, thieves, and pilferers. Or they could leave them locked tight, trading security for a stifling environment that, in summer, could reach an interior temperature of 130 degrees. Within, there was no privacy; the inside was a small open area with bunks and footlockers crowding the space. In summer it was always sweltering. In winter, it was "heated" by an oil stove in the middle of the room.[22]

For any occupant, black or white, the arrangement was miserable. But white hutments had four occupants; colored hutments held five men or six women (fig. 32). The hutments measured 16 x 16 feet. With six bunks and six footlockers crammed into them, there was barely enough room to maneuver around the stove, which, in order to heat the drafty, uninsulated space in winter, often glowed red-hot.[23]

White workers with families lived in houses. Black workers were separated from their families (until late in the war) and treated as single men and women. Single white men and women lived in houses, barracks, or hutments. Single black men and women could live only in hutments. White workers had their housing determined by a complex set of factors; most important was their occupational category and their clout.

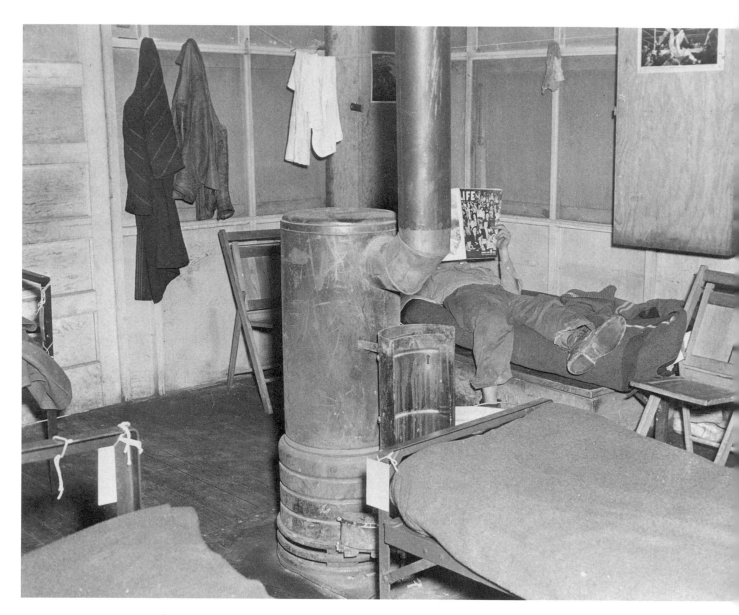

FIG. 32 *Inside Hutment,* Oak Ridge. Photo by James E. Westcott. U.S. Corps of Engineers, Oak Ridge, Tennessee.

Negro operations workers at Oak Ridge could choose one of two job classifications—janitor or laborer. Both were hutment classifications. Negro construction workers worked only the lower classifications; these, too, were hutment classifications. Black workers ended up in the hutments because the District made sure that the lists of accepted black occupations were identical to lists of occupations that destined workers for the hutments.[24]

When, late in the war, the District determined it was necessary to capitulate and provide at least some family housing for Negroes, it converted a string of hutments from the males-only Negro hutment area. There were only enough units converted for twenty-four families, and the entire set had one men's bathhouse and one women's bathhouse. Cooking was done on a coal stove. There was no electricity or running water. Instead of refrigerators, residents used small ice chests. The dangers of sexual assault were high; this was the only area in all of Oak Ridge where women were not separated from single male barracks or hutments by walls and wire fencing.[25]

Throughout Oak Ridge, status lines were roughly drawn by altitude. Those with prestige, high occupational classifications, and clout, lived on what became known as "the Hill"—the hillsides and along the ridges—where they were relatively immune from the cascades of water and the quagmires of dense, claylike mud that covered the lower areas. The Colored Hutment Area was in a lower section, off Scarboro Road, in a mud-encrusted, mosquito-infested swamp of an area. Originally, housing was to be separated from the plant areas, not only by distance but by the expeditious use of ridges to protect the housing areas from possibly catastrophic explosions or noxious emissions. The Colored Hutment Area adjoined the Y-12 electromagnetic uranium enrichment facility. This was not the only time that Negro housing was placed next to a work area in deliberate violation of the instructions of scientists and planners. The District located another colored housing area just outside of the gaseous diffusion enrichment plant.[26]

At Hanford, the housing was generally better throughout, and this applied to the colored facilities, as well. Nonwhite workers had their own areas, but they were located in traditional army-issue barracks. Over the life of Hanford Camp, the District built twenty-one barracks for colored men and seven for colored women; over time, as construction wound down and operations wound up, colored laborers were terminated, while colored women were increasingly needed as maids and domestic help in Richland. So three of the men's barracks were transferred to women.[27]

As at Oak Ridge, however, the hutments were the lowest form of housing, and they were assigned to a far greater proportion of colored than white men—almost exactly three times the percentage of colored men as white men lived in hutments. Hutments offered a convenient means to control the location of colored workers, because they were smaller and easier to build and close up as nonwhite worker populations fluctuated. Since a single barracks held close to two hundred men, opening a new one to accommodate, say, fifty new concrete pourers needed for chemical separations plant construction would be expensive and time consuming. The hutments were prefab, built by Pacific Hutments and easily assembled on the site. In addition, they could be moved and adapted for other uses—hutments served as gasoline stations, as dry cleaners, even as a classified documents storage facility.[28]

The issues surrounding trailers were more complicated, because they were tied in with issues concerning women, children, families, schools—in short, community. Trailers were Hanford's solution to the question of family life on the site. Always an unwilling presence on the District, families introduced nonworkers to the sites, including those expensive inconveniences, children. Families came onto the Hanford site because the original plan to house over half of the workers offsite was an absurd miscalculation, based not only on a major underestimation of the number of construction workers needed, but on an even more unreal picture of the surrounding communities and their abilities to handle those numbers. By mid-spring of 1943, the District knew that Hanford Camp would have to accommodate tens of thousands more than originally estimated, and many of these were families. Trailers were even easier to get than prefab houses, and they were (at least hypothetically) capable of being moved elsewhere once construction was completed. So Du Pont and the District worked together to develop a huge trailer camp.

Cautious about local citizens' reactions to an influx of black families into surrounding communities, the District added a Negro trailer camp to the site, contiguous to the other Negro facilities. But the Negro trailer camp was the last, and smallest, trailer camp built: seventy-six lots. Though black workers comprised about 20 percent of the Hanford construction population at that point, they got only 2 percent of the trailers.[29]

The minimal number of family trailer sites in the Negro area reflected the District's more general attempt to control families via housing policies. With colored families, the issue was complicated by the white stereotype of Negro sexual appetites. Negro families brought Negro women, and District officials were convinced that Negro women would disintegrate the delicate balance keeping Negro male soldiers and workers obedient and civilized.[30]

Bringing Negro families onsite, however, increased the general mass of the nonwhite population, threatening onsite dangers and increasing costs. With the Negro facilities, the District cut costs by offering fewer, and more primitive, facilities—including toilets, urinals, and showers. In the white areas, the District built a bathhouse for every twenty-five residents. In the colored areas, the ratio was 1:38, and the increase meant long lines for showers, even for access to the sinks. Since the laundry tubs were in the bathhouses, the limited number made doing family laundry difficult in the extreme. An SOM report of facilities included a building program change order dated December, 17, 1943; there SOM added "toilet rooms for Negro men and women help" to the stores—"outside, rear access" units shared by men and women and designed to minimize costs and keep the numbers to a minimum, maintaining efficiency and inconveniencing only the Negroes themselves.[31]

District officials used their powers to control, where possible, the type of Negro who lived onsite. Negro workers had to buy their own trailers and bring them onsite—the District did not provide them. And the going rate—about six hundred dollars—helped to limit the camp residents to quiet, responsible, savings-account types.[32]

This sedateness contrasted with the atmosphere within the Negro barracks, where the District allowed a free-for-all atmosphere even more marked than the general laissez-faire attitude within whites-only construction barracks. Here as elsewhere the District distinguished between its responsibilities in the camp and in Richland—Hanford was a wide-open construction camp, controlled by riot squads and police sweeps, while Richland was to be the self-controlled, self-governed middle-class town. In the Negro barracks of Hanford Camp, a third type of law prevailed—the District sought only to prevent violence, lawlessness, and bloodshed from spilling out of the walls and into visible public spaces; it rarely intervened to provide a safe or humane life within the interiors. Nearly forty years after the war was over, Willie Daniels, who had been a laborer, recalled life in the barracks:

> We would go to work and come back and some guy had been there ransacking our room. Once we came back to the barracks, and there were some guys in there scuffling. This guy had another one down, beating him, kicking him with steel-toe shoes, stomping him. He said, "I'll teach you to go in a room and take stuff, I'll bet you won't go in another one." In the barracks, there was drinking and fighting, and carrying on. Oh, man. There'd be gambling in the washrooms, and playing cards. Some of them were professional gamblers, out there to get all the money. I didn't mingle with that bunch, not at all.[33]

Luzell Johnson, also a laborer, confirmed Daniels's report and elaborated on it. He recalled that "every weekend, there was somebody coming through with goods, through the barracks, you understand that? Prostitutes."

Such a lack of policing was distinctly uncharacteristic of the District. Nowhere else on the District except in the Negro quarters was such anarchy permitted, even encouraged; Daniels commented that the barracks were even occupied by nonworkers—apparently the District was not willing to enter the Negro areas to remove those whom it fired or released, as it did with its white workers.

This predominant vision of Negroes as sexual and social savages allowed the District to apply a different standard to the living conditions in the Negro quarters. Recreation for Hanford whites meant a wide diversity of activities, from bowling to elaborate dances with nationally known orchestras. Recreation for Hanford Negroes meant gathering at a primitive drinking-hall with a few add-ons. At the commissaries, whites could play; coloreds could drink.[34]

For all other activities, Negroes went to Mess Hall 5 and to a section of Negro Barracks 201. There (starting in July 1944), they had a recreation hall—a large open area that could be used for "dancing, card games, ping pong, and parties." It was also the site of the "negro church"—although District officials later moved that to what one churchgoer recalled as "an old farmhouse." (By contrast, whites chose among seven different congregations.)[35]

At Oak Ridge, segregation followed the legal mandate of Tennessee's Jim Crow laws, and this made matters clearer and brought into bold relief the differences in life for blacks and whites. At Hanford, there was a Negro area of the movie theaters. At Oak Ridge, Negroes sat on packing crates and a few folding chairs at the colored recreation hall, watching bad 16mm prints of "race" films.[36]

Though the District described the colored recreation hall and the other colored facilities as the equal of their white counterparts, few of those who used them would have agreed. Touring the facilities just after the war's end, the Chicago *Defender* reporter Enoc Waters described the hall as "a large bare barny structure, furnished with a few checkerboards, volleyball net, juke box, dilapidated piano, ping pong table, a few chairs and a projection booth suspended from the ceiling." Mostly, the hall was a place to play cards. In one corner was a punching bag. The usual clientele was almost universally male, and the place was rough. The designation of only one mess hall for Negroes meant that Negroes who missed a meal period or were on odd shifts couldn't go elsewhere to eat; they had to wait for the next meal, which often meant choosing between food and sleep. Recalling the environment decades later, one resident called it, simply, "mean."[37]

Nonwhite children were particularly ill-served by the District. They were doubly unwanted. Children required playgrounds, day-care, and—most difficult of all—schools. At Hanford, there is nothing in the record to suggest how the District dealt with children of black, Hispanic, and Indian workers. Perhaps there were none; perhaps they were segregated in separate classrooms. They do not appear in photographs of children playing in the streets, or in the schools. At Oak Ridge, the record is slightly less cloudy. At first, rather than set up the Jim Crow–mandated separate school, the District just let black children do without. Parents who wanted their children to go to school had to send them to Knoxville's overcrowded colored-only schools twenty-five miles away. Eventually, the District did build a colored elementary school, though high-schoolers always had to endure the daily trip to Knoxville. Girl and Boy Scout troops at Oak Ridge were whites-only. Day-care facilities were whites-only, too.[38]

5. Remain vigilant to limit contact between whites and coloreds. Fear informed labor and racial decisions on the District, particularly a fear of "race riots," of workers in the traditionally racist AFL unions striking to resist working alongside black workers, or of sabotage and subversion brought about by racial strife. Just a month before, the Mobile, Alabama, docks had erupted in a race riot when the WMC integrated work teams at a drydock. District officials feared that the FEPC investigation and the resulting mandate to provide Negro employment and housing on the site would derail progress toward a smooth and efficient workforce by requiring the District to add social and racial justice to the equation.

Their concerns echoed the general tenor of the military concerning nonwhites: fear of insurrection, of riot, of guerrilla warfare and undetermined forms of "unrest which may erupt," and the resulting "necessity of keeping close check on arms and ammunition used by civilian guards in the performance of their duties," to quote a memo to army commanders.[39]

On the sites, District officials shared the suspicion that race bred violence—on both sides. On June 7, 1943, a small pile of papers caught on fire outside Barracks 5-A at Hanford. Quickly doused, it became the focus of an intensive investigation, because Barracks 5-A had been temporarily sequestered for black workers while the Negro camp awaited completion. Reading the fire marshal's report, Colonel Matthias noticed "the peculiar and unusual circumstances of piling paper in such a place," and ordered an investigation by military intelligence. Soon afterward, Matthias noted with what may have been surprise that the "investigation does not disclose any feeling between negroes and whites."[40]

District assumptions about race provoked a gradual shift at Hanford, where (unlike at Oak Ridge) state law did not dictate absolute racial separation. Through the first part of 1943, there had been at least superficial interaction between the races: the Negro barracks were located near to white areas, with a number of shared athletic facilities; Hanford Theater was open to moviegoers of both races; and Negroes were not made to move to the rear when they used the common bus system.

This policy of uneasy integration steadily decreased as Du Pont and Matthias began to open more and more facilities specifically designated for Negroes, in a *de facto* Negro zone. The opening of Mess Hall 5 late in October, for example, enabled the District to cluster Negro social life in a separate area. By the end of 1943, Hanford Camp had its own racial geography.

Still the Hanford Yuletide Carnival that year remained an integrated event. But the actual programs were directed, consciously or not, at white audiences. The "Hilarious full-length 3-act comedy with local cast" that ran for two days was a white hillbilly slapstick. Hanfordites danced nightly to an all-white swing orchestra. And on Wednesday, December 29, the Recreation Program advertised its feature—a "Minstrel Show" with "all the old favorites of blackface comedy." "The treat you've been looking for," bragged the ad, but it was unlikely nonwhite Hanfordites were looking forward to the program, put on by the all-white Clyde and His Dixieland Minstrels.[41]

The next year's carnival was even more elaborate—reflecting the greater urgency of labor retention during the last push of construction. Devising the program required twenty-nine employees plus an advisory committee of thirteen. Planners interspersed a wide variety of temptations, from nationally famous orchestras, puppet troupes, an indoor circus, and local sports contests to "a colorful pageant . . . and a free dinner" on Christmas Day.[42]

But for Negro workers, the program had a different cast. This year, unlike the last, all programs were segregated by race. The promotional brochure graphically pointed up the change; it was set in the form of a calendar, with each day's activities separated into "White" and "Colored" segments. On the first day, white workers got a stage show and a traveling variety show with an all-girl orchestra; colored workers got amateur auditions, a whist and pinochle tournament, and a free movie. That Friday, the celebrity Kay Kyser entertained the whites, followed by a dance to the music of the Weems Orchestra; the colored area featured another whist and pinochle tournament, along with tournaments for checkers and ping pong. In three weeks of intensive entertainment, not once were Negroes offered anything more elaborate than a quiz program and a vaudeville evening with a dance. White children had dances, movies, bingo, caroling, and special programs at their youth center; colored children got nothing.[43]

Because there were no Negroes in the white-collar publicity department, whites wrote the publicity for the colored portion of the programs, and it showed. "Negro actors will present a special pageant . . . on Christmas Eve," announced the *Sage Sentinel*. "Gay music and bright colors will follow at the costume ball to be held the same evening in their Recreation Hall." Yet most of the events relegated for nonwhites lacked the very qualities of gaudiness, of "gay music and bright colors," that District publicists felt were essential to attract colored people. In truth, Negro Christmas at Hanford was a drab, second-class event, done on the cheap.[44]

At Oak Ridge, recreation was a dangerous affair; if you didn't want to get into trouble, black workers recalled later, you stayed away. The Oak Ridge Recreation and Welfare Association administered recreation programs at Oak Ridge; its "volunteer" council was all white. The council worried about wayward youth and juvenile delinquency and funded prevention programs; they were white-only. What programs were planned for Negroes were haphazard and lacked the input of those for whom they were designed. Over the life of the Oak Ridge Recreation and Welfare Association, money entered the coffers disproportionately from colored workers and went out disproportionately to white ones.[45]

6. Prevent the creation of a community. The District sought at each of its sites to sequester blacks in separate facilities, even to the point of setting up separate paths along which workers would walk to and from work. At the same time, the District resisted the conversion of ghetto into community. One way involved simply pretending that there was no Negro community. *Here's Hanford,* the orientation pamphlet given to all arriving workers, described all the facilities but never designated which were for Negroes. Orientation for black arrivees at Oak Ridge was similarly closemouthed.

This policy drove black residents and workers to build counterorganizations, usually covert and informal ones. Over time, these came to serve as nodes for community-building, and that led to protest. District officials viewed these challenges to their authority with alarm and responded quickly. The Oak Ridge Colored Camp Council protested inadequate housing in the fall of 1944; the District reacted by turning the names of the protesters over to military intelligence for investigation. (We can guess their fates, though they are not recorded in the declassified materials.)[46]

By the spring of 1945, the District's Negro community had begun to shrink. This transition placed the District in a difficult position. The previous explosion in demand for Negro workers had produced rough, ill-planned ghettos, populated them with often inadequately screened workers, and engendered the District's policy of using MPs as a sort of border patrol at the edges of the Negro communities and especially the dormitories, resulting in a highly volatile situation. This had been exacerbated by the general tension created through overcrowding, overwork, and inadequate planning. Now the slowdown in construction as the principal plants reached completion meant increased layoffs, higher "standards" for worker behavior, and a new sternness in the workplace and onsite living quarters. Rumors began to circulate that Negroes were being disproportionately fired, and that they were being refused entry into the more desirable housing.

All of this was true, because Negroes lopsidedly filled the ranks of construction laborers and were locked out of the operations skills. The shiftover from construction to operations meant wholesale layoffs of colored workers. Those who remained moved from higher-paying jobs to lower-paying ones—from concrete pouring and truck driving to janitorial and maid work. At Oak Ridge, the District had advertised that managerial families could rest easy: "Separate living quarters in the area will be available for colored maids at a cost of $15.00 per month for single rooms and $10.00 per month each for those occupying double rooms." Now this promise to white employees increasingly underscored the widening gulf between their share of war work and the share designated for colored people. At the Hanford site, construction at Richland ended, and Hanford Camp's closing loomed: Negro workers found they'd become undesirables to be kept out of the new suburban utopia of Richland. In the new paper, the *Richlander,* lively debate about whether Hanfordites making the move from construction to operations should be allowed into the Richland town masked an underlying mandate from Richlanders—keep the Negroes out.

Throughout the District, conflicts soared generally, and racial incidents increased, as Negro workers faced an end to their work and white workers feared they'd be supplanted by cheaper Negro labor shifting over from construction to operations. In Oak Ridge, the conflicts centered on the buses. All the previous summer, the buses (the only place where racial groups were thrust together even minimally) had become increasingly explosive. White riders had begun roughing up Negro workers not quick enough to move to the back of the bus, and Negroes had complained that white bus drivers had refused to pick them up. Rebuffed by District inaction on their complaints, Negroes began to strike back. Rock-throwing incidents by "colored boys," and a series of fracases in which white bus drivers were beaten up and one had his arm broken, signaled the approach to the flashpoint of racial conflict that army officials had identified in an adjutant general's report of January 1945.[47]

That report was a model of sane writing on race in the military. Therein a committee of investigation had urged that the army find ways to bring Negroes a sense of importance, inclusion, and belonging in the wartime military. Move quickly to investigate injustice. Punish quickly and publicly. Open base newspapers and PR materials to Negro news.[48]

The District's own responses rarely followed the sensible recommendations of that report. At Hanford and Oak Ridge, District officials had seized the opportunity afforded by slackening labor demand, and they developed a more punitive style of dealing with "infractions."[49]

Overlaying this harsher style was a patina of public-relations goodwill. Confronted with a racial crisis in the late fall and winter of 1944/45, District officials responded with a public-relations report extolling the adequacy of site facilities for Negroes, dismissing the racial conflicts as isolated "incidents," and declaring the conflicts ended. Luckily for the District, January became August largely without incident, and the war's end changed the context of racial relations at all three sites.[50]

The District's unspoken rules for treatment of minority issues applied with the most force to the industrial sites, and on those sites, to its so-called "colored" and "Negro" populations. But there were others who served similar roles at the margins of District culture. These were "Indians" and "Mexicans"—terms the District used to identify everyone from Navajo and Pueblo traditionalists to Castilian Spanish–Americans.

When labor recruitment was in its worst crisis, the War Manpower Commission had urged that Du Pont recruit Mexicans from the Southwest to the Hanford site, but Matthias pointed out that "the use of this labor will require a third segregation of camp facilities, inasmuch as the Mexicans will not live with the Negroes and the Whites will not live with the Mexicans"—and the WMC had dropped the issue.[51]

As for Native Americans, Hanford's Indian tribe wasn't settled, substantial, or even much known about; indeed, before, during, and after the war, locals and District people alike had a tendency to confuse the local tribe (officially designated the Wanapum, but historically the Chemnapum) with the larger but different Yakima tribe nearby. Mostly the District called the tribe "the Priest Rapids Indians." The tribe consisted of about twenty-five members, loosely affiliated into four families. Too small to serve as a potential source for unskilled or servant labor, the Wanapum became perfect subjects for eviction.

But their culture was alien to the District's—so alien as to make them immune to the District's techniques. They could not be removed by condemnation of their property; the Wanapum had no property. As a District official later reported, "the Priest Rapids Indians . . . believe under their religion that they should not own land." As early as 1855, they had refused to sign reservation and land treaties with the federal and state governments, on the grounds it was sacrilege. They considered the nearby Yakima to be "treaty Indians."[52]

What the Wanapum did own (partly by refusing to sign those treaties) was a set of rights: fishing rights, rights to passage across federal, state, and local lands, rights to harvest certain wild berries and vegetables. Once, long ago (when Lewis and Clark called them the Chemnapum), they had roamed the region in a seasonal movement from one form of food-gathering to another. As white settlement had shrunk their traditional migratory grounds, they had begun to supplement their incomes by working as migratory harvest hands on various crops. Each winter, they returned to the Priest Rapids area, directly opposite the military reservation, living in "thules," reed huts, which they dismantled in the spring. Each fall, they fished the Columbia from land now within the reservation limits, drying and preserving the fish to provide a yearlong source of protein.[53]

When condemnation proceedings began, District officials assumed the Real Estate Branch of the Corps of Engineers would simply "make arrangements" with the Interior Department "to have these fishing rights restricted." But the department refused to act on the District's behalf, and so the District found itself forced "to deal locally," as Matthias wrote in his diary. Negotiations began in February and continued without resolution through September 1943. By that time, the reservation had been emptied, construction was well underway, and the Wanapum were ready for their fall fishing season on the Columbia.[54]

And so the District brought in an intermediary: a Mr. Shotwell, superintendent of the Yakima Indian Agency. Shotwell met first with the tribal family heads, then with the District, and then arranged a meeting of the two sides. From the Wanapum, Shotwell brought "Chief Johnny Buck, Harry Tommy Wash of the tribe, and William Charley, interpreter." Matthias represented the District. The question of winter camping grounds was quickly resolved; the District had no rights (the campground was on the other side of the Columbia from the District's main plot of land), and Matthias graciously ceded those rights in return for complete information on each of the tribe's members, and a promise that those Indians would stay within District-determined geographical parameters. For Matthias and the District, this seemed a small concession; for the Wanapum, who had always before refused to cede their sense of space and the custodianship of land to officials, the agreement may have seemed more momentous.[55]

The matter of fishing rights was far more difficult, and the negotiations revealed with stark clarity the fundamental beliefs of District and Wanapum alike. As Matthias recorded the negotiations in his daily diary: "A number of proposals were offered to the Indians in which they indicated very little interest, among them was a cash settlement equivalent to the value of the fish, a proposal that we deliver to them the amount of fish they would normally catch in a year, [and an agreement] that they would be permitted to fish in the White Bluffs Area this fall, but that they not come back next fall, including a provision for a payment of their fishing privileges."[56]

To Matthias's surprise, the Wanapum representatives refused all three, and the District had to accept a fourth plan:

> It was finally agreed that we provide the Indians with a truck and driver who will, at their request, during the fishing season haul the Indians and the fish from White Bluffs to their camp at Priest Rapids once a day. This would permit the Indians to do their fishing under supervision, it would avoid the necessity of their living and sleeping in the area, and would assure them of as much fish as they now get. A cash settlement, to be paid annually for their privilege to fish and be in that part of the River was rejected by the Chief. His only interest was that he get fish.[57]

Matthias had not understood the core of Wanapum culture: their conjunction of land, space, river, fish, and so much else into a sacred whole that could not be sundered, and from which they themselves could not be excluded. "The earth is the mother of all mankind," Chief Johnny Buck had told a District official, and the Wanapum were tied to their earth through a cycle of migrations and harvests. "We just circle the same way every time," said one Wanapum tribal member. To break that circle was inconceivable. When Johnny Buck refused all three of the District's original offers, he was signaling that belief; it was not a matter of the money, not even a matter of the fish.[58]

Matthias agreed to the compromise; evidence suggests that he and the District saw it as a paper treaty rather than an agreement to be honored. For sometime that winter Johnny Buck wrote a letter detailing the District's failures. The letter, handwritten, went hand to hand from Buck through J. W. May of Priest Rapids, to Mr. Parnell on the reservation, and then to Matthias's assistant, who gave it to the colonel.

> Dear Sir
>
> Why is that we can't go [crossed out] through to Hanford and we'd like you come Sunday because we will be all to gether for a Indians feast so that why we want you to come Sunday and then after that you not see us. We might move for summer stay. We'd like to go through Hanford and Horn where we fish that what we want to know about, and we are stay few more weeks and that why we want you to come Sunday let you see the house we stay in
>
> Must close
> Johnnie
> Buck[59]

Matthias was charmed. On April 2, 1944, he went out to the Priest Rapids area where the Wanapum had built a longhouse. After attending the "Spring Festival," Matthias and Buck discussed the issues of access to the site, and Matthias granted him permission to enter the reservation and arranged for a series of passes to be issued to the tribe as a whole. Afterward, a Wanapum representative named Moody Charley took pictures of the colonel and his adjutant shaking hands with Johnny Buck, with a tribal elder standing by. Less than two weeks later, Charley sent copies of the pictures to Matthias, doubtless as a means of confirming the meeting and the agreement.

The meeting cemented Matthias's relations with the Indians. At the first negotiating session administered by Shotwell, Matthias had commented with surprise that William Charley, the tribal interpreter, "is apparently a man of fair education although his appearance would not indicate as much." That session had suggested that the Wanapum were *good* Indians despite their intransigence. The invitation, the ceremony, and the direct negotiations with Johnny Buck confirmed Matthias's assessment. Buck became, in his eyes, a primitive equivalent of himself. "In general, the Indians are very independent and insist on maintaining that independence and their treaty rights to fish on the Columbia River," Matthias wrote. "At the same time, the Chief and his counsel appeared to be willing to cooperate with us in every possible way and I do not believe that their loyalty can be questioned." These qualities, independence and loyalty, expanded in Matthias's eyes. Buck became a firm leader of a group that needed a firm, patriarchal hand. Years later, Matthias recalled Buck: "I liked him. That guy ruled the tribe. He chased them into the river once a week in the summer." (One assumes that Matthias was admiring Buck's commitment to universal tribal cleanliness.)[60]

Matthias's interest in the tribe approached the obsessional. Matthias often visited the tribe, and one associate recalled that he brought them liquor. When an administrator of the Department of the Interior wrote asking for information on the tribe, Matthias reassigned Community Management Head Norman Fuller to research the matter; Fuller researched at the Yakima Indian Agency, looked into treaties from the nineteenth century, and interviewed "a number of the old timers in this area" to satisfy Matthias's order. When Fuller was done, Matthias sent the report on to the Department of the Interior, along with photostats of the pictures he'd received from Charley. In an interview some forty years after the war, he swelled the tribe to "30 to 50 of them," and remembered Buck producing "a little weatherbeaten treaty which gave them the fishing rights"—despite his investigator's report that they "are not treaty Indians" and actively refused to sign treaties. Matthias also remembered that he had given the tribe "free run" of the reservation.[61]

Matthias's patronizing, patriarchal relation with the Wanapum tribe represented one extreme of the bipolar relationship of the District to its Indians. His was a picture unalloyed by the doubt or self-consciousness that crept into the interactions Los Alamos intellectuals had with the Pueblo natives imported to serve them. At Hanford, Indians were a significant footnote, revealing the way a slip of the tongue is revealing. Negroes were the text itself.

Not so at Los Alamos. There the "colored people" were Mexican, Mexican-American, mestizo, and American Indian—mainly members of the various Pueblo tribes who occupied the mesas near Los Alamos. Together, they played the roles that went to blacks on the other MED sites. They were the maids so necessary at each site to attract and keep qualified managers and professionals and their families. They were the gardeners who made the sites more attractive and began to erase the damage of the Corps of Engineers style of construction. They drove the trucks and poured the concrete. And they stoked the furnaces of the houses, duplexes, and apartment houses.

They formed the bulk of a ragtag assortment of construction and maintenance workers. Phyllis K. Fisher, the wife of the physicist Leon Fisher, was young and relatively sheltered. The visible class striation at Los Alamos surprised her. At the bottom, she recalled, there was the construction and maintenance staff: "some of them lived on the hill. They had the poorest housing of all. They lived in corrugated metal Quonset huts, which had minimal room separation and no insulation from heat or cold. There were never enough resident laborers, nor enough with the proper skills. So daily, from the world outside came a bus with Indian and Spanish-American day-laborers as well as maids. In the late afternoon they vanished by bus to their homes in the valley below."[62]

Most lived down the hill. Many had been sheepherders holding U.S. Forest Service grazing permits to the mesa and now were back as servants. They lived in small communities along Route 1 or in the communities of Indians living at the bases of their ancestral sites. Buses drove them up from the pueblos and villages. In the winter, they waited in the dark along Route 1; like migrant and transient laborers elsewhere in the American landscape, they went from the buses to deployment offices, where they received their assignments. (Writing in 1946, one resident, Kathleen Mark, called them "a troupe of Spanish-Americans.") They worked, usually in a silence enforced by their limited grasp of English and the near-complete ignorance of Spanish and American Indian languages on the part of residents and employers. Then the bus came to take them back, often to subsistence "ranches" in the valley.[63]

Where they differed from other people of color on other sites was in their intimate proximity to the lives of the scientific families who would eventually become heroes. Too close to be threatening, they became exotic; their differentness made them objects of romance in the scientific community, and their mistresses read and wrote about them—in letters, in memoirs, in books published after the war. In these documents, maids, gardeners, and furnace men appeared not as people but as mythic types, drawn from popular literature about the Southwest that passed from household to household.[64]

Phyllis Fisher's naivete was typical in this regard. By the time she wrote her reminiscences in 1983, she had developed a clearer picture of the class stratification at Los Alamos. In November 1944, when she wrote in a letter of her first experience with these workers, she was filled with delight:

> I have household help today for the first time. She came to the house all rolled up in a bright red blanket and smiles. She calls me "Meesie Feesha" and tells me her name is Apolonia. She is a short, middle-aged, stooped Indian woman from a nearby pueblo. She looks as though she couldn't lift a feather. But whether or not she can clean the house is immaterial. I'm sure she'll be worth her wages in entertainment value alone. She is sweet and picturesque, and I love to watch her. If she does nothing more than stand around, I'll find my housework less boring.[65]

With a tourist's attitude toward Native American culture, Los Alamos scientists had little compunction about tromping in on sacred ceremonies and visiting the homes of their maids. On Pueblo turf, they discovered the romantic alternative to their unhappy pursuit of a technology of violence: the same simplicity and purity that had inspired exiles like Georgia O'Keeffe decades earlier. Here is Phyllis Fisher writing her parents of her family's first pueblo visit:

> I never dreamed that an Indian Pueblo could be so attractive. . . . The day was clear and crisp, and the sight of snow-capped mountain peaks above the roofs of the pueblo was really thrilling. . . . The place was immaculate. Booths for the display and sale of pottery were everywhere. . . . The dance was solemn, and the rhythm of the tom-toms and the chant of the singers were punctuated at times by war whoops of the dancing men. I blush to add that our Bobby was quite carried away by it all and finally joined lustily in the war whoops.[66]

Fisher's intimate impression, destined only for her parents, is particularly telling. Her surprise that the pueblo was clean and "attractive"; her focus on the visual qualities of the place; her embarrassment that her son did not maintain the proper distance between performer and audience: all these suggest an attitude alternately reverent and condescending. Other Los Alamos residents confirmed this duality.[67]

Powerless, picturesque, and silent, Indians at Los Alamos became the objects of the collector's mania. Residents acquired Indian art objects with a passion. Some they received from their maids and servants as gifts. Some they purchased while visiting the nearby pueblos. Some they appropriated on their own, from local archaeological sites, in flagrant violation of law. Stern warnings by the authorities, published in the Los Alamos *Bulletin,* did not noticeably diminish what Eleanor Jette called "our Sunday cliff dwelling investigations," although it may have decreased the amount of purloining, and certainly changed the displays in a number of Los Alamos homes. Interest remained high, however. By 1944, the Cultural Arts Group was holding special seminars with experts on Indian art, and a separate pottery group formed.[68]

Often residents sought not objects but experiences to collect. As early as November 3, 1943, the *Bulletin* announced a Sadie Hawkins Day dance would be enlivened by local Indians: "Buffalo Dance—Eagle Dance—War Dance—Real Indians in full war paint," read the announcement. Just what local tribe wore "war paint" or made war dances the paper didn't mention. Usually residents went to the pueblos to watch the dances. They were there for the pageantry, but often they couldn't give themselves up to it; they read up on the subject beforehand, or tried to figure out the rhythmic sequences and symbolism of the music.[69]

Below all this there always lay a certain pool of discomfort with those different ones, and a corresponding picture of them as fundamentally inferior, even distastefully so. Phyllis Fisher recounted her maid Apolonia's fear of electricity and incapacity with machinery. This was romantic—it signaled the gulf between civilizations. But when the garbage men feared her dog, who on two occasions attacked and bit them, she found their differences less charming. Other residents were less tolerant of the failings of their servants. They talked of the inefficiency of those who cleaned the houses before occupancy, of the lackadaisical sense of time and work that characterized the maids, of the inability of furnace men to regulate the heat. When white workers found themselves assigned to housing with Indian workers, they often marched straight to military security to complain. And in this they were supported by their military superiors, men like Security's Maj. Peer de Silva, who busted to private a military scientist who upbraided a WAC for her racial prejudices. The Pueblo maids were nearly always "girls," no matter how old or how high their status within their own communities.[70]

Inside the Los Alamos boundaries, this complex of stereotypes, romantic and otherwise, pervaded the pictures of Indians, and the pictures in which Indians figured. This telling combination of romanticism, condescension, yearning, and contempt was tempered at Los Alamos by something that site had in greater abundance than elsewhere on the District: a particular quality of skepticism and ironic self-scrutiny that characterized the intelligentsia crowded within its fence. Good-hearted and empathic as they might have been, these Los Alamos residents still contributed to the inevitable—they transformed that which they revered, destroying the very aspects of it that were most the object of their longing and their envy. It was at San Ildefonso pueblo that this law of unintended consequences showed itself most boldly, for San Ildefonso was the closest and the most convenient recruiting site for the District. But the phenomenon echoed in other pueblos as well.

The pueblo cultures that surrounded Los Alamos and provided it with the majority of its laborers had existed in complex relationships with Western cultures for centuries. Their religions combined tribal elements with elements drawn from the Catholic church of Spain, which had penetrated to the mesa villages in the seventeenth century, founding their own congregations and building cathedrals of adobe. These pueblo cultures depended on a division of cultural roles between the sexes. Men worked the fields at the mesa's base (or sometimes at greater distances); women remained on the mesas or in the pueblos, where they raised children and did the crucial work of making pottery—pottery that carried in its designs, its glazes, its means of production, and its ritual (and everyday) uses, a significant portion of the pueblo worldview.

Before the war, already, Anglo expatriates had begun to infiltrate the pueblos, and their infiltration changed those sites in complex ways. Probably the most infamous example of that was Pueblo de Taos, where Mabel Dodge Luhan moved, marrying a native man, and bringing a rash of aesthete-expatriates, including D. H. Lawrence, along with her. Her writings, and the writings and paintings of many others, most notably Georgia O'Keeffe, had created a tourist cult of the pueblos, and the incursion of Anglo ideas, Anglo aesthetics, and Anglo economics was noticeable to the more perceptive of Los Alamosans.

Nonetheless, pueblo culture was resilient and the incursions relatively gentle in the areas closest to Los Alamos. The arrival of the MED changed all that. Needing workers whom it could import efficiently and in sufficient numbers, the District looked to the pueblos. In a vast and depopulated region, gathering workers was inherently difficult; a single bus to San Ildefonso could deliver most of the necessary manual laborers.

The results, for the pueblo culture, were profound. The general demand pulled significant numbers of pueblo dwellers out of their traditional work. The men could transfer their agricultural skill to the District and be paid in cash for it. Women recruited to work as housekeepers and maids left their children with grandmothers and took the bus "up the Hill." The pueblo economy made an abrupt shift from subsistence and barter to cash, and became notably more dependent on the outside world for its survival as a result. Los Alamos residents gained picturesque entertainment; Charlie Masters recalled shortly after the war "the kindly, patriarchal face of Chief, an ex-pueblo governor, who substituted a tall, white cap for colored feathers and who stood in the service line pouring soup into thick bowls and handing them across the counter with all the noble solemnity of a cacique handing out judgments." But in truth, the ex-governor was no longer "a cacique handing out judgments"—he was a menial laborer who had lost not only his particular role in the life of his pueblo, not only his power to speak and hence to influence, but even his name, to the well-intentioned romantics of Los Alamos. We do not know his name, now: he is only "Chief," a name given him by some resident, no doubt when his true name was too difficult to pronounce or to remember.[71]

Tied to this shift in the economy (in the largest sense of the term) was another. The Los Alamos site expanded in size, and the proportion of pueblo women's cash earnings outstripped the men's, as the District needed more and more female menials. Absent from the pueblos, bringing in the greater portion of income for families and tribal group alike, the native women laboring at Los Alamos changed delicate cultural balances back at the pueblo—traditions of childrearing, of generational power, of gender relationships. The pottery symbolized this—as lives changed, so did the artifacts central to pueblo culture.

Charlie Masters had lived in the region before Los Alamos and knew whereof she spoke. She described starkly the change in the making of native pottery; it was a shift from "bowls made as gifts of love" to "mass production resulting from the Hill's unprecedented demand": "The best potters . . . fell weeks and even months behind in the filling of orders. A phenomenal amount of black ware was produced, for the Los Alamos folk had an insatiable appetite for these plain, rich bowls, plates, vases, plaques and candlesticks which would not shout 'regional' too loudly when placed next to Wedgwood or pewter back home. It became almost impossible to buy a new piece not sanctioned by the taste of the Hill or to find a potter with the time to make one."[72]

Masters observed two effects: a shift from individual production based upon traditional sources and traditional methods, to mass production aimed at satisfying a compelling demand from outside the culture; at the same time, a shift in the very nature of the artifacts, their style, their iconography, their meaning, to satisfy the call of clients. Suddenly the potters of San Ildefonso were working on commission, and their pottery had become the center of a booming tourist economy.[73]

San Ildefonso was not the only place where such transformations took place. North of Santa Fe was the village of Chimayó. Until Los Alamos began to send buses there to pick up men to work on the Hill, it was legendary for its complex decorative rugs. By the time Los Alamos residents had heard of its artifacts, production had plummeted; Masters reported that one could soon choose only from "a dozen or so, all in commonplace patterns"—the rugmakers had abandoned their craft in favor of "good and steady pay" at Los Alamos.[74]

This change from an indigenous subsistence culture to a tourist culture accelerated as the war ended, and as San Ildefonso and the other indigenous communities had become tourist cultures, dependent economically on the demands of outsiders, their values bound up in the values of Hill culture in the District. A special postwar party at San Ildefonso symbolized the interpenetration; there, square dancers from the Hill performed for the Pueblo natives. They had brought American food with them; at the party, Indians ate "wieners and buns," and drank "cases of Coca-Cola," while the Hill folk ate native Pueblo food. And, at the end, the two danced together in awkward attempts to invent steps that melded the two cultures. Eleanor Jette remembered "a waltz—perfect three-four time" and "a conga line with a young Indian wearing a brand new discharge button" signaling he'd just mustered out of the army. He'd been far away from the pueblo and hadn't seen its changes. What residents had experienced as a continuous process, he perceived as jarring dislocation. "'I never thought I'd live to see anything like this,'" he muttered.[75]

At Los Alamos, the maids were Indians. They were also women, women who worked for women.

Los Alamos was a considerable step down for many of the women who came with their husbands to its closed and secret spaces. Most were college graduates; many had held professional or at least skilled jobs before or during their married lives. Many of them had been working when their husbands got the call—working as scientists, as teachers, as librarians, in a wide variety of the occupations commonly held by highly educated women of the wartime years. Those who weren't working often had left the workforce in order to raise children; a temporary hiatus, they thought—until the District intervened in their lives.[76]

Most were used to active participation in the academic community, not simply in its social life, but in intellectual ways as well. Most had served as the confidantes, critics, and supporters of their scientist-husbands' work, had listened to and understood the often arcane details of their husbands' research and experimentation. Often they'd had scientific training; in any case, they had the benefit of intimacy with their husbands' lives and with the lives of the scientific-academic orbit within which their husbands traveled.

When they arrived at Los Alamos, all this came to an abrupt end. The District hired scientists, it didn't hire families—it didn't even want them onsite, if it could avoid them. It hired individuals, almost always men, and it grudgingly allowed them to bring their wives, but only after trying to persuade or require their new employees to leave the women at home. Women who had worked before found it necessary to choose between family and work.

Phyllis Fisher was newly married when her husband received his recruiting papers for Los Alamos. Decades later, she recalled that first moment of entry into the alien culture of the District: "I had felt a sudden sense of isolation and anger when I discovered that Leon either wouldn't or couldn't answer my questions. . . . Why couldn't I be trusted? . . . In the past, Leon had always patiently described his scientific projects or research to me. But this time he made it absolutely clear that I wasn't to ask and, if I did, he wasn't about to answer. I didn't like the implications, not at all! I felt uncomfortable, sensing a new distance between us, one that might grow larger with the passage of time."[77]

Suddenly sequestered from their husbands, isolated from friends and family, these women strove to discover ways to sustain themselves. Their letters, edited (by them or by military authorities) to pass the censors, reveal a painful combination of loneliness, fortitude, and denial. Writing her first letter home to a friend, Lois Bradbury reported that the living conditions "would be intolerable without a liberal application of the good old sense of humor." "You look from your windows every direction straight into the tenements across from you. . . . we face five other apartments no matter which way we look." Because the apartment walls, floors, and ceilings were paper thin, the noise of crying children "simply drowned out" the wails of her own.[78]

Eleanor Jette's first few hours at shangri-la reflected the experience of most women arriving on the site. The apartment she was assigned was awful. The "soot-covered walls, ceiling, and floor" were the first shock. "There was no linoleum on the bathroom floor. The fixtures were filthy. . . . I stifled an impulse to cry." Within an hour, her husband, Eric, had been summoned to a secret scientific colloquium and he immediately rose from the dinner table and left Eleanor to "the mess in the apartment." "I was thunderstruck," Jette recalled. When she went to see about getting improvements in the apartment, the army WAC "was downright rude. She implied that the scientific staff were nothing but a bunch of prima donnas. [Phyllis Fisher had the same experience more than a year later.] The army provided them with luxurious quarters, but they were constantly making impossible demands. . . . I sizzled with rage."[79]

By the next night, the process of introducing Jette into the exiled spaces of Los Alamos women was complete. Her husband arrived home and handed her "a small tan booklet. I opened it:

RESTRICTED
THIS IS NOT TO BE TAKEN FROM THE SITE
CENSORSHIP REGULATIONS

" 'You'd better study it carefully or G2 will get you,' " he told her. Then he "retired to the living room to stretch out on the cot. He studied the nailholes in the ceiling while he pondered the problems ahead of him," leaving his wife to read the rules. Always before she had been an active participant in her husband's work; now her husband lay "behind an impenetrable wall of silence" built by the regulations in that small tan booklet.[80]

Women weren't just isolated from their husbands. Jette reported that "people from Los Alamos were supposed to cut their own parents if they met them on the street." And the regulations were enforced by the constant indiscreet presence of military intelligence—the "G2" her husband had mentioned. Jette reported that "G2 saw to it that they didn't mail any letter surreptitiously and tailed them into La Cantina (La Fonda's bar [in Santa Fe]). It made sure they didn't divulge any classified information or gather in groups of more than four people, when they bent their elbows." Life was an endless collection of "censorship regulations" and "monitored phone calls [in which] the monitor would cut the connection" if he suspected the slightest possibility of indiscretion; "frequently you never were able to get your connection again."[81]

The scientific wives were the group most alienated. Ruth Marshak wrote of it in 1948, when the pain was still fresh. "The Tech Area was a great pit which swallowed our scientist husbands out of sight, almost out of our lives," she wrote. "They worked at night, and often came home at three or four in the morning. Sometimes, they set up army cots in the laboratories and did not come home at all." "Few women understood what the men were seeking there" at work, Marshak recalled; "the loneliness and heartache of some scientists' wives during the years before the atomic bomb was born were very real."[82]

Some could not bear the strain. Phyllis Fisher recalled "others, like very pretty, very pregnant, and very helpless Margaret." Under the assault of strangeness, the litany of snafus that accompanied every new entrance to the Los Alamos site, she turned for help to those she knew and found she was alone. "She couldn't accept the fact that her Harry, like my Leon, worked late many evenings and she had no idea of the work he was doing. She asked. He clammed up. She had found a wall that never was there before. I felt she was borrowing trouble and I realized she was frightened. She complained about everything. . . . One night, Harry walked out and didn't return until morning and then told her he couldn't stand any more. . . . Margaret couldn't adapt, needed home and mother desperately, and a few weeks later left our mesa, never to return."[83]

Margaret's fate was extreme, but most women experienced the same conditions— isolation, loss of community, loss of love and companionship, and then blame for the loss. Women had to adapt or be treated with condescension or viewed as weaklings. When the Jettes' friend A. B. "Gus" Kinzel arrived at Los Alamos on a consulting trip, he and Eric Jette talked in code about the work in front of Eleanor Jette. When she reacted sharply to their exclusion of her, she received a patronizing instruction to "appreciate the job Eric's doing," and an offer to get her some "things" from New York.[84]

Fisher encapsulated the entire experience with an anecdote that many of the new residents told as their own. She recalled, "At first, I though of Sh-La as a fortress. . . . But gradually I began to suspect that *we* were the prisoners, the dangerous ones, and that 'they' were the safe ones outside."

As in prison camps in many times and places, a hierarchy developed among the prisoners. "As you might expect, the various divisions, both socially and temperamentally lead to much bickering both out in the tech area and socially," Lois Bradbury wrote in a letter in the summer of 1944. "Up on our hill," Phyllis Fisher recalled, "we were told what we needed to know, period. Those who had white badges, Leon included, knew the details of the research going on. Those with blue badges knew what they needed to know for their part of it. And unemployed wives were to know nothing." And like prisoners in those camps, the inmates of Los Alamos who had the least struggled to construct their own worlds within. Fisher wrote to her parents of a typical evening; "Dinner is eaten in a mad rush. The men dash back to work. The wives do the dishes and chat a while. At ten o'clock the men return jabbering a strange language most nearly identified as 'scientese.'" When the men came around, Fisher told her parents, "the only conversation directed my way was 'Hello' and 'Goodbye.'"[85]

Isolation from their families and friends, from their pasts, from the traditions of their communities, had a double-edged effect. It left these women lonely, often depressed, sometimes suicidal. It strained the ties that remained; as happened throughout the homefront, divorces increased. Women reported their feelings that they had been set adrift, without resources. A week after arriving, Lois Bradbury wrote in a letter that she was "practically useless. . . . I'm just completely whipped down."[86]

These emotions intensified if the women were young and their ties with their husbands were still new, and when (as was so often the case) they had recently embarked upon childrearing and were left to learn the hard lessons without the help of parents or friends and without the support of husbands. "Ed and I were the oldsters; I had my 30th birthday up there," Elsie McMillan reported. "At twenty-seven, I felt comfortably middle-aged," recalled Jane Wilson shortly after war's end. Inexperienced, cast adrift without the secure environment of home towns and communities, these women had to cope with new responsibilities and new identities.[87]

But these disruptions had other effects as well, some of them beneficial, even joyous. Because Los Alamos was such a homogeneous environment, because its women were recently out of college or university, because the wartime environment offered a particular rationale for the crises of everyday life, there came into being a peculiar sort of communitarianism. Life came to resemble the sororities of college years, with men absent but powerful, with big sisters to take the new "girls" under their wings, with the eternal party atmosphere and the sense of sisterhood. Eleanor Jette remembered the instant casualness of the Hill as "a welcome change after the formality of university life" as a professor's wife. Phyllis Fisher recalled that "in all matters, emergency and routine, people were the real lifesavers. . . . for me, life was largely confined to close friends."[88]

But this quality was also artificial, a little like the forced conviviality of a long airline flight. "Life at Los Alamos was peculiarly uninhibited and completely unrelaxed. We worked hard and we played hard," reported Jean Bacher. (Her husband ran the Bomb Physics Division). The women were almost entirely responsible for creating a social life that might reconnect them to their husbands, sustain their families, invent their community. Every social institution of import, from the library to the orchestra, was "a result of the spontaneous efforts of private citizens to make of this barren Army Post some sort of real home," Ruth Marshak wrote in 1946.[89]

And these "private citizens" were overwhelmingly female. So women created the community, and they created as well a separate community of their own. The women made the plans for parties, and the women went into Santa Fe to get the liquor that made them successes. They told each other the stories that bound them together. Lois Bradbury wrote a friend that "everyone knows everyone's business; the females including myself hang themselves over their railings and gossip back and forth between apts., shout at children and generally add to the confusion."[90]

It was an intense, close-knit countercommunity that they forged. To read the women's reminiscences—in books, in unpublished manuscripts, in letters to parents and friends that have found their way into newsletters and archives—is to be struck with a triple theme that pervades. One strand involves a sense of uselessness, and a certain suppressed rage at being so close to something so important, yet being so utterly closed off from its nature and from the opportunity to help. Wound around the sense of valuelessness is a second strand: an often-giddy sense of freedom afforded by that exile from importance. Women were free to complain, to gossip, to demand, to organize among themselves. And then there was the third sense, in which they saw, and seized, the opportunity to create their own utopia. If their home was a prison camp, it was a prison camp that went largely unregulated once civilians were ensconced within its walls, and they were thus free to develop their own values and systems within its walls.[91]

By 1944 Los Alamos had a sort of shadow-culture that existed among the women during the day and extended to all the family members at night. "In the evenings the Hill dwellers gathered in groups," reported Jette, and these gatherings were full of rebellious behavior. Jokes and stories of battles, tales of "our former lives in the Out-er World and our adventures prior to our arrival," speculations about the mysterious failures the District refused to acknowledge: these formed the basis for a new com-munity that lay outside of, yet within, the District's boundaries.[92]

And these evening parties offered the chance to regain some measure of potency in a day-to-day life of frustration and impotence. At night, scientists and their wives violated the laws of silence and risked much to recement their broken relations as they "pan-fried" the District, described their battles for a better scientific program, reported their arguments with the District administration, and drank whiskey (the favorite) and rum (the most readily available). They continued these conversations whenever they achieved some measure of isolation—on horseback rides, for example, or on long hikes, far from the observing eyes of Security.

The isolation of men from women only increased as the Manhattan Project ap-proached its culmination and pressures grew. Jette recalled a moment in 1944 when "the atmosphere tightened perceptibly. Eric and the other men disappeared into the Tech Area at strange hours for indefinite periods of time." After that, "the grapevine"—the women's network—"crackled constantly." Men "worked until they were too ill to stand. The Tech Area buzzed with activity day and night; the workers were like crea-tures possessed." Under such pressure, the separation between men and women, the powerlessness of women, the fragility of their community, became increasingly clear.[93]

Scientists' wives were better off, better fed, and better housed than any other women on the District, but only because of their husbands. This was the paradox of the sci-entists' wives. They had built their own coherent, matriarchal society, yet within the patriarchal culture of the District, their community was irrelevant, *they* were irrele-vant. At moments their position beyond the margins became clearer, as when the machinists were granted their own barracks and then, the women learned, they were paid "inducement wages" to come to the Hill *without* their wives and families.[94]

Women's actual status came most clear, however, when they crossed the line and went to work—and, over time, most all of them went to work, as the District realized the need for obedient but unskilled workers to do the white-collar menial labor of running adding machines, of collating data, of reproducing materials, of typing and filing and organizing.

The first public notice that the District was entertaining the possibility of a mass hiring of wives came in January 1944, when the District advertised in the Los Alamos *Bulletin:* "Women who are in a position to work full time or part-time are invited to read the notice which will be posted in the Housing Office (T-133), on various bulle-tin boards in the Tech Area and on the bulletin boards in the Commissary and at the General Store." The message was revealing—women weren't allowed into the Tech Area (they didn't have the clearances), so the notices posted there were really for the benefit of their husbands. Where women *would* read the call was at the store—while shopping, while most aware of their genteel poverty and most forcibly within the walls of women's work. And when they did read the notice, they found no mention of the nature of the work or its potential rewards.[95]

The reason for this omission from the announcement was simple: the pay was lu-dicrously low, the work humiliatingly simpleminded. Richard Feynman described the situation with his characteristic humor. The translation from atomic theory to weapons-grade practicality had reached a stage where the mathematics of the thing had to be determined through an immense amount of calculation, all of which was done on primitive adding machines. Those who did this mind-numbing work were called "computers," and they were all women. They sat in rooms filled with other women doing the same work, and they typed in the endless lists of numbers. They were hired not because they were intelligent, but because they were available. They were never told the rationale behind their work. When the calculations didn't live up to the hopes of the scientists and mathematicians who had devised the theories, they found themselves the butt of anger, contempt, blame. The assumption was: the failure was their fault, not the fault of the theory or the prediction. When they were vindicated, as they often were, they never found out.[96]

The work was numbing. And the process of getting hired was a bit mortifying. Charlotte Serber was a scientific librarian—she described herself later as "one of the few women at Los Alamos who held an important position in the Technical Area." She recalled the recruitment program in an essay written just after the war: "For the working wife, the actual process of being hired in was not very complicated. It entailed filling in a multitude of forms, getting a pass to the Tech Area, listening to a speech on security, hearing an oversimplified version of working conditions on the Hill, and getting her salary set. . . . The working wife's salary, which was set very arbitrarily, was influenced less by her previous work history than by the fact that she really had no bargaining power. She lived, after all, in a sort of company town."[97]

Laura Fermi reminisced about the process in 1975: "I had a part-time job in the technical area, working 3/8ths of the time as a blue badge, who could not be told any secrets. (People who could be told secrets were white badges—physicists and chemists and so on.) The Army encouraged wives to work 'to keep them out of mischief.'" She was not by any means the only Los Alamos woman to surmise that a side benefit of the employment of women was to coopt and control them.[98]

In addition to questions of worth brought on by low pay and low-skill tasks, working brought wracking doubts about a woman's ability to be a mother and wife. Nonetheless, by August 1944, three-quarters of the women were working. Part of the explanation may lie with their feelings of sheer boredom, some with their desperation to find importance in the male world of work; but some of it also lies with the arguments of patriotism that were pressed upon the women by their husbands and their husbands' colleagues. Women's duty was to work, but work didn't free them from other duties. They might go to the Tech Area, within the inner fence, but their clearances were below those of the men. And they still had to shop and cook, clean and comfort.[99]

Yet few could actually do all these things—do them, that is, without a sense of guilt, and without stresses to their identity. The most common impulse among these young working women was to see themselves failing as mothers and helpmeets. To soothe women's fears of abandoning their families, the District offered inducements. One was, as Lois Bradbury wrote in a letter to a friend, "a remarkable arrangement as far as children go—free nursery school run by trained people for all children, from three years on." But the demographics of the women at Los Alamos and the statistics from the maternity wards defy this happy picture—a huge percentage of these women had children under the age of three. *They* needed home care, something the District would not offer. In place of baby-sitters, the District offered maids. Maids could serve as child-care workers without requiring the District to introduce the program of day-care facilities that the Roosevelt administration had attempted to institute on a national level outside the fence, but which had proven expensive, unwieldy, and unpopular. Maids were status symbols. Maids liberated women who were often unused to the sort of constant drudgery of housework characteristic of the wartime Los Alamos house-hold, where coal dust and road dust infiltrated the primitive houses, where cooking on coal stoves and hotplates made meals traumatic adventures, where children reacted predictably to the disruptions of separation from their pasts and their fathers. At the same time, maids reinforced the District's underlying assumptions—that women's work at home wasn't really deserving of respect, and that the women's feelings of inadequacy could be resolved by appeal to an image of leisure-class privilege.[100]

The maid program began as a voluntary effort to provide help for working moth-ers—in May 1943, Charlotte Serber and others petitioned Security to allow them to import women from San Ildefonso pueblo. "The venture was a purely cooperative one," Serber reported in 1946; "aided by a volunteer, non-working wife who made the schedules, met the bus, and assigned the women." But transportation required army assistance. Soon the District had taken it over, and when it did, the rules changed. As the population exploded, there developed a scarcity of maids; while the District did not consider this a crisis, the working mothers, whose maids were often babysitters and nannies, panicked. From a much-desired and scarce commodity administered by women for women, the maid program became a regulated program, subject to the District's general contempt for women and families. Under military administration by WACs, the Housing and Maid Service Office was lowest priority: it was run by buck privates, like Private Wheaton, who served as principal liaison between the office and its clients.[101]

Private Wheaton was one of an entire class of military women brought to the sites to fill the necessary roles as clerks, assistants, and liaisons. Outside of the scientific wives, WACs and WAACs were probably the largest other class of women on the Los Alamos site. They, too, were designated menials. They came to the project because Groves wanted military conscripts to handle what the District official history called "*that* type of clerical work"—work, in other words, that was unskilled and secret. Over time, the WAC numbers rose from six enlisted women and an officer to more than seventy-five by mid-1943. Once the precedent was set, the numbers expanded steadi-ly through war's end, not just at Los Alamos but at all three sites.[102]

WAACs and WACs eventually moved into technical and even scientific areas. They were good workers; they could be controlled, they followed orders, and they kept quiet. Had there been enough of them, perhaps they would have played an important role as laborers in the factories at Hanford and Oak Ridge. As it was, the District sought civilian equivalents of the WACs. Yvette Berry, the operations worker at Hanford, had discovered at her interview that she was overqualified—she knew some chemistry and physics from high school and some math from her first year in college. Had she not already proven herself in Construction, and already received a security clearance, and had the District not been desperate for workers at Chemical Separations, she never would have been hired.[103]

For the District had already begun a debate over which of two types of employee might best serve in the factories and production facilities. One was the educated, scientifically trained professional engineer or technician, who could be cleared for maximum information, briefed on the nature of the procedure, and then given responsibility for the safe and efficient practice of the elaborate processes involved in uranium enrichment and separation, plutonium creation and separation, and the other stages in materials production. This was the type urged upon District officers by the scientific community. To employ such types would require increased security investigation and more elaborate recruitment and training. But it would pay off in safety over the long term, and in the efficiency that comes of dedicated individuals who understand the nature of the work and are committed to its success.[104]

The alternative was to choose workers with little or no knowledge, train them in the rote mechanics of their jobs, and focus supervisory energy on making them docile and obedient—including punishing anyone who asked questions or showed initiative. The advantage here was dual. Such an employee would be easy to train, and discipline was in profusion on the District. But perhaps more important, this employee fit the military culture.

To go that route, however, required that the District design its operations for the maximum of mechanized, automated, assembly-line-style processes. This tack would result in significantly higher costs, because the goal would now have to be development of fail-safe, idiot-proof procedures. And, as the engineer and theorist Charles Perrow has pointed out in *Normal Accidents,* such a philosophy of management carried high risks and ultimate costs when the technologies involved were highly complex and the resultant processes of manufacturing were, in Perrow's phrase, "tightly coupled." (Perrow's models—chemical refineries and nuclear electrical generating plants—form the antecedent and the consequence of the Manhattan District's program.) Designing to avoid human responsibility carried its dangerous consequences.[105]

Yvette Berry's interview reveals the outcome of the debate, at Hanford and elsewhere on the District. At Oak Ridge, the workers for Tennessee Eastman's Y-12 facility were the single most concentrated group fitting the profile. The District's propaganda officer, George O. Robinson, trumpeted the type: "East Tennessee high school girls, with not the faintest idea of what their jobs were about."[106] A District historian paraphrased the official documents to describe the "typical operator trainee":

> a woman, recently graduated from a nearby Tennessee high school, with no scientific training whatsoever. Using one of the XAX electromagnetic tanks in the development plant, the instructional staff taught her how to operate complex control panels in the calutron cubicles adjacent to the racetracks. They gave her only information essential to her task as an operator and, for security reasons, actually misled her as to the real purpose and character of the product. The training program was surprisingly successful, supplying operators on schedule.[107]

At Oak Ridge, and at Hanford, too, this was the nature of "woman's work"—stultifying, repetitive, based upon ignorance and even falsehood, lowest-paid. Here is Robinson reprising the Y-12 achievement: "And all of the production units had to be controlled through amazing automatic mechanisms operated by personnel of average intelligence (many of the employees were high school girls), who had not the faintest idea what their jobs were about, but who operated dials to produce the material which, when used, liberated a part of the power of the universe."[108]

Women, like nonwhite workers, were hired to do work deemed too menial and undignified for white men. Nurses, stenographers, stenotypists, telephone operators: these jobs paid the same bottom-level wage as chauffeurs, office boys, and watchmen. Private Wheaton in Los Alamos's Housing and Maid Service Office was like WAAC Corporal Hope Sloan, who was a secretary in military intelligence at Hanford but gravitated eventually into public relations, where she worked with Jane Jones, a former beauty queen; like Annette Heriford, displaced resident of White Bluffs, who returned from college to find her town disappeared and her parents exiled, and who went to work in Recreation, planning activities to keep the boys happy, like so many other women at all three sites.[109]

If it must include women in its plans, the District sought to control their presence through regulation. Women formed a part of the labor force and as such they were treated, like their male colleagues, as commodities. Unlike the men, however, they retained value outside their worth as workers. They offered access to symbolic forces the District both needed and feared: notions of home, of family, of nurturance and warmth on the one hand and the power of sexuality on the other.

The District's response in both areas was to simultaneously exploit and forbid. The second impulse was more powerful—to repress and interdict these areas, fearing they would disrupt the work, divide loyalties, cause a confusion between life on the sites as a means to an end and as an end in itself.

Take the case of housing. Women could come to the site, could work, but they could not be assigned houses or apartments unless they received the specific approval of the district engineer himself. Even when a woman fit the criteria to rent a house, she was denied it, for—as a District memo from the Oak Ridge files put it, in resolving a case— "it is not considered advisable from the standpoint of the mutual interests of the Government and . . . Corporation to assign a house to her or other women under similar circumstances, ipso facto."[110]

If you were a woman, you were to live in dormitories because in dormitories your life could be more strictly regulated—"for your protection," as the recruiting pamphlet *Dear Anne* told them. Contractors responsible for housing and daily life rigidly controlled dormitory life, at the express direction of the District. At Oak Ridge, the site-management firm of Roane-Anderson frankly declared that it regulated dormitory and barracks behavior "to improve the moral aspect" of life on the site. Some regulation was absurdly patronizing and inappropriate—as when Roane-Anderson tried bringing dormitory house mothers from Smith and Bryn Mawr Colleges, to teach their methods to the local dormitory supervisors. Others were more straightforward— publicized threats of eviction from the dormitory and the site for sexual infractions on women's part.[111]

Roane-Anderson was the District's agent to control the moral lives of site residents at Oak Ridge, men and women both. But the nature of morality differed markedly between men and women. Some of the sins were universal—cooking in the rooms, possession of liquor. The first endangered property and lives of employees. The second curtailed the efficiency of workers. Gambling, theft, and con games, and violence as well, were male infractions. For women, sexuality was the primary infraction—allowing men in the living quarters of dormitories and sex-sequestered housing units. Women who violated regulations could be dismissed; scattered statistics suggest that the District considered infractions of sexual codes by women on a par with violent crimes by men. Gambling could be tolerated—sex could not. And when it came to sex, women were the guilty parties, men the victims.[112]

The result of all this was a steady shrinking of hope, possibility, freedom—for women most of all. As a District investigator described it, "Anyone not living that way can't realize how drab existence is there."[113]

What the District wanted in place of impropriety and disruptive sinfulness was a wholesome, desexed environment of happy competition, a life appropriate to prepubescent boarding-school children—similar, perhaps to life at the Los Alamos Ranch School. At both of the industrial sites, the District sponsored contests on cleanliness, tastefulness, and propriety. "Whoops! Argument Is On! Men Versus Women; May the Best 'Housekeepers' Win!" read the headline announcing a contest concerning files and materials left on desks at the end of workday that ran in the Hanford *Sage Sentinel*. Other articles on barracks and hutment interior decorating, on neatness and life with roommates, all stressed a sort of playful camaraderie within the sexes, and a carefully regulated contact between them. Often these articles came with pictures that focused upon this neutered ideal of collective life, presided over by watchful District minions.[114]

Nonetheless the goal of such management was regulation of men's desire, suppression of women's sexuality. (Though not entirely: women were still to look "attractive"—to men, that is—and *Dear Anne* told female recruits to Hanford that "suits are ideal [have plenty of washable blouses!] . . . also sweaters and skirts, and tailored dresses you can sponge and press yourself. . . . slacks are not worn at work.") After all, when representatives from the Pasco Naval Air Station came to meet with Matthias concerning AWOL conscripts, it was the women of Hanford who were to blame, and their presence and behavior that needed to be controlled. Matthias was more graphic and more direct when he recalled the District's program for housing and regulating women's lives. "It's true the women lived behind barb wire," he told an interviewer, S. L. Sanger, "and we tried to control access. We know we didn't succeed 100 percent. They would get the gals and go out in the sage brush, occasionally. And they were free enough, except they lived in these barracks."[115]

The double standard, which saw male sexuality as a health issue and women's as a moral one, extended into material in the medical files concerning venereal disease, and posters and memos, in a broad if carelessly executed program of prevention. That the District saw venereal diseases as unfortunate consequences of the failures of women is implicit, even, in the title District administrators gave to the file on the subject: "Venereal Diseases, Prostitution, etc."[116]

Women were special cases on the District—as workers and as symbols of social forces the District both feared and sought to harness to its end. Once they became part of each site's population, they insinuated themselves into the social fabric. Indeed, the women *made* that social fabric, not just at Los Alamos, but at Hanford and Oak Ridge as well. This was part of their danger to the District—they created a culture on the District that was devoted to the sorts of desires and realities that held sway outside the fences. In so doing, they threatened the larger military program, which promoted the sites as temporary environments notable for their absence of social ties. To allow residents to imagine that they might achieve some measure of stability and happiness was to deflect them from the District's goals—efficient, rapid weapons production at the minimum of cost and the maximum of sacrifice.

Once they were there, women turned out to be profoundly subversive, for precisely this reason. Their danger wasn't in their sexuality so much as it was the cult of domesticity, of family and community happiness, that they brought onto the sites with them. In this, women were like other unwanted but necessary "populations" who came to the sites: Negroes, Indians, Mexicans. Each of these groups brought their own systems of belief and behavior, their own languages and gestures, and as they used them, they threatened to disrupt the District's program of social control.[117]

As the war progressed, there was some movement to make the District a more humane and attractive place for women and others. But to change the treatment of "undesirables" would have required more than altering rules and regulations, as these liberalizing campaigns rather hesitantly suggested. The conflict lay between Groves's conception of the project as a spartan and violent forced program in weapons development and the alternative: a human environment, in which humane life was the primary goal, and efficient, successful weapons production a willing consequence of that humane life.

The general military calls for a more humane workplace arrived late in the war, and the resistance of Groves and his men to their recommendations was particularly ironic. For despite itself, the District *had* become a human place. By 1945, each of the sites had existed for at least two years (in some cases three). The housing units had become homes (the dormitories and barracks too); the clusters of units had become neighborhoods; the townsites had become communities.

And so the District's work became social work. As the District's effort climaxed and the sites matured, the elements that defined this tendency spread across the populations that had come to live their lives at Hanford, at Oak Ridge, and at Los Alamos. Seeking to improve its human machinery, the District had developed into a bureaucracy for the management of human lives and human minds.

The declassified records of the Oak Ridge site contain the transcript of a meeting of the executive committee of the Recreation and Welfare Association, held at Oak Ridge's town hall on December 31, 1943. The committee had asked Mrs. W. B. Brown, a special assistant to the district engineer, to investigate a mysterious malaise striking the women employees at the site and causing lateness, absenteeism, days sick, and unexplained resignations.[1]

Mrs. Brown did not consider the matter mysterious at all; "since I have been here," she told the men arrayed before her at the table, "I have been making a study of some of the reasons for discontent." Life for the women, she said, wasn't really life; it was "drab existence." "They feel they have nothing to do," she reported rather tartly—their lives consisted of work, laundry, sleep, and meals. Most days, she said, "you just get through work, freshen up, eat, and go back there."[2]

Captain P. E. O'Meara, the Oak Ridge town manager, interrupted Mrs. Brown even before she had spoken for a full minute. "I would like to ask you a question," he said. "These girls who feel there is nothing to do: what do they like to do?"

Mrs. Brown's response ranged far from the narrow question of entertainment, past the question of women's place, and on toward a critique of life on the site. The problem wasn't with women—it was with the structure, the very essence of Oak Ridge as a community, as a culture. To compare Oak Ridge with "an ordinary town . . . I mean an ordinary town of about 30,000 people" was to recognize how much was missing. Oak Ridge lacked not just "organizations"—"school clubs, college alumni, church groups, YWCA and YMCA," but "all the social groups that are already formed . . . in the average town. Here there are none formed to any degree. People are still strangers."[3]

With characteristic directness, Mrs. Brown had reached to the central quandary of the District as it turned from a military structure to a true place. By sequestering the sites, by evacuating them of their populations and stripping them of their pasts and their histories, by building upon those spaces and then importing tens of thousands to work the factories and live in the dormitories, barracks, hutments, and houses, the Manhattan Engineer District had created instant towns; communities, however, it could not so easily call into being.

Something essential was missing from the sites; the anomie felt by Mrs. Brown's "girls" was only one indication. "Discontent" on the part of workers essential to the program raised absentee rates, sparked labor turnover, and made it difficult to recruit replacements. The problems weren't confined to women, either. At Hanford, the men were drinking, and fighting, and going AWOL—and the results were the same. "From the beginning of the planning of the project," wrote a psychiatrist, Dr. Eric Kent Clarke of Oak Ridge, in a report on mental health in the town, "emphasis has been placed on the development of the material aspects of a new community." But these were not ordinary towns; "from the beginning, the residents have been subjected to many additional stresses absent in the usual community." Overcrowding, "the pressure of work," "the difficulties of housekeeping and the inability of mothers to get away from the constant care of children," culture shock on the part of rural people subjected to industrial work pressures and of urban workers who felt themselves trapped in the countryside: these were "but a few of more important facets of life in Oak Ridge," and on the other sites, as well. "The plan has been excellent from the material viewpoint, but is hampered by the huge problem of satisfying individual emotional needs," Dr. Clarke wrote. Now "the terrific termination rate indicates the necessity for reconsideration of the program."[4]

Mrs. Brown and Dr. Clarke painted essentially similar pictures, of environments so new, so lacking in precedent, administered by a military bureaucracy so inexperienced in the essentials of social life, that they must by necessity be places of unhappy absence—of loneliness, anomie, loss. The result was a disintegration of what little community there was, a disintegration that was as rapid as the construction of physical towns. Workers and their families were hemorrhaging at rates greater than new ones could be returned. If the program was to continue, the District would have to modify its own culture.

Mrs. Brown understood one aspect of the problem: lack of traditions, social circles, institutions to draw together women and women, women and men, men and men. Clarke suggested a more wide-ranging picture—of an environment of "limitations," requiring "the patience, in the face of personal inconvenience, to await maturation of the original plan." Both of them approached something even more wide-reaching—an issue of power, its constant presence as a coercive force, held by superiors who were often absent, always dissatisfied, who set the goals and ordered their achievement. Workers and residents lived under orders to produce, but very few of them knew what they were producing. They had little or no internal stake in the results of their work—as Captain Teeter of Oak Ridge put it, "these people . . . haven't the slightest conception . . . why they are here." And so the District had responded by increasing the external demands, the lists of punishments, the exhortative propaganda, the calls for "sacrifice," the warnings. While the District and its corporate officials called for "individual initiative" ("can't the girls show a little initiative and organize themselves?" asked one of Mrs. Brown's interrogators), the entire system of organization removed the freedom and individual power that might engender such initiative. And each time the statistics showed previous campaigns to have failed, the District raised its stakes, called out more shrilly for results. The effect, Clarke said, was "fatigue," "production under pressure"—"high pressure"—"a sizable morale problem," all of which led to "neurotic reactions," and "psychiatric casualties" among the residents and workers.[5]

Mrs. Brown's inquisitors floundered about, grasping for solutions to this failure of morale. They blamed the workers. ("Here you have the type of person who is an introvert. They stay in their rooms and don't want to go out." Some "think they are too good to associate" with others. These were "the type of person who has to be forced to enjoy themselves.") They blamed the architecture. ("The new Recreation Building is too big, with cold barren rooms and a pool room.") They called for more propaganda. ("I think we are all here to do a job. It might be disagreeable to a lot of us, but we are going to have to put up with inconvenience, and don't you think a little education along that line might help?")[6]

Each voice, each proposal for a program to resolve the issues of social dysfunction, came up against basic barriers—security, parsimony, the District's fear of "socialism." And yet, unwillingly, the District's officers and the corporate officials at each of the sites were discovering an uncomfortable truth. By removing individual power and individual freedoms, by eradicating institutions and traditions, the District had constructed the shell of a social welfare state. Someone within the District would have to bring in the Christmas trees, because the District had abolished free enterprise; someone would have to correct the architecture of the recreation hall; someone within the District would have to start "a hikers club, a fencing club," a "men's basketball league" and a women's, too; someone would have to found "a good lively newspaper where you could say what you wanted to"—when, of course, you *couldn't* say what you wanted to. And all of this would have to be done in such a way that residents believed *they* were the owners, the instigators, the authors, as well as the beneficiaries, of each of these. Having eliminated previous communities, having suppressed the communities residents brought with them, viewing as subversive what social and cultural ties grew spontaneously, the District had to create a substitute: an illusion of that very thing interdicted from its spaces.

RECREATION AND WELFARE

As planned by the District's first chief engineer, Colonel Marshall, Oak Ridge was supposed to have been a civilian community administered by benevolent military authority. In this, the Tennessee site would have resembled the tiny Los Alamos community more closely than the larger and functionally similar Hanford site. A Town Management Division would control the construction of the town and would direct the flow between the town and the outside world—bringing in the blacktop for streets and the tarpaper for roofs, contracting for beer distributorships, and hiring the big band for the Christmas dance.

This worked well from the standpoint of security—it presented a united front to the outside and maintained military control over contact across the fences. But the whole arrangement was uncomfortably too much like socialism to satisfy Marshall's replacement, General Groves. It went against the Corps of Engineers tradition, which was to oversee its projects but distribute the work among corporate contractors.

At Hanford, town administration, community development, all the issues of everyday life went through the prime contractor, Du Pont, thus shielding the District from direct responsibility for matters uncomfortably familiar and intimate. As Colonel Matthias's diary makes clear, as the minutes of numerous meetings between the District and Du Pont officials flesh out, the Hanford communities were company towns.

But Oak Ridge had no Du Pont. Instead, it had a confusing welter of subcontractors, handling townsite construction, plant construction, operations and management, all competing with each other for the scarce resources of a frantically expanding physical and organizational entity.[7]

The entire matter was confused when General Groves took over in the fall and winter of 1942. While Groves settled into his position, Marshall staked out Oak Ridge as his last remaining turf, striving to make it an upper-middle-class community of individuals and families with advanced educations and matching tastes in recreation. In February 1943, three Town Management administrators, Devereux, Teeter, and

O'Meara, proposed a first set of activities: these were relentlessly upper and upper-middle class: golf, tennis, archery, field hockey, soccer, and riding were the principal outdoor sports; indoor activities included handball and volleyball, badminton, an officer's club, a library and reading room, a dance and lecture hall. Lieutenant Colonel Blair, Marshall's executive officer, added some working-class touches—pool, bowling—and more high-toned venues—an art room, a writing room, a dramatic society room, and a music room.[8]

Writing to Marshall with their final proposal, the three men pointed up the presence of other proletarian activities—a bowling alley already planned, a large movie theater—and they also inserted the more upper-class activities like riding in with more mundane ones, like cards and games. With the outlines of social organization set forth, the next problem became how to administer this program.

At first, District officials in Town Management considered these programs to be part of the larger mandate to run everyday life on the site, and they delegated the whole to their division. In the summer of 1943, however, as Marshall began to be further eased out of responsibility, Groves's far more austere and authoritarian rule made itself felt throughout the Oak Ridge site. Groves didn't like military involvement in the happiness of workers, and the Marshall program made him uncomfortable. Consequently he moved the site administration toward his preferred Corps of Engineers paradigm, whereby nearly every aspect of everyday activity fell under the purview of a civilian corporate subcontractor, while the District itself remained aloof, commanding from a distance, protected by a layer of administration from the tussles of day-to-day operations. The District sought a contractor to assume most of the operations of town management, and by September 1943 it had persuaded the Turner Construction Company, one of the Corps's favored corporations, to create a shell company, named Roane-Anderson, to assume town management duties.[9]

Roane-Anderson's role was to supply the physical necessities and amenities—milk and sidewalks, bus service and plumbing repairs. The main function was to buffer the military from its own policies, to absorb criticism by providing a scapegoat, and to sequester the world of everyday life from the military goals of weapons production. And there was also the matter of security; Roane-Anderson agents moved in and out of houses, often without announcement, on a twenty-four-hour-a-day basis, and military intelligence found this a convenient means of maintaining surreptitious surveillance without provoking the rage of civilians.[10]

Roane-Anderson could run the physical and administrative elements of the Oak Ridge community. But it could not create that community. That required something a good deal more disconcerting: a "voluntary" social organization secretly run by the District.

The declassified records don't tell us just who came up with the ingenious solution of the Recreation and Welfare Association. The District's official military historian reported only that "the District, in July 1943, permitted organization of a Recreation and Welfare Association, comprised of residents of the community, to operate theaters, bowling alleys, athletic fields, taverns, library services, and a weekly newspaper."[11]

This elegant description slides lightly over the underlying reasons for this organization. One was legal. Military regulations had mandated that military monies could not be expended upon civilian recreation. At the same time, military authorities were forbidden to run civilian profitmaking enterprises of the type that could subsidize the recreational activities the District now deemed essential to countering the wave of absenteeism and attrition threatening the project. The solution was to create a "voluntary association" of site residents, which could then serve as the contracting arm for beer sales, jukeboxes and cigarette machines, and dance hall management, using those funds to purchase band equipment and sports equipment, underwrite clubs and organizations, and subsidize all the other expenses attendant upon the artificial creation of an instant community.

In fact, the organization consisted of volunteer residents only on paper. The actual running of the organization lay with its executive committee, formed of representatives from each of the primary players on the site: Tennessee Eastman, Clinton Laboratories (the Du Pont semiworks subsidiary), the district engineer's office, the U.S. Engineers Division military personnel, the Civil Service employees, District Town Manager T. E. O'Meara, and a professional business manager hired by the District. (Over time, this list would lengthen, as other contractors took on larger and larger chunks of the site's work.) A bare 110 residents, called to a special meeting by their employers, elected the committee. How they were called, out of the thousands at the site, the record does not tell. The bylaws of the association had already been written, by Town Management, and the nominees for the executive committee were already chosen before the first voters showed up at the meeting.[12]

Once formed, the Recreation and Welfare Association rapidly assumed the guise of a government social agency. One of the executive committee's first acts was to hire a professional to do the actual work of management. By December 1943, the association was managing two recreation halls, a beer tavern, a pool room, movie theaters, juke joints, and a number of other facilities; it was in the process of setting up a subscription library. Within a year, the roster had expanded to include four bowling alleys, two more taverns, a total of five theaters, including a drive-in, a string of "canteens" (snack shops), two skating rinks, a riding academy, a miniature-golf course, a swimming pool, and a dancing school.[13]

These were some of the commercial enterprises that, by the end of 1944, were generating a net income of nearly half a million dollars. They funded an even more expansive collection of recreational programs. Sports activities had one paid director; the association was considering hiring two others (a man and a woman) to supervise organization of other activities—bridge clubs, social clubs, hobby programs, and the like. Croquet, badminton, boxing, tennis, trampoline tumbling, shuffleboard, baseball, softball, handball, and paddle tennis were all part of the budget, and so was a range of what the association rather mysteriously called "quiet games."[14]

The budget proposal for calendar year 1945 reveals the speed and the comprehensiveness with which the association's professionals, aided by the District's Town Management Division and watched over by its advisory executive committee, had succeeded in creating the comprehensive net of clubs, organizations, programs and facilities appropriate to a highly modern, New Deal–style town of seventy thousand. In fact, the rapid development of this network anticipates the sorts of instant-community programs that would characterize the suburban communities that sprang up in the immediate postwar years. With the professional skill expected of a professional staff,

Recreation and Welfare managed to create what, a decade later, would be called a "leisure industry."

Yet its organizational shell remained all along a necessary fiction, designed and operated to avoid the restrictions of law, regulation, and public opinion. Seen from outside the fence, its function was to run programs, make contracts, and the like, without arousing the ire of outsiders against the District itself. When beer distributors from outlying areas objected to alleged monopolies and stifling of trade, the District could reply that the contracts were really just the agreements between residents and breweries, meant to bring to the site brands that local distributors wouldn't stock. When Republican candidates might look to the site as socialistic enterprise, District officials could wash their hands, replying that the social network was voluntary and citizen run.[15]

The association sought to mask its intervention in the social life of the community—not just to further District interests, but to pretend that each activity, each club, each message came not from above but from below. This pretense would provide for residents the comforting fiction that in this area at least their needs and desires were being fulfilled in a familiar and democratic way. As a District representative told the committee at its first meeting, "the Army desired to have civilian executive representation where possible in order not to create the impression of Army domination." And the District's overseer, Colonel Vanden Bulck, sought to order committee members to do the committee's work on their own time, to support the appearance of its voluntary nature. Within weeks, however, the meetings had been shifted back to working hours. When the District objected (in a letter from Colonel Marsden to the committee), its members viewed the matter with something approaching disbelief. R&W was, as one member stated, "primary—official duty," and it would remain that way.[16]

The transcripts of meetings (held on company time, on company property, unattended by the association's titular "members") reveal the extent to which the District was willing to go to maintain this necessary fiction. In October 1944, L. C. Schroeder, the association's recreational director, came before the committee to urge that the council approve use of Grove Hall for an Armistice Day dance sponsored by the American Legion "in the form of a benefit." But when the Roane-Anderson representative, L. D. Worrel, asked who had made the request for the hall, Schroeder admitted that he and his staff "have taken over and are acting as commanders and adjutants" of the American Legion post—they had, in effect, created the post as an arm of Recreation and Welfare. No one was concerned at this—in fact, Schroeder's plan was approved, and he was instructed to return to the legion with a proposal the next night.[17]

Recreation and Welfare served another, perhaps more subcutaneous, function: it kept Groves and the District from recognizing that social welfare had become an important product of the entire enterprise. But behind all the populist touches of the association lay the District's power—the power of the purse, the power of regulation, the power to direct and to request, the power that lay most globally in the fact that the District's bureaucratic landscape surrounded everything done or imagined by the residents and their "associations." When the association's budget did not balance, it was the district engineer's office that could "make available for the use of the Association additional revenues." When District officials disapproved plans or activities, they disappeared with nearly instantaneous dispatch. When issues like the management of colored workers were too volatile for immediate District intervention, the association served well as a front organization. And when voices spoke for the association, they were District voices—except, that is, when the audience required that necessary fiction of volunteer visionaries creating out of whole cloth a new utopian community.[18]

R&W was remarkably successful at creating and funding social institutions—so much so that officials at Hanford wrote for advice on replicating the program at their site. O'Meara's response, typically, stressed the techniques for achieving the legal fiction, and the economic ramifications of the program. But perhaps the most telling part of O'Meara's letter was his response to a particular line of questioning the Hanford officials had introduced. Their interest had lain not so much with how to set up such an organization as with how that organization would deal with cases of individual need—what is commonly defined as "welfare." What of the families of men killed at work? What of individuals needing to return home to attend funerals, wishing to borrow the money to do so? Here is O'Meara's reply: "As to the question of deciding upon the worthiness of individual applications for financial or other assistance, we are not in a position to give the information, for the reason that no applications for such nature have been received. A policy covering this feature of the welfare work has not yet been established."[19]

Evidently two different conceptions of "welfare" were in play here. O'Meara and his cohorts saw welfare in terms appropriate to the employer in a company town. Welfare here had to do with reduction of absenteeism and labor shortages, social control, prevention of crime and "riot" through managed social activities that "channeled" behavior: "the general welfare." The Hanford officials were concerned about individual welfare: the process of helping those in need. O'Meara understood exactly what was being asked of him—but the association had never imagined itself as concerned with the welfare of others, because that was not the concern of its founders: the District, Tennessee Eastman, and Stone and Webster.

Within a matter of months, however, the executive committee found itself forced to swim in these murky waters. Again, the matter arose because the District itself wished to move such cases of charity and welfare from its own shoulders. O'Meara reported at the end of 1943 that the rapid influx of workers onto the site had brought with it the problems attendant with the presence of humans in trouble: cases of sudden illness; school children with no clothes to wear to school; parents of young children who had no experience with their new roles or who had to choose either abandoning their children while they worked or failing to show up on the job.[20]

Under O'Meara's guidance, the executive committee became the agency of record for matters of social welfare; the District's officers and employees, however, did the work and the District paid the bills, passing the money through the association. This resolved the administrative awkwardness. But it did not relieve the District of the larger issue. As with recreation and social life, so also with the care of those in trouble: the fiction was that a community acted, spontaneously and with caring, to provide for its own needs, while the underlying reality was that the District administered the program in order to expedite matters, increase labor efficiency, decrease attrition, and retain the most valuable of its raw materials—workers.

Matters were signally different at Los Alamos, where the scientific community dominated the social structures, and most of the workers knew or guessed why they were there and remained there out of conviction, and where the District had imported a culture rather than eradicating one. There, residents formed their own social networks and, as we have seen, these links were often created in defiance of District wishes. People in trouble turned to their neighbors and friends; in the closeness of that site, you couldn't hide much of anything. (One of the women recounted a case of child abuse; it was a network of residents, meeting informally in their kitchens, who determined the fate of the offender.) But at Hanford and Oak Ridge, the power to define social and cultural life always remained firmly in the hands of the District and its military-corporate bureaucracy. Bridge clubs and softball leagues were easy to form. What could not be forced, and what appeared rarely and tentatively, were the deeper and more powerful rhythms of culture.

Throughout the District's history, there is recorded a somewhat confused, usually muffled debate concerning the meaning of this failure. At one extreme, figures like Mrs. Brown argued that what was needed was simply more—more programs, more social staff, more clubs and organizations. At the other extreme was the argument, usually represented as General Groves's position, that the sites were captives of the military conflict, extreme, perhaps elongated versions of home-front realities, and requiring not coddling but calls and orders to further sacrifice. What is not present is a conception of genuine voluntarism, concern and commitment to the interwoven lives of one's fellows.

One finds this debate underlying much of the discussion of social welfare on the District, generally, and on the Oak Ridge Recreation and Welfare docket particularly. It appears strikingly when the executive committee considered its first welfare cases at the December 31, 1943, meeting that had begun with Mrs. Brown's pessimistic characterization of women workers and their travails.

The discussion starts rather formally: Mr. Warren, Tennessee Eastman's representative, announces he has "asked Mr. Beckstead to bring up a subject which pertains to welfare. He has the details." Beckstead, an official in Tennessee Eastman's Administration Division, begins:

> This case came up. I believe it was west of here, in the farm district on the reservation where a man was taken to the hospital; his wife was taken to the hospital to have a child; they have three children in the family—10, 8, and 4. They needed food and had no one to care for them. We took up a collection and got some money to take care of them. The question comes up—can the Welfare Association take care of cases and emergencies of this type, for instance, who would guarantee the medical bill, doctor bill and see that the children were taken care of and had food? As I understand it, we are still under the jurisdiction of the county, or state, however, they would be much against coming in here as they have no compensation for this area and have no funds available for this type of thing since their funds have been reduced by withdrawing this territory from their taxing authority. What could be done if more of this arose, and they will arise among negroes and laborers especially, on this project.[21]

The formality of Warren's introduction belies Beckstead's disorganization: he doesn't even know if it's the county or the state that should have jurisdiction; no one has investigated matters; he doesn't even mention the most likely reason this has come before R&W—that is, Security's unwillingness to let county social service agencies onsite.

What Brownstead has been empowered to ask the committee is: would they "guarantee" the bills "and see that the children were taken care of and had food?" The committee response is haphazard—Warren reports that they'd already passed children's cases on to the schools; Captain Taylor, District representative, reports, rather defensively: "We got one girl clothes for school." The discussion moves to the question of money: O'Meara wants Recreation and Welfare to pay the bills "if we have the money to do it." Taylor hopes Lanham Act federal funds will pay in; Captain Teeter (the military personnel representative) remembers a health-and-hospitalization plan that was promised, but O'Meara reports it's "not ready."[22]

What comes clear is the dual tussle: each of the institutions (the District, Tennessee Eastman, Roane-Anderson) is striving to avoid responsibility, while the members of the committee are rather frantically seeking alternatives to the proposal that they take it on themselves. Here there seems little but a wish that people wouldn't get into trouble and force these difficult issues.

And then the conversation shifts abruptly. Beckstead moves to discuss another welfare case—the James Nink family and the Red Cross's response to its plight. Captain Teeter then interrupts to announce that he has notes from Colonel Vanden Bulck calling for a number of accountability measures on the part of the association, particularly concerning money. One concerns who will pay for Christmas trees; another the prices charged in the bowling alley's restaurant. Warren then veers the conversation further, reporting a threatening letter from the district engineer's office concerning the fact that meetings are being held on company time. This prompts a flurry of debate: are we doing the District's business here or not? The meeting ends with Mrs. Brown and Mr. Smith, the civilian business manager of R&W, reminding the committee of the reason for the association: "They aren't striking here," says Mrs. Brown; "Just leaving," interjects Mr. Smith. At that, the meeting adjourns.

What has happened to the central question—of those who are without resources, helpless and in need: women giving birth, families without food, children left alone, hungry and unclothed? No one wants to accept the underlying notion, that a society could be required—not by law, but by the sheer necessity of it—to help its individual constituents, that in fact this might constitute a very basis of community. Each of the members seems instead to be arguing exactly *against* the notion that a community exists, a community that enfolds and supersedes the corporations, the military bureaucracy, the employees' associations (however artificially formed).

Warren's response to the question of daytime meetings painfully underscores the point: R&W is just one more of "about six of these meetings a week," for him, "a part of the curricula," the responsibility of the District and not of the individuals. "I personally can't take time at night for the two or three hours, from my family, for this meeting," he tells the others. They agree. This is company work in a company town; it's not the covenant of a community.

So also with the narrow opposition between a mechanistic social-welfare bureaucracy on the one hand and a punitive laissez-faire on the other. What was missing in the debates over James Nink and his children, over the pregnant woman and her abandoned children, over the question of school clothes for recent arrivals, is any deep concern for the welfare of the citizens who live and work on the District and suffer its disregard.

FREE PRESS

Nowhere was the necessary hypocrisy of a culture imposed from above more evident than with the invention and evolution of the newspapers at each of the three sites. As Oak Ridge's R&W manager declared late in 1943, American democratic communities required "a good lively newspaper where you could say what you wanted to." Yet what the District approved, funded, staffed, and produced were increasingly elaborate counterfeits of a free press—"issued weekly to inform, educate, and propagandize all workers" (as the District's official historian put it), but developed with steadily increasing sophistication, as mimics of small-town newspapers appropriate to cities the size of Hanford, Richland, and Oak Ridge.[23]

The newspapers of all three District sites started similarly—as mimeographed information bulletins designed, as a Du Pont corporate historian wrote shortly after the war, "not only to satisfy the natural desire for knowledge of current events, but also to disseminate correct local information instead of unfounded rumor or propaganda." Colonel Matthias was more honest—he called the papers "innocuous propaganda" designed to control and organize residents' knowledge of what was going on, and why.[24]

Los Alamos's stayed primitive. But on the larger sites, the ones that looked and acted like company towns, the newspapers evolved. A complex set of circumstances combined to make the final results: newspapers administered by the employees' association at Hanford and by Recreation and Welfare at Oak Ridge, but actually funded by District and corporation, using public relations staff "on leave" for part of each workday, to produce these new house organs and to disguise them as small-town newspapers.

The process differed at each site: Hanford's *Sage Sentinel,* for example, began as a rough mimeo job but quickly evolved: it was no shabby newsletter. These changes were first visible in January and February 1944, with the addition of stiff, controlled publicity photographs, many of them made for recruiting pamphlets, and the introduction of folksy columns and a more informal writing style. The appearance of a comic strip about life at Hanford, complete with a contest to name its everyman hero, had an enormous effect in transforming the *Sentinel* from its stilted company-organ roots. By March, the cartoon character "Sandy Sage" was a regular feature, and readers found "thumbnail interviews" with Hanfordites, as well as pictures of four who answered "the question of the week" and got little bios at the end.[25]

By the spring of 1944, both the *Sentinel* and the *Oak Ridge Journal* had developed into sophisticated agents of District policy. Now the heavy-handed calls for safety in the workplace and greater commitment to the cause transformed into pictorial sidebars featuring the "Safe Driver of the Week" or "Contributions from Our Readers." The line between the editorial page and the rest of the paper came to seem clearer, and the paper's role as a community booster came to resemble that of any local newspaper in any struggling small town.

By June, the *Sentinel* had begun publishing international news, and with the June 23, 1944, issue it went to a full newspaper size, with an additional allotment of newsprint that signaled a significant change in policy by higher administration officials in the District and beyond. Robley Johnson's pictures took an increasing share of the space, becoming in turn more spontaneous, graceful, and sympathetic. The work of the cartoonist, Berlin, expanded from the "Sandy Sage" comic to editorial cartoons, small illustrative drawings, and caricatures. The paper started to run photographs and graphics from national and international sources, devoting whole pages to international war news. In late October, the *Sentinel* began accepting advertising from local merchants, and with that, its fundamental difference from other papers disappeared under a layout, writing style, and new mix nearly indistinguishable from that of papers in towns of similar size.[26]

In part this convergence resulted from more general changes in American newspapers during the wartime era. In their newsrooms, too, national wartime goals and the long arm of military and government censorship had set managed news above the notions of a free press that formed one of the freedoms for which the war was being fought.

In fact, the role of the District's papers in creating community shaded smoothly into their function as reporters to the community. With the addition of local amateur sports coverage, the *Sentinel* visibly raised interest in group sports at the site; the promise of inclusion in the sports page enticed participants, even as the paper inaugurated bowling, softball, and basketball leagues. Similarly, the newspaper legitimized safety campaigns, rationing and salvaging campaigns, campaigns to persuade workers to commit to remaining onsite for the duration.

Articles themselves increasingly hid their underlying purposes under the human-interest umbrella. A general call for less automobile use arrived as a profile of Jim Morgan, a personnel clerk whose bike came across as the height of efficiency, thriftiness, and general good sense. But the close reader of this article found, as with the "thumbnail interviews," that disturbing disruption of language that marked a fabricated interview. "'For the short haul, that lumbering, thin-soled easy chair—the automobile—cannot even compare with the bike,' Jim says. 'The bike can be stationed near the door. The auto usually has to be parked a good kick and a jump away from the office wherever parking is to be had.'" No one ever really talked that way, and readers were sure to know it, even if District authorities couldn't distinguish the difference.[27]

Like Jim Morgan, the weekly workers in the "thumbnail interviews" found themselves ventriloquist's dummies for the arch, calculating language of District public relations officers. Questions invariably supported District programs—"What New Year's Resolutions have you made?" resulted in a series of commitments "just to keep on with war work until the fight is over," "to stay on this job until it's finished," or "to achieve a perfect record in 1945." Whether cheerfully accepting shortages, committing to the site until war's end, contributing to the March of Dimes, buying War Bonds, or lauding District recreation programs, workers invariably spoke that stilted tongue that marks the propagandist. And victims of the column sacrificed their own speech—

salty, personal, idiosyncratic—for District-speak, receiving notoriety and a picture to send back home in return.[28]

As the deadline for evacuation of Hanford grew nearer, these interviews took on an increasingly elegiac tone. Interviewers asked, "What has been your favorite recreation at H.E.W.?" (January 19), and "What have you found most outstanding at Hanford?" (February 2). February 9, 1945, was the date of the *Sage Sentinel*'s last issue; the Hanford Employees' Association was disbanding, and the *Richland Villager* was about to begin printing. This last issue was a reminiscing pictorial, depicting scenes and events "not soon to be forgotten."[29]

The effect of this nostalgic tenor was to encourage those needed for the last stages of construction and operations to remain with the District, and at the same time to recast the site, first for its conversion to a production site populated by technocrats, bureaucrats, and managers, and then in preparation for its apotheosis when the bombs went off. With the majority of workers leaving before they ever understood what it was their project had been made to produce, with a new class of worker dominating the new Richland community and rendering the older Hanford worker not just obsolete but inferior, *Sentinel* writers sought to draw a picture of the site that would retain the silenced obedience of soon-to-be-separated workers. Even Sandy Sage and his Negro sidekick, thickset and thick-lipped Otto, accepted their ROF (Reduction of Force) documents with regret and a certain longing.[30]

In place of Hanford, now, was Richland; in place of the *Sentinel* was the *Richland Villager,* sponsored not by an employees' association, but by Villagers, Inc.—more genteel and middle-class versions of their working-class predecessors. The newspaper itself reflected the way the community of Richland had been constructed as a reflection of middle-class American towns of the wartime period. With its front-page Red Cross appeal, its group and individual photographs of community "leaders," its mixture of news and announcements of local activities, its ads for clothes and jewelry, drugstores and milk, its focus on children: this newspaper seems typical.

But Richland as it revealed itself in the *Villager* was not a model town of the thirties and forties. It was, rather, a presage of the postwar decades. Community connections were defined not around personal roots or complex family, neighborhood, and religious bonds, but around recently invented social organizations, like the Meistersingers, or the Richland Radio Club. To read the newspaper next to similar examples from outside the fence is to see curious anomalies. Where is the "Police Blotter"? Where the expressions of resentment and of hope, of nostalgia and of memory, that characterize the pages of newspapers for towns of equivalent size at the same time? What is visible in the pages of the *Villager* is a town without trouble, a town without poverty, a town without crime, and a town without history.[31]

On the pages of the *Villager,* Richland is also a town built around middle-class material values, even though, at that moment, almost nothing material could be had, or had easily. The District assigned houses; new cars and most other high-status purchases simply weren't available; and most goods were heavily rationed. As a result, those goods that *were* available took on increased symbolic significance. Full- and half-page ads for furs appeared in issue after issue throughout the spring of 1945; similarly, ads for men's fraternal rings, tie clasps, key chains, and silver jewelry, for lockets, pendants, bracelets, and rings for women and girls, appeared prominently.

The *Villager* proposed a sedate affluence, in which the narrow band of class differences within the planned community gave added cultural value to the symbols of prosperity. Yet this was not the heady boomtown economy of Hanford Camp; *that place* remained legendary across the pages of the *Villager* as a cautionary example of uncontrolled prosperity; its famous bar brawls, its eating contests, its prodigiousness in general, represented the feared alternative to self-controlled behavior.

The Hanford *Sage Sentinel*'s themes were distinctly different than those of the *Villager*. Across the pages of the *Sentinel* the District's propagandists struggled, in happy-face, to control and channel Hanford's "destructive" social tendencies. Their pages overflowed with exemplary people, with the modest heroism of individuals doing their jobs, giving 110 percent, staying late and cleaning up, watching for spies, slackers, and agitators, squirreling wages away in war stamps and war bonds, saving up for the postwar American utopia.

By comparison, the *Villager* had little of this, and the reason is simple enough; Du Pont and the District had conceived Richland differently from the start, planned and built it to assure that the disruptive social forces needing to be held in check at Hanford would never enter the city limits of Richland. Hanford's unruly workers would build the facilities, and they would build Richland, too. As Hanford construction workers finished the Richland houses, sometimes three or four per block per day, they filled with good managers, supervisors, technocrats, recruited from other Du Pont divisions or from similar projects, arriving with their families and their furniture.

As a result, the District needed to intervene little if at all in the making of the *Richland Villager*. It was the product of Villagers, Inc., another "voluntary" organization, but one very different from the old Hanford Employees' Association that had made the *Sage Sentinel*. To organize Villagers, Inc., Du Pont and the District had gone to the clubs and organizations that had already formed in Richland—the Boy Scouts, the PTA, Beta Sigma Phi sorority, the Jaycees, the American Red Cross chapter, the Masons; they had also looked to the Castle Club, the Army Corps of Engineers service club. This new community had been built and occupied by the District's ideal workers; little wonder that they had already internalized the District's values and were ready, even eager, to propound those values in print.[32]

Villagers, Inc., thus came into being primarily as a superorganization made up of the most virtuous and stable of American community groups. That they were on District lands at all, however, was the result of District sanction and District wish. District endorsement went further; by District fiat, most of these groups received equipment, tools, portable buildings, and especially money, transferred from their counterparts at the old Hanford Camp. Organizations dedicated to middle-class status and middle-class values cannibalized the remnants of Hanford's working-class organization. The picture was not lost on ex-Hanfordites who had been relocated into the "prefab" and "trailer" areas at the edges of Richland—an unpredicted consequence of the District's failure to engineer a perfect shift from construction to production, and of the failure of earlier planners to realize that even a managerial community would need custodians and plumbers, housepainters and domestics. An opening letter to the editors of the *Villager* spoke politely of the resentment. "It was my pleasure to canvass part of the prefab area for Villagers, Inc. . . . I am sure you are interested in hearing some of the comments. . . . It was felt that the majority of benefits from the organization would be for the areas other than the prefab section. This was a very strong point and it is believed we should make some definite plans to assure the villagers in that area that they will receive the same privileges as those living in other sections of the village."[33]

The letter is rich in its implications. It tells us that as early as January and February 1945, the village had already segmented by class, and that Richland had come into being with its own ready-made ghetto: "the prefab section." Already, class resentment and suspicion was an open matter: prefab people felt themselves pushed to the margins, potential victims of discrimination; well-meaning outsiders with condescension in their voices saw fit to speak for these, believing them incapable of speaking for themselves.

But the matter is richer. Remember that this letter appeared in the opening issue of the *Villager*. And it was published as the opening to an editorial by Don Graham, the president of Villagers, Inc. "We are glad this question has been raised," Graham wrote, "for it provides an opportunity for your present officers and board to go on record as definitely stating that the plans for utilizing athletic equipment, musical instruments, the library and any other properties of activities of Villagers Inc., will be used in a manner to benefit the greatest number of village residents, regardless of the type home, the job they hold or the location in town. . . . It is realized that many people in town were not signed up as members. This was solely because of the lack of time and canvassers—not because we didn't want them. We do want them—all of them. In fact, I now urge everyone to use the membership form in this issue of The Villager to become a member. We want Villagers, Inc., to include all residents of Richland."[34]

Graham's reply bespoke a number of underlying issues, none directly addressed, all neutralized by his oblique approach. First, we must recognize that the letter was itself a sort of sham, written and run on the front page in order to allay fears that Villagers, Inc., representatives believed were widespread enough and threatening enough to merit immediate attention. We may note, for example, that no author is attributed to the letter (unlike all the letters thereafter); that it was the sole letter; that Graham began his response by admitting that it provided the excuse to "go on record." So at the same time that Graham reassured his readers, he also confronted them with the issue itself. Why do this?

The answer lies in the nature of the Villagers, Inc., mission. Whatever its later plans, its initial purpose was to provide the legal fiction necessary to allow the District to transfer equipment and materials from the Hanford Engineer Works Employees' Association—to redistribute wealth from a now-banished working class to a now-triumphant technocratic community.

The true owners of this wealth, however, weren't in fact all gone—they had been moved to the edges of Richland Village. Their presence made the villagers uneasy, even as they sought to enforce the distinction between the true Richlanders and the unfortunate ex-Hanfordites. Graham's letter confirmed this in another way when he admitted that he and his canvassers had slighted the prefab areas and focused their canvassing resources primarily in the permanent housing areas.

Now, however, he was uneasy, and so his language showed more than he might have wished. "We do want them—all of them," he wrote—but who were "we," and who were "they"? Graham answered this question; in fact, he extended the letter's rather primitive split of prefab versus permanent dwellers into a more telling and accurate distinction. Everyone should join, he said, "regardless of the type home, the job they hold or the location in town." Housing, occupation, physical geography: these were to be the determinants of status in Richland. Even if everyone did sign up, "we" and "they" would always be a distinction.

The move from *Sentinel* to *Villager* presents a paradox. On the one side, Richland's paper, the organization behind it, and the town itself were far freer from military and bureaucratic control, more the products of their constituents and less of their employers. And this was the case because Richland had been well planned from the start, with the goal of producing a community for a specific type of resident, a type of resident far more sympathetic to the cast of mind of corps and corporation alike. These were people who could be trusted to run their own newspaper and their own community. And they did it well. But the resulting institutions showed as little lively controversy, as little of what we might conceive as the free inquiry of a free press, as did the tightly controlled institutions of Hanford. The *Villager* was free from censorship and external control in proportion to the success with which the community and its members had already internalized the culture of Du Pont and the District.

TOWN COUNCIL

On November 18, 1944, Hanford's Colonel Matthias reported approvingly in his diary that democracy had come to the site. "At the end of the week of youth activities," he wrote, "the Hanford trailer camp is being operated today with a mayor, assistant mayor, chief of police, safety director and other city officials chosen from the youth of the trailer camp. The children are from sixth grade and have indicated a lot of interest in this activity."[35]

The children of Hanford needed this opportunity because they existed in a place devoid of democracy; the youngest ones had lived their entire lives outside of American political institutions, as had their counterparts at Los Alamos and Oak Ridge. The *Information Bulletin for Oak Ridge Residents* put it in an understated way. "In the city from which you come you were governed by a mayor, city council, city manager and council or other form of Municipal Government, and you were served by privately or publicly owned utility companies. In Oak Ridge, the situation is somewhat different." The difference was this: residents on the District had no power and no authority and few rights not ceded them by the District on a case-by-case basis. Of institutional democracy, there was none.[36]

The parents of Hanford's children's government were closed out from traditional American politics, yet they had their own political institutions, hybrids of small-town participatory democracy and the sort of figurehead assemblies characteristic of governments run by military fiat. In cause and in effect they differed signally from their counterparts outside the fence, offering the comforting appearance of democracy with none of its inefficiencies or uncontrollable effects. They were, in a word, powerless.

The Oak Ridge Town Council, founded in February 1944, illustrates. The town council could be elected, could meet, could pass resolutions and laws, could mandate actions of citizens and institutions alike, but it could never turn voice to action. It was purely "advisory." From the District's point of view, the policy was ideal. It enabled District officials to garner information about the complaints concerning life at Oak Ridge, and to note the identity of the complainers. It provided an entity through which the District could funnel community law and regulation, both by using its representatives to introduce legislation and by selecting from town council resolutions those it would support, allowing the rest to disappear into the files with all the other "advisory" materials that came up from below. And it provided a means of channeling frustration without directly implicating either the District or its contractors. The list of functions envisioned for the council reveals a caricature of a make-work organization designed to siphon off political conflict and absorb complaint and debate, isolating it from the sphere of action. All of this, the District declared, would make Oak Ridgers "good citizens."[37]

The origins of the Los Alamos Town Council were quite different, and so was the tone of council meetings and the flavor of council resolutions. The differences came, naturally enough, out of the fundamental distinctions between the populations of the two sites, their size, and their organization. Los Alamos was far smaller, more homogeneous, its population younger, more highly educated, more likely to have high expectations of government, more supportive of the New Deal, and more likely to question authority. University government, with its strong flavor of voluntarism and participatory democracy, tended to be stronger in residents' memories than American peacetime government; indeed, many had never voted in a presidential election—they were too young.

Los Alamos's town council derived from the same District form as had Oak Ridge's. But action within the town council was far different. Los Alamosans saw the council as an extension of the daily life of the site community, and they made it a lively and disputatious forum for airing views, making complaints, lobbying District officials, and, more broadly, forming the unspoken (and sometimes spoken) bonds of community.[38]

Alice Kimball Smith was one of the six elected council members in the January–July 1945 session. She remembered the audience as "mostly women delayed by putting babies to bed and washing dishes," who "drifted in after the meeting began, sat around the second table as long as the chairs lasted or perched along the raised hearth of the big stone fireplace, and took out their knitting." The council served as court for traffic offenses; it was through the council that you registered your dog, and if your neighbor's dog was a night barker or bit your child, it was the council to whom you turned. The official military historians of Los Alamos called most agenda items "minor administrative problems," but to the residents they were anything but. Every failure related to nonworking life on the site eventually ended up in the council meetings—from short supplies in the PX to questions of sexual freedom among consenting adults. Some meetings were quiet, many were noisy, packed town meetings, lasting far into the night. It was the town council that attempted to intervene in matters relegated to the housing office; fought arbitrary reassignment of residents from one house to another; debated the price, availability and rationing of milk; took on development of playlots and a nursery school; and attempted to deal with the issue of maids and child care more generally. Out of its meetings came the real cultural institutions characteristic of most American communities:

schools, laws regulating behavior (from desecration of lawns to determination of what constituted unseemly noise), discussion of the location of a line between individual rights and community responsibilities.[39]

Alice Smith recalled that, "perhaps twice in each Council's term, the meetings verged on the sensational; feeling ran high, and between bursts of oratory a star performer would plunge the audience into gales of laughter." These were not simple releases of resentment (as the District observers seemed to think); they were the expressions of deep issues. Two of them, both from 1944, afford us clear sight into the heart of the Los Alamos community, and the often-suppressed antithesis between its members' utopian yearnings, and the desires of the District.

One concerned sex, the other housing—or at least, these were the issues on the surface. The first was precipitated by the sudden appearance of military police stationed at the entrances to each of the dormitories where single men and women, especially the clerical and technological workers, primarily, were housed. The reason the District gave for this was a series of problems related to illicit liaisons in the dormitories. One correspondent later reported that the woman alleged to be in the men's dorm turned out to be a horse; another recalled rumors that one of the women's dormitories had served as a brothel. Richard Feynman had been at his pranks, too, putting women's lingerie on the top bunk in his room to discourage the assignment of a roommate. No specific incidents surfaced that would explain the District's sudden squeamishness.[40]

But there were the MP's stationed at the doorways. Had the dormitory residents all been low-level help, the matter might have gone relatively unremarked. But the dormitories also housed scientists, and members of the SED—the Special Engineer Detachment under which many of the younger engineers, technicians, and scientists were organized. As the town council's speakers saw it, this event represented not necessary protection, but unwarranted intrusion into the lives of civilians. It was too much like the gestapo techniques of the enemy. The women scientists, especially, were insulted at this impugning of their morals. They saw the entire issue as an attempt to create by external force a moral climate that was the province of internal, and individual, moral fabric. When a District official suggested at one such meeting that the dorm girls were spreading syphilis, he drove a speaker to tears, and assured the solidarity of the community behind the dorm residents.[41]

The scientists were quick to take the side of the oppressed, and to see principles in the issue. For the scientific community (whose members dominated the town council), the matter focused on individual and civil rights; the conflict lay between militaristic government by authority, and democratic government by individual will, community debate, and consensus. Debate was lively, but in the end, the District only took the complaints under advisement; after a time, the MPs were removed, for the District believed they had done the job of disrupting immoral traffic and were needed elsewhere for more important things.

Within the scientific community, housing was probably the most volatile issue of all, and it was housing policy that brought the second controversy. Scientific residents were used to adequate housing; most of them had risen above graduate student housing while civilians, and they'd been promised something close to what they were leaving behind. When, on July 5, 1944, District officials announced that fourteen families would be forced to move from their apartments into newly built smaller quarters, the entire scientific community rose up in protest. This was an issue that hit directly at each person, for it involved the violation of a covenant struck between the District and the individual, under which each of them had come, accepting hardship and loss, but granted in return some dignity, some sense of specialness. Nothing except the scenery had turned out as planned (the scenery—at least outside the fence—was better than promised), but individually and as a community, Los Alamosans had compromised and accepted this. They had done so partly by forging a community of adversity, and partly by developing a self-identity of sacrifice and a certain measure of secretly cherished heroicism. They were different, and their renunciations had proven it. Now they were being treated as minions, employees. The case of the "Fourteen, Furious, Fighting Families," as they were called, struck a near-unanimous chord of revolt and outrage because it spoke so directly to the real conditions of power at the site.[42]

Their weapon was talk; their only place to speak loudly was the town council. Already the housing office and the commanding officer had refused the appeal. Eleanor Jette was one of the intended victims; she recalled one of the town council meetings that resulted. "The rafters of the big dining room rang with impassioned oratory," she wrote. "Our foreign-born scientists leaped up and down waving the Constitution and Bill of Rights. (They had powerful ammunition in those documents; after the meeting I went home and became a student of early American history.) The sound and fury were impressive."[43]

Unspoken in Jette's description was the second half of Shakespeare's phrase: the council debate signified nothing to the District—nothing more than a minor annoyance. In this case, the rebels won, but the reasons were never clear. The fourteen families represented a small segment of the population, and perhaps it was easier to change the ruling and redirect the scientists' energy to weapons production. The community celebrated, but most of those involved recognized that they had won because the issue was small potatoes to the District. Smith was pretty direct on this count—"the Town Council didn't govern," she said; but "as a place for letting off steam it was a great success. . . . A representative from Post Command became an important figure in Council transactions, explaining why some innocent request could not be granted and, on occasion, convincing his superiors that those confounded civilians had a good case. His presence, however helpful, made clear what we already knew."[44]

As the site expanded, as residents' tenure there continued far beyond original expectations, the cultural roots of the Los Alamos community grew deeper, its distinctions became more clear and more important, and the conflict between a culture directed from above and one that grew from below became more and more pointed. Town council became an increasingly lively place, and its powers changed proportionally. Eleanor Jette was elected to replace Alice Kimball Smith in early 1945; she reported that "the council faced an audience of aroused citizenry at every meeting." In part, the intensity—the urgency—with which residents came to treat the council devolved from their need to voice frustration at the steadily encroaching authoritarianism that characterized their lives. Eleanor Jette described the situation with economy and force:

> I was aware of some of the problems in the town even before I took my
> seat on the council. I soon learned that morale for the town was even

lower than I guessed. . . . The unhappy arrangement, wherein our
ensealed civilian population was dominated by an antagonistic Washington administration, created a situation so delicate and touchy that it
seemed about to explode at any moment. . . . It will do no harm to reiterate that the Council had no real authority and no funds other than
those collected from traffic fines. As a body it heard and tried to arbitrate
matters brought to its attention, among which were many minor matters
in addition to grave, major problems.[45]

Over the span of its career, the council came to have a strange dual life. On one
hand, it was the cap of an increasingly democratic community, a community rooted
in voluntarism, which had produced institutions, from libraries to a radio station,
staffed and funded them, and made them meaningful to the constituency. But whenever this community came into conflict with District culture, with its rules and regulations, and its commitment to power hoarded above and doled out as dispensation,
the limits of the Los Alamos utopia became clear.

The meetings of the town council, on this and so many other issues, evoked a double
effect. From the standpoint of genuine action on a political level, they were exercises in
frustrating impotence. Grown people, lively, independent, used to governing themselves
and controlling their own lives, now could see themselves as petitioners to a paternalistic
authority. Too unimportant even to speak directly to the boss, they acted out a charade of
democratic debate for the benefit of an audience of one—the post representative—who
might or might not deem the performance sufficiently compelling to merit a mention to
the post commander who might, or might not, grant their petitions.

Yet these theatrical exercises, frustrating though they were, had powerful benefits
to the community members themselves. As Eleanor Jette recalled, they were reminders of what might otherwise have been forgotten; they illustrated the difference between an illusion of power and the real thing. And they encouraged the development
of a countercommunity, based not in power but in powerlessness. To confront the
condescending silence of the military was to understand the marvel of true speech
among equals. To encounter the mechanistic social welfare of the District was to be
reminded of the value of something more spontaneous and deeper.[46]

This was the fundamental paradox of culture on the District's sites—not just Los
Alamos, but Richland and Oak Ridge, as well (though to a distinctly lesser extent).
As the project itself wound on and on, the District's bureaucratic attention became
both more powerful and more diffuse as the structures along which it traveled became
increasingly huge, complex, even Byzantine. There grew up in response to the combination of time and unselfconscious tyranny a counteracting indigenous culture, a
counterculture, for which there was no social work; there was only the activity that
comprises living in social conditions—in a community.

At all three sites, these countercommunities coexisted uneasily with the District's
attempts at something more efficient, something controllable and obedient to laws
of military structure. But they did exist. The letters and journals that remain from that
time, the reminiscences of later moments, the oral histories made recently, all convey
residents' sense, often surprised, that life on the site had brought them a feeling of
connection to others, of social belonging, that lay in almost perfect balance to the
anomie and social dislocation of the sites.

Over time, the District's authoritarian social welfare state became the despised antithesis against which residents of the sites strove to make something better. Often this process was unconscious, and often it was surreptitious. "In all matters, emergency and routine, people were the real lifesavers," reported Phyllis Fisher, and the interaction, ranging in formality from drunken brawl to town council protest, created lines of communication and connection that ran counter to the District's pyramid—that snaked around its barriers or hid underneath them. "Without this release," confirmed Jean Bacher, "we would have gone mad." "At our evening meetings," Eleanor Jette recalled, "we pan-fried the Washington Administration and the restrictions on our lives. . . . We seized any conversational gambit available to divert the men from the grim atmosphere in the Tech Area."[47]

But the countercommunity was more than a diversion *from*. It was also a redirection *toward* something else—toward what Alice Kimball Smith described as "that clumsier system represented by the spontaneous, if at times unproductive leadership of the Town Council"; toward the egalitarianism of shared opposition and the discovery of shared beliefs. Such a counterculture cannot, however, survive long without creating its own institutions, rituals, and beliefs. And these appeared not just at the privileged site of Los Alamos, but at all three locations where the District sought to enforce its rule.

One of these counterinstitutions was language. Language was not just the symbol of District power and a weapon in its opposition, it was also the conduit for both authority and resistance. The District's experiments in social work had focused on institutions, while the social work of its countercommunities had focused on more spontaneous, malleable, and intrinsic elements. Both, however, framed their interactions in words, symbols, phrases, sentences, and documents. And there the fundamental differences between a culture of authority and a culture of community became most clear.

On September 4, 1943, the first issue of the *Oak Ridge Journal* appeared, bearing on its mimeographed cover "A Message from Lt. Col. Crenshaw." Crenshaw was about to be appointed head of the Central Facilities Division of the Clinton Engineer Works. At that time he would command the entire Oak Ridge community's development, overseeing recreation and welfare, town planning, town management, and most town construction. At this moment, though, he was formally head of the Feed Materials division, the District's code for uranium metal production.

Here is the letter in its entirety:

4 September 1943   No. 1

A MESSAGE FROM LT. COL. CRENSHAW

The advent of the first issue of the Oak Ridge Journal might properly mark the first stage in the development of the town. In the first few months, the "pioneers" established themselves, and helped to gain a foothold for those who followed them.

At this time, the family units are moving into their permanent quarters, and the town is more and more taking on the aspect of a regular community. The Area Engineer knows how important it is that each of you give your utmost to help advance the work at this project. He also knows how important it is that reasonably satisfactory living quarters be available to you so that you may be comfortable and happy.

It is hoped that all of you will strive to advance the development of the Clinton Engineer Works and the town of Oak Ridge, in order that the war effort may go on at full pace.[1]

Crenshaw's letter took pride of place in the first issue of the *Journal.* It was tantamount to a folksy front-page editorial from the publisher, or an open letter from the mayor. But try as he might, the military man just couldn't muster the right tone. He'd been too long in the military world, spoken its language too long. And what a language it was. Appropriate, perhaps, to the world of marching orders and munitions procurement, it grated harshly when Crenshaw tried to apply it to the world of daily work, homes and families.

Not that he didn't work at it. In his opening paragraph, he tried to evoke the image of American pioneers pushing back a frontier, building a fortress-town in the wilderness, setting up a new outpost for civilization. By the second paragraph, however, he'd lapsed back into military-speak. He couldn't say *families,* he had to say *family units.*

Equally revealing, however, was his next sentence: "The Area Engineer knows how important it is that each of you give your utmost to help advance the work at this project." Suddenly Crenshaw himself transmogrified, from the benevolent bureaucrat to the mouthpiece for a disembodied superior, a superior who was, on top of it, omniscient, able to see into the minds and hearts of the components making up his "family units."

In between the small issue of words and the large issues of power and authority came an intervening grammar of disconnection. In this, the entire last paragraph is redolent. "It is hoped that . . ." Hoped by whom? By the Area Engineer? By the District generally? And what was hoped? That "all of you will strive to advance the development of the Clinton Engineer Works and the town of Oak Ridge, in order that the war effort may go on at full pace." This was not a hope. It was an order, presented by an underling speaking for a disembodied Authority, now not just omniscient, but even omnipotent. "Strive to advance" the District's imperatives, and the Area Engineer will assure "that you may be comfortable and happy."

New words, and old words appropriated and reapplied; new phrases, and old phrases transformed; a new grammar, made by adapting and transforming the multiple American grammars to better fit the needs of a new system of authority; old myths, American myths, retold to have a different lesson: with these, the District moved into the most profound yet subtle means by which thought itself—and by extension, the thoughts of its subjects—came to be structured. Here was deep control, deeper than law, custom, or ritual.

It wasn't a conspiracy to appropriate language—at least, not in the sense that we normally think of conspiracy. What took place on the District was more subtle, haphazard, and ultimately, perhaps, more disturbing. The process of language-invention had its stages. First came deliberate obfuscation—from the creation of code words, to the doling out of pseudonyms, to the generation of a grammar that masked or disintegrated actions and their consequences. As this process grew pervasive, it began to subtract from the environment of discourse (of arguments, instructions, daily chat) element after element of traditional, colloquial, speech. And the *free* speech of individuals was replaced by a new system of language based in the invisible pyramid of the District's bureaucracy, in the areas of security and intelligence, public affairs, and public relations. Creating codes—codes of obfuscation, codes of instruction, codes of punishment—the District developed one of its most powerful but least visible weapons.

ROOTS

Every locale, social group, and profession has its private language, some of it conscious and devoted to streamlining communication among cohorts. Meaning and intention shift as words connect with gestures, are delivered ironically, humorously, conditionally, are changed in their pronunciation. Even as new vocabularies spread to larger and larger populations, they become paradoxically more local, for they move into enclaves (laboratories, subdisciplines, small countries with their own religions and currencies). In these places, meaning becomes particular, merging with the vernacular. Language isn't easy to control.

The District's task—scientific, technological, and military—was the most powerful source for its initial, precise, military and scientific codes. Scientists trained in European and American universities formed the top echelon at Los Alamos. To enter their disciplines each had learned the international shorthand of pure science, and its particular local variants. Often their spouses, even their children, also learned the code of science. Because they were thrust together at the site, in many cases working with others whose native tongues were different than their own, and because they worked at tasks derived from their scientific disciplines, they spoke their vernacular with each other.[2]

At Hanford and Oak Ridge, matters were somewhat different. The elite were often scientific, but they also came from engineering and technological professions, most commonly from the ranks of the major American corporations that served as subcontractors to the Manhattan District. Theirs was a variant of scientific jargon, shot through with language "efficiencies."

Over time, the commonality of languages brought grudging respect between the scientists and the engineers of corporations like Du Pont. Not so with the military culture that dominated all three of the sites. Like the scientific and engineering communities, the military had a rich and deeply personal vernacular, with its own codes, grammar, and artifacts. It, too, had a long history behind it, requiring apprenticeship and initiation into the profession before one could trust oneself to be heard or to feel assured of understanding what others were saying. But military-speak was essentially more rigid, more conservative. Like scientific language, military language described an idealized universe, but this one was social rather than scientific. Military language reflected and enforced an authoritarian utopia where orders passed down from the top, marked by obedience, protocol, and hierarchy.

Despite their obvious differences, the languages of science, engineering, and the military shared certain grammatical and stylistic traits. They were pared down to avoid ambiguity and achieve efficiency, though the nature and goals of efficiency were different in each case. These professional languages quickly became immersed in a babel of other tongues that contested for a place on the sites.

At Los Alamos, the language differences were literal—the lowest-status workers spoke Spanish and dialects of the Pueblo Indian languages. At Hanford and Oak Ridge, there were more subtle variations of race and class. As the hiring calls and recruitment programs reached out across the nation, the resulting influx of workers from every region compressed regional America into the hutments and dormitories. The wide variety of crafts and jobs brought different verbal shorthands; and three races brought their surreptitious codes for talking within themselves, and for talking about each other. Black workers spoke one language within their own ranks, another among their working-class fellows, and a third when importuning the District and its officials.

Overshadowing all other codes and colloquials was the pervasive official bureaucratic-speak, the authorized tongue spoken by government officials and corporate subcontractors and the Corps of Engineer, the language of the powerful, those who could approve contracts, hire and fire, transfer and demote. Similar to yet essentially different from military-speak, it would eventually blend with the other elite languages to form a particular Manhattan District dialect that pervaded the paperwork of the District and, over time, moved into the interviews and meetings, becoming a spoken as well as a written tongue, its advocates battling to ensure its dominance within the boundaries (physical and metaphysical) of the District.

Yet the result was never that neat. Though there came to be a District language, it was a hybrid—unique, but patched rather than invented, the result of conflict and compromise.

WORDS

Everything important at Los Alamos had another name. Atoms were *tops*. Bombs were *boats*. An atomic bomb was a *topic boat*. Plutonium was *product*. Uranium fission was *urchin fashion*. But uranium was given the designation *T*. It was *tube-alloy*; sometimes it had *tuballyl compounds*. To chemically formulate uranium, one stepped back a letter in the alphabet—U235 became T235. Uranium oxyfluoride was TO_2F_2; uranium oxide was TO_3. Sometimes U235 was *tenure*: 2 + 3 + 5 = ten; uranium = ure.[3]

Peer de Silva, the top intelligence officer at Los Alamos, sent a memo on March 27, 1945:

> 1. Effective at once, it is requested that all personnel concerned be advised that the following names or applications will be referred to by the code which is indicated. This applies to oral discussion and teletype messages.
> —Mare Island Navy Yard—"627A" or "The Yard"
> —Port Chicago—"Three Igloo Job" or "Kinne's Place"
> —Outbound Navy Shipments originated by Colonel Lockridge—
>   "Batch"
> —All Other Shipments—"Collection"
> —Shipments by Water—"Freight"
> —Shipments by Air—"Air"
> 2. Attention is invited to the distribution of this memorandum.[4]

Everything important lost its ordinary name and gained an extraordinary one. Once in a while, things were what they were. When they were—when "air" was "air"—that, too, required a code announcement. Behind this burgeoning world of code lay the military obsession with secrecy: its belief, hyperaccentuated on the District, that secrecy could be built into the culture of the sites and the personalities of its residents if only one could order them to use the right codes.

On the District, the premise was particularly difficult to put into effect. Logically, codes of this sort were designed to limit knowledge to those few who held the key. But having a key meant disseminating it, too. The danger that someone might break the code or obtain the key required that it be changed, updated, preferably often. So new memos went out, explaining the new codes. Had the audience been small, there might have been hope that the process could remain secret, and do its job. On the District, the audience was large.

One way to get around this was to instruct smaller work groups to devise their own languages and keep them to themselves. An early memo, dated November 27, 1943, argued for this strategy: "Since employees must necessarily talk with one another concerning problems related to the work in the performance of their duties, it is advisable to invent fictitious terms or code names, which are not descriptive, for reference to secret or confidential matters which it is necessary to discuss. The invention of such language is left to the individual organization so that the terms used will not be uniform throughout all phases of the general project."[5]

But this decentralization went against the heart of the District. This clash of values—on the one hand the universal cryptographic rule that codes are least breakable when known by the fewest, on the other the call of Groves's centralizing campaign for all matters to be well-documented, approved from above, regularly reviewed and as regularly reauthorized—made a shambles of the secret languages of this military science.

Code names and numbers abounded at the District; so also did letters from one group to another attempting to regularize the changes in codes, as well as letters from the Manhattan office instructing changes in codes: Miami Powder was to become Powder A, and the K-1 Barrier transformed to DA, as of November 15, 1944, under a letter from Capt. N. Randolph Archer to Colonel Marsden in Oak Ridge; or, "in all communications with the Chicago Area of the Metallurgical Laboratory, University of Chicago . . . P-9 [is to] be referred to by code name 'Product 644.'" But (for reasons not shared with recipients of the memo) this change was not complete; "the designation P-9 should still be used, however, within your plant or in communications with du Pont." Codes changed in one place were to remain unchanged in others; codes used in some forms of discourse could not be used in others.[6]

Confusion abounded; codeholders found themselves violating their codes in order to explain to others on the Project just what each code meant. Once such a letter arrived at the central headquarters, it meant the code was self-broken; the breaker of code was reprimanded, a new code invented. When new codes arrived, scientists and technicians strove to remember the changes, with mixed success. That was the reason codemakers attempted to make the system rational—it wasn't any good if it couldn't be remembered, and in the face of so many codes, often so fluid, few found the task easy. The more rational the process of constructing the code, the more transparent it became, the easier to break. Most of the scientific codes were transparent to anyone with a college-level background in chemistry and physics and the desire to make sense of the project. Just one memo from the Medical Section concerning toxicology listed enough different uranium compounds that an astute detective could determine the chemical bonds of the substances in question and surmise that the material was uranium.[7]

Despite these many contradictions and difficulties, the District strove, usually haplessly, to make its system of codes serviceable, built and based upon military encryption protocols applicable to simpler matters than the formulation of a new applied physics. As District officials moved to control the speech of scientists outside of the Tech Areas, the role of encryption changed; it became something closer to territorial conflict. With each memo expanding the role of Intelligence and Security, Groves's minions further staked their claim to control over words, in the workplace at least. Capt. W. W. Teeter was a cryptographic officer on the District in the summer of 1944 when he passed on an earlier memo about encryption, from August 26, 1943, which had originated with the adjutant general. This memo warned against the use of certain "extremely stereotyped" words that "should never be used at the beginning or end of a message." These the memo divided into "types of words . . . Compass directions (north, east, etc.), Correspondence symbols (SPSIC, etc.), Months and dates (July, etc.), Numbers (One, two, etc.), Phonetic alphabet components (Able, baker, etc.), Ranks, grades, titles (Commanding general, captain, private, etc.), [and] "Re" words (Reurad, retel, reference, reply, requests, receipt, etc.) at the beginning of messages," and "Individual Words . . . Acknowledge, Action, Advise, Attention, Authority, Cite,

Condition, Date, Desired, Duty, Effective, End, Enemy, Following, For, From, Head-quarters, Information, In Reply, Main, Message, Our, Package, Paraphrase, Paren, Period, Quote, Radio, Shipment, Signed, Stop, System, Your, Unquote."[8]

To follow such a list would have eviscerated communication between the District and all outside sources; within the District it would have made even the simplest discussions tortuously difficult. At the same time, the evidence of countless memos from Groves's own office reveals that Teeter's superiors (and even Teeter himself) paid no attention to the letter or spirit of the memo. This was natural, for the forbidden, potentially threatening words reached far beyond the workplace; though they may have been relevant to District work, they were also crucial to most forms of communication. If you wanted to follow Teeter's prescriptions, you would be vigilant in all contact, no matter how far-flung the subject or innocent the conversation.

The powerful could except themselves or supersede their own orders; for the rest, though, the illogic and rigidity of the new language became the rationale for further punitive expansions of Security into their lives. This was entirely consistent with the District's tendency to expand security protocol to the furthest reaches and smallest details of the Project. In the interest of security, more than technical words had to change. If you worked at the heart of the District, and if your name meant anything, you lost it. Your new name came in a letter from the District—complete with instructions on how to use it. Many of the principal scientists forgot who they were, to the annoyance of District security officers. Enrico Fermi was *Mr. Farmer,* though he used to stand obstinately inattentive at train stations and bus stops while his code name was called, until the security officer sent to pick him up would give up and hiss the physicist's true name. Niels Bohr was *Nicholas Baker;* his son was *James Baker.* The physicist Arthur Holly Compton was *Mr. Holly.* Harold Urey was *Mr. Smith.* School-age children of the scientists registered at school under first names only; they weren't to mention their identities to anyone.[9]

In this quest to own and control unruly language, two quite different goals clashed. One involved protecting the real work of the project from crippling losses—of confidentiality on the one hand, and of efficiency on the other. Its line of attack followed the geographical logic of Los Alamos: find a way to allow the scientists to speak and think freely without endangering the results. The other goal was pure silence. It involved a wholesale clampdown on language, with District security officers monitoring all forms of speech, even the most casual and intimate, while at the same time seeking within the sacrosanct regions of the plants and Tech Areas (where security clearances were, presumably, sufficient) to fragment groups of people and disconnect individuals one from the other—through compartmentalization, and through other more immediate interventions into the everyday lives of scientists and workers. Atomized and isolated, ordered into silence, they couldn't reveal what they didn't know, and they couldn't band together to counter the regimented pressures of the District.

Though both these impulses coexisted throughout the history of the District, the general trend moved from isolating and protecting highly sensitive speech, to limiting more rigorously and rigidly all discourse, except within the highly controlled vocabulary of the District itself.

Science and scientists constituted the subjects for a Districtwide pilot project to turn "free" speech into a commodity only affordable by the District and its obedient servants. At the Met Lab in Chicago in the summer of 1943, the scientists began a sort of free-speech movement. To meet together, the scientists had first to elicit permission from the District authorities. Then they found guards in the meeting rooms—not to protect, but to monitor and intimidate them. Despite this, the scientists met and assembled a petition to their superiors with close to fifty signatures on it. They moved to a more general discussion of the proper atmosphere for success and the need for what was called "open discussion." At one meeting, an exile from Germany spoke about the atmosphere at Nazi-supervised labs. It impressed the young scientists who were unfamiliar with the realities of authoritarian rule—they understood that they were being asked to defend vigilantly their own freedoms against a similar authoritarianism, to avoid becoming the enemy. The speech, and its message, also impressed District authorities, who had been monitoring the entire democratic experiment through their informants. Alice Kimball Smith described the outcome: "Things reached a climax when a local deputy of General Leslie R. Groves . . . interrupted a conference between one of the laboratory leaders and the young scientists to say that they had better disband unless they wanted to be shipped off to Guadalcanal. Although Compton, as Project director, intervened to assure them that this would not happen, the movement was brought to an end."[10]

At all three sites, the District tried to get its workers to internalize these strictures against free speech. One of the most important weapons in this campaign was the "security declaration." Every District worker, whether scientist or construction worker, had to sign a form swearing fealty to the District.[11]

But Security forms weren't enough. The District's security and intelligence agency accepted Groves's fear that randomly dropped phrases, bits of knowledge, names or places, their significance unknown to the speaker, might "fall into the hands" of some centralized enemy spy network, where it might then enable reconstruction of the Project. To combat such a nebulous possibility required vast expansion of the District's controls on the way people talked and wrote, and on the way they thought of the acts of talking and writing. And so the District moved from science and scientists, beyond work and workers, and into lives and minds.

It was a quick transition. By mid-September 1943, in a bulletin to all MED area engineers and their intelligence officers, Capt. H. K. Calvert, the new District intelligence officer, gave instructions on the proper attitude toward language and its most dangerous manifestation, "loose talk." Focusing on an imaginary discussion between an insider and an outsider, Calvert described the string of words that makes up a conversation. It was always an adversarial conflict, he said, in which one side held the goods and the other wanted them. Even the most friendly of talk should be seen as a process of "acquiring bits of information from this, that and other sources," by enemy agents on one side, and, on the other, by the haplessly knowledgeable worker who, with every word, "has lost control of his information; he has set it in motion, and he cannot be sure that the recipient will not in some way disclose it to another whose carelessness will cause it to fall into the hands of the enemy."[12]

Calvert's argument was wily. He proposed that his local officers present this new policy in public meetings, framing it as a sort of morality play, meant to change the worldview of audience members by dramatizing their lives in burlesque, as it were. Indeed, Calvert's memo was actually part of a larger program he was planning, to persuade Manhattan District workers to a thoroughly paranoid worldview, in which everyone, even one's spouses and children, should be treated with suspicion. Under Calvert's program, each site would have its cadre of "security educational agents," roving propagandists for silence and suspicion, drawn from the staff of intelligence officers. These new reeducation officers would themselves have to be faultlessly persuasive, used-car salesmen par excellence. Each one "should be tactful," Calvert wrote, "a promoter, possessing ability to sell himself and his work to all concerned. Further, he should have personal address, some flair for public speaking, [and be] possessed of imagination and some ability to dramatize." From dorm to dorm, neighborhood to neighborhood, worksite to worksite, agents would fan out, bringing the District's message of self-consciousness, suspicion, and silence to every resident of the District.[13]

Calvert's program expanded the District's focus from the highest scientists and most sensitive of workplaces to the lowest minions at the furthest remove from the center of power and danger. The goal was to prevent even the hint of a hint from passing the lips of anyone. Since compartmentalization and enforced ignorance meant that few people could have any inkling of what about their work was "sensitive" and what was routine and harmless, the District's plan was to have everyone simply shut up or talk code. Dramatic exhortations from "security educational agents" were only part of this larger campaign. On one side were the programs to persuade Districtites to self-censorship; on the other, the more direct procedures to stop loose talk from getting anywhere. (And behind both of these was the steady expansion of what constituted loose talk—from speech about atomic weaponry all the way down to those words that began with "re".)

At every site, posters festooned the walls, inside and out, workplace and dormitory, shoeshop and pool hall. Designed in blocky, supersimplified graphic styles, their imagery replete with metaphors for danger or with heavy-handed attempts at cuteness, the posters hammered home their message: shut up. In one, the long shadow of a bowler-hatted spy loomed across a flight of stairs, each step labeled "loose talk" (fig. 33). Another reminded you that Hanford's "know-how" wasn't yours—it was the "Property of U.S.A." "Careless conversation" was equivalent to theft (fig. 34).[14]

Posters like these represented the extreme arm of a nationwide campaign that inundated wartime Americans with imperatives: buy war bonds, save scrap metal, keep your loose lips zipped. But the District's posters worked very differently than the ones that went out into the larger American community. National poster campaigns to keep ship sailings and troop movements secret focused on specific tragic effects—soldiers drowning as their troop ships were sunk, paratroopers shot as they attempted to land. These worked by appealing to group loyalty, to personal sentiment, to identification with potential victims. Manhattan District posters were focused, instead, on inanimate objects—books, stairs, walls, buildings, pieces of furniture. They worked not by arousing sympathy or sentiment, but by threat.[15]

At the same time, wartime posters in an open American community had radically different meanings than they did at the sites. Outside the fences, government instructions competed with commercial ads, with the loud headlines of local newspapers, with the hum of workplace conversation and the buzz of neighborhood gossip. Out there, government and military posters had to contest with the opposing conserva-

FIG. 33 *[right]* Large poster made in 700-Area sign shop, Hanford. Manhattan District History, courtesy National Archives.

FIG. 34 *[below]* Small poster made in 700-Area sign shop, Hanford. Manhattan District History, courtesy National Archives.

tive power of those cultural traditions, or use it. On the District, this competition was severely limited; even so, the volume of propaganda reached new levels.

Not just posters made the point. Films, jumbo signboards, "literature" (meaning everything from brochures to mimeographed reminders tucked into handouts), even special desktop blotters emblazoned with warnings, and disk-inserts for the dials of rotary phones: all repeated the message.[16]

The Hanford newspaper was emblematic. Its very first issues had a military-chosen title that summed up the general tone: "Let's all HEW to the Line." A sidebar on page 3 of the premiere issue instructed readers: "Kill that Rumor As you Would a Snake!" The message here drew upon other campaigns already in place on the sites; the "Loose Lips" directive from a poster campaign, as well as the slogan "Whatever You See Here, Whatever You Hear Here, Keep it Here!" that resided at the top of the newspaper, appeared in most bulletins, and periodically went out in memos as well. Interspersed between columns and short articles in this and later issues were other remonstrances, in small type and often inserted between American flags: "Caution Leaves No Regrets!" "Not Rationed—Buy Bonds!" and various safety slogans. Brief sidebars and column fillers repeated the warnings: "MUZZLE UP!!!! There are at least three occasions when the mouth should be kept shut—when swimming, when angry, and WHEN OUR COUNTRY IS AT WAR!!"[17]

Implicit in these warnings was the continually enforced distinction between official and unofficial language. In an editorial diatribe against rumor, *Let's All HEW to the Line* called for workers to "heed the FACT, it is authentic; enjoy the FICTION; it is funny; turn a deaf ear to RUMOR, it is worthless and dangerous!" But it is in the definition of "FACT" that the newspaper made the implicit explicit: "FACTS are judiciously and *officially* [my emphasis] released so as not to give aid or comfort to the enemy," the editorial writer, Edward P. Schwartz, opined.[18]

The dangers of being caught committing rumor were very real. District policy declared it "the patriotic duty of every employee to report such rumors to superiors, to the security Agent, or to the Military Intelligence Office at once, without repeating them to others." Security officers then interrogated each succeeding individual on the rumor chain, making each both a security risk and an informer.[19]

"Security of this project and of the nation is jeopardized by careless work, careless talk, outright sabotage and loose thinking," wrote Colonel Matthias in the *Sage Sentinel*. There it was, on the front page: a warning against "loose thinking," more dangerous even than "outright sabotage," if Matthias's list followed logic.[20]

But what was "loose thinking," and how could the District control it? The Hanford security booklet in which Matthias's statement also appeared gave an indication. There a Du Pont official warned against "releasing information through thoughtless talking which may be based on over-enthusiasm in the work one is doing, conceited boasting, or simply falling sucker to enemy agents." If you wanted to speak freely, you must be prone to distinct moral failings—conceit, over-enthusiasm, and stupidity. "Loose thinking" was thinking that you had the right to speak freely and openly, that you could engage in acts of trust with others, that you could be neighborly. The brochure echoed a central tenet of the District's campaign: self-censorship didn't involve just silence about your work. It required "eternal vigilance" in all forms of speech and action.[21]

The brochure pointed directly to the most fundamental equation of all: language control was thought control. You could control your own words, keep your thoughts to yourself, but you'd be better off controlling your thoughts. If you didn't, the authorities would do it for you.

While the District called for silence on the part of its workers, its representatives moved from site to site promoting official speech and drawing powerful words from the American past into the accepted lexicon—words like "slave" and "free," "community," "neighbor," "family." At a rally at Hanford early in January 1944, Lt. Col. H. R. Kadlec, one of Matthias's most favored assistants, spoke. "Our ruthless enemies have plenty of labor and it is slave labor," Colonel Kadlec said. "You are here as free American citizens without being forced into your jobs, and the issue is whether free American labor is going to let Nazi slave labor build and win out." (Kadlec had apparently forgotten the purpose and effect of the Statement of Availability program at Hanford, and the contract with Prison Industries, Inc.) Kadlec's words echoed numerous similar wartime propaganda statements, but in the super-restricted environment of the Hanford site, where the work was on a weapon never destined for the European theater, they took on a more sinister meaning. Nonetheless, his speech ran in the *Sentinel,* hammering the message home.[22]

The water tower at Hanford, with its indelible message, "Silence Means Security," formed the most powerful metaphor for the program of language control within the fences. But silence *within* the fences wasn't enough. There was also the rest of America to silence. From the earliest moments of the Project, Groves and his assistants had envisioned a security bureaucracy devoted to monitoring newspapers, radio stations, public speeches, even science fiction novels and short stories, and jumping to prevent anyone from mentioning atomic energy or the possibility of an atomic bomb, and to punish any infractions, no matter how casual or accidental. As early as November 1942, security officials were monitoring periodicals as wide ranging as *Life, Popular Mechanics,* and the *Oil, Paint and Drug Reporter.*[23]

By early spring of 1943, Vannevar Bush and General Groves had forged an agreement with high military officials granting the District the right to run its own censorship program, drawing upon the expertise and the data of the military Office of Censorship, but going much further—using the punishment provisions of the Code of Wartime Practices to threaten "columnists and radio commentators," who were "difficult to control," as the Los Alamos commandant, Whitney Ashbridge, put it.[24]

There were two ways this program could go. One involved maintaining friendly contact with the press—in the words of Colonel Matthias's appeal to General Groves, offering "a minimum of information of a general innocuous nature . . . so that the beneficiaries would "be of aid in controlling really harmful publicity." The other called for absolute silence and harsh punishment; it required a small army of monitors to watch over the newspapers and the airwaves, backed up by army officers ready to take over a radio station or newspaper bullpen that committed infractions, knowingly or not. That was Groves's plan.[25]

To make his policy work, Groves authorized a new security and surveillance bureaucracy. In its first months, this involved a rather haphazard and decentralized program whereby security officers on the sites reviewed the local newspapers, looking for hints of District activity. By the end of 1943, however, its scope had begun to expand dramatically. Within a few months, the District was running its own censorship office, populated by a cadre of observers, many of them WACs, monitoring close to 370 newspapers and 70 magazines, not to mention the countless radio broadcasts that required legions of far-flung informers.[26]

From the first, the program was fraught with irony and paradox. We can begin with the security problems involved in sending out a statement that all discussion of the Project is forbidden, an announcement reaching thousands of broadcasters, radio stations, newspaper editors, reporters, and publishers—and not just one, but a series of such statements, sent out about every six months to an ever-widening audience.

The first went out on June 28, 1943, from Byron Price, Director of Censorship, in the form of a "confidential letter to the Nation's editors and broadcasters."

Confidential and not for publication:

> The codes of wartime practices for the American broadcasters request that nothing be published or broadcast about new or secret military weapons . . . [or] experiments. In extension of this highly vital precaution, you are asked not to publish or broadcast any information whatever regarding war experiments involving:
>
> Production or utilization of atom smashing, atomic energy, atomic fission, atom splitting, or any of their equivalents.
>
> The use for military purpose of radium or radioactive materials, heavy water, high voltage discharge equipment, cyclotrons.
>
> The following elements or any of their compounds: Polonium, uranium, ytterbium, hafnium, protactinium, radium, thorium, deuterium.[27]

Had the District sought purposely to violate its own restrictions on loose talk and tell a wide audience its goals and purposes, it could hardly have done a better job. The blanket nature of the embargo offended editors and journalists, some of whom decided to test the program's limits. District officials slammed down hard on these individuals. The rather benign series on land condemnation planned by the *Seattle Times* gives some indication of the strategy. In the long run these heavy-handed techniques promoted the very knowledge they were supposed to prevent. Warnings, threats, regulations, all pointed the finger at sites, at subjects, at people.[28]

Consider the matter of Los Alamos, its location and its significance: more suggestive because it was there that the District worked hardest to keep the lid on any information—denying the existence of the site at all, creating a shadow location (the famed "Box 1663, Santa Fe, New Mexico"), requiring pseudonyms of workers, severely limiting access to the site and movement from it, and so forth. But to look at the record, you'd think everyone knew where it was, who was there, and what they were doing. For one thing, Santa Fe was rife with rumors about the site, its function and "product." All one had to do was take an afternoon drink in the bar at La Fonda to gather a good deal of juicy information about the presence of a supersecret military site up the road. Condemnation proceedings, land disputes, courtroom controversies: these the District had instigated in its search for parsimony and in its opposition to compromise; the result was a busy rumor machine fueled by disgruntled opponents of the District.

The newspapers often got their information from politicians, government officials, and bureaucracies. One flurry of leaks happened at Hanford in the spring of 1944. The first leak was perhaps the most bizarre; it concerned Morrison-Knudson, one of the contractors for Richland. On April 12, Security's Colonel Lansdale called Colonel Matthias to report that the company had published "an Annual Report to Stockholders which included a large amount of classified information regarding war construction projects, of which the housing in Richland Village was cited together with cost figures." Here was a tempest in a teapot: by 1944, who *didn't* know of Hanford's existence? There was even an article about it in *Business Week* by this time. But Lansdale was livid; three days later he was still ranting to Matthias that the company had compromised "a number of many very embarrassing and illuminating bits of information about our project as well as many other war projects both here and abroad."[29]

In the midst of this came a second "violation," this time committed by the War Manpower Commission. On April 20, in response to complaints from Matthias and Groves that recruiting wasn't going well, the commission published one of its hiring calls for the site. Unfortunately for the commission, someone had decided that the way to improve recruitment was to provide "specific information as to the hiring need of this project and . . . the importance of the work," in Matthias's words. The wording was direct enough that it was picked up by the Associated Press and went out over the wire.[30]

The violation precipitated general rebellion among newspaper editors who had been held to secrecy in part by District promises that no one else would "scoop" them. Once the commission breached that wall of secrecy, the newspapers considered the agreement abrogated. Threatened by Groves's security men, they didn't back down; instead, they told the District that "they were released from any promises that they had made to us to keep information out of the papers." "At this point," Matthias rather dolefully reported, "there appears to be very little that can be done to control either the immediate publications that are coming out or future ones as the newspapers now feel that we have no ability to control releases from Washington." Groves's campaign for complete silence outside the fences had failed.[31]

Matthias moved swiftly to accommodate the change in circumstances. Hanford was obviously not a secret base any more. What it produced, and why, however, remained shrouded in darkness, and Matthias planned to keep it that way. By forbidding journalists access to the site, and then mollifying reporters and their editors with a stream of managed information and pseudo-events that could satisfy their hunger for stories, he and his men controlled with precision just what it was they knew. By the early summer of 1944, Matthias's position had spread Districtwide, and in June, he and Nichols both hired experienced newspapermen to serve as public relations officers for the Hanford and Oak Ridge sites.[32]

From now on, it was honey first, hammers later. At Hanford, Matthias stayed right in there, working out the parameters for press meetings, mixing affably with the press when they got there. The deal would be relatively straightforward—trade information and other perks in order to gain a "cooperative" relationship, in which the District could have final say over the texts of any articles that came out concerning its sites.

The first test of this involved a truly made-for-PR phenomenon: the Day's Pay Bomber—a B-29 that was bought by contributions from workers at Hanford. The whole program was a triumph of public relations: from its inception at the hands of "a Mr. Dougherty from the Utilities setup," as Matthias called him, through its conversion from a grassroots idea to a smoothly orchestrated District morale-booster (still appearing as a spontaneous popular program), until its culmination with the dedication ceremonies—truly a pseudo-event, as Daniel Boorstin has characterized these manufactured happy-face rituals. The idea couldn't have come at a better time—Matthias met with Dougherty on the same day he first interviewed for a PR officer, and Matthias and Lieutenant Christian, the new hire, arranged the dedication ceremony so that it could serve as the symbol of the District's new policy of managed openness. Matthias loved the result, and well he should have: it served double duty, boosting worker morale with an uplifting rally, while introducing the press to the site and its workers under the most photogenic of lights. "The program was apparently very popular with the crowd," he wrote in his diary the evening afterward. Lieutenant Christian proved his mettle. Matthias noted: "A number of officers appeared and all of the talks were short, direct and to the point. The newspaper correspondents that were here were talked to in Richland at 8 and they all agreed to cooperate with us to do just what we wanted them to do. Generally speaking it appears that the experiment of getting these newspaper correspondents in was very successful and I think we can look forward to much closer cooperation than we have received in the past."[33]

Security and Intelligence cast its baleful eye on publishers, editors, broadcasters, and reporters; meanwhile politicians, bureaucrats, gas station attendants, barflies, curious onlookers, and the like were letting go of information at a pace that left the security officials furious but impotent. Then, as they lost control over the large purveyors of information, they focused more and more obsessively on individual workers and residents.

Early in the war, military authorities had moved to declare their right to "effect . . . military censorship over all communications entering, leaving, and within any area, or to or from any personnel, under military jurisdiction within the continental limits of the United States." Hanford was a military reservation; it fell neatly under the regulation. There may have been some question whether it applied to Oak Ridge, never formally given over by the state of Tennessee to military reservation status, but District officials appear to have interpreted the regulation broadly. In both cases, however, the censorship of incoming and outgoing mail was surreptitious and relatively unsystematic. It was a part of the larger process of security investigation; it wasn't meant to control the word-by-word flow of information out of the site, but to discover dangerous security risks—people who needed to be silenced or dismissed. Two examples from the files give us the flavor of this policy. One involved an Oak Ridge medical officer who discovered his mail was being read when a Security and Information agent called on him at the Oak Ridge hospital and confronted him with a letter containing a suspicious reference. The letter wasn't *from* the doctor—it was intercepted on its way *to* him, and it appears to have been the first time the Oak Ridger realized his mail was being steamed open and read. In another case, an Oak Ridge employee who lost a letter she was mailing to her uncle found that Security had scooped it up, opened it, and determined that its contents violated self-censorship regulations; military intelligence agents haled her into the office, browbeat her for some time, required that she confess to what the file called her "foolish" behavior, and then had her "promptly terminated by the company for this indiscretion."[34]

At Los Alamos, though, a far different climate prevailed. Compact, relatively small in population, loaded with highly sensitive information, the Los Alamos site was an ideal candidate for traditional wartime military censorship. But there the District confronted two powerful quandaries. One was the high price the intellectual and scientific population placed on the democratic values for which they were sacrificing themselves; foreign-born and refugee scientists, especially, treasured the freedoms of speech and assembly, and they showed remarkable tenacity in questioning infringements.

But that was only half of it. The other issue concerned the *type* of secrecy the District decided it wanted out of Los Alamos. Not just quiet about what was going on, or even who was doing it: Groves and his associates early declared that Los Alamos should be utterly invisible, not simply in the mundane issues of location or population, but even on the importance of the work at all. To engage in traditional censorship of the military sort would be to draw attention to the site. No letters with rectangular holes in them, no censor stamps, no envelopes with their flaps resealed: all that would alert recipients to the fact that something was going on somewhere. Instead, Los Alamosans would have to censor themselves, and then have their outgoing letters monitored and, if necessary, corrected by vigilant military censors.

One resident, Bernice Brode, recalled the first moment: "In the fall of 1943 the daily bulletin delivered by a soldier and thrust in the kitchen door suddenly announced that all mail, incoming and outgoing, would be censored. The announcement caused quite a stir. . . . We had to apply for cards to send to relatives stating that mail was being opened for security purposes and asking that they destroy the cards and not mention the censorship ever." Immediate relatives thus were forewarned that, from that moment forward, all communication would be observed, and thus all speech would be stilted, artificial, incomplete. Telephone calls would be monitored; Brode wrote, "We sent our mail unsealed with the understanding that it would be read, sealed up and sent on."[35]

"The shadow of Security lay everywhere," recalled Jane Wilson in 1946. Some residents tried to humanize the process, to see the censors as "our guardians," in Wilson's phrase, but it wasn't really possible. "We wanted to cooperate with them, heaven knows, but often rules were contradictory or vague. Sometimes the restrictions seemed arbitrary." And so the program remained a shadow across daily lives, its perpetrators invisible judges whose goal was to find one's speech or thoughts "loose."[36]

As with so much that clustered around language, speech, and thought within the District's limits, the censorship program at Los Alamos focused on forcing residents to internalize the correct codes of speech and action. The instructions were authoritarian in their tone, and infuriatingly imprecise in their content. Here is the opening of the formal set of censorship regulations: "It is deemed necessary in the interests of security to institute censorship over all personal communications to or from any personnel at Site Y. Censorship will accordingly be instituted, effective immediately, over all such communications under provisions of paragraph 3d of War Department Training Circular No. 15 dated 16 February 1943, which provides as follows."[37]

The regulations continued, "Censorship will be conducted at a point outside the limits of Site Y and will be done by persons who are not known to you and whom you do not know." To satisfy these invisible judges, residents were to deposit their letters "only in receptacles provided for such purpose on the Post." Almost everything that made for natural speech was forbidden in the letters. People couldn't talk about where they were, or who they were with, what they were doing, or why, of for how long, or for what pay. They couldn't even discuss the weather or the mountains.[38]

To succeed at the language game, one would finally have had to embrace, rather than mimic, the authoritarian mindset that lay behind the regulations. And so residents failed; their letters revealed too much, or were too stiff, to satisfy the needs of Security and Intelligence. So amended regulations, explanatory memos, appeared. Jane Wilson mused: "Security occasionally issued pamphlets which were supposed to orient the utterances of the citizenry. They only confused me. 'Don't mention the topographical details which are essential to the Project,' one pamphlet warned. 'What detail?' thought I, feeling like a child who has had one too many rides on a merry-go-round. Were the sunsets essential to the Project? Were the mountains? The canyons?"[39]

The censorship regulations undermined the sense of self, and it showed in language: "The result of Security's noncommittal policy," said Wilson, "was that for fear of saying the wrong thing, one said as little as possible. Letters home were inclined to be terse and in my case, anyhow, painfully self-conscious. I couldn't write a letter without seeing a censor poring over it. I couldn't go to Santa Fe without being aware of hidden eyes upon me, watching, waiting to pounce on that inevitable misstep. It wasn't a pleasant feeling."[40]

The entire process was peculiarly disembodied. Once you put the letter in the censorship box, it disappeared. You might hear from your correspondent that it had arrived; it might be delayed for days or weeks at the censorship office. The question of delays generated high tension—residents pretty uniformly agreed that their mail was held back, while the District insisted that delays were minimal. But you couldn't really know. It wasn't until your letter was deemed unacceptable that the machinery intervened. If you spoke out of turn, the invisible censor didn't become visible. Instead, your letter came back to you, with an enclosed set of instructions telling you what you needed to change to make it acceptable. Only if your failure was particularly egregious were you brought down to the office to meet with a living, breathing censor.

Separated from family and loved ones, forbidden to allow them to come and visit, proscribed from leaving the site except under unusual circumstances, Los Alamos residents acted out their lives across a gulf of silence. Telephone calls were difficult, expensive—and you knew they were monitored. That left letters. But to write directly, to imagine your correspondent across the room from you, to look over her shoulder, as she read your letter, became almost impossible when you were writing for the censor's approval first, just in order to get the letter offsite. And repeated experiences with returned letters soon made letter writing an exercise, not like love but like school—elementary school. Soon, you wrote for the teacher, and not your mother, lover, or friend.

"Actually, anyone who had wanted to could have given away secrets," Bernice Brode told her audience at a seminar in the late 1970s. Censorship of this sort wasn't aimed at stopping spies, or eliminating sabotage, or anything of the sort. None of it came near to impeding the spy network that actually operated out of Los Alamos. It wasn't even really aimed at hiding secrets, but at something more complex: creating a persuasive fictitious world, into which Los Alamos residents were to immerse themselves, pretending it was their reality.

Laura Fermi pulled no punches when she described the way the scientific community, particularly the foreign-born exiles, saw this experiment in social control. "None of us had lived in such conditions," she recalled, "conditions so similar to those of a concentration camp that some European-born scientists could not stand them and quit. It was not only the barbed-wire fence, the passes and the badges, and the inspections of cars going in and out of town. It was also the Army running the town uncontested and on a socialist basis."[41]

Such an atmosphere must necessarily place immense pressures on individual workers, demanding that they choose between allegiance to the project, and intimacy of any sort. Small wonder, then, that the District's consulting military psychiatrist found Los Alamos awash in mental conflict, neurosis, and unhappiness.[42]

Few of the Los Alamos intelligentsia found this acceptable; they fought back, some surreptitiously, some with humor, and some with anger and self-righteous idealism. Mail censorship became one of the flashpoints of conflict, and the impotence of "victims" to change the system inspired subversion and pranks—fictitious enclosures of money, envelopes filled with various unsavory substances, letters with made-up serial dramas meant to keep the censor's interest. Stories of triumph over the censors vied with disgusted anecdotes about the absurdity of the program—the letter from a teenager sent back because it mentioned that amoebas reproduced by fission; the young woman whose painful secrets, poured into a letter, went to the censor and then from the censor became a matter of casual conversation at a party. Some of these reports seem unlikely, but what mattered was the way these stories focused and defused resentments over the larger ways the District cut the cords of intimacy. To tell others of the most outrageous violations of privacy, to brag of one's small triumphs over the system, was to recognize and, to some small extent, resist, the process.[43]

Of all the tricksters, the greatest was the bizarrely brilliant Richard Feynman. A true iconoclast, and a very young man, Feynman had a streak of rebellion against authority and, especially, mindless, inefficient authority, which could not help but be constantly piqued while on the District. It was he who reveled in telling off the managers of Oak Ridge, reasserting the prominence of the scientist in the development of atomic weapons. If someone picked the lock on your desk and stole highly sensitive documents; if someone locked the safe whose combination you'd forgotten; if you heard about someone trafficking in ladies' underwear—rest easy and laugh: it was Feynman.[44]

But Feynman's practical jokes usually had behind them a hint of his idealistic fervor. He hated the possibility that something might really get out through security lapses; but he hated even more the smug officiousness of the Security and Intelligence officials who manipulated the lives of Districtites, shrank their liberties and appropriated their freedoms, when real dangers of espionage and security failure went unnoticed.

Censorship was his *bête noir*. It was, he said, "utterly illegal," something "they have no right to do." Feynman was almost certainly the first to be called down to the censors' office—on the very first day the program went into effect. He and his father had a tradition of sending each other messages in codes the sender would invent, and the recipient would then struggle to crack. His wife, dying in a tuberculosis sanitarium in Albuquerque, had taken up the habit. Both letters arrived that first day, and of course they weren't acceptable. The censors insisted that future letters would have to include the key to the code. But Feynman didn't want to see the key—it would ruin the game. So Feynman and the censors compromised: he told his family to include keys; the censors agreed to remove the keys when they read the letters.[45]

Feynman seemed to excel at passive-aggressive strategies that forced the absurdity of authoritarian systems into the open. His battle with the censors resulted in near-weekly events. When his wife wrote, "It's very difficult writing because I feel that the [censor] is looking over my shoulder," the censors clumsily attempted to remove the word *censor* with ink eradicator. The result was a series of letters between Feynman and his wife concerning the issue of censorship—the very thing they weren't supposed to talk about. Only now the censors had to allow the exchange, because their ineptitude had created the difficulty. Feynman recalled the result decades later, "Finally they sent me a note that said, 'Please inform your wife not to mention censorship in her letters.' So I start my letter: 'I have been instructed to inform you not to mention censorship in your letters.' *Phoom, Phoooom*, it comes right back! So I write, 'I have been instructed to inform my wife not to mention censorship. How in the heck am I going to do it? Furthermore, *why* do I have to instruct her not to mention censorship? You keeping something from me?' "[46]

Feynman's strategy resulted in an uncharacteristic response from Security and Intelligence: they were frank, telling him they feared letters would be intercepted. Unexpected honesty disarmed Feynman, and so he and his wife worked out a secret code so that they might speak frankly without the censors' knowledge. Feynman wasn't happy that the program had pressed him to choose between loving intimacy and "something illegal," and so he and his wife worked out a series of sabotages, most of them uninflicted, but fun to plan; one involved sending letters on jigsaw puzzles, another the inclusion of messy pink Pepto Bismol powder, which, when the censors opened the mail, was sure to powder clothes, floor, and furniture, and require that the censors find a source for replacement powder so as to keep the letter intact.[47]

Feynman's pranks sought "to point . . . things out in a non-direct manner." Around the site, they became legendary, yet for us they raise another and more complex question. Like so much of the folklore of resistance to censorship and social control, Feynman's battles defused his anger, turned the anger of others into laughter and amused resignation, and allowed the District to continue its programs without creating an explosive conflict between the residents' call for individual and collective rights, and the District's desire to use their talents and control their minds at the same time. Rather than boycott the program, rather than move actively against the District's appropriation of the project, these scientists came to accept their increasing powerlessness. When, in 1945, the time came to fight hard to prevent the weapons from being used except as a "last recourse," the men and women of the scientific community found they had been shunted far, far to the side. Over the years, the District had learned how to manage them, and they had learned how to maintain their dignity, and even a posture of resistance, while they were being managed. Little by little, they had learned to keep their thoughts to themselves, they had learned to talk the language of the District until, at the end, it seemed they had forgotten how to speak in any other way.[48]

GRAMMAR

Information officers, programs, and policies all reinforced the District's steady encroachment on the word-landscape. Boundaries separated the spaces of the District, where only sanctioned language was allowed, from the outside territories, where freedom, loquacity, "loose talk," represented danger. The District's landscapes were festooned with the signs of the District's language-colonizing. Look at the office walls shown in official pictures—at the tidy signs asking: "Are your drawers shut?" Look—more closely still—at what's printed on the outside of a trailer in which one might live at Oak Ridge (fig. 35). You won't find the names of its occupants, or the address, or any of the homely signs that people put on the outsides of their houses. In place of these, there is a string of numbers and letters: 810, W2192, F, 16902, 19-30. These are, in their own way, declarations of the District's hegemony over the sense of place, reminders of who owns what. But they are also directives of a sort: if you wish to describe where you live, you have to use this clipped, official code to explain it—not just because these are the only signs permitted on District trailers, but because the street, the subdivision, the entire city are similarly organized and named.

This particular photograph is, itself, a document that reinforces the District's grammar—though the way this grammar is imbedded in visual form is clearer in another, equally prosaic picture, also made by Du Pont's official site photographer, Ed Westcott, to illustrate the workings of the K-25 master control room (fig. 36).

Reading the photograph as a distinct document, one can recognize the District's extension of written grammar into visual grammar. Yet the brilliance of the method manifests itself in the way the picture seems not to *tell* but to *show*. Even though, to a careful eye, it's an obviously managed, set-up picture, still the impression persists that the result is natural. The obsessional orderliness of the workplace seems incontrovertible. It seems simply to show the control desk with its banks of switches and the supervisor's desk with its paperwork, with everything lined up parallel and neatly diagonal to the walls filled with their workstation graph-paper plotters and their own cruciform arrangements of gleaming lights. The people, too, are nicely symmetrical—two men, two women; two engrossed in tasks, two awaiting orders. The desks are orderly, reassuringly so. Underneath the details is a message: Everything's under control in the control room.

Of course this conclusion is abetted by Ed Westcott's crisp, businesslike efficiency as staff photographer following orders. Most likely, Westcott has augmented the existing order: he's brought the men and women together at the central area. (He's probably the one who decided that two women should round out the group, and that all four will act out the comfortable roles of men and women in the workplace, with the men the bosses and the women their secretaries, receptionists, assistants.)

Westcott has manipulated the circumstances; yet, at the same time, that's the way things *are* in the master control room. All Westcott has done is make it particularly clear and unambiguous. Similarly with the bland, even lighting. He's combined flash-

FIG. 35 *Trailer in Trailer Camp,* Oak Ridge. Photo by James E. Westcott. U.S. Corps of Engineers, Oak Ridge, Tennessee.

FIG. 36 *Control Desk in the Master Control Room, K-25,* Oak Ridge. Photo by James E. Westcott. U.S. Corps of Engineers, Oak Ridge, Tennessee.

bulbs and ambient light in the right mix to give the faces that washed-out generality that allows the specific people to become Everyman and Everywoman. But no matter how he might have lit them it's doubtful you would be able to pick them out in a lineup. That's the result not just of Westcott's choice of models; its also the result of the District's choice of employees—good, average, white men and women.

Even Westcott's work isn't really his. He has worked the changes in this photograph on orders. The district information officer who ordered this photograph had ideas in mind about what would look right, and he'd schooled Westcott long ago, so now the photographer knew what was wanted and could do it with the minimum of instruction. So the picture satisfies the District's own need for order; otherwise, Westcott wouldn't have made this picture or perhaps even have achieved his position as chief photographer for the Clinton Engineer Works.

Behind Westcott's professionalism lies the repertoire of conventions he learned as he mastered the job of staff photographer. So also with the conventions learned by the architect-engineers of the master control room and transmitted to their plans: that the control room should have even, revealing lighting, and that such lighting came best from multiple panels in the ceiling; that the plotters for each K-25 cubicle should properly be lined up in even rows where they could be easily seen. (This arrangement is orderly, but it isn't necessarily intelligent; looking at the control panel of the Hanford pile for the first time in the fall of 1991, I was struck with an immediate and palpable anxiety, for each of the control stations looked like each of the others—in a crisis, how could the operators, assured by the law of compartmentalization that they would never know the logic that lay beneath the dials, distinguish between one dial and the next in a row of some 100 identical dials? Equally so with the dials and plotters in this master control room.)

Grammar is description, and it is call to action. Grammar takes data and makes it information, connects it into an order to emulate or to learn from. The District's grammar depicted a world far different than the one its occupants might have known outside the fences. And that grammar was imbedded in everything it made or modified to its will. At its most insistent, it broadcast in declaratives and imperatives. The security posters convey one side of it: "ESPIONAGE IS ALWAYS A THREAT. DON'T DISCUSS YOUR WORK OFF THE JOB!" "Don't Open THE BOOK with CARELESS CONVERSATION"; also isolated phrases, pieces of fact strewn about the surface: H.E.W. KNOW HOW SECURITY PROPERTY OF U.S.A. LOOSE TALK. These messages bespoke a need for the reassuring order of declarations and instructions.

District memos carry the other side of the District's grammar—its relentless occupation of the passive voice. The passive voice tells two lies. First, it inverts the chain of causality. The object of action becomes the subject. Then the cause of action somehow disappears from the scene. "I dropped the cup, daddy," says the two year old. "The cup fell over," says the three year old. "The cup got dropped," says the six year old, shielding his sister without taking the blame. Somewhere along the line, the action disappears. No one dropped the cup—it fell on its own or, more distantly, it "was dropped," but the initiator of the causal chain disappears. When this happens, there develops an aura of inevitability to events. No one can be blamed; nothing can be stopped, or changed.

"It is deemed necessary in the interests of security to institute censorship," read the first sentence of the Los Alamos censorship regulations. "Security of this project and of the nation is jeopardized by careless work, careless talk, outright sabotage and loose thinking," read Colonel Matthias's opening to the Hanford security booklet. "You are advised that it has been determined necessary to the interests of the United States in the prosecution of the War that the property of the Los Alamos Ranch School be acquired for military purposes," read the opening sentence of the Los Alamos condemnation letter. At Hanford and Oak Ridge, the Land Acquisition Section filed "Declarations of Taking" to mark legal authority to expropriate specific parcels of land. "With the development of the MED project, the need for insuring uninterrupted production at key facilities becomes increasingly important," read part of a memo on production schedules sent out on "28 June 1944."[49]

Here's an entire memo, from Capt. R. A. Larkin to Col. A. W. Betts, headed "Classified Communications Facilities":

> 1. Attached herewith is a copy of a letter from the Commanding Officer, NOTS, Inyokern, with CNO dispatch 112009 of September.
> 2. It is understood that the Signal Officer at Site Y now has in his possession cryptographic systems for use in communicating with NOTS, Inyokern. However, it is further understood that this channel may not yet be used until approval has been obtained from the Commanding General, Manhattan Engineer District.
> 3. It is requested that a decision on this matter be obtained in order that a reply may be made to the request contained in the attached papers.
> 4. It is requested that the letter from the Commanding Officer, NOTS, Inyokern, and CNO dispatch #112009 of September be returned to this office.[50]

This is the language of bureaucracies, social systems that carry out orders in part by removing the source of orders, thereby deflecting opposition and making obedience easier than interrogation or resistance. Even time is magically neutralized, pressed into an eternal present, a distant past, or an indeterminate future. District Engineer Nichols of headquarters sent out a "Revision of Security Policy" on August 9, 1945, the day Hanford's plutonium bomb exploded, destroying Nagasaki. "Restriction against personnel revealing the fact that they are connected with the project will be removed," he wrote. "Restrictions against divulging general organizational structure of the project will be modified." "Security will be relaxed." Nichols wasn't the instigator of these revolutionary changes. Groves wasn't either. No one was, really—unless it was the explosion at Hiroshima, or the "collective will" of the nation, or of the District. And when would matters change and breathing become easier? Sometime; not now, not yet. Nichols and Ruhoff would remain safe.[51]

Grammar of this sort disembodies power; Captain Larkin disappears, Groves disappears, Nichols disappears, even when the signatory to a memo. It's appropriate to a geography where everything is ordered, everything is to be orderly, a geography devoted to creating weaponry that would kill with a burst of light and heat from above, kill with invisible force waves, with invisible death rays, kill now or kill, mysteriously, days, weeks, months later. It is a grammar directed from above, so to speak.

Disembodied grammar pervaded the artifacts of the District, subsuming words, pictures, physical spaces. When Robley Johnson received orders to make aerial photographs of the Hanford site and its immediate surroundings, they appeared in the form of long lists, marking out the focal length of the lens, the focus point, the longitude and latitude, time of day, comments. From these came a photographic grid: thousands, perhaps tens of thousands of photographs demarcating every inch of a space as big as Rhode Island, updated at intervals, the film processed, the prints made and marked to correspond to the orders, sent to headquarters, filed. Purpose unknown. Purpose: documentation.[52]

Behind the specific orders was a more general one. A district circular letter from Security Officer W. A. Fogg, Manhattan office, stated that "Photographs . . . will be made only by expressed permission of the authorized representative of the District Engineer having jurisdiction of the subject matter, for the purpose of recording progress of the work or of preserving for future reference special or unique conditions encountered in the prosecution of the work."[53]

The individual order forms sprawled past aerial photography and into routine pictures of each building, from each side, at each stage, made at each site. For these, too, the photographer worked by orders to achieve an uninflected, neutral deadness—pictures without interpretation, pictures without meanings.

For us, today, the resulting photographs have an eerie quality; they appear to be preparatory evidence for reconstructing the site after a holocaust. But this is our projection. Something more purposeful was at work. The photographs were often sequential; Johnson's crew took dozens of photographs of a single trench at Hanford. In some cases, someone instructed the photographers to mark on the negative not just the date and camera location and angle, but the time, and to make photographs at minute-by-minute intervals. One sequence detailed each of the original buildings left in Richland after condemnation, demolition, and construction of the new town. Johnson went down one side of the street and up the other, replicating the grid of the new street-plan, even when it disturbed the logic of the sequence. He used a placard that held removable type. In front of each ordered subject he'd place the placard, pushing its metal standard into the ground, and putting on it the proper identifying code—D-7937, D-7938, D-7939, and so forth (fig. 37). He'd been trained at Du Pont as an industrial photographer; he knew how to make pictures so lucid as to seem transparent. "These were records," he told me, in Richland, at eighty-two—"I don't know why they wanted them; they were evidence for some purpose, I guess."[54]

The pictures, making the pictures, blended into the life. Sitting in his living room in Richland in 1990, in the house the District had made for him, Robley Johnson recalled the grammar of everyday life on the District. Who determined what pictures should be shot? "Orders came down. That's all." Who determined how they were to be done? "I was expected to do my job." What was the Photography Section like? "So many workers; something like twenty workers. Just the making of ID photographs occupied much of the time. The photos were made when workers arrived, as part of the processing: intake information and papers check; medical exam; ID photo. Each night the film processed and ID cards made up; workers picked them up next morning before reporting to work."[55]

Sometimes the pictures were even more precise, more imperative. Remember, Johnson took the photographs of the test smoke patterns that recorded the future path

FIG. 37 *D-229: Shoe Repair, 11-8-43.* Photo by Robley Johnson. Richland Operations, Department of Energy.

of iodine 131, the radioactive isotope that spilled out of the furnace-chimneys of Chemical Separations. The aerial pictures, their stamps marking the precise time of the shutter's release, seem so innocent of causality. In them, the chain is broken and we see white clouds patterned across a clear sky. Under such a program of photographs, everything is normalized, even the military knowledge of tragedies that will be allowed to occur in the name of efficiency or "military necessity."

The work blurred into the life.

> I came out in May of '43; my wife and family didn't come until September of '43, and by that time we'd built the houses. Whether you got a house early or later depended on where you were in the heap, and they gave you what was suitable for your family at the time; $37.50 a month and no electric meter and no water meter and if you needed coal, you'd just call up and they'd deliver it.
>
> They didn't tell you anything; you didn't know what you were doing, but you did it faster then anywhere else. You worked all the time; you couldn't talk about anything you did—you mention the word "atom" and you'd have the FBI on your tail. You didn't have anything to do, so they had clubs for everything—stamp clubs, horsemanship clubs.[56]

Johnson told this story in 1990. His wife, Ruby, was there too: "You had no choice; you just took what they gave you; coming out here, getting into Pasco at three o'clock in the morning—well it just seemed like such a godforsaken place. We'd never been in a government town before—we'd been places with Du Pont and this seemed so small and so much emptiness."[57]

The grammar of living played out on a landscape with a similar grammar: so small and so much emptiness at first, then gridded off with streets; and the streets, first denominated by number and letter, then given the names of Corps of Engineers luminaries unknown to anyone but a historian of military engineering. At Hanford Camp the landscape of sameness continued—regulation layout, furnishings, occupants. The men and women Robley Johnson photographed for the *Sage Sentinel* were the winners of Clean Desk contests, Good Housekeeper contests, productivity contests, Miss Hanford contests. Meant to satisfy the corporate desire to create a stage-set normalcy on the sites and thereby reduce employee dissatisfaction and anomie, these last photographs appeared in recruiting pamphlets and booster publications for the sites, and in the house organs at each site. In subject, they sought to provide residents and potential recruits with the illusion that life at the sites was no different than anywhere else in America (fig. 38). In style, they drew from the discourse of mass-culture photography of the thirties and forties—not only newspaper and newsweekly journalism, but the "documentary" photographs of government agencies like the Farm Security Administration and the Office of War Information. But their goals were far more carefully defined, their production more carefully supervised, than were the pictures made in those earlier government programs. Security dictated that there be no exterior shots except for one or two general views, in which the camera angle prevented the viewer from identifying even the ecological zone in which the picture was made. Instead, the pictures were views of social interiors—housing units, recreational facilities—with stock characters acting out their roles in the too-empty pool hall or seated on the tightly folded blankets covering

FIG. 38 Thanksgiving dinner, Hanford. Photo by Robley Johnson. Richland Operations, Department of Energy.

bunks in the hutments (fig. 39). With their carefully organized compositions, stagy smiles, and pseudoevents (fig. 40), all illuminated by an open flash, they seemed readily able to slip into the picture files of wartime picture agencies, governmental or private. But again, they defined themselves by their absences as well. There were no people in these photographs—only virtuous types. Johnson and Westcott justifiably prided themselves on these pictures, and they bear similarity to the work of official armed service photographers released to the big national picture weeklies. The pictures normalized activity at the site; they conflated activities there with activities in the freer world outside the barbed wire and guardhouses. But they also inured their viewers to the circumstances in which they lived, by celebrating as freedom what was often simply obedience—the purchase of war bonds, the conversion of barracks rooms into "homey" quarters, always neat, always marked by propaganda posters or maps of the war zones or similar indexes to wartime will (fig. 41).

With the photographs it is sometimes difficult to locate the passive, imperative grammar: is it in the pictures, or in the things the pictures depict? Most of the time, it was both. Even G. Albin Pehrson's humanized plans for Richland homes or SOM's plans for Oak Ridge fit this vast implacable grammar—fit or had their structures changed, their vernacular idiosyncrasies limited or forbidden (at Groves's meeting with SOM he had decreed: "24 wash bowls too many, to be reduced. . . . Oil burners are out. Can use fireplaces."[58]

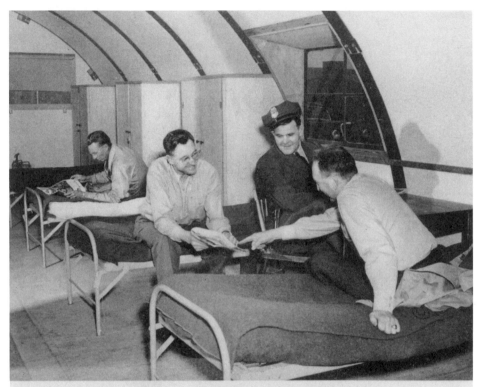

Huttments are cleaned daily and linens are changed once a week.

Is the Food Good?

You won't find any fancy cooking here, but it's good, wholesome food for hearty men. You'll eat in a Mess Hall, family style, and you'll always get plenty to eat. Meal tickets, for 21 meals, cost $12.98, but they punch your meal ticket only when you're there, so you don't pay for any meals you miss.

If you work out in the field, you take a box lunch with you from the Mess Hall in the mornings. You'll want your own thermos bottle for the coffee.

FIG. 39 Page from *Highlights of Hanford*. Richland Operations, Department of Energy.

FIG. 40 Cover, *Highlights of Hanford*. Richland Operations, Department of Energy.

D 7992

FIG. 41 Barracks interior, Hanford. Photo by Robley Johnson. Richland Operations, Department of Energy.

   Return to the sites, their geography, their settlement and their physical presence. Compartmentalization pervaded knowledge, action, the things you touched and the places you lived and worked on the District. This, too, is a grammar. It is the same grammar found in the condemnation notices and the encryption memos and security notices and the house-organ articles about life on the site, illustrated by staged promotional photographs. It is the same grammar, writ larger, large enough to seem invisible down at ground level.

It is deemed necessary. You are advised that it has been determined necessary to the interests of the United States in the prosecution of the War. There is a military necessity. You are to go. Return. Stand for Bus. Sit Only Where. A military necessity exists.

In the record boxes containing the accumulated files of the Manhattan Engineer District at the Southeast Regional Depository of the National Archives, there are folders marked "Medicine—Hygiene" and "General Medical Reports." Inside, one might expect a fat collection of carbons, reports, letters, memos, and the like. After all, the Medical Section of the Manhattan Engineer District employed hundreds of doctors over its wartime life, treated hundreds of thousands of District residents, engaged in significant basic research into the dangers of radiation, of uranium ingestion and inhalation, of plutonium poisoning.[1]

The files are virtually empty—not just there, but throughout the public archives that hold District materials. The records have been destroyed, hidden, or remain classified. Medical records, released to the workers whose names are on the files, would have represented what Colonel Stafford L. Warren, head of the Medical Section of the MED, called "medico-legal" complications.[2]

(Even as late as 1996, with the Department of Energy going so far as to open an Internet website for declassified records of the cold-war medical experiments using atomics and radiation, few new materials have appeared—covers for reports, summaries, but not the reports.)

In the handful of documents in the file is a letter from Dr. Joseph Hamilton, a researcher for the District in Berkeley, to Dr. Robert S. Stone, head of the medical sections of the Metallurgical Laboratory at the University of Chicago and the visionary originator of the District's medical research and hazards-prevention programs.

"I am writing," said Dr. Hamilton, "concerning our experimental subject, Mr. Stephens, who was given the 50 micrograms equivalent of Pu^{238} [radioactive plutonium] approximately two months ago. This man has formerly been a painter by trade but due to his illness, his economic condition is somewhat difficult. . . . Kenneth [Scott, Hamilton's coexperimenter] and I are very much afraid that the man may sell his house and go to live at some distant point which would, of course, put an end to our most interesting set of experiments." Hamilton wanted to offer a proposal that "may be totally irregular and out of keeping with army policy"—to pay this victim of plutonium poisoning to stay nearby and allow Hamilton and Scott to continue tracing the progress of the plutonium through his body. "I think this end could be accomplished if we could pay the man fifty dollars per month," Hamilton estimated.[3]

Hamilton sent a copy of the letter to Colonel Warren, Stone's military superior, and he took the opportunity to bring the two men up to date on other experiments he was supervising. One concerned the rapidity with which certain decay products from "the Uranium solution" reacted over time; another involved the development of "a better method of large scale removal of Product from biological material"— urine and feces, and (presumably) tissue samples. This second matter promised a more efficient way of determining just how much radioactive poison individual workers on the District had ingested, whether in the course of everyday work, or as a result of "incidents."

Hamilton ended his letter with a throwaway: He reported to Stone and Warren that Scott "has also checked the urines of Connick, Hamacker, Kosah, McVey, King, and Koch. Twenty-four-hour urine samples have been counted and the entire output of Plutonium ranged from .004 to .0185 counts per second, including background. The background of the counter plus chemicals gave blank values of .004 to .020 counts per second so as a result, I think we can conclude that these individuals are not contaminated with more than 0.1 microgram of Plutonium"—one five-hundredth the dosage of Stephens—"and probably much less." Hamilton signed off "with very best regards."[4]

Hamilton's letter is a fragment from a vast and still hidden archive documenting the attempts of the District's medical workers to determine what constituted a dangerous dose of the many radioactive materials on the District, to trace the etiology of radioactivity injury, and to find some hints as to how to treat the injured. This fragment deserves attention, and not just because of its rarity. Its language, the circumstances implied in the four experiments it reports, and the very nature of its request concerning the fate of the shadowy "Mr. Stephens" provide us with the wedge to open up an understanding, even if incomplete, concerning the relations between the most basic conceptions of humane responsibility to one's fellow men and the dictates of military expediency during the close of a war.

We can know these few facts. Seven individuals have been somehow contaminated with plutonium—all have ingested it, by either inhaling or swallowing it. One of them, it seems, has been deliberately administered a dose many times that which his cohort received by accident. Plutonium that enters the body stays there—as one of the District's researchers noted, "nearly 90 percent of the plutonium entering the body is retained for many years." Plutonium is a notorious "bone-seeker," that is, it migrates quickly to the human skeleton, where it lodges in the bone marrow. There its damaging effects are complex. It continues to irradiate the surrounding tissue for the duration of its radioactive life (plutonium's half-life is 24,000 years), and the likelihood of cancer increases dramatically. Sustained radiation of this sort also increases the speed and number of genetic mutations in surrounding cells. At the same time, its presence in the blood-manufacturing zone of the human body interferes with the production of certain blood components. As the amount rises, the damage rapidly escalates: leucopenia (drastically reduced white-blood cell count), reticulocyte reduction, platelet deficiency, anemia. "It caused early death in rats and mice," reported one MED researcher.[5]

Plutonium is a deadly poison, and its effects can be painful and debilitating for the victim. Yet Hamilton's letter seems on the surface curiously devoid of Hippocratic concern. Stephens somehow "was given the 50 micrograms equivalent of Pu^{238}"—fifty times the "body tolerance limit" determined by the District's medical research team. For Dr. Hamilton, "Mr. Stephens" is not a patient; he is "our experimental subject." His illness, never detailed in the letter, is important to Hamilton and Scott because it may "put an end to our most interesting series of experiments."[6]

(The use of the term "interesting" was characteristic of District medicine. Capt. John L. Ferry, Corps of Engineers Medical Section, U.S. Engineers Office, Manhattan District, in a similar report to Dr. A. G. Kammer of Carbide and Carbon Chemicals Corporation, the K-25 contractor, reported a Mr. James Bradham who had symptoms "presumably following an exposure at S-50 to material." Ferry ended his letter by noting: "It might be interesting to watch this man to see whether or not recurrences are encountered.")[7]

Mr. Stephens's doctors present him to District officers as the bodily landscape upon which to impose their "most interesting series of experiments." They have depended upon his complaisance (induced in part, perhaps, by the enervating effects of plutonium poisoning itself). Unlike a real landscape, this human subject has announced his intention to leave them; even then they do not think of him as a human being with human needs. He is a commodity, an experimental subject.

The story of medicine and the Manhattan District ties the abstractions of language, social theory, and bureaucracy to mortal bodies. Unpacking its story, fragmentary and incomplete, returns us to the center of this moral history and prepares us for what always lies at the end of the history of the bomb: nearly two hundred thousand civilians, *the enemy,* faces melted, skins crackled and in places still aflame, waiting and perhaps wishing to die and be freed of the body: the consequences of war and victory.[8]

We don't know what happened to Mr. Stephens. But we do know the fate of Dr. Hamilton's request that he be permitted to pay his experimental subject fifty dollars a month to remain a part of the experiment. On July 27, 1945, Lt. Col. Hymer L. Friedell, Colonel Warren's deputy and a radiologist who had studied under Hamilton and Stone at Berkeley before the war but who had, since 1942, served as General Groves's military spokesman in medical affairs, wrote a response. It didn't go to Hamilton but to the area engineer for the California zone. Hamilton can't have the money, Friedell wrote. "However, if it does become necessary to provide Mr. Stephens with some sort of retainer, Lt. Col. Vanden Bulck recommends that *a value be assigned to each specimen obtained and purchase orders issued to pay for the samples* [italics added]. It is requested that this office be informed if payment for specimens is instituted." The District's bureaucracy declared Mr. Stephens only as valuable as his plutonium-laced human wastes.[9]

The medical program began at the Metallurgical Laboratory at the University of Chicago in the spring of 1942. Arthur Holly Compton, director of the Met Lab at this early stage, recalled the circumstances: "Our physicists became worried. They knew what happened to the early experimenters with radioactive materials. Not many of them had lived very long. They were themselves to work with materials millions of times more active than those of these early experimenters. What was their own life expectancy?"[10]

Met Lab physicists knew about the early European researchers with X rays and radium who had been injured or died as a result of their scientific labors (some of the Met Lab scientists had known them personally). And they knew about the workers painting radium on watch faces at United States Radium in New Jersey who became the victims of bizarre illnesses—rotting bone and bone marrow, acute long-term anemia, weakness, infections, cancers of all sorts.[11]

The radium dial scandal conclusively linked ingestion of radioactive materials with a wide variety of injuries and illnesses—some immediate, some delayed. Doctors in the New Jersey area saw, treated, and reported to the medical community at large the bone necrosis—decay of jaws, in this case—the failure of marrow to produce blood cells, the longer-term likelihood of cancer. A New Jersey health official reported in the *Journal of the American Medical Association* as early as 1925 precise outlines of the cases; by 1930, he reported further effects in graphic detail. By 1933, records of cancer, anemia, and a host of other radiation-induced illnesses and fatalities had appeared in leading national medical and public health journals.[12]

The National Bureau of Standards published a handbook in 1941 that detailed the dangers of a wide variety of radiation exposures applicable to the Manhattan District: handling of radioactive materials; bombardment by proximity to materials; breathing of dusts; breathing of gases; ingestion of the elements by mouth or by skin contact. Even more important, the research upon which this handbook was based confirmed that cancer could appear some years after exposure to radiation.

But a dark possibility asserted itself during the same decade. All proposed standards assumed a threshold below which cells healed themselves or were simply not affected. The question of an adequate standard revolved around determining that threshold. But evidence from the field of genetics revealed that minuscule doses could result in genetic damage and mutation. There seemed no threshold to this phenomenon, and the evidence suggested, as one historian of science has noted, that "what looked like tolerance could simply reflect effects too subtle for current techniques to detect." Though the National Bureau of Standards committee could not agree on new, significantly lower limits (from .1 roentgen to .02r "tolerance dose"—that is, the total amount received each day), the controversy within the committee entered the public forum and the medical literature as well.[13]

The Met Lab program early sought a medical representative to join the team, primarily to monitor the medical condition of the scientists. From this came the plan for a health division with a far more extensive mandate, and Compton found an appropriate leader in the University of California's most prominent radiologist, Dr. Robert S. Stone.

The choice was fortuitous. Radiology was not a "developed" medical specialty—in fact, it was rare that one could even do a residency in the field before the war. The Met Lab was a very enticing opportunity, indeed. Within months after recruiting Stone, Compton had staffed his nascent Health Division.[14]

Compton had given the new division a dual mission: "protection of the health of the workers on the Project," and "protection of the public from any hazards arising from the operation of the Project." From the first, everyone involved knew this would require high-level research "to establish tolerance doses, to predict more accurately what might happen in the future, to devise means of detecting ill effects to personnel, and to discover methods of treating any person who might be injured," as Stone wrote, shortly after the war.[15]

At the center of Stone's program was the notion that the University of Chicago, the Met Lab, and its participants had a "moral obligation to the personnel and the community," and this moral obligation was to make certain that the weapons being developed would be forces for good, that workers and citizens would not end up the unwitting victims of state imperatives, even in wartime.[16]

Within the young health division, there prevailed a philosophy both moral and scientific. Medical research and medical supervision of the industrial process were essential to ensure that the Project would move forward with full knowledge of the risks and with adequate plans for coping with those risks, rather than bumbling forward in a state of hopeful ignorance. Yet fundamental problems bedeviled the program from the start. First among them was its clash with the District's deeply imbedded obsession with rapid "progress" in weapons production, and its desire to cast unfortunate side effects—like what to do with the toxic, radioactive effluent of plutonium production—off onto some hypothetical rosy future, when undisclosed (and as yet unfunded) scientific research and development would come up with solutions.

This was surely a David–Goliath conflict; Stone's Chicago Health Division was small, isolated from the centers of power, and nascent, while the District itself was already mature and had behind it all the weight of the Corps of Engineers and the army. In addition, the medical section was a supplicant to the District—for funding and for permission to pursue its research program. To achieve its goals of ensuring safe practices in the short and long term, the medical section would have to beg the District's military, industrial, and production sections to tailor their programs to the dictates and the schedules of a tiny group of white-coated civilian research doctors from the University of Chicago.

From the first, the medical section was behind the curve, and that effectively doomed its program to the margins. It would have been hard enough to persuade architects and engineers to modify their plans and corporations their manufacturing procedures; it was another thing entirely to ask them to change what they were already doing. With workers already handling uranium, and with plans for the first piles and programs for factory production already in the development stages, the medical division faced the fact that there wasn't even an agreement about what constituted a hazardous radiation dose—and this line between *safe* and *dangerous* defined everything, from the type of gloves to be worn by experimenters to the thickness of walls in factory settings.

Outside the Met Lab, the pressure was simply to accept the dosage levels that had been set as industrial standards before the war. Upon the timely determination of "tolerance doses" would rest millions of dollars worth of construction and quite possibly many months' difference in production time. Unfortunately, the X-ray and gamma-ray "tolerance dosages" established by prewar industry were based on "rather poor experimental evidence," as Stone understated it. Moreover, "there was little knowledge of the tolerance for fast neutrons, and none for slow and thermal neutrons, or for alpha or beta rays," and these were all constituents of the radioactive emissions that were likely to result from the program. Even before the Manhattan District had assumed control of the Medical Section, Stone and his new colleagues were torn between the dictates of scientific accuracy and the calls of District higher-ups for military expediency.[17]

The problem was compounded by the disarray that accompanied helter-skelter excursion into a radically new scientific endeavor. Everything interconnected, and most of it was in a state of rudimentary development. There were few instruments for measuring radiation, none at all for measuring certain of the most dangerous. Much of the medical research had been based on the so-called "erythremic dose"— sufficient exposure to cause visible reddening of the skin: a nuclear sunburn. But it was one thing to apply such a standard to radium dial workers who were in contact with the hazardous material, another to apply it to people exposed to whole-body radiation, or radiation primarily to feet or face, or to the lungs as a result of inhaling uranium or plutonium dust. And there was the entire question of contact with "fission products"—radiation emitters, rather than radiation itself. The production program was destined to produce a complex "soup" of these incredibly rare elements, some of which (like plutonium) had never existed in nature before the arrival of the Project. But no one yet knew much at all about their medical dangers.

Working rapidly, facing deadlines that branded the scientific method an impediment rather than a necessity, reminded often of the imperatives of wartime, the men and women of Stone's Health Division often made decisions based upon incomplete knowledge and an imprecise definition of what constituted danger to those exposed. For workers and planners, there appears to have grown up a particular sort of doubled vision: the more terrifying the prospects—sterility, infertility, long-term cancers, debilitating illness long after exposure, genetic mutation producing damaged children—the more potent the repression and denial that accompanied it. The record is rife with stories of scientists, many of them brilliant, who took immense risks, routinely overexposing themselves under the pressures of the moment and the demands of the program. Their doctors, too, were not immune from this psychic numbing.

By the spring of 1943, as Groves moved to assume control over every aspect of the program, the Metallurgical Lab was one of the prime sites toward which he aimed his attention. Groves's contempt for intellectuals affected the medical programs, too. Because these individuals attempted to define and defend against still-abstract hazards, and because they threatened to slow weapons development (and, perhaps, because they set moral imperatives into the same arena as military-tactical issues), the Medical Section was particularly vulnerable to "conversion."

The process began with Groves's decision to build a separate military medical program within the District, independent of the Chicago program and superseding its powers, its military staff owing unconditional allegiance to the military-industrial culture and to Groves. The person Groves and his men chose to run their program was Stafford Warren. Warren was probably as skilled and knowledgeable as Stone, but he had a more attractive credential for the Army Corps of Engineers—he had worked extensively as a consultant for the Eastman Company in Rochester, was familiar with the dictates of industrial production, and had the endorsement of Eastman's corporate policymakers.

It was in April 1943, in a meeting with Stone and his staff at the Met Lab, that Warren first learned the important details of the program. From that point on, his relations with Stone, and the relations between the District and Stone's Health Division, grew strained. Warren had corporate and industrial allegiances; he served Groves directly; his early actions strongly suggested his commitment to the military expediency of the project. More than that: he became one of Groves's few confidantes, as well as the general's personal physician. Groves obviously trusted him; knowing the general, it is hard to imagine that such trust could have come without proof of the doctor's absolute loyalty. (Even the fact that Warren, a radiologist, would end up serving as a general practitioner suggests something of the inappropriate medical demands that Groves made of Warren, and to which Warren acceded.)[18]

The division between military medicine and Hippocratic medicine, between Warren and Stone, focused itself in controversies over the mission and the independence of Stone's medical research team. At the forefront was the question of the independence of Stone's group from military authority. But that was in some ways secondary to the two deeper philosophical issues: the role and importance of high-level scientific research into the effects of radiation and "emission products," and the overall mission of the military medical division. Stone was always troubled by the question of melding the demands of wartime with the scientific method and with the ethics of medicine. His reports concerning such matters as the amount of radiation to allow workers to experience under "emergency" circumstances show him agonizing over the proper balance of war and humanitarianism, as he sought to define for his frontline physicians and health officers the compromises they might allow their patients to take, "this being a *war* project and speed being a necessary factor." "In answer to your specific question— 'what dose of gamma radiation may an area superintendent order one of his men to be exposed to with reasonable assurance that the chance of any permanent damage occurring is extremely slight?'" Stone wrote in October 1944 to Hanford's Dr. Norwood. "My personal opinion is that an area superintendent should not *order* a man to expose himself to other than tolerance except in cases of grave emergency when *time* is the most important element. Before a man is *asked* to do a job requiring overexposure," Stone continued pointedly, there would have to be close determination of the dangers, by a senior radiologist. Wartime allowed for greater hazards to workers, as long as they were fully informed of the dangers and volunteered, he concluded. His was a vision of a democracy at war, in which the balance between liberty and patriotic self-sacrifice were determined through open discussion and voluntary action.[19]

All available evidence suggests Warren had a different concept of the rights of those subjected. From the first, he was Groves's man; while still a consultant, he presided over the militarization of medicine on the Project; he even wrote the "statement of mission" that K. D. Nichols sent out over the signature of the district engineer. When the medical office was ready, in October 1943, Warren arranged to be commissioned a colonel in the army, named the head of the Section, and designated as Groves's official medical adviser.[20]

Warren's mission statement for his new medical division was particularly revealing. Early in his stint as a civilian consultant, he had called for "the supervision of research designed to establish the presence of hazards and limitations to be set up for the elimination of health hazards in the various aspects of the project." His new mission statement substituted a critical variant. There Warren called on the medical division to determine "what protective measures should be taken to eliminate *or protect* against any *specific* health hazard *of a serious nature*" [italics added]. The addition of the word "specific" gutted the Chicago program of its focus on low-level radiation and toxicity studies, branding it a fishing expedition. Adding the phrase "of a serious nature" to the end of the statement further separated the medical research program from the study of long-term effects, for it required some predetermination that the health hazards were, indeed, already serious. And that the medical division was now forbidden to undertake the experiments to determine.[21]

It was a classic Catch-22. Warren took away from the Medical Division the mandate and the power to mitigate the very health hazards that would later prove to be most characteristic of radiation and atomic injury.

Eventually, Warren's demotion of medicine went even further. Stone's team, and the larger medical bureaucracy Warren himself would supervise, became the inspectors of all the factories and sites. They were "expected to give assistance and cooperation . . . by making periodic inspections to check on the working out in actual practice of the protective measures devised"—but their power was advisory only. They had no powers of enforcement, no authority to halt dangerous practices or order changes in the procedures. Warren's program left the doctors and researchers diffident servants to the contracting corporations and the district engineer's office.

Warren's recommendations were draconian, but they weren't enough for Groves. He wanted further guarantees that the doctors themselves would not let humanitarian concerns get in the way of their duty. He sought an authority that could supersede the Hippocratic oath. Three months after Warren—by now a lieutenant colonel—took over the Medical Section, Groves acted decisively. He wrote to the head of the Army Service Forces urging that the entire medical program be militarized.

His argument was pure Groves: the issue, for him, was control. Militarize the doctors and you have the means to prevent unwanted information from leaking out of the Project. Doctors under military control could be forbidden to report any hazards to either patients or the broader medical community, inside the Project or outside. Equally important, military doctors would serve at the direction of the commanding officer, staying put, doing their work, quiet.

Groves's way of putting this last stipulation summed up his argument. He requested "that the Medical Department Personnel . . . be not transferred to or from the control of the District Engineer . . . in order to control the security of classified information and in order to ensure that the especially selected medical personnel will be retained on their presently assigned tasks." This last stipulation meant that the medical staff—doctors, nurses, orderlies, and aides—would remain virtual prisoners with the Project for its duration.[22]

The reasons concerned more than the fear that they might deliver secrets. Groves's letter began with a statement regarding "the unique occupational hazards which will be encountered in the operations of the projects under the control of the Manhattan District of the Corps of Engineers." Groves wanted to be sure that doctors confronting these "unique occupational hazards" could not endanger the continuation of the Project, whether by requiring more extensive medical and occupational safeguards (threatening the cost efficiency of the Project and slowing its progress) or by injecting a dangerous ethical debate over means and ends. Shortly thereafter, Groves got his way, and Warren took over supervision of a military section.[23]

Despite his clear allegiance to the District and the military, Warren still began his tenure believing that military and health dictates could be pursued concurrently. Early on, Warren had hoped to "see that there are no health hazards in any of the operations of the Manhattan District." But his commanding officer was Groves; the general looked for *limitation of hazards,* insofar as the commanding officer determined was pragmatic. By militarizing the medical section Groves assured that individual doctors could not concern themselves with ethical matters.[24]

This clash of values was fundamental to the troubled history of the Medical Section. On one extreme was Dr. Stone, and his Met Lab colleagues, who saw themselves as founders of the medical program, and conceived their responsibilities on the project as extensions of their medical and scientific responsibilities outside the District: to the welfare of their patients, to the good of humankind more generally, and to the furtherance of scientific and medical knowledge on the assumption that this would eventually lead to safer conditions and better forms of treatment for those who might be injured. At the other extreme was Groves, whose concern was with keeping a lid on information should there be (in Lieutenant Colonel Warren's words) "accidents with radiation exposure."[25]

Warren may have started off on Stone's side; once head of the section, he gravitated rapidly to Groves's camp. For him, safety practices became "a primary requirement, quite apart from humane considerations," because of "the necessity of maintaining absolute secrecy." His explanation of the way secrecy determined safety, written decades after the end of the Project, is revealing:

> 1. If scientists or workers in any part of the project should receive enough radiation, or should absorb enough radioactive material, to produce physiologic damage, it would be impossible either to keep the project secret or to procure enough employees to carry on with it.
>
> 2. If controls over radioactive materials in effluent air and water and on contaminated clothing were not strict, radioactivity might become measurable in the surrounding community and the knowledge might leak out that a secret government project was operating on a large scale with radioactive materials.[26]

"Directly or indirectly," Warren boasted, some thirty years later, "security . . . was the original driving force that made the most hazardous, and probably the single largest, industry under one control in World War II the safest of all wartime enterprises." Warren's was an empty swagger. As we shall see, even he never knew the extent of immediate injury on the Manhattan District, let alone the longer-term injuries to workers, environments, and surrounding populations that District policy simply eliminated from consideration, only coming to light in the last decade. But it was under his orders that the Medical Section shifted away from its mandate for the elimination of health hazards, and to the control of "medico-legal" complications for the District.[27]

It took nearly a year for the consequences of this shift in power to surface. In February 1944, Stone's Chicago Health Division finally received enough plutonium from the military division to begin research on the hazardous effects of the metal. It would be months before the first results would begin to trickle in; pragmatically, it might be years before truly conclusive evidence could be garnered. That August, Stone confronted Warren directly over his continued refusal to fund research into low-level emissions and long-term effects, and Stone was utterly routed. Warren ordered that no long-term studies should be initiated, no new facilities built, and all research redirected to focus solely on producing clear, usable information on "acute" illness.[28]

What for Warren seems to have been clear-cut was, for Stone, painfully complex. In his letter of protest to Colonel Warren, Stone exposed the ethical core of the District—the balance of life against life, of injury against injury, that lay behind each decision: soldiers against workers; District employees against true civilians unknowing of their danger; those killed or injured today against those struck down later, years, perhaps decades later. And Stone's last-ditch attempt to return the Medical Division to what he saw as a truly medical mission may well have been motivated by the disturbing results he was beginning to receive from his team's research. Warren's mandated experimental plan wasn't yielding the relevant information. There simply wasn't time to wait for latency effects to show up, and so the data was transparently optimistic, in light of previous evidence that short-term recovery masked long-term damage that eventually resulted in terminal conditions like leukemia.[29]

Stone was in evident distress; he understood that the experimental method used was inappropriate to the problem, and that conclusions drawn from the experiments were colored by the momentum of the Project and the ambition of its military directors. Nonetheless, there was the equally agonizing fact that this program was a wartime weapons program, and it was going to continue whether or not Stone had qualms about possible injury to a few, or a few thousand, workers. Stone had hoped to use sophisticated research to discover "the means by which radiations, no matter what their origin, caused the changes in biological matter." From this, everything else would follow. "If this mechanism could have been discovered," Stone wistfully recalled, "many of the problems would have been simpler." And this was the core that Warren removed from consideration by the militarized medical section, and placed off limits to Stone's division as well.[30]

By the middle of 1944, the Medical Section's path was clearly set. It was a military entity, split off from any allegiance to or supervision by the surgeon general. Using contracts, budgets, and the exigencies of day-to-day work on the Project, Warren had successfully reoriented Stone's lab from basic research toward short-term studies. Perhaps most important, Warren's own emphasis had evolved into an echo of his mentor Groves's focus on immediate results, minimal costs, and a narrow conception of cost-benefit analysis. But there was something less obvious and more pernicious also at work. The Medical Section had begun to embrace a philosophy of purposeful ignorance, of knowledge control, which sought to limit research into atomic hazards in order to prevent revelations that might hamper the project. Warren's administrative and philosophical changes now began to affect the day-to-day workings of the District.

From a military standpoint, the dangers of unlimited medical research were multiple. Experimental results might leak out to workers, spreading panic and causing boycotts of production, both by scientists and by line workers. Compartmentalization was the prime weapon to counter this danger. But while limited knowledge was adequate for line workers already relegated to ignorance and silence, Warren's adaptation of the compartmentalization program couldn't work on top-level scientists, simply because they already had knowledge, if incomplete, of the nature of the tasks and the potential dangers of their work. For them, the District held a different kind of duplicity: let the scientists think that sophisticated medical research was underway or already complete, that hazards were understood and responses mapped.

This was the situation graphically illustrated by a series of catastrophes at Los Alamos in 1944 and 1945. As early as February 1944, Oppenheimer himself had written to the Chicago group, rather plaintively reminding the scientists that they were "in a far better position than ours to undertake" the work of devising ways to detect and measure radiation and its causative poisons. A year earlier, Oppenheimer had hired a self-professed neophyte, a twenty-nine-year-old internist only four years out of medical school, to run his health-hazards section at Los Alamos. As had occurred at the Met Lab, Dr. Louis H. Hempelmann and his associate Dr. James F. Nolan didn't even arrive on the site until after work was well under way. Nolan took over general health care; Hempelmann devoted himself to the dangers of the Tech Area.[31]

From the first, Hempelmann had depended upon Stone's group to do the elaborate medical research necessary for his task. Even before going to Los Alamos, he had made a pilgrimage to Stone's laboratories. Unfortunately, he arrived at a time when the members of Stone's group believed they had control over the outline and direction of medical research, and believed as well that they had an adequate program mapped out to assure a realistic safety program. Hempelmann arrived, in other words, at the worst possible moment, while hopes were high but before the truly daunting problems of long-term, low-level hazards research had yet become clear, and—perhaps more important—before Warren had entered the scene to put his peculiar stamp on the enterprise. Hempelmann left Chicago for Los Alamos convinced that the Met Lab would handle research; as a result, Los Alamos never developed its own research program.[32]

Over the next eighteen months, Hempelmann and his colleagues would grow to regret the decision. Unable to get the information they needed from Chicago and its subsidiary laboratories, they began to suspect that something was amiss. Compartmentalization successfully hampered the rapid exchange of information between sites—requests had to travel up the ladder of command, in this case reaching up to Warren and perhaps to Groves before being redirected to their actual recipient; responses moved the same way. No one had told Hempelmann and the Los Alamos people that Warren and Groves had shifted the focus of the medical program, eliminating most of the medical research, underfunding other projects, and redirecting the entire program to pragmatic industrial-medicine issues.[33]

The bloody consequences of this change became clear in August 1944, when a vial of plutonium compound exploded in the face of a Los Alamos chemist, and the victim spontaneously gasped and swallowed, taking the material into his respiratory and digestive systems. The Los Alamos doctors immediately called Chicago: How do we determine how much he has ingested? they asked; What are his risks, and what are his chances? What do we do to save him? In vain they waited for a response. Even now, with production of huge quantities of plutonium at the Hanford factories just four months away, Met Lab's Health Division could not answer the questions. Medicine had failed in its mission to find the necessary knowledge to understand radiation injury and develop the techniques to deal with it.[34]

The accident and its consequences provoked Hempelmann and Oppenheimer to confront General Groves. He, in turn, sent Warren down to confer. Faced with a revolt, Warren acceded to the Los Alamos demands for an accelerated medical research program—at Los Alamos. But Warren's concession was smoke and mirrors. Stone's Met Lab medical team had the training, the experience, and the expertise to mount and supervise such a program, and the commitment to see it through to completion. But Warren didn't give the program to Stone; he gave it to Hempelmann, an inexperienced young doctor supervising a multitude of medical programs, from routine hospitalization to medical monitoring of an upcoming atomic test. In fact, the timing of the battle between Stone and Warren suggests that the Los Alamos accident may well have precipitated Stone's confrontation of Warren, the confrontation that resulted in the Chicago medical team's forced shift to a search for "quick useful results."[35]

Why was this? One answer lies in Warren's own description of the role of medical research, pieced together from his memos during and after the war. As he reiterated his position to Stone in 1945 (when, it seems, Stone was once again questioning the wisdom of District policy on medical research), the medical section was "charged with conducting operations which will be valuable in the present war effort; . . . all accessory and auxiliary functions should be directed and oriented so that they are in direct support of this premise." When it came to medical research, the prime focus was "medico-legal"—the function of research was to prevent, not injuries, but lawsuits resulting from injuries. If the Medical Section unearthed evidence supporting radiation dangers and long-term injury on the part of workers exposed to materials and their radioactivity, that knowledge could be used to support legal claims of negligence against the District.[36]

Over time, Warren's attitude trickled down to the line researchers. In his reminiscences, the colonel described the effect: "The pace and pressure were usually so great that there was little time for speculation, and the general attitude of the medicobiologic research workers was 'If this is all we need to know, we don't want the responsibility of knowing any more.'" Here was the goal of compartmentalization realized in a new and chilling way.[37]

From a medico-legal standpoint, ignorance was bliss. Stone and his people never grasped this concept. They were trapped in a different paradigm, in which the saving of human life, the elimination of health hazards, and the development of sophisticated scientific understanding of this new and terrifying world were prime parts of their moral mission. Their reports, written during and immediately after the war, reiterate this focus. Stone's researchers took every opportunity to recount the differences between acute injuries and chronic ones, and between the types of research necessary to each. Long-term injury could not be simply deduced by subtracting from the acute dose and its effects, nor could these effects be as easily deduced from the sorts of experiments the District was willing to fund—animal studies where the metabolism, skin thickness, amount of fur, and the like interfered with direct inference, and human studies where high-level doses brought immediate and visible effects. If you wanted to determine reasonable and necessary precautions in the workplace, first you had to have a clear understanding of what constituted a "tolerance dose"; to do that, you had to understand how long-term, low-level exposure might affect the lifetime health patterns of workers. Behind this was the purely scientific question of the "mechanism" behind radiation injury. But the research necessary to this goal must inevitably slow production. To know the dangers and to order workers to endure them nonetheless was a textbook definition of negligence and liability. If you didn't find out the hazards, though, you were safe.[38]

It was not just in the area of long-term medical research that the District confronted unresolvable conflicts. There was also the matter of day-to-day industrial medicine, where District medical officers, Stone's researchers, and the health-and-safety people within the corporations overlapped and clashed—and where radiation dangers mixed with other hazards.

The District's official history, written in 1945 and 1946, reports that the electromagnetic process at the Oak Ridge site included "phosgene and dusts containing uranium, but numerous other hazards were also present." The doctors and their associates weren't dealing only with radiation and its mysteries, but with whole cities full of profoundly hazardous industrial processes in factories often working round-the-clock—circumstances that invited traditional industrial accidents. The diffusion processes used dangerous uranium hexafluoride gas, and uranium oxyfluorine as well. Just how volatile these processes were is indicated by the official historian's 1946 statement that Tennessee Eastman's electromagnetic process resulted in "an average of 150 cases of occupational injury or illness . . . every 24 hours" when the process was in full production. And these were only the cases treated by the Tennessee Eastman Corporation medical team; lower-level injuries, such as skin rashes from contact with radioactive and toxic materials, may have been much higher.[39]

The District Medical Section's responsibilities in this regard started with the task of determining what constituted a safety hazard in each of the toxic materials that seemed to permeate the site, and in each of the complex processes where, in one plant, hundreds of different toxic materials might be produced at different stages and in different places. In addition, the possibility of accidental interactive contaminations could not be discounted; a worker might carry one material, on his skin, or imbedded in his shirt or even his face mask, and then touch or inhale toxic materials from another area. And the inclusion of radiation danger only made the calculus more complex. Different types of particles—slow and fast neutrons, X rays, gamma rays— all had different effects at different distances and were neutralized by different materials. (Fast-neutron radiation, for example, was unimpeded by lead, but could be stopped by paraffin.)

Everything conspired to pressure the Medical Section investigators into hasty, ad hoc decisions. For there was always the District's own insistent haste, coupled with its unwillingness to fund or staff projects that did not have immediate and visible effects in speeding up weapon production. The size of the medical program suggests how low a priority it was: the research group reached its peak in 1945 with 72 medical officers, 3 dentists, 3 medical administrators, 1 veterinarian, and 1 sanitary-corps officer.[40]

By the middle of 1944, Medical Section doctors found themselves with multiple responsibilities. In order to determine the nature of the dangers, they needed to inspect and become intimately familiar with each factory and each process. From these inspections, they hoped to devise efficient and safety-conscious programs to replace the haphazard conditions that predominated. Concurrently, they needed to teach workers and management how to implement the health and safety regulations already in place, to lessen the dangers until they could get new procedures worked out. In addition, it was the Medical Section that was responsible for monitoring all radiation and toxic emissions to air and water, including such programs as the salmon-irradiation experiments in the Columbia River at Hanford and the testing of mud and water in White Oak Creek at Oak Ridge.[41]

In the face of this, the Medical Section managed to devise a remarkable set of programs—on paper, at least. But imbedded in the culture of the corporations and the military, doctors and scientists came increasingly to shift their allegiances. Slowly, steadily, the language of medicine became infected with the attitudes of military efficiency, and with District habits of speech.

This process came painfully to the fore in the matter of health-and-safety inspections of sites and factories. Consider an inspection visit to "Dr. Spedding's Institute" in Ames, Iowa, made by Doctors Watson and Tannenbaum early in February 1944. Spedding was a metallurgist with the Iowa State University, and his program was to experiment with means of efficiently extracting uranium. Watson and Tannenbaum "questioned" and "examined" "a number of the men who had possibly been exposed either to chemicals of one sort or another or to excess radiation." They inspected the program and the plant, and they reported back to the Medical Section with recommendations for changes in the District plant safety program, the production layout, working conditions, medical treatment, and more specific diagnoses, prognoses, and treatment plans for those found to be injured. It was a daunting task, and they did it in a single day.[42]

The lab was fine, but the plant at Ames presented a harsh lesson in sloppy and dangerous working conditions. Space was inadequate, "the potential dust hazard . . . considerable," and the two doctors "observed many workmen whose skin was slightly green in many areas because of exposure to this dust." In addition, the factory's "safety man," a Mr. Gladrow, was primarily a laboratory researcher who spent "only about two half-days weekly on the safety problem." There was no program for monitoring radiation laboratories "where hot [i.e., radioactive] material was being handled," and "no regular desk or hand inspection in progress." Not only that, but the safety officer himself was one of the men inspected for radiation and uranium contamination after "he spilled a rather hot sample, as he described it, on his hands."[43]

Watson and Tannenbaum "questioned and examined a number of the men who had possibly been exposed either to chemicals of one sort or another or to excess radiation"—eight of them. (How many of the Ames workers had in fact been contaminated the report didn't say. It seems clear that the two doctors examined as many as they had time to see, but they didn't get to all of those waiting in the hall outside the examining room.) The exams bore stark witness to the importance of the now-moribund basic research program and warned how fundamentally its foreclosure was to alter the prospects for safety for workers. Mr. Warp "came in contact with the metal only with his hands and no dust exposure," but his urine had shown indications of contamination, possibly of kidney damage. Yet the doctors had no more sophisticated way of determining contamination and radiation injury—they were reduced to gross physical examination, looking for erythremia, hair loss, weight loss, and the like. "Examination revealed nothing significant," they wrote, and sent Mr. Warp back to work. Mr. Kempt had been working with "hot metal shipped from Argonne," studying "volatilization of fission products." He "was apt to be careless." Again, however, the doctors had no way of knowing whether any injury had been sustained; they noticed "a very small area of reddening over the dorsum of the right fourth finger," reddening that could have been evidence of continued contamination, a precursor to tumor. But it might have been the result of Mr. Kempt's having closed his hand in a window, nervously picked at his fingers, or any number of other reasons too trivial for the subject to remember. The doctors could only recommend that this symptom "should be watched."[44]

Every single case the doctors looked at that day mirrored this quandary: these workers had been exposed to "material," in some cases considerable exposure to considerable amounts of it, but their condition simply couldn't be assessed with the techniques for determining "acute" injury that the District was promoting. Mr. Ayers, for example, "had had some exposure to radioactive iodine and xenon for about one year" and "is now working with tracer amounts of 49." Right away, the imprecision of his contact with these materials, and the fact that he had been working on three different contaminants, made his case useless from an experimental point of view, and problematic from a diagnostic standpoint as well. Nonetheless, as doctors knew then, radioactive iodine is particularly pernicious, because it lodges in the thyroid, resulting in the short term (in acute cases) in thyroid irregularities; in the long term, it can bring thyroid cancer. But the doctors had no means of determining what might have happened as a result of the exposure, beyond asking the man if he'd had any weight change, looking in his throat, at his mouth, and checking his "general appearance" for abnormalities.

Against this, compare Mr. Sleight.

> This man had been handling fission products for a number of months. He extracts hot metal with ether. On three or four occasions, this had come in contact with his hands. He had not always got his hands back to background after scrubbing.
>
> [This was an ominous admission on Mr. Sleight's part. His hands had knocked the needle on a Geiger counter; even after he'd gone through the specified scrubbing routines, his hands were still emitting measurable radiation.]
>
> On a few occasions, he may have contacted radioactive gases, but if so, he was not aware of it. He states that he feels very well, his appetite is good but he says that he thinks he has lost about five pounds weight. This man has a rather constant eosinophilia, ranging from 6 to 12 per cent. He does also have a number of allergies with intermittent asthma which almost certainly accounts for the eosinophilia. Examination was negative.[45]

Here again, the doctors had no way of determining what condition Mr. Sleight was in; one of their cardinal indications—weight loss—was disturbingly present, and so was the even more foreboding eosinophilia—a readily recognizable abnormality in the blood chemistry that, research was beginning to show, can indicate the body's reaction to radiation injury. Their conclusion that the matter could be dismissed as a matter of allergies may have been a result of their lack of knowledge about this link, it may have been wishful thinking on their part—or it could have been a perceptive diagnosis. At any rate, they did not order the more complicated, costly and time-consuming blood tests, "leucocyte determinations and differentials at monthly intervals" that Stone's researchers would eventually decide were essential in cases of this sort.[46]

There is something else to notice here: the matter of worker safety. Mr. Sleight worked under conditions so haphazard that he could only guess that he'd been exposed to radioactive gas leaks; he, himself, couldn't tell for sure. And he'd allowed "hot metal with ether" to "come in contact with his hands" because he wasn't wearing the gloves that Warren had prescribed for Manhattan District workers handling "material." Similarly with <u>Mr. Ahman</u>, who "had shown frequent traces of albumen in the urine since 1942" and for whom "there had been considerable handling of T and Hg, also Bismuth, without gloves." Not only that, but "there had been occasional fires in making the amalgams," but Mr. Ahman "thought he had been well shielded by the hood." Here were all the ingredients for catastrophe—chaotic, dirty, unsafe working conditions; careless, even reckless workers; consequential accidents; evidence of real injuries. One might have expected the two doctors to have rung alarm bells up and down the District's bureaucracy. Instead, they diffidently reported that "it would seem best, if at all possible, to protect the workers from the hazard." In any case, they thanked Dr. Spedding for "a very pleasant and instructive day."[47]

Despite their list of dangers, the two doctors bent over backwards to soften the blow. "Although we have no doubt of Dr. Spedding's real interest in safety, and his sincere intention to further it insofar as possible, we do not feel that sufficient attention is being given to safety measures," they wrote, in the closest thing to a real indictment. Of the greenish skin of contaminated workers, they hastened to note that "it is quite possible, of course, that this does not represent a hazard at all because of the insolubility of the material." Still, in calling for further protections, they added: "We fully realize that this would offer difficulties, and that to do so might well interfere with the present efficiency; but looking at it purely from the safety standpoint, we have no other suggestion to make. We do not believe that ventilation is adequate in the plant."

In fact, the team wasn't even able to force the Ames facility to conform to the most basic of safety programs. More than a year later, Warren wrote to Dr. Stone that, "for 'T' exposure, the Ames Group probably represented the worst exposure." Yet "we have been unable to arrange for good urine collections yet at any of the plants." Ames had received its vastly expanded mandate, working with even more hazardous materials, yet the safety program remained utterly inadequate—even Warren confessed to Stone that "the plant doctor has no personnel to take care of this and, in general, is occupied with other things."[48]

By this time, Warren was reaping the bitter fruits of his own campaign for military efficiency and military allegiance in the medical sphere. Now even he couldn't get action from the steadily expanding number of plants under his care; he didn't have the authority to override the contractors, even when violations were blatant or life threatening. At one site: "Many obstacles prevent a good series [of test samples] being obtained because the contractor does not wish to have his men disturbed about their exposure." The plant operator, afraid that the results of tests would panic his workers, had vetoed the medical monitoring program.[49]

The effect on safety at the plants themselves was palpable. Fanning out from their headquarters at Los Alamos, Oak Ridge, or the University of Chicago's Met Lab, the roving medical officers sought to develop a clear picture of hazards and, wherever possible, to pressure military commanders or industrial subcontractors to change their practices. At site after site, the medical teams found dosages far above the allowable maximum. Ames was just one example. The Port Hope Refinery showed numerous violations of the Medical Section's protocols. There exposures reached as much as 160 times the maximum allowable dosages. To comply with the regulations, workers would have to have been limited to no more than three minutes of work per day if they were not to exceed dosage limits. So also at Hanford, where Hempelmann, on loan from

Los Alamos, reported areas of exposure as high as thirty-two times the maximum dosage of radiation; the center of the small fractionating and intubation laboratory read 1,666 micromicrocuries per liter of air—more than sixteen times the maximum allowable dosage.[50]

The District's response to the reported dangers at the Hanford site stripped away any pretense of concern for health and safety. The Manhattan District engineer, K. D. Nichols, recommended that maximum permissible dosages be increased. This statistical sleight-of-hand would magically make the site safe again.[51]

Similarly with the issue of safety gloves all up and down the District. Stone and Warren had sparred over the inadequacy of Warren's decision to allow workers to handle uranium and other highly radioactive materials using only cotton-lined leather gloves. Stone reported that Warren's glove program "reduced the radiation received by the skin of the hand by 50 per cent" only, when the material was uranium—grossly inadequate under many conditions routine for District workers. Yet Warren's standard was only "usually followed"; in most situations where workers were inconvenienced or work was slowed by the use of gloves, employers and employees left the gloves in the box. The case of machinists was both typical and troubling: "almost to a man" they "flatly refused . . . saying it was impossible to operate a machine tool while wearing gloves." Stone retorted, "Experience at the Hanford Engineer works showed that it is perfectly possible to do machine work while wearing gloves," but the medical officers had no power to effect changes. Workers rejected the gloves because they were cumbersome, and because they were forbidden to know why they needed to wear them. Supervisors allowed the violation, because it sped operations—and because, perhaps, their corporation had shifted liability from itself to the government.[52]

Warren was able to still his own disquietude with these failures, and he sought to do the same to Stone. After all, he wrote, medical effects "which are present now in the plants [of the MED] are sub-clinical." Stone had asked permission to move more aggressively against safety violations, and Warren rebuffed him, replying, "If any cases of acute or chronic exposure come to our attention in the future, we will contact you." Here again, however, the lack of medical research defining any but the most "acute or chronic exposure" limited the Medical Division's capacity to notice injury.[53]

Stone had predicted in 1944 that the consequences of the District's medical philosophy would show up as the project moved to maturity and the effects of low-level injury began to surface. He was right. On July 26, 1945, exactly ten days after the first atomic bomb had lit the desert near Alamogordo, New Mexico, Philip J. Close, a second lieutenant in the Judge Advocate-General Division on loan to the District, reported on a meeting at Oak Ridge between "officers of the Insurance Section and the Medical Section." The doctors had apparently convened the meeting, because they had come upon the first manifestation of a radiation injury among the workers under their care: "a case of nephritis"—kidney failure—"in which it appears with some degree of probability that the disease was occasioned by exposure."

> The plant involved is Tennessee-Eastman Corporation. The woman plant
> worker involved was assigned to chemical recovery. She cleaned D units

[where uranium was enriched] as they came from the tracks [the high-speed "racetracks" of the electromagnetic separation plant]. These units are still warm and fumes from "T" materials [uranium and enriched uranium] as well as HCL [hydrochloric acid] and CL [chlorine gas] are present during this operation. The worker began her employment in 1943 without pre-employment examination and has had almost two years of exposure. She is unaware of her condition which now shows up on routine physical check and urinalysis.[54]

Here was a complete breakdown of the reassuring fantasies of Warren and his military officers, that safety procedures were being properly implemented in the factories. Moreover, since Warren's own division was responsible for periodic inspections of these factory processes, his officers either had been deceived by Tennessee Eastman or had deliberately overlooked a profound health hazard. No one had rotated this woman off her dangerous job; no one had monitored her safety procedures; when she underwent monthly physicals, the medical officers hadn't flagged her case, even though they must have seen the sort of changes in blood chemistry the physical exams were designed to detect. Now that she was incurably ill with radiation poisoning, no one had even told her of her condition.

Instead, the medical officers had approached the legal and insurance representatives of the District. Close's report of that meeting is stark testimony:

> The medical officers anticipate that we will have continued cases of this character. In some cases there will be a permanent impairment of kidney functions. In simple terms, the filtering efficiency of the kidneys is impaired to the extent that there is a beginning trace of albumin in the urine and progressive uremic poisoning in the system which ultimately produces a high degree of toxicity. The patient in this condition is more vulnerable to increase in kidney damage from such conditions as strep throat or similar infections.

In addition, the representative from the judge advocate-general's office reported that "the incidence of discovered tuberculosis among employees is becoming manifest." Radiation wasn't directly causing this outbreak, but "in the opinion of the medical officers . . . we will face difficulty in disproving aggravation" as a result of lowered resistance brought on by radiation injury.

Now, finally, the MED doctors were insisting on action: "the employees must necessarily be rotated out, and not permitted to resume further exposure," wrote Close to Maj. C. A. Taney of the New York office of the MED. But Close framed the demands of the doctors as a response to the legal consequences of the case. "In frequent instances," he wrote, "no other type of employment is available" to those suffering industrial illnesses. "Claims and litigation will necessarily flow from the circumstances outlined."

The rest of the letter focused relentlessly on the medico-legal consequences. Lieutenant Close turned to the New York office for "determination of policy and guidance"; he pointed to five essential questions for which the District's "higher authority" must now take responsibility. First on his list was the certainty that, while "rotation is vital to the physical welfare of the workers," it "will undoubtedly invite suspicion and doubt in the minds of others about continuing their work." How not to "disturb . . . relations between employer and employee"?

Second was the question of "morale." Close put it bleakly: "a knowledge on their part that their health is being or may be permanently impaired will have a drastic effect upon the spirit and willingness of the workers. What program or policy may be adopted so that morale may be maintained to the maximum efficiency possible?"

Then came "litigation and claims"—"a chronic problem of industry" made critical here because of the threats to the cone of silence surrounding the program. "Can we successfully fend off and postpone trial of numbers of cases?" Close asked. "How, by whom, and in what manner are the benefits of the health and hazards clause of the contract to be extended to such affected employees?"

Then there was the danger to security—if the employee was rotated off a high-paying job, he or she might leave the District and, once beyond the immediate control of the District, "will doubtless seek independent medical attention which will result in inquiries about the manner and type of exposure." Terminated employees might "invite comment and questioning by friends, neighbors and relatives." Eventually, they were sure to turn to the American legal system. Injury suits, particularly concerning injury in which the victims had been questionably treated by District doctors—allowed to remain at tasks sure to increase their injury, told nothing of their sickness until it was severe enough that it could not be denied any longer—would assuredly be scandalous, and it was hard to imagine how such cases could help but breach the District's security program, or so Close thought.

Last on Close's list was a phrase utterly foreign to the discourse of the District, a phrase I have seen nowhere else in the tens of thousands of documents that comprise my five-years' excursion into the files: the phrase "Ethical Considerations."

But Close's concern wasn't with the ethics of the situation, or the ethical responsibilities of the District, as it turned out. He was talking about the legal conflict for the doctors themselves between "their canons of ethics" and those of the District. It seems clear from his phrasing that Close was warning his superiors of a further security danger: that the doctors might well decide to "advise the patient of his true condition, its cause, effect and probable prognosis, . . . if not on ethical grounds," and "if not on moral grounds," then quite possibly "under penalty of liability for malpractice or proceeding for revocation of license for their failure to do so."

But it seems more likely that Close wasn't understanding the nature of the medical workers' revolt. Being a District minion, he understood the issue in District terms. For doctors and nurses, trained to give help, to cure disease, to palliate suffering, the implications of this woman's injury were in fact ethical, moral, and personal. It seems likely that the case of nephritis, plus the tuberculosis epidemic, had emboldened the physicians, and they had threatened to revolt unless something were done, not only to relieve them of responsibility, but to confront this new and ominous trend. Compartmentalization of the medical area had conspired to mask from these doctors earlier evidence of this epidemic-to-be. Oak Ridge medical officers didn't know of the rash of radiation injuries at Los Alamos in 1944 that culminated in the "acute radiation exposure" of four tech workers, and the death of a fifth. Nor did they necessarily know of industrial injuries at Oak Ridge factories. Medical officers under District authority were largely separated from the medical officers for the contracting corporations, and often had little or no knowledge of the inner workings of the factories. We know that those ordered out on factory inspection tours didn't necessarily look carefully. The case of Ames, Iowa, wasn't isolated; the army's own historian reported that "frequency and thoroughness of inspections varied" depending on whether the District "had complete financial responsibility," in which case "the operating practices of the contractor . . . were likely to receive very close scrutiny," or whether the corporation itself was financially responsible for safety, in which case "inspections were more infrequent and less rigorous." Copies of pre- and postemployment physicals made by the corporations went to "the District Engineer, Attention: Medical Section, along with copies of the previous examinations for filing," as the instructions put it. The most important word in this phrase is "filing"; there appears to have been no settled procedure for investigating the reports that came in, or for comparing early and later physicals. The reports just went into the steel filing cabinets.[55]

For the doctors themselves, radiation injury provided a particularly troubling matter. On the one hand, they had no idea how to treat the disease; in fact, they might not even be able to make an informed diagnosis, thanks in part to the District's orders limiting research. What were they to tell those patients who came to them with symptoms of severe radiation illness?

According to the District: nothing. The case of one Oak Ridge worker, Spencer Lusk, some four months before, provides a telling indicator. Lusk had worked for Tennessee Eastman and had then left both the company and the site. Early in April 1945, he had checked into the Duke University hospital suffering from "a skin abnormality of unknown type." He told the doctors there that he'd been working with highly secret materials. As a result, Duke's Dr. J. Lamar Callaway wrote to Tennessee Eastman asking for Lusk's medical records and for information concerning the materials to which he had been exposed. The letter made its way to Dr. James M. Sterner, the medical director for the corporation. He wrote back to Dr. Calloway denying his request and dismissing the possibility that the problem was industrial in origin.[56]

But Sterner was lying. In a letter written that same day, he told Warren he was convinced that Lusk's disease was "definitely related to his work"—that contact exposure to "tuballoy oxide (TO_3) [uranium oxide]" was the cause of his "severe eczematoid dermatitis." Sterner's concern with this case lay not with the patient but with the question of the method for determining liability—he told Colonel Warren that "I do not see that much benefit can be gained by patch testing so far as identification of this case is concerned."[57]

This was only one of a series of such questions that had arisen in the months before the medical officers forced Close and his people to call in the military lawyers. At around that time, "a confidential informant" had written to District security officials to report that ten employees suffering from body rashes had surfaced in medical clinics outside the District. Like Lusk, these victims had gone first to District doctors at Oak Ridge, telling them that their conditions were the result of occupational hazards. The doctors had kept their mouths closed, and the men had agreed among themselves to seek "satisfactory care" elsewhere.[58]

This time, it was the informer's report to the security police that brought action, rather than a request from the "outside" physicians. But the response was the same: the District treated the case as proof of the need for better medical training—in propaganda. "To prevent patients from consulting 'off area' physicians in the future and thereby disclosing classified information by describing their working conditions and materials used," the authors of the District's own history reported, "the hospital was requested to assure such patients that Oak Ridge medical authorities were best equipped and trained to treat any cases arising out of the peculiar working conditions of the area. The operating companies were also asked to stress this fact to their personnel."[59]

There appears no evidence that the District addressed the causes of these accidents and injuries, many of them at the Tennessee Eastman facility supervised by the very contractor who had recommended Warren in the first place, and for whom Warren had worked before joining the District. Indeed, an accidentally declassified document, in an otherwise empty file marked "Records and Reports of Fires and Other Accidents," reports two cases at Tennessee Eastman in the month of May alone:

3 MAY 1945 IN Y-12 AREA AT 1550 HOURS.

"Stainless steel burner used to ignite contaminated process carbons for recovery of tuballoy" exploded—"three women operators in the room were slightly injured and another woman operator in an outside room fainted. It was estimated . . . that 2 to 5 milligrams of Beta re-cycle tuballoy was lost."

21 MAY 1945 AT 1300 HOURS.

Tank 609 in track 6 exploded, blowing a trap: "the arms, legs and heads of two process operators were singed."[60]

These were obviously cases in which contamination and consequent radiation injury were inevitable. But the recurrence of such accidents indicated that the cases medical officers were now seeing were only the beginning of what would almost certainly approach an epidemic of radiation injury and radioactive-substance poisoning. These doctors had no known cures for this epidemic; moreover, they were ordered to tell victims the incidents were not District-caused yet could best be treated only by District doctors.

And so by the summer of 1945 the District had begun to see the dark consequences of its most basic tenets: efficiency, secrecy, obedience, military discipline, compartmentalization. Of course the architects of these policies, and their most powerful advocates, were not the ones injured. The bureaucratic pyramid of the District insulated them from the workplaces where their decisions had their effects on the health and safety of workers.

The District had severely restricted medical experiments, particularly those that studied contaminated subjects. Instead, the District itself had become a vast medical experiment in the effects of radiation exposure, of plutonium and uranium inhalation and ingestion, of phosgene gas poisoning, of uranium hexafluorine inhalation, of beryllium overexposure.[61]

But it was an experiment conducted without controls, without adequate scientific supervision, and—perhaps most important—without the access to information needed by the medical research teams to determine the scientific causes and effects they hoped to understand. For now, within the District, the issue was damage control, and the methods belonged to the heart of the District: calls for loyalty in a climate of secrecy, then censorship, dissimulation, threats.

Writing after the war, Stafford Warren bragged that the Manhattan Engineer District was "the safest of all wartime enterprises." The representatives of the District and the army presented the program as one beset by the extraordinary circumstances of wartime and the radically new hazards of atomic energy, striving successfully to balance wartime necessities and the humane practices of the Hippocratic ideal of medicine, with the result that health and safety were never more than minimally compromised. But the truth is that, once the District went into production, it was an extremely dangerous place to work and live—worse than the civilian chemical industry (a notoriously dangerous sector), worse than Army Ordnance (the ammunition and explosives division), worse even than Chemical Warfare.[62]

The campaign of duplicity concerning the dangers continues today. It began as soon as the first true cases of radiation injury surfaced. Four days after Close's memo on the medical rebellion at Oak Ridge went out, Warren wrote his own extraordinary memo to the files, a "history" of the District's medical operations. Warren's document reinvented the medical program, placed him at the center, downgraded Stone's Health Division, and presented the mission of the entire medical program as necessarily and solely focused on "the direct winning of the war." Again and again, Warren's memo reiterated that medicine was, from the start, subservient to the larger goal of "winning the present war." "All . . . functions" of the MED, Warren stated, "should be directed and oriented so that they are in direct support of . . . the present war effort." Finally, Warren presented the medical research program as funded and directed to "strengthen the Government interests," from a "medico-legal point of view."[63]

Closer to the bone was Warren's belief that the atomic-weapons industry should be treated as simply another industrial program, under which, as the DOE historian Barton Hacker paraphrased the memo, "normal industrial safety practices were good enough. Special standards should apply only upon proof of prompt, clear-cut biological changes or health threats." Yet we must not forget that it was Warren himself who gutted the medical research program and prevented the development of the means of detecting such injury. And he had done so in the face of strong evidence, dating back to the 1920s, that most fatal injuries in this field would never be marked by "prompt, clear-cut biological changes," but would instead appear only after a lengthy latency.[64]

It is hard not to read Warren's memo as an attempt to rewrite the history of the District to counter the threat of "medico-legal" complications. He himself said so in his memo; his voice was strong enough to elicit an unprecedented response from Stone, in which the doctor set the issue as a fundamental clash of values. "I do not believe that any research should be done to 'strengthen the Government interests' from the medico-legal point of view," Stone wrote. "Research should be done to establish the facts, if these are in the employee's interest they should be done equally as much as if they are in the Government's interests, because the two interests should be the same. No biological investigation should be carried on from a purely medico-legal standpoint. If the health and welfare of the workers are the main objects, the medico-legal aspect is automatically taken care of."[65]

But Stone was either immensely naive or was engaged in his own form of historical revisionism. As we know, he, too, had sought a compromise position between military necessity and human safety. But now he was writing a letter of rebuttal just days after the Oak Ridge uranium bomb and the Hanford–Los Alamos plutonium bomb had done their wartime work, had ended the war and ushered in a new wave of global terror and moral consequence. Like Warren, and so many of those deeply involved in the Manhattan District, Stone was seeking some way, if not to undo what had been done, perhaps to remake the narrative and his place within it.

The District's convoluted policies on medical research, radioactivity and radiation safety, industrial injury and treatment seem to set up a harsh dichotomy between industrial medicine and general health care. The official histories and the reminiscences of District officers like Groves and Nichols glowingly portray a utopian program of universal health care for all who lived and labored within the fences—a health plan subsuming prevention, family medicine, and hospitalization, so complete that it courted accusations of "socialized medicine."

But a closer study of this civilian health program reveals a disturbing unity of purpose and execution. Though opposite in technique, both the industrial and the family health plans were designed to ensure a compliant, efficient, high-functioning workforce. "Socialized medicine" and "industrial medicine" were both subsets of "state medicine," which set the goals of the state as the dominant—even, perhaps, the prime—factors in determining policy. Medical care, District officials reported in 1946, was "an inducement" so that "workmen could be attracted to the isolated site" of Hanford, or the unattractive site of Oak Ridge. In addition, complete, comprehensive, low-cost or no-cost medical care served the goal of "mandatory . . . extreme secrecy." This mandated "all medical facilities being under Government control . . . to prevent leaks in information." Off the job as well as on, medicine was an adjunct to security and industrial efficiency.[66]

The nature of the Oak Ridge medical plan reveals how clearly the District distinguished between productive workers and unfortunately necessary families, and how strictly the separation of workers from residents would be enforced. Memberships in the Oak Ridge health plan were limited to individual workers ($2 a month) and to families ($4 a month). But family memberships entitled only the *worker* to comprehensive medical care; the plan restricted family members solely to hospital care. Such a program kept costs minimal, kept workers healthy, and provided some assurance that serious medical problems would be treated before they might spread to the general population and impair efficiency.[67]

The program also sequestered intractable illnesses; once diagnosed, "nervous, mental and tuberculosis cases" found their medical coverage abruptly terminated. So also with cases of drug addiction and alcoholism. This policy assured that the District would not have to build or staff facilities for these difficult, long-term illnesses and could rid itself of such troublesome citizens by shipping them off the site.

Health, like happiness, was a subsidiary goal. What mattered was work. Consider, for example, the Du Pont strategy for dealing with injured workers or medical malingerers. Both were entered into a program of "guided work" under which they continued to labor forty-five hours a week at tasks designated to be unrelated to the injury or incapacitation. The idea, District officials wrote, was to find "another means of conserving manpower," and the program "acted as an incentive to the employee to recover his total ability to return to his regular job." What went unspoken here was the economic incentive that also played in guided work—workers received no compensation without working, and they worked at less "demanding" tasks that inevitably seemed to carry significantly lower wage rates.[68]

Again we may ask: what was missing as a result of this forceful truncation of human vision and ethical responsibility? The Medical Section and, even Dr. Stone's Health Division, regarded the Manhattan District as an industrial program. No one spoke of it as a weapons program, devoted to inventing a radically new weapon, a weapon that would change the face of human warfare—and its victims.

Blast Effects. Acute, chronic, and lingering radiation. Fallout. Colonel Warren reported later on the moment when these matters first entered the District lexicon:

> The chief effort at Los Alamos was devoted to the design and fabrication of a successful atomic bomb. Scientists and engineers engaged in this effort were, understandably, so immersed in their own problems that it was difficult to persuade any of them even to speculate on what the after effects of the detonation might be. Their concern was whether any one of their several designs for the bomb would actually detonate, and, if the detonation did occur, how massive it would be.
>
> Little attention was therefore paid to the possible effects of the detonation of the bomb until the spring of 1945, when the Medical Section of the Manhattan Engineer District raised the question with General Groves and was given the mission to investigate the whole matter.[69]

Warren's description was typically self-serving. In fact, it was the Los Alamos scientific community that forced the issue. As the Los Alamos physicists reached the end of their work, they began to raise their heads from the microscopic tasks to which they had devoted themselves, and the enormity of what they had done began to strike them. Their first response was fear for themselves if the test explosion set for Alamogordo in the summer of 1945 produced the sort of dangers they now began to imagine it would. They turned to their medical team, which responded true to Warren's predilection—by treating the issue as it might result in lawsuits and damages. At a meeting in March, the physicists and their medical man, Dr. Hempelmann, began to discuss the test and its implications. Hempelmann summarized the discussion: "(1) danger to personnel at the site and in the neighboring areas during and after the shot, (2) medico-legal aspects of these hazards and (3) instruments and organization needed to cope with the above hazards."[70]

The scientists' worries about their own safety were quickly laid to rest, as the District developed plans to build thick, supersafe shelters far from the tower where the test bomb at Alamogordo would detonate. The District's own focus quickly turned to making sure that there was a set of "permanent records . . . for future reference," in the case of future lawsuits. A test shot in May, using conventional explosives but scattering radioactive materials in order to watch the effects, resulted in a cloud of highly radioactive debris. This cloud rose into the air and moved east. Hours later and over a hundred miles downwind, the cloud was still intact and clearly visible. No one measured its contents; no one followed it as it headed past Roswell, New Mexico. Even with the cloud marring a clear sky, no one was yet ready to imagine the medical consequences of this new form of warfare.

EPILOGUE

In 1996, the President's Advisory Committee on Human Radiation Experiments submitted a report detailing its findings. Though the committee had focused primarily on cold-war abuses, its researchers had access to all archives, including the still-hidden medical reports from the Manhattan Engineer District. Their demands for material brought back to public light some of the documents that had long ago disappeared from the medical files.[71]

One of the documents released to the committee by the Department of Energy concerned Dr. Hamilton's "experimental subject," "Mr. Stephens," and that "most interesting set of experiments" involving the effects of massive plutonium ingestion on human subjects—the story with which we began this chapter. Dr. Hamilton had apparently misspelled the subject's name in his original letter—he was "fifty-eight-year-old Albert Stevens, designated CAL-1" in Hamilton's experimental protocol. Stevens had been diagnosed with stomach cancer; shortly after Hamilton injected him with plutonium—without Mr. Stevens's knowledge or permission—the doctors discovered that he suffered instead from a benign stomach ulcer. After the injection, Hamilton's team operated on Stevens, removing samples of bone and spleen to test for plutonium retention.

Stevens was only one of more than fifty such "subjects"; almost all the rest came from the University of Rochester, from Dr. Stafford Warren's old laboratories. As the 1996 report put it, the "patient-subjects . . . were never told that the injections were part of a medical experiment for which there was no expectation that they would benefit, and they never consented to this use of their bodies." Like the conscientious objectors of the prison camp in the shadow of Hanford's radiation-spewing smokestacks, they were expendable.

Perhaps the most shocking new case to surface in the report concerned an Oak Ridge worker, Ebb Cade, a "colored male," aged fifty-three, the victim of an auto accident. Hospitalized with a broken arm and leg, he was given plutonium, apparently on the orders of Dr. Hymer Friedell. The District's doctors pulled out fifteen of his teeth and tested them for plutonium; they also took unspecified "bone samples," probably from his broken limbs. Sometime later, Ebb Cade sneaked out of the hospital and disappeared from sight.

Even this tale, with its powerful stench of the Tuskeegee syphilis experiments, took further turns. When the researchers sought the urine samples used to monitor the progress of the plutonium through Mr. Cade's body, they found that laboratory workers, compartmentalized into ignorance about the experiment, had mixed the samples together, rendering the results of the experiment moot. When, in 1974, Atomic Energy Commission interviewers sought information on Mr. Cade from the doctors involved, they found themselves in a quagmire of accusations, counteraccusations, and denials. Dr. Joseph Howland, the administering physician, insisted he had acted only after his objections were overruled by Dr. Friedell's direct orders; Friedell denied ever having given such orders and, paradoxically, charged that it wasn't Howland but another doctor entirely who had given the injection.

Readers of this book will not be surprised by the revelations. But in its report, the advisory committee covered only scientific experimentation on human subjects; it did not reach out into the surrounding terrain to examine the ground from which these events sprang. And so the committee could not guess the sad significance in the fact that Dr. Hamilton was Dr. Robert S. Stone's partner in experimentation and that Stone himself had authorized the protocol on "Stephens"; readers of the report could not realize the larger meaning of Dr. Louis Hempelmann's decision—facing the horror of unknown injuries to his own scientists and colleagues from these new poisons— to encourage, even authorize, experiments on others less prestigious, less powerful, less knowledgeable.

Nor should it be surprising that the report itself told its stories in the bland, reassuring, passive voice that is the contemporary offspring of District-speak. Thereby the committee seemed to enervate its own findings. These seemed tailored not to shock but to reassure the public, offering the comfort of a present government dedicated to "Lifting the Veil of Secrecy" (in the cliché of a chapter head) and recasting the excesses of the past in a romanticized wartime atmosphere of sacrifice and heroics.

We might also note significant absences from the report. Because they were not the victims of deliberate scientific experiments, none of the workers who were unwittingly exposed to "*T*" and "Product" appear; nor do the children who drank the milk of the cows east of Hanford after the chemical separations plants began operations; nor those who looked toward the sky near Alamogordo on the morning of July 16, 1945, and felt a snowfall of hot ash flakes falling on their faces.

SILENCE

METERS

JULY 16, 1945

Ground zero. For a little while, all geography emanates from this point. Silence surrounds it.

In the narratives written, spoken, recalled by eyewitnesses, a space appears, pressed out between the preparation and the enactment. Men are huddled around their recording instruments; some are hillside-bound, holding in front of their eyes army-issue welding glass. Bets have been made, arguments temporarily suspended; all wait to see what will happen when the transubstantiation of this enterprise remakes the world. A voice carried over a microphone punctuates the desert air.

Remembering this countdown, physicists, soldiers, generals recall the last moment as a moment of silence.

This silence is mythic. Within the body, the blood still rushes. There is breath, a cough, the faint sound of wind, the hum of the tubes in the amplifier to which the microphone and speaker horns are connected. But for those who have written of this moment, this experience, there is in their story nonetheless the urge to describe a powerful, essential tear in the continuity of the everyday, into which silence rushed.

ORIGINATION

By the spring of 1944, the scientists at Los Alamos had decided on a test, codenamed Trinity. The primitive "gun" design used to achieve instantaneous criticality with the uranium bomb didn't work with the plutonium weapon; yet there was too much money and military capital expended on plutonium to abandon that material. A second, far more complex system came out of Los Alamos specialist George Kistiakowsky's Explosives Division. Proposals made originally by a Cal Tech physicist, Seth Neddermeyer, and the mathematicians Stanislau Ulam and John von Neumann proposed a process of superpressure through implosion, using "shaped charges" to produce "explosive lenses" that would impel the plutonium in upon itself with such force and speed that it would go instantaneously critical and explode.

But this process involved what one Trinity planner, Kenneth Bainbridge, called an "enormous step from the differential and integral experiments, and theory, to a practical gadget." Whereas the uranium gun design was logical and could be practically conceived, the implosion design employed radically new theoretical principles and immensely complex mathematics.[1]

Early on, Groves opposed the idea of a test. He saw a potentially devastating waste of plutonium and a shameful exhibition should it fail, an unnecessary exercise should it succeed. But Groves's obsession with getting the weapon *used* before the war ended eventually prevailed, as it became clear that a successful test would consolidate his position, raise his capital, and virtually assure that military authorities would include atomic weapons within their planning for a Japanese defeat.[2]

Led by Bainbridge, Los Alamos Group X-2 developed the site requirements in March and April of 1944. The site had to be flat, "to minimize extraneous effects on blast," Bainbridge wrote—to make the scientific measurements more precise, in other words. "The large amount of optical information desired required that, on the average, the weather should be good, with small and infrequent amounts of haze or dust and relatively light winds." The site should be close to Los Alamos, to minimize "loss of time in travel by personnel and transportation of equipment." And, as always, there was "the question of security and complete isolation of the activities of the test site from activities at Project Y."[3]

Military security officials had their own list of site requirements. The explosion must be as distant from "settlements" as possible, to keep to a minimum the number of people who might see the flash of light, hear the thunder, feel the shiver of the earth. Impinging on Mormon settlements, even individual Mormon ranches, was out of the question. Mormons were too politically savvy, too resistant, too powerful. Nor could Indians be moved—the Secretary of the Interior wouldn't have it.[4]

Bainbridge, Robert Henderson, and Oppenheimer, along with Maj. W. A. Stevens, the District's military liaison with the scientists, and Maj. Peer de Silva, the Los Alamos security head, searched for sites, but the social, physical, and environmental consequences of their quest lay at the periphery of their vision. (In this, they recapitulated the history of the District.) From the first they sought the vast, hostile zones, places already inhospitable, already lit by a harsh and unrelenting light, already written out of the mythology of redemption. No amount of cultivation would turn these deserts into gardens. They were the sites of the American sublime, places where people came to test themselves against the harshness of nature, places of tenuous human settlement or of utter isolation.

The men focused their search on natural monuments of vast scale and near-infinite hostility. Jornada del Muerto: the Journey of Death (some call it the Road of the Dead Man), near Alamogordo, New Mexico; "the lava region south of Grants, New Mexico"; "Sand bars, which form the coast of southern Texas, located 10 miles from the main coast"; a region "near the Great Sand Dunes National Monument."[5]

Then they surveyed from above, in a borrowed C-45 transport plane. They had detailed aerial photographs made, photographs that revealed the sites as rectangles inscribed by the pencil lines of roads and the tidy, tiny rectangles of ranch houses and outbuildings. They rode by car, singly or in groups, speeding along those straight lines of the desert roads, in the midsummer heat, in closed cars and open jeeps.

The quality of harsh sublimity, of entering an awesome, hostile landscape, abandoned for millennia, stuck with Bainbridge. Remembering the search process decades later, he wrote that one site "looked much like a smooth area of the Moon, desolate and forbidding." The land, vast in scale, its horizons hundreds of miles away, cut by mountains, by mesas, by huge thunderheads that promised heavy weather: this was one picture of the test region—as a place too monumental ever to be injured by human depredations. Here was a landscape where the time scale of the physicist, measured in millions of years, could be graphically seen. Here, Bainbridge implied, was a landscape suited to the new atomic sublime he and his colleagues would create.[6]

(A botanist, a biologist, an ecologist would have seen a very different picture—of land not sterile, "desolate and forbidding," but teeming with life, marvelously adapted to this particular environment, fragile yet enduring.)

Another trek took the site search party along "unmapped ranch trails, past deserted areas of dry farming lands beaten by too many years of drought and high winds." Entering the Jornada del Muerto desert for the first time, they came upon a ranch they assumed was abandoned. They were wrong. "Armed with rifles, two boys 12 and 14 years old circled on horseback our two military vehicles." Bainbridge's final survey of the Alamogordo site involved another prophetic incident. "Major Stevens and I looked up to see a flight of B-17 bombers approaching with black underbellies, bomb bay doors open." Surrounding the men were the craters of bomb runs.[7]

In the fall of 1944, Bainbridge, Stevens, de Silva, and the group chose a section of the Jornada for their Trinity shot. Sometime soon afterward, Groves accepted the recommendation of the search committee.[8]

INCORPORATION

The search party's composition suggests the forces coalescing around the atomic test. Bainbridge was the scientist rewarded with this assignment for his fluid adaptation to the role of technologist. He understood what wasn't known, and what the test was designed to determine. Oppenheimer was the scientist-administrator, mediator between scientific interest and military necessity. Major Stevens's wartime role on the District had been (and would continue to be) to force progress from the scientists. Lately he had taken over the construction program at Los Alamos; he was serving as the consummate Corps of Engineer officer, supervising construction crews from the corps's detachment, transforming scientific experimentation into practical weapons development. The presence of Major de Silva, as head security officer for the Los Alamos site, ensured that the District would remain tightly sealed, isolated from its surroundings. And above them all, increasingly active in their involvement, were General Groves and his deputy, Brig. Gen. Thomas F. Farrell.[9]

As matters moved forward, Trinity recapitulated the structure and the history of the District. Groves determined to use nonmilitary contractors to do the construction and site treatment work, choosing familiar Corps of Engineers companies. Los Alamos, too, operated as a subcontractor, providing the elite of white-collar workers. Below them were the SED workers and the MPs, and then, at the very bottom, the workers for the subcontracting companies.

The result was a pyramid of power, exceedingly effective from the standpoint of authority but destructive in other ways. By Trinity's time, the success of the District's policies of centralization and compartmentalization left few people with the inclination, and none with the power, to question the self-imposed picture of the project and its mission promulgated by the District. Writing in 1957, James Nolan, the head of safety planning for Alamogordo, put it baldly: "Possible hazards were not too important in those days. There was a war going on," and the army engineers "were interested in having a usable bomb and protecting security. . . . Radiation hazards were entirely secondary."[10]

CONDEMNATION

The stark, clear emptiness of the Alamogordo area as it appeared on the aerial photographs and the maps belied the reality of the site as a landscape occupied, transformed, and owned by others. Groves had chosen the site because he could get the land from the air force, more or less; but the air force itself held contested territory. It wasn't owned; it was leased—from the state of New Mexico, and from individual landholders, who had been promised they'd get their lands back when the war was over.[11]

To appropriate the lands still in private hands, the District might have applied its old condemnation methods. But without the time to go through legal proceedings for "taking," the District's people moved instead to lease (or re-lease) the land, promising (or perhaps only implying) its eventual return. The plan was excellent from the District's point of view, for it gained the land without paying full purchase price. And the District's agreements were careful to allow perpetual renewal of those leases, without obligation to the landowners. Calling upon their patriotism and the "emergency military necessity" of the secret program, the District's representatives negotiated the landowners into contracts most would regret forever.

Preliminary and highly speculative estimates of blast efficiency, combined with Groves's desire to minimize land-lease and Security's desire to make as little fuss as possible, determined a twelve-mile boundary—lease, expropriate, and evacuate an area twelve miles from the epicenter. Already issues of legal action and security were rising on the list of priorities. Bainbridge wrote in his official report that "12 miles to the nearest habitation . . . was great enough so that no trouble could be expected from shattering of ranchers' windows by the blast even under conditions of 100% yield." Mainly this meant assuming the air force and army leases on ranches; it also seems to have required that the District close the lands to herders, some of whom had legal grazing rights, some of whom simply considered the lands open to them.[12]

Even the ranchers moved off by lease for the bombing range weren't really gone. The McDonald family had ranched the site since the cowboy-and-gunslinger days at the end of the nineteenth century. They had built their ranch to last, built it of stone; they returned periodically, before and after the test, to tend their property and keep up their claims. It was probably McDonald children who had surrounded the search party and then "drew down" on them with their rifles before they were sure Bainbridge and his people weren't thieves or claimjumpers.[13]

As the McDonalds and other ranch owners understood it at the time, the arrival of the District was simply a short-term transfer of a temporary leasing arrangement. District negotiators didn't disabuse them of this notion. Partly it was a matter of ignorance within the District. Compartmentalization meant that only a scattered few knew, even speculatively, that there might be permanent and irreversible damage to the land, that the ranches would be sowed with something more toxic than salt, and infinitely longer-lasting. The land-use negotiators had little or no idea what they were doing beyond following orders.

The District leased only the land within its twelve-mile boundaries. Most of the District planners assumed the only real danger lay with the potential blasting of incompletely alchemized plutonium all over the landscape, where cattle and sheep might get hold of it, or where it might contaminate the rare water sources dotting the desert spaces.[14]

District officials hadn't yet thought of fallout. That concern came in the spring of 1945, when two scientists, Joseph Hirschfelder and John Magee, were between important assignments, and Hans Bethe gave them the task of looking over *all* the effects of the explosion. Sometime in April, Hirschfelder and Magee put together the deathly equation. The blast would—in Hirschfelder's words—"pick up dirt, rocks, and assorted debris, some of which [would] pass through the fire ball and get plated with radioactive materials." As these two physicists frantically began to read up on wind patterns, weather, dust behavior, precipitation, the likelihood of dust devils, thunderheads, tornadoes (the esoteric physics of everyday life), they also began to play with dust, dirt, fans and winds, water vapor and rain, in order to approximate the physical effects of the blast. That was when they first came to understand the consequences of radioactive clouds, held aloft by their own heat, wafted by currents utterly unpredictable because they were created by such complex interactions of blast effects, weather, wind, time of day, season, and much more, eventually depositing their contents in a microscopic dust across the earth.[15]

Hirschfelder and Magee's early predictions, sent up the District pyramid in mid-June 1945, declared that immense quantities of toxic radioactive dust would drop from the clouds onto nearby towns, while an undetermined amount would drift unpredictably for much longer. Though Trinity historian Ferenc Szasz declared that the physicists' prediction represented a revelation of dangers "so lethal as to make the test virtually impossible," no one talked of canceling, or even significantly modifying, the test program.[16]

After a month of intense work, Hirschfelder and Magee were able to lower their estimates by half, or further. By then the Alamogordo group had seen fallout at first-hand. Test teams had produced a dry-run explosion at the site, using TNT and plutonium. Observers from Los Alamos then watched the wind carry their plutonium-salted cloud right over the town of Carrizozo and then eastward. Suddenly everything depended on the wind. If it blew properly (that is, as they wished it to), the cloud would move over unoccupied lands until it had dropped its heaviest matter to the earth and dispersed its dusts over wider and wider air masses, diluting it until no one could recognize its source. Perhaps its danger would diminish as well. If it didn't, it would threaten lives and permanently contaminate the Mescalero Apache Reservation, routes 70 and 380, close to ten smaller communities, and the substantial town of Roswell. It would also deposit radioactive materials in a number of rivers and streams, including the Rio Penasco, the Rio Felix, the Rio Hondo, and the Rio Bonito, and the river into which they fed—the Pecos.[17]

Again, compartmentalization prevented the results of this dry run from reaching the specialists who might understand its significance and lobby for cancellation of the test, or emasculated those who did. The doctors of the Los Alamos Health Physics Group, especially Hempelmann and Nolan, quickly understood the dangers Hirschfelder and Magee had mapped out. But the structure of the District, which had placed Health Physics far down and to the side of the power pyramid, militated against their drawing much attention to these critical discoveries. Hirschfelder recalls it: "In spite of all this work, very few people believed us when we predicted radiation fallout from the atom bomb. . . . We had such low priority that the best transportation we could get was an old automobile which we borrowed from Jim Tuck."[18]

Because their discoveries originated at the margins of the District's pyramid, by definition they couldn't be important. Yet, as Hirschfelder noted, the District's officers "did not dare to ignore this possibility"—the possibility of wholesale catastrophe. Groves sent the problem to Col. Stafford Warren, his specialist in medico-legal issues. Warren expanded the safety boundaries from twelve miles to thirty. But by this time it was too late to condemn and expropriate or lease out to the new border. (Besides, the new circle took in most of the Mescalero Apache Reservation and a number of smaller towns.) Instead, Warren instructed the District to develop an evacuation plan for those who lived, ranched, herded, and passed through this far larger area.[19]

Though no one seems to have thought so at the time, Groves and the District got off easy under Warren's plan. A circular buffer zone with a thirty-mile radius may look good on a map or in a memorandum, but it doesn't bear much scrutiny in the wind and the weather, the dry washes and ravines with their sudden floods, the scrub and cactus surrounding ground zero. Warren's buffer zone conveniently excluded Carrizozo and Roswell, for example—in fact, it missed most of the area that scientists had mapped out as most likely to be inundated by fallout. And the predictions themselves were highly imprecise. For it is in the nature of fallout clouds to be unpredictable, to rise or ride or drop to the earth as randomness and not military orders dictate. Colonel Warren's plan seems the work not of a scientist or a doctor, but a lawyer concerned with "medico-legal consequences."

CONSTRUCTION

Following precedent, the District turned to military, corporate, and governmental agencies to whom it could parcel out the work of the test. The first step was to turn construction over to the regional engineer for the Army Corps of Engineers. He, in turn, looked to outside contractors on his list, settling on New Mexico's largest construction corporation, run by Albuquerque's Ted Brown. The company had a branch in Lubbock, Texas, as well; from the entire region, Brown brought in two hundred workers, housing them at the site, where they worked nonstop for the month of March. Then Brown sent them home—back to their communities. Word of the site began to spread. Brown called an equally big crew for another month of round-the-clock work. Then he sent them home. Word spread further. A third crew worked the same shifts in May.[20]

Corps-scavenged workers and Brown employees replicated on the Jornada del Muerto the atomic spaces of the other District sites. First they dug big holes, graded roadways, generated dust storms visible from the air and the ground for hundreds of miles. Then they paved roads to crisscross the site (at five thousand dollars a mile in wartime dollars), connecting distant observation posts, security posts, measurement bunkers, Temporary Dwelling Units (Quonset huts and portables, like the ones at Hanford, Oak Ridge, and Los Alamos), dining halls, latrines, garbage dumps. New roads ran from Tularosa and U.S. 54 to the southeast, from U.S. 380 ten miles east of San Antonio, from Truth or Consequences on U.S. 85 to the southwest, and from Pope Siding, where Jumbo, Babcock and Wilcox's huge and heavy never-to-be-used containment vessel sat on a siding until they trucked it in and dumped it near the epicenter.[21]

By April, construction had thoroughly transformed the space. Low-slung electrical, phone, and test-equipment wire crisscrossed the place, breaking up the paths of the antelope herds that normally ran, faster than a car, across the vacant land. The construction workers themselves had to be housed, fed, latrined, so they constructed their own plywood-and-canvas frontier town. In a photograph made by the District for its official files, the scene looks remarkably like a location-set for a Hollywood Western (fig. 42). The MPs took over one of the McDonald ranch houses, swimming in the cattle cistern, setting up a rec room. Volleyball, horseshoes: the MP commander was a polo nut, and he had his underlings team up and play. Construction workers brought in the equipment for the test, and they brought in the equipment necessary to bring in *that* equipment. (More than a hundred trucks, cars, back-hoes, loaders, even a pair of lead-lined tanks, ended up strewn around the landscape, in parking lots, and by the sides of roads.) They built repair shops for the trucks and cars. There was a quartermaster's office, to make sure that requisitions went out and came in, to keep track of the wires and the voltmeters and the horseshoes.[22]

COMPARTMENTALIZATION

Construction broke the landscape into segments. On the official maps, red circles mark out the space in radial zones: 10,000 yards, 10 miles, 20 miles, 30 miles. The construction crews built to comply with these limits, but they didn't know those invisible red target-circles were there, or what the limits meant. Three basic shelters, bunkers made of concrete and covered with dirt, lay outside the 10,000-yard line. Base camp was just beyond the ten-mile marker. At ground zero, the April crew built a wooden tower. While they were out on furlough, the Los Alamos explosives team came in and set off the pretest explosion, the one with TNT and plutonium. On the vaporized remains of the first tower, the May crew built a second, made of steel. If the two construction crews hadn't been substantially the same, the significance of this might have escaped them. By June, the news was spreading that the Journey of Death site was a test ground for some new explosive, and the geography of the site had coalesced around ground zero.[23]

The stringing of wire now took on a pattern—it, too, pointed toward the center, even as it connected the bunkers with one another and with the base camp. The overall network of wires closely resembled a spider's web. Yet even then the base camp loomed largest, with eleven big Quonset huts and a number of smaller temporary buildings and tents, serviced by two or three roads.

The physical compartmentalization of the site belied the chaotic conditions beneath the roofs, just as the organizational map belied the sprawling expansion and confused system of command, and just as the security regulations belied the reality that every order for secrecy and security was rapidly and repeatedly broken. (Perhaps the metaphor most apt was the storehouse for the test site. Originally a neat prefab structure, its insides grew so incoherent and disorganized it gained the name FUBAR: fucked up beyond all recognition.)[24]

At base camp, everyone congregated by rank. MPs were in one area; SEDs in

FIG. 42 Trinity Base Camp, 1945. Archives, Los Alamos National Laboratory.

another; construction workers over here; scientists over there. The basic break was between the military-scientific elite, and the grunts. Val L. Fitch was a member of the SED, a uniformed enlisted man with technical expertise, closed out by Security from putting in for combat duty or applying to Officer Candidate School. He was one of the first of the Los Alamos contingent to work at the Alamogordo site. "As little time as possible was spent at Trinity," he recalled, lapsing into District-speak, "because the working and living conditions there were highly uncomfortable." Temperatures in the living quarters shot as high as 130 degrees; dust was everywhere. Fitch remained far from the luminaries. He was introduced to most of the physicists, but he was, as he put it, one of "the individuals present . . . outside the spotlight, on historically important occasions . . . one of that anonymous 'handful of soldiers' mentioned by General Farrell," in *his* official report. One soldier told Eleanor Jette how "the Brass" arrived and "we had to make room for them." Grunts would watch the test from the twenty-mile shelter.[25]

Your place on the pyramid also determined how early you arrived and how long you stayed at Alamogordo. Ultimately, "distinguished visitors," as the Atomic Energy Commission's official historians called them, "checked in" the day before the test—on Sunday. That was when Groves came, with Farrell at his heels. It was also the day that Vannevar Bush, James B. Conant, and others whose importance was ceremonial and administrative showed up to watch. A caravan moved from Los Alamos in the late afternoon, went on to Santa Fe and then Albuquerque, to pick up the official journalist, William L. Laurence of the *New York Times,* along with the British team's titular head, Sir James Chadwick.[26]

Scientists commuted back and forth between Los Alamos and the site. Grunts stayed onsite. The lowest on the chain were the MPs. They were the security arm of Groves's team; he handpicked them just before Christmas 1945, the story goes, from MP squads nationwide, and sent them straight to the site. There were forty-five of them, in living conditions closer to those of prison inmates than prison guards. As the spring approached, the temperatures soared, and the contingent suffered a series of skin diseases brought on by hot weather, no bath or shower facilities, and alkali water.[27]

As the camp filled up, the plight of Trinity residents took on greater importance. SEDs and MPs benefited, albeit indirectly, from the demands of the scientists, engineers, and security officers who settled onsite. Making the site more livable mean that more toilet paper, disinfectant, and ammunition went into the FUBAR. Brown's construction men added new buildings to the base camp. It sprawled; by May, you could see it from quite a distance. By plane, by car, on horseback, from the freight cars of the Santa Fe Railroad, some part of it was visible. This was the paradox of Hanford all over again—to make it even marginally humane was to make it visible.

Compartmentalization was supposed to resolve this issue, by separating trivial knowledge from significant knowledge, keeping the significant information within the paths of the District's authority. Locals and passersby might discover the site from its clouds of dust or its furloughed construction workers; if the underlying knowledge of what was to be tested remained secure, the District's mandate stayed secure.[28]

The core of compartmentalization at Alamogordo was its communication system, designed to facilitate the movement of information within the pyramid of authority, and to prevent information from leaking outside the District or traveling along unauthorized lines. It was an attempt to turn into physical form, into wires and radios, microphones and speakers and headsets, the District's larger program of security control and managed efficiency.

The system had five parts; every one of them compromised the secrecy of the test. The public-address system was the most rudimentary system; it was meant to boom out instructions, orders, and warnings. It used telephone wire and telephone poles (albeit short ones). Allied to it was a second, portable PA system, hooked to jeeps, ready for use if the winds went bad and the clouds went townward, and evacuation became a necessity.

Classified communication went out over the truly secret system, available only to the powerful—the portable short-wave radio system, with its special secret frequency. Hirschfelder, working on fallout management, had one of those radio sets—he called it his "unreliable walkie-talkie." Right before the bomb went off, he watched as his superior, Col. Stafford L. Warren, sent his fallout and radiation monitors *upwind* rather than *downwind* of ground zero. Hirschfelder tried to call Warren to explain the colonel's mistake, but the radio couldn't convey his message. "By the time that this got straightened out," he recalled, "it was too late to move the monitors to places where they would be useful."[29]

The radio frequency for internal communications was supposed to be secret, and it had been chosen to keep others from listening in. But Intelligence chose a band also in use by the Santa Fe Railroad freight switchyard radios in San Antonio, Texas. Throughout the night, Feynman and Hirschfelder and the rest listened for messages and heard the sounds of the moving trains and the desultory conversations of switchyard engineers and trainmen. The airport at Socorro listened in as well.[30]

Bainbridge ended up using the phone lines to set up the timing sequence that culminated in the explosion. It was a lucky decision. As Sam Allison called the countdown into the radio, radio station KCBA in Delano, California, went on the air with the traditional recording of the Star Spangled Banner. Its frequency was the same as Allison's, and so the national anthem drowned out the count.[31]

A fourth communications system went from ground to air, to the specially modified B-29 bombers that were supposed to circle in just the right places over the site, then follow the radioactive cloud, sampling it as they went. But it, too, was wide open, in and out. The frequency was Voice of America's. Listeners to the early morning broadcasts tuned in about 6:00 and heard the call-and-response of the pilots of the planes attempting to track the fallout cloud. The pilots had been briefed, but, as one of them later told Ferenc Szasz, "we didn't know exactly what to expect." When he saw "that huge mushroom cloud boiling up" out of the predawn darkness, he knew what he was to follow. For the next hours he and his colleague in the other B-29 would drone across the sky, watching as the radioactive cloud split into three parts and began to drop its contents across New Mexico and Colorado. If you listened to Voice of America that day, you might have heard them talking to each other and to base.[32]

And then there was the radio frequency assigned to the two lead-shielded tanks that were to take samples from ground zero immediately after the explosion; the tank drivers shared it with the taxi company in nearby Carrizozo, New Mexico.[33]

In the end, the District's systems to ensure secrecy and control of information proved too complex. As they failed, they provided a space for disruption, indeterminacy, luck (good and bad), even resistance. While Groves raged against the wind and rain and weather, seeking to order its compliance, threatening the weatherman with a prison sentence if things didn't go as the general wished them to, those outside his magisterial gaze took over the test, at some, perhaps mundane, level.[34]

OTHERS: SOCIAL WORK

Groves hated the weather, and the weathermen; they represented chaos and the messengers of chaos. Weather violated boundaries, ignored walls and gates, failed to adhere to deadlines, disobeyed orders. Weather caused delays.[35]

The weather forecasters had opposed the test date for months—it was set within a window of unfavorable conditions: thunderstorms, rain, high winds, inversion layers. Groves had overridden them. Now they were onsite, and conditions were exactly the worst possible, with an electrical storm the night before the test date threatening not just the test, but the lives of those setting it up. Groves saw it as a matter of insubordination when the weather forecasters refused to forecast good weather for the test. In the office where he took Oppenheimer, the chief meteorologist, Jack Hubbard, reiterated the unpredictability of the weather.

The accounts of the principals as to what happened next are wildly at odds with each other. Groves's account came decades after the test, in his published memoirs. He reported that it was the weathermen and not the military men who had ignored the weather predictions. His recollections demoted the meteorologists: they were "some weather forecasters whom we called in." They were overly emotional and unable to contribute to a rational decision. "Since it was obvious that they were completely upset by the failure of the long-range predictions, I soon excused them. . . . After that," he wrote, "it was necessary for me to make my own weather predictions—a field in which I had nothing more than very general knowledge."[36]

Hubbard's picture of the circumstances differed markedly. He wrote his report in a diary at the time. Here is Hubbard's account: Oppenheimer and Hubbard were already in the ranch house, had already discussed the weather, had even decided how to proceed under the current weather, when Groves stormed in, asking, "What the hell is wrong with the weather?" Hubbard reminded Groves of his perpetual opposition to the date on the grounds it was inappropriate for proper weather. Groves insisted upon a firm prediction as to when the storm would pass. Hubbard tried to explain that the volatility of the season made such prediction impossible. Groves became increasingly abusive; he insisted again on a specific time. Oppenheimer tried to calm Groves, at the same time supporting Hubbard's expertise. Groves insisted upon a signed weather forecast. He warned Hubbard that if he was wrong, "I will hang you." Hubbard signed the report.[37]

Groves's performance with Hubbard wasn't private. Soldiers, engineers, scientists, fellow-workers saw it, or heard about it on that night.

The MPs had been disobeying Groves for months. They were supposed to remain at the site, completely isolated, until the spring. But the MPs were resourceful; their plight wasn't secret, and their friendships and camaraderie didn't stop when they went out to the desert. So on Christmas 1944, not long after the guards were assigned, a group of WACs drove down from Los Alamos to entertain the MPs, drawing a red line on the map from the secret city to the secret site.[38]

Women weren't to know. But the women knew. Eleanor Jette found out almost from the moment the test was planned. People disappeared and returned to the site, disrupting work and town council meetings, and their whereabouts didn't remain secret from "the Grapevine," as Jette always called the informal community of resistance at Los Alamos. When "a whole contingent of mounted MPs disappeared," she recalled, it was hard to miss.[39]

Elsie McMillan remembered that everyone at Los Alamos knew there would be a test at Alamogordo; everyone knew when it would be. Those who'd come to understand what was being built in their town understood what it meant. McMillan recalled her husband telling her that "we will all be blown to bits if it is more powerful than we expect." Eric Jette told Eleanor about the betting pool on the megatonnage output. Ruth Haley told her: "if the gadget is a flop, Congress will be on our necks. The next time you take a long ride pick out a couple of wee, roomy caves for the Jettes and the Haleys." McMillan's husband told her: "Be sure to look out of the baby's window toward Alamogordo."[40]

McMillan remembered "a light tap on my door. There stood Lois Bradbury, my friend and neighbour. She knew. Her husband was out there too." (After the war, Norris Bradbury would run the Los Alamos weapons program.) Together the two women stayed up the night, watching out the window.[41]

Someone told Dorothy McGibbon, who had done yeoman's work at the Santa Fe office and had organized so much of the life at Los Alamos; she drove to the top of Sandia Peak late that night and watched the sky to the southeast. She wasn't alone. Sandia Peak was the rendezvous for official tourists who were in the loop, who knew, but who weren't important enough to make it onto the site.

Even the authorized ones behaved in unauthorized ways. The instructions were: travel by the military bus caravan, leaving Los Alamos with a motorcycle escort in the afternoon. But many of the scientists understood this to be a field trip; they left earlier in the day, heading down by car into Albuquerque, so they could shop and get a restaurant lunch. They'd arranged for the caravan to pick them up at the Hilton. The caravan stopped first at the airport, to pick up the visiting firemen—including Groves. The sight of an entourage standing around the airport infuriated Groves, who summarily ordered his subordinates to forget their luggage and get into the cars. Then they went on to Albuquerque, to the Hilton to pick up the rest of the scientific community. There much of Los Alamos stood or sat in the lobby, waiting for the buses until Groves, sensing a gross breach of security, ordered them out.[42]

At the test site a loose community developed. As at the parent site of Los Alamos, this was a comradeship that often cut across the boundaries of status. Partly it was the result of preexisting friendships built up at Los Alamos through the town council, through the complex network of whiskey smuggling and the many shared annoyances. Partly it was the result of that growing sense of united purpose, purpose often set in opposition to the demands of the District: to see things through despite the snafu, to make things work, to see what would happen. After years together, high-ranking scientists and lowly enlisted men shared a commitment that their exile in Los Alamos would bear fruit.

By the time of the Trinity test, even the local security officers had shifted their allegiance. Eleanor Jette recalled that Groves ordered Security to keep the test results "SECRET—particularly from the wives at Los Alamos." But the security officers refused—behind the general's back, of course. One said: "'The next thing he'll ask me to do, is keep the Mississippi River secret.'" Not Security (the bureaucracy) but individual security officers let the information slip out to women, to members of the Los Alamos "family."[43]

When Groves arrived onsite, he brought the entire Trinity society into relief, because every sign of its existence infuriated him. He forbad everything: no betting on the outcome; no speculation on the test; no fraternizing among the different groups. He took Oppenheimer out of that environment, and into his own; later he wrote that he'd done this in the name of better decisionmaking: "I felt that no sound decision could ever be reached amidst such confusion."[44]

This process played itself out in the geography of the site. Before Groves's arrival, the privilege of a good viewing spot went to those who'd worked hard—grunts, scientists, MPs, or administrators. One enlisted man told Eleanor Jette that he and his buddies had "sweated in the blazing sun . . . in the hope they'd be allowed to view it from headquarters," and the scientific community had rewarded them accordingly with spots by their sides. When Groves arrived, he summarily evicted them from the spots they'd earned. As they were leaving, some sympathetic MP told them Groves was trying to sleep in a tent; just hours before the test, they revved their engines and did what they could to pay him back. (Groves bragged later that he was sound asleep the whole time.) Groves evicted Val Fitch too, but Fitch's superior, the British scientist Ernest Titterton, dismissed him from his duties and sent him out to watch the explosion, anyway. Another scientist had already given Fitch one of the special protective glass viewers that had been handed out to the big shots.[45]

In the hours before the test, some of the scientists remembered discerning their true place in the District culture in a series of epiphanies. Hirschfelder and Magee, the long-marginalized experts on fallout, were among the most blunt in their debate. Ferenc Szasz interviewed Hirschfelder in 1982; Hirschfelder remembered Magee listening to the rain and telling him the brass couldn't run the test under conditions so dangerous. "The hell they can't," Hirschfelder remembered telling Magee; "they've brought in all these high officials, and they can't delay. It's going."[46]

Kistiakowsky, Bainbridge, the chief Trinity officer Bush, and two assistants had their place pointed out in a different way. Groves sent them up onto the bomb tower itself, to prevent potential sabotage. Kistiakowsky understood that this was, in his recollection, "a perfectly idiotic idea," especially as lightning was playing around the tower, and the dangers were profound. Nonetheless, he and his team stood watch, "with a sub-machine gun in the hands of Captain Bush and that sort of thing." From eminent genius and deviser of the implosion concept, Kistiakowsky had been demoted to security guard.[47]

The Trinity community's symbolic location was Compania Hill—the hill of companions. This was where the bus caravan stopped: it was the bleachers. There, those not big enough to watch with Oppenheimer and Groves stood in a group, holding their special-issue welding-glass strips and listening to the erratic countdown, as the radio kept breaking down and various of them tried to repair it. This was the place to which Eleanor Jette's rebellious GI had been exiled; Richard Feynman was there, and so were most of the top scientists; also present was William Laurence, the official journalist Groves had picked to write the postwar stories. (Laurence, too, was furious that he'd been brought in to do this job and then stuck far from the action.) Laurence was sleeping in a car at 5:00 A.M. Edward Teller offered suntan lotion to everyone, regardless of rank. At the moment before 5:30 A.M.., some were lying around on the slope, some with their faces away from ground zero, others, defying the regulations, facing the test; some were standing; some were inside the cars and trucks; some were leaning against them, using them as shields.[48]

But perhaps the most striking expression of this disintegration of authority that countered the hardening of conditions is the story of José Miera. He owned a bar in San Antonio, a bar expressly off limits to travelers between Los Alamos and Trinity. The only legal stopping point was a place called Roy's Café, in the tiny town of Belen. But Miera's café had become an accepted part of life at Trinity. In the days before the test, a military detail had arrived to rent the cabins behind the bar. In the night hours just before the test, Miera's daughter was in the process of giving birth. Sometime in the early morning the MPs assigned to prepare for the evacuation of San Antonio went over to Miera's and woke him up, telling him to come outside and see the first new thing since Creation.[49]

ENCRYPTION: SPEAKING IN TONGUES

A Glossary (incomplete):

Aches: radio code name of Bainbridge follow-up team member Julian Mack (see *Pains,* below)[50]

Arming Party: group responsible for climbing the tower and arming the trigger; also responsible for climbing the tower and removing the trigger in the event of a misfire or canceled test

Base Camp: where you stayed

Brass: see *Distinguished Visitors*

Broadway: code name for principal route through base camp

Compania Hill: where you stood if you weren't a "Distinguished Visitor," but it was still your project

Casuals: unexpected victims of fallout not previously located by surveillance

Cowpuncher: the supervising committee for the test

Distinguished Visitors: see *Brass*

J. R. Oppenheimer	Major General Leslie R. Groves
R. C. Tolman	C. C. Lauritsen
Vannevar Bush	I. I. Rabi
J. B. Conant	Sir Geoffrey I. Taylor
Brigadier General T. F. Farrell	Sir James Chadwick

Gadget: the test weapon

Ground Zero: site of explosion

Groups: code names for scientific teams with particular tasks

CM-10	G-4	O-4
F-4	G-11	R-1 through R-4

S-45   X-2A   X-2C
X-2   X-2B

HE: high explosives—used in the non-atomic dry run

Hot Run: assembly of the bomb

Jornada del Muerto: Journey of Death

Jumbo: containment vessel insisted upon by Groves but never used

"the 'Malpais' area": region to the east of the Jornada[51]

Material: plutonium

the Oscuras: mountains to the east of site[52]

Pains: Berlyn Brixner's code name (see *Aches,* above)[53]

Proper Authorities: meaning unclear, but certainly not oneself; used as in "to notify proper authorities when such dangers exist" (Hempelmann)[54]

Rehearsal: non-atomic dry run

Safe: meaning unclear; used as in "Persons will not be permitted to leave along Broadway until all danger of contamination has passed and the monitors have declared it *safe.* This may take several hours" (Bainbridge, "Directions for Personnel at Base Camp at Time of Shot").[55]

Trinity: the test

TR: site for the test

Voice of America: government propaganda radio

Zero: moment of detonation

As throughout the District, at Trinity there was legitimate speech and there was illegitimate speech. Legitimate speech was confused, arbitrary, misdirected; illegitimate speech was direct, immediate, necessary. When Aches and Pains tried to speak to each other in code over their 25-W Motorola FM radios in order to co-ordinate the electronic and photographic monitoring of the explosion, something went wrong; Mack switched from code to direct speech. Security was monitoring the radio to prevent such occurrences; the two scientists were ordered to resume code.[56]

Code was necessary to prevent spies from understanding what was going on. The spy Klaus Fuchs knew anyway; he was there onsite, watching the test. Code was necessary to prevent casuals from realizing there was a secret military test going on. Security had assigned radio frequencies that left the supersecret radio transmissions wide open. Casuals listening in on Voice of America (or from the railyards) would have heard code: they would presumably not have watched the many spy movies or listened to the many radio plays of the wartime years in which just this sort of military code meant a supersecret military event was going on. (Of course, this assumed as well that most curious people in New Mexico or northwest Texas hadn't already heard from the construction workers or the rural grapevine that there was a top-secret weapons test going on in the desert south of Albuquerque.)

William Laurence had been instructed to produce a series of press releases for use when the test occurred. Each word was numbered, and the entire set was sent off to the Alamogordo air base. Once the test was completed, Groves and his men would call the air base, instruct its press office which words were to go into the press release, and then order it sent out.[57]

There were four releases, code-named Contingency Releases A, B, C, and D. The most innocuous of the four formed the bulk of the press release used:

> Several inquiries have been received concerning a heavy explosion which occurred on the Alamogordo Air Base reservation this morning.
>
> A remotely located ammunition magazine containing a considerable amount of high explosives and pyrotechnics exploded.
>
> There was no loss of life or injury to anyone, and the property damage outside of the explosives magazine itself was negligible.[58]

The wind was uncertain, the explosion very, very big. After consulting with the medico-legal men, Groves had a sentence added: "Weather conditions affecting the content of gas shells exploded by the blast may make it desirable for the Army to evacuate temporarily a few civilians from their homes." Release B would have reported "severe" damage to surrounding property; Release C, some loss of life; the last release would have reported "widespread destruction of property and great loss of life" and included the obituaries of all the distinguished visitors (including Groves, even Laurence himself).[59]

MEDICINE

Hempelmann's description of the Medical Department for the official set of Trinity plans pulled no punches: "It is the purpose of the Medical Department to anticipate possible dangers to the health of scientific personnel, residents of nearby towns, and of casuals, to provide means of detection of these dangers, and to notify proper authorities when such dangers exist. It is also necessary to obtain records which may have medico-legal bearing for future reference."[60]

At Alamogordo, Medicine wasn't medicine but surveillance. Without the power to prevent injury, without the facilities, staff, training, research, or knowledge to treat, Medicine was left to "anticipate," to "detect," to "notify." And it was to "collect"—to keep the records that might protect the District from later lawsuits.

Hempelmann's dour fatalism may have been the result of further failed expectations. As had the scientists responsible for planning the test, he had assumed that his preparations were to account for a worst-possible-scenario based upon the minimal safe conditions the meteorologist Hubbard had set out and the Cowpuncher group had originally set as criteria for testing. Under those circumstances, Hempelmann believed dangers would be minimal, and the relegation of his division to observe-and-advise status made sense. For a scientist too often confronted with experiments gone wrong, Trinity must have seemed—at first—to be a welcome return to the ideal of scientific research. For a few months, Hempelmann and his crew were to be part of the experimental assessment team at the culmination of Los Alamos's labors, not a force for catastrophe management.[61]

When the reality of the actual circumstances hit Dr. Hempelmann, it was too late to fight back, and besides, there was no one to fight. Two issues moved the dangers of Trinity into glaring relief. One was the issue of explosive release. What if the bomb turned out thousands of times more powerful than predicted? What if it ignited the upper atmosphere? Both of these were questions debated right up to the explosion. But they weren't particularly useful to Hempelmann, because—like most everyone else on the project—he assumed that there was no way to prepare for such catastrophe.

The immediate issue was fallout. Fallout presented a far more disturbing epidemiological picture, for it offered a wide range of human dangers and spread them over a wide geographical area, threatening people hundreds of miles away, with injuries no one had as yet observed and had barely predicted. Virtually all the experimental and predictive material collected by the District's various medical divisions had focused on injury to scientists exposed to radiation from plutonium or uranium. The danger of highly radioactive particles, ranging from atoms through molecules and dust motes to fragments the size of snowflakes, rising in the wind and traveling until weather or gravity caused them to descend: this was an unexpected condition.

But the reality of fallout didn't come home to the medical people until late in the spring of 1945, weeks before the test. By that time, the medical team's manpower was set. So was most of its equipment allocation. Groves gave to the medical team the role of advising on the possibility of evacuation—no more. When Hubbard's weather team warned that the wind might send fallout in any direction, Hempelmann had to spread his troops even more thinly. The new dangers brought a concomitant reorganization of Medicine; Stafford Warren and his assistant, Hymer Friedell, came in from Groves's offices and took on the decisionmaking. As had occurred with the dangers of working at Hanford, now at Alamogordo there had appeared a potentially nettlesome local team with strong allegiance to its constituency and the power to make real trouble—by strike or boycott, or simply by warning in writing (and thus in medico-legal documentation). Warren's appearance coopted Hempelmann, relegating him and his group to "observer" status.

We can see this written against the geography of the Trinity site. Warren was at base camp, "with the high command" (Hirschfelder's words), along with Oppenheimer and Groves. Friedell was in Albuquerque. The lines of communication went to Warren or to Friedell. If something went wrong, Friedell would handle the evacuation, on the orders of Warren. Hempelmann was at S-10,000—the South 10,000 observation post—giving salve to a scientist with an eye infection. Hirschfelder and Magee, in their beat-up sedan borrowed from Jim Tuck back at Los Alamos, waited with the rest of the scientific rabble at Compania Hill, waited for the explosion so they could lead "the convoy of soldiers into the desert" to see what had happened.[62]

By the time things happened, the entire medical program was far from the center of things. Four hundred twenty-five people were scattered across the site, and the Medical Division officially numbered four, including Warren. The rest of the monitoring team—a few men with Geiger counters, a couple of drivers, Hirschfelder's ironically named "convoy of soldiers," and so on—brought the total on the roster to 44, but that number conflated workers on a variety of missions at different times over the next days and weeks. Medicine had the following at its disposal: 100 radiation-monitoring film badges; a "Hand and Swipe Counter" designed to determine radioactive dust-fall; 200 "pencils" (radiation monitors); 112 gas masks, only twelve of which were adequate to filter radioactive gases; 100 sets of coveralls, caps, booties and gloves; 2 ambulances; 2 four-wheel drive vehicles; a beat-up, borrowed sedan for the roving radiation monitors—that is, Hirschfelder and Magee.[63]

Hempelmann divided his small cadre into smaller groups. One member of the medical team at each shelter to monitor conditions and report on instruments. One at base camp, to monitor all instruments, protect observers, check tolerances, and maintain radio contact with the town monitors. One borrowed observer roving along highway 54 between Carrizozo and Oscura, Three Rivers and Tularosa. No radio— only pay-phone contact with Dr. Friedell in Albuquerque. One borrowed observer roving highway 285 between Carlsbad and Roosevelt. One along highway 85, checking San Antonio. One town monitor at Carrizozo.[64]

SILENCES

HIRSCHFELDER: "We were all cold and tired and very, very nervous. . . . The explosion took place just before dawn with the sky still dark. All of a sudden."[65]

KISTIAKOWSKY: "I had nothing to do and so just before the time counting came to zero I went up to the top of the control bunker, put on dark glasses and turned away from the tower. I didn't think anything would happen to me."[66]

FEYNMAN: "But just a few minutes before it was supposed to go off the radio started to work, and they told us there were 20 seconds or something to go. . . . I got behind a truck windshield, because the ultraviolet can't go through glass, so that would be safe, and so I could *see* the damn thing. O.K. Time comes, and this *tremendous* flash."[67]

BOYCE MCDANIEL: "Finally at T-ten minutes, all of us at the base site crouched on the ground behind an earthen barricade watching the light glowing on top of the tower. The first gray of dawn was making its way through the clouds, I remember thinking, 'this is a very dramatic moment. I must concentrate on it so that I can remember it.' I looked around me at the leaders of the program and at my friends. I remember especially I. I. Rabi, Fermi, and Bacher, each staring intently into the darkness. Then came the last minute countdown with the switch to automatic time out. Finally, the brilliant flash of an ever growing sphere was followed by the billowing flame of an orange ball rising above the plain."[68]

VAL FITCH: "Over to the east of the bunker I lay on the ground and peered over the top of a mound of earth, my hands tightly cupping the glass in front of my eyes. I was joined by three or four others. I waited with my line of sight not directed due north toward the tower but rather northeast toward the mountains where the dawn was breaking. At the moment of detonation I did not want to be looking directly at the source. Then, 10,000 yards (six miles) to the north that indescribable flash of light occurred."[69]

OTTO FRISCH (1945): "I watched the explosion from a point said to be about 20 (or 25) miles away and about north of it, together with the members of the coordinating council. Fearing to be dazzled and to be burned by ultraviolet rays, I stood with my back to the gadget, and behind the radio truck. I looked at the hills, which were visible in the first faint light of dawn (0530 M. W. Time). Suddenly and without any sound, the hills were bathed in brilliant light, as if somebody had turned the sun on with a switch."[70]

JOHN H. MANLEY: "[I had] an eye infection which was miserable, but through which I could still see the blinding flash at time zero, 10,000 yards away from the west bunker that was my command."[71]

KENNETH BAINBRIDGE: "The bomb detonated at T=0=5:29:45 A.M. I felt the heat on the back of my neck, disturbingly warm."[72]

J. O. ACKERMAN, Major, Corps of Engineers: "4. The initial white flash and the following brilliant colors were amazing even when expected."[73]

I. I. RABI (1970): "We were lying there very tense, in the early dawn, and there were just a few streaks of gold in the east; you could see your neighbor very dimly. Those ten seconds were the longest ten seconds that I ever experienced. Suddenly, there was an enormous flash of light, the brightest light I have ever seen or that I think anyone has ever seen. It blasted; it pounced; it bored its way right through you. It was a vision which was seen with more than the eye. It was seen to last forever. You would wish it would stop; altogether it lasted about two seconds. Finally it was over, diminishing, and we looked toward the place where the bomb had been; there was an enormous ball of fire which grew and grew and rolled as it grew; it went up into the air, in yellow flashes and into scarlet and green. It looked menacing. It seemed to come toward one.

"A new thing had just been born; a new control; a new understanding of man, which man had acquired over nature."[74]

LESLIE R. GROVES (July 18, 1945): "At 0530, 16 July, 1945, in a remote section of the Alamogordo Air Base, New Mexico, the first full-scale test was made of the implosion of the atomic fission bomb. For the first time in history there was a nuclear explosion. And what an explosion! . . . The test was successful beyond the most optimistic expectations of anyone. Based on the data which it has been possible to work up to date, I estimate the energy generated to be in excess of the equivalent of 15,000 to 20,000 tons of TNT; and this is a conservative estimate. Data based on measurements which we have not yet been able to reconcile would make the energy release several times the conservative figure. . . . Huge concentrations of highly radioactive materials resulted from the fission and were contained in this cloud. . . .

"4. A crater from which all vegetation had vanished, with a diameter of 1200 feet and a slight slope toward the center, was formed. . . .

"5. One-half mile from the explosion there was a massive steel test cylinder weighing 220 tons. The base of the cylinder was solidly encased in concrete. Surrounding the cylinder was a strong steel tower 70 feet high, firmly anchored in concrete foundations. This tower is comparable to a steel building bay that would be found in typical 15 or 20 story skyscraper or in warehouse construction. . . . The effects on the tower indicate that, at that distance, unshielded permanent steel and masonry buildings would have been destroyed. I no longer consider the Pentagon a safe shelter from such a bomb."[75]

LESLIE R. GROVES (1962): "As I lay there, in the final seconds, I thought only of what I would do if, when the countdown got to zero, nothing happened.

"I was spared this embarrassment, for the blast came promptly with the zero count, at 5:30 A.M., on July 16, 1945.

"My first impression was one of tremendous light, and then as I turned, I saw the now familiar fireball. As Bush, Conant and I sat on the ground looking at this phenomenon, the first reactions of the three of us were expressed in a silent exchange of handclasps. We all arose so that by the time the shock wave arrived we were standing.

"I was surprised by its comparative gentleness when it reached us almost fifty seconds later. As I look back on it now, I realize that the shock was very impressive, but the light had been so much greater than any human had previously experienced or even than we had anticipated that we did not shake off the experience quickly.

"Unknown to me and I think to everyone, Fermi was prepared to measure the blast by a very simple device. He had a handful of torn paper scraps and, as it came time for the shock wave to approach, I saw him dribbling them from his hand toward the ground. There was no ground wind, so that when the shock wave hit it knocked some of the scraps several feet away."[76]

HERBERT L. ANDERSON: "I had persuaded Fermi to come down from Los Alamos and to give us a hand with the tanks we had prepared to gather samples of radioactive dirt after the explosion. At the moment of the explosion he stood with the others at an observation point some 10,000 feet away from the steel tower supporting the atomic device. He later related that he did not hear the sound of the explosion, so great was his concentration on the simple experiment he was performing: he dropped small pieces of paper and watched them fall. When the blast of the explosion hit them, it dragged them along, and they fell to the ground at some distance. He measured this distance and used the result to calculate the power of the explosion. His results turned out to agree well with those obtained with more elaborate preparation, including ours. The successful Trinity test was the climax of the Los Alamos wartime period."[77]

ENRICO FERMI (late July 1945): "About 40 seconds after the explosion the air blast reached me. I tried to estimate its strength by dropping from about six feet small pieces of paper before, during and after the passage of the blast wave. Since, at the time, there was no wind I could observe very distinctly and actually measure the displacement of the pieces of paper that were in the process of falling while the blast was passing. The shift was about 2½ meters, which, at the time, I estimated to correspond to the blast that would be produced by ten thousand tons of T.N.T."[78]

JACK AEBY, watching Fermi: "That man has flung clear off his rocker."[79]

ROBERT SERBER (1945): "The grandeur and magnitude of the phenomenon were completely breathtaking."[80]

BRIG. GEN. THOMAS F. FARRELL (1945): "The scene inside the shelter was dramatic beyond words. For some hectic two hours preceding the blast, General Groves stayed with the Director, walking with him and steadying his tense excitement. Every time the Director would be about to explode because of some untoward happening General Groves would take him off and walk with him in the rain, counselling with him and reassuring him that everything would be all right. . . . We were reaching into the unknown and we did not know what might come of it. It can be safely said that most of those present—Christian, Jew and Atheist—were praying and praying harder than they had ever prayed before. If the shot were successful, it was a justification of the several years of intensive effort by tens of thousands of people—statesmen, scientists, engineers, manufacturers, soldiers, and many others in every walk of life.

"In that brief instant in the remote New Mexico desert the tremendous effort of the brains and brawn of all these people came suddenly and startlingly to the fullest fruition. . . . And then the announcer shouted 'Now!' and there came this tremendous burst of light followed shortly thereafter by the deep growling roar of the explosion. . . . Several of the observers standing back of the shelter to watch the lighting effects were knocked flat by the blast. . . .

"The effects could well be called unprecedented, magnificent, beautiful, stupendous and terrifying. No man-made phenomenon of such tremendous power had ever occurred before. The lighting effects beggared description. The whole country was lighted by a searing light with the intensity many times that of the midday sun. It was golden, purple, violet, gray and blue. It lighted every peak, crevasse and ridge of the nearby mountain range with a clarity and beauty that cannot be described but must be seen to be imagined. It was that beauty the great poets dream about but describe most poorly and inadequately. Thirty seconds after the explosion came first, the air blast pressing hard against the people and things, to be followed almost immediately by the strong, sustained, awesome roar which warned of doomsday and made us feel that we puny things were blasphemous to dare tamper with the forces heretofore reserved to The Almighty. Words are inadequate tools for the job of acquainting those not present with the physical, mental and psychological effects."[81]

KENNETH BAINBRIDGE (1974): The bomb detonated at T=0=5:29:45 A.M. I felt the heat on the back of my neck, disturbingly warm. Much more light was emitted by the bomb than predicted, the only important prediction that was off by a good factor. When the reflected flare died down, I looked at Oscuro Peak which was nearer Zero. When the reflected light diminished there I looked directly at the ball of fire through the goggles. Finally I could remove the goggles and watched the ball of fire rise rapidly. It was surrounded by a huge cloud of transparent purplish air produced in part by the radiations from the bomb and its fission products. No one who saw it could forget it, a foul and awesome display."[82]

EDWIN MCMILLAN July 19, 1945: "The whole spectacle was so tremendous and one might almost say fantastic that the immediate reaction of the watchers was one of awe rather than excitement."[83]

FRANK OPPENHEIMER (1980): "And so there was this sense of this ominous cloud hanging over us. It was so brilliant purple, with all the radioactive glowing. And it just seemed to hang there forever. Of course it didn't. It must have been just a very short time until it went up. It was very terrifying."[84]

ELSIE MCMILLAN: "We were in Dave's room. He awakened and wanted a bottle. Lois watched out of the window as I heated the bottle as quickly as possible in the kitchen. It was 5:15 A.M. and we began to wonder. Had weather conditions been wrong? Had it been a dud? I sat at the window feeding Ed's and my baby. Lois stood staring out. There was such quiet in that room. Suddenly there was a flash and the whole sky lit up. The time was 5:30 A.M. The baby didn't notice. We were too fearful and awed to speak."[85]

CONTINUATION

Between the first blinding flash and the rumble, "like huge noisy waggons running around in the hills," there was that space of silence. At the principal observation sites,

10,000 yards away, about 5½ miles from ground zero, it lasted half a minute. At base camp, it was about a minute. At Compania Hills, two minutes.[86]

Into that space of silence other spaces insert themselves. One is the space of memory; between the moment experienced and the moment remembered is a space that grows increasingly wide. Into it can be inserted guilt, rationalization, anger, loss, responsibility, but also a complex transformation of things, of memory and experience, so that *what happened* changes. Everyone remembers clearly; but they remember differently.

Some remember momentary silence and then prolonged cheering. Some remember solemnity, others exuberance—line dances in the bunkers, tangoes on the roof. Not just social comportment lay at issue: the experience of the explosion itself became the prize in an increasingly intense struggle to own, in memory, in reminiscence, and in published account, the nature and significance—the power—of the first atomic blast. What each person said to the other; what the words actually meant: these became skirmishes in a larger war to shape the flow of events and meanings that led from that moment.[87]

Over time, men and women fought their earlier selves to produce a convincing picture of the past, a picture that could resonate with the present—whichever present they were in, at the time. Parts of the story faded, others appeared with new clarity, some came into being for the first time, as the story became myth.

Perhaps the most remarkable of all these were the official journalist William Laurence's accounts. He wrote at least two reports. One appeared just after the end of the war, the other in his first book on the subject of the atomic bomb, *Dawn over Zero*, published in 1946.

Here is Laurence's account written in the summer of 1945:

> The Atomic Age began at exactly 5:30 Mountain War Time on the morning of July 16, 1945, on a stretch of semi-desert land about 50 airline miles from Alamogordo, N.M., just a few minutes before the dawn of a new day on that part of the earth.
>
> Just at that instant there rose from the bowels of the earth a light not of this world, the light of many suns in one. It was a sunrise such as the world had never seen, a great green super-sun climbing in a fraction of a second to a height of more than 8,000 feet, rising ever higher until it touched the clouds, lighting up earth and sky all around with a dazzling luminosity.
>
> Up it went, a great ball of fire about a mile in diameter, changing colors as it kept shooting upward from deep purple to orange, expanding, growing bigger, rising as it was expanding, an elemental force freed from its bonds after being chained for billions of years.
>
> For a fleeting instant the color was unearthly green, such as one sees only in the corona of the sun during a total eclipse. It was as though the earth had opened and the skies had split.
>
> One felt as though he had been privileged to witness the Birth of the World—to be present at the moment of Creation when the Lord said: "Let There Be Light."[88]

Here is Laurence less than a year later:

The atomic flash in New Mexico came as a great affirmation to the prodigious labors of our scientists during the past four years. It came as the affirmative answer to the until then unanswered question: Will it work?

With the flash came a delayed roll of mighty thunder, heard, just as the flash was seen, for hundreds of miles. The roar echoed and reverberated from the distant hills and the Sierra Oscuro range near by, sounding as though it came from some supramundane source as well as from the bowels of the earth. The hills said yes and the mountains chimed in yes. It was as if the earth had spoken and the suddenly iridescent clouds and sky had joined in one affirmative answer. Atomic energy—yes. It was like the grand finale of a mighty symphony of the elements, fascinating and terrifying, uplifting and crushing, ominous, devastating, full of great promise and great forebodings.

I watched the birth of the era of atomic power from the slope of a hill in the desert land of New Mexico, on the northwestern corner of the Alamogordo Air Base, about 125 miles southeast of Albuquerque.[89]

It requires no real training in rhetoric to understand how six months had changed the reporter's picture; how the Promethean picture of elemental nature unchained, of the earth "opened up" and the sky split, became "a mighty symphony . . . joined in one affirmative answer": "Atomic energy—yes." And how an atomic explosion became, by the end, not death but opportunity, became "atomic power," with its vastly different implications; and how the particularity of the moment faded into controlled abstractions, "great promise and great forebodings."

There it was: one minute or ten, in which to interject the human dominion over this new thing of nature, this new Nature. Then came the sound itself, sound and blast roughly simultaneous. At the near sites, the blast was strong enough to flatten those who stood up to watch the light effects. Kistiakowsky (at S-10,000) was knocked down. The sound effects varied depending on where you were. At Compania Hill it began as "a tremendous noise—BANG" and then reverberated off the hills and mountains at greater and greater distance. This was Otto Frisch's "long rumble like heavy traffic far away," as he heard it through plugged ears.[90]

Light, heat, force, sound. Directly beneath the blast, the desert sand, the metal tower, the concrete supports for the tower, fused into a green glass later named *trinitite*. About an hour and a half after the blast and sound waves had passed, two lead-lined tanks lumbered toward ground zero. One quickly broke down. The other continued. Inside was Herbert Anderson from Los Alamos; he looked through his periscope and told headquarters that the landscape had turned entirely green. But the tank didn't make it far; Geiger counters revealed that the two inches of lead lining were nowhere near sufficient to shield the occupants of its interior from the devastating radioactivity.[91]

(Enrico Fermi was supposed to go along. One set of reports has him making the trip and bringing back the samples; another has him in the stalled tank, disgustedly getting out and walking back to the bunker. By 1983, Anderson remembered it differently: in his picture, Fermi had been too sick to go along at all.)[92]

What Anderson saw in that brief moment was a striking transformation in the landscape of the earth—a new ground at ground zero. Interviewed by Lansing Lamont in the early 1960s, he remembered (in Lamont's paraphrase) "what looked like a great jade blossom amid the coppery sands of the desert. Where the shot tower had once stood, a crater of green ceramic-like glass glistened in the sun . . . a 1200-foot-wide saucer some twenty-five feet deep at the center." After gathering his samples, Anderson recalled that he "lingered for a moment, gazing through his periscope at the thousands of emerald beads" over which his tank was to return.[93]

Groves sent his report on to the secretary of war; he reported observing "a crater from which all vegetation had vanished, with a diameter of 1200 feet and a slight slope toward the center." Stafford Warren reported in 1945 on the biological consequences visible in a circle expanding from ground zero: "Partially eviscerated dead wild jack rabbits were found more than 800 yards from zero, presumably killed by the blast." Lansing Lamont interviewed those who did the biological searches after the blast. Here is his précis: "The stench of death clung to the desert in the vicinity of the detonation. No rattlesnake or lizard—nothing that could crawl or fly—was left. Here and there carbonized shadows of tiny animals had been etched in the hard-packed caliche, where the rampaging blaze had emulsified them. . . . The yuccas and Joshua trees had disappeared in the heat storm; no solitary blade of grass was visible."[94]

These are pictures of the ground spreading from ground zero; a newscape to which scientists, military men and visitors would return obsessively over the next days, months and years. The trinitite turned out to have saved the observers from lethal doses of radioactivity. It sealed the ground, preventing a dust storm of particles that would have killed, quickly or slowly, all who had no masks, who had inadequate masks, or who didn't use their masks scrupulously—just about everyone, in that hyperactive environment.

Not all the plutonium (half-life: 24,000 years) bedded in the glass. To leeward of ground zero, in a stretched oval, the plutonium struck, stuck or fell upon thousands of acres of New Mexico grazing, ranching, and desert land.[95]

When the District sought to capture and record the visible consequences of Trinity, it sent an aerial photography team over the site. The resulting image (fig. 43) showed not a uniform crater but a baleful eye staring back at the camera, the plane, the photographer, the viewer. At the bottom of the photograph are the data of the aerial camera, reporting the number of hours after Zero, telling which way is north, and providing a scale chart in meters. These words, numbers, and signs etched on the negative seem to float above that eye, which stares and stares until we turn the page or flip the photograph on its face.

The picture was made two days after the test, probably to assure that airborne travel through the atmosphere above ground zero had become safe. On July 16, Zero Day, this atmosphere was a foil for the new ground beneath it. First there were the awesome, the sublime visual effects—purple clouds, tinged with silver, rising and mutating into new forms as each minute passed. And then the physical contents of those purple, red, awesome clouds began to move. For a short time, the observer planes hung back, tracking the cloud visually. Then it melded into the dawn-tinged thunderheads of summer in New Mexico.

It is in the nature of radioactivity not to end but to continue. The implications of this at Alamogordo were slow to arrive. There was plenty of time for elation and for

FIG. 43 Aerial photograph of crater, first atomic explosion, Alamogordo, New Mexico, 1945. Archives, Los Alamos National Laboratory.

the contest for a piece of the triumph. Then the monitors Hempelmann had sent out along the roads, and the ones Warren had sent in the wrong direction, too, began to report their tallies. At N-10,000 (two miles north of ground zero), celebration ceased when one of the medical men ordered immediate evacuation. Outside the shelter, a seething red cloud full of what one observer called "stuff" headed for them. Inside, the principal meter went hot. The danger was less than they thought: it was the meter that was faulty—a fact whose foreboding implications doubtless weren't lost on Hempelmann. S-10,000 had a partial evacuation. Remaining observers described that cloud as more like dirty fog. Some left; the rest put on masks and waited for the danger to pass over them and onward to the north. As the early morning sun rose, so did the fallout readings. Hirschfelder and Magee, in their borrowed car, headed north. At Bingham, New Mexico, they said nothing to the residents, but they bought all the food off the shelves—a pair of actions right in line with the demands of Security and of Warren's medico-legal orders. Further along, a team of GIs manning a searchlight had made a campfire and some of the men were roasting steaks. But, said one of them, there were "small flaky dust particles gently settling on the ground"—all that was left of the tower, the bomb itself, the sand, dirt, and dust, the vegetation, the living things, great and small, that had chirped and cheeped, quivered in the wind (or just stood before it), wet and glistening in the rain of July 16 before 5:29:30. Hirshfelder reported that "the radiation level was quite high"—two roentgen an hour, nearly five hundred times the tolerance dose, and rising. On orders from the monitors, the two men instructed the soldiers to abandon their celebration and their steaks; they "buried them and pulled out."[96]

The monitors moved further; they found higher and higher radioactivity readings, readings at the edge of the District's already extremely liberal allowances. Their radios, bad at first, died completely. Highway 380 cuts to the north of ground zero (it was the route the WACs took into the site when they visited at Christmas)—it ran from San Antonio to Bingham, New Mexico, and beyond. Along the way, two searchlight posts had been set up in hopes of illuminating the fallout cloud in the predawn darkness. Radiation levels at those sites were the responsibility of a monitor named Arthur Breslow. Driving 380 toward Bingham, he came upon a surreal landscape dusted with a silvery coat of radioactivity. He'd left his mask at one of the searchlight sites after telling the men to get out. Now he had to drive through the valley with his windows rolled up, breathing through a slice of bread.[97]

Breslow was one of the monitors who converged on Bingham to guess at the outcome of this plague of roentgens. As the cloud passed northwesterly, local readings dropped, and the monitoring group decided Groves's dreaded evacuation would not have to take place. Then one set of monitors left to follow the airborne radioactivity, tracing out the invisible, elastic contours of this atomic newscape.

John Magee rapidly came upon what would later be named "Hot Canyon"—an ancient geological declivity transformed into something entirely new with the arrival of Zero's residues. Three hours after the explosion, he watched his meter reading 20 roentgens per *hour* (a year's maximum dose in less than two hours); this time there wasn't anything wrong with the meter, either—Hempelmann told him to check the area again and to use another meter. The ratings were steady. Hempelmann called Friedell; Friedell came down from Albuquerque. Over the next few hours, Hot Canyon got something over 200 roentgens total—about 300 times the wartime maximum dose for an equivalent period of time, 40 times more than postwar limits allowed in an entire year. Even the monitors had to be monitored, their clothes tossed, their cars abandoned, scrubbing showers required. John Magee refused to check his readings after all that. He just didn't want to know.[98]

When Ferenc Szasz wrote his compelling account of the discovery of Hot Canyon, he depended on interviews with those monitors still living in 1983. They mentioned what the DOE historian Barton Hacker discovered in detail: Hot Canyon wasn't un-occupied, it wasn't evacuated, and it wasn't closely monitored after the decision not to evacuate the surrounding towns and ranches. Unknown to the monitors, the District had missed a family—the Raitliffs, with their grandson, dogs, and livestock. Monitors found them on July 17, the day after the cloud had descended upon them—too late for preemptive evacuation. Consulting with Col. Stafford Warren, the observers decided, not surprisingly, to leave them there.[99]

(Colonel Warren's own public record didn't mention any people at all, and he pushed the discovery of Hot Canyon forward a few days. "Fallout was found in some canyons north of . . . the important east-west highway between Socorro and Carri-zozo . . . about 30 miles away from the area of the crater," he wrote. "Some was also found at the base of the Chupadera Mesa, but the high cliffs and lack of roads prevented further exploration at this time, in addition to the fact that preparations had to be made for the departure of the survey team that had been ordered to leave for Japan on 13 August, to study the effects of the bombs that had been dropped on Hiroshima and Nagasaki." Warren's account conveniently modified the chronology, com-pressing a month of District inaction and medical inattention into a few hasty mo-ments.)[100]

Apparently those first casual observers of Hot Canyon didn't ask the Raitliffs if they had neighbors. Had they done so, they'd have learned of the Wilsons, who ranched up the road. In August, Hempelmann followed up on these two families. (Stafford Warren had come along—to supervise, presumably—but he didn't stay long, and he didn't go into Hot Canyon or its surrounding areas himself.) Hempelmann returned to Hot Canyon seeking to determine just how bad the news might be. (By then, the injuries from Hiroshima and Nagasaki had shown the extent of nuclear horror, and its inexorable creeping human consequences.) That was when old man Raitliff told him just what it had been like to be the first victim of fallout. He'd been outside the whole day, he told Hempelmann; his grandson had left the ranch early in the morn-ing, going in to Bingham for the day. Hempelmann reported back that the boy "missed most of the heavy exposure of the first day in the 'Hot Canyon.'" Today, the conclu-sion seems curious. For the grandfather told Hempelmann that "the ground imme-diately after the shot" looked like it was "covered with light snow"—highly radioac-tive flakes of explosion trash, including plutonium and materials that would, in a day or so, mutate into strontium 90. That residue remained for days. Raitliff's grandson had left "early in the morning—" but not before that fall of deadly snow. And the boy had retraced the path of the explosion, out of Hot Canyon and into Bingham. No one reports checking his boots, or his feet, or the saddle of the horse he'd ridden in to town; no District official recalls asking (as parents would ask, knowing children) if he'd worn the same pair of pants, the same shirt, for days afterward.[101]

None of this appears in Warren's report.

In Hot Canyon, at Raitliff's ranch, Hempelmann saw striking evidence of the effects of fallout, not on the people, but on the animals. Some had "beta burns" (radiation burns familiar to those who have steeled themselves sufficiently to stare at the photographs of survivors of Hiroshima and Nagasaki), bleeding, and loss of hair. It seems that Hempelmann didn't tell the Raitliffs or the Morgans to slaughter their cattle or their milk cows; probably he didn't know how deadly his silence might be (because, after all, research in this area hadn't been sanctioned by Warren—it wasn't of immediate "medico-legal" significance). But there at Hot Canyon and throughout its surroundings, cattle grazed on the fallout grass, and the cows made milk, and the milk—some of it—went the path of the Hanford milk. Here, however, that milk wasn't so likely to be mixed with the milk of thousands of other cows in dairy cooperatives, thus diluting its effects. And here, where subsistence ranching was the norm, the milk was far more likely to be drunk, day after day, by the same people—the Raitliffs and the Wilsons, the Raitliffs' grandson and their two-year-old niece, who came to live with them that fall of 1945. In December, after other, more prosperous and influential ranchers threatened to sue over the damage to their cattle, the army sent its people out to buy up the most obviously afflicted animals—not to get them out of the food chain, but to quiet the complaints of locals by creating an observation program. They bought seventy-five of the six hundred worst. The rest remained, gave milk, were fattened, slaughtered, and went to market.[102]

Hempelmann's reports may have disheartened him, but to the District's administration they were undeniably reassuring. No one then knew just how limited was Hempelmann's knowledge of radiation effects—limited in part by the haste and drive for economy imbedded in the District, in part by Warren's more deliberate reorientation of research away from long-term effects. Hempelmann looked for gross injury and found none in the human population. And he concluded that, since most people change their clothes and bathe often, the dangers of fallout remaining on the skin were minimal, and therefore that the correlation between animals and humans couldn't be made.

But just how to calculate the formula for injury—and just who determined that formula—remains unclear. Dr. Stone came down to Los Alamos from Berkeley in February 1946 and saw the cattle the army had bought. He estimated that they had received "between 4,000 roentgens and 50,000 roentgens, probably about 20,000 roentgens." What fraction of that dosage went to people, what fraction remained on the land, on the foliage and the grazing lands: unknown.[103]

Lest we forget: the maximum human dosage considered safe as of 1936 was .10 of a roentgen per day, with an annual total of 36.5 roentgens; after the war, with the discovery of radiation-induced leukemia, it dropped to 5 roentgens, or rems, a year. Had the people received just a tenth of the animal dosage, 2,000 rems, they would have received four hundred times the postwar annual dose.[104]

Hempelmann and Stone both seem to have missed the dangerous pathway traced at Hanford—the path from sky to grass, to cows, to milk, and then to humans vulnerable to the dangers: the iodine 131 and strontium 90 path. So did the full-bore survey of the residual effects on the landscape, begun some three years later. The survey was contracted out by the new Atomic Energy Commission—contracted to a team connected with Stafford Warren, now dean of the medical school at UCLA. Not surprisingly, the conclusions were optimistic, though the survey team observed hot mesa grass surrounding Hot Canyon.[105]

We don't know what happened to the Raitliff family or the Wilsons; to the children and adults who drank the milk from cows grazing the sparse grass of the region, and ate the meat from slaughtered cattle; to the transient sheepherders and cowboys who worked the region. The records are classified, or lost. Even Hempelmann's reports stayed carefully sequestered from the other reports that emanated from Trinity, in order "to safeguard the project against being sued by people claiming to have been damaged," as a 1946 report phrased it. To read Hempelmann's reports now is to see why they stayed hidden: to read, for example, that the Raitliff family collected their drinking water from a cistern that drew rainwater from the roof, to know, then, that hard rain fell and they drank the hard rain. Or to read the rancher Ted Coker's recollection of standing underneath the raining fallout cloud as it passed over him, his recollection that "it smelled funny." To read, and to know that Coker died of cancer, one of a cluster of cancer deaths in the area, a statistical "hot spot."[106]

Over the next years, a series of ecological studies sponsored by the Atomic Energy Commission sought rather straightforwardly to reassure everyone concerned that the land was not sowed with salt, that ranchers were not endangering themselves or their families or customers by staying in the region. But concern with "medico-legal effects" required that there be some sort of cautionary statement in the reports. With the District's legacy intact, indeed continuing both in the AEC's own staff and in the subcontracting investigators under Stafford Warren, the reports continued to speak the District's twisted tongue. "In the absence of better information," said one, "it would seem logical to suspect that conditions hazardous to man are not absent from the areas." By 1956, with no major legal claims, the AEC turned its attention to rather more violent depredations at the postwar South Sea test sites. There the effects on humans were far more severe, approximating the symptoms of the cattle and sheep in Hot Canyon and the surrounding Chupadera Mesa. Blessedly for the District, however, these were (in District eyes) powerless native peoples; army information officers softened them up with fairly heavy doses of propaganda before the atomic tests emulsified, or merely irradiated to sterility, their tropical paradises. By comparison, Alamogordo didn't look so bad; the ecological surveys ended.[107]

In 1983 Ferenc Szasz thought to ask just what happened to all the green glass fused from the sand at ground zero, ringing the eye of the explosion and covering more than seventy acres. Like so many of us who were children or came of age after the war, he remembered the exotic sheen that new substance, that trinitite, had on the imagination. Here is what he found: Motels and banks gave away samples to customers; women made necklaces of trinitite; a gas station owner's wife kept a box of the stuff in her closet; reporters and photographers, brought to the site by Groves in September 1945 to "prove" that there were no lingering aftereffects to atomic warfare, still held onto some of the surreally shaped trinitite globules they had grabbed to keep as souvenirs; streams of atomic tourists came to see ground zero and to take away a little something.[108]

That newspaperman's excursion dreamed up by Groves included Geiger counter demonstrations. Readings at the site were about twelve roentgens per hour—one-fiftieth of the lethal lifetime dose the District projected at that time, and one-third the annual dose. (Apparently the group stayed at ground zero long enough that Oppenheimer received an eighteen-roentgen dose and had to be warned off the area.) Nonetheless, Szasz also noted a strange and lucky quirk of the creation of trinitite. As a glassy sand, it didn't act as it should have when humans or animals ingested it. It didn't serve as a "bone-seeker," because the glass served as a sort of barrier. It passed through the digestive system, emitting its radiation, was excreted, and that was it.[109]

In some poetic way, the trinitite that traveled around the country and around the world, in pockets and jewelry and bank souvenirs and shoeboxes, replicated the globalizing of the atomic landscape. The explosion at Alamogordo swept up the earth of the Great American Desert, the Journey of Death itself; swept it up and transmuted it into elements and compounds never before known.

C O N S E Q U E N C E

PICTURES

On August 14, 1945, Ed Westcott climbed above a crowd of Oak Ridge workers assembled for his camera and photographed them holding up copies of the *Knoxville Journal* carrying the banner headline, WAR ENDS (fig. 44).

It is an arresting picture, a contrast of brightly lit faces and newspapers against black shadows and unreadable backgrounds, full of jubilation, apparently artless. It is an image that seems quintessentially to celebrate the joy of workers returned triumphant to their country after a long exile. Even its style—so much a part of popular journalism in 1945, so similar to photographs made all over the United States—inserts the Manhattan District into the national celebration, wild, free, exultant at the triumph of democracy over tyranny.

This is an image made, not merely at the end of something, but also at the beginning of something else. War ends, and so does the need for secrecy, for long workdays, for the voices of authority intoning their calls for greater efficiency, greater fealty to the District and its goals, for isolation from friends, relatives, other people, other places, other possibilities than are held inside the fences.

At the other end of the transition from war to peace, from the Manhattan Engineer District to the Atomic Energy Commission, is another image, on first glance remarkably similar. It, too, is a news image, destined to be seen by millions, part of the mass culture of the atomic age. This one is a newsreel, released on the first anniversary of the Hiroshima bombing, August 8, 1946. Here's the way the advance press release described the reel: "'Atom Bomb Birthplace,' Oak Ridge, Tenn.—First pictures of the Manhattan Project—home of the atom bomb. In these dramatic films you will see men at work on the epochal process, and the homes in which the workers live. Wartime censorship has been lifted, as Uncle Sam releases small quantities of by-products for medical science."[1]

The press release alone is a remarkable précis of the District's mythology regarding its own end. Now what was secret and suppressed has become public—become, moreover, the object of celebration and veneration. The eras of repression and secrecy have ended, and now the poisons of war are magically, alchemically converted to the potions of peace.

The newsreel itself confirms this promise. "Atomic Aid for Science" is its title. A voice familiar from radio and newsreels booms out the text across footage drawn from the District's public relations department, footage shot between the spring of 1944 and war's end.

> Atomic capital of the world, Oak Ridge Tennessee. Home of the Manhattan Project, birthplace of the atomic bomb, and the spot where 50,000 persons kept the war's greatest secret. In this mile-and-a-half-square, the foundation of a new age was laid. But Oak Ridge beat its swords into plowshares, and for the first time, the press is admitted to the closely

FIG. 44 *War Ends. Oak Ridge, 1945.* Photo by James E. Westcott, U.S. Corps of Engineers, Oak Ridge, Tennessee.

guarded plant. All visitors receive meters, to determine any radioactivity they may have acquired during their stay in the plant—a wartime rule to protect workers. Upon entering, they see the lead and concrete shields, behind which the atomic pile generates enormous radioactivity. The first step in peacetime use of the atom.[2]

The newsreel's visuals break the narrative into a sequence of emblematic images. First: fences, barbed wire. Then: the gate, a smiling official among smiling officials cutting a ribbon across a main street. Then: a sign—"Visitors: Obtain meters here before entering." Then: images of factories.

The final shot describes the core message—so well that Ed Westcott reproduced the filmmaker's stance in making four photographs, an establishing shot, a pan, and two "takes" of the proper PR shot (figs. 45, 46). We see, on a platform, men clustered in two groups. Both are in uniform. On one side, the uniforms are military. On the other, medical—white lab coats over suits, perhaps even a stethoscope. After an awkward pause, the high military official hands the test tubes of radioactive isotopes to the high medical official. The voice swells, recapitulating the message carried by the event. "At Oak Ridge today, it is: Operation Healing."

To look at the newsreel once is to return to the everyday world of Ed Westcott's picture, to be immersed in the life of the site, finally free to look. But look again and again at those three-or-so minutes and the newsreel changes. Its artlessness fades. The film footage seems not spontaneous but coached and canned. The image—of an official cutting the ribbon to make Oak Ridge "just another American town" (in the words of the voiceover)—betrays not the ceremonial quality of the event, but its stilted origins in the District's public relations departments. As the scenes shift, the falseness of that moment comes to pervade other images. Despite the benevolent thrust of the narrative, the matériel of war, danger, and injury impinge: the warning signs, the shielding, the clichés of the narrator. And the final event, the ceremonial handing of a test tube full of radioisotopes, at first so apt, seems, over time, *too* apt, another example of Daniel Boorstin's "pseudo-event."[3]

In fact, this newsreel is the near-literal translation of a series of releases from the War Department Public Relations Division that began on June 14, 1946, and culminated with an August 2 release to commemorate the first formal transfer of radioactive material from military to civilian hands. The releases celebrated "a program for the nationwide distribution of the beneficial radioactive isotopes to be produced from the uranium chain-reacting 'atom pile' at the Clinton Engineer Laboratories, Oak Ridge, Tennessee." Behind this transfer, as each of the releases is careful to observe, is the benevolent arm of the military. Each of the releases also mentions "life," "the dynamic processes of living," and the "therapeutic . . . treatment of certain special diseases."[4]

This newsreel and the propaganda program behind it are not isolated media events; they are parts of a larger tapestry of public presentations that sought to define the cold-war atomic culture as both a continuation and a transformation of the Manhattan Project.

On the Saturday before "Operation Healing," the newsreel of the week recorded another, darker scene, dubbed "Operation Crossroads." That newsreel's title was "Underwater Atom Blast," and the release sent out to newspapers promised the film was

FIG. 45 *Sale of First Radioisotope, August 2, 1946*, Oak Ridge. Photo by James E. Westcott, courtesy National Archives.

FIG. 46 *Sale of First Radioisotope, August 2, 1946,* Oak Ridge. Photo by James E. Westcott, courtesy National Archives.

"a graphic record of one of the most terrifying happenings in world events." Here is the narration:

> These are the instruments that will loose the bomb in the target area. . . . The signal: Two minutes to go! and everyone in the fleet stands by to picture history in the making—a scene that excites even the most experienced newsman. . . . All eyes are trained on the blast point . . . Deadly radioactive water . . . in a deadly mist . . . seen from the air the towering waves set in motion appear to be only shallow ripples. The beach at Bikini gets a pounding. A television screen records an on-the-spot picture story. . . . deadly with its radioactive gases . . . and for days it was not safe for salvage crews to board the ships. Geiger counters record the intense rays, which would have proved fatal if the ship had been manned.
>
> And now are shown the most dramatic pictures of the underwater blast, taken from an underwater plane [*sic*]. Here is the motion picture spectacle of all time! A million tons of water alive with deadly rays. Awe-inspiring in its significance for man, who learned how to control the atom, but must now learn to control himself. There is but one defense against the atom bomb, and that is distance, and distance will mean nothing without world peace. This is—*Crossroads.*[5]

Here is the dark sublime that the District sought to banish the next week with its image of Operation Healing. Or perhaps not banish; perhaps, instead, to balance two necessary mythologies, one of terror, the other of renewal, with the District and its successors (overt and covert) at the fulcrum.

And so these two documents of transition—Westcott's photograph and Universal's newsreel—might be seen as residing at opposite ends of a process. It is a process of transition, not simply from wartime to peacetime, but from one form of social and cultural control to another—from a closed cultural space ruled by direct and indirect intervention in the social fabric, to an opened culture ruled by the covert creation and manipulation of mythology, linking the closed atomic spaces with the open American spaces surrounding them in a new, coercive American culture.[6]

DECONSTRUCTION

In Richland, the same day that Ed Westcott made his photograph, Maj. William Sapper, Colonel Matthias's principal assistant, wandered through the clubs where engineers and officers and their wives had assembled to celebrate. He carried a primitive recording machine—some cross between a Dictaphone and a record player—and he recorded a series of mock-interviews, he mimicking the stentorian voice and officious style of the radio interviewer. His subjects, most of them friends and acquaintances of long standing, emerge from the scratchy, incoherent background and then recede again. Every once in a while, some other sound will appear with startling clarity: the scrape of a highball glass across a table; the tap of a spoon nervously, repetitively hit against the side of a chair. The voices, too: people seem dazed, drunk, unable to fit themselves neatly into Bill Sapper's usual ironic, joking frame.[7]

For nearly everyone, this loss of identity, this sense of a seismic shift, seems to have prevailed. In Los Alamos, Phyllis Fisher wrote her parents of the sudden and disorienting experience of the first days after the end of the war. Suddenly Los Alamos was public knowledge, and it seemed alternately a liberation and a violation. "The radio announcers . . . told the whole story," she wrote. "How had they gotten the information so quickly? They named names! Who had told them? They described our hill, *our* hill. They located us on a barren plateau in the mountains north and west of Santa Fe. They identified us as LOS ALAMOS!"[8]

For Fisher this new state of public adulation and relief brought with it a deep disturbance; "part of me keeps saying, 'This can't be real,'" she wrote. "After months of caution and secrecy, it's too much." For weeks, even months, Los Alamos became a place of "emotional bits," of the terror aroused by a traveling salesman, of "Scotty, who lives next door," found "nauseated, dizzy, and completely hysterical . . . sobbing convulsively into his pillow," of a husband who "gets up and wanders around at night when he should be sleeping." At Los Alamos, the medical team ran out of "headache pills, sleeping pills and medicine for nausea" three days after Hiroshima, and faced a mob of desperate patients.[9]

"Women wanted to know. Everything. At once." That was Laura Fermi's remembrance. "Children celebrated noisily, paraded through every single home, led by a band playing on pots and pans with lids and spoons. Men viewed the consequences of their work, and suddenly they became vocal." After years of enforced silence, the men overflowed with manic talk, talk that started with atomic physics and spread to the global consequences of their work. "Now the entire world was their concern," Fermi wrote.[10]

And now there was a chance to recement what had been broken by the District. Marriages, loves could be rediscovered. Phyllis Fisher and her husband looked at each other again. "Suddenly there was no longer any need for a wall of silence between us. Ahead of us stretched hours and hours of trying to sift through our tangled feelings of hope for peace and of despair for the world. Night after night we talked. We explored the silence between us that had affected our lives for a year. We spoke of the additional loneliness that silence had caused." That was Phyllis Fisher's memory of the first nights after the first days.[11]

Next step was to pack up and leave: throughout the autumn of 1945, the residents of the MED became a sort of willing diaspora, taking their celebrity with them out into a world newly opened by the lifting of censorship and the abandonment of regulations that had kept them onsite. At Los Alamos, Eleanor Jette reported, "the stream of departing trailers almost blocked The Hill road." At Oak Ridge, the population dropped from close to 80,000 to 52,000 in the fall months succeeding V-J Day. At Hanford, the exodus was as large or larger.[12]

Los Alamos came close to disintegrating entirely. How to keep residents? The District ran a survey. It revealed an overwhelming consensus on the way the future of the site should be assured. End military control over the site, and replace it with "civilian administration of project and community." Build a new and more humane environment; equalize wages; spread power and decisionmaking out among the populace; retool to convert weapons of war into tools of peace.[13]

Many responded with their own utopian visions for an ideal postwar American community. But this was just one of the ways citizen-residents sought to gain or regain control of these atomic spaces. Theirs was an effort built first of all on the euphoria of war's end and the declared triumph of the atomic mission. It was built as well on a quickened sense of responsibility, particularly among those within the fence, to make the new world better than the old. For some, this meant moving forward aggressively—it meant progress. For others it meant the opposite: a nostalgic return to the safety of a preatomic America.

Now that the fences were unnecessary, cultural forces from outside sought to take back what had been removed from them with the expropriation of the sites. Local residents called for the reopening of roads that had long been closed, while the District sought ways to keep control over their spaces and the routes to and from them. The District's continued appropriation of the roads signaled to outsiders a broken promise and a dangerous precedent for retaining or even expanding the mandate and the style of the secret wartime facility. Writing to Congressman Jennings, once the firebrand populist in the real-estate battles of 1943, Scott E. Williamson, a resident of Oliver Springs, Tennessee, put it bluntly: "apparently some of the Big Brass of CEW don't know the war is over."[14]

For the most part, however, the District sought a strategy of outward conciliation covering and softening inner implacability. Matthias was the most successful; he traveled from town to town speaking at Kiwanis clubs and Jaycee meetings, recasting the story of the war and the site to make it seem inevitable, more humane, more heroic than it might have seemed to his audiences just a few weeks or months before. (Throughout this, he was in touch with Washington public relations officials to make certain exactly what he could and could not say.) In the process, he offered cooperation with local officials—gifts from the site, expert advice, tightly controlled site visits. The result was to keep the site *the site,* separate and inviolate, while laying the foundation for a postwar Manhattan District, regulating to eternity the created sites and cities of Hanford, Richland, and the great spaces compassed by the wartime boundaries.[15]

Matthias's strategy was a slightly more folksy, less authoritative version of the tactics throughout the District. As the MED saw it, the District had nothing to gain and much to lose by exposing the sites to democracy, to openness, to the ebb and flow of American life and American institutions. Retain power; control information; draw a convincing but thoroughly happy picture of the program: that was the best way.

Circumstances hardened this position rather quickly. For even as District officials basked in the celebration of their heroism, other pictures of the project, and of them, began to percolate into the public arena. As early as August, rumors and newspaper stories had begun to surface suggesting health hazards to the workers at Hanford and residents surrounding it, radiation leakage into the Columbia, and heating of the river. Matthias wrote to Groves urging that someone issue "authoritative statements from some high official in the War Department covering the steps that had been taken to protect the health of workers at Hanford and the steps that had been taken to insure that no damage had been done to the fishing industry in the Columbia River."[16]

Similarly with the environmental dangers. By midfall of 1945, Matthias and Groves knew something of the ecological troubles they had wrought. Despite the clear evidence of iodine 131 contamination of the exhaust gases from Chemical Separation, the District had continued, even expanded, its separations program. So also with releases into the Columbia; though the war was over, the District continued to release wastewater too rapidly into the river, failing to wait for the short-lived fission products to decay.[17]

More important than these sins was the discovery that the jerry-built storage tanks and reservoirs were beginning to fail, releasing unknown amounts of toxic and hazardous materials into soils and water. In late October, Matthias arranged for the return of a Major White to the Hanford site from Oak Ridge, where he had been on assignment. Matthias noted in his diary that he needed White, "for a short period at least, to review the apparent implications involved in noticeable leaking from some of the 107 reservoirs." It was also on that day that Hanford received word of its first claim of radioactivity injury by a worker. Matthias wrote:

> Miss Anthon of the *Yakima Daily Republic* called this morning to report that a news service release indicated that a Mr. James W. Darling was claiming publicly that he was slowly burning to death because of mysterious burns encountered while he was working in a maintenance shop at Hanford on November 29, 1943. Further investigation indicated that the probabilities are that the acid with which he was burned was sulfuric acid common to machine shops. It was done at a time when no radioactive materials were at Hanford. He is represented by a Mr. Kavanay, Attorney, who apparently is not well known in this area.[18]

The case went before the State Compensation Commission on November 13, and "it was agreed by the Commission that there was no legitimate claim in connection with radioactivity that contributed to Darling's disability."

The combination of these two events brought home the threat to the reputation of the District, and of its officers, and the potential threat on legal grounds, as well. Opened sites, the taking down of fences, meant a tremendous potential increase in the number of people exposed to the toxicity lacing the sites; opened files and open government promised an equivalent increase in revelations and lawsuits—justified or not.

By the end of 1945, District officials at the Oak Ridge site had discovered that even the land acquisition program remained a live issue; locals sought the return of their property and the privatization of the site. There, too, issues of radiation danger and of toxic spills had resurfaced; the "medico-legal implications" of demilitarizing the site must have been on the minds of many District officers. On this, the District was unequivocal: the lands were taken in perpetuity; the lands belonged to the District and its successors.[19]

But to keep the sites intact was only part of the larger program of continuation. Bringing the Manhattan Engineer District from a wartime to a postwar America meant perpetuating production of plutonium, enriched uranium, and the mechanical assemblies for the bombs themselves. It meant retaining, as much as possible, the production facilities and the workers to staff them. It meant preserving the fundamental bureaucratic structure, the program of compartmentalization, control over information and speech, cooperation among corporate, government, military and labor institutions—in short, all the weapons the District had developed during the war. Perhaps most important, those first weeks and months of continuation indicated clearly that Groves and his forces planned to retain as much as possible of their wartime atomic culture, to transform what surrounded the District rather than transforming the District itself.

Writing his memoirs in the early 1960s, Groves was relatively direct in his appraisal of the postwar program. His first concern, he wrote, had lain with keeping his staff together, and with recruiting new staff as rapidly as possible to replace those who left. He envisioned a cadre of new officers, ready to join the technocratic elite that would revolutionize military affairs and international politics in the postwar atomic culture— he wanted "men who were young enough to break into the atomic field, but who were senior enough in rank to have demonstrated their ability to accept heavy responsibilities, and whose age would be an asset in their dealings with our scientific personnel, almost all of whom were extremely young." Groves looked to West Point for officer recruits who were "young," full of "mental alertness," "among the first five or ten of their class," but also with "a successful athletic career, demonstrating a more than average determination and will to win." In his military and scientific elite, he sought aggressive, competitive men capable of seeing the cold war as a contest, but at the same time ready to subsume their individuality to a more general "team spirit."[20]

For Groves, the end of the war provided the opportunity to centralize and enforce control over those sites the District would retain—under its current identity, or under whatever new configuration of military, governmental, and corporate collaboration would take the District's place. Not surprisingly, Groves sought to rid the District of the subsites at key academic centers, particularly the University of Chicago's Met Lab and the site at Columbia University. The northern California site of Ernest Lawrence's lab would continue, because it was closely focused around a safe individual: Groves wrote in 1962 that the Berkeley lab "would continue as long as Ernest Lawrence would live."[21]

Los Alamos would remain central to the postwar atomic culture, Groves decreed, despite a significant body of sentiment among major scientific and administrative staff that this was a mistake—that the site was too isolated, too topographically limited, too arid, and too primitively built to be salvaged for the new postwar environment. Behind this was a general assessment that the site was too disreputable ever to attract a postwar scientific force of real stature. Groves decided otherwise; he began to expand the site, building family housing to attract a new generation of young scientists and seeking to restructure the leadership.[22]

At Los Alamos especially, a new site commander would have to serve as actual and symbolic representative of the new atomic culture. How to replace Oppenheimer? became the question. Groves pulled off a major coup by hiring Norris Bradbury. A veteran of the site, Bradbury was both an academic physicist and a military man. Here was an administrator perfectly suited to bring the Los Alamos site smoothly from world war to cold war without danger of losing its essential flavor as a military weapons development, testing, and production facility. Bradbury had overseen the delicate setup of the Alamogordo bomb on the tower, and he had supervised the assembly of Fat Man, the plutonium weapon. His appointment brought Groves a man dedicated to the site and ready to find new programs and problems to attract a new generation of physicists.[23]

Bradbury proved Groves right in his choice. While Oppenheimer's final speech to his assembled troops bemoaned a world in danger from the demotion of science into technology and its conversion into an inventing-ground for consumer culture, Bradbury worked assiduously to bring about just such a shift. He saw the new Los Alamos as a place where technologically oriented physicists would find a happy home, full of interesting technical problems and full as well of "toys," to use the Los Alamos parlance for their products. At a meeting on October 1, Bradbury had started from Groves's insistence: that "the project cannot neglect the stockpiling or the development of atomic *weapons* [and it was Bradbury who put the emphasis on this word] in this interim period. Strongly as we suspect that these weapons will never be used, much as we dislike the implications contained in this procedure, we have an obligation to the nation never to permit it to be in the position of saying it has something which it has not got." To propose otherwise would be "to weaken the nation's bargaining power in the next few months," Bradbury warned, and he made it clear such a proposal would be "suicidal" for the nation and seditious for the individual or group proposing it.[24]

That wasn't all. It was Bradbury who, in his first meetings with his staff, pressed the idea of future atomic tests, on the grounds that the tests would serve as "a goal to stimulate the staff." His weight behind an accelerated weapons-test program was essential to the decisions that led to Operation Crossroads and the tests, in the summer of 1946, that eliminated at least one South Sea island from the face of the earth and permanently poisoned others.[25]

Bradbury was, in these regards, an ideal scientific leader to direct Los Alamos under a cold-war military establishment. But there is evidence that Bradbury also envisioned the shift from wartime to postwar community as the opportunity to return to the older, never-achieved scientific utopia of independence, cooperation, and self-determination. Had matters evolved unimpeded, this would quite possibly have happened; with the scientific community shifted directly from Groves to the new civilian AEC, its leaders would have been in a position to demand and receive a central place at the table.

But Groves appears to have anticipated this possibility, and he worked, ingeniously, to thwart it. To do this, he had to reroute the scientific administration from his own jurisdiction *before* the transfer of powers from his office to the AEC. This he did, reorganizing the maps of power so that Los Alamos lay under a military commander and thus was removed from the transfer from Groves's authority to that of the commission.[26]

Groves's activities during those months provide us with the picture of a District committed to maintaining, even extending, its reach. But to focus too closely on Groves would be to miss the larger reality of a more powerful and more amorphous set of forces—the metaphysical geography of the District—equally committed to self-preservation and self-perpetuation. Scientists like Bradbury and Jette who thought they could push their rights as civilians misapprehended the circumstances; in particular, they underestimated the power of the District's traditions, its history, its momentum, and its culture.

But Groves developed a changed demeanor; his softened and more conciliatory voice reflected two fundamental shifts in the politics of the atomic program. One was the emergence of a powerful lobby for civilian control of the atomic age, the other the inevitable transformation that came when the scientists had the freedom to bargain for their services and the temerity to press for changes in the philosophy of the entire program. Groves's solution—to defer to the scientists in language and rhetoric, but to retain control over the program wherever possible—represented a compromise.

In all these ways, Groves and the District moved practically and pragmatically to ensure its own perpetuation in the postwar era—even if this occurred under the titular administration of a civilian agency. At the industrial sites of Oak Ridge and Hanford, however, this process took place with different emphases and different strategies—strategies more appropriate to their industrial and manufacturing character.

Groves recognized that the logic of war's end would, sooner or later, result in calls to curtail drastically, or even mothball, the production facilities. Nevertheless, he decided to continue plant expansion. It was a highly controversial decision, and Groves remained silent on his rationale. Indeed, his autobiographical account veers abruptly into a discussion of the confusing chain of command during the interregnum, and a defense of his own unparalleled power over the program and the lack of accountability to accompany his power.[27]

We can speculate over the reasons. Increasing production provided the materials for a significant stockpile of atomic bombs. Such a stockpile shifted the balance of military force toward the new atomic military; this shift in balance moved Manhattan closer and closer to the center of American military, political, and international life. Such an explanation gives logic to Groves's otherwise rambling accounts of internal political power struggles and his declarations of his own irreplaceability. The product Groves was interested in consolidating and streamlining wasn't just uranium, and the power it produced wasn't just atomic: politics and political power lay at the center of things.

This, then, became Groves's mission: to keep the boundaries fixed and the walls high; to replace independent-minded scientists with patriotic technologists; to expand production of atomic weapons and thus to make the atomic culture an indispensable part of American life in the postwar years.

But Groves was no longer an omnipotent being overseeing a vast empire invisible to all but the highest federal officials. The end of the war made the program manifest, and now those whom he had silenced in the name of wartime security believed they could speak again.

EMPLOYEES

Probably the most prominent of these voices belonged to the labor movement. By the end of the war, grassroots local union activity had largely ceased on the District sites. Groves's labor plan had involved three steps to control union activity on the District: first to bring about a transfer of union power from local to national and "international" headquarters; then to negotiate cooperative agreements with these large-scale union corporations; and finally to offer a trade-off in which the Internationals gave labor peace in return for a place at the table and the promise of postwar rights to organize in the new sites and the new industries that came with atomic technologies.

Now the war was over, and it was time to cash in the chips. District officials were understandably reluctant to give up all they had gained; but how were they to retain control over the process and mold it to their goals without at the same time seeming like antidemocratic obstructionists?

One tactic was to move the discussion from pragmatic realities to highflown ideals—to control the mythology and thereby control the way the conflict was pictured. In this, labor was only one part of a larger strategy. Long before the end of the war, District flak-catchers were hard at work preparing press releases to handle every aspect of the conversion from secrecy to celebrity. One of these concerned the labor movement: its headline read "Labor Plays Vital Role in Activity of Manhattan District." Written for release on the day of the first atomic bombing of Japan, it was probably the product of William Laurence's pen.

The theme was cooperation among the District, the unions, and the War Manpower Commission, who "teamed up to achieve what at times seemed impossible." But this teamwork was not meant to imply egalitarianism. The unions were loyal subjects. "On several occasions it was necessary that Judge Robert Patterson, the Under Secretary of War, call in the leaders, including the President of the A.F. of L., Mr. William Green, and the General Presidents of several Building Trades Unions, to seek their cooperation and to give them a better understanding of the problems involved. Mr. Philip Murray, CIO Chief, aided greatly. They, in a great many instances, broke down conditions of long standing in order that the completion on schedule be not interfered with."[28]

Behind this praise of the unions lay the outlines of a program for postwar relations between management and workers in the postwar atomic spaces. Efficiency, "completion on schedule," was the ideal. Old union activities had been devoted to interference in the production process; the new unions sat down at the table and "broke down conditions of long standing"—work rules, safety rules, rights to organize, rights in general. In return, the new government-corporate management partnership took the welfare of workers to heart, remaking the landscape of the company town in a more benevolent form. At the sites, the PR man wrote, "the Army attempted to make conditions more normal by providing recreation facilities [such] as movie houses, baseball diamonds, tennis courts and recreation halls. These facilities greatly assisted in keeping workers on the job. The Army also provided subsidized transportation, nursery schools to release working mothers, tire and gasoline rationing boards and conveniently located shopping facilities."[29]

To read this release was to see the District cast as the new American utopia, in which technological progress, managerial cooperation, and government paternalism all combined to provide for a new environment beneficial to all. Emanating from Washington, celebrating the largest and most centralized Internationals (the press release ended with a list of "unions . . . most closely associated with the construction phases of the project," and all were Internationals or the equivalent), the release presented a compelling case for the benevolent paternalism of the District.[30]

But on the sites themselves, a far more disturbing picture was coming into focus: a picture of District officials using every power within their means to obstruct and delay the process of unionization, to control the unions that did manage to organize onsite, and to influence the resulting elections, negotiations, and contracts to keep labor influence to a minimum.

The change in relations began even before war's end. Some union officials had been let in on the secret as a condition for allowing the District to control the labor process. As construction wound down and production began, however, they recognized that the end was soon to be at hand. They had been promised first rights to organize after the war, and they wanted to begin.

The District was Janus-faced in responding to this change in circumstances. On the surface, District officials seemed to accept unionization as an inevitable consequence; they sought only to assure that there would be no violation of security as union organizing occurred. But in fact this was not the District's real policy. Instead, dismemberment of worker organizations, eviction of unions from the Project, the interdiction of strikes and labor activities, and the disenfranchisement of workers as such were all, *in themselves*, goals of the Project, independent of the end of winning the war.

Even before war's end, District labor specialists had been at work on a stew of strategies. The most extreme was to "federalize" the sites, permanently if possible, or if not, for long enough to afford a shield of secrecy while District officials eliminated the scourge of unions and labor organizing from the sites.[31]

This draconian plan never came to be policy. It was probably too extreme even for District officials; certainly someone recognized how dim was the likelihood of getting Truman to come in on such a plan, thereby risking his political currency with union supporters. But in place of this direct and public strategy came more covert and ad hoc campaigns with the same general goals in mind. The District worked actively to destabilize union organizing, to prevent, stymie, or at least postpone activities, to maintain control over the site wherever possible and, where organizing was a fait accompli, to keep organizing with the nationals, and to prevent "off-project union influence" by locals. At Hanford, for example, the District refused all requests for permission to distribute literature to workers during shift changes, and it forbad all union meetings in Richland. "Ground rules" prevented any grassroots organizing by unions and guaranteed that only "approved" groups could assemble within the city, could hold parades, meetings or rallies, or even use soundmakers or distribute literature without a permit. District officials insisted that their representatives be present at all meetings, and that all information and communications—from union recruit lists to routine mail to brochures and pamphlets—be open to District scrutiny and subject to District censorship.[32]

For insurance, District security officials laced the unions and their organizing meetings with informers who funneled information to the proper District officials and pressed the discourse in directions desired by security officers, wherever possible. A November 25, 1946, memo to Col. Arthur Frye from John H. Mahoney, chief of the security division at Argonne in Chicago, gives some indication of the reach of these informant networks. There Mahoney revealed he was using his informers' reports to set union against union; when one union appeared to be successfully organizing, he passed along the information his people had gathered to competing unions, to foment conflict and to prevent successful unionization.[33]

At Oak Ridge, the policy of foot-dragging and bureaucratic disruption reached down to the most petty of levels. No loudspeakers could be used at union meetings; Groves himself expressly forbad picketing of all sorts; "parades" were outlawed as potential "public nuisances"; District officials even refused to sell ad space in the Oak Ridge *Journal* to unions, even though they sold space to churches and social organizations.[34]

Over the succeeding months, the security and labor specialists for the District ran a remarkable performance, leading local organizers, various unions, even the Internationals in a complicated dance of promises, threats, manipulated allegiances, betrayals, and naked power-games. The result was a collection of union locals and their people intimidated, confused, and disorganized, and a collection of Internationals alternately played against each other, or played against their own locals, and their patriotism and self-interest challenged to the ultimate benefit of the District. By the end of 1945 it was clear that the Hanford workforce would enter the AEC civilian era still unprotected by union representation.[35]

This, then, was to be the District's heritage in labor relations as the sites prepared for conversion from military to civilian authority: it would fight to maintain its control over its workers and the production process, would resist the return to normal industrial labor relations, and would strive on the contrary to forge a new labor-management-government relationship appropriate to the ideal of an efficient, streamlined atomic manufactory.

MAKING HISTORY

The battle over labor organization suggests the more general process of centripetal force that countered the explosive centrifugal force of exodus and abandonment during the months immediately after the war. Residents and workers left, taking their families and their trailers with them; representatives of democratic institutions sought to sweep in, bringing a new era of openness and freedom to the sites themselves. In all its most mundane and many of its most disturbing ways, the District sought to stop both these movements. Its goal was different: not simply to maintain itself on its present lands and spaces, even under different names, even civilian institutions; but to expand its culture outward from the sites.

The years between V-J Day and the arrival of the Atomic Energy Commission as replacement and continuation of the older military District were years of remembrance, self-definition, and planning—the construction of a past, a present, and a future. This construction happened at the level of pragmatics, of labor law and road designations, of corporate contracts and waste-tank repairs. Yet it was also a construction made out of fact and mythology. But as with the spaces themselves, owned by others before the war, then claimed by the District in the name of war, and now, after war's end, claimed—reclaimed—by others from outside the fences, so too with the mythologies of the atomic culture. Others—workers and women, unions, companies, blacks, Hispanos, Indians—also laid their claims by telling their own stories and making their own myths, which became part of the larger stories of American democracy, American labor, American capitalism.[36]

Against these outer, older cultures and their claims, the District countered by presenting as historical truth its own mythology, forged and brought to maturity on the sites over the years from 1942 to 1946. We might look for this in the stories told by the atomic corporations of the Manhattan District as they made their work public, in special publications and in corporate annual reports. When Du Pont recounted its narrative of "action, sacrifice, high morale, and loyal, hard-working employees," it became "the epic of American industry's and American workers' answer to the challenge of a great emergency." This was nothing new—it was just the District's press release rhetoric from the days and weeks after Nagasaki, appropriated and applied to the corporation. So also with Stone and Webster, whose *Report to the People* had as its epigraph this excerpt from a speech by Harry Truman: "The people of the United States know that the overwhelming power we have developed in this war is due in large measure to American science and American industry, consisting of management and labor."[37]

Those words of Truman, borrowed by Stone and Webster, were not exactly his own—they, like the words used in Du Pont's report, originated with the District's propagandist William L. Laurence, this time filtered through Groves to the press releases, from the press releases to the ears of Truman's speechwriters, and thence to the president's own voice and the authority of his office. In the original draft, atomic energy was "the culmination of years of Herculean effort on the part of science and industry working in cooperation with the military authorities." The version Groves approved changed it to "the greatest achievement of the combined efforts of science, industry, labor, and the military in all history."[38]

The District's versions presented a picture of atomic energy—in Truman's rendition "a harnessing of the basic power of the universe," and "the force from which the sun draws its power"—as the product of a brilliant cooperative triad: science, corporate capitalism, and the military. Truman's speechwriters expanded upon this: under their pens, it became a uniquely *American* cooperation. "It is doubtful such another combination could be got together in the world," Truman told his national and international audience that August day.[39]

Truman's radio speech was the equivalent of the piece by Du Pont and Stone and Webster—it presented the claim by the government and the military to a stake in the postwar atomic culture. The speech went out to the press as one part of a large packet of materials upon which District officials had been working for more than a year. Individual portions of the packet had been researched and written by local District public relations officers at the sites (including George O. Robinson at Oak Ridge), then passed through the filters of other officers and officials of the District, including William Laurence (who also wrote some of the most important parts from scratch). Then they went up to Groves, who approved or disapproved them and, in his fashion, often rewrote them himself. These then went to the proper officials or their staffs for signatory approval—commanding officers of the individual sites, Secretary of War Stimson, President Truman. Finally, District publicity and public information officers assembled the packet itself for release.[40]

In each of the stages District officials organized and controlled the substance and the tone of information released. Laurence was Groves's choice, recommended to him by an official in the office of censorship. It was Groves who pressed to have Laurence attached to the District, Groves who arranged for what he later called Laurence's "indoctrination," and Groves who made it possible for the reporter to visit each of the sites, interview prominent figures, travel to Alamogordo to witness the first atomic explosion, and ride in the planes that released the new weapon on Japan. Laurence wrote the official statements of various officials on the District, in the military, and in government. They then went to the interim committee, then to Groves's and Stimson's staffs. In some cases, it is highly doubtful that the signatories ever read their own words until they appeared in print after August 6, 1945.[41]

The District's public relations campaign was a triumph. The MED had arranged for a primary packet to be released immediately after the explosion; all this, including Truman's speech, had been written months before. Besides the Truman text, the first packet contained a further text from the secretary of war, a release from Alamogordo, New Mexico, concerning the test (and including excerpts of General Farrell's glowing, poetic response to the explosion), and releases by Laurence concerning the physics of the explosion, the role of labor in the production, the nature of each of the three sites, and other special-interest releases.

It was in this first collection that the triad of military, corporate, and scientific establishments first appeared publicly as the fundamental force behind American victory. Again and again in these releases, it was the military authorities who served as heroic mediators, expediters, facilitators. Each party benefited. Truman's release recast the scientists as larger-than-life figures, "scientists of distinction" fighting "the battle of the laboratories." And American capitalism, with its "tremendous industrial and financial resources," made success possible.

But ghosts also crept into even these first releases. American geography was one of these. Truman's release insisted that the project could not have occurred anywhere else, because the immensity of the natural forces and the attendant dangers demanded vast spaces, and the American interior afforded protection from prying eyes and enemy bombers. And Truman's speech introduced a new American technological and industrial sublime to accompany and to supplant the older geographical sublime invoked elsewhere in the release—"two great plants and many lesser works devoted to the production of atomic power" where "employment during peak construction numbered 125,000" and where, "even now . . . 65,000 individuals . . . are engaged in operating the plants."[42]

In Truman's release, America's Manifest Destiny reappeared in miniature: that myth of a vast unpeopled tabula rasa upon which heroic settlers carved out a heroic new enterprise, steadily transformed by the forces of scientific and technological progress into an urban-industrial civilization of equally vast scale. The press release emanating from Secretary of War Stimson's office, far more detailed than the others, extended this theme, and brought it to the three sites themselves. Oak Ridge, a city of "large size and isolated location," was a community of dedicated Americans who "live under normal conditions in modest houses, dormitories, hutments, and trailers, and have for their use all the religious, recreational educational, medical and other facilities of a modern small city," thanks to government ownership and management. Hanford appeared as a similarly vast space "in an isolated area" occupied by "a Government-owned and operated town."[43]

In these releases, however, we might find evidence of a sort of leakage between the metaphysical geography of the District and the physical geographies of the sites. Under the pens of the District's propagandists, nature has left these places. Nature has become "Atomic Energy," the "Source of Inexhaustible Power."[44]

In place of the American sublime of spaces and sites, of natural events to which man is awestruck witness and diminished spectator, there is in this first public literature of the atomic culture a new sublime, an atomic sublime whose signal importance lies in the very fact that it is manmade, and whose beauty is partly a product of its source in that American triad of science, capital, and military government. It appears with greatest clarity in the release concerning Alamogordo, the release that reproduces Farrell's description of the bomb: "unprecedented, magnificent, beautiful, stupendous and terrifying." "No man-made phenomenon of such tremendous power had ever occurred before," comments the general in the midst of his paean. The tone is millennarian, drawing from sources in Protestant sermons of apocalypse. Atomic power granted omniscience to its witnesses; "it lighted every peak, crevasse and ridge of the nearby mountain range with a clarity and beauty that cannot be described but must be seen to be imagined. It was that beauty the great poets dream about but describe most poorly and inadequately."[45]

"Thirty seconds after the explosion came first, the air blast pressing hard against the people and things, to be followed almost immediately by the strong, sustained, awesome roar which warned of doomsday and made us feel that we puny things were blasphemous to dare tamper with the forces heretofore reserved to The Almighty." That was Farrell's warning, but he took it back just a second later—took it back by urging all to experience this "awesome . . . doomsday" and its pleasures. "Words are inadequate tools for the job of acquainting those not present with the physical, mental and psychological effects," he wrote. "It had to be witnessed to be realized."[46]

Here, then, was the new sublime, brought into being by a new relationship between man and nature, in which man was the instigator, the audacious, even "blasphemous" usurper of the power of the Almighty, alternately "puny" and omnipotent. But something was missing, and that something was, indeed, what the new atomic sublime took away. Remember: this was a press release to accompany the Hiroshima bomb, to presage Nagasaki. Nowhere is there mention of the dead, of those bombed back from civilization to desperate, short-lived primitive scavenging, on the way to pain and death.

This is the first literature of the atomic culture, its first aesthetics, its religion and its poetry. But this is a mythology under construction, written and managed by officials of the state, closely observed by state security and military officials. Some of it is unearthly and deeply unsettling: in the Alamogordo release, Groves tells how, "at about two minutes of the scheduled firing time, all persons lay face down with their feet pointing towards the explosion." It is a peculiar image, peculiar in itself and peculiar as something Groves would have seen fit to describe, the interim committee to pass upon, and the American population to read as part of its first introduction to the secret culture of the Manhattan District. Yet there it is.[47]

As the first days passed into weeks and months, this new cultural geography evolved, returning at each new incarnation richer, more complete, better knit to other and older strains of American space and its significance. In the late summer or early fall, the District began to let groups of reporters on its sites. New and larger packets awaited them: packets that boasted of the journalists' unique privilege to be allowed access, and at the same time took away that privilege with stern warnings about the covenant made with the forces of security; packets that substituted a wealth of controlled, District-released information for the more dangerously uncontrolled data reporters might gather on their own. In each of these packets, reporters found recapitulated the story of American progress mutated to the story of the District.[48]

What is perhaps most striking about this picture of a new American community is how little the losses of personal and social identity by District residents seem to matter. Here is the extreme extension of American industrial progress—workers in cookie-cutter assembly-line jobs, fed selected bits of information and instructions by an all-powerful state apparatus that controlled every aspect of public and most elements of private life. And yet under these circumstances (even Oak Ridge's publicist Robinson admitted in his official press release on the city that there was "an atmosphere of unreality, in which giant plants worked day and night to produce nothing that could be seen or touched"), there grew up an American community little different than any other—except, perhaps, improved over the older model. Writing of Oak Ridge, Robinson waxed poetic: "With the bulldozers, the carpenters, plumbers, and electricians also came books, musical instruments, artists' paints and brushes and all the other paraphernalia of American culture—a culture reflecting every section of the country, for Oak Ridge is an extremely cosmopolitan place, its residents coming from virtually every state in the Union."[49]

The reporters who received this Oak Ridge press packet were visiting Oak Ridge in the fall of 1945, and they received as well the photographs of Ed Westcott and Hedrich-Blessing, photographs alternately folksy and eerily artificial (fig. 47). Armed with their packets, they moved in groups from locale to locale within the District site, watched over by a benevolent "guide" who would offer and control access to the various parts of the site, or by "dormitory advisors" who "are on duty at Casper Dormitory

FIG. 47 *Sadie Hawkins Day, Oak Ridge.* Photo by James E. Westcott, U.S. Corps of Engineers, Oak Ridge, Tennessee.

to assist you and to make your stay as comfortable as possible." "Tours of the Area will be conducted for your pleasure and information," promised one of the handouts.[50]

To write the story of the present and predict the future, the District found it necessary also to rewrite its past. In handouts to reporters, the story of the District's relation to the region and the past received a treatment quite different than the one we have come to know. Condemnation of property went smoothly and was ultimately beneficial to all: "The area was among the first in Tennessee to be settled and the Government went to great pains to resettle these uprooted families. Many of them took jobs on the site." Construction occurred with penurious economy: "Most of the automotive and construction equipment (light and heavy) was obtained from previously-completed war construction jobs by Government transfer, with practically all the major construction pieces obtained from other Corps of Engineer construction jobs." Residents lived in accommodations that might "vary in size, but are comfortable, roomy and homey." No discussion of the Negro areas appeared, and reporters traversed along paths far from those hutments and trailers and prefabs. Pleasure and culture were the responsibilities of "the Oak Ridge Recreation and Welfare Association, a non-profit citizens' organization which derives its revenue from self-liquidating recreational enterprises." (Here Robinson made an in-joke; much of the ORRWA money came from beer sales, a particular sort of "self-liquidating enterprise.")[51]

Hanford's tours involved an equivalent reconstruction of history and control of present circumstances. Hanford Village, by the late summer of 1945 a ghost town, appeared nowhere in the packets; the latest ideal community was Richland, a "newly-built, pleasant little town 15 miles northwest of Pasco," where "the inhabitants have good jobs and pleasant Government-owned homes on the banks of the swiftly flowing Columbia River." Los Alamos was "not unlike any other community of similar population in the United States . . . housewives shop for food for daily meals at an Army commissary where ration points are just as important as elsewhere and a 'trading post' offers items needed in everyday life and there are the usual Post Exchange stores."[52]

(Here we might see multiple programs at work, not just to direct the press and its national audience to the legitimacy of the community, but to defuse anticipated suspicions of elitism and privilege for these superheroes of science.)

Having read the site packets, reporters and visitors found themselves acting out the District's mythology in ritual acts—sleeping in a special barracks; walking along controlled vectors, accompanied by "guides"; observing the rote, unknowing assembly-line work of laborers and the hygiene of the factories; seeing the proof that here poverty and unhappiness had been banished by a benevolent patriarchal bureaucracy, and yet life remained normal, just a few steps closer to the dream of the ideal American community.

For the most part, the press reporters took up the District's picture of its past, present, and future, and within months they had woven it into the fabric of American culture. From the first days after the first bomb until January 1, 1947, the day the Atomic Energy Commission took over the atomic spaces, the story the District told became the origin myth of the new atomic culture.

LANDSCAPES OF THE DEAD

The District's postwar project extended far beyond the three sites. Countering the District picture of the atomic age as one of global security, orderly and efficient technological progress, and even a new atomic aesthetic, there lay after August 6, 1945, a terrifying alternative—an image of the dead at Hiroshima and Nagasaki, sprawled randomly about a flattened plain of destroyed city, and the near-dead and soon-to-die, winding their way in irregular file out of that plain, seeking help from the inexorable progress of that atomic plague.

With Hiroshima and Nagasaki, the District added a new landscape to its atomic spaces. Alamogordo had done the same. But there, at Trinity site, the blast and its effects settled into the larger mythology of the desolated Western wastelands known in the nineteenth century as the Great American Desert. And General Farrell's description just as firmly planted the explosion in the American heritage of the sublime.

Central to the American sublime aesthetic was the fact that, while Nature might threaten man, it stayed its hand, and in that forbearance revealed the divine sanctioning of American expansion, American progress. The plains of death where once Hiroshima and Nagasaki had stood might fit this vision of American destiny. Certainly Truman's speech presented it in that way—as the national incarnation of the Angel of Vengeance. Laurence had carefully crafted Truman's words in this regard. "The Japanese began the war from the air at Pearl Harbor," Truman told the world. "They have been repaid many fold. And the end is not yet. . . . They may expect a rain of ruin from the air, the like of which has never been seen on this earth."[53]

This picture of a new landscape of salted earth, sowed by the righteous to strike down the unrighteous, resonated well with the prevailing American Protestant imagery that had come down since Governor Winthrop at Puritan Massachusetts Bay. It was continuous with the warlong campaign to set the Japanese as inhuman masses. But it could not sustain the assaultive images of what Warren's onsite assessment group called the "devastated area," or its survivors, predominantly women and children, who came to seem not perpetrators of evil but evil's victims.

The District responded quickly to prevent that second image from dominating American and international consciousness. One strategy was suppression—of stories, through censorship, and of images like those made by the survivors, which remained uncirculated for years.[54]

But suppression of individual images could never erase the larger picture. Groves and the District administration knew this well. From the first, they moved to provide a reassuring set of counterassertions. Probably the most controversial of these concerned the new atomic spaces at Hiroshima and Nagasaki, and the medical effects of the blasts. When Japanese radio reported that relief workers were dying of some unknown disease; when authoritative voices within the American scientific community suggested that the sites would remain uninhabitably dangerous for decades, perhaps centuries; when the Japanese made a formal charge that the atomic bomb was a violation of the Geneva Conventions: the result was a fundamental threat to the benevolent image of the District.

The Manhattan District's public relations specialists leapt into action to reverse this unhappy direction of public discourse. The counterattack brought even "Dr. J. R. Oppenheimer, the head of this phase of the work," into the fray, defending the bombings and reasserting the impermanence of the injury. But this was on paper; what the District needed was something more active, more dramatic, more reputable than a press release. As Groves's medical assessment team wended its way across the Pacific arena, the national and international response to the bombings at Hiroshima and Nagasaki increasingly fulfilled his nightmares.[55]

By the end of August, the general's concern had escalated to something approaching panic. On the morning of August 25, Groves, like millions of other Americans, read a newspaper report of the sort increasingly cropping up as reporters and scientists teamed up to assess the effects, both short- and long-term, of the new atomic weapons. Within minutes, he was on the phone to Oak Ridge, to Lieutenant Colonel Rea of the Oak Ridge hospital. The newspaper report, released by the Associated Press, had gone out nationally and been picked up by newspapers all over the country. Groves understood that the resulting articles were immensely damaging: they focused on the long-term consequences of radiation exposure and painted with graphic urgency the terrible effects. Groves read the most damning passages to Rea, including the now-famous passage: "So painful are these injuries that sufferers plead, 'Please kill me.'... No one can ever completely recover."[56]

Groves's concern lay not only with the picture of suffering on the part of the Japanese—a matter he dismissed as "a good dose of propaganda." It focused as well on the reports that relief workers and soldiers at the sites were suffering severe lowering of white- and red-blood cell counts, "various sicknesses and ill health." Clearly this would affect the army's ability to keep soldiers in those cities. Groves also reported that it was threatening Hanford. "You see what we are faced with," he told Rea; "Matthias is having trouble holding his people out there."[57]

The memos of the conversation between Groves and Rea reveal an unsettling duality. On one side, here were two men groping with the enormity of what they had wrought. Both of them grasped rather desperately at the explanation of the deaths as the result of "good old thermal burns," in Rea's words. (What might they have been imagining, that the hideousness of burning to death might become comforting by comparison?) The lowered blood counts, too, they sought to assure themselves, were simply normal variations or the creation of propaganda. Their conversation was a deeply personal version of a larger cultural phenomenon: the struggle to force the realities of atomic war into the old conditions of conventional warfare.[58]

But their other desire was to counter propaganda with propaganda. Rea told Groves early on: "I think you had better get the anti-propagandists out." But Groves pointed out the problem—"We can't, you see," he told the doctor, "because the whole damage has been done by our own people. There is nothing we can do except sit tight." Rea reiterated his position: "I would say this," he told Groves: "You will have to get some big-wig to put a counterstatement in the paper." Groves wanted something more direct: he wanted to get the AP science editor and put the screws on him.

Groves sought scientific reports to counter the reports coming back from the hot cities of Japan. Rea suggested Warren's reports on Alamogordo, and Friedell's follow-ups. But they weren't as useful as Rea remembered them—they conveyed much more than Groves was willing to release. Groves had sent Warren to Hiroshima and Nagasaki as part of a hand-picked investigating group; now he waited for its "counterstatements" from Japan.

For this, the makeup of Groves's team was perfect—his assistant, Farrell, and his personal physician and the head of the military medical division, Colonel Warren. Farrell was the master of the atomic sublime, Warren was the progenitor of an atomic medicine that suppressed the Hippocratic responsibilities of medicine in favor of the tactical necessities of warfare and the good of the state. Arriving in Japan in early September, the two men vindicated Groves's faith, in spades. Farrell described the new atomic landscapes: Hiroshima was "awe inspiring and tremendous. A city of approx imately 300,000 was essentially destroyed. While there were many buildings standing around the outer part of the city, its center was leveled." Nagasaki revealed "more spectacular effects." Farrell even described the Nagasaki terrain in language lifted from the nineteenth-century travel literature of the sublime: "the rugged terrain, including steep hills and deep ravines," he said, "provided much shielding," and so "Nagasaki is still alive and functioning, while Hiroshima is flat and dead." Almost as a sidelight, he reported "no evidence of any radioactivity" at either city.[59]

In this matter, Warren backed Farrell all the way. He reported, in his words, "an extensive survey of the detonation area in Nagasaki and a somewhat less complete survey of the Hiroshima area." "In all the areas examined," he wrote, "ground contamination with radioactive materials was found to be below the hazardous limit; when the readings were extrapolated back to zero hour, the levels were not considered to be of great significance." Warren provided that ideal combination: a reassuring authority with a plausible explanation—"that the detonation occurred at about 1,800 ft., and the fireball therefore did not actually touch the ground." At Nagasaki, Warren did note "induced radioactivity from neutron bombardment . . . in sulfur insulators, copper wires, and brass objects, in human and animal bones, and in the silver amalgam in human teeth." In that list, "human and animal bones" lost their terrifying implications, becoming evidence and not metaphor.[60]

The program followed by the investigating group was brilliantly conceived and executed. For if the primary emphasis went to the blast effects, then long-term study of long-term effects became unnecessary. Similarly, if the District's medical studies were quickly completed and as quickly reported, they could not be faulted for failing to take into account those long-term effects—and rapid reporting was essential under Groves's directive, because one of the investigation's purposes was to reassure military leaders and their soldiers that it was not dangerous to enter and patrol the blasted zones. Once again, medical study focused not on the long-term effects of low-dose radiation, but on the short-term effects of high dosages. Genetic-injury studies would wait for more than a decade.[61]

The group's work—rapid, sketchy, deliberately narrow in its breadth—might be seen as a brilliant countertactic designed to complement the District's larger program to evolve and publicize a series of reassuring pictures of the postwar atomic culture. Certainly the combination of Farrell's hyperactive aesthetic language and Warren's vision of a terrible swift sword proposed a radically different atomic landscape than that other, more ominous one the historian Paul Boyer has argued remained at the edge of consciousness, and perhaps the center of the unconscious, of most postwar citizens of the world.[62]

From the District's point of view, the dead were dead, the survivors healed. We can see this portrayed in a single photograph made by the group and reproduced by Warren in his report (fig. 48). Warren's caption, reproduced in his later recasting of the report, went like this:

> Figure 307.—Healed flash burn of back. This man, wearing khaki cotton clothing, was standing in the open, as shown in posed photograph. The blast threw him to the ground, and his cotton clothing was scorched and destroyed. His burns healed, and he recovered from mild radiation symptoms which he showed. This view shows scars of healed flash burns on back, elbows, and lateral aspect of right arm. The rest of the body was unhurt. Note huts in background, built for temporary housing after bomb was dropped. Note also, on horizon, trunks of trees denuded of branches by blast. Bushes and grass in ditch have begun to grow.[63]

Warren presented the victim's body as a surface torn and injured, now healing; so also, he urged, were the landscapes of Hiroshima and Nagasaki rapidly healing from the cataclysmic violence of atomic blast, as "bushes and grass . . . have begun to grow." The picture, however, has for us perhaps a different flavor. The man whose back we see has been posed at the spot where he experienced the violence of the blast. He has taken off his shirt for the camera. He is subservient to the authority of the camera

FIG. 48 *Healed Flash Burn on Back.* Photo by Stafford Warren. From Stafford Warren, "Role of Radiology," in *Radiology in World War II.*

FIG. 49 *Two Members of the Atomic Bomb Casualty Commission.* Photo by Stafford Warren. From Stafford Warren, "Role of Radiology," in *Radiology in World War II.*

and its wielder—a man who is both scientist and victor. The photograph seems, in other words, to tell us more about this postwar moment than it intends to. This quality is reinforced by the appearance in Warren's account of another photograph; "Figure 297.—Two members of the Atomic Bomb Casualty Commission, Dr. John S. Lawrence and Dr. Herman E. Pearse, Jr. visit ground center of atomic bomb detonation. Hiroshima, Japan, June 1947" (fig. 49). It shows two men, one in uniform, field glasses slung across his shoulder, the other in mufti, a camera around his neck. It is a tourist picture of visitors at the site. It suggests a new future for these places: as locations for a form of atomic tourism that will, in fact, resurface in the 1950s, when atomic tests become part of Nevada's repertoire of tourist events, to be marketed along with its Wild West history and its gambling cities.[64]

These two photographs encapsulate a mythology of atomic spaces that emanated from the District in the months between Hiroshima and the takeover of the atomic spaces by the Atomic Energy Commission. The land is injured but will heal. The occupants, too, will heal. The bomb was not pernicious, morally ambiguous, physiologically or ecologically mysterious. Rather it was clear, direct, thoroughly rational and predictable, a vindication of the District's theology of efficiency, productivity, obedience.

CONTINUATION

Within the older atomic spaces, this mythology also dominated. It dominated at Alamogordo, where Groves and his minions arranged for managed tours by reporters, complete with scientist-tourguides and souvenirs of trinitite. And it dominated there in the plans to make the Trinity site into a national park, complete with "a sheltered walk" and an "atomsite exhibit in place under glass"—plans deflected only after it became clear that the radioactivity levels were so high that a Park Service employee might expect to get a lethal dose in as little as fifty hours.[65]

It dominated at Los Alamos, where the questions of toxic waste and worker exposure gave way to conflicts over water and housing, where Groves succeeded in marketing an aggressive expansion plan that turned the atomic city into one more American town suffering the growing pains of postwar suburban growth. It dominated at Hanford, where elimination of the once-rowdy worker community of Hanford Camp through rapid-fire and near-complete demolition left only the idyllic middle-class town of Richland as the model for the plutonium place. And when Du Pont left the site, Groves found a mirror-image replacement more eager to partake of the promise of a postwar, cold-war atomic utopia—General Electric, corporate symbol of benevolent energy and beneficent technology.[66]

And it dominated in the negotiations that took the Manhattan Engineer District from a military culture to a civilian one. There Groves managed a holding action against congressional, scientific, and grassroots forces urging control and eventual elimination of the atomic threat. By the time the transfer occurred, on January 1, 1947, Groves had rendered non-negotiable most of what the military wished to keep. In addition, the negotiation process had so demoralized and disheveled the AEC's nascent forces that the new commissioners took the reins without having even seen all the sites—took the reins, in other words, without the knowledge or power necessary to manage what they had inherited. In that way, Groves virtually guaranteed that he and the military culture he represented would long—perhaps always—remain *de facto* mentors and powers in the postwar atomic culture.[67]

So the atomic culture of the Manhattan District entered postwar American culture, blending with it, transforming, mutating. But as it did so, the sites themselves came to seem, to many of their residents, places emptied of significance, shells of a once-heroic landscape of power and possibility. At Hanford, Du Pont backed out, and General Electric stepped in. GE courted engineers, scientists, technicians, and skilled workers to stay. What the company had to offer was money.

In Richland, a hard-partying martini crowd of scientist-engineers and their families had coalesced around Roy Hageman, Charlie Wende, Bill Overbeck, and Bill Milton, among others. Together they wrote, played, and sang a series of wonderful, sardonic anthems to wartime and postwar Hanford. In "The Milton Jubilee," Bill Milton told of GE's recruitment campaign:

> We'll polish up their egos
> and we'll help them in adversity;
> if only we can find a dean
> we'll found a university.

Here beneath the desert skies,
amid this land of sand and sage,
unfurl the GE banner
and proclaim the new atomic age . . .

Come all youse lads who long have worn
the badges of the clan Du Pont;
see if General Electric
hasn't got the very job you want . . .

We were all so hypnotized,
'twas not till later that we thought
perhaps we'd better take a look
at this new Gospel we have bought.[68]

But Milton's "jubilee" was very different from other pictures that appear on the scratched, difficult-to-hear recordings that Major Sapper made of the crowd during the transition. Charlie Wende, in particular, described the scene in darker and more sardonic terms. Here is his "Plutonium Blues":

I got those blues,
those Hanford blues;
I've got
[radio?]activity I've got to lose.
I've got those blues,
those plutonium blues.

It's those plutonium blues
from those piles up high,
send those neutrons galloping
up and down my spine.
I've got atomic fire
[stakes up higher] in my hold,
but in the dark
you ought to see me glow.[69]

Even more unnerving is an unnamed song sung on the recording by Hageman:

Working Hanford, working in the sand,
all I got to show is this bottle in my hand.
My feet are all dusty, my tonsils are dry.
If I don't drink this whiskey I surely will die.

Go along little [neutrons?], go along,
we're going to Richland where desert winds blow.

Stayed in Richland till the bitter end,
everyone's gone and I haven't got a friend.
Everything's gone but this bottle of corn.
I'm going to get plastered as sure as you're born.

Go along little moving van,

take it slow.
You'll never find housing
wherever you go.

Rode the bus for a weary mile
out to 100 to operate the pile;
back to Separation to make a hellish brew.
We should have made whiskey instead of Pu,
we should have made whiskey,
not nearly so risky,
we should have made whiskey instead of Pu.

Went to Pasco to the liquor store,
all the cowpunchers got no punches anymore.
There may come a day
when you die on my door . . .

Here the tape becomes unintelligible—the pentimenti of time distort the singing, and the voice fades into incomprehensibility.

MEDITATION

Here is the beginning of Groves's farewell speech to the Manhattan Engineer District, given to his officers and men on December 23, 1946, and made public as a press release by the War Department on December 31, 1946:

> Five years ago, the idea of Atomic Power was only a dream. You have made that dream a reality. You have seized upon the most nebulous of ideas and translated them into actualities. You have built cities where none were known before. You have constructed industrial plants of a magnitude and to a precision heretofore deemed impossible. You built the weapon which ended the War and thereby saved countless American lives. With regard to peacetime applications, you have raised the curtain on vistas of a new world.[70]

These words of Groves encapsulate the District's ideology: the conversion of scientific fantasies into hard, conclusive physicality—what Groves calls, tellingly, "reality." This reality *was* the reality of the sites—their physical presence, as "cities where none were known before" and "industrial plants of a magnitude and to a precision heretofore deemed impossible." In this vision, Manhattan is the triumph of the industrial revolution, its capstone and its transformation into something more. Yet much is absent from Groves's picture of the District's accomplishments. There are no people, there is no society, no system of beliefs, no ideology.

In Groves's revealing description, the Manhattan Engineer District was the apotheosis of modernity and its unspoken ends: progress, practicality, efficiency, the production of things by which, then, power might be accumulated and held. Groves didn't just see this landscape of cities and factories as a goal in itself. It was also the means to further progress, to "vistas of a new world."

But Groves's final analogy included something further: an audience to whom the District "lifted the curtain" on this new world, this utopia of infinite power and the society that would devolve from it. This, too, is revealing. For it intimates that the District's victory might be incomplete, might, finally, depend upon the support of others for its continuation.

In the atomic spaces this had always been the case. The District had needed many who could not be fully brought within its network: scientists whose loyalty remained divided; workers manipulated but always held outside; marginal groups, suspect groups, nonetheless necessary to build its factories and staff them; women and chil dren essential to the social cohesion of the places, but antithetical to its ethos of efficiency and coercion.

And so, in the end, Groves admitted the necessity for a continuing mythos to ac company the physical realities of those sites, cities, factories, transferred to the AEC but still controlled and owned in the most basic sense by the District and the forces it represented. To keep things working, the District and its successors would have to continue to "lift the curtain," persuading those outside the bureaucracies, outside the physical geography of sites and spaces, that what was contained within was right, and must continue as it was.

The close of the Manhattan Engineer District on January 1, 1947, meant, then, some thing richer and more complicated than an ending, something closer to its diffusion from the sites and spaces to the culture that surrounded it—physically and ideolog ically. As the membrane between site and nonsite grew increasingly porous, what was outside crept in, and what was within leaked out and diffused itself into the larger world. During the first years, the District and its remnants sought to control and di rect that process of incursion and diffusion. Men like Groves, Nichols, and Matthias had a stake in what they had built; it exemplified their beliefs just as the men them selves embodied the beliefs of the spheres within which they operated.

So also with scientists like Leo Szilard and Kenneth Bainbridge, residents like Elean or Jette and Phyllis Fisher, laborers like Luzell Johnson, plant operators like Yvette Berry. They, too, had pictures of the forced spaces they had occupied at the behest of the District and they, too, sought more or less consciously to influence the debate of the postwar atomic culture. Some worked directly, founding groups, such as the Atom ic Scientists, and publications, among them the *Bulletin of the Atomic Scientists.* But their influence was perhaps greater at the level of less conscious behavior and belief. When the women who wrote their memoirs of Los Alamos in 1948 found no pub lisher, their pictures of life at that site shrank from public view. When those memoirs finally appeared, in the 1970s and 1980s, they meant something different than they might have thirty years before. Today, they are woven into the fabric of belief that forms the historical discourse of contemporary culture. They feed our nostalgia, and our cynicism, about the past.

After 1947 the District—its spaces, its places, buildings, people, its orders and reg ulations, meetings and memos—lost the clear demarcations that had made cultiva tion of a new atomic culture possible. No longer secret, the District became, to some extent, accountable to outside forces and opinions. No longer closed to interaction, the District could not pilot its ideology in the social sphere with the same experimental purity. No longer fully the property of the military, corporate, and scientific elites who had formed the kernel of its enterprise, the District became to some extent the property of other, often conflicting ideals and agendas.

But at the same time, the systems of behavior and belief that guided the actors and participants of the District spread from the sites and spaces as the fences came down. The Manhattan District influenced the course of America and of international civilization in important ways; we cannot yet define that influence with precision. We seek, and find at intervals, evidence, but may not yet marshal that evidence into something clear or unambiguous.

Atomic spaces interpenetrated, perhaps even became, American spaces—like the brown clouds that rose from the chemical separations plant, to fall abruptly to the desert floor or perhaps be taken by the high winds far from the fences. Or the liquid effluent that leaked from the waste tanks at Hanford, into the waters of the Columbia, and from the Columbia to the sea. Or the "hot mud" deposited in the creeks at Oak Ridge—mud that might be washed away by spring floods or might be covered, season after season, by accretions, over the span of geological time compressing into the bones of the earth, a marker to someone, perhaps, of the moment between two epochs, preatomic and postatomic. Or like the cloud of radioactivity that rose from Alamogordo, to be tracked by airmen as it twice circled the globe, merging imperceptibly into the earth, the seas, and the air we breathe.

MEDITATION

Eleven Pictures

1990–95

by Peter Bacon Hales

Roadway Signs along Bethel Valley Road near Oak Ridge, Tennessee, 1991.

Billboard along Restricted Roadway, Hanford Engineer Works Site, 1990.

Cleanup Crew, Chemical Separations Plant, Hanford Engineer Works Site, 1990.

Toxic Radioactive Waste Barrel Storage Trench with Required Safety Equipment—
a Chemical Fire Extinguisher—Hanford Engineer Works Site, 1990.

Single-Walled Tank Farm Cleanup Facility, Hanford Engineer Works Site, 1990.

Site of Hanford Village, Hanford Engineer Works Site, 1990.

Richland Village Town Center, Richland, Washington, 1990.

Yard Sale Sign and "D" Houses, Richland, Washington, 1990.

Intact Cemesto House, Oak Ridge, Tennessee, 1991.

Prefab House, Richland, Washington, 1990.

Interactive Exhibit, "World War II: Fighting for Freedom," Bradbury Science Museum,
Community Involvement Office ("To carry out the Laboratory's corporate citizenship
responsibilities"), Los Alamos National Laboratory, Department of Energy Facility,
Los Alamos, New Mexico, 1995.

This project began as a brief introductory passage in a book about the postwar American landscape, for which research and writing was funded by a fellowship from the National Endowment for the Humanities. NEH has supported intellectual and historical adventure in many guises, and I am grateful for its support on this and other projects.

Once it became clear that I was writing something closer to an epic than a preface, I turned to the Campus Research Board of the University of Illinois, Chicago, for interim funding. A sabbatical leave from the History of Architecture and Art Department enabled me to immerse myself in the archives. A generous fellowship from the Institute for the Humanities of UIC enabled me to write the first sprawling draft, and to begin the process of excision and revision. The continued encouragement and support of the institute and its director, Gene Ruoff, made the book possible.

ACKNOWLEDGMENTS

Work of this sort cannot take place without the support of archivists and librarians. At the university, Kathy Kilian's assiduous tracking of interlibrary loan sources enabled me to use archival materials that would otherwise have been difficult to find. My gratitude goes to the various public officials who provided me access to the vast archives of the Manhattan Engineer District: Ed Reese at the National Archives; Ms. Marchiante at the Department of Energy facilities in Oak Ridge and Kenneth Morgan at DOE Hanford/Richland; Mollie Rodriguez at the Los Alamos National Laboratory; Heddy Dunn, Rebecca Collinsworth, and Theresa Strottman at the Los Alamos Historical Museum; and Gayle Peters and Charles Reeves at the Regional Depository of the National Archives at East Point, Georgia, where Dr. Reeves, especially, guided me among labyrinthine walls of record boxes. At Hanford, William Heine kindly toured me around the site and explained some of the arcane matters of waste treatment bureaucracy. Annette Heriford and Robley Johnson, two Hanford MED veterans who shared their memories, have my gratitude. At Oak Ridge, Ed Westcott treated me with kindness and tolerance. Patrick Nagatani, a photographer and historian of atomic consequences, lent me important books and suggested ways to extend my analysis. These were only some of those who gave so kindly of their time and knowledge

This book was written not only in the silence of the academic's study but in the noisy environs of a lived life as well: at swim meets and practices where my son, Taylor, came to depend on my presence in the official's booth; at daughter Molly's ballet classes and violin lessons; in airports and subway stations. But my students, colleagues, and neighbors know where the bulk of this came into being: in the tolerant environs of Evanston's Café Express, where Jeff Ayoub and Randy Barangos, the co-owners, came to view me as something closer to a piece of furniture than a patron, and where their successor, Brent Johnson, acquired me along with the fixtures when he bought the place in 1995. These people and the men and women that worked there (as patrons and as employees) have taken a lively and encouraging interest. Beth, Kathy, Jillian, Cathy, Allison, Bonnie, Tony, Nancy, Todd, Anna, Patrick, George: thanks.

Thanks also to my colleagues in the Art History Department at the University of Illinois, Chicago, for viewing my excursions into cultural history as a natural part of our intellectual work; thanks especially to David Sokol, chair of the department and tireless champion of its faculty. Graduate students in various seminars contributed comments, critiques, and enthusiasm, providing me with a sense of connection between the arts of teaching, writing, and the making of photographs.

Early drafts of this book went through a few select and stringent hands. Gail Siegel, Bradford Collins, Robert Bruegmann, Barbara Monier, James McKerrow, Milton Hales, David Follmer, and Jeffrey Meikle all read large segments of the book and provided important suggestions. Paul Boyer and Hal Rothman, who served as readers, took me to task and pressed me in new directions. Finally, Senior Editor Karen Hewitt of the University of Illinois Press gently hectored me to allow her to read it for the press, and showed herself a wise and encouraging voice, an editor who weighed each word, probing for the best. Then, when I thought I was done, Carol Betts, my copy editor, showed me the error of my ways and helped make order and coherence where there had been something less. None of these people fully prevailed upon my hardheadedness; where the book is good, they deserve credit, where it is headstrong or ill-considered, I am fully responsible.

Acknowledgments

380

NOTES

CHAPTER 1: ORIGINATION

1. Orrin Thacker Jr., "Gross Appraisal Proposed Site for Kingston Army Camp Kingston, Tennessee," Cincinnati, Ohio, Ohio River Division, Army Corps of Engineers, typescript, p. 1, file 601.1, box 5, RG 4nn-326-8505, National Archives and Records Administration, Southeast Region Depository, East Point, Georgia (hereafter, NARD).

2. Ibid.

3. Ibid., p. 9.

4. Ibid., pp. 10–11.

5. Ibid., pp. 7–8.

6. James A. Young, four articles on original communities of Wheat, Robertsville, Elza, and Scarboro, first published in the *Nuclear Division News,* c. 1975–76, republished by Martin Marietta Corporation as *An Historical View of Oak Ridge* (Oak Ridge, Tenn.: Martin Marietta, n.d.). My thanks to J. L. Langford, Technical Information Officer, Martin Marietta Energy Systems, for providing me with this material.

7. The exact number of these photographs is a mystery; the original report had pictures glued onto its back pages, singly and in groups two and three. Many of these photographs had become detached; some were still in the report or its folder, while others had fallen into the record box in which the folder was kept with hundreds of others. Their source, too, is unexplained. The numbers on them suggest a range of some four hundred negatives made in the region. It is unlikely that Thacker himself made these during the ten days he devoted to the appraisal. Rather, these may have been file photographs found in the TVA land evaluation files, which Thacker then used to illustrate (and thus transform) his report.

8. Photographs of the region include "Field of Rye—Roane County," 11011-C; "River Bottom Hay Field—Knox County Near Reservoir Area," 7692-F; Tobacco Patch—Roane County," 8804-F; and "Clinch River—Bottom and Adjacent Upland Roane County," 11018-B: all are located in the file holding Thacker's "Gross Appraisal," either in the unpaginated portion at the rear of the report, or in the back of the file.

9. Thacker, "Gross Appraisal," p. 16.

10. This paragraph quotes from the phrases used in the "Site Selection Criteria" of the Manhattan Engineer District (MED), reproduced in Edith C. Truslow, *Manhattan District History: Nonscientific Aspects of Los Alamos Project Y, 1942 through 1946* (Los Alamos: Los Alamos National Scientific Laboratory, 1973 [based on unpublished 1946 work]), p. 1. The debate concerning the nature of the site and its selection is recorded in Leslie R. Groves, *Now It Can Be Told: The Story of the Manhattan Project* (New York: Harper and Row, 1962); John H. Dudley, "Ranch School to Secret City," in *Reminiscences of Los Alamos, 1943–1945,* ed. Lawrence Badash, Joseph O. Hirschfelder, and Herbert P. Broida (Boston: D. Reidel, 1980), pp. 1–11; and Bernie E. White, "Preliminary Real Estate Report, Los Alamos Project, Los Alamos, New Mexico," Albuquerque, Army Corps of Engineers Division Real Estate Suboffice, 1942, prepared by White for Lt. Col. Leonard Cowley, Army Corps of Engineers (hereafter ACE), a copy of which is held in file MD 680.1, NARD.

11. The best general source for information concerning the geological and paleontological history of the region is Roland A. Pettitt, *Los Alamos before the Dawn* (Los Alamos: Pajarito Publications, 1972), pp. 12–19.

12. Truslow, *Nonscientific Aspects,* p. 1; Vincent Jones, *Manhattan: The Army and the Atomic Bomb* (Washington, D.C.: Center of Military History, 1985), pp. 82–88.

13. Warner's life is chronicled, and her letters reproduced, in Peggy Pond Church's *The House at Otowi Bridge* (Albuquerque: University of New Mexico Press, 1959, 1960); the quote is from p. 33.

14. Ibid., pp. 41, 52, 66, 69. Warner was only one of these expatriates. The most famous— Mabel Dodge Luhan, Dorothy Brett, D. H. Lawrence—clustered in Taos. But the experience was the same: writing in the preface to her book about Lawrence, *Lorenzo in Taos,* Luhan (who married "her" Indian) declared that her book "tells of the process of change, of the permutations of the spirit worked upon by spirit. It does not end happily . . . for life is not concerned with results, but only with Being and Becoming" (Luhan, *Lorenzo in Taos* [New York: Knopf, 1932]; Lawrence's letter to Luhan is quoted on p. 6). Similar experiences are contained in the archive materials on Dorothy Brett held in the Special Collections Department of Northwestern University Library. Her descriptions of the land are found in her diary report of a horseback trip with D. H. Lawrence in May 1924; of the Indians, in a letter dated Oct. 15, 1946.

15. Church, *House at Otowi Bridge,* p. 6; on the Ranch School, see the compilation of materials by Fermor S. Church and Peggy Pond Church, *When Los Alamos Was a Ranch School* (Los Alamos: Los Alamos Historical Society, 1974); for general information about the school, see also A. J. Connell, *Los Alamos Ranch School, Otowi, Sandoval County, New Mexico* [ca. 1935], the school's thirty-five-page recruiting pamphlet, a copy of which is held in the Archives of the Los Alamos Historical Society (hereafter LAHS).

16. Pond, quoted in Church, *House at Otowi Bridge,* p. 6.

17. Letter, Douglass Campbell to his mother, undated [probably Jan. 1935]: "We went without our shirts, et al." (LAHS).

18. Manuscript notebook held in the Meyer Collection, LAHS; for further information on Connell and his philosophy, see also Connell, *Los Alamos Ranch School;* and Church and Church, *When Los Alamos Was a Ranch School,* esp. pp. 8–9: "One of the reasons for building a boys' school in such a remote location was the conviction that boys become men more easily when separated from oversolicitous mothers. . . . There was a legend that faculty wives would be expected to produce only sons."

19. Manuscript of reminiscences held in the Meyer Collection, LAHS.

20. Connell, *Los Alamos Ranch School.* Probably the most illustrious MED officer to have graduated from the Ranch School was the Los Alamos site's first commander, Whitney Ashbridge.

21. White, "Preliminary Real Estate Report." For general information on the social history of the region, see also Hal Rothman, *On Rims and Ridges: The Los Alamos Area since 1880* (Lincoln: University of Nebraska Press, 1992), pp. 24–33, 128–31.

22. Pettitt, *Los Alamos before the Dawn,* pp. 38–45.

23. White, "Preliminary Real Estate Report," pp. 4–10. Pettitt, *Los Alamos before the Dawn,* pp. 45–46, describes the Baca scheme; Hal Rothman presents a lacing analysis of the Los Alamos landholder Frank Bond's adaptation of *partido* to make it something closer to a cross between urban contract labor and Southern-style sharecropping, in *On Rims and Ridges,* esp. pp. 128–31.

24. White, "Preliminary Real Estate Report," pp. 10, 12–13.

25. Files marked "Hanford History Display," "Miscellaneous Files," Hanford Science Center of the Department of Energy, Richland, Washington; see also Mary Powell Harris, *Goodbye, White Bluffs* (Yakima, Wash.: Franklin Press, 1981), and Martha Berry Parker, *Tales of Richland, White Bluffs, and Hanford, 1805–1943* (Fairfield, Wash.: Ye Galleon Press, 1986); copies of these two publications are also held in the center.

26. Rainfall data from "Construction: Hanford Engineer Works, U.S. Contract No. W-7412-ENG-1; DuPont Project 9536, History of the Project, Start March 22, 1943, Complete

March 31, 1945," 4 vols., typescript, Wilmington, Del.: E. I. du Pont, Aug. 9, 1945, pp. 6–7. This construction history is held in the Department of Energy (DOE) Records Office at Richland, Washington.

27. Segments of the homesteader's diary were reproduced for an exhibit at the Hanford Science Center, where they are held in the "Miscellaneous Files."

28. Haynes file, "Family Histories" notebooks, Hanford Science Center.

29. Materials on the Northern Pacific Company's land-development schemes can be found in the library of the Montana Historical Society, Helena, Montana. One of the richest sources is the archive related to Frank Jay Haynes. This conglomerate founded the Hanford Power and Irrigation Company to dam the Columbia at the Priest Rapids and provide both electricity and irrigation water to the entire region. But Judge Hanford and his colleagues quarreled; the result was the founding of Hanford, and the appearance of the rival White Bluffs Land and Irrigation Company. The best general histories of water and irrigation in the American West are Marc Reisner, *Cadillac Desert: The American West and Its Disappearing Water* (New York: Penguin, 1987), pp. 114–21; and Donald Worster, *Rivers of Empire: Water, Aridity, and the Growth of the American West* (New York: Pantheon, 1985), pp. 156–78. On the local history, see Harris, *Goodbye, White Bluffs,* pp. 100–105.

30. "Local History" file, Hanford Science Center; see esp. clipping from the Hanford *Columbia,* marked "Apr. 1908," in clippings section.

31. See "Family Histories" notebooks, esp. Bash and Moffatt histories, Hanford Science Center; Parker, *Tales of Richland.*

32. Miscellaneous materials held in files at Hanford Science Center; file marked "Hanford History Display"; Parker, *Tales of Richland;* Harris, *Goodbye, White Bluffs,* pp. 101–23.

33. "Settlers Wanted," pamphlet, dated 1922, Hanford Science Center.

34. Ibid.; untitled leaflet, undated [ca. 1923]; materials held in the miscellaneous local history files in Hanford Science Center.

35. Miscellaneous materials held in Hanford Science Center.

36. Bash file, "Family Histories" notebooks, miscellaneous files, Hanford Science Center; Parker, *Tales of Richland;* Harris, *Goodbye, White Bluffs.* Information on the Wanapum is found in Richard Reierson's file, "Family Histories" notebooks, Hanford Science Center; in the recollections of Frank Buck, a Wanapum tribal member, recorded in *Hanford and the Bomb: An Oral History of World War II,* ed. S. L. Sanger (Seattle: Living History Press, 1989), p. 12; and in files on the tribe assembled for Colonel Matthias during the war years and still held in the "Miscellaneous Files," Hanford Science Center.

37. "Miscellaneous Information" files, Hanford Science Center; Harris, *Goodbye, White Bluffs,* pp. 130–51; Kolar reminiscences, "Family Histories" notebooks, Hanford Science Center; interview with Annette Heriford, 1992.

38. Movie footage provided by Harry Anderson to the Hanford Science Center and transferred to video.

39. "Family Histories" notebooks, Hanford Science Center.

40. This account of the apple growers is a composite of stories held in the "Family Histories" notebooks, Hanford Science Center, or described in Parker, *Tales of Richland,* and Harris, *Goodbye, White Bluffs.* These stories were in many cases collected decades after the District condemned the lands, and hence are colored by nostalgia and regret; yet the picture that underlies them is consistent with the history of the region and regions like it during this period.

41. Bessie Whitwer file, "Family Histories" notebooks, Hanford Science Center.

42. Esther Krug Schultz file, "Family Histories" notebooks, Hanford Science Center.

43. Clark file, "Family Histories" notebooks, Hanford Science Center.

44. The Coulee was so huge that its concrete would have required hundreds of years to solidify by conventional means, so grandiose that it even had its own hired troubadour, a hayseed Marxist folksinger named Woody Guthrie, who traveled the region in a chauffeured car and wrote a string of songs praising a new Eden of managed land, managed energy, and managed society, a utopia "run by E-lectricity," in the words of the song "Talking Columbia." Guthrie

took the Washington desert to a national audience with his songs; "your power is turning our darkness to dawn," he sang, promising "atomic bedrooms, and plastic" in a new consumer culture of plenty managed by hidden but benevolent bureaucrats. Marc Reisner tells the story of Guthrie's chauffeur in *Cadillac Desert,* p. 167; Guthrie's Columbia River songs have been assembled on CD as *Columbia River Collection* (Rounder CD 1036), which includes an excellent set of notes on the history of the project.

45. Matthias reminiscence, in Sanger, *Hanford and the Bomb,* pp. 6–7.

CHAPTER 2: INCORPORATION

1. Richard Feynman, *Surely You're Joking, Mr. Feynman* (New York: Norton, 1985), p. 53.

2. Ibid.

3. The literature of the history of science provides a rich background for understanding these trends. See especially the following: Michael Polanyi, *Science, Faith and Society* (1946; rpt. Chicago: University of Chicago Press, 1964), pp. 43–44, describes the process of discovery in a manner that focuses the activity more sharply on the individual and the mentor, but the essential elements are there; Thomas Kuhn, *The Structure of Scientific Revolutions* (Chicago: University of Chicago Press, 1962); Charles Weiner, "A New Site for the Seminar: The Refugees and American Physics in the Thirties," in *The Intellectual Migration: Europe and America, 1930–1960,* ed. Donald Fleming and Bernard Bailyn (Cambridge, Mass.: Harvard University Press, 1969), pp. 191–234; Laura Fermi, *Illustrious Immigrants: The Intellectual Migration from Europe, 1930–1941* (Chicago: University of Chicago Press, 1968), p. 39; Leo Szilard, "Reminiscences," in Fleming and Bailyn, *The Intellectual Migration,* p. 95; Robert K. Merton, in *Social Theory and Social Structure: Toward the Codification of Theory and Research* (Glencoe, Ill.: Free Press, 1957); Bernard Barber, in *Science and the Social Order* (New York: Collier, 1962); Gerald Holton, ed., *The Twentieth Century Sciences: Studies in the Biography of Ideas* (New York: Norton, 1972).

4. Alice Kimball Smith and Charles Weiner, "Robert Oppenheimer: The Los Alamos Years," *Bulletin of the Atomic Scientists* 36, no. 6 (June 1980): 11–17, esp. 14–17.

5. Otto Frisch, *What Little I Remember* (Cambridge: Cambridge University Press, 1979), pp. 113–19; Lise Meitner, "Looking Back," *Bulletin of the Atomic Scientists* 20, no. 9 (Nov. 1964): 7.

6. Ibid.

7. Because European intellectuals generally defined their roles in terms not simply of their professions but more broadly, in a critical and skeptical frame of reference that could be applied not only to science but to politics and philosophy as well, they were early targets for Fascist and Nazi scapegoating. And because the universities and the intellectual professions contained a disproportionate number of Jews, the argument for racial purity shaded easily into the attack on intellectuals and their institutions. See L. Fermi, *Illustrious Immigrants,* p. 41.

In the words of one group of pure scientists protesting the shift from pure science to useful engineering, "only such investigations are favored which are likely to bring about a direct technical advance." The quote is from "A Call to Scientists," published in *The New Republic* in 1934 and signed by a host of luminaries; it is quoted in Weiner, "A New Site," p. 209. In 1937, the sociologist Robert Merton delivered a paper on the subject of the threat to science by the totalitarian regime in Germany; republished in his *Social Theory and Social Structure* (New York: Free Press, 1968), pp. 591–603, it remains an impassioned and valuable description of the general effects of Nazism on scientific endeavor.

8. Letter, Selig Hecht to Leslie C. Dunn, June 20, 1933, quoted in Weiner, "A New Site," p. 205.

9. On the movement from Europe to America, see Weiner, "A New Site," pp. 196–228.

10. Daniel Boorstin, *The Americans: The Democratic Experience* (New York: Random House, 1973), p. 1.

11. Weiner, "A New Site," p. 223.

12. Laura Fermi, *Atoms in the Family* (1954; rpt. Chicago: University of Chicago Press, 1987), p. 145.

13. Polanyi is quoted in Richard Rhodes, *The Making of the Atomic Bomb* (New York: Simon and Schuster, 1986), p. 34.

14. James B. Conant, *My Several Lives* (New York: Harper and Row, 1970), pp. 234–36; Donald K. Price, *The Scientific Estate* (Cambridge, Mass.: Harvard University Press, 1965), p. 65.

15. The individual elements of this system were still loosely coupled, open to innovation and capable of being flexed by individuals with sufficient stubbornness and ingenuity, and were often adapted by both the NDRC and the laboratory during the contract negotiations. Taking over the Uranium Committee in mid-June of 1940, the NDRC made it purely scientific; now connection with the military occurred through the institution of the NDRC. And a new "Advisory Committee," chaired by the physicist Harold Urey, took over the role of long-range planning for this immensely complex and still largely opaque program of atomic weapons research and development. But this new committee's first activity was a restrictive one; by dint of the immensely prestigious scientists among its ranks, it was able to ram through a policy of restriction on all publication of atomic matters in scientific journals. See Spencer R. Weart and Gertrud Weiss Szilard, eds., *Leo Szilard: His Version of the Facts* (Cambridge, Mass.: MIT Press, 1978), pp. 118–19, 126–33.

16. Jones, *Manhattan,* p. 27.

17. This schedule of managerial responsibilities is drawn from a number of sources: they include James Phinney Baxter III, *Scientists against Time* (Boston: Little Brown, 1946) pp. 421–44); Jones, *Manhattan,* pp. 19–39; Conant, *My Several Lives,* pp. 234–85; Richard G. Hewlett and Oscar E. Anderson Jr., *The New World, 1939–1946* (University Park, Pa.: Pennsylvania State University Press, 1962), pp. 49–52.

18. Jones, *Manhattan,* p. 34; Hewlett and Anderson, *New World,* pp. 44–45.

19. Jones, *Manhattan,* p. 34, Conant, *My Several Lives,* pp. 236–37; Hewlett and Anderson, *New World,* p. 50.

20. Hewlett and Anderson, *New World,* p. 62. James Phinney Baxter III, in his *Scientists against Time,* describes the planning board's role as one of "recommending diffusion and centrifuge contracts to Bush"; see pp. 421–44.

21. Hewlett and Anderson, *New World,* pp. 65, 66.

22. By the lights of the scientists, the entire project was in shambles. Wheeler Loomis, head of the physics department at the University of Illinois, told a youthful John Manley (who'd been recruited by the pioneering atomic physicist Leo Szilard for work at Columbia), "that stuff is so terribly poorly organized that I won't let you go; that's all there is to it" (John H. Manley, "A New Laboratory Is Born," in Badash, Hirschfelder, and Broida, *Reminiscences,* p. 22).

23. Jones, *Manhattan,* p. 34, explains the various responsibilities of the three program chiefs.

24. Compton's and Lawrence's memos to Conant, Jan. 22 and 24, 1942, respectively, are quoted in Hewlett and Anderson, *New World,* pp. 54–56. Manley talks of the effect of joining the Met Lab after this stage as "thrilling, hectic and varied. I got back into the swing of the neutron physics that had been going on at Columbia . . . with old colleagues . . . like Szilard, Zionn, George Weil and Herb Anderson" (Manley, "A New Laboratory," p. 23).

25. Letter, Marshall to Lenore Fine and Jesse Remington, Jan. 15, 1968, quoted in Fine and Remington, *The Corps of Engineers: Construction in the United States* (Washington, D.C.: Office of the Chief of Military History, U.S. Army, 1972), p. 652.

26. K. D. Nichols, *The Road to Trinity* (New York: Morrow, 1987), p. 36.

27. For a general history of the Army Corps of Engineers, see Daniel A. Mazmanian and Jeanne Nienaber, *Can Organizations Change? Environmental Protection, Citizen Participation, and the Corps of Engineers* (Washington, D.C.: Brookings Institution, 1979), pp. 8–19; Arthur Ernest Morgan, *Dams and Other Disasters: A Century of the Army Corps of Engineers in Civil Works* (Boston: P. Sargent, 1971), passim; Fine and Remington, *Corps of Engineers,* passim. An acerbic analysis of the Corps of Engineers and dam-building in the West is found in Reisner's *Cadillac Desert.*

28. Fine and Remington, *Corps of Engineers,* pp. 33, 42–110, passim.

29. For a management analysis of the Corps of Engineers, see Mazmanian and Nienaber,

Can Organizations Change? pp. 8–19; see also the lacing polemic presented in Morgan's *Dams and Other Disasters,* pp. 69–70.

30. Fine and Remington, *Corps of Engineers,* pp. 661–63. Nichols echoed this position in his own memoirs: "We needed a separate command structure with adequate capabilities to perform all functions, independent of existing organizations. A corollary to this is to accept cooperation only when it is available without any infringement on our independence. We definitely needed cooperation, but only on our terms, and fortunately we got it" (Nichols, *Road To Trinity,* pp. 52–53).

31. Fine and Remington, *Corps of Engineers,* p. 659; Jones, *Manhattan,* p. 43; Groves, *Now It Can Be Told,* pp. 13, 17.

32. Groves, *Now It Can Be Told,* pp. 13, 17.

33. Ibid., p. 17; the quote is from Groves, in Groves-Haley interviews, Dec. 11, 1957, transcript, box 2, RG 200, National Archives, Washington, D.C. (hereafter NA).

34. Fine and Remington, *Corps of Engineers,* p. 661. The orders stated that he would "report to the Commanding General, Services of Supply" and would "operate in close conjunction with the Construction Division of your office and other facilities of the Corps of Engineers" (Orders from Somervell's memo to Gen. Reybold, quoted in Fine and Remington, *Corps of Engineers,* p. 661; Groves's characterization of the orders came in an interview with army historians in 1967 that is quoted on pp. 661–62). See also Groves-Haley interviews, Dec. 11, 1957, transcript, box 2, RG 200, NA. Col. K. D. Nichols, Groves's immediate underling, even found it necessary to devise a separate page on his organization chart in his memoirs to account for Groves (Nichols, *Road to Trinity,* pp. 15–17). See also Groves's own description of the advantages of having Marshall as his front, in the Groves-Haley interviews, Dec. 11, 1957, transcript, box 2, RG 200, NA.

35. See Nichols's comments about the battle between Marshall and Groves over living conditions at Oak Ridge and Los Alamos, in *Road to Trinity,* p. 59; his reports concerning Marshall's inability to forgive Groves's unrelenting criticism and faultfinding are detailed on pp. 102–3. On this vexing obsession of Groves's, see Col. Franklin T. Matthias's diary, Hanford Science Center Reading Room.

36. Letter, Einstein to Briggs, Apr. 25, 1940, reprinted in *Einstein on Peace* (New York: Schocken, 1968), pp. 300–301.

37. Szilard, "What Is Wrong with Us," typescript [Sept. 1942], held in the declassified documents of the Los Alamos National Scientific Laboratory Records Center/Archive, Los Alamos, New Mexico (hereafter LASL).

38. Ibid.

39. Leona Marshall Libby, *The Uranium People* (New York: Crane Russak/Scribner's, 1979), pp. 90–91.

40. In his often very fine popular study of the Manhattan Project, *The Making of the Atomic Bomb,* Richard Rhodes inverts the chronology (placing Szilard's manifesto *before* Bush's call for a new authoritarianism and Groves's appointment to the District), and thereby confuses the issue—which, as I see it, signals the way that the scientific community was already far outside the decisionmaking loop, and concurrently, the way that Bush's argument exactly opposed Szilard's. See Rhodes, *Making of the Atomic Bomb,* pp. 421–28.

41. Groves, *Now It Can Be Told,* pp. 43–47; Arthur Holly Compton, *Atomic Quest: A Personal Narrative* (New York: Oxford University Press, 1956), pp. 113–14. Interestingly, Groves blamed the restiveness of the scientists on the presence of foreign agitators among them (he was thinking of Szilard and Fermi, no doubt). His nativist intolerance may have accidentally hit the mark. As others have noted (and I have echoed), American science was far less experienced with the sort of radical democracy I have characterized at the opening of this chapter, and far more familiar with the industrial-technological R&D arrangement that the District eventually imposed on the program; that was part of the reason why so little of true importance in the world of atomic physics happened in America at the instigation of Americans.

42. See Groves, *Now It Can Be Told,* pp. 41–43, 55; Compton, *Atomic Quest,* pp. 105–25; Lib-

by, *Uranium People,* pp. 91–93. As Rhodes points out in a footnote (*Making of the Atomic Bomb,* p. 823), Compton's account is extremely garbled, conflating meetings, reversing events, imputing to the past what was understood only much later.

43. Compton, *Atomic Quest,* p. 108.

44. As early as January 1940, the company had begun contracting for new smokeless powder plants; by the end of 1943, it would have fifty-four new plants, 95 percent funded by $1 billion in government monies. Between 1941, itself a boom year, and 1946, operating income would rise by 46 percent, employee population by 20 percent, and operating investment by more than 42 percent. Between 1940 and 1944, the rise was even more dramatic—a 60 percent jump in operating profits. Gerard Colby, *Du Pont Dynasty: Behind the Nylon Curtain* (Secaucus, N.J.: Lyle Stuart, 1984), p. 183; ibid., p. 388, citing pages 16–17 of the 1943 Senate Special Committee on Post-War Economic Policy and Planning "Report" of 1943; David A. Hounshell and John Kenly Smith Jr., *Science and Corporate Strategy: du Pont R&D, 1902–1980* (Cambridge: Cambridge University Press, 1988), p. 328; Colby, *Du Pont Dynasty,* p. 394.

45. Hounshell and Smith, *Science and Corporate Strategy,* p. 334.

46. Lammot du Pont, quoted in Colby, *Du Pont Dynasty,* pp. 391–92.

47. Ibid., p. 388; Hounshell and Smith, in their Du Pont–approved history of R&D at the corporation, were more muted: "Du Pont's executives took the position that the company would cooperate fully with the government as requested but that they wished to keep the company on its highly successful track of commercial development as much as possible" (*Science and Corporate Strategy,* p. 333). See also Groves, *Now It Can Be Told,* pp. 46–52, for his own reminiscence of the decision.

48. Greenewalt summed up his thinking in July 1944, when he wrote a lengthy memo to Roger Williams, then the head of the plutonium project. But his thinking along these lines extended back to 1942, as his diary reveals. See Hounshell and Smith, *Science and Corporate Strategy,* pp. 340–45, for a detailed discussion of the issue; Greenewalt's remark, which first appeared in his diary, is quoted on p. 341.

49. In 1957, Groves reiterated how large this dark possibility loomed at the time. In a preliminary interview for a projected television series, Groves told his interviewer: "Remember we are dealing with a field that is brand new and people don't understand and therefore they can make mistakes. They can make serious ones. The next thing that happened with this was that DuPont could have gotten a terrific black eye. That might have severe financial losses even to the point where the company could have been wiped out. It may seem strange but it could have happened if we had had the wrong kind of an accident. Today I would say no, but as we knew it then it could have happened" (Groves-Haley interview, Dec. 27, 1957, transcript, p. J-1, box 2, RG 200, NA).

50. Jones, *Manhattan,* pp. 99, 105–7; Groves, *Now It Can Be Told,* pp. 56–59. Jones's report presents Du Pont as already determined to have nothing to do with atomics ("du Pont did not want to manufacture plutonium after the war and made clear it was agreeing to do so now only because of the expressed desire of the Army" [p. 106]); his argument confuses Du Pont's bargaining strategy with the corporation's internal decisions.

51. "Report to the President by the Military Policy Committee, 15 December, 1942," in Manhattan District History (hereafter MDH), "Annexes to the Diplomatic History of the Manhattan Project" (unpaginated). The contract and its predecessor "letter of understanding" are found in a file marked "Record of Preliminary Negotiations," RG 77, Military Division, NA.

The Manhattan District History is in fact a huge multivolume and multiauthor compendium of narratives, produced at the order of General Groves, during the interregnum between the end of the war and the transfer of power to the Atomic Energy Commission. Portions of the Manhattan Project's history were parceled out to continuing members of Groves's team, scientists remaining with the District, army officers, and the like, depending on their area of expertise or their place in the scheme. The result was a polyglot work, sometimes pure propaganda, sometimes serious research, sometimes haphazard compendium. In addition, the "History" was full of appendices into which were squirreled photographs, charts, letters, copies of memos, and reports: all forms of documentation. The result, a typescript with carbon copies, was declassified and microfilmed in the late 1950s or early 1960s. One twelve-reel microfilm copy is held by the Collections Research Libraries in Chicago; in addition I consulted copies at the Richland DOE facility and at the National Archives, Washington, D.C. It is not clear that all copies of the MDH are identical; in a few cases where there seem to have been discrepancies, I have listed the specific copy from which I drew the citation or document.

52. Groves's understanding of the agreement is found in the file "General—Views," Groves miscellany, box 6, RG 200, NA. Also see Hounshell and Smith, *Science and Corporate Strategy*, p. 342: "Greenewalt suggested that Du Pont [*sic*] could gain prestige and improve its university relations through publications in nuclear physics. . . . Greenewalt had sought to recruit first-class Chicago physicists to enter the employ of du Pont on a temporary basis to serve as experts at Hanford."

53. Hounshell and Smith, *Science and Corporate Strategy*, p. 342. I am referring here to the meetings held at Met Lab in 1943, at which guards were posted and Groves's assistant threatened the participants with assignment as "grunts" to Guadalcanal; and to the attempt to petition the executive branch to maintain surveillance over the Du Pont programs at Oak Ridge. On this, see Alice Kimball Smith, *A Peril and a Hope: The Scientists' Movement in America, 1945–47* (Chicago: University of Chicago Press, 1965), pp. 15–17.

54. John H. Manley, recruited to the Met Lab early on and soon assigned to Oppenheimer as his principal aide, described one small subprogram in which the frustration of this interim system is neatly illustrated. He reported that he and Oppenheimer moved into the study of fast neutrons after the physicist originally assigned to the task resigned from the group: "I had to chase around the country because there were, I think, nine separate contracts with universities that had accelerators which could be used as neutron sources . . . everywhere from Washington, D.C., to Rice to Minnesota, Wisconsin, Purdue and so on. Oppenheimer, on the other hand, had a small group in Berkeley which was concentrating on the theoretical problems and calculating with the data which the experimental programs would feed him" (Manley, "A New Laboratory," pp. 21–38, esp. p. 25.)

55. Groves, *Now It Can Be Told*, p. 55.

56. Manley, "A New Laboratory," p. 26.

57. Letter, Oppenheimer to Manley, Oct. 12, 1942, in *Robert Oppenheimer: Letters and Recollections*, ed. Alice Kimball Smith and Charles Weiner (Cambridge, Mass.: Harvard University Press, 1980), p. 42.

58. Dudley, "Ranch School to Secret City," pp. 3–4.

59. Ibid., p. 4.

60. Letter, Oppenheimer to Manley, Nov. 6, 1942, in Smith and Weiner, *Robert Oppenheimer*, p. 236.

61. Edward McMillan, "Early Days at Los Alamos," in Badash, Hirschfelder, and Broida, *Reminiscences*, pp. 14–15.

62. Ibid., p. 15.

63. William Lawren, *The General and the Bomb* (New York: Dodd, Mead, 1988), pp. 46–47. Lawren reports on Groves's upbringing but soft-pedals the psychological brutality of it; the facts are horrifying to anyone familiar with the psychological development of children. Nichols's statement is found in his *Road to Trinity*, p. 71; Groves's recollections are found in his *Now It Can Be Told*, pp. 66–67.

64. Minutes of the Military Policy Committee, quoted by Jones, *Manhattan*, p. 109.

65. Fine and Remington (*Corps of Engineers*, p. 667) provide a relatively precise chronology of the site-selection process; unfortunately, it appears to conflict with Matthias's own report in his diary for the period, which strongly suggests that the preliminary site criteria were defined before the MPC meeting. Matthias is firm that the team chose Hanford by the end of December. See Matthias diary, opening pages marked "prior to Feb. 1, 1943."

66. See the "Site Selection Criteria" materials, MDH, bk. 4, vol. 3, "Design," esp. pp. S-1–S-3, pp. 2.1–2.8.

67. Ibid.

68. The words concerning haste are from Groves, *Now It Can Be Told,* p. 71; he was echoing the original site selection criteria reproduced in MDH, bk. 4, vol. 3, p. S-2.

69. Groves, *Now It Can Be Told,* pp. 74–75.

70. Reybold's "General Order" is found in the special introductory section of the copy of the MDH held in the DOE archive at the Hanford facility, Richland, Washington.

CHAPTER 3: CONDEMNATION

1. Memo, Fred Morgan, Project Manager, to Division Engineer, Ohio River Division, ACE: "Report of Hearing Before House Military Affairs Sub-Committee in Connection with Land Acquisition at Harriman, Tennessee," entry for Aug. 13, 1943, N3-326-87-07, NARD.

2. These matters are detailed in documents assembled as appendix 2 of MDH, bk. 1, vol. 10, and in materials located in files catalogued as N3-326-87-07, NARD. See especially Morgan, "Report of Hearing"; the lengthy typescript synopsis of the hearings provided by Col. R. G. West to the chief of engineers and dated Aug. 30, 1943; and the reports in both the *Knoxville News-Sentinel* (Aug. 13, 1943) and the *Knoxville Journal* (Aug. 12, 1943, p. 1). The précis that follows is drawn from these sources.

3. Morgan, "Report of Hearing"; West, synopsis, Aug. 30, 1943, and the reports in both the *Knoxville News-Sentinel* (Aug. 13, 1943) and the *Knoxville Journal* (Aug. 12, 1943, p. 1).

4. An account of the event was published in the *Knoxville Journal,* Aug. 12, 1943, p. 1. The *Journal* gave Griffith's first name as "Dicie"; Fred Morgan, Corps of Engineers project manager, spelled it "Dicey" in his "Report of Hearing."

5. Report of Morgan on hearings, Aug. 11, 12, 1943, MDH, bk. 1, vol. 10, appendix 2; "Appraisers Criticized in Land Price Hearing," *Knoxville Journal,* Aug. 12, 1943, reproduced in MDH, bk. 1, vol. 10, appendix B-2-3.

6. "Clinton Probers Score U.S. Appraisers' Acts," *Knoxville Journal,* Aug. 12, 1943, reproduced in MDH, bk. 1, vol. 10, appendix B-2-J. The materials presented in the appendix include letters from Jennings and responses by representatives of the District; these letters suggest that Jennings was not blameless in the controversy over what facts were accurate in case after case.

7. The process of land acquisition is described, if incompletely, in Jones, *Manhattan,* pp. 319–43. But I have drawn the vast majority of information concerning land condemnation and acquisition from the original documents. Such materials concerning the Clinton Engineer Works are held in boxes 6 and 7, RG N3-326-87-07, NARD. Pertinent materials about Hanford are assembled in the Du Pont "Construction: Hanford Engineer Works," and in other miscellaneous files in that archive. In addition, a detailed chronology of the process was included in the District's 1946 self-history; see MDH, bk. 1, vol. 4, S-1–13. The bulk of condemnation materials concerning Los Alamos is held in the LAHS archive. This includes a manuscript in the Meyer Collection by an unknown author, a narrative based on interviews conducted in 1948 with residents and workers at the Ranch School, including Peggy Pond Church, Bences Gonzales, and Aline Nusbaum O'Brien; and the general file of materials concerning condemnation, assembled as Collection 1989.006.

8. At Kingston, the legal directive from an undersecretary of the army came on September 29, 1942. But by then the Real Estate Branch had opened its office; even earlier, its appraisers had canvassed the region. Many of these appraisers came from the Ohio River Division of the Corps. But these weren't enough for a site containing about 850 individual pieces of land, some in town, some rural, some so isolated that no formal roads reached back to their doorways and even Rural Free Delivery had no record of their location. So Real Estate recruited appraisers from the Federal Land Bank and the Tennessee Valley Authority, and from the War Department itself. See condemnation records compiled as appendix B of the MDH, bk. 1, vol. 10, p. 2.29.

9. Groves, *Now It Can Be Told,* pp. 25–26; Jones, *Manhattan,* pp. 78, 319; Charles W. Johnson and Charles O. Jackson, *City behind a Fence: Oak Ridge, Tennessee, 1942–1946* (Knoxville: Uni-

versity of Tennessee Press, 1981), p. 8. The authors of *City behind a Fence* include a précis of an interview with a wartime resident who reported of the "Clinton Demolition Range" that "the name sounded ominous" (p. 207), suggesting it served its purpose. Nancy May's report was delivered to the House Military Affairs Subcommittee on Aug. 11 and 12, 1943, and summarized in Morgan, "Report of Hearing," p. 2.

10. MDH, bk. 1, vol. 10, appendices B, C; declassified files and condemnation-appraisal notebooks for the Clinton site are located in the misnamed "Records of the Atomic Energy Commission," boxes 6 and 7, RG N3-326-87-07, NARD. There are eleven condemnation-appraisal notebooks, containing negative photocopies of typescript tract valuation forms, and photographs of all buildings on each tract, a minimum of one photo per building. The valuation forms list tract number, beginning with A-1, name of owner, valuation of improvements: replacement less depreciation basis, type of building, size, construction type, roof type, foundation type, condition, value, and salvage value. The photographs are from negatives approximately 2¾" x 3¾" in size, each bearing the number assigned to the corresponding building listed in the appraisal form (negative A-1-1, for example, showed the farmhouse of the W. B. Thacker family, tract A-1).

11. Appraisal notebooks, "Records of Atomic Energy Commission."

12. Ibid.

13. The appraisers determined the value of land not by crop yield or extent of improvements, but by location and by conformity to the ideal of the suburban brick cottage with its neatly tended garden and lawn. Explaining the surprisingly high assessment of E-443 (the owner's name illegible), the appraiser wrote that a "large number of dwellings in area are owned by people who work outside of farm and due to proximity to available outside work, buildings usually carry a high value to the property." There was no "comparable" to support the claim; the appraiser just knew that suburban houses were "highly desirable." By contrast, farm owners off the principal highways who took pride in their property and who strove to make them neat and well-tended found themselves punished by the appraiser's accusation that the land was "overimproved." This was the case with E-441, Edgar F. Ford's farm: "This property is considerably overimproved and good portion of building value could not be obtained through a reasonable sale." J. A. Gamble's tract was "somewhat over built, but owner's two sons make their homes on it. They work other nearby land." Not that this explanation availed in the matter of value: the appraiser rated the entire parcel at $850.

14. Reports of the process and its abuse fill the land acquisition records of all three sites; the single most comprehensive collection of these is found in box 5, RG 4nn-326-8505, NARD; see, for example, file 601, "Request for Easement, Sherman F. Owen, Tract E-416," letters dated Jan. 25 and 27, 1943. A more confusing example (to the historian, at least) is the case of the Wilson and Roberts ranches at the Hanford, Washington, site; mentioned in passing in the Matthias diary, it appears to represent a case where individual army officers sought to manipulate the process to make personal exemptions and special rights possible for favored landowners. See Matthias diary, Aug. 31, 1943.

15. Morgan, "Report of Hearing."

16. This act of charity is recorded in MDH, bk. 1, vol. 10, sec. 2 and appendices A through E.

17. On the "Requests to Vacate," see MDH, bk. 1, vol. 10, sec. 2 and appendices.

18. Eviction notice for Parlee Raby, Route 1, Oliver Springs, held by Oak Ridge Children's Museum, Oak Ridge, Tennessee.

19. Appraisal notebooks, "Records of the Atomic Energy Commission."

20. Letter, A. J. Connell to Col. Lawrence S. Hitchcock, Apr. 12, 1943, LAHS. This case is almost certainly one of those argued before the Supreme Court by O'Brien's mentor, Norman Littell, and discussed by him in his book *My Roosevelt Years* (Seattle: University of Washington Press, 1987).

21. Recorded in MDH, bk. 1, vol. 10, p. 2; ibid., S-8.

22. This figure is reported in the MDH, bk. 1, vol. 10, p. 2.

23. Thacker, "Gross Appraisal," p. 8. Quixotically, Thacker estimated a total of 900 tracts, 1,100 families, and a total population of 4,400.

24. This material is drawn from an anonymous typescript narrative with interviews, including those with Peggy Pond Church, Bences Gonzales, and Aline Nusbaum O'Brien, held in the Meyer Collection, LAHS archives.

25. Letter of condemnation from Stimson, Dec. 1, 1942, Meyer Collection, LAHS archives.

26. Ibid.

27. Dudley, "Ranch School to Secret City," pp. 1–11.

28. Church and Church, *When Los Alamos Was a Ranch School*, pp. 20–23; Church, *House at Otowi Bridge*; assorted letters and reminiscences, LAHS archives.

29. See letters, Connell to Hitchcock, May 9 (from which quote is drawn), May 24, and June 11, 1943, LAHS; in the June 11 letter Connell gave the name of the Washington supervisor of the condemnation proceedings and included the warning that "I am not sure whether it would be proper for you in your position to approach him." See also undated letter, Connell to Hitchcock, marked on top in Hitchcock's handwriting, "ans[wered] 19 June on rev[erse]," also in LAHS.

30. Letter, Connell to Hitchcock, June 19, 1943, LAHS. The property appraisals are in the LAHS; a preliminary estimate also appears in White, "Preliminary Real Estate Report."

31. See letter, "Fred" to Hitchcock, Jan. 24, 1944, LAHS. This reports receipt of a check for $60,000 and the failure to pay the $7,800 in interest. Jones and virtually all other historians report the sale of the school at $350,000—see Jones, *Manhattan*, p. 329, and Truslow, *Nonscientific Aspects*, p. 9. The burial wishes, and the response, are discussed in another letter, "Fred" to Hitchcock, Feb. 11, 1944, LAHS.

32. Real Estate's principal justification for its appraisal—that the prime value lay with "improvements" and not with land itself—is only marginally convincing. For while the Ranch School had fifty-four buildings, its own power plant, water and sewer systems, roads and road-building equipment, and farm implements, and held grazing rights to an 800-acre tract in the National Forest, many of the small farmers were themselves not so small. The report of the ownership of these grazing rights and properties is included in White's "Preliminary Real Estate Report" and in the final real estate reports and the appraisals.

33. These figures are drawn from White, "Preliminary Real Estate Report"; from the Albuquerque Engineer District's *Report on Proposed Site for a Military Project at the Los Alamos Ranch School* (both held in the land acquisition files, NARD), and from an undated page titled "Names and Addresses of Purported Owners," A-84-019-73-1, LASL.

34. See "Names and Addresses of Purported Owners," LASL.

35. Truslow, *Nonscientific Aspects*, p. 9.

36. These brochures, bills, and labels are all among the materials held in the miscellaneous files of the Hanford Science Center, many in the file drawers of the Public Information Office.

37. On the Hanford land valuation question, see the Du Pont "Construction: Hanford Engineer Works," vol. 1. See also the "Family Histories" notebooks, Hanford Science Center.

38. The last major government condemnations for which the Washington Land Bank office had supplied appraisers had been Camp White and Camp Adair, both of which were in far different economic and ecological environments in Oregon. MDH, bk. 4, vol. 4, appendix D, provides information on the appraisers and their experience.

39. A representative sample of condemnation appraisal forms is reproduced in MDH, bk. 4, vol. 4, appendix C-4. My description of the grounds is drawn from the appraisal photographs made of the sites; some are reproduced in appendix D of MDH, bk. 4, vol. 4; others are scattered in the archives at DOE, at the Hanford Science Center, and in the Richland DOE Public Information Office.

40. Du Pont, "Construction: Hanford Engineer Works," vol. 1, pp. 8–9. This "Du Pont construction history," as it is informally called, includes a précis of documents provided for the condemnation, including Land Bank appraisal records and similar materials.

41. The residents' views are drawn from the "Family Histories" notebooks, Hanford Science Center.

42. "Family Histories" notebooks, Hanford Science Center; Du Pont, "Construction: Han-

ford Engineer Works," vol. 1; MDH, bk. 1, vol. 4, passim. The Kennewick *Courier-Reporter* article is included in the "Family Histories" notebooks.

43. MDH, bk. 4, vol. 4, appendix D; Du Pont, "Construction: Hanford Engineer Works," vol. 1, pp. 8–11, and appendix.

44. See sample appraisal forms, lists of comparables and their valuations, and general explanations of the appraisal process, MDH, bk. 4, vol. 4, appendix D; see also condemnation and valuation materials in the Du Pont "Construction: Hanford Engineer Works," vol. 1, pp. 6–8. The matter of the crop valuations is obliquely mentioned in the MDH, bk. 4, vol. 4, sec. S-2, and appendix C.

45. Du Pont, "Construction: Hanford Engineer Works," vol. 1, p. 6.

46. The first order of business was a complete tour of the site, according to the Matthias diary entry for March 24, 1943: "Pasco to Richland and all around the village; to Yakima River Bend; to Benson Ranch via 'Rattlesnake Blvd.'; to Vernita and Priest Rapids; back through White Bluffs; Hanford; across on ferry to top of bluff opposite White Bluffs; to limit of B area on Hanford-Connell road; and back along east side of river to Pasco. That evening, held a discussion with General Groves, Mr. Church [Du Pont's top executive on the project], Col. O'Brien and Real Estate people—Mr. Farrell, Mr. Burton, etc.—in my office. Many points still remain to be crystallized; but in general the basic points were settled."

47. Reierson file, "Family Histories" notebooks, Hanford Science Center. Readers of John Steinbeck's *Grapes of Wrath* will recognize this rural legend of the thirties, updated and used by a government man.

48. Matthias diary, Mar. 26, Apr. 13, 1942; Jones, *Manhattan,* p. 335.

49. Reierson file, "Family Histories" notebooks, Hanford Science Center; Matthias diary, Mar. 30, 1943; letter, Board of Directors, Richland Irrigation District, to Richland Land Owners, Apr. 23, 1943, MDH, bk. 4, vol. 4, appendix C.

50. Matthias diary, Apr. 24, 1943.

51. Robinson's story is quoted by James A. Young in his article "Bring Them Home Sooner," *Nuclear Division News,* reprinted by the Oak Ridge Operations Office of Public Information as a pamphlet. Its genealogy is unknown.

52. Matthias diary, June 1, 4, 7, 8, 12, 16, 18, 22, and Aug. 9, 1943.

53. Ibid., June 18, 21, July 5, 1943.

54. Ibid., July 5, 7, 1943.

55. Ibid., Aug. 28, 1943. A day earlier, Matthias had admitted to Schwellenbach that payments were still not being made. The judge had been told—probably by lawyers for the complainants in the condemnation trials—that the withheld payments were limited to lands in disputes. See Matthias diary, Aug. 27, 1943.

56. Matthias diary, Aug. 27, 1943.

57. The stories of the District's attempts to influence the judicial process are interwoven through Colonel Matthias's diary for the years 1943–45. Specific documents relating to condemnation matters are found in the MDH, vol. 4, p. 4, appendix C. There is also significant data in the letters, journals, and reminiscences of Norman Littell, who was eventually fired through the intervention of District officials. Some of these accounts are excerpted in his book, *My Roosevelt Years.* See also Wiehl interview, in Sanger, *Hanford and the Bomb,* pp. 11–12. See Matthias diary, Oct. 14–Nov. 7, 1944; see also cable, Matthias to District Engineer, Oct. 24, 1944, box 9, RG 326-83-005, box 8, NARD; Littell diary, Oct. 19, Nov. 18, 19, 21, 22, 24, Dec. 6, 1944, reproduced in *My Roosevelt Years,* pp. 319–20.

58. Jones, *Manhattan,* p. 337; Harvey Bundy, "Remembered Words," *Atlantic Monthly,* Mar. 1957.

59. Matthias diary, Dec. 17, 1944.

60. Ibid., Dec. 17, 18, 1944.

61. "Letter to guard officers re evacuation of farmhouses in TNX area 3 Nov. 43," box 5, RG 4nn-326-8505, NARD.

CHAPTER 4: CONSTRUCTION

1. Ruth Marshak, "Secret City," in *Standing By and Making Do: Women of Wartime Los Alamos,* ed. Jane S. Wilson and Charlotte Serber (Los Alamos: Los Alamos Historical Society, 1988), p. 4. Marshak's reminiscence was originally completed for publication in 1946.

2. Ibid., p. 5

3. Eleanor Jette, *Inside Box 1663* (Los Alamos: Los Alamos Historical Society, 1977), p. 15.

4. Ibid.

5. Matthias, quoted in Sanger, *Hanford and the Bomb,* p. 57; Staub, quoted in Bernice Brode, "Tales of Los Alamos," *LASL Community News,* June 2, 1960, p. 8.

6. L. Fermi, *Atoms in the Family,* p. 207.

7. Manley, "A New Laboratory," pp. 32–33; letter of permission, Groves to Albuquerque District Engineer, Nov. 30, 1942, and memo, Groves to Albuquerque District Engineer, "Construction of Project at Los Alamos," Dec. 2, 1942, both in file MD 600.1, box 41, RG 4nn-326-8505, NARD.

8. Truslow, *Nonscientific Aspects,* pp. 11–40.

9. Memo, Matthias for Groves to District Engineer, Albuquerque, Dec. 2, 1942, file MD 600.1, box 41, RG 4nn-326-8505, NARD.

10. See Manley, "A New Laboratory," passim; see also memorandum, Oppenheimer/David Dow[illegible] to General Groves, "Housing," Sept. 20, 1944, document A-87-019, 18-7, LASL.

11. Brode, "Tales of Los Alamos," p. 7.

12. One of the earliest examples of conflict concerns Groves's discovery in September 1942 that the University of Chicago scientists could make approximations only within a power of ten on the most basic questions. Instead of awaiting further scientific development, Groves concluded that the scientists were simply incompetent ("nincompoops," one informant remembered as his phrase) and used the circumstances as justification to move without them. The program would not wait for knowledge or accuracy; the scientists could catch up later (Groves, *Now It Can Be Told,* p. 40; Libby, *Uranium People,* pp. 90, 95–96). In his autobiography, Groves was quick to assert that his meeting with the Chicago scientists left him "with a very high opinion of the scientific attainments of the Chicago group" (p. 40); all other reports dispute this claim.

13. Manley, "A New Laboratory," pp. 29–31.

14. Concerning the road, see James W. Kunetka, *City of Fire: Los Alamos and the Birth of the Atomic Age, 1943–1945* (Englewood Cliffs, N.J.: Prentice-Hall, 1978), pp. 91–92; Truslow, *Nonscientific Aspects,* p. 24.

15. Truslow, *Nonscientific Aspects,* pp. 11–61. The housing conditions, interior and exterior, were photographed immediately after the war; these photographs are in the LASL and LAHS archives.

16. Jette, *Inside Box 1663,* p. 15; Marshak, "Secret City," p. 3.

17. Truslow, *Nonscientific Aspects,* pp. 11–61.

18. Marshak, "Secret City," p. 8.

19. MDH, bk. 8, vol. 2, 6.2.

20. Memo, Oppenheimer/David Dow[illegible] to General Groves, Sept. 20, 1944, document A-84-019-18-7, LASL; letter, E. Segre to Major McGavock, Dec. 18, 1943, document A-84-019-18-7; letter, McGavock to Segre, Dec. 16, 1943, in file A-84-019-18.

21. Marshall's diary entry for Sept. 24, 1942, is quoted in Jones, *Manhattan,* p. 434.

22. Jones, *Manhattan,* p. 434; see also "Notes on Conference in Dist. Office, 9:45 A.M. Oct. 26, 1942," in file MD 337, "Meetings and Conferences," box 28, RG 4nn-326-8505, NARD. The physical results of this early stage are best documented in the photographs made of the site; some are held in the Oak Ridge Children's Museum, some in the site progress reports files at NARD.

23. "Notes on Conference in District Office, 9:45 A.M., Oct. 26, 1942," in file MD 337, "Meetings and Conferences," box 28, RG 4nn-326-8505, NARD.

24. The exact numbers are confirmed in a letter, Blair to Klein/Stone and Webster, Dec. 18, 1942, file MD 624, "Housing," box 52, RG 4nn-326-8505, NARD.

25. "Notes on Conference in District Office, 9:45 A.M., Oct. 26, 1942," in file MD 337, "Meetings and Conferences," box 28, RG 4nn-326-8505, NARD.

26. The materials concerning Norris Village are held in the TVA files, NARD. See also Walter Creese, *TVA's Public Planning: The Vision, the Reality* (Knoxville: University of Tennessee Press, 1990), pp. 239–60.

27. Transcript of conversation between Klein and Marshall, Dec. 18, 1942, file MD 600.1, "Construction and Installations," box 41, RG 4nn-326-8505, NARD.

28. Capt. E. J. Bloch, "Conference with J. B. Pierce Foundation with Reference to Town Planning and Housing Development," Jan. 29, 1943, in file "Meetings and Conferences: J. B. Pierce Foundation," box 29, RG 4nn-326-8505, NARD.

29. Ibid.; letter, O'Brien to Capt. Bloch, Mar. 3, 1943, box 52, RG 4nn-326-8505, NARD; Lt. Col. Robert C. Blair, memorandum to the files, Feb. 10, 1943, file MD 600.1, "Construction and Installations," box 41, RG 4nn-326-8505, NARD.

30. Letter, Nichols to Russell T. Branch, Vice Pres., Stone and Webster, Feb. 17, 1943, file MD 600.1, box 41, RG 4nn-326-8505, NARD.

31. Warren George, "Report on Progress of Pierce Foundation Housing Group," Mar. 17, 1943, file MD 624, "Housing," box 52, RG 4nn-326-8505, NARD.

32. Nathaniel Owings, *The Spaces in Between: An Architect's Journey* (Boston: Houghton Mifflin, 1973), pp. 80–82.

33. *Completion Report: Portion of Townsite Planning of Oak Ridge, Tennessee . . .* (Oak Ridge: U.S. Engineer Office, Sept. 2, 1944).

34. Owings, *Spaces in Between,* p. 95.

35. Ibid., p. 93.

36. Ibid., p. 95.

37. Ibid., p. 93.

38. Ibid., p. 90.

39. The Hedrich-Blessing archive has been given to the Chicago Historical Society, to which the first of its negatives and files were transferred from the company's vaults in 1991.

40. *Housing for Clinton Engineer Works* (Oak Ridge: Clinton Engineer Works, 1943).

41. Jones, *Manhattan,* p. 130, 158, 178.

42. That revealing moment in the unveiling of Stone and Webster's housing plan on Oct. 26, 1942, speaks to this with unplanned eloquence:
"Discussion of access of workers to work area.
(1) Negroes to have separate clock alley opposite village."
"Notes on Conference in District Office, 9:45 A.M., October 26, 1942," MD 337 (District 6), X624, box 28, NARD.

43. MDH, bk. 4, vol. 3, pp. S-2–S-3.

44. Ibid., vol. 5, pp. 5.1–5.3. Du Pont had originally drawn three development plans; in all of them, housing sites were either too near the production facilities for operators to live safely, or too far for construction workers to travel efficiently between work and living quarters.

45. This decisionmaking process is described, in quite different terms, in the two military histories of the District—MDH, bk. 4, vol. 5, and Jones's *Manhattan* (pp. 450–51). The various original documents—the "Site Selection Criteria" list (see chapter 1, n. 10), the reports of the Mar. 2, 1943, meeting of Matthias and the Du Pont representatives, and Matthias's diary for the period up to the end of March—provide a different set of circumstances. Du Pont's own "Construction: Hanford Engineer Works" drew from Du Pont's minutes of another site-selection meeting, on Dec. 12, 1942, between the military and the Du Pont staff, at which "it was pointed out that the nature of the plant and the product to be manufactured required that no living or housing facilities could be located closer than 10 miles up-wind from a 105 or a 221 bldg. Although this condition was later modified in a letter from A. H. Compton of the University of Chicago, to 7 miles from a 221 building and three miles from a 105 building this,

naturally eliminated all possible sites in that portion of the project known as land Area 'A.'" (vol. 1, p. 102).

46. Du Pont, "Construction: Hanford Engineer Works," vol. 1, p. 87; Matthias diary, Mar. 2, 1943; "Memorandum of Conference, 4/1/43 Groves, Nichols, Matthias, Pardee, Daniels, Yancey, Roger Williams, Crawford Greenewalt," MD 600.1, "Construction and Installations," box 41, RG 4nn-326-8505, NARD.

47. Matthias diary, Mar. 2, 1943.

48. Ibid., Mar. 2, 3, 1943; memo, Church to Matthias, Mar. 11, 1943, MD 600.1, "Construction and Installations," box 41, RG 4nn-326-8505, NARD; memo, Major J. E. Travis to Nichols, "Hanford Engineer Works Townsite," Apr. 19, 1943, file MD 337, "Meetings and Conferences Clinton Engineer Works [sic]," box 28, RG 4nn-326-8505, NARD.

49. G. Albin Pehrson [actual author unknown], "Report on the Hanford Engineer Works Village," Nov. 1943, pp. 5–6; letter, Church to Pehrson, Mar. 16, 1943; both in Hanford Science Center.

50. Pehrson, "Report," p. 1.

51. On the matter of the philosophy behind the Richland plan, see the Du Pont "Construction: Hanford Engineer Works," esp. vol. 1, pp. 102–55. The Du Pont philosophy is threaded throughout the company's negotiations with the District proper, in the memos and reports previously cited, as well as in the daily meetings with Matthias, especially, recorded in his diary throughout 1943, 1944, and into 1945. It is also described in Pehrson's "Report."

52. Pehrson, "Report," p. 42.

53. Ibid.

54. Ibid., p. 27.

55. Ibid., p. 1.

56. Ibid., pp. 51–52.

57. Groves's beliefs are found in his spontaneous comments at various meetings at which the Richland plans were hashed out or presented for approval, including the meeting of Apr. 1, 1943, where the original plan came up for review. See especially "Notes of Conference, 4/1/43 Groves, Nichols, Matthias, Pardee, Daniels, Yancey, Roger Williams, Crawford Greenewalt," file MD337, "Meetings and Conferences Clinton Engineer Works [sic]," box 29, RG 4nn-326-8505, NARD. Something of the battle can be found by looking at Pehrson's own defense, in his "Report," pp. 55–56. See also Matthias's diary entries in which he records negotiating among the various players in the controversy, esp. those for Apr. 12, 16, 17, June 24, July 23, 26, 1943.

58. See esp. Matthias diary, July 23, 1943.

59. See Matthias, diary, Apr. 12, 16, June 24, 1943; Du Pont's appeal to satisfy "qualified workers" came on April 16, and by the nineteenth, Matthias had caved in, approving more large houses. But even as this compromise was reached, Matthias discovered that Du Pont's Engineering Department had illicitly upgraded the specs for wiring and electrical fixtures in the houses. Groves was obsessed by the issue of downscaling Du Pont's profligate plans; throughout June 1943 he spent much of his time kvetching to Matthias about the intransigence of Du Pont designers, and browbeating Du Pont's Wilmington planner Yancey to downgrade the buildings. See Matthias's entry for June 27, 1943, especially.

60. MDH, bk. 4, vol. 5, pp. 5.1–5.8.

61. Ibid., bk. 5, vol. 5, p. 5.

62. Ibid., pp. 5, 5.6; see the following chapter for a more detailed discussion of the segregation of the sites.

63. Johnson, quoted in Sanger, *Hanford and the Bomb,* p. 85; Ted Van Arsdol, *Hanford: The Big Secret* (Richland: Columbia Basin News, 1958), pp. 50–51.

64. The lyrics come from a recording made by Maj. William Sapper, Colonel Matthias's principal assistant. The recordings are held by Major Sapper's grandson, Jay Needham, who kindly allowed me to transcribe them. Needham is working on a large multimedia project using these and other recordings, as well as additional materials, from the Hanford site.

65. Much has been written about emissions and their human consequences at Hanford. See

especially Daniel P. Grossman, "A Policy History of Hanford's Atmospheric Releases" (Ph.D. diss., Massachusetts Institute of Technology, 1994); on groundwater contamination, see Michael James Graham, "Hydrogeochemical and Mathematical Analyses of Aquifer Intercommunication, Hanford Site, Washington State" (Ph.D. diss., Indiana University, 1983), and Daniel Kao Sun Ting, "The Far Field Migration of Radionuclides in Groundwater through Geologic Media" (Ph.D. diss., University of California, Berkeley, 1981). A scientifically astute and complete analysis of the entire Hanford emissions history is found in Michele Stenehjem Gerber, *On the Home Front: The Cold War Legacy of the Hanford Nuclear Site* (Lincoln: University of Nebraska Press, 1992).

66. These films are still held by the successor to the Manhattan Engineer District's Richland headquarters—the Richland facility of the Department of Energy—where they are retained in the restricted areas of the facility. Some have been released through Freedom of Information requests; pieces of these were included, for example, in Noel Buckner and Rob Whittlesey's documentary film on Hanford, *The Bomb's Lethal Legacy,* WGBH/Nova, Boston, 1990. In addition, a number of them are held in uncatalogued form at the Hanford Science Center.

67. Fine and Remington, *Corps of Engineers,* p. 681; Libby, *Uranium People,* p. 167.

68. Regarding offsite housing, see Matthias diary, Sept. 1, 1943. On the Hanford Camp, see the Du Pont "Construction: Hanford Engineer Works," vol. 1, p. 87; MDH, bk. 4, vol. 5, pp. 4.2–4.5; Jones, *Manhattan,* pp. 453–56 (Jones's description of an orderly and safe community [p. 455] pertains to a different time and a different part of the Hanford Camp—see below); Fine and Remington, *Corps of Engineers,* p. 681.

69. MDH, bk. 5, vol. 5, pp. 5, 5.8.

70. Matthias diary, Apr. 14, 23, May 6, 13, 20, 1943. Copies of the recruiting pamphlets are located in the scrapbooks and uncatalogued folders in the Public Information Office of the Richland facility of the DOE.

71. Matthias diary, May 18, Sept. 1, 1943.

72. Du Pont, "Construction: Hanford Engineer Works," vol. 1, pp. 86–90. Jones reports that "Du Pont and the Army decided reluctantly to permit them in the trailer camps and provided schools for their children, but the policy remained to discourage family groups" (Jones, *Manhattan,* pp. 461–62). See also Matthias diary, May 6, 18, June 3, Aug. 21, 1943.

73. Du Pont, "Construction: Hanford Engineer Works," vol. 1, p. 86.

74. Interview with Robley Johnson, Sept. 11, 1990.

75. Letter, Capt. Samuel Baxter to SOM and Andrews, Nov. 12, 1943, file 624, box 52, RG 4nn-326-8505, NARD. On the search for trailers, see summary of conversation between Warren George and R. K. Creighton, NHA Regional Director, Atlanta, May 21, 1943, file 624, box 52, RG 4nn-326-8505, NARD. The one-every-thirty-minutes statistic is from George O. Robinson, *The Oak Ridge Story* (Kingsport, Tenn.: Southern Publishers, 1950), pp. 49–50.

76. Letter, Kelley to James Ellis, Ass't Works MGR, TEC, Sept. 15, 1943, file 624, box 5, RG 4nn-326-8505, NARD.

77. Memo, Kelley to Nichols, file 624, box 5, RG 4nn-326-8505, NARD.

78. Owings, *Spaces in Between,* pp. 96–97.

79. George O. Robinson Jr., public relations officer, report, "Public Relations Procedure and Problems at Clinton Engineer Works," Aug. 14, 1944, box 10, RG 4nn-326-8505, NARD. Robinson's *Oak Ridge Story,* published immediately after the war, was the first history of Oak Ridge; appropriately enough, Robinson didn't mention his particular responsibilities with the District, or the fact that the book was itself a direct extension of those responsibilities.

80. Jones, *Manhattan,* p. 150.

81. On this expansion, see the SOM *Completion Report;* see also Jones, *Manhattan,* pp. 437–39.

82. Owings, *Spaces in Between,* p. 97.

83. The nicknames for the ridge cemesto communities were recorded by Johnson and Jackson, *City behind a Fence,* p. 105.

CHAPTER 5: COMPARTMENTALIZATION

1. Letters, Jan. 25 and 27, 1943, file 601, "Request for Easement, Sherman F. Owen, Tract E-416," box 5, RG 4nn-326-8505, NARD. It is from these letters that the subsequent quotes are drawn. Some information on Owen's farm is scattered in the condemnation and land acquisition records, boxes 6 and 7, N3-326-87-07, NARD.

2. Ibid.; Waller's was another of the prosperous farms, valued at 2,919, with fifteen structures on the site, including a large frame house.

3. These various administrative units are described in the elaborate organizational charts the District obligated each of its areas to produce and reproduce every time a new institutional entity was created. They are strewn throughout the District records; an idealized description of the program as of August 1943 is found in chart 2 of Jones, *Manhattan,* opposite p. 90.

4. But for George, such a determination was a logical one. Institutions and bureaucracies could be understood and controlled. Individuals could not.

5. Letter, Jan. 27, 1943, file 601, "Request for Easement, Sherman F. Owen, Tract E-416," box 5, RG 4nn-326-8505, NARD. The quotation in the next paragraph is from this same source.

6. See Robinson, *Oak Ridge Story,* pp. 77–78; Jones, *Manhattan,* pp. 141–42.

7. This story is drawn from an interview a local journalist, Ted Van Arsdol, did for the *Columbia Basin News* in 1958, later assembled into his *Hanford: The Big Secret,* pp. 65–70. The interviews were apparently heavily rewritten by Van Arsdol. In this interview, for example, Yvette Berry is quoted as "blurting" out questions to the "personable young recruiter," and as telling Van Arsdol, "I thought I was Lady Macbeth washing away imaginary blood," when describing the process of washing up after work. Corrupted as they are, however, the interviews provide glimpses, like this one, into the early days of construction and production.

8. Van Arsdol, *Hanford: The Big Secret,* p. 69.

9. Jones, *Manhattan,* pp. 269–70; Libby, *Uranium People,* p. 179.

10. Libby, *Uranium People,* p. 179; the punishments for infractions are detailed in numerous security documents held in the Hanford Science Center.

11. Groves, *Now It Can Be Told,* p. 140. The Groves testimony is included in the transcripts of the Oppenheimer security hearing, published as *In the Matter of J. Robert Oppenheimer: Transcript of Hearing before Personnel Security Board and Texts of Principal Documents and Letters* (Cambridge, Mass.: MIT Press, 1971).

12. The photograph is held in the collection of the Hanford Office, DOE, Richland. It is reproduced in Jones, *Manhattan,* p. 215.

13. MDH, bk. 4, vol. 5, p. 5.1 and appendix B-2.

14. Having to cover an average distance of 60 miles daily, and with mandated six-day workweeks, each car would travel nearly 1,500 miles a month; the highest gasoline appropriation allowed by the Office of Price Administration was 225 miles a month. See the chart marked as appendix B-2 in MDH, bk. 4, vol. 5.

15. Eventually, federal money to compensate local school boards for new pupils would be forthcoming; but when tiny districts had to increase their teaching staffs tenfold, with equivalent increases in school classrooms, initial outlay was catastrophically high, and reimbursement was traditionally slow.

16. See, for example, the report titled "No. 1 Job Priority: Thousands of War Project Workers, Hundreds of Tradesmen Are Sought for Richland, Wash. Job Recruiting Is Difficult," *Business Week,* July 1, 1944, pp. 22–23.

17. The nature of this document is defined in MDH, bk. 1, vol. 12, pp. 1.5–1.6.

18. This account is a composite from three sources; Leonard's own report on the meeting, as recorded by Johnson and Jackson, *City behind a Fence,* pp. 48–49 (the original memo disappeared in the transfer of files from Oak Ridge to NARD); Nichols's *Road to Trinity,* pp. 99–100, 116–18; and Groves's memoir, *Now It Can Be Told,* pp. 26–27.

19. This account is drawn almost entirely from Nichols's reminiscence, *Road to Trinity,* pp. 115–18.

20. Ibid., pp. 119.

21. Ibid., p. 120.

22. MDH, bk. 4, vol. 6, p. 10.

23. Solway and Edgemoor bridges lay just outside the Clinton Engineer Works, on roads through the regions now appropriated by the District. These routes became, in the eyes of locals, roads to nowhere, eliminating important access across the valley regions and between the hinterlands and the nearest important city—Knoxville. The extraordinarily complex process by which local officials fought back is recorded, in somewhat garbled form, in Nichols, *Road to Trinity,* pp. 117–19; I have depended on the reconstruction of documents held in the Oak Ridge Children's Museum, confirmed by Johnson and Jackson, in *City behind a Fence,* pp. 60–63, which draws on the original documents, some of which I have seen at the National Archives, others of which are held in the Oak Ridge Children's Museum, Oak Ridge, Tennessee.

24. On the Bonneville Power Administration's role, see Oregon Representative Homer Angell's speech in favor of increasing the appropriation for the BPA, *Congressional Record,* Apr. 27, 1944, p. 3815: "it will consume more power than Portland, representing a population of around a half-million." The reclamation project was an interesting case of a previous era's governmental programs now working against the needs of the District. In Depression times, the project had promised federally funded irrigation waters and a bureau-constructed irrigation canal, to run northward of the Columbia along the so-called Wahluke Slope. But the section of the project condemned by the District sliced across the proposed irrigation canal, halting all development. And the closing of the state road through the slope placed a wall between the farming area and the prime market city of Yakima due west. On the reclamation project, see MDH, bk. 4, vol. 6, sec. 10.

25. A letter of thanks from the chief engineer of the BPA to Colonel Matthias in late October 1943 made clear the relationship between Bonneville and the MED. See Schultz, Chief Engineer of BPA, to Matthias, Oct. 22, 1943, in Matthias diary for same date. A meeting on Oct. 23, 1943 is particularly edifying. Its subject was a bridge or crossing for a new irrigation ditch that had been constructed to circumvent the Hanford site and replace the lost canal of the Columbia Basin Project. The function of the ditch was to keep farmers who were already dependent on Columbia River irrigation from losing their water—and their farms and livelihoods. Attached to the proposal was a plan for a road that would allow farm-to-market access. The meeting brought together the Federal Bureau of Reclamation (which built the ditch), the Roads Department of Washington, the federal Public Roads Administration, and Hanford officials. There it was Colonel Matthias who engineered an agreement: the state would complete road construction; the Bureau of Reclamation and the District would provide the engineering (with the District in charge, of course); the Bureau of Reclamation would supply the concrete necessary for the road; and the Public Roads Administration would pay for it all. It was a perfect solution; the District controlled the program, paid little or nothing, in money, land, or ceded authority, and left local officials and individual farmers and residents supplicated but not empowered.

26. Matthias diary, Feb. 25, 1944.

27. On the responses to regions surrounding the Tennessee site, see the "Knoxville-Clinton, Tennessee, Progress Report II," prepared by the Federal Security Agency's Office of Community War Services, Region 7, Oct. 14, 1944. A copy is held in file MD 624, NARD.

28. For the Tennessee site, see the "Progress Reports" of the Federal Security Agency's Office of Community War Services, dated Feb. 1, May 20, and Oct. 14, 1944, and held in file MD 624, NARD. For Hanford, evidence of nearly identical programs is found in the daily notes of programs and reports filed by the HEW, and of meetings with local, state and federal officials, dotting the Matthias diary.

29. "Knoxville-Clinton, Tennessee, Progress Report II," Oct. 14, 1944, p. iv., file MD 624, NARD.

30. Army Corps of Engineers, "Memorandum on the Los Alamos Project," ca. 1943, reproduced in its entirety in Jette, *Inside Box 1663,* pp. 125–28; Oppenheimer, "Note on Security," May 22, 1943, LAHS archives.

31. Jane S. Wilson, "Not Quite Eden," in Wilson and Serber, *Standing By and Making Do,* pp. 44–45.

32. Jette, *Inside Box 1663,* p. 13; Marshak, "Secret City," p. 2; Jette, *Inside Box 1663,* p. 10.

33. As Oppenheimer explained it in a universally distributed memo in 1943, "if you are employed on the project you are not permitted to leave Los Alamos and its neighboring communities without special permission" (Robert Oppenheimer, "Memorandum on the Los Alamos Project," pp. 5–6, LASL archives).

34. On the boundaries, see Harlow W. Russ, *Project Alberta: The Preparation of Atomic Bombs for Use in World War II* (Los Alamos, N.M.: Exceptional Books, 1990), p. 5; Clint Gass's comments are found in the typescript "Reminiscences," LAHS. Oppenheimer's sole authority to allow visitors is detailed in a memo, "Authorization for Visits to Zia Site," Feb. 15, 1943, LASL archives. The District circular rescinding Oppenheimer's power is marked "District Circular, MED NY division, 5/8/43," box 1, "Protective Security," RG 326-83-007, NARD.

35. Transcript, untitled speech by McGibbon, LAHS archives.

36. Security Committee (Joseph Kennedy, David Hawkins, John Manley), "Memorandum," Oct. 5, 1943, p. 1, file A-84-019, 64-24, LASL archives.

37. Draft of letter, Lois Bradbury to her family, held in the LAHS, and published in the *LAHS Newsletter* 10, no. 4 (Dec. 1989): 2–6; the quotation is from page 3.

38. Security Committee "Memorandum," Oct. 5, 1943, p. 2. The security committee's experiments in fence-breaking were early examples of what became, at times, a residents' game: sneaking through the fences. One Los Alamosan speculated that the obvious holes in the perimeter remained, month after month, because the guards wanted to provide convenient access to otherwise interdicted visitors—prostitutes, perhaps, or maids, or children (Frisch, *What Little I Remember,* p. 154).

39. Richard Feynman, "Los Alamos from Below," in Badash, Hirschfelder, and Broida, *Reminiscences,* p. 115.

40. The letter is reproduced in Phyllis K. Fisher, *Los Alamos Experience* (Tokyo: Japan Publications, 1985), pp. 46–47.

41. Letter, Blair to Klein, Jan. 21, 1943, box 53, RG 4nn-326-8505, NARD. Major Warren George, who supervised an earlier perimeter fence report, called for "650 . . . trespass signs . . . 3 feet by 5 feet . . . of a permanent type of construction . . . with spacing of 500 feet" ("Perimeter Fencing Report," undated, box 53, RG 4nn-326-8505, NARD); letter, W. R. Burton, Tennessee Eastman Corporation, to Kelley, Apr. 13, 1943, box 53, RG 4nn-326-8505, NARD.

42. Phyllis K. Fisher recounts the distinction between badges, in *Los Alamos Experience,* p. 40.

43. See Matthias diary, Sept. 7, 1943.

44. Ibid.

45. Libby, *Uranium People,* pp. 174–75.

46. See the MED's undated recruitment brochure, titled *Here's Hanford,* esp. photograph captioned "HEW buses take you to and from your job and operate in the Hanford Area for your convenience free of charge—for example they take you from your barracks to the movies and the dances." Petcher's recollections are found in Sanger, *Hanford and the Bomb,* pp. 76–77.

47. Transportation plans for the area involved a highway grid for autos, bus service, and some rail service using existing rail lines. Rail service, however, was entirely planned for transcontinental travelers, recruits arriving from all over, who would exit at Pasco. Local transportation was planned based on buses and cars, and in the process, the lines between private and public were significantly blurred. Not only did the District supervise road improvements for autos, but they also turned over many of their own passenger buses to private lines "in an effort to keep that private service up to the required capacity" (Matthias diary, Nov. 16, 1943).

48. A series of photographs of the Y-12 area, as well as some descriptions of its site, appear in MDH, bk. 5, vol. 1, appendix B.

49. Robinson (*Oak Ridge Story,* p. 78) reports these statistics on the Y-12 facility, drawn from

press releases after the site went public; see also MDH, bk. 5, vol. 3, appendix C, from which the quote is drawn.

50. MDH, bk. 5, vol. 6, p. 7.3.

51. Ibid., bk. 1, vol. 7, p. 2.7.

52. On the interiors, see, for example, the photograph C3, captioned "Vacuum Distillation (Sublimation), Bldg. 9202," and with the legend "Still and associated equipment as used in Alpha feed preparation," in MDH, bk. 5, vol. 3, appendix C. On the liquid diffusion plant, see ibid., bk. 6, vol. 4, sec. 4.

53. Libby, *Uranium People*, p. 171.

54. MDH, bk. 6, vol. 4, sec. 4.

55. Ibid., bk. 4, vol. 6, sec. 2; the flow circuit chart appears in bk. 4, vol. 6, sec. A-11.

56. The medical literature on the radiation exposure level is aptly summed up in Barton C. Hacker's *The Dragon's Tail: Radiation Safety in the Manhattan Project, 1942–1946* (Berkeley: University of California Press, 1987), pp. 21–27; see also Robert Spencer Stone, ed., *Industrial Medicine on the Plutonium Project* (New York: McGraw-Hill, 1951); Averill A. Liebow et al., "Pathology of Atomic Bomb Casualties," *American Journal of Pathology* 25, no. 5 (1949): 853–1027.

57. Sanger has interviewed the fisheries expert Donaldson and reports on the icthyologist Foster's experiences in *Hanford and the Bomb*, pp. 184–85. See MDH, bk. 1, vol. 7, pp. 5.13–5.14; see also Matthias diary, Mar. 30, 31, May 10, 1944; Sanger, *Hanford and the Bomb*, pp. 181–85.

58. MDH, bk. 1, vol. 6, 2.16–2.18; Foster, quoted in Sanger, *Hanford and the Bomb*, pp. 184–85.

59. Foster's report, presented to the State of Washington Ecological Commission in Richland on Dec. 15, 1970, is selectively quoted in Sanger, *Hanford and the Bomb*, pp. 184–85. In the mid-1990s, the federal government, in concert with the state of Washington, began a larger "dose reconstruction project"; data on that project is available through the numerous newsletters and regular reports that have been issued, all of which are held at the Hanford Science Center.

60. Groves, *Now It Can Be Told*, p. 83; MDH, bk. 1, vol. 7, p. 5.13–5.14.

61. Letter, Matthias to Groves, quoted in Sanger, *Hanford and the Bomb*, p. 182.

62. Genereaux's reminiscence appears in Sanger, *Hanford and the Bomb*, pp. 42–46. The chemical-separation program itself is well described in Hewlett and Anderson, *New World*, pp. 219–22, 309, and 374; significantly, there is no mention of the fate of waste byproducts. The program is extremely well analyzed in Gerber's *On the Home Front*. Gerber's book, by far the most balanced and sophisticated analysis of the Hanford environmental disaster, appeared after the bulk of my research and two early drafts of this book had been completed. I have relied on her work to clarify and complete my analysis of the documents.

63. Genereaux, in Sanger, *Hanford and the Bomb*, p. 45; MDH, bk. 4, vol. 6, pp. 2.20–2.24. Gerber has reviewed the scientific apologia for these propositions in *On the Home Front*. Her conclusions are perhaps best summed up in the aphorism that begins her chapter on groundwater contamination (p. 143): it is the Hanford hydrologist Randall Brown's comment that "we used to have a joke that there was no sense in doing a percolation test because you couldn't drop to your knees fast enough to measure any water before it all disappeared into the ground."

64. MDH, bk. 4, vol. 6, 18.62, 2.20–23.

65. The story of the hydrogen-bubbling dangers remains one of the most powerful in the annals of atomic muckraking. The District's successors eventually admitted that this was sufficiently dangerous that they halted some recovery programs, but only after years of official denials and punitive reassignments of scientists and engineers who pointed out the dangers.

66. MDH, bk. 4, vol. 6, 18.62; the weld joints are discussed more fully later in this chapter.

67. Ibid., 18.62, 2.24, 4.20–4.21. Gerber's *On the Home Front* describes in detail the internal documents concerning the search for dilution.

68. In fact, the final programs ended up jetting amounts of radioactive and toxic waste into

Columbia River water, where it was taken up by the water systems of nearby towns like Pasco and Kennewick (Kennewick didn't even have water treatment during the early fifties), channeled into the river bed, and carried to the sea, where it had measurable effect on ocean mollusks and other sea life up and down the Washington and Oregon shorelines. See Gerber, *On the Home Front,* pp. 115, 127, 129, 131, 137, and passim.

69. Matthias diary, Jan. 5, 1944, reports on the meeting with Preload.

70. Ibid., Apr. 5, 1944.

71. Ibid., May 27, 1944.

72. Ibid.

73. MDH, bk. 4, vol. 6, 18.62; Matthias diary, May 27, 1944.

74. Matthias diary, Aug. 27, 1944.

75. Ibid., Sept. 5, 1944.

76. Ibid., Feb. 24, 1943; MDH, bk. 4, vol. 6, p. 9.8.

77. MDH, bk. 4, vol. 6, pp. 4.20–4.21.

78. This particular incident is described, albeit circumspectly, in MDH, bk. 4, vol. 6, pp. 4.20–4.21.

79. Memo, Stafford L. Warren to District Engineer, Oct. 25, 1944, held in file 700.2, "Medical Records," box 54, RG 4nn-326-8505, NARD.

80. MDH, bk. 4, vol. 6, appendix A, p. A-70.

81. "Memorandum to the File: Meteorological Studies at H.E.W.," p. 3, held in "Miscellaneous Files" boxes, Hanford Operations Office, Richland DOE facility.

82. Ibid.

83. Notes attached to the set of aerial views state they were made at intervals of as short as three days throughout May and on June 1 and 3, 1944. See notes and photographs, held in the miscellaneous files at the Hanford Science Center.

84. "Memorandum to the File: Meteorological Studies at H.E.W.," p. 6, "Miscellaneous Files" boxes, Hanford Operations Office, Richland DOE facility; see also the report of Roger Hultgren, a member of the meteorological team, in Sanger, *Hanford and the Bomb,* pp. 182–83.

85. Matthias diary, Feb. 21, 1944.

86. Ibid., Mar. 1, 1944.

87. "Operation of Hanford Engineer Works, Memorandum for the File: 200 Areas—Isolation Operations to July 1, 1945," typescript, Aug. 22, 1945, p. 3, Reading Room, Hanford Science Center.

88. "Continuous operation of this system is vital to the safe operation of the process hoods, since an interruption in service would permit production-contaminated air to escape outside the vessels and process hoods" (ibid.).

89. Libby, *Uranium People,* p. 174.

90. Ibid.

91. See MDH, bk. 4, vol. 6, p. 5.14; see also Sanger, *Hanford and the Bomb,* p. 183.

92. *Draft Air Pathway Report: Phase I of the Hanford Environmental Dose Reconstruction Project* (Richland, Wash.: Pacific Northwest Laboratory, for the Hanford Environmental Dose Reconstruction Project, July 1990) reports that the possibility of transport through milk was not reported until 1956 and 1957 (p. 1.7). This is surprising, considering that the coyote studies were already exploring food-chain transportation.

93. Berry is quoted in Van Arsdol, *Hanford: The Big Secret,* pp. 65–70.

94. At Richland, the prefab builders filled one out of every six-or-so houses with the furniture for all of them and then distributed the furnishings (those that weren't broken by rough travel) when the shipment arrived.

95. Johnson and Jackson (*City behind a Fence,* pp. 103–5) mention this process of distinguishing neighborhoods by class.

96. Du Pont, "Construction: Hanford Engineer Works," vol. 1, p. 88.

97. Los Alamos *Bulletin,* Dec. 8, 1943; "Olympic Commissary Operations," in "Miscellaneous Files," Richland Science Center; Du Pont, "Construction: Hanford Engineer Works," vol. 1, pp. 113–14. Matthias's comments are from his diary, May 26, 1943.

98. *Highlights of Hanford,* unpaginated. Colonel Matthias worked hard to make this distinction even more prominent, by arranging to have one of the cafeterias turned into an executive dining area for "office people and other casuals. This may be converted to permit the preparation of meals more suitable for office workers and to permit adjustments in prices for office workers" (Matthias diary, June 22, 1943).

99. See Matthias diary, June 10, 1943 entry; Johnson and Jackson, *City behind a Fence,* pp. 105–6. The Matthias diary entry for June 28, 1943, reports that Du Pont's Yancey told Matthias he had argued in a meeting with Groves that "people out here would not be satisfied unless they had at least the bare essentials of normal small cities."

CHAPTER 6: WORKERS

1. Comparison figures come from Eli Ginzberg and Hyman Berman, *The American Worker in the Twentieth Century* (New York: Free Press/Macmillan, 1963) pp. 266–67, except for the number of army soldiers at Okinawa, which comes from Ron E. Appleman et al., *Okinawa: The Last Battle* (Washington, D.C.: Historical Division, Department of the Army, 1948), appendix C, table 1, p. 488; the District's employee numbers (the exact figure is 125,310) come from MDH, bk. 1, vol. 8, appendix A-1. See also George Q. Flynn, *The Mess in Washington: Manpower Mobilization in World War II* (Westport, Conn.: Greenwood, 1979), pp. 189–91. Vincent Jones calculates the peak at 129,000, with 84,500 construction workers, 40,500 operating employees, 1,800 military, and "an equal number of civil service employees" (Jones, *Manhattan,* p. 344).

2. The literature on labor-management relations is wide and deep. I have depended upon two seminal (if opposed) texts: Nelson Lichtenstein's *Labor's War at Home: The CIO in World War II* (Cambridge: Cambridge University Press, 1982) and Howell John Harris's *The Right to Manage: Industrial Relations Policies of American Business in the 1940s* (Madison: University of Wisconsin Press, 1982). Robert H. Zieger's *American Workers, American Unions, 1920–1985* (Baltimore: Johns Hopkins University Press, 1986) is a general survey written from a labor perspective; it includes a solid chapter on the wartime years, "The Unions Go to War," pp. 62–99. Herbert Northrup and Gordon Bloom, *Government and Labor: The Role of Government in Union-Management Relations* (Homewood, Ill.: Richard D. Irwin, 1963), offers a gloss on the role of government in managing labor markets. Melvyn Dubofsky's edited anthology, *American Labor since the New Deal* (Chicago: Quadrangle, 1971), provides valuable primary sources from the era. Allan M. Winkler's *Home Front U.S.A.: America during World War II* (Arlington Heights, Ill.: Harlan Davidson, 1986), has a brief general discussion in the first chapter, "The Arsenal of Democracy."

3. Harris, *Right to Manage,* pp. 23–40; Sanford M. Jacoby, *Employing Bureaucracy: Managers, Unions, and the Transformation of Work in American Industry, 1900–1945* (New York: Columbia University Press, 1985), pp. 223–39, 241–60.

4. Jacoby, *Employing Bureaucracy,* esp. pp. 207–75. See also Zieger, *American Workers, American Unions,* pp. 35–74; Winkler, *Home Front U.S.A.,* pp. 10–23.

5. Jacoby, *Employing Bureaucracy,* pp. 262–74; Harris, *Right to Manage,* pp. 37–44; Lichtenstein, *Labor's War,* pp. 26–66.

6. A brief survey of the relations among military, industrial, and union forces during the war is Paul A. C. Koistinen's "Mobilizing the World War II Economy: Labor and the Industrial-Military Alliance," *Pacific Historical Review* 42, no. 4 (Nov. 1973): 443–78. Condensing his dissertation ("The Hammer and the Sword: Labor, the Military, and Industrial Mobilization, 1920–1945" [University of California, Berkeley, 1964]), Koistinen's article provides an excellent overview of the broader circumstances within which the Manhattan Engineer District was both an example and a special case. Koistinen's argument—that, finally, the labor unions came out of the war less rather than more powerful, despite the illusions of inclusion at the tables of power—is confirmed by the MED.

7. The national context for the District's labor battles is ably discussed in Flynn's *Mess in Washington.*

8. Richard Polenberg, *War and Society: The United States, 1941–1945* (Philadelphia: Lippincott, 1972), pp. 20–22; Jacoby, *Employing Bureaucracy*, pp. 262–69; Byron Fairchild and Jonathan Grossman, *The Army and Industrial Manpower* (Washington, D.C.: Office of the Chief of Military History, Department of the Army, 1959), pp. 131–49. Matthias reported on the attempts by competing labor markets to close Hanford; diary, June 27, 1943.

9. On the statistics of labor recruitment at Hanford, see Du Pont, "Construction: Hanford Engineer Works," vol. 1, passim. An ad placed in the Baton Rouge *State Times Morning Advocate* suggested how successfully local interests were able to manipulate the system. Appearing twenty-four times between mid-November and mid-December 1943, the ad called for carpenters and laborers on a "Pacific Northwest Construction Project"—Hanford. But near the bottom of the advertisement was a caveat: "NOTICE TO LOCAL EMPLOYERS Should you require the services of workers listed above, please call the local U.S. Employment Service Office and your order will be given preference over the employer sponsoring this advertisement, if you have a priority which equals the one held by this employer" (Du Pont, "Construction: Hanford Engineer Works," vol. 1, p. 59). Matthias reports the recruiting failures at Hanford in his diary entry for Sept. 23, 1943.

10. MDH, bk. 4, vol. 5, appendix D, p. 6.; Jones, *Manhattan*, p. 352.

11. A Matthias diary entry for June 28, 1943, reports on a meeting at which the outlines of the plan were hammered out for Hanford recruiters. As Matthias noted there, "no clearance for employment from any other sources will be honored in those areas" where a labor surplus had been indicated.

12. Matthias (diary, Nov. 2, 1943) recounts the meeting in Washington at which this was worked out.

13. Complaints from District officials concerning the unwillingness of USES officials to follow protocol are scattered in the District files. See also the reports of resistance in the Du Pont "Construction: Hanford Engineer Works," vol. 1, pp. 55–60, and passim.

14. At Hanford, the plan had been to hire three hundred workers a week for the last six months of 1943. By the end of October, Hanford's Colonel Matthias reported in his diary that each of Du Pont's field recruiters was getting just over three recruits per day. Through the summer and fall, Du Pont had dealt with the low success rate by increasing the number of recruiters. But the labor requirement had leaped, and recruiting continued to fall behind. Matthias diary, Sept. 23, Oct. 12, 1943.

15. Ibid., June 7, Oct. 20, 1943; MDH, bk. 1, vol. 8, sec. 2.

16. Each region of the nation would be "allotted a certain number of people of each craft, and . . . each region . . . told that they are expected to produce that many" (Matthias diary, Sept. 9, 1943).

17. On union locals and "Internationals," see Leonard R. Sayles and George Strauss, *The Local Union: Its Place in the Industrial Plant* (New York: Harper, 1953), esp. pp. 3–4, 7, 65–69. Lichtenstein describes the conflict between local and "international" organizations by focusing on the Brewster Aeronautical Corporation conflicts and the clash between the CIO and Local 365; see Lichtenstein, *Labor's War*, esp. pp. 127–35. See also Bruno Stein, "Labor's Role in Government Agencies," *Journal of Economic History* 17 (1957): 389–408, and Nelson Lichtenstein, "Ambiguous Legacy: The Union Security Problem during World War II," *Labor History* 18 (1977): 214–38; Lichtenstein's position is also represented in a review essay by Joshua Freeman, "Delivering the Goods: Industrial Unionism during World War II," *Labor History* 19 (1978): 570–93, esp. 572–74.

18. After the September meeting with Flaherty, Matthias reported that "it was also felt that the heads of the Unions involved should be contacted by Colonel Barker's office or by Mr. Flaherty and also by du Pont Company to enlist their aid in sending men to this project" (Matthias diary, Sept. 9, 1943).

19. Lichtenstein gives some idea of the ways that union-local stridency and activism impelled the NWLB and the CIO in particular into each others' arms; see *Labor's War*, pp. 131–35.

20. Matthias reported as early as September 1 that Major Jacobs, a labor specialist, had found

steamfitters, plumbers, and carpenters via the "International Union headquarters" and "he was going to check with the WMC immediately to find out what arrangements can be worked out to insure that we obtain the labor we need. He will report to us any pools of available labor for which clearances can be obtained." On September 2, Matthias called Jacobs "concerning the labor recruiting program. He has not been wholly successful in lining up labor and skilled craft pools through the unions. He has, however, been working with the WMC to get the same priority on skilled crafts that we had for labor" (Matthias diary, Sept. 1, 2, 1943). The decision to leave the WMC out of the equation came in a Oct. 6, 1943, diary entry.

21. Lichtenstein, *Labor's War*, pp. 127–35. Sayles and Strauss, *The Local Union*, is a valuable primary source on union locals. A textbook on industrial management and industrial relations, it is loaded with anecdotes and interview materials with workers. Also useful, though more clearly a product of the postwar years, is Arnold S. Tannenbaum and Robert L. Kahn, *Participation in Union Locals* (Evanston, Ill.: Row, Peterson, 1958).

22. The Charles O. Walgreen Foundation Lecture delivered by Charles O. Gregory at the University of Chicago in 1943 is a remarkable document concerning the ways that labor rights were curtailed by wartime conditions. It was republished as "Law and Labor Relations in Wartime," in *War and the Law,* ed. Ernst W. Puttkammer (Chicago: University of Chicago Press, 1944), pp. 92–116. A general analysis is found in Polenberg, *War and Society,* pp. 20–27. See also Lichtenstein, *Labor's War,* esp. pp. 178–202.

23. Fairchild and Grossman, *Army and Industrial Manpower,* pp. 129–31.

24. Ibid., pp. 129–30.

25. See MDH, bk. 1, vol. 8, appendix B.

26. Ibid., bk. 4, vol. 5, sec. 4; ibid., bk. 1, vol. 8, secs. S, 2; Jones, *Manhattan,* pp. 344–48.

27. On the Brown-Patterson program, see MDH, bk. 1, vol. 8, appendix B; ibid., bk. 4, vol. 5, pp. 4.7–4.10. A further analysis of the Certificate of Availability Program follows.

28. Brown-Patterson was what the District termed an "extraordinary" stage in the larger process of recruitment and retention. District officials later presented the plan as primarily voluntary on the part of workers, involving forced sacrifice by their original employers, who lost labor for ninety days and were obligated to retain seniority positions for those who went to Hanford. However, the agreement wasn't with employer associations but with the IBEW, and the reason lies in the way these workers were to be chosen—by direct intervention on the part of union workers, probably shop stewards on the designated "lower-priority" jobsites. District officials implied that they left the recruitment up to union representatives, but a passing reference to "selected Labor Relations Officers" who made "personal visits to union offices" suggests that pressure on the union officials formed the fulcrum to pry workers out of less-arduous work and into the high-pressure 54- and 60-hour weeks common in crisis-driven Hanford and Oak Ridge. Almost no information on the Brown-Patterson Agreement exists.

What remains mysterious about the Brown-Patterson Agreement was how union officials were able to persuade workers to leave. The answer probably lay in the slackening pace of employment as most other military construction programs reached completion, while civilian construction remained halted. By targeting job sites where work was nearing completion, union representatives had the threat of a hiring-hall freeze-out at their disposal. Go here now, they could say, and we will find you work now and later. Refuse, and your favored place in the hiring hall will be gone. In any case, the Brown-Patterson agreement unambiguously moved the labor unions into management's role, leaving only the increasingly spavined locals to stand up for workers' rights. (I am grateful to the political scientist and labor historian Peter Swenson for suggesting this hypothesis to me.) Certainly the District offered a sweetened travel arrangement to electricians and linemen: round-trip fare and a travel subsidy of $2.50 per day, plus "a certificate of service signed by the Under Secretary of War." (The *Manhattan District History* reports on the circumstances of the agreement but fails to mention just how workers were recruited. See MDH, bk. 4, vol. 5, pp. 4.7–4.13. See also the materials on labor recruiting in RG 4nn-326-8505, NARD, and discussions of labor in the Du Pont "Construction: Hanford Engineer Works.")

"This plan . . . was continued to provide replacements at Clinton Engineer Works," reported the District historian in 1946. Then, when Los Alamos needed 190 more machinists and toolmakers late in 1944, the War Manpower Commission followed the Brown-Patterson Agreement in sending a directive declaring all workers in these trades "available," even if their employers refused to release them. MDH, bk. 4, vol. 5, pp. 2.6, 4.10–4.15.; ibid., bk. 1, vol. 8, p. 2.6.

29. The ticketing provision is mentioned in a press release dated June 21, 1944; it appears as appendix B-7 in MDH, bk. 1, vol. 8.

30. See the recruiter-profile abstract in Sanger, *Hanford and the Bomb,* p. 48; see also the segments on recruiting in the MDH for each site.

31. Overstreet tells his own story in an interview in Sanger, *Hanford and the Bomb,* pp. 66–69.

32. Du Pont, "Construction: Hanford Engineer Works," vol. 1, p. 70.

33. Matthias *Diary,* entries for July 21, Aug. 5, 1943. The new treatment for workers was touted in *Dear Anne,* 1944 recruiting pamphlet, p. 2, "Miscellaneous Files," DOE, Richland Operations Office.

34. MDH, bk. 1, vol. 8, sec. 3 and appendix 5; the statistics for other wartime plants come from Fairchild and Grossman, *Army and Industrial Manpower,* p. 141.

35. Absentee statistics are found in the *Labor Status Reports,* in box 2, RG 4nn-326-8505, NARD. On August 3, 1943, for example, the Oak Ridge contractor, Stone and Webster, reported 29.2 percent of its nonskilled workers were absent on average at any given time in the past month; Clinton Home Builders, the housing subcontractor putting up SOM's designs, reported a similar rate, 25.1 percent.

36. The original memo concerning "exit interviews" is recapitulated in a longer "Office Bulletin #72," released by Blair's office in Knoxville on July 3, 1943, and held in box 7, RG 326-83-008, NARD. An optimistic description of the process is found in Jones, *Manhattan,* pp. 363–65.

37. See, for example, Van Arsdol, *Hanford: The Big Secret;* Robinson, *Oak Ridge Story;* Sanger, *Hanford and the Bomb;* and Johnson and Jackson, *City behind a Fence.*

38. MDH, bk. 1, vol. 8, secs. 3, 6, appendix A; see also Johnson and Jackson, *City behind a Fence,* pp. 90–92. On Hanford, see Matthias diary, Oct. 13, 1943. Unfortunately, the notes from these interviews have disappeared from the Hanford archive.

39. Johnson and Jackson, in fact, report that food was the number-one reason workers cited on exit interview forms. See *City behind a Fence,* p. 91.

40. See Matthias diary, Oct. 15, 1943, Jan. 7, 8, 1944.

41. Matthias diary, Oct. 11, 13, 1943.

42. File MD 600.914, "Records and Reports of Fires and Other Accidents," box 43, RG 4nn-326-8505, NARD. The second report was written by Maj. R. F. Gornall, the Area Protective Security Officer.

43. The crime, fire, and accident reports for the sites are loaded with these episodes; see file MD 600.914, "Records and Reports of Fires and Other Accidents," box 43, RG 4nn-326-8505, NARD. Robley Johnson mentioned the Hanford road's wrecks in an interview I held with him in September 1990.

44. Libby, *Uranium People,* p. 67; photographs in the Richland office of the Department of Energy show the crowds outside the Hanford tavern; see DeWitt Bailey's reminiscence in Sanger, *Hanford and the Bomb,* pp. 108–9, for a vivid description of the atmosphere inside.

45. MDH, bk. 1, vol. 8, p. 3; ibid., bk. 4, vol. 5, pp. 4.22–4.29. Leon Overstreet tells the story of the dentures in Sanger, *Hanford and the Bomb,* pp. 67–68.

46. Groves, memo to the Deputy Director of the Army Service Forces Production Division, Nov. 10, 1943, file 624, box 52, RG 4nn-326-8505, NARD.

47. Ibid.

48. Matthias diary, Oct. 11, 16, 1943.

49. See on this the "Manual of Operations—War Manpower Commission," Feb. 5, 1943, in box 1, RG 326-83-008, NARD. Once the chairman of the WMC had designated a workplace,

an industry, a trade, or even a geographical area to be "a critical labor shortage area," the directives asserted that "all hiring, rehiring, solicitation and recruitment of workers for specified employments shall be conducted solely through the United States Employment Service" or through a special program controlled by the WMC. "The Civil Service Commission will *not* approve for employment any new employee who, during the preceding 30-day period, was engaged in an essential activity, unless a statement of availability is secured from the employer or, where applicable, the United States Employment Service" (MED Circular, June 11, 1943, p. 1, NARD).

50. Ibid.; the quote is from the MED circular dated June 11, 1943, p. 1.

51. Lt. Col. John S. Hodgson, "Campaign to Obtain Maximum Labor Efficiency—Field and Office, Clinton Engineer Works," June 14, 1944, box 2, RG 326-83-008, NARD.

52. Over the life of the District, Intelligence and Security expanded at a furious pace. Recruits came from within and outside the District. Some were assigned to the security inspection of plants; some did undercover investigations of suspected subversives; some formed a secret army set with the task of protecting plants and sites, independent of the military police and the perimeter guards. At the same time, the Division spawned its own pyramid of bureaucracy.

And then there were the "creeps." This was an ironic term within the District hierarchy. To some, it meant simply those who worked in Security or its various offshoots. For others, it meant the counterintelligence forces, the spies and informers within the workplaces and living spaces, and the figures who were planted within the work and living environments for the purpose of cheerleading District goals and pushing from within for greater productivity, greater obedience, more patriotic behavior. Groves reported in *Now It Can Be Told* that there were 485 "creeps" by the end of the war; which definition he was using is unclear.

These were part of a surreptitious force of much greater size. If the Counterintelligence Corps's boast that one out of every thirty workers was an informant for military intelligence, then the District should have had as many as three thousand informants in its ranks. Certainly the range of informants' reports retained by the District confirms a vast network of secret observers—intelligence workers who not only reported but also acted to foment crisis where desired, to prevent it where desired.

Part of this program was based on a more imprecise and less conscious application of corporate paternalism to the workplaces and living environments. Similarly with the arguments over who should staff and supervise the plant security patrols. The corporations most experienced in operating company towns (Du Pont was the premiere corporation in this regard) were enthusiastic about expanding their own security forces to serve in this capacity. Within the district's reservations, these might not have been noticeable violations of the Pinkerton Act; there was the question of jurisdiction in such legal environments, and there was also the simple fact that the wider net of security and the programs of individual and press censorship would discourage awareness of the circumstances on the sites.

On the subject of wartime security generally, see Joan Jensen's *Army Surveillance in America, 1775–1980* (New Haven: Yale University Press, 1991), pp. 211–29. On the District's security apparatus, see Groves, *Now It Can Be Told*, pp. 138–40; Jones, *Manhattan*, pp. 254–58; MDH, bk. 1, vol. 14, pp. 7.7–7.8. A significant amount of raw documentation is found in NARD records; see, especially, box 7, RG 326-83-008.

53. These examples are drawn from cases discussed in various documents, including appeals, or from warnings by the District released in memos and circulars. See "Regulations Issued by the Chairman of the WMC on Apr. 18, 1943 in Conformity with Section 3 of Executive Order No. 9238"; "Manual of Operations—War Manpower Commission," Feb. 5, 1943; "Policy: Employment Stabilization Programs," Feb. 1, 1943; and sample "Statement of Availability" provided by Civil Service Commission for duplication by employing agencies, all in box 1, RG 326-83-008, NARD. See also memo dated July 20, 1945, in box 6, RG 326-83-008, NARD; "Public Proclamation #2," Mar. 25, 1943, and letter Nichols to Merritt, Feb. 19, 1944, in file CEW 624, "Housing—Policy in ORO facilities and Services Division," box 3, RG 326-83-008, NARD.

54. Du Pont, "Construction: Hanford Engineer Works," vol. 1, p. 70.

55. *Let's All HEW to the Line!* July 23, 1943 (second issue), p. 2.

56. See, for example, Matthias diary, Sept. 7, 8, 1944, for discussion of these tactics.

57. Harris emphasizes the response of management in this shift (*The Right to Manage,* pp. 58–60), citing Thomas Roy Jones's warning to the National Association of Manufacturers that they faced incipient labor-directed socialism if they weren't vigilant.

58. Quoted in Harris, *Right to Manage,* p. 63.

59. Sanger, *Hanford and the Bomb,* pp. 57–58.

60. For the context of labor programs in World War II, see Fairchild and Grossman, *Army and Industrial Manpower,* esp. pp. 129–30.

61. Matthias diary, Sept. 3, 1943.

62. Ibid., Apr. 11–12, 1944. A marvelous document in the history of Dave Beck is *Life*'s postwar profile, which called Beck "public goon No. 1" and documented his millionaire status, but presented him overall in a grudgingly admiring light; the profile ended with a quote from the Seattle *Times:* "Many are wishing that there could be more Dave Becks in the national labor picture." See "The Boss of the Teamsters Rides High: Once Called Goon No. 1, Dave Beck Adds Respectability to His Power as Head of World's Biggest Union," *Life,* Apr. 19, 1945, pp. 122–30.

63. See file ORDO-015.1, "Union Activity," box 103, RG 326-8505, NARD; see also Matthias diary, Dec. 28, 1943.

64. Telephone transcript from unnamed informant, Oct. 23, 1944, box 103, RG 326-8505, NARD.

65. File CEW 624, "Houses, Dorms, Furniture, etc.," box 3, RG 326, Facilities and Services Division records.

66. Libby, *Uranium People,* pp. 169–71.

67. Matthias exacted from the union reps an agreement whereby unions could meet onsite, but only if the gatherings were "informative meetings held by prominent members of the union of the grade of International Representatives"—thereby closing out representatives of locals, and preventing not just business meetings, but also meetings concerning grievances over safety and worksite conditions, from being held onsite. The meetings that *were* allowed, as it turned out, were those at which union representatives from the International offices explained Du Pont and District policies to workers.

68. Matthias diary, June 10–20, 1944.

69. This strategy was s.o.p. throughout the Project—see, for example, the response of Groves to problems with the Carpenters' Union, recounted in Matthias diary, Sept. 1, 1944.

70. Matthias diary, July 20, 1944. The fact that Groves knew the details of a state labor convention suggests how extensive was the District's surveillance of labor.

71. Ibid., July 26, 1944.

72. Certainly incidents such as the deaths of the seven men crushed by the falling tank could be attributed to the sheer size of the project—by the large number of workers alone. After all, Hanford had a far better safety record than virtually any other industrial project of its kind in history, and to prove it would be a simple enough matter. This was the position of the *Manhattan District History,* for example.

73. On this entire issue, Matthias's diary provides perhaps the clearest indications; incidents and controversies concerning congressmen and their committees and investigating teams bedeviled the Hanford site, and Matthias was outspoken in his description of the policy he and Groves devised to cope with the intervention of the legislative branch. See, for example, Matthias diary, Oct. 15, 1943; May 25, Jan. 7, 8, July 16, 24, Sept. 25, 1944; Apr. 11, Oct. 9, 26, 1945.

74. Ibid., Aug. 9, 1944.

75. Ibid.

76. Ibid., Sept. 7, 8, 1944.

77. R. R. Wilson, "A Recruit for Los Alamos," in *All in Our Time,* ed. Jane Wilson (Chicago: Bulletin of the Atomic Scientists, 1975), p. 158.

78. Ibid.

79. Meeting with Church, Matthias diary, Sept. 4, 1944.

80. Ibid., Sept. 21, 1944.

81. Ibid., Sept. 14, 1943; Mar. 3, Nov. 14, 1944; Feb. 1, 17, 1945.

82. Ibid., June 10, 11, July 7, 1943; MDH, bk. 4, vol. 6, sec. 10-7.

83. Matthias diary, Mar. 3, 1944.

84. Ibid., Jan. 31, Feb. 1, 1945.

85. Ibid., Feb. 17, 1945.

86. Ibid., May 21, 1945.

87. Ibid., Oct. 26, 31, 1945.

88. Ibid., Dec. 6, 1945.

89. MDH, bk. 4, vol. 6, sec. 10-7.

90. Du Pont, "Construction: Hanford Engineer Works," vol. 4, 1348.

CHAPTER 7: OTHERS

1. Readers will note the reappearance of the anachronisms "colored" and "Negro" interspersed in this chapter. I have chosen to use the District's terms when closely paraphrasing District mandates or memos, here as throughout the book. This is not simply a matter of stylistic oddity; District racial categories were more fluid than those used today. "Colored" was a term principally used to denominate an amorphous amalgam of unwelcome dark-skinned people. "Negroes" was a more respectful term for a more "respectable" (in District officials' eyes) and clearly delineated entity. In quotations, I have, of course, followed capitalization exactly, as this, too, is significant. Further discussion of issues of language as a part of the District's ideology is found in chapter 9, "Speaking in Tongues."

2. A solid background source concerning race relations on the home front is found in Polenberg, *War and Society,* especially pp. 99–130. Two essays in *Working for Democracy: American Workers from the Revolution to the Present,* ed. Paul Buhle and Alan Dawley (Urbana: University of Illinois Press, 1985), provide context as well: Nell Irvin Painter, "Black Workers from Reconstruction to the Great Depression" (pp. 63–72), and Richard Thomas, "Blacks and the CIO" (pp. 93–102). See also the chapter "John Henry and War Work" in Flynn, *Mess in Washington,* pp. 149–71.

3. Telling early racial statistics are found in the Oak Ridge Monthly Field Progress Reports, 1943–44, listed in two files as 600.914, "JBP Housing," in box 49, RG 4nn-326-8505, NARD.

4. On the FEPC accusation, see Matthias diary, June 14, 1943; the Du Pont monthly labor statistics are reproduced in the MDH, bk. 4, vol. 5, appendix B. This record is confusing. It reports the number of "colored workers" "*sleeping*" [italics added] on the site at zero. On the surface, this would seem to imply only that the District was requiring colored workers to live offsite. But this was the only statistical recording by race for the Hanford site at this time—and the surrounding communities were not equipped to accept nonwhite workers, as we shall see. So it seems almost certain that failing to house Negro workers was equivalent to keeping them off the job entirely (though the District could, under these conditions, absolve itself of blame for the lack of Negro workers—as Matthias did).

5. Flynn, *Mess in Washington,* pp. 161–62.

6. Matthias reported that the FEPC was "requesting [a] report on racial discrimination against negroes." He and Du Pont's Mr. Church responded by drafting a reply that went to Groves in Washington; a copy went to Du Pont in Wilmington, "for their comments and remarks" (Matthias diary, June 14, 1943). The FEPC's complex relation with the WMC is detailed in Flynn, *Mess in Washington,* pp. 154–62. Even as late as the end of July, Matthias reported that "it will be several days before the negro camp will be ready for use" (Matthias diary July 23, 1943).

7. Itinerants who traveled where pay was highest and overtime most likely, the "boomers" drawn to the work at Hanford were mostly from the middle areas of the South: Texas, Oklahoma, Arkansas, and southern Missouri. Even those recruited from the two top recruiting states

(Washington and California) had often come to the West Coast from the South, in search of work in the defense industries. The statistics on labor origins are found in the MDH; they are excerpted in Van Arsdol, *Hanford: The Big Secret*. All the Hanford residents I interviewed commented at one point or another on the "Okie" flavor of the Hanford Camp. In addition, the entertainment programs (found in the miscellaneous files at the Richland DOE facility) show a marked leaning toward hillbilly music (though not as prevalent as at Oak Ridge).

8. The housing-need reports of May and August 1943 attest to the precision of racial planning on that site; each segment of the operations estimates—that is, both separate employers and separate operations facilities—showed Negro workers at 10 percent. The suggestion that this represents an unwritten compact to limit colored employment in operations to 10 percent is underscored by Tennessee Eastman's operations housing estimate. There, Capt. D. C. Moore of the Corps of Engineers' Y-12 operations division left the numbers raw, rather than publishing percentages of white and black workers. Out of 7,078 total payroll, he listed 6,370 white employees; he did not mention Negro employees, but simple subtraction left 708 Negroes—precisely 10 percent. Month after month, these numbers hewed to the 10 percent rule in the reports of each area and contractor. In October, Carbide and Carbon Chemicals Corporation sent its workforce estimates to the New York office of the MED; again, the Negro workforce worked out to 10 percent on the nose. See file 624, box 5, RG 4nn-326-8505, NARD, especially C&CCC's letter to Lt. Col. J. C. Stowers of the New York office of MED, Oct. 6, 1943.

9. Matthias diary, Apr. 11, 1945.

10. Ibid.

11. Flynn reports the statistics: As the war began, blacks made up 3 percent of the war labor force; by September 1942 the figure rose to 5.7 percent, and by the end of 1944 it stood at 8.4 percent. Flynn, *Mess in Washington,* pp. 153–54.

12. See the memorandum and attachments called "Decision of the Secretary" concerning the Davis-Bacon Act, Feb. 18, 1943; see also the updated wage schedule for 1945 from the same source. The percentages of whites, blacks, and others hired in each job classification can be found in the monthly employment reports for each subcontractor, in RG 4nn-326-8505, NARD, whence comes the statistic for cement finishers.

13. Johnson and Jackson argue that the barring of blacks from "other than very low level jobs" at Oak Ridge was an effect of generalized racial attitudes of employers—see *City behind a Fence,* pp. 112–13. Polenberg (*War and Society,* pp. 114–16) discusses the union programs of the AFL. The case of nurses and janitors at Oak Ridge is detailed in Enoc P. Waters, "Negro Kids Can't Go to School at Biggest Brain Center," Chicago *Defender,* Dec. 29, 1945, pp. 1, 6.

14. Matthias diary, Aug. 18, 1943.

15. This was also the policy of the USES at the beginning of the war—George Flynn reports the story of WMC director McNutt's horror at discovering that his own organization was complying with employer requests for workers of specific races. Even as late as August 1942, while McNutt's Fair Employment Practice Commission was investigating racial discrimination, "the USES policy continued to emphasize persuasion . . . [and] if persuasion failed . . . was under orders to refer workers as requested" (Flynn, *Mess in Washington,* pp. 153–55, esp. p. 155).

16. At a meeting on October 26, Groves had instructed his people on this matter: "Start negro town, with dormitories and houses. . . . Same construction for same class of employee, black and white." Notes on conference, Oct. 26, 1942, file MD 337, "Meetings and Conferences, District Office," p. 2, box 29, RG 4nn-326-8505, NARD.

17. Letter, Blair to A. C. Klein, Stone and Webster, Boston, Nov. 21, 1942, file MD 624, "Housing I," box 52, RG 4nn-326-8505, NARD. The SOM plans are found in files marked "CEW 600.914, Field Progress Reports," box 4, RG 4nn-326-8505, NARD.

18. Lt. Col. Crenshaw's post-mortem report on Negro Village, addressed to the District Engineer, Nov. 2, 1943, is found in RG 2nn-326, NARD.

19. Notes on conference, Oct. 26, 1942, file MD 337, "Meetings and Conferences, District Office," p. 2, box 29, RG 4nn-326-8505, NARD.

20. Quoted in Johnson and Jackson, *City behind a Fence*, p. 118.

21. According to one official line, "Although the colored people of their own volition requested separate barracks, mess and recreational facilities, they were in no way prohibited from frequenting any of the areas in the camp or attending any of the recreational facilities available" (MDH, bk. 4, vol. 5, p. 5.6). As of the late 1980s, Colonel Matthias continued to report to interviewers, "It wasn't more than a few weeks after we started getting people in our camp that I had a visit from a whole bunch of black guys led by a black minister who said they would rather have their own barracks. They hadn't had any real trouble, but they figured they would" (Sanger, *Hanford and the Bomb*, p. 57). No such visit is recorded in his diary. In addition, Du Pont reported in its June 1943 statistics that there were no "colored men sleeping on plant site"; see MDH, bk. 4, vol. 5, appendix B, for a copy of this report. Housing estimates are in file 624, box 5, RG 4nn-326-8505, NARD.

22. Descriptions of the Oak Ridge hutments are found in Johnson and Jackson, *City behind a Fence*, p. 87, and in Enoc P. Waters, "Negroes Live in Modern 'Hoovervilles' at Atom City," Chicago *Defender*, Jan. 5, 1946, pp. 1, 8.

23. On the hutments of Oak Ridge, see Johnson and Jackson, *City behind a Fence*, pp. 87, 112; see also Waters, "Negroes Live in Modern 'Hoovervilles' at Atom City." Interestingly, the latter account reported that each hutment had "four steel cots," contradicting the District's own reports and suggesting that postwar conditions were marginally improved over wartime ones. Johnson and Jackson (*City behind a Fence*, pp. 212–15) paraphrase an interview with an African-American hutment resident.

24. Johnson and Jackson, *City behind a Fence*, p. 212. The categorization of race, occupational classification, and housing is found in the file "Housing Status of Trailers, Huts and Barracks," box 3, RG 2nn-326, "Operations Boxes," NARD. See also Waters, "Negro Kids Can't Go to School," and idem, "Negroes Live in Modern 'Hoovervilles' at Atom City."

25. On this, see Waters, "Negro Kids Can't Go to School"; see also Johnson and Jackson, *City behind a Fence*, p. 113.

26. See Jones, *Manhattan*, p. 426; Johnson and Jackson, *City behind a Fence*, map p. 34.

27. MDH, bk. 4, vol. 5, appendix A-40.

28. Ibid., appendix A-40, also sec. 5.

29. Ibid., bk. 4, vol. 5.

30. Matthias's diary entry for Aug. 10, 1944, offers a telling fragment: Matthias met with representatives of the Pasco Naval Air Station "to discuss the present colored problem in Pasco. They were particularly interested in knowing how long we will have colored women at Hanford."

31. Skidmore, Owings, and Merrill, "Report of Facilities for Town of Oak Ridge, Tennessee," July 1, 1944, appendix 2, Change Order; bus station change order dated 4 Jan. 1944, in file "Building Program—(Brown's File)," box 4, RG 326, ORO Gen. Council Files, NARD. See also MDH, bk 4, vol. 5, passim.

32. Interview with Willie Daniels, in Sanger, *Hanford and the Bomb*, pp. 87–91.

33. Ibid., p. 89; the subsequent remark by Luzell Johnson comes from p. 104.

34. MDH, bk. 4, vol. 5, appendix A.

35. Information on Negro recreation at Hanford is found in a typewritten list, "Facilities Available in the Negro Area," reproduced in the MDH, bk. 4, vol. 5, as Exhibit O; see also the recollections of Willie Daniels in Sanger, *Hanford and the Bomb*, pp. 87–91. See also *Here's Hanford*, passim.

36. Johnson and Jackson discuss the matter of movies (*City behind a Fence*, pp. 116–17).

37. Waters, "Negroes Live in Modern 'Hoovervilles,'" p. 1; Johnson and Jackson, *City behind a Fence*, pp. 212–14.

38. Waters, "Negro Kids Can't Go to School."

39. D. McCoach Jr., memo, "Negro Troops," July 16, 1943, file MD 291.1, box 23, RG 4nn-326-8505, NARD.

40. Report on fire, Matthias to Travis in New York, June 12, 1943, file MD 600.913, "Records and Reports of Fires and Other Accidents," box 43, RG 4nn-326-8505, NARD.

41. "Day by Day Program, Hanford Yuletide Carnival," miscellaneous files, DOE Public Information Officer file cabinet, Richland Operations Office, DOE.

42. See the ads and announcements for the carnival in the *Sage Sentinel,* Dec. 1, 7, 1944, both p. 1.

43. "Christmas 1944 Schedule," in files at Richland DOE facility. Robley Johnson's personal memorabilia contain materials related to this carnival.

44. An undated *Sage Sentinel* article taped into Robley Johnson's scrapbook is the source of the quotations. See also *Sage Sentinel,* Dec. 1, 8, 1944, both p. 1.

45. This was the result of the way money was gathered for the association—it came from vending machines and juke boxes, and from beer sales, all revenue sources that District officials pushed disproportionately on the Negro recreation facilities. See the Recreation and Welfare Association Council minutes, passim, RG 326, NARD.

46. Recounted in Johnson and Jackson, *City behind a Fence,* pp. 113–14.

47. The story of the racial incidents at Oak Ridge is told by Johnson and Jackson (*City behind a Fence,* pp. 114–15); the original materials concerning the incidents have been lost in the files at the National Archives, probably during the move from Oak Ridge to the NA facility at East Point, Georgia, shortly after the authors completed their research. The adjutant general's report, "Problems Relating to Negro Military Personnel," specifically warned that bus service was a dangerous area in which inequities were likely to occur; see also Ivy Lee and T. J. Ross, "A Public Relations Study of the Clinton Engineer Works Project, December, 1944–January, 1945," unnumbered box, RG 326, NARD.

48. Adjutant general's report, "Problems Relating to Negro Military Personnel," unnumbered box, RG 326, NARD.

49. On this, see Waters, "Negro Kids Can't Go to School," and idem, "Negroes Live in Modern 'Hoovervilles' at Atom City."

50. Lee and Ross, "Public Relations"; Johnson and Jackson, *City behind a Fence,* 114–17.

51. Matthias diary, Aug. 29, 1943.

52. See Chief Johnny Buck's affidavit on land status, and also Fowler's report to Matthias concerning the "Pom Pom religion," both in the Hanford Science Center Archives.

53. Ibid.

54. Matthias diary, Sept. 14, 1943; materials on "Priest Rapids Indians [Wanapum]" in file marked "Housing and Indians," Hanford Science Center Archives.

55. Matthias diary, Sept. 14, 1943.

56. Ibid.

57. Ibid.

58. Frank Buck interview, in Sanger, *Hanford and the Bomb,* p. 12.

59. This letter is part of a packet in the "Housing and Indians" file at the Hanford Science Center Archives.

60. Matthias interview, in Sanger, *Hanford and the Bomb,* pp. 59.

61. Maj. William Sapper recalled the alcohol incident in a phone interview with me in 1992; Matthias interview, in Sanger, *Hanford and the Bomb,* p. 59.

62. Fisher, *Los Alamos Experience,* pp. 43–44.

63. Information on these workers is remarkably absent from the official records. Partly this is a result of the informal nature of the maid service—it was, for some time, a volunteer-run service coordinated by Los Alamos wives but was later taken over by the Housing Office. Gardeners fell under the purview of the army, apparently; so did the furnace stokers for the housing. Some information is found in the reminiscences of site residents—see, for example, Fisher, *Los Alamos Experience,* esp. pp. 44–45, 137; Jette, *Inside Box 1663;* and the reminiscences found in Wilson and Serber, *Standing By and Making Do.*

64. The myth of maids and gardeners pervades many of the reminiscences of Los Alamos, particularly by women. See Jette, *Inside Box 1663,* esp. pp. 33, 37, 40–42, 95. The furnace men are remembered by Jette, and by Wilson, "Not Quite Eden," p. 48.

65. Fisher, *Los Alamos Experience,* p. 44.

66. Ibid., pp. 47–48.

67. Jette, *Inside Box 1663*, pp. 42–43.

68. Ibid., p. 42; Los Alamos *Bulletin,* Feb. 10, 1944.

69. Jette, *Inside Box 1663*, p. 42.

70. Ibid., pp. 40–41; the incident with de Silva is recounted in Fisher, *Los Alamos Experience,* pp. 142–43.

71. Charlie Masters, "Going Native," in Wilson and Serber, *Standing By and Making Do,* p. 122.

72. Ibid., p. 124.

73. The effect of this change on the pueblo itself was significant. Traditional pottery virtually disappeared from the vocabulary of the potters. Masters knew the native pottery well; when she herself sought a "genuine" piece, she could not find one. Nor could she even find a potter able to make one. It was only after traveling from potter to potter throughout the entire pueblo that Masters was able to find one who would even consider her request. And then it took months and four separate visits to the pueblo to get the piece. Masters, "Going Native," pp. 124–27.

74. Ibid., p. 127.

75. Jette, *Inside Box 1663*, pp. 116–19; Masters, "Going Native," pp. 127–29.

76. A solid general history of working women in the United States is Alice Kessler-Harris, *Out to Work: A History of Wage-Earning Women in the United States* (New York: Oxford University Press, 1983).

77. Fisher, *Los Alamos Experience*, p. 26.

78. Letter, Lois Bradbury to unnamed friend, Aug. 4, 1944, reproduced in *LAHS Newsletter* 9, no. 4 (Dec. 1989): 2–6.

79. Jette, *Inside Box 1663*, pp. 16, 19.

80. Ibid., p. 24. For a few, it was possible to place the change in a positive light. Enrico Fermi was highly secretive about his work, both at the Met Lab and at Los Alamos. Laura Fermi reported some decades after the war that while others suffered, "as for myself, I greatly enjoyed my vacation from physics. Only physicists think that physics *must* be the main topic of conversation in a family." With Enrico forbidden to talk about his work, Laura found a new position of equality and power. L. Fermi, "The Fermis' Path," pp. 95–96.

81. Jette, *Inside Box 1663*, p. 25.

82. Ibid., p. 24; Marshak, "Secret City," p. 10–11.

83. Fisher, *Los Alamos Experience*, pp. 62–63.

84. Jette, *Inside Box 1663*, p. 39.

85. Letter, Bradbury to unnamed friend, Aug. 4, 1944, reproduced in *LAHS Newsletter* 9, no. 4 (Dec. 1989): 3; Fisher, *Los Alamos Experience*, pp. 78–80.

86. Letter, Bradbury to unnamed friend, Aug. 4, 1944, *LAHS Newsletter*, p. 2.

87. Elsie McMillan, "Outside the Inner Fence," in Badash, Hirschfelder, and Broida, *Reminiscences,* p. 43; Wilson, "Not Quite Eden," p. 53.

88. Jette, *Inside Box 1663*, pp. 20–21; Fisher, *Los Alamos Experience*, p. 60.

89. Jean Bacher, "Fresh Air and Alcohol," in Wilson and Serber, *Standing By and Making Do,* p. 103; Marshak, "Secret City," p. 16.

90. Jette, *Inside Box 1663*, p. 22; letter, Bradbury to unnamed friend, Aug. 4, 1944, *LAHS Newsletter,* p. 3.

91. McMillan, "Outside the Inner Fence," p. 42.

92. Jette, *Inside Box 1663*, p. 34.

93. Ibid., pp. 85, 88.

94. Ibid., p. 86.

95. Los Alamos *Bulletin,* Jan. 28, 1944.

96. Feynman, *Surely You're Joking,* pp. 125–26, provides an excellent description of the conditions under which women worked at Los Alamos.

97. Charlotte Serber, "Labor Pains," manuscript, LAHS archives.

98. Letter, Robert Sproul to Robert Oppenheimer, Feb. 19, 1943, file A-84-019-4-3, LANL Archives; L. Fermi, "The Fermis' Path," p. 96.

99. According to Lois Bradbury, "About seventy-five percent of the wives work" (Bradbury, letter to unnamed friend, Aug. 4, 1944, *LAHS Newsletter,* p. 4); Jette, *Inside Box 1663,* p. 29.

100. Bradbury, letter to unnamed friend, Aug. 4, 1944, p. 4; see also Phyllis Fisher's letters to her parents celebrating her culinary triumphs, in *Los Alamos Experience.* A general discussion of the federal daycare center debacle is found in Alice Kessler-Harris, "Women, Work, and War," in Thomas R. Frazier, *The Private Side of American History: Readings in Everyday Life,* ed. Gary B. Nash and Cynthia J. Shelton, 2 vols. (San Diego: Harcourt Brace Jovanovich, 1987), vol. 2, pp. 281–300.

101. Serber, "Labor Pains," p. 69; Alice Kimball Smith, "Law and Order," manuscript, 1946, in LAHS archives; the petition for greater order in maid service and transfer of duties to the Housing Office is found in a memo titled "Household Help" held by the LAHS; "Memo on Maids," undated, file 86.989, NARD.

102. Company D WAC detachment file A-84-019, LANL archives.

103. Yvette Berry's interview is found in Van Arsdol, *Hanford: The Big Secret,* pp. 64–70.

104. This, for example, was Feynman's argument when he trained his SED employees at Los Alamos. See Feynman, *Surely You're Joking,* pp. 127–32.

105. Charles Perrow, *Normal Accidents: Living with High Risk Technologies* (New York: Basic Books, 1984).

106. Robinson, *Oak Ridge Story,* pp. 77–78.

107. Jones, *Manhattan,* p. 142.

108. Robinson, *Oak Ridge Story,* p. 87.

109. The statistics on pay levels are found in a memo, "Contractor salaries allowed by MED as of 5/13/43," in "Circular from Labor Relations Branch 16," ACE, #2390, box 1, RG 326-830-008, NARD. On Hope Sloan Amacker, see her interview in Sanger, *Hanford and the Bomb,* pp. 105–7. In the fall of 1990 I interviewed Annette Heriford, who still works at Hanford; the story of her eviction from White Bluffs also appears in Sanger's book, pp. 7–9.

110. This memo, now lost, is quoted in Johnson and Jackson, *City behind a Fence* p. 80.

111. Ibid.

112. Some of this is detailed in Johnson and Jackson's *City behind a Fence,* pp. 82–85; see also the files on housing and Roane-Anderson, file 624, box 5, RG 4nn-326-8505 NARD.

113. *Dear Anne,* 1944 recruiting pamphlet, "Miscellaneous Files," DOE, Richland Operations Office; "Minutes of Meeting—Executive Committee—Recreation and Welfare Association," Oak Ridge, Dec. 31, 1943, box marked "AEC OROO, Community Affairs City Management Division," RG 326, NARD.

114. Copies of the *Sage Sentinel* are held in the Hanford Science Center. Robley Johnson's publicity photographs are held in various files and offices of the Richland DOE installation and the Hanford Science Center; in addition, the photographer very kindly showed me many of his own copies of photographs made for the District.

115. Sanger, *Hanford and the Bomb,* p. 57.

116. File, "Venereal Diseases, Prostitution, etc.," MD 726.1, NARD.

117. Probably the single most revealing indication of this change can be found in a memo on recruitment and retention held as District Circular letter from Lt. Col. Curtis A. Nelson, ACE, Feb. 23, 1945, box 1, RG 326-83-008, NARD.

CHAPTER 8: SOCIAL WORK

1. "Minutes of Meeting, Executive Committee, Recreation and Welfare Association, 12/13/43," RG 4nn-326-88-004, NARD; transcripts of the meetings are in box marked "AEC OROO, Community Affairs City Management Division," RG 326, NARD.

2. Brown report, R&W Association Executive Committee Minutes, Dec. 31, 1943, p. 1, RG 326, AEC OROO, Community Affairs City Management Division, NARD.

3. Ibid., p. 2.

4. Dr. Eric Kent Clarke, "Report on Existing Psychiatric Facilities and Suggested Necessary Additions," Oak Ridge, Tennessee, Oct. 31, 1944, file MD 701, "Medical Attendance," pp. 1, 2, J-364-5, NARD.

5. Ibid., pp. 1–3.

6. "Minutes of Meeting, Executive Committee, Recreation and Welfare Association, 12/31/43," pp. 5–7, RG 4nn-326-88-004, NARD.

7. Letter, Harry S. Traynor, Oak Ridge, to P. E. O'Meara, Town Manager, re: Community Welfare Activities, Oct. 29, 1943, box 2, RG 4nn-326-8505; file MD 631, "Administration and Recreation Buildings," box 52, RG 4nn-326-8505, both in NARD.

8. Ibid.

9. The history of Roane-Anderson is fully and well told in Johnson and Jackson, *City behind a Fence*, pp. 65–98.

10. *Information Bulletin for Oak Ridge Residents*, Dec. 8, 1943, pp. 1–2, box marked "OR Operations Facilities and Service Division Records," RG 326, NARD. See also "Intelligence and Security Activities, Clinton Engineer Works," box 2 and box 7, RG 326-83-008, NARD. More general information on security is found in the memo from the New York office, "Organization for Protective Security," box 1, RG 326-83-008, NARD, which details the earliest stages of security. Founded in January 1942, the Security section was authorized "to establish and maintain confidential sources of information within the District Office . . . concerning acts, utterances or personal backgrounds indicative of disloyalty or any disposition thereto, of dishonesty or impropriety in the transaction of official business by or with the office, and of subversive inclination or activity." This established a complex net of interwoven policing, social control, and anti-espionage forces—ranging from the FBI's specially assigned forces at each site, to the ACE's own security section, to the safety and security forces of the subcontractors, especially Du Pont, to the Military Police, to the Military Intelligence section, and finally to all the other local policing agencies, from local police through county sheriffs to state police. This sprawl of jurisdictions resulted, by late 1943 in a consolidation of Military Intelligence and Protective Security into one Intelligence and Security Division, headed first by Capt. H. K. Calvert, District Intelligence Officer, and in 1944 by Lt. Col. W. B. Parsons; a Nov. 12, 1944, memo from Lt. Col. Thomas T. Crenshaw announced the consolidation (see memo, "Intelligence and Security Activities, Clinton Engineer Works," and also memo of Mar. 13, 1944, concerning office hours of the division, both in box 2, RG 326-83-008, NARD).

11. Jones, *Manhattan*, p. 445.

12. The agenda and minutes for this meeting, dated July 21, 1943, appear in the Recreation and Welfare files, file 310.1, box 4, RG 4nn-32-88-004 ["Town Management"], NARD. See also letter, Harry S. Traynor, Oak Ridge, to P. E. O'Meara, Town Manager, re: Community Welfare Activities, Oct. 29, 1943, box 2, RG 4nn-326-8505, NARD. A copy of the agenda held in the file contains handwritten notes suggesting that designees had already been approached to serve.

13. See the proposed budget for calendar year 1945, in file 121.7 (CEW [R&W]), box 4, RG 4nn-326-88-004, NARD.

14. Ibid.

15. Minutes of R&W Council, passim, 4nn-326-88-004, NARD; transcripts of the meetings are in box marked "RG 326 AEC OROO Community Affairs City MGMT Division," NARD. The story of the beer complaint is reported in Johnson and Jackson, *City behind a Fence*, pp. 58–59.

16. Minutes, R&W Association Executive Committee for 1943, box 4, RG 4nn-326-88-004 ["Town Management"], NARD.

17. Recreation and Welfare Executive Committee, transcript of Oct. 11, 1944, meeting, box marked "RG 326 AEC OROO Community Affairs City MGMT Division," NARD.

18. See the minutes of the Recreation and Welfare Association Executive Committee meeting, Dec. 31, 1943, pp. 18–20, which detail Colonel Vanden Bulck's attempts, through his agents on the committee, to regulate, without regulating, the activities of R&W.

19. Letter, Harry S. Traynor, Oak Ridge, to P. E. O'Meara, Town Manager, re: Community Welfare Activities, Oct. 29, 1943, box 2, RG 4nn-326-8505, NARD.

20. Transcript of the Recreation and Welfare Association Executive Committee meeting, Dec. 31, 1943, pp. 13–17.

21. Ibid., pp. 13–14.

22. Ibid., pp. 14–16.

23. Matthias diary, Sept. 4, 1944; MDH, bk. 4, vol. 5, appendix 8.

24. Du Pont, "Construction: Hanford Engineer Works," vol. 4, pp. 1342–44, in declassified but restricted materials archive, Richland office, DOE; Matthias diary, Sept. 4, 1944; MDH, bk. 4, vol. 5, 4.43–4.25.

25. Du Pont, "Construction: Hanford Engineer Works," vol. 4, pp. 1342–44; Robley Johnson interview, Sept. 11, 1990; copies of the *Sage Sentinel* are held in the Hanford Science Center, and some have been microfilmed.

26. *Sage Sentinel*, June 9, 23, 1944, Hanford Science Center Archives.

27. "Recommends Wheels for Ails," *Sage Sentinel*, Jan. 19, 1945, p. 6.

28. *Sage Sentinel*, Dec. 29, 1944, p. 3.

29. Ibid., Jan. 19, Feb. 2, 9, 1945.

30. Ibid., Feb. 9, 1945, passim.

31. See "News of Richland Clubs," *Richland Villager*, Mar. 8, 1945, p. 8.

32. "Board Acts Quickly on Paper and Library," ibid., pp. 1–2.

33. Ibid., p. 4.

34. Ibid.

35. Matthias diary, Nov. 18, 1944.

36. *Information Bulletin for Oak Ridge Residents*, p. 1–2.

37. *Oak Ridge Journal*, Feb. 26, 1944, p. 3.

38. Almost from the first arrivals, Los Alamos recruits agitated for representative democracy on the site. Promised freedoms commensurate with offsite peacetime life in return for removal to the isolation of the Los Alamos site, they were disconcerted by their status as clients of a welfare state in which they had little say, and whose workings were almost entirely invisible to them. Alice Kimball Smith, a town council representative, recalled in 1946 that "the novelty of life at Los Alamos made every man his own politician. . . . we were gripped by the panic that so easily besets a civilian confronted by the stern exigencies of military discipline" (Alice Kimball Smith, "Law and Order," in Wilson and Serber, *Standing By and Making Do*, p. 74).

The District's first response was to create an advisory council, with its members appointed by the military. Few of the civilians recognized this as democracy; Oppenheimer agitated to the site's military commander and the result, in August 1943, was a new, democratically constituted town council. But "its status is purely advisory," as an official election notice put it (Los Alamos *Bulletin*, Dec. 11, 1943; this was the call for the election of the second biannual council).

39. See Truslow, *Nonscientific Aspects*, p. 99; Smith, "Law and Order," pp. 73–87; Los Alamos *Bulletin* June 23, 1944; ibid., Dec. 11, 1943.

40. Smith, "Law and Order," pp. 77–78; Feynman, *Surely You're Joking*, pp. 125–26.

41. Smith, "Law and Order," p. 78.

42. Jette, *Inside Box 1663*, pp. 55–59.

43. Smith, "Law and Order," p. 77; Jette, *Inside Box 1663*, p. 59.

44. Smith, "Law and Order," p. 77.

45. Jette, *Inside Box 1663*, p. 90.

46. Eleanor Jette had her own analogy for the distinction: "Los Alamos was like a giant ant hill. The atom bomb was its queen and the Tech Area was her nest" (Jette, *Inside Box 1663*, p. 42).

47. Fisher, *Los Alamos Experience*, p. 60; Bacher, "Fresh Air and Alcohol," p. 115; Jette, *Inside Box 1663*, p. 36.

1. *Oak Ridge Journal,* Sept. 4, 1943, p. 1.

2. I have drawn information on the languages of Los Alamos principally from the published reminiscences of scientists on the site, as well as from materials in the LASL archives.

3. On the codes, see Daniel Lang, *Early Tales of the Atomic Age* (Garden City, N.Y.: Doubleday, 1948), p. 19; Matthias diary, for example, Feb. 26, 1945; see also memo from Dr. Carl Voegtlin and Dr. Harold C. Hodge to Lt. Col. H. L. Friedell, "Medical Division Report on Toxicology," Apr. 26, 1945, file MD 700, box 54, RG 4nn-326-8505, NARD.

4. "Memorandum for Captain W. S. Parson, USN, Subject: Code Designations for Use at Site Y," Mar. 27, 1945, file A-84-019-7-5, LANL Archives.

5. "Safeguarding Military Information: Regulations. Intelligence Bulletin No. 5," Nov. 27, 1943, revised Sept. 1, 1944, in *MDH,* bk. 1, vol. 14, appendix B-7.

6. Letter, Capt. M. J. Barnett, to Dr. C. H. Wright, Consolidated Mining and Smelting Co., Trail, B.C., re: changes in "nomenclature and terminology," file MD 312.7, box 7, RG 4nn-326-8505; letter, Capt. N. Randolph Archer to Col. Marsden in Oak Ridge, file "Nomenclature and Terminology," box 23, RG 4nn-326-8505, both NARD.

7. See the letter, University of Rochester School of Medicine and Dentistry, Andrew W. Dowdy to Col. Stafford L. Warren, Mar. 17, 1944; see also Dr. Carl Voegtlin and Dr. Harold C. Hodge to Lt. Col. H. L. Friedell, "Medical Division Report on Toxicology," Apr. 26, 1945, both in file MD 700, box 54, RG 4nn-326-8505, NARD. Both of these scrupulously followed the code requirements; both are also transparent.

8. Memo, "13 July 44, W. W. Teeter, Captain, Cryptographic Officer," box 2, RG 326-83-008, NARD.

9. See, for example, Stafford Warren's reminiscence, "The Role of Radiology in the Development of the Atomic Bomb," in *Radiology in World War II,* ed. Arnold Lorenz Ahnfeldt, Kenneth D. A. Allen, et al. (Washington, D.C.: Office of the Surgeon General, Department of the Army, 1966), p. 850.

10. Smith, *Peril and a Hope,* pp. 15–17. On this incident, see also Aaron Novick, "A Plea for Atomic Freedom," *New Republic,* Mar. 25, 1946, pp. 399–400. The rest of the information on the meeting is from interviews Smith did with the scientists Coryell and Sugarman in 1959, which formed the basis for her reconstruction in *Peril.*

11. "Declaration 'C'" and "Declaration of Secrecy 'A' Designed for Execution by all Physicists, Chemists, and other Employees of Similar Professional or Scientific Caliber," both in "War Dept. Circular, Oak Ridge, Oct. 15, 1943," box 1, RG 328-83-008, NARD.

12. H. K. Calvert, *Intelligence Bulletin No. 3,* Oak Ridge, Sept. 1943, p. 2, reprinted in *MDH,* bk. 1, vol. 14, as appendix B-8.

13. Ibid.

14. *MDH,* bk. 4, vol. 6, appendix B.

15. On this subject, see Zbynek Zeman, *Selling the War: Art and Propaganda in World War II* (London: Orbis, 1978), especially the chapter titled "You Never Know Who's Listening," pp. 49–61; also Denis Judd, *Posters of World War II* (London: Wayland, 1972).

16. Du Pont, "Construction: Hanford Engineer Works," vol. 1, p. 49.

17. *Let's All HEW to the Line!* July 23, 1943, p. 1.

18. Ibid.

19. *Sage Sentinel,* Feb. 4, 1944, p. 1.

20. Ibid., Dec. 31, 1943, p. 3; Feb. 4, 1944, p. 4; Dec. 31, 1943, p. 1.

21. Ibid., Dec. 31, 1943, p. 3; *Security Bulletin,* p. 4, in "Miscellaneous Files," Hanford Science Center.

22. *Sage Sentinel,* Jan. 14, 1944, p. 1.

23. Letter, Fogg to Bright, Nov. 28, 1942, "Publicity and Public Relations" file, box 10, RG 4nn-326-8505, NARD.

24. Ashbridge is quoted in a letter, Capt. R. J. McLeod, Assistant District Intelligence Offic-

er, to Col. Marshall, Mar. 9, 1943; "Publicity and Public Relations" file, box 10, RG 4nn-326-8505, NARD.

25. Letter, Matthias to Groves, Apr. 9, 1943, box 10, RG 4nn-326-8505, NARD.

26. *MDH,* bk. 1, vol. 14, pp. S-9, 6.15–6.16.

27. Letter, Byron Price to editors and broadcasters, June 28, 1943, ibid.

28. One "security breach" was particularly laughable: in June 1945, Dr. Arthur Holly Compton of the Met Lab took a call from a Mr. Brown, the editor of a farm journal in Asheville, North Carolina. Brown wanted Compton to tell him where he could get some U235 in order to create "a sensation in lectures he frequently gave," in the words of the District's Security historian. Brown had read a number of prewar articles about uranium; when he got his copy of the Confidential Censorship Directive, he concluded that the U.S. was involved in a supersecret atomic bomb project. Brown had met Compton casually some years before; he had tracked down the physicist's location by using the most rudimentary of reporter's techniques, and put two and two together. *MDH,* bk. 1, vol. 14, pp. S-9, 6.15–6.16.

29. "Future Assured," *Business Week,* Feb. 3, 1945, p. 41; Matthias diary, Apr. 12, 15, 1944.

30. Matthias diary, Apr. 20, 1944.

31. Ibid. and Apr. 29, 1944, entry.

32. Ibid., June 8, 1944; Robinson, "Public Relations Procedure and Problems at Clinton Engineer Works," Aug. 14, 1944, box 10, RG 4nn-326-8505, NARD.

33. Matthias diary, July 23, 1944.

34. The quoted passages as well as a sample of Security censorship cases were reproduced in *MDH,* bk. 1, vol. 14, in an appendix titled "Typical leakage of Information Cases," pp. 3–5.

35. Brode, "Tales of Los Alamos," p. 140; Fisher, *Los Alamos Experience,* pp. 39–40; Wilson, "Not Quite Eden," pp. 44–46; Brode, "Tales of Los Alamos," p. 140.

36. Wilson, "Not Quite Eden," p. 44.

37. "Censorship Regulations," quoted in Jette, *Inside Box 1663,* pp. 129–32.

38. Ibid.

39. Wilson, "Not Quite Eden," p. 44.

40. Ibid.

41. L. Fermi, "The Fermis' Path," p. 93.

42. Memorandum from Dr. Eric Kent Clark to Col. S. L. Warren, 29 Aug. 1944, "Mental Hygiene Survey at 'Y' August 23–27, 1944," file MD 330.11, "Morale and Welfare," box 28, RG 4nn-326-8505, NARD.

43. The first anecdote is mentioned in Joseph O. Hirschfelder, "The Scientific-Technological Miracle at Los Alamos," in Badash, Hirschfelder, and Broida, *Reminiscences,* p. 87; Feynman's *Surely You're Joking* contains accounts of a number of the anticensorship pranks.

44. Feynman, *Surely You're Joking,* pp. 121–23, 113, 119–20.

45. Feynman, "Los Alamos from Below," pp. 112–13.

46. Ibid., p. 114.

47. Ibid., pp. 114–15.

48. Ibid., p. 119.

49. "Censorship Regulations," p. 1, file A-84-019-30-3, LANL Archives; Matthias, *Security Bulletin,* p. 1, miscellaneous files, Hanford Science Center; "Notice of Condemnation," LAHS; "Intelligence Bulletin No. 7, 28 June 1944," file location not noted, NARD.

50. Memo, Larkin to Betts, "Classified Communications Facilities," date illegible on photocopy, file A-84-019-7-5, LANL Archives.

51. Memo, Colonel Nichols, "Revision of Security Policy," Aug. 9, 1945, location of original lost, photocopy marked "319.27," NARD.

52. Carbon copies of the order forms are held in the "Miscellaneous Files" of the Hanford Science Center.

53. District Circular Letter, W. A. Fogg, Manhattan office, MED, Oct. 23, 1942, RG 326-83-008, NARD. This was further explained by Lt. Col. Warren George in a letter transmitting "photographic album no. 2 of pictures depicting the construction phase of the Clinton Engineer

Works, covering the period from Mar. 19, 1943 through May 10, 1943. The pictures are incorporated so as to furnish adequate photographic records of the class of such work" (file, "charts, maps, photographs, blueprints, drawings," box 11, RG 4nn-326-8505, NARD).

54. Interview with Robley Johnson, Sept. 11, 1990.

55. Ibid.

56. Ibid.

57. Interview with Ruby Johnson, Sept. 11, 1990.

58. "Notes on Conference in District Office, 9:45 A.M., October 26, 1942," file MD 337, "Meetings and Conferences," box 28, RG 4nn-326-8505, NARD.

CHAPTER 10: MEDICINE

1. These files are found in "General Medical Reports," MD 700.1, and "Medicine—Hygiene," MD 700, both in box 54, RG 4nn-326-8505, DOE, NARD. In addition, there is a strange file in the separate records collection of the Department of Energy, Dr. Joseph D. Mastromonaco, M.D., subcontract no. 117, box 24, RG 236, DOE, NARD.

2. Clifford T. Honicker has detailed his tenacious attempts to receive information on the Los Alamos medical files, in his exposé, "The Hidden Files," *New York Times Magazine,* Nov. 19, 1989, pp. 38–41, 98–103, 120. Stafford Warren's concern with "medico-legal" consequences is detailed in an exchange between Warren and Dr. Stone of the Met Lab and is discussed later in this chapter. See memo, Warren, "Purposes and Limitations of the Biological and Health-Physics Program," quoted in Hacker, *Dragon's Tail* pp. 50–51.

3. Letter, Hamilton to Stone, July 7, 1945, file 700.1, "General Medical Reports," box 54, RG 4nn-326-8505, NARD.

4. Ibid.

5. Jacobson, Marks, and Lorenz, "Hematological Effects of Ionizing Radiations," in Stone, *Industrial Medicine,* pp. 186–87; Russell and Nickson, "Distribution and Excretion of Plutonium," ibid., pp. 257, 258, 260; on the incidence of carcinoma, see Jacobson and Marks, "Clinical Laboratory Examination of Plutonium Project Personnel," ibid., esp. pp. 132–35. See also Schubert, "Treatment of Plutonium Poisoning by Metal Displacement," ibid., p. 472. All but the last are versions of MED reports rewritten to remove classified references.

6. Letter, Hamilton to Stone, July 7, 1945, file 700.1, "General Medical Reports," box 54, RG 4nn-326-8505, NARD.

7. Letter, Ferry to Kammer, Feb. 8, 1945, MD 726.2, box 55, RG 4nn-326-8505, NARD; Russell and Nickson, "Distribution and Excretion of Plutonium," p. 258.

8. The full range of effects of bomb blast on human subjects was first scientifically presented in Averill A. Liebow, M.D., Shields Warren, M.D., and Elbert DeCoursey, "Pathology of Atomic Bomb Casualties," *American Journal of Pathology* 25, no. 5 (May 1949): 853–1027.

9. Letter, Friedell to California Area Engineer, July 27, 1945, file 100.1, "General Medical Reports," box 54, RG 4nn-326-8505, NARD. Hacker reports Friedell's relationship to Hamilton and Stone, in *Dragon's Tail,* p. 46.

10. Compton, *Atomic Quest,* p. 177.

11. This story is well told in Hacker's *Dragon's Tail,* pp. 19–29. An account by MED officials is Cantril and Parker, "Status of Health and Protection at the Hanford Engineer Works," declassified revision of Met Lab report CH-3570, in Stone, *Industrial Medicine,* pp. 477–79.

12. Hacker, *Dragon's Tail,* pp. 21–27.

13. Ibid., pp. 15–15, 26 (quote); *MDH,* bk. 1, vol. 7, p. 2.1; "Hazards of Radioactivity," ibid., pp. 5.1–5.15.

14. Warren, "Role of Radiology," pp. 831–936, esp. p. 834.

15. Stone, *Industrial Medicine,* p. 2.

16. Robert S. Stone, "Memo to Files: Colonel Stafford L. Warren's memo entitled 'Purposes and Limitations of the Biological and Health-Physics Program,'" Aug. 17, 1945, file MD 700.2, box 54, RG 4nn-326-8505, NARD (quote); Stone, "Introduction," *Industrial Medicine,* p. 4; Hacker, *Dragon's Tail,* pp. 29–31; Warren, "Role of Radiology," pp. 841, 864–65.

17. Robert S. Stone, "Health Protection Activities of the Plutonium Project," *Proceedings of the American Philosophical Society* 90, no. 1 (Jan. 1946): 16–17.

18. Ferenc Szasz discusses Groves's trust in Warren as his personal physician, in *The Day the Sun Rose Twice* (Albuquerque: University of New Mexico Press, 1984), pp. 64–65.

19. Letter, Stone to Norwood, Oct. 25, 1944, in file MD 700.2, "Medical Records," box 54, RG 4nn-326-8505, NARD.

20. Warren, "Role of Radiology," p. 843; Hacker, *Dragon's Tail*, pp. 49–50.

21. Letter, Nichols to Warren, Aug. 10, 1943, *MDH*, bk. 1, vol. 7, appendix A-1. Warren himself displays a conveniently edited rewrite of this document in his "Role of Radiology," p. 843, including a footnote reporting that the document remained classified.

22. Letter, Groves to the Commanding General, Army Service Forces, Sept. 21, 1943, file MD 700, "Medicine—Hygiene," box 54, RG 4nn-326-8505, NARD.

23. Ibid.

24. Warren's memo to the District Engineer, June 17, 1943, is evidence of his early commitment to health-hazards management. In it he lays out the ways the District should respond to contractor inquiries regarding health hazards. But it is also worth noting that his approach was reactive. On the one hand he promised that "if the question cannot be answered because of lack of information, such research as seems indicated will then be allotted to a definite group" and the results passed back to the contractor "and to all other companies to which such a ruling may apply." But such a program set the companies' concerns as the trigger, and, as we shall see, the companies themselves were usually the least likely to introduce issues of safety. See memo, June 17, 1943, Warren to District Engineer, "Procedures for Answering Medical Questions Received from Companies Associated with the Project," file 700, box 54, RG 4nn-326-8505, NARD.

25. Warren, "Role of Radiology," pp. 846–48.

26. Ibid., pp. 848–49.

27. Ibid., p. 848.

28. Hacker, *Dragon's Tail*, pp. 50–51.

29. Letter, Dr. Stone to Dr. Norwood of the Richland Hospital, concerning "exposures exceeding tolerance," Oct. 25, 1944, p. 2, file 700.2, box 54, RG 4nn-326-8505, NARD.

30. Ibid., p. 4.

31. Warren, "Role of Radiology," pp. 846, 879, 881; Jones, *Manhattan*, pp. 416–17; Hacker, *Dragon's Tail*, pp. 59–61.

32. Hacker, *Dragon's Tail*, pp. 59–61.

33. Ibid., p. 67.

34. This story is pieced together by Barton Hacker from a series of memos and reports to which he had access as the official DOE historian; I have been unable to find them, probably because they remain classified or restricted. Hacker reports that the chemist's ingestion was only by swallowing, but Hempelmann's request to Oppenheimer for research approval specifically asked for permission to study how plutonium in the lung could be measured, indicating that the chemist breathed as well as swallowed. His or her name and fate remain part of the closed record. See Hacker, *Dragon's Tail*, pp. 65–67.

35. Hacker cites Stone's memo to Hamilton, Aug. 14, 1944, announcing the reorientation; see Hacker, *Dragon's Tail*, pp. 50–51 and p. 178, n. 87.

36. Hacker cites Warren's actual memo to the files, "Purposes and Limitations of the Biological and Health-Physics Program," which is still classified or has disappeared from the Medical Division records of the MED; see Hacker, *Dragon's Tail*, pp. 50–51. Surprisingly, Stone's extraordinary response to Warren's memo has survived; see Stone, "Memo to Files: Colonel Stafford L. Warren's Memo Entitled 'Purposes and Limitations of the Biological and Health-Physics Program,'" Aug. 17, 1945, file 700.2, box 54, RG 4nn-326-8505, NARD.

37. Warren, "Role of Radiology," p. 848.

38. Stone, *Industrial Medicine*, pp. 8–16, reiterating reports of spring 1944, Mar. 1945, esp. Mar. 23, 1945, and also pp. 34, 56, 57, 58, 69; see also S. T. Cantril, "Industrial Medical Program—Hanford Engineer Works," a declassified revision of Met Lab report CH-3553, written around

August 1945, ibid., in Stone, *Industrial Medicine,* pp. 289–307; and Cantril and Parker, "Status of Health and Protection at the Hanford Engineer Works," ibid., pp. 476–84.

39. *MDH,* bk. 1, vol. 7, S-8.

40. Ibid., sec. 6.2.

41. Clinton Laboratory, for example, was responsible for determining maximum dosages of a number of substances, while at the same time instituting measures "to cover all likely possibilities of exposure and to safeguard the workers." But the lab also "assumed responsibility for the medical supervision and protection of all workers at Clinton Laboratories, both by monitoring the plant and making physical and laboratory studies of the workers at frequent regular intervals" (*MDH,* bk. 1, vol. 7, pp. 5.15–16).

42. Report, Watson and Tannenbaum to Dr. R. S. Stone, Feb. 6, 1944, box 5, RG 4nn-326-8505, NARD.

43. Ibid.

44. Ibid. The underlining of the patients' names in my text follows the form used in the original report.

45. Ibid.

46. See Jacobson and Marks, "Clinical Laboratory Examination of Plutonium Project Personnel," p. 120.

47. Report, Watson and Tannenbaum to Dr. R. S. Stone, Feb. 6, 1944, box 5, RG 4nn-326-8505, NARD; the quotation in the next paragraph is also from this source.

48. Letter, Warren to Stone, Apr. 25, 1945 (also dated Apr. 20, 1945), file MD 700.2, box 5, RG 2nn-326-8505, NARD.

49. Ibid.

50. *Report of Survey Made at the Port Hope Refinery,* June 14, 15, 1944, file 319.1 (Medical), box 54; and Report, "Radiation hazards—Hanford," Sept. 1, 1944, file 700, "Medical Reports," box 82, both in Decimel File 5, RG77, NA.

51. Report, "Radiation hazards—Hanford," Sept. 1, 1944, in file 700, "Medical Reports," box 82, Decimel File 5, RG 77, NA.

52. Warren's "recommendations" regarding the use of gloves when handling uranium are found in the memo "Procedure for Answering Medical Questions Received from Companies Associated with the Project," Warren to Dist. Eng. Manhattan, June 17, 1943, file MD 700, box 54, RG 4nn-326-8505, NARD. Stone's reply is found in his memo "Protective Measures for Personnel," in Stone, *Industrial Medicine,* p. 90.

53. Warren to Stone, "Protective Measures," file 700, box 54, RG 4nn-326-8505, NARD.

54. Letter, Close to Taney, "Determination of Policy on Cases of Exposure to Occupational Disease," July 26, 1945, file MD 726.2, "Occupational Diseases," box 55, RG 2nn-326, NARD. The quotations from Close in the following paragraphs came from the same source.

55. Jones, *Manhattan,* pp. 417–18, 420; memo to Brush Labs, Cleveland, Aug. 11, 1943, box 54, RG 4nn-326-8505, NARD.

56. Letter, Dr. J. Lamar Callaway to Dr. James M. Sterner, Apr. 3, 1945, and reply, Sterner to Callaway, Apr. 7, 1945, both in file MD 726.2, "Occupational Diseases," box 55, RG 4nn-326-8505, NARD. Sterner was medical director for Tennessee Eastman Corporation.

57. Letter, Sterner to Warren, Apr. 7, 1945, file MD 726.2, "Occupational Diseases," box 55, RG 4nn-326-8505, NARD.

58. *MDH,* bk. 1, vol. 14, appendix, "Typical Leakage of Information Cases," p. 2.

59. Ibid., pp. 2–3.

60. File MD 600.913, "Records and Reports of Fires and Other Accidents," box 43, RG 4nn-326-8505, NARD.

61. In fact, it was in April 1945 that Dr. Schwartz of Stone's group wrote to Stone begging for information concerning cases of beryllium exposure injuries at the MIT research facilities and requesting that the District pass to the research division urine and blood samples so that scientists there could build from those a scientific data base. Schwartz's request signaled an odd turn of events. The need for human experimental subjects had ended by April 1945. Stone

passed the request on to Warren, who denied it. One of the victims, Warren reported, "is in extremis from some obscure acute disease," but "the other two are only mild exposures." On top of it, he wrote, MIT had no medical officer, and the Medical Section had "no easy way of getting urines from these men unless Schwartz went there himself." In addition, Warren wrote, other plants from which useful urine samples might come were likely to be rejected by the corporations themselves, because "the contractor does not wish to have his men disturbed about their exposure." Letter, Dr. Schwartz to Dr. Stone, Apr. 2, 1945, and reply, Warren to Stone, Apr. 25, 1945, file MD 700.2, box 55, RG 2nn-326-8505, NARD.

62. Warren, "Role of Radiology," p. 848; *MDH*, bk. 1, vol. 11, pp. 5.1–5.5. The army-sponsored reports tout the accident rates on the Manhattan District by comparing them with these industries—by far the most dangerous of the war years. But the comparisons always weighed the District *before* startup against military and chemical industries in full wartime production. Look, instead, to the first six months of 1945, and the contrast is stark: the District's rate for the first half of the year was 6.78, while Ordnance's was 4.3 and Chemical Warfare's was 6.

63. See Stone, "Memo to Files," Aug. 17, 1945, box 54, RG 2nn-326–8505, NARD, and Hacker, *Dragon's Tail*, pp. 50–51.

64. Quoted in Stone, "Memo to Files," Aug. 17, 1945.

65. Stone, "Memo to Files," Aug. 17, 1945.

66. *MDH*, bk. 1, vol. 7, pp. 4.10–4.15, 4.23–4.25.

67. Ibid., p. 4.4.

68. Ibid., p. 4.28.

69. Warren, "Role of Radiology," p. 881.

70. Hempelmann, memo, quoted in Hacker, *Dragon's Tail*, p. 77.

71. Quotations in this epilogue are drawn from Ruth R. Faden et al., *Advisory Committee on Human Radiation Experiments—Final Report* (Washington, D.C.: Government Printing Office, 1996), reproduced on Internet at http://nattie.eh.doe.gov/systems/hrad/report.html.

CHAPTER 11: ALAMOGORDO, 5:29 A.M.

1. Kenneth Bainbridge, *Trinity* (Los Alamos: Los Alamos Scientific Laboratory, 1976), p. 1. This publication is a reissue of the declassified portions of the original report Bainbridge wrote shortly after the test, probably in late July 1945.

2. Ferenc Szasz, the preeminent historian of the Trinity explosion at Alamogordo, was more blunt in his assessment of Groves: "He lived in constant fear of facing congressional investigating committees if the Manhattan Project did not succeed in time to help end the war" (Szasz, *Day the Sun Rose*, p. 26). Ruth Marshak confirms this: "Groves was an authority on Congressional investigations, and some of us thought that this was one reason he had been chosen for this job. Had the atomic bomb not materialized, there was always the possibility of Congress investigating the reason why millions and millions of dollars had been spent on a boondoggle. So we lived in anticipation of a Congressional investigation" (Marshak, "Secret City," p. 10).

3. Bainbridge, *Trinity*, p. 3.

4. Szasz, *Day the Sun Rose*, pp. 26–27. Writing in the summer of 1945, Bainbridge did report one further requirement: "Ranches and settlements should be distant to avoid possible danger from the products of the fission bomb." But his report projected onto the spring of 1944 discoveries of a year later. As Barton Hacker has pointed out, this concern surfaced after the testing program was far along. The evidence shows that at the outset, planners and physicists stubbornly refused to consider what Groves himself called "toxic effects." Hacker, *Dragon's Tail*, pp. 85–86.

5. Bainbridge, *Trinity*, p. 3.

6. Kenneth Bainbridge, "Orchestrating the Test," in Wilson, *All in Our Time*, pp. 209–15.

7. Ibid.

8. Bainbridge, *Trinity*, pp. 3–4; Szasz, *Day the Sun Rose*, pp. 27–31; George Kistiakowsky,

"Reminiscences of Wartime Los Alamos," in Badash, Hirschfelder, and Broida, *Reminiscences,* pp. 55–56.

9. On Stevens, see Jones, *Manhattan,* pp. 500, 507.

10. Letter, James Nolan to Richard F. Newcomb, Aug. 12, 1957, quoted in Hacker, *Dragon's Tail,* p. 84.

11. See Szasz, *Day the Sun Rose,* pp. 30–31.

12. Bainbridge, *Trinity,* p. 3.

13. On the McDonalds, see Szasz, *Day the Sun Rose,* pp. 29–31; and Bainbridge, "Preparations," in Wilson, *All in Our Time,* p. 212.

14. Hacker, *Dragon's Tail,* pp. 77–78.

15. Hirschfelder, "Scientific-Technological Miracle," pp. 73–76; Szasz, *Day the Sun Rose,* pp. 62–66.

16. Szasz, *Day the Sun Rose,* p. 63.

17. Ibid., p. 64.

18. Hirschfelder, "Scientific-Technological Miracle," pp. 74–76.

19. Ibid.; see also Hacker, *Dragon's Tail,* pp. 88–92. The geography of the new area is shown on the map of Trinity in Jones, *Manhattan,* p. 479.

20. Bainbridge, *Trinity,* pp. 4, 15–27; Szasz, *Day the Sun Rose,* p. 32; Fine and Remington, *Corps of Engineers,* p. 71; Jones, *Manhattan,* pp. 478–79.

21. See map of Trinity in Jones, *Manhattan,* p. 479.

22. Perhaps the most graphic description of Trinity, gleaned from interviews, is in Lansing Lamont, *Day of Trinity* (New York: Signet/New American Library, 1965), pp. 82–83.

23. Szasz, *Day the Sun Rose,* p. 33; Lamont, *Day of Trinity,* p. 87; Val L. Fitch, "Soldier in the Ranks," in Wilson, *All in Our Time,* p. 196.

24. Szasz provides a bowdlerized version of FUBAR, in *Day the Sun Rose,* p. 32.

25. Fitch, "Soldier in the Ranks," pp. 189–96; Jette, *Inside Box 1663,* pp. 105–6.

26. Hewlett and Anderson, *New World,* pp. 378–79.

27. Lamont, *Day of Trinity,* pp. 81–82.

28. On this, see Bainbridge, "Orchestrating the Test," pp. 220–21.

29. Hirschfelder, "Scientific-Technological Miracle," p. 76. Richard Feynman was one of the scientists allowed to witness the test. "We had a radio," he reports, "and they were supposed to tell us when the thing was going to go off and so forth, but the radio wouldn't work, so we never knew what was happening." In one of so many miraculous coincidences, the situation righted itself. "Just a few minutes before it was supposed to go off the radio started to work, and they told us there was 20 seconds or something to go" (Feynman, "Los Alamos from Below," p. 130).

30. Szasz, *Day the Sun Rose,* pp. 79–80; Bainbridge, "Orchestrating the Test," pp. 225, 227–29.

31. Kunetka, *City of Fire,* p. 168, reports the radio station's interference, while Lamont gives the call numbers, in *Day of Trinity,* p. 170.

32. Szasz, *Day the Sun Rose,* pp. 85, 115–17.

33. Lamont, *Day of Trinity,* p. 188.

34. On Groves's behavior with the meteorologist Hubbard, see Szasz, *Day the Sun Rose,* pp. 76–77; Groves, "Some Recollections of July 16, 1945," *Bulletin of the Atomic Scientists* 26 (June 1970): 21–28.

35. Groves, "Some Recollections," 27.

36. Groves, *Now It Can Be Told,* p. 292.

37. Szasz, *Day the Sun Rose,* pp. 76–77.

38. Lamont, *Day of Trinity,* pp. 81–82; Kunetka, *City of Fire,* pp. 145–49; Jones, *Manhattan,* pp. 478–80; *MDH,* bk. 8, vol. 2, pp. xviii.2–xviii.4.

39. Jette, *Inside Box 1663,* pp. 94, 97.

40. McMillan, "Outside the Inner Fence," pp. 45–47.

41. Ibid., pp. 46–47.

42. Lamont, *Day of Trinity,* pp. 149–51; Groves mentions none of this in his accounts.

43. Jette, *Inside Box 1663,* p. 104.

44. Groves, *Now It Can Be Told*, p. 292.

45. Jette, *Inside Box 1663*, pp. 105–6; Groves, *Now It Can Be Told*, pp. 293–94; Fitch, "Soldier in the Ranks," pp. 189–91.

46. Szasz, *Day the Sun Rose*, pp. 73–74.

47. Kistiakowsky, "Reminiscences," p. 59.

48. Lamont, *Day of Trinity*, p. 170.

49. Kunetka, *City of Fire*, pp. 152, 156; Lamont, *Day of Trinity*, p. 176.

50. Lamont, *Day of Trinity*, pp. 172–73.

51. Bainbridge, *Trinity*, p. 3.

52. Lamont, *Day of Trinity*, p. 176.

53. Ibid., pp. 172–73.

54. Hempelmann, "Health and Monitoring Organization and Preparations," in Bainbridge, *Trinity*, p. 131.

55. Bainbridge, "Final Preparations for Rehearsals and Test," handed out to Trinity personnel, reproduced in Bainbridge, *Trinity*, p. 31.

56. Lamont, *Day of Trinity*, pp. 172–73.

57. Groves, *Now It Can Be Told*, pp. 300–301; Szasz, *Day the Sun Rose*, pp. 85–86.

58. Cited in Groves, *Now It Can Be Told*, p. 301; Lamont, *Day of Trinity*, p. 192; Szasz, *Day the Sun Rose*, pp. 85–86; Kunetka, *City of Fire*, p. 171.

59. Szasz, *Day the Sun Rose*, pp. 85–86; Lamont, *Day of Trinity*, p. 90.

60. Hempelmann, "Health and Monitoring Organization and Preparations," p. 31.

61. Hacker, *Dragon's Tail*, p. 87–88.

62. Hirschfelder, "Scientific-Technological Miracle," 76–77.

63. Szasz gives the number of workers monitoring radiation as forty-four, in *Day the Sun Rose*, pp. 123–24; Hempelmann, "Health and Monitoring Organization and Preparations," pp. 32–33.

64. Hempelmann, "Health and Monitoring Organization and Preparations," pp. 33–37.

65. Hirschfelder, "Scientific-Technological Miracle," p. 76.

66. Kistiakowsky, "Reminiscences," pp. 59–60.

67. Feynman, "Los Alamos from Below," pp. 130–31.

68. Boyce McDaniel, "Journeyman Physicist," in Wilson, *All in Our Time*, pp. 187–88.

69. Fitch, "Soldier in the Ranks," pp. 190–91.

70. Otto Frisch (probably 1945), "Foreign Relations of the United States," reprinted in *American Atom: A Documentary History of Nuclear Policies*, ed. Philip L. Cantelon, Richard J. Hewlett, and Robert C. Williams (Philadelphia: University of Pennsylvania Press, 1991), pp. 50–51.

71. John H. Manley, "Organizing a Wartime Laboratory," in Wilson, *All in Our Time*, p. 139.

72. Bainbridge, "Orchestrating the Test," p. 229.

73. Memo, J. O. Ackerman to Capt. T. O. Jones, "Recollections on TR Shot," July 27, 1945, file 319.1, "Trinity Test Records (Miscellaneous)," box 56, Decimel File 5, RG 77, NA.

74. I. I. Rabi, from *Science: The Center of Culture* (1970), quoted in Rhodes, *Making of the Atomic Bomb*, p. 672.

75. Groves, from original report to the Secretary of War, reprinted in Cantelon, Hewlett, and Williams, *American Atom*, pp. 51–54.

76. Groves, *Now It Can Be Told*, p. 296.

77. Herbert L. Anderson, "Assisting Fermi," in Wilson, *All in Our Time*, p. 102.

78. Enrico Fermi, "My Observations during the Explosion at Trinity on July 16, 1945," file 319.1, "Trinity Test Reports (Miscellaneous)," box 56, Decimel File 5, RG 77, NA.

79. Quoted in Lamont, *Day of Trinity*, p. 182.

80. Quoted in Rhodes, *Making of the Atomic Bomb*, p. 673.

81. Farrell's report is included in its entirety by Groves in his "Memorandum for the Secretary of War," July 18, 1945, which is reprinted in Cantelon, Hewlett, and Williams, *American Atom*, pp. 51–59.

82. Bainbridge, "Orchestrating the Test," pp. 229–30.

83. McMillan memo, July 19, 1945, file 319.1, "Trinity Test Reports (Miscellaneous)," box 56, Decimel File 5, RG 77, NA.

84. Television interview with Frank Oppenheimer, 1980, quoted in Rhodes, *Making of the Atomic Bomb,* pp. 674–75.

85. McMillan, "Outside the Inner Fence," p. 47.

86. The quote is from Frisch, "Foreign Relations of the United States," pp. 50–51.

87. Cyril Smith wrote his account to Taylor, July 25, 1945, file 319.1, "Trinity Test Reports (Miscellaneous)," box 56, Decimel File 5, RG 77, NA; Groves tells his version once in *Now It Can Be Told,* p. 296; Hewlett and Anderson recount some of the stories from interviews done in the forties and fifties, in *New World,* p. 379; Ed Oppenheimer is quoted in Rhodes, *Making of the Atomic Bomb,* p. 675; Kistiakowsky, "Reminiscences," p. 60. Probably the most hotly fought contest over the meaning of words concerned Bainbridge's "Now we are all sons of bitches," allegedly spoken to Oppenheimer. Lansing Lamont, a journalist, interpreted it; Bernard Feld, a witness, took exception; eventually Bainbridge himself intervened to regain ownership of his words and their possible meanings. See Lamont, *Day of Trinity,* p. 186; Bernard T. Feld, "The Nagasaki Binge," *Bulletin of the Atomic Scientists* (Feb. 1966): 35; and Bainbridge, "Orchestrating the Test," p. 230.

88. Oddly enough, Laurence's account was apparently never published in the *Times* that summer. Instead, the Alamogordo test received a truncated story patched together from official press releases. It was finally published on Sept. 26, 1945, pp. 1, 16, as "Drama of the Atomic Bomb Found Climax in July 16 Test."

89. William Laurence, *Dawn over Zero: The Story of the Atomic Bomb* (New York: Knopf, 1946), p. 4.

90. Feynman, *Surely You're Joking,* p. 135; Frisch, *What Little I Remember,* p. 164.

91. Anderson was interviewed by Szasz; this is his recollection. See Szasz, *Day the Sun Rose,* pp. 116–17.

92. Kunetka reports Fermi made the trip (*City of Fire,* p. 173); Rhodes (following Lamont, *Day of Trinity,* p. 188) has Fermi walking back (*Making of the Atomic Bomb,* p. 677); Anderson's remembrance comes from a 1983 interview condensed in Szasz, *Day the Sun Rose,* p. 117. Anderson himself didn't mention Fermi's role in this when he wrote about the test for the *Bulletin of the Atomic Scientists* in the early 1970s.

93. Lamont, *Day of Trinity,* pp. 188–89.

94. Groves, quoted by Rhodes, *Making of the Atomic Bomb,* p. 677; Warren's comment comes from a memo to the file by Warren in MED records, file 319.1, box 27, RG 4nn-326-8505; Lamont, *Day of Trinity,* p. 189.

95. Szasz, *Day the Sun Rose,* pp. 119–22, provides an excellent précis of the plutonium effects.

96. This narrative is heavily drawn from Hacker's *Dragon's Tail,* pp. 101–8; see also Szasz, *Day the Sun Rose,* esp. pp. 122–29.

97. This story is cited by Szasz, in *Day the Sun Rose,* p. 125.

98. Szasz traced the July 16 events concerning Hot Canyon through interviews with the survivors, in 1983, combined with close readings of technical reports in the Los Alamos National Laboratory files. See Szasz, *Day the Sun Rose,* pp. 126–28.

99. Hacker, *Dragon's Tail,* p. 104.

100. Warren, "Role of Radiology," p. 885.

101. Hempelmann's report is quoted in Hacker, *Dragon's Tail,* pp. 104–5; the conclusions are mine.

102. Ibid., p. 106.

103. Stone's estimate is quoted in Hacker, *Dragon's Tail,* p. 106.

104. Szasz, *Day the Sun Rose,* p. 118.

105. The UCLA report is condensed in Hacker, *Dragon's Tail,* pp. 106–7.

106. Memo, Mullaney to Norris E. Bradbury, "Report by J. G. Hoffman on 'Biological Effects of July 16th Explosion,'" Jan. 3, 1946, quoted in Hacker, *Dragon's Tail,* p. 106, and discussion by Szasz in *Day the Sun Rose,* pp. 142–43.

107. Szasz, *Day the Sun Rose,* pp. 139–41.

108. Ibid., pp. 124–15, 136, 161.

109. Ibid., pp. 161–62, quoting from a 1981 interview with Hempelmann.

CHAPTER 12: CONTINUATION

1. *Atom Bomb Birthplace,* Universal Newsreel, Aug. 8, 1946, and advanced information for newspaper publicity release, Universal Newsreels archives, NA.

2. Ibid.

3. Daniel Boorstin, *The Image: A Guide to Pseudo-Events in America* (New York: Harper and Row, 1964).

4. This press release is reproduced in the *MDH,* bk. 1, vol. 4, chap. 8.

5. *Underwater Atom Blast,* Universal Newsreel, Aug. 5, 1946, Universal Newsreels archives, NA.

6. On the subject of postwar American culture and the atomic bomb, four works stand out. Paul Boyer, *By the Bomb's Early Light: American Thought and Culture at the Dawning of the Atomic Age* (New York: Pantheon, 1985); Spencer Weart, *Nuclear Fear: A History of Images* (Cambridge, Mass.: Harvard University Press, 1988); and Allan Winkler, *Life under a Cloud: American Anxiety About the Atom* (London: Oxford University Press, 1993), are important cultural histories with varying methodologies. Most recent, and most radical of the four, is Alan Nadel, *Containment Culture: American Narratives, Postmodernism, and the Atomic Age* (Durham, N.C.: Duke University Press, 1995).

7. These recordings are the property of William Sapper's grandson, Jay Needham; he and his grandfather very kindly let me listen to and transcribe sections of the tapes.

8. Fisher, *Los Alamos Experience,* p. 116.

9. Ibid., pp. 116–17, 122–23.

10. L. Fermi, *Atoms in the Family,* pp. 237–42.

11. Fisher, *Los Alamos Experience,* p. 12.

12. Jette, *Inside Box 1663,* p. 111; Johnson and Jackson, *City behind a Fence,* pp. 168–69.

13. "Some Comments on the Results of the Questionnaire," Mar. 14, 1946, unidentified author or recipient, LANL Archives.

14. Hanford's roads and their fates are detailed in Matthias's diary; see especially the entries for Feb. 1 and Sept. 24, 1945. Concerning Oak Ridge's highways, see letter, Williamson to Jennings, Jan. 14, 1946, file now lost, quoted in Johnson and Jackson, *City behind a Fence,* pp. 176, 232.

15. Matthias diary, Sept. 11, 17, 21, 24, Nov. 10, 1945.

16. Ibid., Aug. 12, 1945.

17. These matters remain highly controversial; District representatives interviewed by S. L. Sanger in the 1980s argued that this process occurred only while the District was on wartime alert and while the dangers of I-131 and other effluents remained unknown. (See Sanger, *Hanford and the Bomb,* pp. 153–54, 156, 181–86.) Against this, evidence contained in the DOE library in Richmond suggests the programs of waiting until wind conditions were safe were not followed through 1945. The Hanford Dose Reconstruction Project, while remaining relatively understated in its attribution of blame, has tended to support the latter position. Gerber has fully aired this matter in *On the Home Front;* her documentation is exhaustive and her conclusions unequivocal.

18. Matthias diary, Nov. 13, 1945. The following quotation is from the same source.

19. See Johnson and Jackson, *City behind a Fence,* p. 176.

20. Groves, *Now It Can Be Told,* pp. 374, 377.

21. Ibid., p. 377.

22. The most significant alternative proposal involved moving the site to Southern California and dividing it into two parts—an urban laboratory setting near academic centers, and a remote experimental site at Inyokern, in the desert to the east of the mountains. But Groves rejected the plan, and his reasons were revealing. One, of course, was cost: Groves didn't want to

abandon his investment in Los Alamos or spend the cash necessary to build a state-of-the-art lab in an urban center with urban expenses. And the general believed that the pragmatics of a site separated into two parts would discourage the sort of rough-and-ready experimental field-work that characterized weapons development—the hotshots would stay in their labs near L.A. and their allegiance would swerve from the army to the academy. See Groves, *Now It Can Be Told,* pp. 378–79.

23. Groves, *Now It Can Be Told,* p. 378; Hewlett and Anderson, *New World,* pp. 310, 319, 378.

24. Bradbury's speech is quoted in appendix A of Edith C. Truslow and Ralph Carlisle Smith's "Beyond Trinity" (originally included in the *MDH*), in *Project Y: The Los Alamos Story* (Los Angeles: Tomash, 1983), pp. 356–68.

25. Ibid., pp. 362–63. See also Kunetka's assessment of the rationale behind this call for new weapons development and testing (*City of Fire,* pp. 201–2). Portions of Bradbury's speech are also found in Hewlett and Anderson, *New World,* pp. 626–30.

26. Kunetka, *City of Fire,* pp. 198–99; letter and memo exchanges, Bradbury, Groves, Col. Seeman, Nichols, Col. Roper, and Bradbury's assistants, Eric Jette and A. W. Betts, dated between Sept. 7 and Oct. 24, 1946, LANL Archives. These include memo from Jette as Acting Director in Bradbury's absence, Sept. 6, 1946; letter, Bradbury to Nichols, Dec. 11, 1946.

27. Groves, *Now It Can Be Told,* pp. 379–81.

28. "Labor Plays Vital Role in Activity of Manhattan District," press release probably by Laurence, *MDH,* bk. 1, vol. 4, p. 8.

29. Ibid.

30. Ibid.

31. Memo, John J. Flaherty to Col. Nichols, "Labor Policy," Aug. 9, 1945, file MD 004.06, "Labor Conditions and Statistics," box 10, RG 4nn-326-8505, NARD. Here Flaherty suggested the full strategy, warning at the same time that the unions were "waiting in the wings" for the District to show weakness.

32. See various labor-related materials interspersed in file MD 004.06, "Labor Conditions and Statistics," box 10, RG 4nn-326-8505, NARD.

33. Memo, John H. Mahoney to Col. Arthur Frye, Nov. 26, 1946, box 11, RG 4nn-326-8505, NARD. See also letter, Capt. H. C. Calvert, Dist. Intelligence Officer, to Lt. Col. John Lansdale Jr., Chief, Investigation and Review Branch, Counterintelligence Group, Military Intelligence Service, Washington, D.C., July 23, 1943, file MD 004.06, "Labor Conditions and Statistics," box 10, RG 4nn-326-8505, NARD. The District could not afford to have this potentially explosive information leak out, and officials were diligent to keep things quiet. Even the filing of this material was circumspect—MED clerks filed all reports of union-delaying and union-spying activities not under "union organizing" but under the category of "Societies and Associations"—along with items about the Elks Club and the Boy Scouts and Girl Scouts. See the files, box 11, RG 4nn-326-8505, NARD.

34. All these examples are drawn from Johnson and Jackson's culling of files in the old Oak Ridge archives, reported in their *City behind a Fence,* pp. 179–85.

35. The story of Hanford's union activities after the war is traced out in the daily entries of Colonel Matthias's diary, especially those for Jan. 29, Feb. 9, Mar. 3, 22, 27, Apr. 2, 12, 19, 21, 23, 24, May 4, 14, 15, June 9, 14, 16, 22, July 4, 10, 17, Sept. 6, and Dec. 20, 1945, and scattered throughout entries for the first months of 1946.

36. The *New Yorker,* in late September 1945, found that, while "the Army may not know it . . . it is operating Oak Ridge on a downright radical principle"; the magazine called it "one of the better tries at a classless society," as a result of which there is "full employment," a crime rate that "is one of the lowest in the country," "no panhandlers," a population that "is extraordinarily healthy, . . . [with] universal commitment to education," an urban socialist utopia, in other words. See Daniel Lang, "The Atomic City," *New Yorker,* Sept. 29, 1945, pp. 48–54.

37. *The Du Pont Company's Part in the National Security Program, 1940–1945* (Wilmington, Del.: E. I. du Pont de Nemours, 1946), p. 63; *A Report to the People: Stone and Webster Engi-*

neering Corporation in World War II (N.p.: Stone and Webster Engineering Corporation, 1946), pp. 2, 5.

38. Press release sent by District under imprint of Secretary of War to accompany Truman's announcement, reproduced in *MDH*, bk. 1, vol. 4, chap. 8.

39. "Statement by the President of the United States," *MDH*, bk. 1, vol. 4, chap. 8, sec. 1.

40. This material is documented in *MDH*, bk. 1, vol. 4, chap. 8, sec. 1; it is also recounted in Jones, *Manhattan*, pp. 554–57. A draft of the proposal for writing the *MDH* itself, held in the LANL, is particularly engrossing—it suggests some of the ways in which history might also be created by a similar team, with a similar goal.

41. See Groves, *Now It Can Be Told*, pp. 323–32.

42. "Statement by the President of the United States," *MDH*, bk. 1, vol. 4, chap. 8, sec. 1.

43. Ibid.

44. This is the title of a press release issued among that first set of materials on the Manhattan Project, and reproduced in *MDH*, bk. 1, vol. 4, chap. 8, sec. 1.

45. Farrell's text is reproduced in Cantelon, Hewlett, et al., *American Atom*, pp. 56–57.

46. Ibid.

47. Groves's description is republished in the appendix to *Now It Can Be Told*, p. 438.

48. Robinson, press release on Oak Ridge, *MDH*, bk. 1, vol. 4, chap. 8, sec. 1.

49. Ibid.

50. Ibid.

51. Ibid.

52. Hanford press packet, reproduced in *MDH*, bk. 1, vol. 4, chap. 8, sec. 1.

53. "Statement by the President of the United States, August 6, 1945: Immediate Release," *MDH*, bk. 1, vol. 4, chap. 8, sec. 1.

54. "When Atom Bomb Struck: Uncensored," *Life*, Sept. 29, 1952, pp. 19–25. I have written about this suppression and recovery of photographs, in "The Mass Aesthetic of Holocaust: American Media Construct the Atomic Bomb," *Bulletin of the Center for American Studies of the University of Tokyo* 17 (1995): 1–16.

55. Hacker provides this scenario in *Dragon's Tail*, pp. 109–11. See also press release, Aug. 8, 1945, *MDH*, bk. 1, vol. 4, p. 8; for Oppenheimer's comments see also the Aug. 8 press release.

56. "Memorandum of Telephone Conversation between General Groves and Lt. Col. Rea, Oak Ridge Hospital, 9:00 A.M., Aug. 25, 1945," RG 77, NA.

57. Ibid.

58. Ibid.

59. Farrell's words are reported in Hacker, *Dragon's Tail*, p. 111.

60. Warren paraphrased his earlier report in "Role of Radiology," pp. 888–93. Most scientists since have vindicated Farrell's argument that radiation at the Japanese sites was significantly lessened by the decision to detonate well above the ground. But to say that is to miss the larger issue—the question of how much radiation actually was released, how long-lived it was, how many were its victims, how long and how painfully they suffered, and—from this— whether, indeed, the atomic bomb was inhumane or even a violation of the rules of war. In this, Farrell's expedition was not a fact-finding mission. It was sent for the purpose of producing a convincing and authoritative work of propaganda supporting the District's denial that radioactivity was a compelling concern. Indeed, Ferenc Szasz reports that Farrell gave precise instructions to the investigators that their mission was "to prove that there was no radioactivity left from the bomb" (Szasz, *Day the Sun Rose*, p. 160).

Warren and Farrell's investigating group released a series of reports that formed the basis for a blitz of reassuring publicity emanating from the District through 1945 and 1946. Warren's reports went to the District, where they were edited and made public as press releases in the early summer of 1946. Warren testified in a boldly assertive manner before Congress: radiation was a minimal cause of death and injury—only 8 percent of the deaths, he said, were caused by radiation. His testimony, and the supporting words of General Farrell, placed the bombed-out cities of Hiroshima and Nagasaki in the context of conventional warfare, variations on the fire-bombing of Dresden or, more significantly, the destruction of London. The group's reports reconfirmed the District's words, spoken by Truman when he declared the bombing both a great vengeance upon the unrighteous and a viable form of conventional warfare. Missing was the ghost sickness; missing were the hairless, lesion-riddled, weakened survivors, who would die of other plagues in the months after the bombing; missing also were the bodies of those who vomited out their lives in the first hours and days. Warren admitted as much, decades later, when he reported that "no count could be made of those who died outside of the devastated area, in public schools or other buildings to which they had been taken for care." Even within the central zones, "bodies were hastily cremated . . . the destruction and overwhelming chaos made orderly counting impossible." See Hacker, *Dragon's Tail,* pp. 112–15; Warren, "Role of Radiology," pp. 895–903.

61. Hacker, *Dragon's Tail,* pp. 115–16.

62. See Boyer, *By the Bomb's Early Light.*

63. Warren, "Role of Radiology," p. 907.

64. On this subject, see Peter Hales, "The Atomic Sublime," *American Studies* 32, no. 1 (Spring 1991): 5–12; idem, "Mass Aesthetic of Holocaust."

65. Szasz, *Day the Sun Rose,* pp. 160–68.

66. On Los Alamos, see Jette, *Inside Box 1663,* pp. 109–23; Hewlett and Anderson, *New World,* pp. 630–31; Jones, *Manhattan,* pp. 579–96; Groves, *Now It Can Be Told,* pp. 378–79, 381–84. On Hanford, see *MDH,* bk. 4, vol. 6, sec. 15; Hewlett and Anderson, *New World,* pp. 629–30; Jones, *Manhattan,* pp. 591–94. The letters between Groves and C. E. Wilson, president of GE, that trace the negotiations with that corporation are noted in Jones, *Manhattan,* p. 592.

67. See Hewlett and Anderson, *New World,* pp. 639–45, for an account of the transition that is sympathetic to the District.

68. The lyrics to "The Milton Jubilee" are approximate; they come from a tape provided me by Jay Needham, grandson of Major Sapper. Sapper's primitive recorder, something like an early Dictaphone, with which he recorded parts of the life at Hanford, produced vinyl records that were then transferred to tape. I owe a special debt of gratitude to Major Sapper, who allowed me to interview him shortly before his death, and to his grandson, for permitting me to use the tapes.

69. This, too, comes from Sapper's recordings, as does the following lyric.

70. Quoted in Hewlett and Anderson, *New World,* p. 655.

INDEX

mos, 283–84; on the MED, 159–60, 273–98; and morality on MED, 275; and postwar MED, 336–39; on Trinity test, 317–19

Medico-legal liability: Matthias warning regarding Hanford emissions, 137–38; and MED regulations, 284–85; and Oak Ridge radiation illnesses, 291

Meitner, Lise: contributes to discovery of atomic fission, 26

Memos: MED, 264–65

Merrill, John, 112

Mescalero Apache Reservation: included in Trinity danger zone, 306

Mess halls: racial separation of, 201

Metal Hydrides, Inc.: relation to early atomic weapons research, 30

Metallurgical Laboratory, 247; and early opposition to Groves, 37; founded at University of Chicago, 32; Groves seeks to close, 344; hires Dr. Robert S. Stone, 276; Medical program origins in, 275–79; plans for toxic, radioactive gas releases, 144; prime site for Groves's restructuring, 278; reorientation after Du Pont takeover, 41; scientists assist in Hanford site plans, 93; scientists revolt against District security, 249; scientists try to solve Hanford airborne emissions crisis, 148; and Stone and Webster visit, 38

Meteorological tower, Hanford, 148

Met Lab. See Metallurgical Laboratory

"Mexicans," 153; as District term, 203. See also Hispanos

Miera, Jose, 315

Militarization: of MED workforce, 163–64

Military Affairs Subcommittee, House of Representatives: investigates land acquisition at Clinton, 47–49

Military Police: assigned to patrol dormitories at Los Alamos, 239; at Los Alamos, 128; take over Alamogordo's McDonald Ranch, 307; at Trinity, 312–13; and Trinity housing, 310

Military Policy Committee: supports separation of plutonium project from uranium programs, 44

Milk: and radioactive iodine, 149

Milton, Bill, 360–61

Mobile, Alabama: dock riots, 200

Moller, Christian: contributes to discovery of nuclear fission, 26

Monitors, radiation: at Trinity test, 327–28

Moody Charlie, 205–6

Morey, Herb: farm condemned for Hanford site, 63

Morgan, Fred: and land acquisition appeals, 115–16; represents District at Clinton land scandal hearings, 48; signs Clinton "request to vacate" form, 54–55

Morgan, J. E., and Sons. See J. E. Morgan and Sons

Morgan, Jim, 233

Morganville: housing at Los Alamos, 77–78

Mormons: and location of Trinity test site, 302

Morrison-Knudson Company, 140, 141; requests abeyance of X-ray tank inspections, 142; violates MED censorship regulations, 255

MPs. See Military Police

Mud: at Oak Ridge, 112

Murray, Cornelius, 174

Nagasaki, 328; destruction of, 1; images of, in postwar MED publications, 355–59

NAM. See National Association of Manufacturers

National Association of Manufacturers, 164

National Bureau of Standards: contributes to early weapons research, 29; handbook of radiation exposure dangers, 276; sets prewar radiation exposure standards, 276

National Defense Research Committee: and codes of secrecy proposed for weapons development, 31; founded, 28; reorganizes, 29

National Housing Authority, 99, 106

National Labor Relations Board, 164–65, 178; District limits on, 170–71

National Park Service: dissuaded from building monument at Ground Zero, 360

National War Labor Board, 165

Native Americans: arts collected at Los Alamos, 20; and Los Alamos scientists, 207–11; at Los Alamos, 206–11. See also "Indians"

Necrosis, bone: resulting from radium-dial painters' ingestion, 275–76

Neddermeyer, Seth: and plutonium bomb design, 301

"Negro Area," Hanford, 102–3

"Negro" barracks, at Hanford, 198–99

"Negroes," 152–53; army plans for inclusion, 203; and MED, 191–202; myths about, 199; special Oak Ridge clock alley for, 92; as unnamed evictees of Clinton site, 56–57

X ray: for inspection of Hanford waste tanks, 140–42
X-10: siting of, 91
X-2, Los Alamos Group: Develops Trinity test site requirements, 302

Y-12, 30, 92, 115–16, 131; described, 91–92; employment statistics, 131; ideal employee, 218; proximity to Colored Hutment Area, 197; siting of, 91

Yakima Daily Republic: reports on first Hanford claims of radiation injury, 342–43
Yakima Indian Agency, 204
Yuletide Carnival, Hanford: programs described, 201; and racial separation, 201

Zero. *See* Ground zero

PETER BACON HALES is a professor in the History of Architecture and Art Department, a University Scholar, and the director of the American Studies Institute at the University of Illinois, Chicago. He is the author of several books, including *Silver Cities: The Photography of American Urbanization, 1839–1915* and *William Henry Jackson and the Transformation of the American Landscape, 1843–1942*.